Digital Coins &

Cryptocurrencies,

Law & Regulation

Digital Coins & Cryptocurrencies, Law & Regulation

Cases & Problems

Felix Shipkevich

SPECIAL PROFESSOR OF LAW

MAURICE A. DEANE SCHOOL OF LAW, HOFSTRA UNIVERSITY

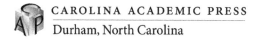
CAROLINA ACADEMIC PRESS
Durham, North Carolina

Names: Shipkevich, Felix, author.
Title: Digital coins and cryptocurrencies law and regulation : cases and problems /
    Felix Shipkevich.
Description: Durham, North Carolina : Carolina Academic Press, 2023. | Securities — Money
    transmission laws — Commodities — Custody of digital assets — Decentraliazed
    finance — Stablecoins — Central bank digital currency — Anti-money
    laundering — International laws. | Includes bibliographical references and index.
Identifiers: LCCN 2023027607 | ISBN 9781531027612 (paperback) | ISBN 9781531027629 (ebook)
Subjects: LCSH: Cryptocurrencies — Law and legislation — United States. |
    Bitcoin — United States. | Electronic funds transfers — Law and legislation — United States. |
    Blockchains (Databases) — Law and legislation — United States. |
    Cryptocurrencies — Law and legislation.
Classification: LCC KF6208 .S55 2023 | DDC 343.73/032 — dc23/eng/20230609
LC record available at https://lccn.loc.gov/2023027607

Carolina Academic Press
700 Kent Street
Durham, North Carolina 27701
(919) 489-7486
www.cap-press.com

Printed in the United States of America

To my parents Emil and Larisa Shipkevich
*   for teaching me about life, hard work, and perseverance*

To my wife Evelina
*   for being my partner, best friend, and beshert*

To my children Ethan, Amelia, and Ellie
*   for making me a better human*

To my students
*   for inspiring my passion for teaching*

Contents

Digital Coins &

Cryptocurrencies,

Law & Regulation

One

Introduction

I. Pre-Modern Era Medium of Exchange

A. The Barter System

Money has value because people have come to understand and accept it as a medium of exchange. However, items that are used as money, such as the paper that is used to print money, are not exceptionally valuable in and of themselves. Once a bill or coin is accepted by everyone as having value, it can be used as a form of payment to purchase goods and services.

Money has been a part of human history for the past 5,000 years. Before money, people acquired and exchanged goods through bartering, a system of exchange. Specifically, bartering is a direct trade for goods and services between two parties for other goods and services, without using money to facilitate the transaction. Bartering is a reciprocal exchange that typically occurs on a bilateral basis. It is argued that the barter system is inefficient because there needs to be a "double coincidence of wants," where the two parties in a barter transaction need to have what the other wants. However, the barter system is advantageous in that it does not require payments to be made using money. Thus, bartering can be utilized when money is in short supply or in hyperinflation situations where money becomes quickly devalued.

Between 1690 to 1710, colonial governments began issuing paper money in the form of bills of credit. In the seventeenth century, however, the colonial economy was troubled by a severe shortage of a circulating medium of exchange. This scarcity limited government power. New England colonial governments often required taxes to be levied in commodity currencies, including corn and wheat. However, a lack of currency made it challenging to satisfy tax obligations. As a result, barter transactions became favored among the colonists as a means to avoid taxation.

B. The Challenges of the Barter System

Facilitating a system of barter exchange is challenging, and the colonists adopted a variety of mechanisms to surpass direct barter. First, they used things such as corn, wheat and tobacco as "commodity money." These were "money substitutes" that functioned as cash. Laborers were compensated with shop notes, and colonists created and entered into networks of debt relationships such as book accounts that allowed members of a community to buy and sell goods without using cash, functioning as a system of tabs.

A pure barter system creates two obstacles to economic activity: First, the requirement for a "double coincidence of wants," and second, informational problems associated with a lack of monetary prices. The first obstacle, the need for a "double coincidence of wants" means that exchanges can only occur when individuals want to exchange the precise goods they possess, and agree on a value, quantity, and time to make an exchange. As you can imagine, this limits transactions greatly.

A double coincidence problem poses three obstacles that must be overcome. The first obstacle is known as "incommensurability," meaning the goods of one of the potential parties to a transaction is unable to be divided to match the value of the goods of the other by quantity or according value. Many exchanges, therefore, do not occur because it is impossible to exchange at a fair value or quantity. The second obstacle is referred to as an "incompatibility of wants," meaning a potential party desires to trade a specific item of his for a specific item of someone else's, and no one has the item he wants to exchange his for. This limits transactions unless one party is willing to compromise. The third obstacle is "synchronization," a situation where the parties may want to make an exchange, but they don't have the exact goods desired by the other at the exact time the other wants to make the exchange.

A lack of monetary prices also negatively affects transactions that occur via bartering. A price establishes a good's value in relation to all other goods, and a general value is established. In a barter system, this is not the case; in a barter system, the parties to a transaction have to seek out information to determine the common cost of the specific good they are trading. The use of money to facilitate transactions eliminates this problem because it allows for payments according to the precise value of the goods being exchanged.

C. Silver and Gold Coins

Massachusetts was among the first colonies to have a mixed coin and barter economy when silver and gold coins began to circulate throughout the colonies before the widespread circulation of government issued paper money. Silver and gold coins, however, were scarce and not used in many transactions due to their high value. Gold and silver were extraordinarily valuable because European governments believed that policies adopted to prohibit the export and encourage the import of coins would provide a readily available medium of exchange. In 1695, the English Parliament prohibited all export of the English Sterling to the colonies. Portugal also prohibited the export of coins. These prohibitions on coin exportation caused a high demand for currency.

D. The Transition to Paper Money

In the seventeenth and early eighteenth centuries, the cost of war efforts caused the colonial governments to print paper money in the form of bills of credit. From 1710 onward, colonial economies transformed into economies that used government issued paper money. The new paper money system had drastic benefits to the colonial economies. For one thing, the adoption of paper money empowered legislatures and governments to finance transactions which greatly lowered the cost of transacting. Governments were also able to raise funds quickly by printing and issuing bills. Taxation also became a more efficient practice since levying taxes in bills of credit was more efficient than taxing in corn or wheat. The development of paper money meant that more people were exchanging and transacting, and the market development began to proliferate.

II. The Modern Era: Pre-Bitcoin

A. The Coinage Clause

[The Congress shall have Power . . .] To coin Money, regulate the Value thereof, and of foreign Coin, and fix the Standard of Weights and Measures; . . .

U.S. Constitution, article 1, section 8, clause 5.

The power to coin money and regulate the value thereof has been broadly construed to authorize regulation of every phase of the subject of currency. Congress may charter banks and endow them with the right to issue circulating notes,[1] and it may restrain the circulation of notes not issued under its own authority.[2] To this end, it may impose a prohibitive tax upon the circulation of the notes of state banks[3] or of municipal corporations.[4] It may require the surrender of gold coin and of gold certificates in exchange for other currency not redeemable in gold. A plaintiff who sought payment for the gold coin and certificates thus surrendered in an amount measured by the higher market value of gold was denied recovery on the ground that he had not proved that he would suffer any actual loss by being compelled to accept an equivalent amount of other currency.[5] Inasmuch as every contract for the payment of money, simply, is necessarily subject to the constitutional power of the government over the currency, whatever that power may be, and the obligation of the parties is, therefore, assumed with reference to that power,[6] the Supreme Court sustained the power of Congress to make Treasury notes legal tender in satisfaction of antecedent debts,[7] and, many years later, to abrogate the clauses in private contracts calling for payment in gold coin, even though such contracts were executed before

---

1. McCulloch v. Maryland, 17 U.S. (4 Wheat.) 316 (1819).
2. Veazie Bank v. Fenno, 75 U.S. (8 Wall.) 533 (1869).
3. 75 U.S. at 548.
4. National Bank v. United States, 101 U.S. 1 (1880).
5. Nortz v. United States, 249 U.S. 317 (1935).
6. Legal Tender Cases (Knox v. Lee), 79 U.S. (12 Wall.) 457, 549 (1871); Juilliard v. Greenman, 110 U.S. 421, 449 (1884).
7. Legal Tender Cases (Knox v. Lee), 79 U.S. (12 Wall.) 457 (1871).

the legislation was passed.[8] The power to coin money also imports authority to maintain such coinage as a medium of exchange at home, and to forbid its diversion to other uses by defacement, melting or exportation.[9]

Article I, section 8, clause 5 of the United States Constitution is known as the "Coinage Clause," and gives the power to "coin Money, regulate the Value thereof, and of foreign Coin, and fix the Standard of Weights and Measures" to the United States Congress.[10] The purpose of the Coinage Clause was to create a system of uniformity and surety in U.S. currency. The benefit of a uniform U.S. currency was that it allowed all individual states to participate in interstate commerce, without trade barriers. A uniform currency also facilitates travel, credit, and commerce.

Before the Constitution, each state issued its own currency, and the nominal values of these currencies varied from state to state. Nonetheless, gold and silver coins remained as the U.S. currency until the Legal Tender Act of February 25, 1862, when Congress passed a law authorizing the issues of $150,000,000 of paper notes (commonly called "greenbacks"), which sparked major controversy.

The interpretation of the Coinage Clause caused controversy regarding Congress's power to coin money, which was litigated in the Supreme Court in the 19th century. Beginning in 1869, the Supreme Court upheld the authority of Congress to issue and regulate paper money in *Veazie Bank v. Fenno*. Veazie Bank, chartered by the State of Maine, challenged the constitutionality of a law passed on July 13, 1866, which provided that all banks were required to pay a 10% tax (previously 1%) on their notes used for circulation. Laws imposing taxation on bank notes were first adopted in 1863, and required the banks to provide monthly reports to the government about the amount of notes in circulation. However, Veazie Bank argued that the increased tax percentage was unconstitutional.

Veazie Bank v. Fenno

75 U.S. (8 Wall.) 533

Supreme Court of the United States (December 13, 1869)

The CHIEF JUSTICE delivered the opinion of the court.

The necessity of adequate provision for the financial exigencies created by the late rebellion, suggested to the administrative and legislative departments of the government important changes in the systems of currency and taxation which had hitherto prevailed. These changes, more or less distinctly shown in administrative recommendations, took form and substance in legislative acts. We have now to con-

---

8. Norman v. Baltimore & Ohio R.R., 294 U.S. 240 (1935).
9. Ling Su Fan v. United States, 218 U.S. 302 (1910).
10. U.S. Const. art. 1, § 8, cl. 5.

sider, within a limited range, those which relate to circulating notes and the taxation of circulation.

At the beginning of the rebellion the circulating medium consisted almost entirely of bank notes issued by numerous independent corporations variously organized under State legislation, of various degrees of credit, and very unequal resources, administered often with great, and not unfrequently, with little skill, prudence, and integrity. The acts of Congress, then in force, prohibiting the receipt or disbursement, in the transactions of the National government, of anything except gold and silver, and the laws of the States requiring the redemption of bank notes in coin on demand, prevented the disappearance of gold and silver from circulation. There was, then, no National currency except coin; there was no general regulation of any other by National legislation; and no National taxation was imposed in any form on the State bank circulation.

The first act authorizing the emission of notes by the Treasury Department for circulation was that of July 17th, 1961. The notes issued under this act were treasury notes, payable on demand in coin. The amount authorized by it was $50,000,000, and was increased by the act of February 12th, 1862, to $60,000,000.

On the 31st of December, 1861, the State banks suspended specie payment. Until this time the expenses of the war had been paid in coin, or in the demand notes just referred to; and, for some time afterwards, they continued to be paid in these notes, which, if not redeemed in coin, were received as coin in the payment of duties.

Subsequently, on the 25th of February, 1862, a new policy became necessary in consequence of the suspension and of the condition of the country, and was adopted. The notes hitherto issued, as has just been stated, were called treasury notes, and were payable on demand in coin. The act now passed authorized the issue of bills for circulation under the name of United States notes, made payable to bearer, but not expressed to be payable on demand, to the amount of $150,000,000; and this amount was increased by subsequent acts to $450,000,000, of which $50,000,000 were to be held in reserve, and only to be issued for a special purpose, and under special directions as to their withdrawal from circulation. These notes, until after the close of the war, were always convertible into, or receivable at par for bonds payable in coin, and bearing coin interest, at a rate not less than five per cent., and the acts by which they were authorized, declared them to be lawful money and a legal tender.

This currency, issued directly by the government for the disbursement of the war and other expenditures, could not, obviously, be a proper object of taxation.

But on the 25th of February, 1863, the act authorizing National banking associations was passed, in which, for the first time during many years, Congress recognized the expediency and duty of imposing a tax upon currency. By this act a tax of two per cent. annually was imposed on the circulation of the associations authorized by it. Soon after, by the act of March 3d, 1863, a similar but lighter tax of one per cent. annually was imposed on the circulation of State banks in certain proportions to their capital, and of two per cent. on the excess; and the tax on the National associations was reduced to the same rates.

Both acts also imposed taxes on capital and deposits, which need not be noticed here.

At a later date, by the act of June 3d, 1864, which was substituted for the act of February 25t, 1863, authorizing National banking associations, the rate of tax on circulation was continued and applied to the whole amount of it, and the shares of their stockholders were also subjected to taxation by the States; and a few days afterwards, by the act of June 30, 1864, to provide ways and means for the support of the government, the tax on the circulation of the State banks was also continued at the same annual rate of one per cent., as before, but payment was required in monthly instalments of one-twelfth of one percent., with monthly reports from each State bank of the amount in circulation.

It can hardly be doubted that the object of this provision was to inform the proper authorities of the exact amount of paper money in circulation, with a view to its regulation by law.

The first step taken by Congress in that direction was by the act of July 17, 1862, prohibiting the issue and circulation of notes under one dollar by any person or corporation. The act just referred to was the next, and it was followed some months later by the act of March 3d, 1865, amendatory of the prior internal revenue acts, the sixth section of which provides, "that every National banking association, State bank, or State banking association, shall pay a tax of ten per centum on the amount of the notes of any State bank, or State banking association, paid out by them after the 1st day of July, 1866."

The same provision was re-enacted, with a more extended application, on the 13th of July, 1866, in these words: "Every National banking association, State bank, or State banking association, shall pay a tax of ten per centum on the amount of notes of any person, State bank, or State banking association used for circulation, and paid out by them after the first day of August, 1866, and such tax shall be assessed and paid in such manner as shall be prescribed by the Commissioner of Internal Revenue."

The constitutionality of this last provision is now drawn in question, and this brief statement of the recent legislation of Congress has been made for the purpose of placing in a clear light its scope and bearing, especially as developed in the provisions just cited. It will be seen that when the policy of taxing bank circulation was first adopted in 1863, Congress was inclined to discriminate for, rather than against, the circulation of the State banks; but that when the country had been sufficiently furnished with a National currency by the issues of United States notes and of National bank notes, the discrimination was turned, and very decidedly turned, in the opposite direction.

The general question now before us is, whether or not the tax of ten per cent., imposed on State banks or National banks paying out the notes of individuals or State banks used for circulation, is repugnant to the Constitution of the United States.

In support of the position that the act of Congress, so far as it provides for the levy and collection of this tax, is repugnant to the Constitution, two propositions have been argued with much force and earnestness.

The first is that the tax in question is a direct tax, and has not been apportioned among the States agreeably to the Constitution.

The second is that the act imposing the tax impairs a franchise granted by the State, and that Congress has no power to pass any law with that intent or effect.

The first of these propositions will be first examined.

The difficulty of defining with accuracy the terms used in the clause of the Constitution which confers the power of taxation upon Congress, was felt in the Convention which framed that instrument, and has always been experienced by courts when called upon to determine their meaning.

The general intent of the Constitution, however, seems plain. The General Government, administered by the Congress of the Confederation, had been reduced to the verge of impotency by the necessity of relying for revenue upon requisitions on the States, and it was a leading object in the adoption of the Constitution to relieve the government, to be organized under it, from this necessity, and confer upon it ample power to provide revenue by the taxation of persons and property. And nothing is clearer, from the discussions in the Convention and the discussions which preceded final ratification by the necessary number of States, than the purpose to give this power to Congress, as to the taxation of everything except exports, in its fullest extent.

This purpose is apparent, also, from the terms in which the taxing power is granted. The power is "to lay and collect taxes, duties, imposts, and excises, to pay the debt and provide for the common defence and general welfare of the United States." More comprehensive words could not have been used. Exports only are by another provision excluded from its application.

There are, indeed, certain virtual limitations, arising from the principles of the Constitution itself. It would undoubtedly be an abuse of the power if so exercised as to impair the separate existence and independent self-government of the States, or if exercised for ends inconsistent with the limited grants of power in the Constitution.

And there are directions as to the mode of exercising the power. If Congress sees fit to impose a capitation, or other direct tax, it must be laid in proportion to the census; if Congress determines to impose duties, imposts, and excises, they must be uniform throughout the United States. These are not strictly limitations of power. They are rules prescribing the mode in which it shall be exercised. It still extends to every object of taxation, except exports, and may be applied to every object of taxation, to which it extends, in such measure as Congress may determine.

The comprehensiveness of the power, thus given to Congress, may serve to explain, at least, the absence of any attempt by members of the Convention to define, even in debate, the terms of the grant. The words used certainly describe the whole power, and it was the intention of the Convention that the whole poser should be conferred. The definition of particular words, therefore, became unimportant.

It may be said, indeed, that this observation, however just in its application to the general grant to power, cannot be applied to the rules by which different descriptions of taxes are directed to be laid and collected.

Direct taxes must be laid and collected by the rule of apportionment; duties, imposts, and excises must be laid and collected under the rule of uniformity.

Much diversity of opinion has always prevailed upon the question, what are direct taxes? Attempts to answer it by reference to the definitions of political economists have been frequently made, but without satisfactory results. The enumeration of the different kinds of taxes which Congress was authorized to impose was probably made with very little reference to their speculations. The great work of Adam Smith, the first comprehensive treatise on political economy in the English language, had then been recently published; but in this work, though there are passages which refer to the characteristic difference between direct and indirect taxation, there is nothing which affords any valuable light on the use of the words "direct taxes" in the Constitution.

We are obliged, therefore, to resort to historical evidence, and to seek the meaning of the words in the use and in the opinion of those whose relations to the government, and means of knowledge, warranted them in speaking with authority.

And, considered in this light, the meaning and application of the rule, as to direct taxes, appears to us quite clear.

It is, as we think, distinctly shown in every act of Congress on the subject.

In each of these acts, a gross sum was laid upon the United States, and the total amount was apportioned to the several States, according to their respective numbers of inhabitants, as ascertained by the last preceding census. Having been apportioned, provision was made for the imposition of the tax upon the subjects specified in the act, fixing its total sum.

In 1798, when the first direct tax was imposed, the total amount was fixed at two millions of dollars; in 1813, the amount of the second direct tax was fixed at three millions; in 1815, the amount of the third at six millions, and it was made an annual tax; in 1816, the provision making the tax annual was repealed by the repeal of the first section of the act of 1815, and the total amount was fixed for that year at three millions of dollars. No other direct tax was imposed until 1861, when a direct tax of twenty millions of dollars was laid and made annual; but the provision making it annual was suspended, and no tax, except that first laid was ever apportioned. In each instance, the total sum was apportioned among the States, by the constitutional rule, and was assessed at prescribed rates, on the subjects of the tax. These subjects, in 1798, 1813, 1815, 1816, were lands, improvements, dwelling-houses, and slaves; and in 1861, lands, improvements, and dwelling-houses only. Under the act of 1798, slaves were assessed at fifty cents on each; under the other acts, according to valuation by assessors.

This review shows that personal property, contracts, occupations, and the like, have never been regarded by Congress as proper subjects of direct tax. It has been supposed that slaves must be considered as an exception to this observation. But the exception is rather apparent than real. As persons, slaves were proper subjects of a capitation tax, which is described in the Constitution as a direct tax; as property they were, by the laws of some, if not most of the States, classed as real property, descendible to heirs. Under the first view, they would be subject to the tax of 1798, as a capitation tax; under the latter, they would be subject to the taxation of the other years as realty. That the latter view was that taken by the framers of the acts after 1798, becomes highly probable, when it is considered, that in the States where slaves were held, much of the value which would otherwise have attached to land passed into the slaves. If, indeed, the land only had been valued without the slaves, the land would have been subject to much heavier proportional imposition in those States than in States where there were no slaves; for the proportion of tax imposed on each State was determined by population, without reference to the subjects on which it was to be assessed.

The fact, then, that slaves were valued, under the acts referred to, far from showing, as some have supposed, that Congress regarded personal property as a proper object of direct taxation under the Constitution, shows only that Congress, after 1798, regarded slaves, for the purposes of taxation, as realty.

It may be rightly affirmed, therefore, that in the practical construction of the Constitution by Congress, direct taxes have been limited to taxes on land and appurtenances, and taxes on polls, or capitation taxes.

And this construction is entitled to great consideration, especially in the absence of anything adverse to it in the discussions of the Convention which framed, and of the conventions which ratified, the Constitution.

What does appear in those discussions, on the contrary, supports the construction. Mr. Madison informs us, that Mr. King asked what was the precise meaning of direct taxation, and no one answered. On another day, when the question of proportioning representation to taxation, and both to the white and three-fifths of the slave inhabitants, was under consideration, Mr. Ellsworth said: "In case of a poll tax, there would be no difficulty;" and, speaking doubtless of direct taxation, he went on to observe: "The sum allotted to a State may be levied without difficulty, according to the plan used in the State for raising its own supplies." All this doubtless shows uncertainty as to the true meaning of the term direct tax; but it indicates, also, an understanding that direct taxes were such as may be levied by capitation, and on lands and appurtenances; or, perhaps, by valuation and assessment of personal property upon general lists. For these were the subjects from which the States at that time usually raised their principal supplies.

This view received the sanction of this court two years before the enactment of the first law imposing direct taxes eo nomine.

During the February Term, 1796, the constitutionality of the act of 1794, imposing a duty on carriages, came under consideration in the case of *Hylton v. The United States.* Suit was brought by the United States against Daniel Hylton, to recover the penalty imposed by the act for not returning and paying duty on a number of carriages, for the conveyance of persons, kept by the defendant for his own use. The law did not provide for the apportionment of the tax, and, if it was a direct tax, the law was confessedly unwarranted by the Constitution. The only question in the case, therefore, was, whether or not the tax was a direct tax.

The case was one of great expectation, and a general interest was felt in its determination. It was argued, in support of the tax, by Lee, Attorney-General, and Hamilton, recently Secretary of the Treasury; in opposition to the tax, by Campbell, Attorney for the Virginia District, and Ingersoll, Attorney-General of Pennsylvania.

Of the justices who then filled this bench, Ellsworth, Paterson, and Wilson had been members, and conspicuous members, of the Constitutional Convention, and each of the three had taken part in the discussions relating to direct taxation. Ellsworth, the Chief Justice, sworn into office that morning, not having heard the whole argument, declined taking part in the decision. Cushing, senior Associate Justice, having been prevented, by indisposition, from attending to the argument, also refrained from expressing an opinion. The other judges delivered their opinions in succession, the youngest in commission delivering the first, and the oldest the last.

They all held that the tax on carriages was not a direct tax, within the meaning of the Constitution. Chase, Justice, was inclined to think that the direct taxes contemplated by the Constitution are only two: a capitation or poll tax, and a tax on land. He doubted whether a tax by a general assessment of personal property can be included within the term direct tax. Paterson, who had taken a leading part in the Constitutional Convention, went more fully into the sense in which the words, giving the power of taxation, were used by that body. In the course of this examination he said:

"Whether direct taxes, in the sense of the Constitution, comprehend any other tax than a capitation tax, and tax on land, is a questionable point. If Congress, for instance, should tax, in the aggregate or mass, things that generally pervade all the States in the Union, then, perhaps, the rule of apportionment would be the most proper, especially if an assessment was to intervene. This appears from the practice of some of the States to have been considered and a direct tax. Whether it be so, under the Constitution of the United States, is a matter of some difficulty; but as it is not before the court, it would be improper to give any decisive opinion upon it. I never entertained a doubt that the principal—I will not say the only—objects that the framers of the Constitution contemplated as falling within the rule of apportionment, were a capitation tax and a tax on land."

Iredell, J., delivering his opinion at length, concurred generally in the views of Justices Chase and Paterson. Wilson had expressed his opinion to the same general effect, when giving the decision upon the circuit, and did not now repeat them. Neither Chief Justice Ellsworth nor Justice Cushing expressed any dissent; and it cannot be supposed if, in a case so important, their judgments had differed from those announced, that an opportunity would not have been given them by an order for reargument to participate in the decision.

It may be safely assumed, therefore, as the unanimous judgment of the court, that a tax on carriages is not a direct tax. And it may further be taken as established upon the testimony of Paterson, that the words direct taxes, as used in the Constitution, comprehended only capitation taxes, and taxes on land, and perhaps taxes on personal property by general valuation and assessment of the various descriptions possessed within the several States.

If follows necessarily that the power to tax without apportionment extends to all other objects. Taxes on other objects are included under the heads of taxes not direct, duties, imposts, and excises, and must be laid and collected by the rule of uniformity. The tax under consideration is a tax on bank circulation, and may very well be classed under the head of duties. Certainly it is not, in the sense of the Constitution, a direct tax. It may be said to come within the same category of taxation as the tax on incomes of insurance companies, which this court, at the last term, in the case of *Pacific Insurance Company v. Soule* held not to be a direct tax.

Is it, then, a tax on a franchise granted by a State, which Congress, upon any principle exempting the reserved powers of the States from impairment by taxation, must be held to have no authority to lay and collect?

We do not say that there may not be such a tax. It may be admitted that the reserved rights of the States, such as the right to pass laws, to give effect to laws through executive action, to administer justice through the courts, and to employ all necessary agencies for legitimate purposes of State government, are not proper subjects of the taxing power of Congress. But it cannot be admitted that franchises granted by a State are necessarily exempt from taxation; for franchises are property, often very valuable and productive property; and when not conferred for the purpose of giving effect to some reserved power of a State, seem to be as properly objects of taxation as any other property.

But in the case before us the object of taxation is not the franchise of the bank, but property created, or contracts made and issued under the franchise, or power to issue bank bills. A railroad company, in the exercise of its corporate franchises, issues freight receipts, bills of lading, and passenger tickets; and it cannot be doubted that the organization of railroads is quite as important to the State as the organization of banks. But it will hardly be questioned that these contracts of the company are objects of taxation within the powers of Congress, and not exempted by any relation to the State which granted the charter of the railroad. And it seems difficult to distinguish the taxation of notes issued for circulation from the taxation of these railroad contracts. Both descriptions of contracts are means of profit to the corporations which issue them; and both, as we think, may properly be made contributory to the public revenue.

It is insisted, however, that the tax in the case before us is excessive, and so excessive as to indicate a purpose on the part of Congress to destroy the franchise of the bank, and is, therefore, beyond the constitutional power of Congress.

The first answer to this is that the judicial cannot prescribe to the legislative departments of the government limitations upon the exercise of its acknowledged powers. The power to tax may be exercised oppressively upon persons, but the responsibility of the legislature is not to the courts, but to the people by whom its members are elected. So if a particular tax bears heavily upon a corporation, or a class of corporations, it cannot, for that reason only, be pronounced contrary to the Constitution.

But there is another answer which vindicates equally the wisdom and the power of Congress.

It cannot be doubted that under the Constitution the power to provide a circulation of coin is given to Congress. And it is settled by the uniform practice of the government and by repeated decisions, that Congress may constitutionally authorize the emission of bills of credit. It is not important here, to decide whether the quality of legal tender, in payment of debts, can be constitutionally imparted to these bills; it is enough to say, that there can be no question of the power of the government to emit them; to make them receivable in payment of debts to itself; to fit them for use by those who see fit to use them in all the transactions of commerce; to provide for their redemption; to make them a currency, uniform in value and description, and convenient and useful for circulation. These powers, until recently, were only partially and occasionally exercised. Lately, however, they have been called into full activity, and Congress has undertaken to supply a currency for the entire country.

The methods adopted for the supply of this currency were briefly explained in the first part of this opinion. It now consists of coin, of United States notes, and of the notes of the National banks. Both descriptions of notes may be properly described as bills of credit, for both are furnished by the government; both are issued on the credit of the government; and the government is responsible for the redemption of both;

primarily as to the first description, and immediately upon default of the bank, as to the second. When these bills shall be made convertible into coin, at the will of the holder, this currency will, perhaps, satisfy the wants of the community, in respect to a circulating medium, as perfectly as any mixed currency that can be devised.

Having thus, in the exercise of undisputed constitutional powers, undertaken to provide a currency for the whole country, it cannot be questioned that Congress may, constitutionally, secure the benefit of it to the people by appropriate legislation. To this end, Congress has denied the quality of legal tender to foreign coins, and has provided by law against the imposition of counterfeit and base coin on the community. To the same end, Congress may restrain, by suitable enactments, the circulation as money of any notes not issued under its own authority. Without this power, indeed, its attempts to secure a sound and uniform currency for the country must be futile.

Viewed in this light, as well as in the other light of a duty on contracts of property, we cannot doubt the constitutionality of the tax under consideration.

The three questions certified from the Circuit Court of the District of Maine must, therefore, be answered

AFFIRMATIVELY.

Close to when the Supreme Court decided *Veazie Bank v. Fenmo,* it ruled in *Hepburn v. Griswold* that Congress did *not* have the authority to make paper money legal tender for a debt that had arisen before the legal tender law.[11]

This case involved a promissory note made by a certain Mrs. Hepburn on June 20, 1860, by which she promised to pay Henry Griswold $11,250.00 on February 20, 1862 (at which time, the only lawful money of the United States that could be used to pay private debts was gold and silver coins).[12] On February 25, 1862, five days after Mrs. Hepburn's note was due, Congress passed a law authorizing the issues of $150,000,000 of its own notes (or "greenbacks") and provided that these notes would be now used to pay all personal debts.[13] When Mrs. Hepburn still hadn't paid the promissory note by March of 1864, Henry Griswold brought suit seeking payment, at which point Mrs. Griswold paid the promissory note using other government notes (pursuant to the 1862 legal tender law).[14]

---

11. *Hepburn,* 75 U.S. at 625–46.
12. *Id.* at 603.
13. *Id.*
14. *Id.*

Hepburn v. Griswold

75 U.S. (8 Wall.) 603

Supreme Court of the United States (February 7, 1870)

The CHIEF JUSTICE delivered the opinion of the court.

The question presented for our determination by the record in this case is, whether or not the payee or assignee of a note, made before the 25th of February, 1862, is obliged by law to accept in payment United States notes, equal in nominal amount to the sum due according to its terms, when tendered by the maker or other party bound to pay it? And this requires, in the first place, a construction of that clause of the first section of the act of Congress passed on that day, which declares the United States notes, the issue of which was authorized by the statute, to be a legal tender in payment of debts. The clause has already received much consideration here, and this court has held that, upon a sound construction, neither taxes imposed by State legislation, nor demands upon contracts which stipulate in terms for the payment or delivery of coin or bullion, are included by legislative intention under the description of debts public and private. We are now to determine whether this description embraces debts contracted before as well as after the date of the act.

It is an established rule for the construction of statutes, that the terms employed by the legislature are not to receive an interpretation which conflicts with acknowledged principles of justice and equity, if another sense, consonant with those principles, can be given to them. But this rule cannot prevail where the intent is clear. Except in the scarcely supposable case where a statute sets at nought the plainest precepts of morality and social obligation, courts must give effect to the clearly ascertained legislative intent, if not repugnant to the fundamental law ordained in the Constitution.

Applying the rule just stated to the act under consideration, there appears to be strong reason for construing the word debts as having reference only to debts contracted subsequent to the enactment of the law. For no one will question that the United States notes, which the act makes a legal tender in payment, are essentially unlike in nature, and, being irredeemable in coin, are necessarily unlike in value, to the lawful money intended by parties to contracts for the payment of money made before its passage. The lawful money then in use and made a legal tender in payment, consisted of gold and silver coin. The currency in use under the act, and declared by its terms to be lawful money and a legal tender, consists of notes or promises to pay impressed upon paper, prepared in convenient form for circulation, and protected against counterfeiting by suitable devices and penalties. The former possess intrinsic value, determined by the weight and fineness of the metal; the latter have no intrinsic value, but a purchasing value, determined by the quantity in circulation, by general consent to its currency in payments, and by opinion as to the probability of redemption in coin. Both derive, in different degrees, a certain additional value from their adaptation to circulation by the form and impress given to them under National authority, and from the acts making them respectively a legal tender.

Contracts for the payment of money, made before the act of 1862, had reference to coined money, and could not be discharged, unless by consent, otherwise than by tender of the sum due in coin. Every such contract, therefore, was, in legal import, a contract for the payment of coin.

There is a well-known law of currency, that notes or promises to pay, unless made conveniently and promptly convertible into coin at the will of the holder, can never, except under unusual and abnormal conditions, be at par in circulation with coin. It is an equally well-known law, that depreciation of notes must increase with the increase of the quantity put in circulation and the diminution of confidence in the ability or disposition to redeem. Their appreciation follows the reversal of these conditions. No act making them a legal tender can change materially the operation of these laws. Their force has been strikingly exemplified in the history of the United States notes. Beginning with a very slight depreciation when first issued, in March, 1862, they sank in July, 1864, to the rate of two dollars and eighty-five cents for a dollar in gold, and then rose until recently a dollar and twenty cents in paper became equal to a gold dollar.

Admitting, then, that prior contracts are within the intention of the act, and assuming that the act is warranted by the Constitution, it follows that the holder of a promissory note, made before the act, for a thousand dollars, payable, as we have just seen, according to the law and according to the intent of the parties, in coin, was required, when depreciation reached its lowest point, to accept in payment a thousand note dollars, although with the thousand coin dollars, due under the contract, he could have purchased on that day two thousand eight hundred and fifty such dollars. Every payment, since the passage of the act, of a note of earlier date, has presented similar, though less striking features.

Now, it certainly needs no argument to prove that an act, compelling acceptance in satisfaction of any other than stipulated payment, alters arbitrarily the terms of the contract and impairs its obligation, and that the extent of impairment is in the proportion of the inequality of the payment accepted under the constraint of the law to the payment due under the contract. Nor does it need argument to prove that the practical operation of such an act is contrary to justice and equity. It follows that no construction which attributes such practical operation to an act of Congress is to be favored, or indeed to be admitted, if any other can be reconciled with the manifest intent of the legislature.

What, then, is that manifest intent? Are we at liberty, upon a fair and reasonable construction of the act, to say that Congress meant that the word "debts" used in the act should not include debts contracted prior to its passage?

In the case of Bronson v. Rodes, we thought ourselves warranted in holding that this word, as used in the statute, does not include obligations created by express contracts for the payment of gold and silver, whether coined or in bullion. This conclusion rested, however, mainly on the terms of the act, which not only allow, but require payments in coin by or to the government, and may be fairly considered, independently of considerations belonging to the law of contracts for the delivery of specified articles, as sanctioning special private contracts for like payments; without which, indeed, the provisions relating to government payments could hardly have practical effect. This consideration, however, does not apply to the matter now before us. There is nothing in the terms of the act which looks to any difference in its operation on different descriptions of debts payable generally in money—that is to say, in dollars and parts of a dollar. These terms, on the contrary, in their obvious import, include equally all debts not specially expressed to be payable in gold or silver, whether arising under past contracts and already due, or arising under such contracts and to become due at a future day, or arising and becoming due under subsequent contracts. A strict and literal construction indeed would, as suggested by Mr. Justice Story, in respect to the same word used in the Constitution, limit the word "debts" to debts existing; and if this construction cannot be accepted because the limitation sanctioned by it cannot be reconciled with the obvious scope and purpose of the act, it is certainly conclusive against any interpretation which will exclude existing debts from its operation. The same conclusion results from the exception of interest on loans and duties on imports from the effect of the legal tender clause. This exception affords an irresistible implication that no description of debts, whenever contracted, can be withdrawn from the effect of the act if not included within the terms or the reasonable intent of the exception. And it is worthy of observation in this connection, that in all the debates to which the act gave occasion in Congress, no suggestion was ever made that the legal tender clause did not apply as fully to contracts made before as to contracts made after its passage.

These considerations seem to us conclusive. We do not think ourselves at liberty, therefore, to say that Congress did not intend to make the notes authorized by it a legal tender in payment of debts contracted before the passage of the act.

We are thus brought to the question, whether Congress has power to make notes issued under its authority a legal tender in payment of debts, which, when contracted, were payable by law in gold and silver coin.

The delicacy and importance of this question has not been overstated in the argument. This court always approaches the consideration of questions of this nature reluctantly; and its constant rule of decision has been, and is, that acts of Congress must be regarded as constitutional, unless clearly shown to be otherwise.

But the Constitution is the fundamental law of the United States. By it the people have created a government, defined its powers, prescribed their limits, distributed them among the different departments, and directed, in general, the manner of their exercise. No department of the government has any other powers than those thus delegated to it by the people. All the legislative power granted by the Constitution belongs to Congress; but it has no legislative power which is not thus granted. And the same observation is equally true in its application to the executive and judicial powers granted respectively to the President and the courts. All these powers differ in kind, but not in source or in limitation. They all arise from the Constitution, and are limited by its terms.

It is the function of the judiciary to interpret and apply the law to cases between parties as they arise for judgment. It can only declare what the law is, and enforce, by proper process, the law thus declared. But, in ascertaining the respective rights of parties, it frequently becomes necessary to consult the Constitution. For there can be no law inconsistent with the fundamental law. No enactment not in pursuance of the authority conferred by it can create obligations or confer rights. For such is the express declaration of the Constitution itself in these words:

"The Constitution, and the laws of the United States which shall be made in pursuance thereof, and all treaties made, or which shall be made under the authority of the United States, shall be the supreme law of the land; and the judges of every State shall be bound thereby, anything in the constitution or laws of any State to the contrary notwithstanding."

Not every act of Congress, then, is to be regarded as the supreme law of the land; nor is it by every act of Congress that the judges are bound. This character and this force belong only to such acts as are "made in pursuance of the Constitution."

When, therefore, a case arises for judicial determination, and the decision depends on the alleged inconsistency of a legislative provision with the fundamental law, it is the plain duty of the court to compare the act with the Constitution, and if the former cannot, upon a fair construction, be reconciled with the latter, to give effect to the Constitution rather than the statute. This seems so plain that it is impossible to make it plainer by argument. If it be otherwise the Constitution is not the supreme law; it is neither necessary or useful, in any case, to inquire whether or not any act of Congress was passed in pursuance of it; and the oath which every member of this court is required to take, that he "will administer justice without respect to persons, and do equal right to the poor and the rich, and faithfully perform the duties incumbent upon him to the best of his ability and understanding, agreeably to the Constitution and laws of the United States," becomes an idle and unmeaning form.

The case before us is one of private right. The plaintiff in the court below sought to recover of the defendants a certain sum expressed on the face of a promissory note. The defendants insisted on the right, under the act of February 25th, 1862, to acquit themselves of their obligation by tendering in payment a sum nominally equal in United States notes. But the note had been executed before the passage of the act, and the plaintiff insisted on his right under the Constitution to be paid the amount due in gold and silver. And it has not been, and cannot be, denied that the plaintiff was entitled to judgment according to his claim, unless bound by a constitutional law to accept the notes as coin.

Thus two questions were directly presented: Were the defendants relieved by the act from the obligation assumed in the contract? Could the plaintiff be compelled, by a judgment of the court, to receive in payment a currency of different nature and value from that which was in the contemplation of the parties when the contract was made?

The Court of Appeals resolved both questions in the negative, and the defendants, in the original suit, seek the reversal of that judgment by writ of error.

It becomes our duty, therefore, to determine whether the act of February 25th, 1862, so far as it makes United States notes a legal tender in payment of debts contracted prior to its passage, is constitutional and valid or otherwise. Under a deep sense of our obligation to perform this duty to the best of our ability and understanding, we shall proceed to dispose of the case presented by the record.

We have already said, and it is generally, if not universally, conceded, that the government of the United States is one of limited powers, and that no department possesses any authority not granted by the Constitution.

It is not necessary, however, in order to prove the existence of a particular authority to show a particular and express grant. The design of the Constitution was to establish a government competent to the direction and administration of the affairs of a great nation, and, at the same time, to mark, by sufficiently definite lines, the sphere of its operations. To this end it was needful only to make express grants of general powers, coupled with a further grant of such incidental and auxiliary powers as might be required for the exercise of the powers expressly granted. These powers are necessarily extensive. It has been found, indeed, in the practical administration of the government, that a very large part, if not the largest part, of its functions have been performed in the exercise of powers thus implied.

But the extension of power by implication was regarded with some apprehension by the wise men who framed, and by the intelligent citizens who adopted, the Constitution. This apprehension is manifest in the terms by which the grant of incidental and auxiliary powers is made. All powers of this nature are included under the description of "power to make all laws necessary and proper for carrying into execution the powers expressly granted to Congress or vested by the Constitution in the government or in any of its departments or officers."

The same apprehension is equally apparent in the tenth article of the amendments, which declares that "the powers not delegated to the United States by the Constitution, nor prohibited by it to the States, are reserved to the States or the people."

We do not mean to say that either of these constitutional provisions is to be taken as restricting any exercise of power fairly warranted by legitimate derivation from one of the enumerated or express powers. The first was undoubtedly introduced to exclude all doubt in respect to the existence of implied powers; while the words "necessary and proper" were intended to have a "sense," to use the words of Mr. Justice Story, "at once admonitory and directory," and to require that the means used in the execution of an express power "should be bona fide, appropriate to the end." The second provision was intended to have a like admonitory and directory sense, and to restrain the limited government established under the Constitution from the exercise of powers not clearly delegated or derived by just inference from powers so delegated.

It has not been maintained in argument, nor, indeed, would any one, however slightly conversant with constitutional law, think of maintaining that there is in the Constitution any express grant of legislative power to make any description of credit currency a legal tender in payment of debts.

We must inquire then whether this can be done in the exercise of an implied power.

The rule for determining whether a legislative enactment can be supported as an exercise of an implied power was stated by Chief Justice Marshall, speaking for the whole court, in the case of *McCullough v. The State of Maryland*; and the statement then made has ever since been accepted as a correct exposition of the Constitution. His words were these: "Let the end be legitimate, let it be within the scope of the Constitution, and all means which are appropriate, which are plainly adapted to that end, which are not prohibited, but consistent with the letter and spirit of the Constitution, are constitutional." And in another part of the same opinion the practical application of this rule was thus illustrated: "Should Congress, in the execution of its powers, adopt measures which are prohibited by the Constitution, or should Congress, under the pretext of executing its powers, pass laws for the accomplishment of objects not entrusted to the government, it would be the painful duty of this tribunal, should a case requiring such a decision come before it, to say that such an act was not the law of the land. But where the law is not prohibited, and is really calculated to effect any of the objects entrusted to the government, to undertake here to inquire into the degree of its necessity would be to pass the line which circumscribes the judicial department, and tread on legislative ground."

It must be taken then as finally settled, so far as judicial decisions can settle anything, that the words "all laws necessary and proper for carrying into execution" powers expressly granted or vested, have, in the Constitution, a sense equivalent to that of the words, laws, not absolutely necessary indeed, but appropriate, plainly adapted to constitutional and legitimate ends; laws not prohibited, but consistent with the letter and spirit of the Constitution; laws really calculated to effect objects entrusted to the government.

The question before us, then, resolves itself into this: "Is the clause which makes United States notes a legal tender for debts contracted prior to its enactment, a law of the description stated in the rule?"

It is not doubted that the power to establish a standard of value by which all other values may be measured, or, in other words, to determine what shall be lawful money and a legal tender, is in its nature, and of necessity, a governmental power. It is in all countries exercised by the government. In the United States, so far as it relates to the precious metals, it is vested in Congress by the grant of the power to coin money. But can a power to impart these qualities to notes, or promises to pay money, when offered in discharge of pre-existing debts, be derived from the coinage power, or from any other power expressly given?

It is certainly not the same power as the power to coin money. Nor is it in any reasonable or satisfactory sense an appropriate or plainly adapted means to the exercise of that power. Nor is there more reason for saying that it is implied in, or incidental to, the power to regulate the value of coined money of the United States, or of foreign coins. This power of regulation is a power to determine the weight, purity, form, impression, and denomination of the several coins, and their relation to each other, and the relations of foreign coins to the monetary unit of the United States.

Nor is the power to make notes a legal tender the same as the power to issue notes to be used as currency. The old Congress, under the Articles of Confederation, was clothed by express grant with the power to emit bills of credit, which are in fact notes for circulation as currency; and yet that Congress was not clothed with the power to make these bills a legal tender in payment. And this court has recently held that the Congress, under the Constitution, possesses, as incidental to other powers, the same power as the old Congress to emit bills or notes; but it was expressly declared at the same time that this decision concluded nothing on the question of legal tender. Indeed, we are not aware that it has ever been claimed that the power to issue bills or notes has any identity with the power to make them a legal tender. On the contrary, the whole history of the country refutes that notion. The States have always been held to possess the power to authorized and regulate the issue of bills for circulation by banks or individuals, subject, as has been lately determined, to the control of Congress, for the purpose of establishing and securing a National currency; and yet the States are expressly prohibited by the Constitution from making anything but gold and silver coin a legal tender. This seems decisive on the point that the power to issue notes and the power to make them a legal tender are not the same power, and that they have no necessary connection with each other.

But it has been maintained in argument that the power to make United States notes a legal tender in payment of all debts is a means appropriate and plainly adapted to the execution of the power to carry on war, of the power to regulate commerce, and of the power to borrow money. If it is, and is not prohibited, nor inconsistent with the letter or spirit of the Constitution, then the act which makes them such legal tender must be held to be constitutional.

Let us, then, first inquire whether it is an appropriate and plainly adapted means for carrying on war? The affirmative argument may be thus stated: Congress has power to declare and provide for carrying on war; Congress has also power to emit bills of credit, or circulating notes receivable for government dues and payable, so far at least as parties are willing to receive them, in discharge of government obligations; it will facilitate the use of such notes in disbursements to make them a legal tender in payment of existing debts; therefore, Congress may make such notes a legal tender.

It is difficult to say to what express power the authority to make notes a legal tender in payment of pre-existing debts may not be upheld as incidental, upon the principles of this argument. Is there any power which does not involve the use of money? And is there any doubt that Congress may issue and use bills of credit as money in the execution of any power? The power to establish post-offices and post-roads, for example, involves the collection and disbursement of a great revenue. Is not the power to make notes a legal tender as clearly incidental to this power as to the war power?

The answer to this question does not appear to us doubtful. The argument, therefore, seems to prove too much. It carries the doctrine of implied powers very far beyond any extent hitherto given to it. It asserts that whatever in any degree promotes an end within the scope of a general power, whether, in the correct sense of the word, appropriate or not, may be done in the exercise of an implied power.

Can this proposition be maintained?

It is said that this is not a question for the court deciding a cause, but for Congress exercising the power. But the decisive answer to this is that the admission of a legislative power to determine finally what powers have the described relation as means to the execution of other powers plainly granted, and, then, to exercise absolutely and without liability to question, in cases involving private rights, the powers thus determined to have that relation, would completely change the nature of American government. It would convert the government, which the people ordained as a government of limited powers, into a government of unlimited powers. It would confuse the boundaries which separate the executive and judicial from the legislative authority. It would obliterate every criterion which this court, speaking through the venerated Chief Justice in the case already cited, established for the determination of the question whether legislative acts are constitutional or unconstitutional.

Undoubtedly among means appropriate, plainly adapted, really calculated, the legislature has unrestricted choice. But there can be no implied power to use means not within the description.

Now, then, let it be considered what has actually been done in the provision of a National currency. In July and August, 1861, and February, 1862, the issue of sixty millions of dollars in United States notes, payable on demand, was authorized. They were made receivable in payments, but were not declared a legal tender until March, 1862, when the amount in circulation had been greatly reduced by receipt and cancellation. In 1862 and 1863 the issue of four hundred and fifty millions in United States notes, payable not on demand, but, in effect, at the convenience of the government, was authorized, subject to certain restrictions as to fifty millions. These notes were made receivable for the bonds of the National loans, for all debts due to or from the United States, except duties on imports and interest on the public debt, and were also declared a legal tender. In March, 1863, the issue of notes for parts of a dollar was authorized to an amount not exceeding fifty millions of dollars. These notes were not declared a legal tender, but were made redeemable under regulations to be prescribed by the Secretary of the Treasury. In February, 1863, the issue of three hundred millions of dollars in notes of the National banking associations was authorized. These notes were made receivable to the same extent as United States notes, and provision was made to secure their redemption, but they were not made a legal tender.

The several descriptions of notes have since constituted, under the various acts of Congress, the common currency of the United States. The notes which were not declared a legal tender have circulated with those which were so declared without unfavorable discrimination.

It may be added as a part of the history that other issues, bearing interest at various rates, were authorized and made a legal tender, except in redemption of bank notes, for face amount exclusive of interest. Such were the one and two years five per cent. Notes and three years compound interest notes. These notes never entered largely or permanently into the circulation; and there is no reason to think that their utility was increased or diminished by the act which declared them a legal tender for face amount. They need not be further considered here. They serve only to illustrate the tendency remarked by all who have investigated the subject of paper money, to increase the volume of irredeemable issues, and to extend indefinitely the application of the quality of legal tender. That it was carried no farther during the recent civil war, and has been carried no farther since, is due to circumstances, the consideration of which does not belong to this discussion.

We recur, then, to the question under consideration. No one questions the general constitutionality, and not very many, perhaps, the general expediency of the legislation by which a note currency has been authorized in recent years. The doubt is as to the power to declare a particular class of these notes to be a legal tender in payment of pre-existing debts.

The only ground upon which this power is asserted is, not that the issue of notes was an appropriate and plainly adapted means for carrying on the war, for that is admitted; but that the making of them a legal tender to the extent mentioned was such a means.

Now, we have seen that of all the notes issued those not declared a legal tender at all constituted a very large proportion, and that they circulated freely and without discount.

It may be said that their equality in circulation and credit was due to the provision made by law for the redemption of this paper in legal tender notes. But this provision, if at all useful in this respect, was of trifling importance compared with that which made them receivable for government dues. All modern history testifies that, in time of war especially, when taxes are augmented, large loans negotiated, and heavy disbursements made, notes issued by the authority of the government, and made receivable for dues of the government, always obtain at first a ready circulation; and even when not redeemable in coin, on demand, are as little and usually less subject to depreciation than any other description of notes, for the redemption of which no better provision is made. And the history of the legislation under consideration is, that it was upon this quality of receivability, and not upon the quality of legal tender, that reliance for circulation was originally placed; for the receivability clause appears to have been in the original draft of the bill, while the legal tender clause seems to have been introduced at a later stage of its progress.

These facts certainly are not without weight as evidence that all the useful purposes of the notes would have been fully answered without making them a legal tender for pre-existing debts. It is denied, indeed, by eminent writers, that the quality of legal tender adds anything at all to the credit or usefulness of government notes. They insist, on the contrary, that it impairs both. However this may be, it must be remembered that it is as a means to an end to be attained by the action of the government, that the implied power of making notes a legal tender in all payments is claimed under the Constitution. Now, how far is the government helped by this means? Certainly it cannot obtain new supplies or services at a cheaper rate, for no one will take the notes for more than they are worth at the time of the new contract. The price will rise in the ratio of the depreciation, and this is all that could happen if the notes were not made a legal tender. But it may be said that the depreciation will be less to him who takes them from the government, if the government will pledge to him its power to compel his creditors to receive them at par in payments. This is, as we have seen, by no means certain. If the quantity issued be excessive, and redemption uncertain and remote, great depreciation will take place; if, on the other hand, the quantity is only adequate to the demands of business, and confidence in early redemption is strong, the notes will circulate freely, whether made a legal tender or not.

But if it be admitted that some increase of availability is derived from making the notes a legal tender under new contracts, it by no means follows that any appreciable advantage is gained by compelling creditors to receive them in satisfaction of pre-existing debts. And there is abundant evidence, that whatever benefit is possible from that compulsion to some individuals or to the government, is far more than outweighed by the losses of property, the derangement of business, the fluctuations of currency and values, and the increase of prices to the people and the government, and the long train of evils which flow from the use of irredeemable paper money. It is true that these evils are not to be attributed altogether to making it a legal tender. But this increases these evils. It certainly widens their extent and protracts their continuance.

We are unable to persuade ourselves that an expedient of this sort is an appropriate and plainly adapted means for the execution of the power to declare and carry on war. If it adds nothing to the utility of the notes, it cannot be upheld as a means to the end in furtherance of which the notes are issued. Nor can it, in our judgment, be upheld as such, if, while facilitating in some degree the circulation of the notes, it debases and injures the currency in its proper use to a much greater degree. And these considerations seem to us equally applicable to the powers to regulate commerce and to borrow money. Both powers necessarily involve the use of money by the people and by the government, but neither, as we think, carries with it as an appropriate and plainly adapted means to its exercise, the power of making circulating notes a legal tender in payment of pre-existing debts.

But there is another view, which seems to us decisive, to whatever express power the supposed implied power in question may be referred. In the rule stated by Chief Justice Marshall, the words appropriate, plainly adapted, really calculated, are qualified by the limitation that the means must be not prohibited, but consistent with the letter and spirit of the Constitution. Nothing so prohibited or inconsistent can be regarded as appropriate, or plainly adapted, or really calculated means to any end.

Let us inquire, then, first whether making bills of credit a legal tender, to the extent indicated, is consistent with the spirit of the Constitution.

Among the great cardinal principles of that instrument, no one is more conspicuous or more venerable than the establishment of justice. And what was intended by the establishment of justice in the minds of the people who ordained it is, happily, not a matter of disputation. It is not left to inference or conjecture, especially in its relations to contracts.

When the Constitution was undergoing discussion in the Convention, the Congress of the Confederation was engaged in the consideration of the ordinance for the government of the territory northwest of the Ohio, the only territory subject at that time to its regulation and control. By this ordinance certain fundamental articles of compact were established between the original States and the people and States of the territory, for the purpose, to use its own language, "of extending the fundamental principles of civil and religious liberty, whereon these republics" (the States united under the Confederation), "their laws, and constitutions are erected." Among these fundamental principles was this: "And in the just preservation of rights and property it is understood and declared that no law ought ever to be made, or have force in the said territory, that shall in any manner whatever interfere with or affect private contracts or engagements bona fide and without fraud previously formed."

The same principle found more condensed expression in that most valuable provision of the Constitution of the United States, ever recognized as an efficient safeguard against injustice, that "no State shall pass any law impairing the obligation of contracts."

It is true that this prohibition is not applied in terms to the government of the United States. Congress has express power to enact bankruptcy laws, and we do not say that a law made in the execution of any other express power, which, incidentally only, impairs the obligation of a contract, can be held to be unconstitutional for that reason.

But we think it clear that those who framed and those who adopted the Constitution, intended that the spirit of this prohibition should pervade the entire body of legislation, and that the justice which the Constitution was ordained to establish was not thought by them to be compatible with legislation of an opposite tendency. In other words, we cannot doubt that a law not made in pursuance of an express power, which necessarily and in its direct operation impairs the obligation of contracts, is inconsistent with the spirit of the Constitution.

Another provision, found in the fifth amendment, must be considered in this connection. We refer to that which ordains that private property shall not be taken for public use without compensation. This provision is kindred in spirit to that which forbids legislation impairing the obligation of contracts; but, unlike that, it is addressed directly and solely to the National government. It does not, in terms, prohibit legislation which appropriates the private property of one class of citizens to the use of another class; but if such property cannot be taken for the benefit of all, without compensation, it is difficult to understand how it can be so taken for the benefit of a part without violating the spirit of the prohibition.

But there is another provision in the same amendment, which, in our judgment, cannot have its full and intended effect unless construed as a direct prohibition of the legislation which we have been considering. It is that which declares that "no person shall be deprived of life, liberty, or property, without due process of law."

It is not doubted that all the provisions of this amendment operate directly in limitation and restraint of the legislative powers conferred by the Constitution. The only question is, whether an act which compels all those who hold contracts for the payment of gold and silver money to accept in payment a currency of inferior value deprives such persons of property without due process of law.

It is quite clear, that whatever may be the operation of such an act, due process of law makes no part of it. Does it deprive any person of property? A very large proportion of the property of civilized men exists in the form of contracts. These contracts almost invariably stipulate for the payment of money. And we have already seen that contracts in the United States, prior to the act under consideration, for the payment of money, were contracts to pay the sums specified in gold and silver coin. And it is beyond doubt that the holders of these contracts were and are as fully entitled to the protection of this constitutional provision as the holders of any other description of property.

But it may be said that the holders of no description of property are protected by it from legislation which incidentally only impairs its value. And it may be urged in illustration that the holders of stock in a turnpike, a bridge, or a manufacturing corporation, or an insurance company, or a bank, cannot invoke its protection against legislation which, by authorizing similar works or corporations, reduces its price in the market. But all this does not appear to meet the real difficulty. In the cases mentioned the injury is purely contingent and incidental. In the case we are considering it is direct and inevitable.

If in the cases mentioned the holders of the stock were required by law to convey it on demand to any one who should think fit to offer half its value for it, the analogy would be more obvious. No one probably could be found to contend that an act enforcing the acceptance of fifty or seventy-five acres of land in satisfaction of a contract to convey a hundred would not come within the prohibition against arbitrary privation of property.

We confess ourselves unable to perceive any solid distinction between such an act and an act compelling all citizens to accept, in satisfaction of all contracts for money, half or three-quarters or any other proportion less than the whole of the value actually due, according to their terms. It is difficult to conceive what act would take private property without process of law if such an act would not.

We are obliged to conclude that an act making mere promises to pay dollars a legal tender in payment of debts previously contracted, is not a means appropriate, plainly adapted, really calculated to carry into effect any express power vested in Congress; that such an act is inconsistent with the spirit of the Constitution; and that it is prohibited by the Constitution.

It is not surprising that amid the tumult of the late civil war, and under the influence of apprehensions for the safety of the Republic almost universal, different views, never before entertained by American statesman or jurists, were adopted by many. The time was not favorable to considerate reflection upon the constitutional limits of legislative or executive authority. If power was assumed from patriotic motives, the assumption found ready justification in patriotic hearts. Many who doubted yielded their doubts; many who did not doubt were silent. Some who were strongly averse to making government notes a legal tender felt themselves constrained to acquiesce in the views of the advocates of the measure. Not a few who then insisted upon its necessity, or acquiesced in that view, have, since the return of peace, and under the influence of the calmer time, reconsidered their conclusions, and now concur in those which we have just announced. These conclusions seem to us to be fully sanctioned by the letter and spirit of the Constitution.

We are obliged, therefore, to hold that the defendant in error was not bound to receive from the plaintiffs the currency tendered to him in payment of their note, made before the passage of the act of February 25th, 1862. It follows that the judgment of the Court of Appeals of Kentucky must be affirmed.

It is proper to say that Mr. Justice Grier, who was a member of the court when this cause was decided in conference, and when this opinion was directed to be read, stated his judgment to be that the legal tender clause, properly construed, has no application to debts contracted prior to its enactment; but that upon the construction given to the act by the other judges he concurred in the opinion that the clause, so far as it makes United States notes a legal tender for such debts, is not warranted by the Constitution.

Discussion Points

1. *Overruled.* The law established in *Hepburn* did not last long. Soon after, in 1871, the Supreme Court overruled *Hepburn* in the Legal Tender cases, *Knox v. Lee* and *Parker v. Davis*, 79 U.S. (12 Wall.) 457 (1871).

2. *CBDC:* Do you think the U.S. government will issue a central bank digital currency (CBDC) similar to how it did with paper money? Do you think the issue of CBDC's validity under the Coinage Clause or challenges of whether or not it can be classified as legal tender would be argued before the U.S. Supreme Court?

3. Regarding legal tender, what was the key issue analyzed by the U.S. Supreme Court in *Hepburn v. Griswold*?

4. On what legal basis did the plaintiff, Hepburn, challenge the constitutionality of the Legal Tender Act of 1862?

5. Explain the majority's legal analysis that led to the U.S. Supreme Court upholding the constitutionality of the Legal Tender Act in *Hepburn v. Griswold.*

6. What is the significance of the U.S. Supreme Court's decision to distinguish the power to issue legal tender and the power to make it a legal tender for both public and private debts?

7. Describe the legal reasoning provided by the majority's interpretation of the Necessary and Proper Clause as it relates to the constitutionality of the Legal Tender Act.

8. How did the U.S. Supreme Court's legal analysis and decision to uphold the constitutionality of legal tender in *Hepburn v. Griswold* affect U.S. legal tender laws in the long term?

In 1884, the Supreme Court followed the ongoing trend and upheld another tender law, enacted May 31, 1878. In *Juilliard v. Greenman*, it was held that Congress was allowed to reissue greenbacks into circulation during periods of peacetime, expanding Congress' power even further given that the previous cases had only applied to Congress' power during war-time and the time immediately following war-time.

Juilliard v. Greenman

110 U.S. 421

Supreme Court of the United States (March 3, 1884)

MR. JUSTICE GRAY delivered the opinion of the court.

The amount which the plaintiff seeks to recover, and which, if the tender pleaded is insufficient in law, he is entitled to recover, is $5,100. There can, therefore, be no doubt of the jurisdiction of this court to revise the judgment of the Circuit Court. Act of February 16th, 1875, ch. 77, § 3; 18 Stat. 315.

The notes of the United States, tendered in payment of the defendant's debt to the plaintiff, were originally issued under the acts of Congress of February 25th, 1862, ch. 33, July 11th, 1862, ch. 142, and March 3d, 1863, ch. 73, passed during the war of the rebellion, and enacting that these notes should "be lawful money and a legal tender in payment of all debts, public and private, within the United States," except for duties on imports and interest on the public debt. 12 Stat. 345, 532, 709.

The provisions of the earlier acts of Congress, so far as it is necessary, for the understanding of the recent statutes, to quote them, are re-enacted in the following provisions of the Revised Statutes:

"SECT. 3579. When any United States notes are returned to the Treasury, they may be reissued, from time to time, as the exigencies of the public interest may require.

"SECT. 3580. When any United States notes returned to the Treasury are so mutilated or otherwise injured as to be unfit for use, the Secretary of the Treasury is authorized to replace the same with others of the same character and amounts.

"SECT. 3581. Mutilated United States notes, when replaced according to law, and all other notes which by law are required to be taken up and not reissued, when taken up shall be destroyed in such manner and under such regulations as the Secretary of the Treasury may prescribe.

"SECT. 3582. The authority given to the Secretary of the Treasury to make any reduction of the currency, by retiring and cancelling United States notes, is suspended."

"SECT. 3588. United States notes shall be lawful money and a legal tender in payment of all debts, public and private, within the United States, except for duties on imports and interest on the public debt."

The act of January 14th, 1875, ch. 15, "to provide for the resumption of specie payments," enacted that on and after January 1st, 1879, "the Secretary of the Treasury shall redeem in coin the United States legal tender notes then outstanding, on their presentation for redemption at the office of the Assistant Treasurer of the

United States in the City of New York, in sums of not less than fifty dollars," and authorized him to use for that purpose any surplus revenues in the Treasury and the proceeds of the sales of certain bonds of the United States. 18 Stat. 296.

The act of May 31st, 1878, ch. 146, under which the notes in question were reissued, is entitled "An act to forbid the further retirement of United States legal tender notes," and enacts as follows:

> "From and after the passage of this act it shall not be lawful for the Secretary of the Treasury or other officer under him to cancel or retire any more of the United States legal tender notes. And when any of said notes may be redeemed or be received into the Treasury under any law from any source whatever and shall belong to the United States, they shall not be retired, cancelled or destroyed, but they shall be reissued and paid out again and kept in circulation: Provided, that nothing herein shall prohibit the cancellation and destruction of mutilated notes and the issue of other notes of like denomination in their stead, as now provided by law. All acts and parts of acts in conflict herewith are hereby repealed." 20 Stat. 87.

The manifest intention of this act is that the notes which it directs, after having been redeemed, to be reissued and kept in circulation, shall retain their original quality of being a legal tender.

The single question, therefore, to be considered, and upon the answer to which the judgment to be rendered between these parties depends, is whether notes of the United States, issued in time of war, under acts of Congress declaring them to be a legal tender in payment of private debts, and afterwards in time of peace redeemed and paid in gold coin at the Treasury, and then reissued under the act of 1878, can, under the Constitution of the United States, be a legal tender in payment of such debts.

Upon full consideration of the case, the court is unanimously of opinion that it cannot be distinguished in principle from the cases heretofore determined, reported under the names of the *Legal Tender Cases*, 12 Wall. 457; *Dooley v. Smith*, 13 Wall. 604; *Railroad Company v. Johnson*, 15 Wall. 195; and *Maryland v. Railroad Company*, 22 Wall. 105; and all the judges, except Mr. Justice Field, who adheres to the views expressed in his dissenting opinions in those cases, are of the opinion that they were rightly decided.

The elaborate printed briefs submitted by counsel in this case, and the opinions delivered in the Legal Tender Cases, and in the earlier case of *Hepburn v. Griswold*, 8 Wall. 603, which those cases overruled, forcibly present the arguments on either side of the question of the power of Congress to make the notes of the United States a legal tender in payment of private debts. Without undertaking to deal with all those arguments, the court has thought it fit that the grounds of its judgment in the case at bar should be fully stated.

No question of the scope and extent of the implied powers of Congress under the Constitution can be satisfactorily discussed without repeating much of the reasoning of Chief Justice Marshall in the great judgment in *McCulloch v. Maryland*, 4 Wheat. 316, by which the power of Congress to incorporate a bank was demonstrated and affirmed, notwithstanding the Constitution does not enumerate, among the powers granted, that of establishing a bank or creating a corporation.

The people of the United States by the Constitution established a national government, with sovereign powers, legislative, executive and judicial. "The government of the Union," said Chief Justice Marshall, "though limited in its powers, is supreme within its sphere of action;" "and its laws, when made in pursuance of the Constitution, form the supreme law of the land." "Among the enumerated powers of government, we find the great powers to lay and collect taxes; to borrow money; to regulate commerce; to declare and conduct a war; and to raise and support armies and navies. The sword and the purse, all the external relations, and no inconsiderable portion of the industry of the nation, are entrusted to its government." 4 Wheat. 405, 406, 407.

A constitution, establishing a frame of government, declaring fundamental principles, and creating a national sovereignty, and intended to endure for ages and to be adapted to the various crises of human affairs, is not to be interpreted with the strictness of a private contract. The Constitution of the United States, by apt words of designation or genera description, marks the outlines of the powers granted to the national legislature; but it does not undertake, with the precision and detail of a code of laws, to enumerate the subdivisions of those powers, or to specify all the means by which they may be carried into execution. Chief Justice Marshall, after dwelling upon this view, as required by the very nature of the Constitution, by the language in which it is framed, by the limitations upon the general powers of Congress introduced in the ninth section of the first article, and by the omission to use any restrictive term which might prevent its receiving a fair and just interpretation, added these emphatic words: "In considering the question, then, we must never forget that it is a constitution we are expounding." 4 Wheat. 407. See also page 415.

The breadth and comprehensiveness of the words of the Constitution are nowhere more strikingly exhibited than in regard to the powers over the subjects of revenue, finance, and currency, of which there is no other express grant than may be found in these few brief clauses:

> "The Congress shall have power
>
> "To lay and collect taxes, duties, imposts and excises, to pay the debts and provide for the common defence and general welfare of the United States; but all duties, imposts and excises shall be uniform throughout the United States;
>
> "To borrow money on the credit of the United States;
>
> "To regulate commerce with foreign nations, and among the several States, and with the Indian tribes;"

"To coin money, regulate the value thereof, and of foreign coin, and fix the standard of weights and measures."

The section which contains the grant of these and other principal legislative powers concludes by declaring that the Congress shall have power "To make all laws which shall be necessary and proper for carrying into execution the foregoing powers, and all other powers vested by this Constitution in the government of the United States, or in any department or officer thereof."

By the settled construction and the only reasonable interpretation of this clause, the words "necessary and proper" are not limited to such measures as are absolutely and indispensably necessary, without which the powers granted must fail of execution; but they include all appropriate means which are conducive or adapted to the end to be accomplished, and which in the judgment of Congress will most advantageously effect it.

That clause of the Constitution which declares that "the Congress shall have the power to lay and collect taxes, duties, imposts and excises, to pay the debts and provide for the common defence and general welfare of the United States," either embodies a grant of power to pay the debts of the United States, or presupposes and assumes that power as inherent in the United States as a sovereign government. But, in which ever aspect it be considered, neither this nor any other clause of the Constitution makes any mention of priority or preference of the United States as a creditor over other creditors of an individual debtor. Yet this court, in the early case of *United States v. Fisher*, 2 Cranch, 358, held that, under the power to pay the debts of the United States, Congress had the power to enact that debts due to the United States should have that priority of payment out of the estate of an insolvent debtor, which the law of England gave to debts due the Crown.

In delivering judgment in that case, Chief Justice Marshall expounded the clause giving Congress power to make all necessary and proper laws, as follows: "In construing this clause, it would be incorrect, and would produce endless difficulties, if the opinion should be maintained that no law was authorized which was not indispensably necessary to give effect to a specified power. Where various systems might be adopted for that purpose, it might be said with respect to each, that it was not necessary, because the end might be obtained by other means. Congress must possess the choice of means, and must be empowered to use any means which are in fact conducive to the exercise of a power granted by the Constitution. The government is to pay the debt of the Union, and must be authorized to use the means which appear to itself the most eligible to effect that object." 2 Cranch, 396.

In *McCulloch v. Maryland*, he more fully developed the same view, concluding thus: "We admit, as all must admit, that the powers of the government are limited, and that its limits are not to be transcended. But we think the sound construction of the Constitution must allow to the national legislature that discretion, with respect to the means by which the powers it confers are to be carried into execution, which will enable that body to perform the high duties assigned to it, in the manner most beneficial to the people. Let the end be legitimate, let it be within the scope of the Constitution, and all means which are appropriate, which are plainly adapted to that end, which are not prohibited, but consist with the letter and spirit of the Constitution, are constitutional." 4 Wheat. 421.

The rule of interpretation thus laid down has been constantly adhered to and acted on by this court, and was accepted as expressing the true test by all the judges who took part in the former discussions of the power of Congress to make the treasury notes of the United States a legal tender in payment of private debts.

The other judgments delivered by Chief Justice Marshall contain nothing adverse to the power of Congress to issue legal tender notes.

By the Articles of Confederation of 1777, the United States in Congress assembled were authorized "to borrow money or emit bills on the credit of the United States;" but it was declared that "each State retains its sovereignty, freedom and independence, and every power, jurisdiction and right which is not by this confederation expressly delegated to the United States in Congress assembled." Art. 2; art. 9, § 5; 1 Stat. 4, 7. Yet, upon the question whether, under those articles, Congress, by virtue of the power to emit bills on the credit of the United States, had the power to make bills so emitted a legal tender, Chief Justice Marshall spoke very guardedly, saying: "Congress emitted bills of credit to a large amount, and did not, perhaps could not, make them a legal tender. This power resided in the States" *Craig v. Missouri*, 4 Pet. 410, 435. But in the Constitution, as he had before observed in *McCulloch v. Maryland*, "there is no phrase which, like the Articles of Confederation, excludes incidental or implied powers; and which requires that everything granted shall be expressly and minutely described. Even the Tenth Amendment, which was framed for the purpose of quieting the excessive jealousies which had been excited, omits the word 'expressly,' and declares only that the powers 'not delegated to the United States, nor prohibited to the States, are reserved to the States or to the people;' thus leaving the question, whether the particular power which may become the subject of contest has been delegated to the one government or prohibited to the other, to depend on a fair construction of the whole instrument. The men who drew and adopted this amendment had experienced the embarrassments resulting from the insertion of this word in the Articles of Confederation, and probably omitted it to avoid those embarrassments." 4 Wheat. 406, 407.

The sentence sometimes quoted from his opinion in *Sturges v. Crowninshield* had exclusive relation to the restrictions imposed by the Constitution on the powers of the States, and especial reference to the effect of the clause prohibiting the States from passing laws impairing the obligation of contracts, as will clearly appear by quoting the whole paragraph: "Was this general prohibition intended to prevent paper money? We are not allowed to say so, because it is expressly provided that no State shall 'emit bills of credit;' neither could these words be intended to restrain the States from enabling debtors to discharge their debts by the tender of property of no real value to the creditor, because for that subject also particular provision is made. Nothing but gold and silver coin can be made a tender in payment of debts." 4 Wheat. 122, 204.

Such reports as have come down to us of the debates in the Convention that framed the Constitution afford no proof of any general concurrence of opinion upon the subject before us. The adoption of the motion to strike out the words "and emit bills" from the clause "to borrow money and emit bills on the credit of the United States" is quite inconclusive. The philippic delivered before the Assembly of Maryland by Mr. Martin, one of the delegates from that State, who voted against the motion, and who declined to sign the Constitution, can hardly be accepted as satisfactory evidence of the reasons or the motives of the majority of the Convention. See 1 Elliot's Debates, 345, 370, 376. Some of the members of the Convention, indeed, as appears by Mr. Madison's minutes of the debates, expressed the strongest opposition to paper money. And Mr. Madison has disclosed the grounds of his own action, by recording that "this vote in the affirmative by Virginia was occasioned by the acquiescence of Mr. Madison, who became satisfied that striking out the words would not disable the government from the use of public notes, so far as they could be safe and proper; and would only cut off the pretext for a paper currency, and particularly for making the bills a tender, either for public or private debts." But he has not explained why he thought that striking out the words "and emit bills" would leave the power to emit bills, and deny the power to make them a tender in payment of debts. And it cannot be known how many of the other delegates, by whose vote the motion was adopted, intended neither to proclaim nor to deny the power to emit paper money, and were influenced by the argument of Mr. Gorham, who "was for striking out, without inserting any prohibition," and who said: "If the words stand, they may suggest and lead to the emission." "The power, so far as it will be necessary or safe, will be involved in that of borrowing." 5 Elliot's Debates, 434, 435, and note. And after the first clause of the tenth section of the first article had been reported in the form in which it now stands, forbidding the States to make anything but gold or silver coin a tender in payment of debts, or to pass any law impairing the obligation of contracts, when Mr. Gerry, as reported by Mr. Madison, "entered into observations inculcating the importance of public faith, and the propriety of the restraint put on the States from impairing the obligation of contracts, alleging that Congress ought to be laid under the like prohibitions," and made a motion to that effect, he was not seconded. Ib. 546. As an illustration of the danger of giving too much weight, upon such a question, to the debates and the votes in the Convention, it may also be observed that propositions to authorize Congress to grant charters of incorporation for national objects were strongly opposed, especially as regarded banks, and defeated. Ib. 440, 543, 544. The power of Congress to emit bills of credit, as well as to incorporate national banks, is now clearly established by decisions to which we shall presently refer.

The words "to borrow money," as used in the Constitution, to designate a power vested in the national government, for the safety and welfare of the whole people, are not to receive that limited and restricted interpretation and meaning which they would have in a penal statute, or in an authority conferred, by law or by contract, upon trustees or agents for private purposes.

The power "to borrow money on the credit of the United States" is the power to raise money for the public use on a pledge of the public credit, and may be exercised to meet either present or anticipated expenses and liabilities of the government. It includes the power to issue, in return for the money borrowed, the obligations of the United States in any appropriate form, of stock, bonds, bills or notes; and in whatever form they are issued, being instruments of the national government, they are exempt from taxation by the governments of the several States. *Weston v. Charleston City Council*, 2 Pet. 449; *Banks v. Mayor*, 7 Wall. 16; *Bank v. Supervisors*, 7 Wall. 26. Congress has authority to issue these obligations in a form adapted to circulation from hand to hand in the ordinary transactions of commerce and business. In order to promote and facilitate such circulation, to adapt them to use as currency, and to make them more current in the market, it may provide for their redemption in coin or bonds, and may make them receivable in payment of debts to the government. So much is settled beyond doubt, and was asserted or distinctly admitted by the judges who dissented from the decision in the *Legal Tender Cases*, as well as by those who concurred in that decision. *Veazie Bank v. Fenno*, 8 Wall. 533, 548; *Hepburn v. Griswold*, 8 Wall. 616, 636; *Legal Tender Cases*, 12 Wall. 543, 544, 560, 582, 610, 613, 637.

It is equally well settled that Congress has the power to incorporate national banks, with the capacity, for their own profit as well as for the use of the government in its money transactions, of issuing bills which under ordinary circumstances pass from hand to hand as money at their nominal value, and which, when so current, the law has always recognized as a good tender in payment of money debts, unless specifically objected to at the time of the tender. *United States Bank v. Bank of Georgia*, 10 Wheat. 333, 347; *Ward v. Smith*, 7 Wall. 447, 451. The power of Congress to charter a bank was maintained in *McCulloch v. Maryland*, 4 Wheat. 316, and in *Osborn v. United States Bank*, 9 Wheat. 738, chiefly upon the ground that it was an appropriate means for carrying on the money transactions of the government. But Chief Justice Marshall said: "The currency which it circulates, by means of its trade with individuals, is believed to make it a more fit instrument for the purposes of government than it could otherwise be; and if this be true, the capacity to carry on this trade is a faculty indispensable to the character and objects of the institution." 9 Wheat. 864. And Mr. Justice Johnson, who concurred with the rest of the court in upholding the power to incorporate a bank, gave the further reason that it tended to give effect to "that power over the currency of the country, which the framers of the Constitution evidently intended to give to Congress alone." Ib. 873.

The constitutional authority of Congress to provide a currency for the whole country is now firmly established. In *Veazie Bank v. Fenno*, 8 Wall. 533, 548, Chief Justice Chase, in delivering the opinion of the court, said: "It cannot be doubted that under the Constitution the power to provide a circulation of coin is given to Congress. And it is settled by the uniform practice of the government, and by repeated decisions, that Congress may constitutionally authorize the emission of bills of credit." Congress, having undertaken to supply a national currency, consisting of coin, of treasury notes of the United States, and of the bills of national banks, is authorized to impose on all State banks, or national banks, or private bankers, paying out the notes of individuals or of State banks, a tax of ten per cent. upon the amount of such notes so paid out. *Veazie Bank v. Fenno*, above cited; *National Bank v. United States*, 101 U.S. 1. The reason for this conclusion was stated by Chief Justice Chase, and repeated by the present Chief Justice, in these words: "Having thus, in the exercise of undisputed constitutional powers, undertaken to provide a currency for the whole country, it cannot be questioned that Congress may, constitutionally, secure the benefit of it to the people by appropriate legislation. To this end, Congress has denied the quality of legal tender to foreign coins, and has provided by law against the imposition of counterfeit and base coin on the community. To the same end, Congress may restrain, by suitable enactments, the circulation as money of any notes not issued under its own authority. Without this power, indeed, its attempts to secure a sound and uniform currency for the country must be futile." 8 Wall. 549; 101 U.S. 6.

By the Constitution of the United States, the several States are prohibited from coining money, emitting bills of credit, or making anything but gold and silver coin a tender in payment of debts. But no intention can be inferred from this to deny to Congress either of these powers. Most of the powers granted to Congress are described in the eighth section of the first article; the limitations intended to be set to its powers, so as to exclude certain things which might otherwise be taken to be included in the general grant, are defined in the ninth section; the tenth section is addressed to the States only. This section prohibits the States from doing some things which the United States are expressly prohibited from doing, as well as from doing some things which the United States are expressly authorized to do, and from doing some things which are neither expressly granted nor expressly denied to the United States. Congress and the States equally are expressly prohibited from passing any bill of attainder or ex post facto law, or granting any title of nobility. The States are forbidden, while the President and Senate are expressly authorized, to make treaties. The States are forbidden, but Congress is expressly authorized, to coin money. The States are prohibited from emitting bills of credit; but Congress, which is neither expressly authorized nor expressly forbidden to do so, has, as we have already seen, been held to have the power of emitting bills of credit, and of making every provision for their circulation as currency, short of giving them the quality of legal tender for private debts—even by those who have denied its authority to give them this quality.

It appears to us to follow, as a logical and necessary consequence, that Congress has the power to issue the obligations of the United States in such form, and to impress upon them such qualities as currency for the purchase of merchandise and the payment of debts, as accord with the usage of sovereign governments. The power, as incident to the power of borrowing money and issuing bills or notes of the government for money borrowed, of impressing upon those bills or notes the quality of being a legal tender for the payment of private debts, was a power universally understood to belong to sovereignty, in Europe and America, at the time of the framing and adoption of the Constitution of the United States. The governments of Europe, acting through the monarch or the legislature, according to the distribution of powers under their respective constitutions, had and have as sovereign a power of issuing paper money as of stamping coin. This power has been distinctly recognized in an important modern case, ably argued and fully considered, in which the Emperor of Austria, as King of Hungary, obtained from the English Court of Chancery an injunction against the issue in England, without his license, of notes purporting to be public paper money of Hungary. *Austria v. Day*, 2 Giff. 628, and 3 D.F. & J. 217. The power of issuing bills of credit, and making them, at the discretion of the legislature, a tender in payment of private debts, had long been exercised in this country by the several Colonies and States; and during the Revolutionary War the States, upon the recommendation of the Congress of the Confederation, had made the bills issued by Congress a legal tender. See *Craig v. Missouri*, 4 Pet. 435, 453; *Briscoe v. Bank of Kentucky*, 11 Pet. 257, 313, 334–336; *Legal Tender Cases*, 12 Wall. 557, 558, 622; Phillips on American Paper Currency, passim. The exercise of this power not being prohibited to Congress by the Constitution, it is included in the power expressly granted to borrow money on the credit of the United States.

This position is fortified by the fact that Congress is vested with the exclusive exercise of the analogous power of coining money and regulating the value of domestic and foreign coin, and also with the paramount power of regulating foreign and interstate commerce. Under the power to borrow money on the credit of the United States, and to issue circulating notes for the money borrowed, its power to define the quality and force of those notes as currency is as broad as the like power over a metallic currency under the power to coin money and to regulate the value thereof. Under the two powers, taken together, Congress is authorized to establish a national currency, either in coin or in paper, and to make that currency lawful money for all purposes, as regards the national government or private individuals.

The power of making the notes of the United States a legal tender in payment of private debts, being included in the power to borrow money and to provide a national currency, is not defeated or restricted by the fact that its exercise may affect the value of private contracts. If, upon a just and fair interpretation of the whole Constitution, a particular power or authority appears to be vested in Congress, it is no constitutional objection to its existence, or to its exercise, that the property or the contracts of individuals may be incidentally affected. The decisions of this court, already cited, afford several examples of this.

Upon the issue of stock, bonds, bills or notes of the United States, the States are deprived of their power of taxation to the extent of the property invested by individuals in such obligations, and the burden of State taxation upon other private property is correspondingly increased. The ten per cent. tax, imposed by Congress on notes of State banks and of private bankers, not only lessens the value of such notes, but tends to drive them, and all State banks of issue, out of existence. The priority given to debts due to the United States over the private debts of an insolvent debtor diminishes the value of these debts, and the amount which their holders may receive out of the debtor's estate.

So, under the power to coin money and to regulate its value, Congress may (as it did with regard to gold by the act of June 28th, 1834, ch. 95, and with regard to silver by the act of February 28th, 1878, ch. 20) issue coins of the same denominations as those already current by law, but of less intrinsic value than those, by reason of containing a less weight of the precious metals, and thereby enable debtors to discharge their debts by the payment of coins of the less real value. A contract to pay a certain sum in money, without any stipulation as to the kind of money in which it shall be paid, may always be satisfied by payment of that sum in any currency which is lawful money at the place and time at which payment is to be made. 1 Hale P.C. 192–194; Bac. Ab. Tender, B. 2; Pothier, Contract of Sale, No. 416; Pardessus, Droit Commercial, Nos. 204, 205; *Searight v. Calbraith*, 4 Dall. 324. As observed by Mr. Justice Strong, in delivering the opinion of the court in the *Legal Tender Cases*, "Every contract for the payment of money, simply, is necessarily subject to the constitutional power of the government over the currency, whatever that power may be, and the obligation of the parties is, therefore, assumed with reference to that power." 12 Wall. 549.

Congress, as the legislature of a sovereign nation, being expressly empowered by the Constitution "to lay and collect taxes, to pay the debts and provide for the common defence and general welfare of the United States," and "to borrow money on the credit of the United States," and "to coin money and regulate the value thereof and of foreign coin;" and being clearly authorized, as incidental to the exercise of those great powers, to emit bills of credit, to charter national banks, and to provide a national currency for the whole people, in the form of coin, treasury notes, and national bank bills; and the power to make the notes of the government a legal tender in payment of private debts being one of the powers belonging to sovereignty in other civilized nations, and not expressly withheld from Congress by the Constitution; we are irresistibly impelled to the conclusion that the impressing upon the treasury notes of the United States the quality of being a legal tender in payment of private debts is an appropriate means, conducive and plainly adapted to the execution of the undoubted powers of Congress, consistent with the letter and spirit of the Constitution, and therefore, within the meaning of that instrument, "necessary and proper for carrying into execution the powers vested by this Constitution in the government of the United States."

Such being our conclusion in matter of law, the question whether at any particular time, in war on in peace, the exigency is such, by reason of unusual and pressing demands on the resources of the government, or of the inadequacy of the supply of gold and silver coin to furnish the currency needed for the uses of the government and of the people, that it is, as matter of fact, wise and expedient to resort to this means, is a political question, to be determined by Congress when the question of exigency arises, and not a judicial question, to be afterwards passed upon by the courts. To quote once more from the judgment in *McCulloch v. Maryland*: "Where the law is not prohibited, and is really calculated to effect any of the objects entrusted to the government, to undertake here to inquire into the degree of its necessity would be to pass the line which circumscribes the judicial department, and to tread on legislative ground." 4 Wheat. 423.

It follows that the act of May 31st, 1878, ch. 146, is constitutional and valid; and that the Circuit Court rightly held that the tender in treasury notes, reissued and kept in circulation under that act, was a tender of lawful money in payment of the defendant's debt to the plaintiff.

Judgment affirmed.

Discussion Points

1. *21st Century.* With the rise of cryptocurrencies in the modern era, are we likely to see a similar case before the U.S. Supreme Court concerning cryptocurrencies or a central bank digital currency (CBDC)? Why or why not?

2. *Cryptocurrency.* How does the legal status of paper money compare to the legal status of cryptocurrencies like Bitcoin? What are the key legal issues surrounding the use of cryptocurrencies as legal tender, and how do they differ from issues surrounding the use of paper money?

3. What was the main issue analyzed by the U.S. Supreme Court in *Juilliard v. Greenman* regarding legal tender?

4. Explain the factual allegations of the case that led to the legal dispute between the plaintiff, Juilliard, and the defendant, Greenman.

5. Describe the legal reasoning and rationale of Juilliard in challenging the constitutionality of the Legal Tender Act of 1862.

6. Discuss the Supreme Court's interpretation of the scope and limitations of Congress's power to issue and make legal tender in the context of the Legal Tender Act of 1862.

7. What was the historical significance of the Supreme Court's ruling in *Juilliard v. Greenman* as it relates to the understanding and interpretation of legal tender laws in the United States?

III. The Internet Age

A. The 1990s

The inception of the internet and widespread use of home computers allowed individuals to access information from across the world in a matter of seconds. With large amounts of data and numerous communications happening concurrently, a need arose for increased security to protect internet communications from outside interception. Essentially, there was now a need to gain and maintain privacy.

As the online community grew, so did subgroups within the online community. One such subgroup was Cypherpunks, a group focused on online digital privacy. Cypherpunks maintained a mailing list for its members, from which sprang discussions of keeping communications confidential. Members even discussed the possibilities of e-cash. It wasn't until 1993 that the "Cypherpunk manifesto" was born. According to Eric Hughes, the writer of the manifesto, the proposal is a great deal of privacy, but a distinction is drawn between privacy and secrecy. "Privacy is not secrecy. A private matter is something one doesn't want the whole world to know, but a secret matter is something one doesn't want anybody to know. Privacy is the power to selectively reveal oneself to the world."[15] According to the manifesto, privacy is ensured by revealing only the information that is necessary for whatever transaction or interaction you hold online. Privacy also allows for anonymity in transactions, so those involved can reveal themselves if they please, or not. To achieve this level of privacy, code had to be written and widely distributed, and encrypting information could allow it to reach a global scale.

At the first meeting of the Cypherpunks, it was evident that these untraceable communications protected against tampering could have a profound effect on governance, regulations, and levels of trust in society. With the advancement of private networks and communications, there was increasing government concern and interference. It was feared that "crypto anarchy would allow national secrets to be traded freely and will allow illicit and stolen materials to be traded."[16] Despite these concerns, the development of cryptography could help broaden access to previous seemingly inaccessible material.

---

15. Eric Hughes, *A Cypherpunk's Manifesto* (March 9, 1993), https://www.activism.net/cypherpunk/manifesto.html.

16. Andrew Fiala, "Anarchism", *Stanford Encyclopedia of Philosophy* (Edward N. Zalta, ed., Spring 2018), https://plato.stanford.edu/entries/anarchism.

Anarchy itself implies no monitoring body, no centralized power, and a form of "rule by all—with consensus and unanimity providing an optimistic goal."[17] The idea of rule by all essentially juxtaposes the traditional role of law which is mostly rule by a few over the majority. As such, crypto anarchists have been seen to have conflicts with the law. It appears that there is a delicate balance in the eyes of the law between radical individual liberties, and state concern/involvement in the execution of these liberties.

Despite being built on the foundation of privacy, the idea of cryptocurrencies and the supporting cryptographic software still faced government scrutiny. As these materials were freely available on a global scale due to the rise of the internet, anyone could have access to encrypted material. An executive order from the office of President Clinton deemed that having encrypted data overseas "could harm national security and foreign policy interests" and having such information available to foreign entities/individuals might lead to the revelation of "classified information that could harm the United States national security and foreign policy interests."[18] This was said to fall under the remit of the Export Administration Regulations.[19] Such export controls on encryption software were a way to control the spread of this phenomenon and the new accompanying technology; though this stemmed from the function of the technology as opposed to the information it held.

The Cypherpunk vision of freedom from government control and towards greater autonomy has been challenged over its course. In *Bernstein v. Department of Justice*,[20] an encrypted code was considered by the government to be a "munition" under the International Traffic in Arms Regulations. The government held that a license was necessary to make the code available outside of the country. The court decided that encryption and the defendant's source code was speech/expression protected under the First Amendment, which was violated by the Export Administration Regulations, and that government regulation preventing publication of the code was unconstitutional. The court did stress, however, that not all software would be considered expression. This decision in a way supports the Cypherpunk notion of individual liberties and freedom of communication through encryption. The fact that the government's actions were considered unconstitutional encouraged greater freedom of expression and demonstrates the importance of minimal government surveillance and control on private transactions. The whole idea of government control of encryption, and thus the ensuing cryptography, could be seen as a huge invasion of privacy, and the antithesis of free will, expression and speech.

---

17. *Id.*

18. Administration of Export Controls on Encryption Products, E.O. 13026 of Nov. 15, 1996, 61 Fed. Reg. 58767, Nov. 19, 1996.

19. 15 C.F.R. Part 730.

20. Bernstein v. Department of Justice, 176 F.3d 1132 (9th Cir. 1999).

Before *Bernstein*, the government had tried to target Philip R. Zimmerman—Cypherpunk and the developer of "Pretty Good Privacy" (PGP). This was an email encryption software package published in 1991 on the internet with international reach. Following this, Zimmerman was the subject of a three-year criminal investigation as the government argued that due to the international spread of the software, US export restrictions for cryptographic software were violated. In 1996, the case against him was dropped.

Despite these apparent targets on Cypherpunks by the government, this did not slow down their development or their growth. In 1997, Hashcash, an anti-spam mechanism developed by Dr. Adam Back, was the initial attempt at an anonymous tracing system. Many present-day cryptocurrencies use similar methods to those previously developed by crypto evangelists, and built on these ideas.

But increased developments saw increased ways in which the government tried to interfere. The US government made an attempt to introduce a key forfeiture system under its "Clipper Chip" (or MYK-78). This was to allow government agencies access to private communications and actions through overriding other people's codes. Cypherpunks, those in the communication and computer industry, and their allies were against this proposal. Cryptography allowed for privacy, but the government's issue was that this privacy was granted to criminals as well as the law abiding, and this chip was a way to circumvent that. The intention was to balance privacy and safety; it was directed to be used as a government standard. But this government system would have introduced a vulnerability to the system, as "any system that relies on trusted third parties is, by definition, weaker than one that does not." Although the Clipper was presented as voluntary, the government essentially flooded the market with the device that would allow it access to communications, and essentially blocked competitors. The Clipper was only the first step in the master plan to give Uncle Sam a key to everyone's cyberspace back door. This very idea threatens the foundations of the Cypherpunks' belief in communication free from government control. By 1995, the initiative failed—it was rejected as a form of "universal surveillance," its messages could be easily forged, and leaked FBI files from 1993 showed plans to ban all other encryption except Clipper.

Government agencies felt the need to regulate this space to prevent crime, as it was believed that through encryption, criminals could hide their activity, and damage couldn't be prevented. The need for regulation and prevention of crime posed a constant battle between the government and Cypherpunks, as the government wanted to protect public safety from potential harm, and Cypherpunks maintained principles of privacy and self-governance.

Since its introduction, cryptography has seen vast amounts of international uptake, and the rapid communication and transfer of information it offers is comparable to the early uptake and function of the internet. Early government internet interception could possibly have been prevented by earlier adoption of cryptography.

The aim of Cypherpunks is to have a global network where only the information which the originator wishes to share is available, and one which intruders and third parties cannot infiltrate. The end result of the conflict between the freedom and elimination of crypto could map out its function in the 21st Century.

B. The 2000s to Present Day

In 2008, bitcoin.org was registered as a domain name. Following that, in 2009, the entity/individual called Satoshi Nakamoto emailed the Cypherpunks addressing the shortcomings of previous crypto developments, in his paper "Bitcoin: A Peer-to-Peer Electronic Cash System."[21] This effectively launched the changes that led to the crypto space we are familiar with today. Nakamoto's Bitcoin emerged as the first cryptocurrency—a peer-to-peer electronic cash system with the aim of increased transactional security, and to arm against inflation.

By 2011, there was a surge in rival cryptocurrencies, and in 2012, cryptocurrency had reached pop culture and was the topic in season three episode 13 of The Good Wife, in the episode entitled "Bitcoin for Dummies." Since then, it has also been mentioned on The Simpsons (no surprise there), House of Cards, Blacklist, and even the TV drama Startup.

Cryptocurrency also has some relationship with the "dark net." The "dark net" or the "dark web," as it is commonly referred to, is a subset of the deep web, which is a network of secret websites existing on an encrypted network. The dark net is encrypted content not generally accessible on the regular internet, and is often used as a guise for criminal activity like exchanging illegal goods, providing anonymity for hackers, hitmen, money launderers, funding terrorism, drug dealing and the like.

With the anonymity the dark net offers, we see a link to cryptocurrencies. To disguise transactions in this arena, cryptocurrency is often used to protect the identities of the buyers and sellers in this space. It is also worth noting that while cryptocurrencies (especially bitcoin) are used to facilitate illegal online trading, it could be argued that they also help detect and trace it as a result of the blockchain. It's a double-edged sword. Nevertheless, for Cypherpunks, these negatives are outweighed by the benefits that spawn from eliminating a state monopoly over currency and state control over markets.

As a result of their centralized and peer to peer nature, Bitcoin and its counterpart cryptocurrencies are able to determine wealth ownership, without any law enforcement. So, the government is effectively out of the loop with the entirety of one's assets and is unable to trace an individual's wealth sources. These cryptocurrencies and their supporting networks and technology are able to evolve past being mere institutions, to being able to create and enforce property rights. As property rights are

---

21. Satoshi Nakamoto, *Bitcoin: A Peer-to-Peer Electronic Cash System*, https://bitcoin.org/bitcoin .pdf.

created in cryptocurrency, there also comes the necessity to protect those rights. How are your rights in your intangible assets enforced without a centralized body? If those rights are infringed, what is the course for reparations?

It appears that government agencies are still scrambling for ways to regulate cryptocurrencies, as there is currently no uniform approach to cryptocurrency regulation in the U.S. In March 2018, the U.S. Securities and Exchange Commission (SEC) categorized cryptocurrencies as securities and demonstrated an intent to apply securities laws to cryptocurrency wallets and exchanges. The Commodities Futures Trading Commission (CFTC), however, takes a more hands off approach, and instead describes bitcoin as a commodity, and allows cryptocurrency derivatives to trade publicly.

What does the future hold for cryptocurrencies? Will they become as commonly used as fiat currency (i.e., regular money)? Will they become so widely used that fiat is looked at the way we see bartering? If cryptocurrency gets to a stage where there is mass adoption, that also attracts increased observance and government scrutiny, which unfortunately undermines the essence of the private network this initially set out to be. Here, it helps to think about the relationships between privacy and government surveillance, between criminal activity and regulations to prevent that, between global decentralized networks and user protection, and much more.

IV. Cryptocurrencies

To better understand the growth of cryptocurrency and digital assets, it is helpful to have some background knowledge of the developments that led to its rise, and the state of the U.S. and world economy prior to its proposal. One major factor in the growth of digital assets is the U.S. financial crisis. By late 2007, housing prices had crashed, bankruptcy filings increased, and interest rates were cut by the Federal Reserve. It was apparent that the U.S. was headed towards financial turmoil.

A number of major centralized financial institutions felt the economic crunch in a big way. For example, Fannie Mae and Freddie Mac are federal mortgage insurers that were created to provide liquidity and stability in the mortgage market. These two federal bodies were at the core of the U.S. housing system. The government made efforts to assist Fannie Mae and Freddie Mac following a spike in mortgage defaults as a result of the housing crisis by passing the Housing and Economic Recovery Act in July 2008. This Act gave the Treasury unlimited investment authority in both firms. However, soon after, both Fannie Mae and Freddie Mac were effectively seized by the government under the Federal Housing Finance Agency (FHFA)—their new regulator. Other major financial institutions underwent major changes. Merrill Lynch ended up selling itself to Bank of America to combat the worsening financial crisis. Lehman Brothers, a key global investment bank and Wall Street staple, filed for bankruptcy after failure to score a buyer, representing what became known as the largest failure of an investment bank. Bear Sterns, one of the largest U.S. investment banks at the time, was forced into mergers, and there was a huge need for government bailouts to help the financial system. Trading froze and the stock market crashed, sending the U.S. economy into a recession.

On the heels of this, the insurers American International Group (AIG) received a $85 billion loan from the Federal Reserve. The loan came at the price of the government taking 79.9% of AIG's liquidity, allowing the government to replace management and exercise veto power over key decisions. The legality of the AIG bailout was later challenged; one of AIG's largest shareholders, former AIG CEO Maurice "Hank" Greenberg's Starr International Co., alleged that the government's actions were unlawful in relation to its acquisition of AIG equity and following actions leading to a stock split. Ultimately, Starr was held to lack standing to allege a Fifth Amendment taking without just compensation.

In an attempt to ease the worsening crisis, the Federal Reserve started making loans to institutions with bailouts for banks, General Motors, and homeowners. A government stimulus package in 2009 allowed for new cash flow in the economy through tax cuts and new spending.

In 2010, financial reform came when the Dodd-Frank Act in 2010 was passed. This Act aimed to increase transparency in the banking sector and reduce the level of risk banks took on. The Act also set up a consumer protection bureau to reduce predatory lending and set parameters so if banks failed, they did so in a predictable way which could be better handled by those involved. It could be said that the crisis existed because the government had previously failed to adequately supervise and control the financial system. Dodd-Frank was eventually rolled back in 2018 following the passing of the Economic Growth, Regulatory Relief, and Consumer Protection Act with changes having the biggest impact on smaller banks, exempting them from the previously imposed regulatory scrutiny.

It is unsurprising that the argument between centralized and decentralized control was gaining traction. The financial crisis demonstrated the far-reaching effects of centralized control and its associated pros and cons. It also showed how with centralized control, there were fewer freedoms with how people could conduct their affairs. This being considered, one could only imagine how well the Cypherpunk evangelists and followers would have reacted to the increased state control. Generally, with every crisis comes a state of innovation leading out of it.

In 2008, on the heels of the financial crisis, a gateway to the future of spending could be seen with Satoshi Nakamoto's white paper to the Cypherpunks. If it is said that the crisis was due to poor government management of the financial system, then it is unsurprising that the government is weary of decentralized private networks that allow the flow of cryptocurrency, and would want to impose more controls on that system—which would be the antithesis of its creation in the first place.

So, this is a constant tug of war. It was concluded that the crisis was partly due to the belief that markets could be self-correcting, and financial institutions could effectively police themselves. As the crash was linked to self-governance of financial institutions, seeing the rise of decentralized networks through blockchain and self-regulating cryptocurrency, it is unsurprising that there are increased concerns in this area. However, as the Inquiry Commission noted "to paraphrase Shakespeare, the fault lies not in the stars, but in us."[22] So, if the crash was created by human error, poor decisions and possibly greed, then a system that tracks every transaction with a clear indication of where the fault lies, might not be such a bad thing and may be easier to grasp.

The Bitcoin system, having no third-party intervention, acts as a parallel economy to the government regulated economy and the decentralized system championed by the Cypherpunks. At the time of this book's creation, the 12th anniversary of Satoshi Nakamoto's white paper had passed in October 2020. This white paper effectively changed the face of online transactions and launched the Bitcoin era that we know of today. Posting the white paper on the Cryptography mailing list made sense as there had been discussions around creating a virtual currency. This agenda was aligned with the Cypherpunk vision of increased privacy away from government control.

Federally and centrally controlled banks had failed the people by making bad bets that led up to the crisis. Skepticism in centrally controlled banking systems or fiat currency (government-issued currency not backed by a commodity, i.e., U.S. Dollar, Pound sterling), is why having assets of gold has been a feature in our economy and in people's investments as a source of value. Similarly, bitcoin acts as a sort of digital gold. The use of fiat currency and its value is solely backed by faith in the government that they will have and maintain value. The aftermath of the financial crisis saw the value of fiat plummet, and as such, the faith in government-controlled institutions to protect assets, fell along with it.

It could be said that the trust regulators had in banks and other financial institutions to properly manage their affairs with little oversight eventually crippled the system. The blockchain system Nakamoto proposed, eliminated the need for trust by way of the transport systems in place via cryptographic proof. Having proof of the transaction history eliminated the blind trust in banks that previously existed. So, transactions could take place peer-to-peer without the need for a trusted third party. Nakamoto's Bitcoin proposed a system that eliminated the risk of double spending, provided the necessary anonymity and protection of personal data, and prevented unauthorized transaction reversals.

---

22. Financial Crisis Inquiry Commission, *The Financial Crisis Inquiry Report: Final Report of the National Commission on the Causes of the Financial and Economic Crisis in the United States* xvii (February 25, 2011), https://www.govinfo.gov/content/pkg/GPO-FCIC/pdf/GPO-FCIC.pdf.

In the simplest of terms, Bitcoin is an online currency. It may be helpful to note that *Bitcoin* is the concept created by Satoshi Nakamoto, whilst *bitcoin* is the unit of currency. Bitcoin is stored on the blockchain which is an open online system that allows users to track the origins of every transaction. Think of the blockchain as a virtual abacus maze: numerous transactions at the same time but you can easily follow or trace the route a transaction takes from the very beginning till the end, so everything is accounted for and there is no third-party intervention needed. Although blockchain is usually mentioned in terms of bitcoin and cryptocurrency, it can be used to store any type of digital information, from certificates and medical records to collector's cards. Blockchain operates as the technology behind bitcoin and is what helps make it work.

Looking at the way in which the Bitcoin system operates, it is unsurprising that it was proposed after the financial crisis. As opposed to a managing central organization, Bitcoin is run by a protocol. Unlike a managing organization, a protocol lacks an easily workable mechanism to change prices, offerings, and rules. It is this stability that was lacking in the centralized financial systems that contributed to the crash. Despite the volatility of bitcoin pricing, the system it runs on, and the processes that make it work, are quite stable and reliable. The limit of bitcoins to be created is capped at 21 million, making a definite supply of the currency. This cap eradicates the risk posed by current fiat currency as the supply of it is known, avoiding any surprises and allowing the certainty that fiat lacks. Limited supply effectively acts to combat inflation which is apparent in fiat. For instance, Zimbabwe saw an average hyperinflation rate of around 69% between 2009 and 2020.

Blockchain are digital blocks that store information. Blockchain was developed as the means through which bitcoin could be facilitated. They were originally created as a timestamp mechanism for digital documents. When you own bitcoin, you essentially have a key or code to prove you own that material—this is what is referred to as the private key, and is half of a digital signature showing proof of ownership. The blockchain is available to anyone who wants to use it—it is an accessible open system. Each block consists of transaction details, previous transaction details and history, a unique hash, a one-of-a-kind code or set of information which identifies that block with all its corresponding history.

There is also a public key linked to your bitcoin and stored in the blockchain. To buy things with bitcoin, you broadcast a request which alerts miners. Blockchain isn't disruptive technology, it is a foundational technology: it has the potential to create new foundations for economic and social systems.

A hash is calculated once a block is created. Hashes help identify changes to the blocks. If a hash changes even in the slightest, it is no longer the same block. The hash and its corresponding data are unique to the block. A block also has the hash of the previous block which creates a string of block information, or a block-chain. This technique and the special characters in the hash, combined with the traceability of the system, helps add surety to the security of transactions and their origins. If one hash is tampered with, the following block's information would not link it to the doctored hash—this shows a break and quickly identifies where the fault is in the system. A change in hash from a block could invalidate the following blocks, as the information they stored from the previous hash wouldn't match that of the tampered hash. The permanent records of these transactions can be verified, stored and shared. If blocks in the chain are linked to one's payment, that acts as verification of the origin of that payment. It is on the blockchain that bitcoin transactions are recorded. The blockchain is maintained openly by computers worldwide. To prevent a situation where a hash is altered, along with the hashes of the following blocks, there exists "proof-of-work."

The electronic cash system proposed in the white paper would allow the direct transfer of payments without a formal financial institution. Nakamoto noted that at the time of their proposal, there was currently no existing system which facilitated payments without a trusted third party. Despite the openness of the blockchain, it still allows for privacy via anonymous public keys. This allows you to see information is being sent, but without revealing said information, and without identifying the parties to the transaction. A sender on the bitcoin blockchain has a public and private key. Ownership of a bitcoin or other coin is transferred from a public address to another. An owner then uses a private key to decrypt the information stored on the coin. Anyone can have access to a public key, but only the user can see the exact information transferred, and this is done through using the private key. The private key is like a secret code that links to and unlocks the Bitcoin address. It helps protect against theft. Funds are deposited in a public address, like a virtual bank account, and the private key is what unlocks the funds. The public key is made from the private key.

The blockchain system that bitcoin flows on is made possible through cryptography. Cryptography is a form of computer security—essentially a secret code. It is through a cryptographic signature that third parties can verify the authorization of transactions from the sender. The public and private keys used to decode transactions on the blockchain, and cryptographic validation of transactions are fundamental cryptographic technologies.

Bitcoin public keys can only be accessed with the owner's private key, and the public key is on the computer's hard drive in "wallets"—a software program that holds and trades bitcoin. It is through a wallet that bitcoin can be sent and received. A bitcoin wallet could also be referred to as a digital wallet. Unlike a physical wallet, a bitcoin wallet stores information for digital transactions like private keys. Wallets can be hosted or un-hosted. A hosted wallet is a centralized modem to store bitcoin. It is a third-party provider which a user entrusts with their virtual assets—much like a bank. An un-hosted wallet, or decentralized wallet, is owned and controlled by only you with a private key, and allows seamless transactions without the need for a third party. An un-hosted wallet eliminates the possibility of funds being seized by third parties.

There is no standalone third party in a decentralized ledger. Instead, a group of online peers, called nodes, reach a uniform agreement on each individual transaction. When a transaction occurs using bitcoin, computers on the bitcoin network will check to ensure the transaction is accurate and complete. If a transaction is deemed accurate and complete, a consensus is reached and the transaction is approved, and added to the block-chain. If it is not approved, the transaction will be rejected. Bitcoin operates on a decentralized ledger, so there is no single entity that controls it, unlike fiat currency and banks. It is a transparent peer-to-peer process available to anybody. Being decentralized, its distribution is neither controlled nor regulated by a third party. The lack of oversight or third-party governance could give rise to concerns over user protection. The lack of a central controlling body allows bitcoin to be an apolitical, borderless global unit of currency. The volatility of bitcoin is also illustrative of its decentralized nature. Unlike fiat currency, there is no central bank for Bitcoin to intervene and stabilize prices, as this would counter its fixed supply nature.

Mining is how coins are introduced to the blockchain. Bitcoin miners solve mathematical problems using special software in return for bitcoins. This system issues the currency and creates an incentive for mining as miners get to keep the coins they crack. Miners approve bitcoin transactions so the more miners there are, the more secure the bitcoin network is. There needs to be a large capacity for mining to take place. With pooled mining, the work of many miners is brought together towards a common goal. This helps find solutions to the mathematical problems faster than individuals would, then each in the pool would be rewarded with bitcoin for their contribution. The new bitcoin is a reward for the miners solving the problem and adding the new block to the blockchain. Miners are essentially the verification process in the blockchain network. They track and verify transactions, and are rewarded in bitcoin. Having numerous miners act as checks for transactions in the system and helps ward off centralized power in the workings of the Bitcoin ecosystem. Mining is open to anyone who has enough internet connection, computer software and capacity to mine (as this is incredibly power consuming). It is miners that provide and maintain the bitcoin payment system infrastructure. Though miners make the bitcoin system work, there is no need for trust in individual miners as it is a collective effort and incentivised by the payments the miners receive. The system as a whole remains reliable and trustworthy since it is computer protocol, and not individuals or organized bodies that govern the system and lay out the rules for miners and users. Miners are the "peers" in the peer-to-peer system.

Miners organize posted transactions into blocks. Miners themselves are not trusted—they are there for their own gain, the "coin reward," and are incentivised to make profits by expanding their mining capabilities. They are also free to start and stop mining at their convenience. The system they mine on however, is secure and trusted, as only legal and authenticated transactions are processed. The mining system also works to combat inflation that was seen around the time of the financial crisis. Since the code governing miners makes it so the reward they get is halved every four years, this helps control inflation. With mining being available to anybody in any region, the system is basically set up in a way that makes it more difficult to regulate miners. What organized body in which location would be suitable to regulate miners worldwide?

Bitcoin transaction logs are maintained on a distributed network that is available to anyone. When a transaction occurs, the transaction information of both the sender and receiver is recorded and added to the digital ledger, a.k.a., the blockchain. Each transaction is verified and authenticated by numerous points in the network to ensure every computer on the blockchain network is using identical copies of the blockchain. This helps ensure the correct information is sent, and confirms proof of ownership and transaction history.

Bitcoin differs from other financial systems in that its governing rules were made by engineers, not lawyers and regulators. The non-legal influence in its workings could also contribute to why it is difficult to regulate. Its borderless nature also contributes to that challenge. Despite the uniformity in the operations of the Bitcoin ecosystem, the regulatory approach has been quite varied. For instance, throughout the Russia-Ukraine War, cryptocurrency has been used to run both countries' financial systems. The Russian Ministry of Finance amended its digital currency bill on April 15, 2022, to include comprehensive rules on cryptocurrency trading and mining. Russia amended the bill to apply regulations in its digital asset mining industry. In Nigeria, bitcoin is legal, but the Nigerian Securities and Exchange Commission warned of investments in cryptocurrency being risky. Whereas in Cyprus, a bitcoin-friendly jurisdiction, bitcoin is yet to be declared a legal tender, and there is no expansive legal framework guiding its operations there. In fact, bitcoin began to be widely embraced in Cyprus following its own financial crisis.

The introduction of Bitcoin on the heels of the financial crisis is not by chance. Bitcoin aimed to create an environment where the creation and market price of currency was outside the reach and control of financial institutions. The peer-to-peer function was to create trust in the workings of the system without the need of a centralized governing body. Essentially, it was theorized that Bitcoin could replace fiat currency and end financial crises, due to high transaction costs and the necessity of placing one's trust in an intermediary. With Bitcoin being borderless, it is worth considering whether regulations on imports or information transfer would be suited to govern its workings. Gray areas such as this make it harder to regulate this system.

A. Satoshi Nakamoto and BTC

Bitcoin: A Peer-to-Peer Electronic Cash System

Satoshi Nakamoto satoshin@gmx.com

https://bitcoin.org/bitcoin.pdf

[Bracketed references appear at end of article]

Abstract. A purely peer-to-peer version of electronic cash would allow online payments to be sent directly from one party to another without going through a financial institution. Digital signatures provide part of the solution, but the main benefits are lost if a trusted third party is still required to prevent double-spending. We propose a solution to the double-spending problem using a peer-to-peer network. The network timestamps transactions by hashing them into an ongoing chain of hash-based proof-of-work, forming a record that cannot be changed without redoing the proof-of-work. The longest chain not only serves as proof of the sequence of events witnessed, but proof that it came from the largest pool of CPU power. As long as a majority of CPU power is controlled by nodes that are not cooperating to attack the network, they'll generate the longest chain and outpace attackers. The network itself requires minimal structure. Messages are broadcast on a best effort basis, and nodes can leave and rejoin the network at will, accepting the longest proof-of-work chain as proof of what happened while they were gone.

1. Introduction

Commerce on the Internet has come to rely almost exclusively on financial institutions serving as trusted third parties to process electronic payments. While the system works well enough for most transactions, it still suffers from the inherent weaknesses of the trust based model. Completely non-reversible transactions are not really possible, since financial institutions cannot avoid mediating disputes. The cost of mediation increases transaction costs, limiting the minimum practical transaction size and cutting off the possibility for small casual transactions, and there is a broader cost in the loss of ability to make non-reversible payments for non- reversible services. With the possibility of reversal, the need for trust spreads. Merchants must be wary of their customers, hassling them for more information than they would otherwise need. A certain percentage of fraud is accepted as unavoidable. These costs and payment uncertainties can be avoided in person by using physical currency, but no mechanism exists to make payments over a communications channel without a trusted party.

What is needed is an electronic payment system based on cryptographic proof instead of trust, allowing any two willing parties to transact directly with each other without the need for a trusted third party. Transactions that are computationally impractical to reverse would protect sellers from fraud, and routine escrow mechanisms could easily be implemented to protect buyers. In this paper, we propose a solution to the double-spending problem using a peer-to-peer distributed time-stamp server to generate computational proof of the chronological order of transactions. The system is secure as long as honest nodes collectively control more CPU power than any cooperating group of attacker nodes.

2. Transactions

We define an electronic coin as a chain of digital signatures. Each owner transfers the coin to the next by digitally signing a hash of the previous transaction and the public key of the next owner and adding these to the end of the coin. A payee can verify the signatures to verify the chain of ownership.

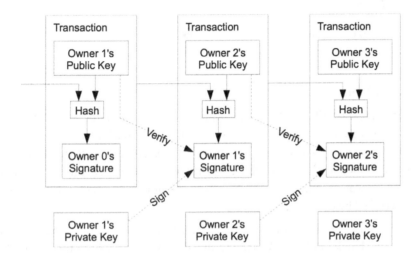

The problem of course is the payee can't verify that one of the owners did not double-spend the coin. A common solution is to introduce a trusted central authority, or mint, that checks every transaction for double spending. After each transaction, the coin must be returned to the mint to issue a new coin, and only coins issued directly from the mint are trusted not to be double-spent. The problem with this solution is that the fate of the entire money system depends on the company running the mint, with every transaction having to go through them, just like a bank.

We need a way for the payee to know that the previous owners did not sign any earlier transactions. For our purposes, the earliest transaction is the one that counts, so we don't care about later attempts to double-spend. The only way to confirm the absence of a transaction is to be aware of all transactions. In the mint based model, the mint was aware of all transactions and decided which arrived first. To accomplish this without a trusted party, transactions must be publicly announced [1], and we need a system for participants to agree on a single history of the order in which they were received. The payee needs proof that at the time of each transaction, the majority of nodes agreed it was the first received.

3. Timestamp Server

The solution we propose begins with a timestamp server. A timestamp server works by taking a hash of a block of items to be timestamped and widely publishing the hash, such as in a newspaper or Usenet post [2–5]. The timestamp proves that the data must have existed at the time, obviously, in order to get into the hash. Each timestamp includes the previous timestamp in its hash, forming a chain, with each additional timestamp reinforcing the ones before it.

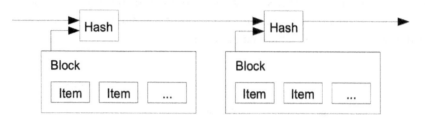

4. Proof-of-Work

To implement a distributed timestamp server on a peer-to-peer basis, we will need to use a proof- of-work system similar to Adam Back's Hashcash [6], rather than newspaper or Usenet posts. The proof-of-work involves scanning for a value that when hashed, such as with SHA-256, the hash begins with a number of zero bits. The average work required is exponential in the number of zero bits required and can be verified by executing a single hash.

For our timestamp network, we implement the proof-of-work by incrementing a nonce in the block until a value is found that gives the block's hash the required zero bits. Once the CPU effort has been expended to make it satisfy the proof-of-work, the block cannot be changed without redoing the work. As later blocks are chained after it, the work to change the block would include redoing all the blocks after it.

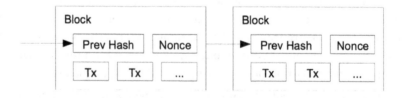

The proof-of-work also solves the problem of determining representation in majority decision making. If the majority were based on one-IP-address-one-vote, it could be subverted by anyone able to allocate many IPs. Proof-of-work is essentially one-CPU-one-vote. The majority decision is represented by the longest chain, which has the greatest proof-of-work effort invested in it. If a majority of CPU power is controlled by honest nodes, the honest chain will grow the fastest and outpace any competing chains. To modify a past block, an attacker would have to redo the proof-of-work of the block and all blocks after it and then catch up with and surpass the work of the honest nodes. We will show later that the probability of a slower attacker catching up diminishes exponentially as subsequent blocks are added.

To compensate for increasing hardware speed and varying interest in running nodes over time, the proof-of-work difficulty is determined by a moving average targeting an average number of blocks per hour. If they're generated too fast, the difficulty increases.

5. Network

The steps to run the network are as follows:

1. New transactions are broadcast to all nodes.
2. Each node collects new transactions into a block.
3. Each node works on finding a difficult proof-of-work for its block.
4. When a node finds a proof-of-work, it broadcasts the block to all nodes.
5. Nodes accept the block only if all transactions in it are valid and not already spent.
6. Nodes express their acceptance of the block by working on creating the next block in the chain, using the hash of the accepted block as the previous hash.

Nodes always consider the longest chain to be the correct one and will keep working on extending it. If two nodes broadcast different versions of the next block simultaneously, some nodes may receive one or the other first. In that case, they work on the first one they received, but save the other branch in case it becomes longer. The tie will be broken when the next proof- of-work is found and one branch becomes longer; the nodes that were working on the other branch will then switch to the longer one.

New transaction broadcasts do not necessarily need to reach all nodes. As long as they reach many nodes, they will get into a block before long. Block broadcasts are also tolerant of dropped messages. If a node does not receive a block, it will request it when it receives the next block and realizes it missed one.

6. Incentive

By convention, the first transaction in a block is a special transaction that starts a new coin owned by the creator of the block. This adds an incentive for nodes to support the network, and provides a way to initially distribute coins into circulation, since there is no central authority to issue them. The steady addition of a constant of amount of new coins is analogous to gold miners expending resources to add gold to circulation. In our case, it is CPU time and electricity that is expended.

The incentive can also be funded with transaction fees. If the output value of a transaction is less than its input value, the difference is a transaction fee that is added to the incentive value of the block containing the transaction. Once a predetermined number of coins have entered circulation, the incentive can transition entirely to transaction fees and be completely inflation free.

The incentive may help encourage nodes to stay honest. If a greedy attacker is able to assemble more CPU power than all the honest nodes, he would have to choose between using it to defraud people by stealing back his payments, or using it to generate new coins. He ought to find it more profitable to play by the rules, such rules that favour him with more new coins than everyone else combined, than to undermine the system and the validity of his own wealth.

7. Reclaiming Disk Space

Once the latest transaction in a coin is buried under enough blocks, the spent transactions before it can be discarded to save disk space. To facilitate this without breaking the block's hash, transactions are hashed in a Merkle Tree [7][2][5], with only the root included in the block's hash. Old blocks can then be compacted by stubbing off branches of the tree. The interior hashes do not need to be stored.

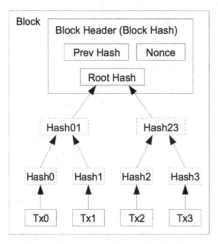 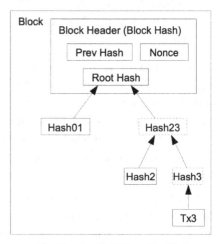

Transactions Hashed in a Merkle Tree   After Pruning Tx0-2 from the Block

A block header with no transactions would be about 80 bytes. If we suppose blocks are generated every 10 minutes, 80 bytes * 6 * 24 * 365 = 4.2MB per year. With computer systems typically selling with 2GB of RAM as of 2008, and Moore's Law predicting current growth of 1.2GB per year, storage should not be a problem even if the block headers must be kept in memory.

8. Simplified Payment Verification

It is possible to verify payments without running a full network node. A user only needs to keep a copy of the block headers of the longest proof-of-work chain, which he can get by querying network nodes until he's convinced he has the longest chain, and obtain the Merkle branch linking the transaction to the block it's timestamped in. He can't check the transaction for himself, but by linking it to a place in the chain, he can see that a network node has accepted it, and blocks added after it further confirm the network has accepted it.

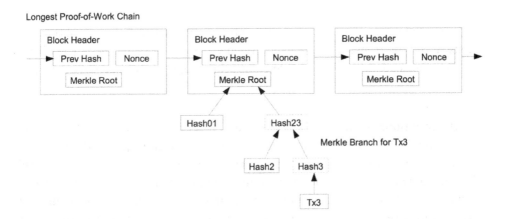

As such, the verification is reliable as long as honest nodes control the network, but is more vulnerable if the network is overpowered by an attacker. While network nodes can verify transactions for themselves, the simplified method can be fooled by an attacker's fabricated transactions for as long as the attacker can continue to overpower the network. One strategy to protect against this would be to accept alerts from network nodes when they detect an invalid block, prompting the user's software to download the full block and alerted transactions to confirm the inconsistency. Businesses that receive frequent payments will probably still want to run their own nodes for more independent security and quicker verification.

9. Combining and Splitting Value

Although it would be possible to handle coins individually, it would be unwieldy to make a separate transaction for every cent in a transfer. To allow value to be split and combined, transactions contain multiple inputs and outputs. Normally there will be either a single input from a larger previous transaction or multiple inputs combining smaller amounts, and at most two outputs: one for the payment, and one returning the change, if any, back to the sender.

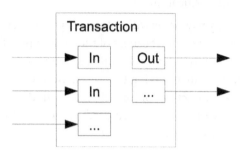

It should be noted that fan-out, where a transaction depends on several transactions, and those transactions depend on many more, is not a problem here. There is never the need to extract a complete standalone copy of a transaction's history.

10. Privacy

The traditional banking model achieves a level of privacy by limiting access to information to the parties involved and the trusted third party. The necessity to announce all transactions publicly precludes this method, but privacy can still be maintained by breaking the flow of information in another place: by keeping public keys anonymous. The public can see that someone is sending an amount to someone else, but without information linking the transaction to anyone. This is similar to the level of information released by stock exchanges, where the time and size of individual trades, the "tape", is made public, but without telling who the parties were.

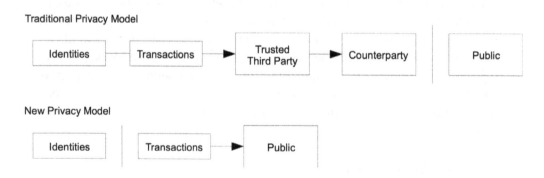

As an additional firewall, a new key pair should be used for each transaction to keep them from being linked to a common owner. Some linking is still unavoidable with multi-input transactions, which necessarily reveal that their inputs were owned by the same owner. The risk is that if the owner of a key is revealed, linking could reveal other transactions that belonged to the same owner.

11. Calculations

We consider the scenario of an attacker trying to generate an alternate chain faster than the honest chain. Even if this is accomplished, it does not throw the system open to arbitrary changes, such as creating value out of thin air or taking money that never belonged to the attacker. Nodes are not going to accept an invalid transaction as payment, and honest nodes will never accept a block containing them. An attacker can only try to change one of his own transactions to take back money he recently spent.

The race between the honest chain and an attacker chain can be characterized as a Binomial Random Walk. The success event is the honest chain being extended by one block, increasing its lead by +1, and the failure event is the attacker's chain being extended by one block, reducing the gap by -1.

The probability of an attacker catching up from a given deficit is analogous to a Gambler's Ruin problem. Suppose a gambler with unlimited credit starts at a deficit and plays potentially an infinite number of trials to try to reach breakeven. We can calculate the probability he ever reaches breakeven, or that an attacker ever catches up with the honest chain, as follows [8]:

p = probability an honest node finds the next block

q = probability the attacker finds the next block

qz = probability the attacker will ever catch up from z blocks behind

$$q_z = \begin{cases} 1 & \text{if } p \leq q \\ (q/p)^z & \text{if } p > q \end{cases}$$

Given our assumption that $p > q$, the probability drops exponentially as the number of blocks the attacker has to catch up with increases. With the odds against him, if he doesn't make a lucky lunge forward early on, his chances become vanishingly small as he falls further behind.

We now consider how long the recipient of a new transaction needs to wait before being sufficiently certain the sender can't change the transaction. We assume the sender is an attacker who wants to make the recipient believe he paid him for a while, then switch it to pay back to himself after some time has passed. The receiver will be alerted when that happens, but the sender hopes it will be too late.

The receiver generates a new key pair and gives the public key to the sender shortly before signing. This prevents the sender from preparing a chain of blocks ahead of time by working on it continuously until he is lucky enough to get far enough ahead, then executing the transaction at that moment. Once the transaction is sent, the dishonest sender starts working in secret on a parallel chain containing an alternate version of his transaction.

The recipient waits until the transaction has been added to a block and z blocks have been linked after it. He doesn't know the exact amount of progress the attacker has made, but assuming the honest blocks took the average expected time per block, the attacker's potential progress will be a Poisson distribution with expected value:

$$\lambda = z \frac{q}{p}$$

To get the probability the attacker could still catch up now, we multiply the Poisson density for each amount of progress he could have made by the probability he could catch up from that point:

$$\sum_{k=0}^{\infty} \frac{\lambda^k e^{-\lambda}}{k!} \cdot \begin{cases} (q/p)^{(z-k)} & \text{if } k \le z \\ 1 & \text{if } k > z \end{cases}$$

Rearranging to avoid summing the infinite tail of the distribution...

$$1 - \sum_{k=0}^{z} \frac{\lambda^k e^{-\lambda}}{k!} \left(1 - (q/p)^{(z-k)}\right)$$

Converting to C code...

```c
#include <math.h>
double AttackerSuccessProbability(double q, int z)
{
        double p = 1.0 - q;
        double lambda = z * (q / p);
        double sum = 1.0;
        int i, k;
        for (k = 0; k <= z; k++)
        {
            double poisson = exp(-lambda);
            for (i = 1; i <= k; i++)
                poisson *= lambda / i;
            sum -= poisson * (1 - pow(q / p, z - k));
        }
return sum;
        }
```

Running some results, we can see the probability drop off exponentially with z.

```
q=0.1
z=0       P=1.0000000
z=1       P=0.2045873
z=2       P=0.0509779
z=3       P=0.0131722
z=4       P=0.0034552
z=5       P=0.0009137
z=6       P=0.0002428
z=7       P=0.0000647
z=8       P=0.0000173
z=9       P=0.0000046
z=10      P=0.0000012
q=0.3
z=0       P=1.0000000
z=5       P=0.1773523
z=10      P=0.0416605
z=15      P=0.0101008
z=20      P=0.0024804
z=25      P=0.0006132
z=30      P=0.0001522
z=35      P=0.0000379
z=40      P=0.0000095
z=45      P=0.0000024
z=50      P=0.0000006
```

Solving for P less than 0.1%…

```
P < 0.001
q=0.10    z=5
q=0.15    z=8
q=0.20    z=11
q=0.25    z=15
q=0.30    z=24
q=0.35    z=41
q=0.40    z=89
q=0.45    z=340
```

12. Conclusion

We have proposed a system for electronic transactions without relying on trust. We started with the usual framework of coins made from digital signatures, which provides strong control of ownership, but is incomplete without a way to prevent double-spending. To solve this, we proposed a peer-to-peer network using proof-of-work to record a public history of transactions that quickly becomes computationally impractical for an attacker to change if honest nodes control a majority of CPU power. The network is robust in its unstructured simplicity. Nodes work all at once with little coordination. They do not need to be identified, since messages are not routed to any particular place and only need to be delivered on a best effort basis. Nodes can leave and rejoin the network at will, accepting the proof-of-work chain as proof of what happened while they were gone. They vote with their CPU power, expressing their acceptance of valid blocks by working on extending them and rejecting invalid blocks by refusing to work on them. Any needed rules and incentives can be enforced with this consensus mechanism.

References

[1] W. Dai, "b-money," http://www.weidai.com/bmoney.txt, 1998.

[2] H. Massias, X.S. Avila, and J.-J. Quisquater, "Design of a secure timestamping service with minimal trust requirements," In *20th Symposium on Information Theory in the Benelux*, May 1999.

[3] S. Haber, W.S. Stornetta, "How to time-stamp a digital document," In *Journal of Cryptology*, vol 3, no 2, pages 99–111, 1991.

[4] D. Bayer, S. Haber, W.S. Stornetta, "Improving the efficiency and reliability of digital time-stamping," In *Sequences II: Methods in Communication, Security and Computer Science*, pages 329–334, 1993.

[5] S. Haber, W.S. Stornetta, "Secure names for bit-strings," In *Proceedings of the 4th ACM Conference on Computer and Communications Security*, pages 28–35, April 1997.

[6] A. Back, "Hashcash—a denial of service counter-measure," http://www.hashcash.org/papers/hashcash.pdf, 2002.

[7] R.C. Merkle, "Protocols for public key cryptosystems," In *Proc. 1980 Symposium on Security and Privacy*, IEEE Computer Society, pages 122–133, April 1980.

[8] W. Feller, "An introduction to probability theory and its applications," 1957.

Discussion Points

1. *Legal Tender.* Other than the *possibility* of the U.S. government adopting a central bank digital currency (CBDC), will other cryptocurrencies ever qualify as legal tender? Why or why not? Will legal tender be redefined be-

cause of the Bitcoin or other virtual currencies adoption in the mainstream? What are the key differences between legal tender, Bitcoin, and other virtual currencies?

2. *Peer-to-Peer Transactions:* Satoshi Nakamoto argues for decentralized peer-to-peer transactions. Do you agree that this would help to improve our financial infrastructure? Does the rise in interest in cryptocurrency used on decentralized networks pose a threat to traditional centralized financial networks in the global banking systems? Why or why not?

3. *Pseudonymous Transactions.* Satoshi Nakamoto emphasized the pseudonymous nature of Bitcoin transactions. What are the potential privacy and security implications of using a pseudonymous wallet address in transactions for value? Consider both the potential benefits and risks associated with transactions of this nature.

4. Discuss the legal implications of establishing a decentralized payment network by omitting a trusted central authority in electronic peer-to-peer cash transactions.

5. Explain the legal advantages and disadvantages of implementing a proof-of-work system in a decentralized payment network. How might a decentralized validation process impact legal issues regarding trust, accountability, and potential regulatory interventions?

6. Regarding the peer-to-peer nature of Bitcoin transactions and the absence of intermediaries, explain the legal issues surrounding consumer protection, dispute resolution, and regulatory oversight.

V. Textbook Overview

The purpose of this textbook is to provide insight into the legal and regulatory issues arising out of cryptocurrencies. After reading this textbook, readers will understand how Bitcoin and other digital currencies are treated under a legal guise by regulators in the U.S. and abroad, and what standard to apply when analyzing blockchain technology and cryptocurrencies issues.

So far, we have discussed the history of money through the pre-modern medium of exchange, the modern era (pre-bitcoin), the internet age, ending with Satoshi's White Paper. Next, we will discuss the existing legal framework of currency and payments, and the application of such a framework with federal and state laws. We will further discuss blockchain technology and the legal and regulatory issues associated with blockchain technology.

Two

Securities

I. The United States Securities and Exchange Commission

The purpose of the United States Securities and Exchange Commission (SEC) is to protect investors, while maintaining a fair and efficient market that facilitates capital formation. The SEC is a federal administrative agency that oversees market monitoring, securities laws, and development of new regulations. The goal of the SEC is to promote full public disclosure, protect investors from fraudulent, manipulative market practices, and monitor corporate takeover actions.[23]

The Securities Act of 1933, 15 U.S.C §77b(1), defines the term "security" to include the commonly known documents traded for speculation or investment.[24] The SEC has the authority to regulate any assets which are deemed a security, which can include cryptocurrencies. A variety of laws govern the securities industry, some of which are included below.

Important Laws and Regulations

1. *The Securities Act of 1933.* This Act has two main goals: First, the Act requires that investors receive financial and other significant information concerning securities being offered for public sale. This enables investors to be able to make an informed decision about whether to purchase a security. Second, the Act prohibits deceit, misrepresentations, and other fraud in the sale of securities. These objectives allow for disclosure of important and accurate financial information through the registration of securities.

   The Securities Act of 1933 also describes the registration process for most securities sold in the United States. Registration requires a description of the company's business, a description of the security to be offered for sale, management information, and financial statements certified by independent accountants. However, not all securities offerings need to be registered. Some exemptions to the registration requirement include private offerings to a limited number of persons, offerings of limited size, and offerings of securities of municipal, state, and federal governments.

---

23. What We Do, https://www.sec.gov/about/what-we-do (last visited May 2, 2022).
24. 15 U.S.C §77b(1).

2. *Securities Exchange Act of 1934.* This Act was passed by Congress to create the Securities and Exchange Commission. The Act gives the SEC broad authority over the securities industry. Such authority includes the power to register, regulate and oversee brokerage firms, transfer agents, clearing agencies, and the nation's securities self-regulatory organizations (SROs). Examples of SROs include the New York Stock Exchange, NASDAQ Stock Market, and Financial Industry Regulatory Authority (FINRA).

The SEC has the power to regulate entities by identifying and prohibiting certain types of market conduct. The SEC also has the power to require periodic reporting of information by companies with publicly traded securities and more than $10 million in assets whose securities are held by more than 500 owners.

3. *Sarbanes-Oxley Act of 2002.* The Sarbanes-Oxley Act of 2002 was signed into law by President Bush on July 30, 2002. The purpose of this Act is to increase corporate responsibility, financial disclosures and combat corporate fraud.

4. *Dodd-Frank Wall Street Reform and Consumer Protection Act of 2010.* The Dodd-Frank Wall Street Reform and Consumer Protection Act was signed into law by President Obama on July 21, 2010. The purpose of this Act is to reshape th e regulatory framework regarding consumer protection, including trading restrictions, credit ratings, and financial products. The Act is also meant to regulate corporate governance, disclosure and transparency.

SEC v. W.J. Howey Co.

328 U.S. 293

Supreme Court of the United States

Decided May 27, 1946

CERTIORARI TO THE CIRCUIT COURT OF APPEALS FOR THE FIFTH CIRCUIT

Syllabus

1. Upon the facts of this case, an offering of units of a citrus grove development, coupled with a contract for cultivating, marketing, and remitting the net proceeds to the investor, was an offering of an "investment contract" within the meaning of that term as used in the provision of § 2(1) of the Securities Act of 1933 defining "security" as including any "investment contract," and was therefore subject to the registration requirements of the Act. Pp. 328 U.S. 294–297, 328 U.S. 299.

2. For purposes of the Securities Act, an investment contract (undefined by the Act) means a contract, transaction, or scheme whereby a person invests his money in a common enterprise and is led to expect profits solely from the efforts of the promoter or a third party, it being immaterial whether the shares in the enterprise

are evidenced by formal certificates or by nominal interests in the physical assets employed in the enterprise. Pp. 328 U.S. 298–299.

3. The fact that some purchasers, by declining to enter into the service contract, chose not to accept the offer of the investment contract in its entirety does not require a different result, since the Securities Act prohibits the offer, as well as the sale, of unregistered non exempt securities. P. 328 U.S. 300.

4. The test of whether there is an "investment contract" under the Securities Act is whether the scheme involves an investment of money in a common enterprise with profits to come solely from the efforts of others; and, if that test be satisfied, it is immaterial whether the enterprise is speculative or non speculative, or whether there is a sale of property with or without intrinsic value. P. 328 U.S. 301.

5. The policy of the Securities Act of affording broad protection to investors is not to be thwarted by unrealistic and irrelevant formulae. P. 328 U.S. 301.

151 F.2d 714 reversed.

The Securities & Exchange Commission sued in the District Court to enjoin respondents from using the mails and instrumentalities of interstate commerce in the offer and sale of unregistered and nonexempt securities in violation of the Securities Act of 1933. The District Court denied the injunction. 60 F. Supp. 440. The Circuit Court of Appeals affirmed. 151 F.2d 714. This Court granted certiorari. 327 U.S. 773. *Reversed*, p. 328 U. S. 301.

MR. JUSTICE MURPHY delivered the opinion of the Court.

This case involves the application of § 2(1) of the Securities Act of 1933[1] to an offering of units of a citrus grove development, coupled with a contract for cultivating, marketing and remitting the net proceeds to the investor.

The Securities and Exchange Commission instituted this action to restrain the respondents from using the mails and instrumentalities of interstate commerce in the offer and sale of unregistered and nonexempt securities in violation of § 5(a) of the Act. The District Court denied the injunction, 60 F. Supp. 440, and the Fifth Circuit Court of Appeals affirmed the judgment, 151 F.2d 714. We granted certiorari, 327 U.S. 773, on a petition alleging that the ruling of the Circuit Court of Appeals conflicted with other federal and state decisions, and that it introduced a novel and unwarranted test under the statute which the Commission regarded as administratively impractical.

Most of the facts are stipulated. The respondents, W.J. Howey Company and Howey-in-the-Hills Service, Inc., are Florida corporations under direct common control and management. The Howey Company owns large tracts of citrus acreage in Lake County, Florida. During the past several years, it has planted about 500 acres

---

1. 48 Stat. 74, 15 U. S. C. § 77b (1).

annually, keeping half of the groves itself and offering the other half to the public "to help us finance additional development." Howey-in-the-Hills Service, Inc., is a service company engaged in cultivating and developing many of these groves, including the harvesting and marketing of the crops.

Each prospective customer is offered both a land sales contract and a service contract, after having been told that it is not feasible to invest in a grove unless service arrangements are made. While the purchaser is free to make arrangements with other service companies, the superiority of Howey-in-the-Hills Service, Inc., is stressed. Indeed, 85% of the acreage sold during the 3-year period ending May 31, 1943, was covered by service contracts with Howey-in-the-Hills Service, Inc.

The land sales contract with the Howey Company provides for a uniform purchase price per acre or fraction thereof, varying in amount only in accordance with the number of years the particular plot has been planted with citrus trees. Upon full payment of the purchase price, the land is conveyed to the purchaser by warranty deed. Purchases are usually made in narrow strips of land arranged so that an acre consists of a row of 48 trees. During the period between February 1, 1941, and May 31, 1943, 31 of the 42 persons making purchases bought less than 5 acres each. The average holding of these 31 persons was 1.33 acres, and sales of as little as O.65, O.7 and O.73 of an acre were made. These tracts are not separately fenced, and the sole indication of several ownership is found in small land marks intelligible only through a plat book record.

The service contract, generally of a 10-year duration without option of cancellation, gives Howey-in-the-Hills Service, Inc., a leasehold interest and "full and complete" possession of the acreage. For a specified fee plus the cost of labor and materials, the company is given full discretion and authority over the cultivation of the groves and the harvest and marketing of the crops. The company is well established in the citrus business, and maintains a large force of skilled personnel and a great deal of equipment, including 75 tractors, sprayer wagons, fertilizer trucks, and the like. Without the consent of the company, the landowner or purchaser has no right of entry to market the crop;[2] thus, there is ordinarily no right to specific fruit. The company is accountable only for an allocation of the net profits based upon a check made at the time of picking. All the produce is pooled by the respondent companies, which do business under their own names.

The purchasers, for the most part, are nonresidents of Florida. They are predominantly business and professional people who lack the knowledge, skill, and equipment necessary for the care and cultivation of citrus trees. They are attracted by the expectation of substantial profits. It was represented, for example, that profits during the 1943–1944 season amounted to 20%, and that even greater profits might be expected during the 1944–1945 season, although only a 10% annual return was to

---

2. Some investors visited their particular plots annually, making suggestions as to care and cultivation, but without any legal rights in the matters.

be expected over a 10-year period. Many of these purchasers are patrons of a resort hotel owned and operated by the Howey Company in a scenic section adjacent to the groves. The hotel's advertising mentions the fine groves in the vicinity, and the attention of the patrons is drawn to the groves as they are being escorted about the surrounding countryside. They are told that the groves are for sale; if they indicate an interest in the matter, they are then given a sales talk.

It is admitted that the mails and instrumentalities of interstate commerce are used in the sale of the land and service contracts, and that no registration statement or letter of notification has ever been filed with the Commission in accordance with the Securities Act of 1933 and the rules and regulations thereunder.

Section 2(1) of the Act defines the term "security" to include the commonly known documents traded for speculation or investment.[3] This definition also includes "securities" of a more variable character, designated by such descriptive terms as "certificate of interest or participation in any profit-sharing agreement," "investment contract," and, "in general, any interest or instrument commonly known as a security." The legal issue in this case turns upon a determination of whether, under the circumstances, the land sales contract, the warranty deed and the service contract together constitute an "investment contract" within the meaning of § 2(1). An affirmative answer brings into operation the registration requirements of § 5(a), unless the security is granted an exemption under § 3(b). The lower courts, in reaching a negative answer to this problem, treated the contracts and deeds as separate transactions involving no more than an ordinary real estate sale and an agreement by the seller to manage the property for the buyer.

The term "investment contract" is undefined by the Securities Act or by relevant legislative reports. But the term was common in many state "blue sky" laws in existence prior to the adoption of the federal statute, and, although the term was also undefined by the state laws, it had been broadly construed by state courts so as to afford the investing public a full measure of protection. Form was disregarded for substance, and emphasis was placed upon economic reality. An investment contract thus came to mean a contract or scheme for "the placing of capital or laying out of money in a way intended to secure income or profit from its employment." *State v. Gopher Tire & Rubber Co.*, 146 Minn. 52, 56, 177 N.W. 937, 938. This definition was uniformly applied by state courts to a variety of situations where individuals were led to invest money in a common enterprise with the expectation that they would

---

3. "The term 'security' means any note, stock, treasury stock, bond, debenture, evidence of indebtedness, certificate of interest or participation in any profit-sharing agreement, collateral-trust certificate, preorganization certificate or subscription, transferable share, investment contract, voting-trust certificate, certificate of deposit for a security, fractional undivided interest in oil, gas, or other mineral rights, or, in general, any interest or instrument commonly known as a 'security,' or any certificate of interest or participation in, temporary or interim certificate for, receipt for, guarantee of, or warrant or right to subscribe to or purchase, any of the foregoing."

earn a profit solely through the efforts of the promoter or of someone other than themselves.[4]

By including an investment contract within the scope of § 2(1) of the Securities Act, Congress was using a term the meaning of which had been crystalized by this prior judicial interpretation. It is therefore reasonable to attach that meaning to the term as used by Congress, especially since such a definition is consistent with the statutory aims. In other words, an investment contract, for purposes of the Securities Act, means a contract, transaction or scheme whereby a person invests his money in a common enterprise and is led to expect profits solely from the efforts of the promoter or a third party, it being immaterial whether the shares in the enterprise are evidenced by formal certificates or by nominal interests in the physical assets employed in the enterprise. Such a definition necessarily underlies this Court's decision in *SEC v. Joiner Corp.*, 320 U.S. 344, and has been enunciated and applied many times by lower federal courts.[5] It permits the fulfillment of the statutory purpose of compelling full and fair disclosure relative to the issuance of "the many types of instruments that, in our commercial world, fall within the ordinary concept of a security." H.Rep. No.85, 73rd Cong., 1st Sess., p. 11. It embodies a flexible, rather than a static, principle, one that is capable of adaptation to meet the countless and variable schemes devised by those who seek the use of the money of others on the promise of profits.

The transactions in this case clearly involve investment contracts, as so defined. The respondent companies are offering something more than fee simple interests in land, something different from a farm or orchard coupled with management services. They are offering an opportunity to contribute money and to share in the profits of a large citrus fruit enterprise managed and partly owned by respondents. They are offering this opportunity to persons who reside in distant localities and who lack the equipment and experience requisite to the cultivation, harvesting, and marketing of the citrus products. Such persons have no desire to occupy the land, or to develop it themselves; they are attracted solely by the prospects of a return on their investment. Indeed, individual development of the plots of land that are offered and sold would seldom be economically feasible, due to their small size. Such tracts gain utility as citrus groves only when cultivated and developed as component parts of a larger area. A common enterprise managed by respondents or third parties

---

4. *State v. Evans*, 154 Minn. 95, 191 N.W. 425; *Klatt v. Guaranteed Bond Co.*, 213 Wis. 12, 250 N.W. 825; *State v. Heath*, 199 N.C. 135, 153 S.E. 855; *Prohaska v. Hemmer-Miller Development Co.*, 256 Ill. App. 331; *People v. White*, 124 Cal. App. 548, 12 P.2d 1078; *Stevens v. Liberty Packing Corp.*, 111 N.J. Eq. 61, 161 A. 193. See also *Moore v. Stella*, 52 Cal. App. 2d 766, 127 P.2d 300.

5. *Atherton v. United States*, 128 F.2d 463; *Penfield Co. v. S.E.C.*, 143 F.2d 746; *S.E.C. v. Universal Service Assn.*, 106 F.2d 232; *S.E.C. v. Crude Oil Corp.*, 93 F.2d 844; *S.E.C. v. Bailey*, 41 F.Supp. 647; *S.E.C. v. Payne*, 35 F.Supp. 873; *S.E.C. v. Bourbon Sales Corp.*, 47 F.Supp. 70; *S.E.C. v. Wickham*, 12 F.Supp. 245; *S.E.C. v. Timetrust, Inc.*, 28 F.Supp. 34; *S.E.C. v. Pyne*, 33 F.Supp. 988. The Commission has followed the same definition in its own administrative proceedings. *In re Natural Resources Corp.*, 8 S.E.C. 635.

with adequate personnel and equipment is therefore essential if the investors are to achieve their paramount aim of a return on their investments. Their respective shares in this enterprise are evidenced by land sales contracts and warranty deeds, which serve as a convenient method of determining the investors' allocable shares of the profits. The resulting transfer of rights in land is purely incidental.

Thus, all the elements of a profit-seeking business venture are present here. The investors provide the capital and share in the earnings and profits; the promoters manage, control, and operate the enterprise. It follows that the arrangements whereby the investors' interests are made manifest involve investment contracts, regardless of the legal terminology in which such contracts are clothed. The investment contracts in this instance take the form of land sales contracts, warranty deeds, and service contracts which respondents offer to prospective investors. And respondents' failure to abide by the statutory and administrative rules in making such offerings, even though the failure result from a *bona fide* mistake as to the law, cannot be sanctioned under the Act.

This conclusion is unaffected by the fact that some purchasers choose not to accept the full offer of an investment contract by declining to enter into a service contract with the respondents. The Securities Act prohibits the offer, as well as the sale, of unregistered, nonexempt securities.[6] Hence, it is enough that the respondents merely offer the essential ingredients of an investment contract.

We reject the suggestion of the Circuit Court of Appeals, 151 F.2d at 717, that an investment contract is necessarily missing where the enterprise is not speculative or promotional in character and where the tangible interest which is sold has intrinsic value independent of the success of the enterprise as a whole. The test is whether the scheme involves an investment of money in a common enterprise with profits to come solely from the efforts of others. If that test be satisfied, it is immaterial whether the enterprise is speculative or non speculative, or whether there is a sale of property with or without intrinsic value. *See SEC v. Joiner Corp., supra,* 320 U.S. 352. The statutory policy of affording broad protection to investors is not to be thwarted by unrealistic and irrelevant formulae.

Reversed.

MR. JUSTICE JACKSON took no part in the consideration or decision of this case.

MR. JUSTICE FRANKFURTER dissenting.

"Investment contract" is not a term of art; it is conception dependent upon the circumstances of a particular situation. If this case came before us on a finding authorized by Congress that the facts disclosed an "investment contract" within the general scope of § 2(1) of the Securities Act, 48 Stat. 74, 15 U.S.C. § 77b(1), the Se-

---

6. The registration requirements of § 5 refer to sales of securities. Section 2(3) defines "sale" to include every "attempt or offer to dispose of, or solicitation of an offer to buy," a security for value.

curities and Exchange Commission's finding would govern unless, on the record, it was wholly unsupported. But that is not the case before us. Here, the ascertainment of the existence of an "investment contract" had to be made independently by the District Court, and it found against its existence. 60 F. Supp. 440. The Circuit Court of Appeals for the Fifth Circuit sustained that finding. 151 F.2d 714. If respect is to be paid to the wise rule of judicial administration under which this Court does not upset concurrent findings of two lower courts in the ascertainment of facts and the relevant inferences to be drawn from them, this case clearly calls for its application. *See Allen v. Trust Co. of Georgia,* 326 U.S. 630. For the crucial issue in this case turns on whether the contracts for the land and the contracts for the management of the property were, in reality, separate agreements, or merely parts of a single transaction. It is clear from its opinion that the District Court was warranted in its conclusion that the record does not establish the existence of an investment contract:

> "... the record in this case shows that not a single sale of citrus grove property was made by the Howey Company during the period involved in this suit, except to purchasers who actually inspected the property before purchasing the same. The record further discloses that no purchaser is required to engage the Service Company to care for his property, and that, of the fifty-one purchasers acquiring property during this period, only forty-two entered into contract with the Service Company for the care of the property."

60 F. Supp. at 442.

Simply because other arrangements may have the appearances of this transaction, but are employed as an evasion of the Securities Act, does not mean that the present contracts were evasive. I find nothing in the Securities Act to indicate that Congress meant to bring every innocent transaction within the scope of the Act simply because a perversion of them is covered by the Act.

Discussion Points

1. *The Howey Test.* How do you think the Howey test would apply to digital tokens today? The Howey test holds that a transaction constitutes an investment contract and triggers regulation by federal securities laws if four elements are met: (1) a person invests money; (2) in a common enterprise; (3) with the expectation of profits; (4) derived solely from the efforts of others. An investment is anything that can be consideration for a bargained for exchange.[25] Which of these four elements would be difficult to meet when

---

25. Framework for "Investment Contract" Analysis of Digital Assets, U.S. Securities and Exchange Commission.

selling digital coins or cryptocurrencies? Should the SEC reconsider using the Howey test in the 21st century?

2. *When does the Howey Test apply?* Does the Howey test apply to products whose function is to be a medium of exchange? Does it apply to peer to peer (p2p) exchanges? Would the Howey test apply to closed loop transactions? Should the Howey test be applicable to cross-border transactions in digital coins and cryptocurrencies?

3. *Cryptocurrencies.* Do cryptocurrencies meet the definition of a security under the federal securities laws? Apply the Howey test to cryptocurrencies. What is the result? If cryptocurrencies do not satisfy the Howey test, which element do they fail to meet?

The DAO Report

Release No. 81207 / July 25, 2017

SECURITIES AND EXCHANGE COMMISSION

SECURITIES EXCHANGE ACT OF 1934

Release No. 81207 / July 25, 2017

Report of Investigation Pursuant to Section 21(a) of the Securities Exchange Act of 1934: The DAO

I. Introduction and Summary

The United States Securities and Exchange Commission's ("Commission") Division of Enforcement ("Division") has investigated whether The DAO, an unincorporated organization; Slock.it UG ("Slock.it"), a German corporation; Slock.it's co-founders; and intermediaries may have violated the federal securities laws. The Commission has determined not to pursue an enforcement action in this matter based on the conduct and activities known to the Commission at this time.

As described more fully below, The DAO is one example of a Decentralized Autonomous Organization, which is a term used to describe a "virtual" organization embodied in computer code and executed on a distributed ledger or blockchain. The DAO was created by Slock.it and Slock.it's co-founders, with the objective of operating as a for-profit entity that would create and hold a corpus of assets through the sale of DAO Tokens to investors, which assets would then be used to fund "projects." The holders of DAO Tokens stood to share in the anticipated earnings from these projects as a return on their investment in DAO Tokens. In addition, DAO Token holders could monetize their investments in DAO Tokens by re-selling DAO Tokens on a number of web-based platforms ("Platforms") that supported secondary trading in the DAO Tokens.

After DAO Tokens were sold, but before The DAO was able to commence funding projects, an attacker used a flaw in The DAO's code to steal approximately one-third of The DAO's assets. Slock.it's co-founders and others responded by creating a work-around whereby DAO Token holders could opt to have their investment returned to them, as described in more detail below.

The investigation raised questions regarding the application of the U.S. federal securities laws to the offer and sale of DAO Tokens, including the threshold question whether DAO Tokens are securities. Based on the investigation, and under the facts presented, the Commission has determined that DAO Tokens are securities under the Securities Act of 1933 ("Securities Act") and the Securities Exchange Act of 1934 ("Exchange Act").[1] The Commission deems it appropriate and in the public interest to issue this report of investigation ("Report") pursuant to

Section 21(a) of the Exchange Act[2] to advise those who would use a Decentralized Autonomous Organization ("DAO Entity"), or other distributed ledger or blockchain-enabled means for capital raising, to take appropriate steps to ensure compliance with the U.S. federal securities laws. All securities offered and sold in the United States must be registered with the Commission or must qualify for an exemption from the registration requirements. In addition, any entity or person engaging in the activities of an exchange must register as a national securities exchange or operate pursuant to an exemption from such registration.

This Report reiterates these fundamental principles of the U.S. federal securities laws and describes their applicability to a new paradigm—virtual organizations or capital raising entities that use distributed ledger or blockchain technology to facilitate capital raising and/or investment and the related offer and sale of securities. The automation of certain functions through this technology, "smart contracts,"[3] or computer code, does not remove conduct from the purview of the U.S. federal

---

1. This Report does not analyze the question whether The DAO was an "investment company," as defined under Section 3(a) of the Investment Company Act of 1940 ("Investment Company Act"), in part, because The DAO never commenced its business operations funding projects. Those who would use virtual organizations should consider their obligations under the Investment Company Act.

2. Section 21(a) of the Exchange Act authorizes the Commission to investigate violations of the federal securities laws and, in its discretion, to "publish information concerning any such violations." This Report does not constitute an adjudication of any fact or issue addressed herein, nor does it make any findings of violations by any individual or entity. The facts discussed in Section II, *infra*, are matters of public record or based on documentary records. We are publishing this Report on the Commission's website to ensure that all market participants have concurrent and equal access to the information contained herein.

3. Computer scientist Nick Szabo described a "smart contract" as:
   a computerized transaction protocol that executes terms of a contract. The general objectives of smart contract design are to satisfy common contractual conditions (such as payment terms, liens, confidentiality, and even enforcement), minimize exceptions both malicious and accidental, and minimize the need for trusted intermediaries. Related economic goals include lowering fraud loss, arbitrations and enforcement costs, and other transaction costs.

See Nick Szabo, *Smart Contracts*, 1994, http://www.virtualschool.edu/mon/Economics/Smart-Contracts.html.

securities laws.[4] This Report also serves to stress the obligation to comply with the registration provisions of the federal securities laws with respect to products and platforms involving emerging technologies and new investor interfaces.

II. Facts

A. Background

From April 30, 2016 through May 28, 2016, The DAO offered and sold approximately 1.15 billion DAO Tokens in exchange for a total of approximately 12 million Ether ("ETH"), a virtual currency[5] used on the Ethereum Blockchain.[6] As of the time the offering closed, the total ETH raised by The DAO was valued in U.S. Dollars ("USD") at approximately $150 million.

The concept of a DAO Entity is memorialized in a document (the "White Paper"), authored by Christoph Jentzsch, the Chief Technology Officer of Slock.it, a "Blockchain and IoT [(internet-of-things)] solution company," incorporated in Germany and co-founded by Christoph Jentzsch, Simon Jentzsch (Christoph Jentzsch's brother), and Stephan Tual ("Tual").[7] The White Paper purports to describe "the first implementation of a [DAO Entity] code to automate organizational governance

---

4. *See SEC v. C.M. Joiner Leasing Corp.*, 320 U.S. 344, 351 (1943) ("[T]he reach of the [Securities] Act does not stop with the obvious and commonplace. Novel, uncommon, or irregular devices, whatever they appear to be, are also reached if it be proved as matter of fact that they were widely offered or dealt in under terms or courses of dealing which established their character in commerce as 'investment contracts,' or as 'any interest or instrument commonly known as a 'security''.); *see also Reves v. Ernst & Young*, 494 U.S. 56, 61 (1990) ("Congress' purpose in enacting the securities laws was to regulate investments, in whatever form they are made and by whatever name they are called.").

5. The Financial Action Task Force defines "virtual currency" as:

a digital representation of value that can be digitally traded and functions as: (1) a medium of exchange; and/or (2) a unit of account; and/or (3) a store of value, but does not have legal tender status (i.e., when tendered to a creditor, is a valid and legal offer of payment) in any jurisdiction. It is not issued or guaranteed by any jurisdiction, and fulfils the above functions only by agreement within the community of users of the virtual currency. Virtual currency is distinguished from fiat currency (a.k.a. "real currency," "real money," or "national currency"), which is the coin and paper money of a country that is designated as its legal tender; circulates; and is customarily used and accepted as a medium of exchange in the issuing country. It is distinct from e-money, which is a digital representation of fiat currency used to electronically transfer value denominated in fiat currency.

FATF Report, Virtual Currencies, Key Definitions and Potential AML/CFT Risks, FINANCIAL ACTION TASK FORCE (June 2014), http://www.fatf-gafi.org/media/fatf/documents/reports/Virtual-currency-key-definitions-and-potential-aml-cft-risks.pdf.

6. Ethereum, developed by the Ethereum Foundation, a Swiss nonprofit organization, is a decentralized platform that runs smart contracts on a blockchain known as the Ethereum Blockchain.

7. Christoph Jentzsch released the final draft of the White Paper on or around March 23, 2016. He introduced his concept of a DAO Entity as early as November 2015 at an Ethereum Developer Conference in London, as a medium to raise funds for Slock.it, a German start-up he co-founded in September 2015. Slock.it purports to create technology that embeds smart contracts that run on the Ethereum Blockchain into real-world devices and, as a result, for example, permits anyone to rent, sell or share physical objects in a decentralized way. *See* SLOCK.IT, https://slock.it/.

and decision making."[8] The White Paper posits that a DAO Entity "can be used by individuals working together collaboratively outside of a traditional corporate form. It can also be used by a registered corporate entity to automate formal governance rules contained in corporate bylaws or imposed by law." The White Paper proposes an entity—a DAO Entity—that would use smart contracts to attempt to solve governance issues it described as inherent in traditional corporations.[9] As described, a DAO Entity purportedly would supplant traditional mechanisms of corporate governance and management with a blockchain such that contractual terms are "formalized, automated and enforced using software."[10]

B. The DAO

"The DAO" is the "first generation" implementation of the White Paper concept of a DAO Entity, and it began as an effort to create a "crowdfunding contract" to raise "funds to grow [a] company in the crypto space."[11] In November 2015, at an Ethereum Developer Conference in London, Christoph Jentzsch described his proposal for The DAO as a "for-profit DAO [Entity]," where participants would send ETH (a virtual currency) to The DAO to purchase DAO Tokens, which would permit the participant to vote and entitle the participant to "rewards."[12] Christoph

---

8. Christoph Jentzsch, *Decentralized Autonomous Organization to Automate Governance Final Draft – Under Review*, https://download.slock.it/public/DAO/WhitePaper.pdf.

9. *Id.*

10. *Id.* The White Paper contained the following statement:

> A word of caution, at the outset: the legal status of [DAO Entities] remains the subject of active and vigorous debate and discussion. Not everyone shares the same definition. Some have said that [DAO Entities] are autonomous code and can operate independently of legal systems; others have said that [DAO Entities] must be owned or operate[d] by humans or human created entities. There will be many use cases, and the DAO [Entity] code will develop over time. Ultimately, how a DAO [Entity] functions and its legal status will depend on many factors, including how DAO [Entity] code is used, where it is used, and who uses it. This paper does not speculate about the legal status of [DAO Entities] worldwide. This paper is not intended to offer legal advice or conclusions. Anyone who uses DAO [Entity] code will do so at their own risk.

Id.

11. Christoph Jentzsch, *The History of the DAO and Lessons Learned*, SLOCK.IT BLOG (Aug. 24, 2016), https://blog.slock.it/the-history-of-the-dao-and-lessons-learned-d06740f8cfa5#.5o62zo8uv. Although The DAO has been described as a "crowdfunding contract," The DAO would not have met the requirements of Regulation Crowdfunding, adopted under Title III of the Jumpstart Our Business Startups (JOBS) Act of 2012 (providing an exemption from registration for certain crowdfunding), because, among other things, it was not a broker-dealer or a funding portal registered with the SEC and the Financial Industry Regulatory Authority ("FINRA"). *See Regulation Crowdfunding: A Small Entity Compliance Guide for Issuers*, SEC (Apr. 5, 2017), https://www.sec.gov/info/smallbus/secg/rccomplianceguide-051316.htm; *Updated Investor Bulletin: Crowdfunding for Investors*, SEC (May 10, 2017), https://www.sec.gov/oiea/investor-alerts-bulletins/ib_crowdfunding-.html.

12. *See* Slockit, *Slock.it DAO demo at Devcon1: IoT + Blockchain*, YOUTUBE (Nov. 13, 2015), https://www.youtube.com/watch?v=49wHQoJxYPo.

Jentzsch likened this to "buying shares in a company and getting…dividends."[13] The DAO was to be "decentralized" in that it would allow for voting by investors holding DAO Tokens.[14] All funds raised were to be held at an Ethereum Blockchain "address" associated with The DAO and DAO Token holders were to vote on contract proposals, including proposals to The DAO to fund projects and distribute The DAO's anticipated earnings from the projects it funded.[15] The DAO was intended to be "autonomous" in that project proposals were in the form of smart contracts that exist on the Ethereum Blockchain and the votes were administered by the code of The DAO.[16]

On or about April 29, 2016, Slock.it deployed The DAO code on the Ethereum Blockchain, as a set of pre-programmed instructions.[17] This code was to govern how The DAO was to operate.

To promote The DAO, Slock.it's co-founders launched a website ("The DAO Website"). The DAO Website included a description of The DAO's intended purpose: "To blaze a new path in business for the betterment of its members, existing simultaneously nowhere and everywhere and operating solely with the steadfast iron will of unstoppable code."[18] The DAO Website also described how The DAO operated, and included a link through which DAO Tokens could be purchased. The DAO Website also included a link to the White Paper, which provided detailed information about a DAO Entity's structure and its source code and, together with The DAO Website, served as the primary source of promotional materials for The DAO. On The DAO Website and elsewhere, Slock.it represented that The DAO's source code had been reviewed by "one of the world's leading security audit companies" and "no stone was left unturned during those five whole days of security analysis."[19]

---

13. *Id.*

14. *See* Jentzsch, *supra* note 8.

15. *Id.* In theory, there was no limitation on the type of project that could be proposed. For example, proposed "projects" could include, among other things, projects that would culminate in the creation of products or services that DAO Token holders could use or charge others for using.

16. *Id.*

17. According to the White Paper, a DAO Entity is "activated by deployment on the Ethereum [B]lockchain. Once deployed, a [DAO Entity's] code requires 'ether' [ETH] to engage in transactions on Ethereum. Ether is the digital fuel that powers the Ethereum Network." The only way to update or alter The DAO's code is to submit a new proposal for voting and achieve a majority consensus on that proposal. *See* Jentzsch, *supra* note 8. According to Slock.it's website, Slock.it gave The DAO code to the Ethereum community, noting that:

The DAO framework is [a] side project of Slock.it UG and a gift to the Ethereum community. It consisted of a definitive whitepaper, smart contract code audited by one of the best security companies in the world and soon, a complete frontend interface. All free and open source for anyone to re-use, it is our way to say 'thank you' to the community.

Slock.it, https://slock.it. The DAO code is publicly-available on GitHub, a host of source code. *See The Standard DAO Framework, Inc., Whitepaper*, GitHub, https://github.com/slockit/DAO.

18. The DAO Website was available at https://daohub.org.

19. Stephen Tual, *Deja Vu DAO Smart Contracts Audit Results*, SLOCK.IT BLOG (Apr. 5, 2016), https://blog.slock.it/deja-vu-dai-smart-contracts-audit-results-d26bc088e32e.

Slock.it's co-founders also promoted The DAO by soliciting media attention and by posting almost daily updates on The DAO's status on The DAO and Slock.it websites and numerous online forums relating to blockchain technology. Slock.it's co-founders used these posts to communicate to the public information about how to participate in The DAO, including: how to create and acquire DAO Tokens; the framework for submitting proposals for projects; and how to vote on proposals. Slock.it also created an online forum on The DAO Website, as well as administered "The DAO Slack" channel, an online messaging platform in which over

5,000 invited "team members" could discuss and exchange ideas about The DAO in real time.

1. DAO Tokens

In exchange for ETH, The DAO created DAO Tokens (proportional to the amount of ETH paid) that were then assigned to the Ethereum Blockchain address of the person or entity remitting the ETH. A DAO Token granted the DAO Token holder certain voting and ownership rights. According to promotional materials, The DAO would earn profits by funding projects that would provide DAO Token holders a return on investment. The various promotional materials disseminated by Slock.it's co-founders touted that DAO Token holders would receive "rewards," which the White Paper defined as, "any [ETH] received by a DAO [Entity] generated from projects the DAO [Entity] funded." DAO Token holders would then vote to either use the rewards to fund new projects or to distribute the ETH to DAO Token holders.

From April 30, 2016 through May 28, 2016 (the "Offering Period"), The DAO offered and sold DAO Tokens. Investments in The DAO were made "pseudonymously" (i.e., an individual's or entity's pseudonym was their Ethereum Blockchain address). To purchase a DAO Token offered for sale by The DAO, an individual or entity sent ETH from their Ethereum Blockchain address to an Ethereum Blockchain address associated with The DAO. All of the ETH raised in the offering as well as any future profits earned by The DAO were to be pooled and held in The DAO's Ethereum Blockchain address. The token price fluctuated in a range of approximately 1 to 1.5 ETH per 100 DAO Tokens, depending on when the tokens were purchased during the Offering Period. Anyone was eligible to purchase DAO Tokens (as long as they paid ETH). There were no limitations placed on the number of DAO Tokens offered for sale, the number of purchasers of DAO Tokens, or the level of sophistication of such purchasers.

DAO Token holders were not restricted from re-selling DAO Tokens acquired in the offering, and DAO Token holders could sell their DAO Tokens in a variety of ways in the secondary market and thereby monetize their investment as discussed below. Prior to the Offering Period, Slock.it solicited at least one U.S. web-based platform to trade DAO Tokens on its system and, at the time of the offering, The DAO Website and other promotional materials disseminated by Slock.it included representations that DAO Tokens would be available for secondary market trading after the Offering Period via several platforms. During the Offering Period and afterwards, the Platforms posted notices on their own websites and on social media that each planned to support secondary market trading of DAO Tokens. [20]

In addition to secondary market trading on the Platforms, after the Offering Period, DAO Tokens were to be freely transferable on the Ethereum Blockchain. DAO Token holders would also be permitted to redeem their DAO Tokens for ETH through a complicated, multi-week (approximately 46-day) process referred to as a DAO Entity "split." [21]

2. Participants in The DAO

According to the White Paper, in order for a project to be considered for funding with "a DAO [Entity]'s [ETH]," a "Contractor" first must submit a proposal to the DAO Entity. Specifically, DAO Token holders expected Contractors to submit proposals for projects that could provide DAO Token holders returns on their investments. Submitting a proposal to The DAO involved: (1) writing a smart contract, and then deploying and publishing it on the Ethereum Blockchain; and (2) posting details about the proposal on The DAO Website, including the Ethereum Blockchain address of the deployed contract and a link to its source code. Proposals could be viewed on The DAO Website as well as other publicly-accessible websites. Per the White Paper, there were two prerequisites for submitting a proposal. An individual or entity must: (1) own at least one DAO Token; and (2) pay a deposit in the form of ETH that would be forfeited to the DAO Entity if the proposal was put up for a vote and failed to achieve a quorum of DAO Token holders. It was publicized that Slock. it would be the first to submit a proposal for funding. [22]

ETH raised by The DAO was to be distributed to a Contractor to fund a proposal only on a majority vote of DAO Token holders. [23] DAO Token holders were to cast votes, which would be weighted by the number of tokens they controlled, for or against the funding of a specific proposal. The voting process, however, was pub-

---

20. The Platforms are registered with FinCEN as "Money Services Businesses" and provide systems whereby customers may exchange virtual currencies for other virtual currencies or fiat currencies.

21. According to the White Paper, the primary purpose of a split is to protect minority shareholders and prevent what is commonly referred to as a "51% Attack," whereby an attacker holding 51% of a DAO Entity's Tokens could create a proposal to send all of the DAO Entity's funds to himself or herself.

22. It was stated on The DAO Website and elsewhere that Slock.it anticipated that it would be the first to submit a proposal for funding. In fact, a draft of Slock.it's proposal for funding for an "Ethereum Computer and Universal Sharing Network" was publicly-available online during the Offering Period.

23. DAO Token holders could vote on proposals, either by direct interaction with the Ethereum Blockchain or by using an application that interfaces with the Ethereum Blockchain. It was generally acknowledged that DAO Token holders needed some technical knowledge in order to submit a vote, and The DAO Website included a link to a step- by-step tutorial describing how to vote on proposals.

licly criticized in that it could incentivize distorted voting behavior and, as a result, would not accurately reflect the consensus of the majority of DAO Token holders. Specifically, as noted in a May 27, 2016 blog post by a group of computer security researchers, The DAO's structure included a "strong positive bias to vote YES on proposals and to suppress NO votes as a side effect of the way in which it restricts users' range of options following the casting of a vote."[24]

Before any proposal was put to a vote by DAO Token holders, it was required to be reviewed by one or more of The DAO's "Curators." At the time of the formation of The DAO, the Curators were a group of individuals chosen by Slock.it.[25] According-ing to the White Paper, the Curators of a DAO Entity had "considerable power." The Curators performed crucial security functions and maintained ultimate control over which proposals could be submitted to, voted on, and funded by The DAO. As stated on The DAO Website during the Offering Period, The DAO relied on its Curators for "failsafe protection" and for protecting The DAO from "malicous [sic] actors." Specifically, per The DAO Website, a Curator was responsible for: (1) confirming that any proposal for funding originated from an identifiable person or organization; and (2) confirming that smart contracts associated with any such proposal properly reflected the code the Contractor claims to have deployed on the Ethereum Blockchain. If a Curator determined that the proposal met these criteria, the Curator could add the proposal to the "whitelist," which was a list of Ethereum Blockchain addresses that could receive ETH from The DAO if the majority of DAO Token holders voted for the proposal.

Curators of The DAO had ultimate discretion as to whether or not to submit a proposal for voting by DAO Token holders. Curators also determined the order and frequency of proposals, and could impose subjective criteria for whether the pro-posal should be whitelisted. One member of the group chosen by Slock.it to serve collectively as the Curator stated publicly that the Curator had "complete control over the whitelist... the order in which things get whitelisted, the duration for which [proposals] get whitelisted, when things get unwhitelisted... [and] clear ability to control the order and frequency of proposals," noting that "curators have tremen-dous power."[26] Another Curator publicly announced his subjective criteria for deter-

---

24. By voting on a proposal, DAO Token holders would "tie up" their tokens until the end of the voting cycle. *See* Jentzsch, *supra* note 8 at 8 ("The tokens used to vote will be blocked, meaning they can not [sic] be transferred until the proposal is closed."). If, however, a DAO Token holder abstained from voting, the DAO Token holder could avoid these restrictions; any DAO Tokens not submitted for a vote could be withdrawn or transferred at any time.

25. At the time of The DAO's launch, The DAO Website identified eleven "high profile" individ-uals as holders of The DAO's Curator "Multisig" (or "private key"). These individuals all appear to live outside of the United States. Many of them were associated with the Ethereum Foundation, and The DAO Website touted the qualifications and trustworthiness of these individuals.

26. Epicenter, *EB134 – Emin Gün Sirer And Vlad Zamfir: On A Rocky DAO*, YouTube (June 6, 2016), https://www.youtube.com/watch?v=ON5GhIQdFU8.

mining whether to whitelist a proposal, which included his personal ethics.[27] Per the White Paper, a Curator also had the power to reduce the voting quorum requirement by 50% every other week. Absent action by a Curator, the quorum could be reduced by 50% only if no proposal had reached the required quorum for 52 weeks.

3. Secondary Market Trading on the Platforms

During the period from May 28, 2016 through early September 2016, the Platforms became the preferred vehicle for DAO Token holders to buy and sell DAO Tokens in the secondary market using virtual or fiat currencies. Specifically, the Platforms used electronic systems that allowed their respective customers to post orders for DAO Tokens on an anonymous basis. For example, customers of each Platform could buy or sell DAO Tokens by entering a market order on the Platform's system, which would then match with orders from other customers residing on the system. Each Platform's system would automatically execute these orders based on pre-programmed order interaction protocols established by the Platform.

None of the Platforms received orders for DAO Tokens from non-Platform customers or routed its respective customers' orders to any other trading destinations. The Platforms publicly displayed all their quotes, trades, and daily trading volume in DAO Tokens on their respective websites. During the period from May 28, 2016 through September 6, 2016, one such Platform executed more than 557,378 buy and sell transactions in DAO Tokens by more than 15,000 of its U.S. and foreign customers. During the period from May 28, 2016 through August 1, 2016, another such Platform executed more than 22,207 buy and sell transactions in DAO Tokens by more than 700 of its U.S. customers.

4. Security Concerns, The "Attack" on The DAO, and The Hard Fork

In late May 2016, just prior to the expiration of the Offering Period, concerns about the safety and security of The DAO's funds began to surface due to vulnerabilities in The DAO's code. On May 26, 2016, in response to these concerns, Slock. it submitted a "DAO Security Proposal" that called for the development of certain updates to The DAO's code and the appointment of a security expert.[28] Further, on June 3, 2016, Christoph Jentzsch, on behalf of Slock.it, proposed a moratorium on

---

27. Andrew Quentson, *Are the DAO Curators Masters or Janitors?*, THE COIN TELEGRAPH (June 12, 2016), https://cointelegraph.com/news/are-the-dao-curators-masters-or-janitors.

28. *See* Stephan Tual, *Proposal #1-DAO Security, Redux*, SLOCK.IT BLOG (May 26, 2016), https://blog.slock.it/both-our-proposals-are-now-out-voting-starts-saturday-morning-ba322d6d3aea. The unnamed security expert would "act as the first point of contact for security disclosures, and continually monitor, pre-empt and avert any potential attack vectors The DAO may face, including social, technical and economic attacks." *Id.* Slock.it initially proposed a much broader security proposal that included the formation of a "DAO Security" group, the establishment of a "Bug Bounty Program," and routine external audits of The DAO's code. However, the cost of the proposal (125,000 ETH), which would be paid from The DAO's funds, was immediately criticized as too high and Slock.it decided instead to submit the revised proposal described above. *See* Stephan Tual, *DAO.*

all proposals until alterations to The DAO's code to fix vulnerabilities in The DAO's code had been implemented.[29]

On June 17, 2016, an unknown individual or group (the "Attacker") began rapidly diverting ETH from The DAO, causing approximately 3.6 million ETH—1/3 of the total ETH raised by The DAO offering—to move from The DAO's Ethereum Blockchain address to an Ethereum Blockchain address controlled by the Attacker (the "Attack").[30] Although the diverted ETH was then held in an address controlled by the Attacker, the Attacker was prevented by The DAO's code from moving the ETH from that address for 27 days.[31]

In order to secure the diverted ETH and return it to DAO Token holders, Slock. it's co-founders and others endorsed a "Hard Fork" to the Ethereum Blockchain. The "Hard Fork," called for a change in the Ethereum protocol on a going forward basis that would restore the DAO Token holders' investments as if the Attack had not occurred. On July 20, 2016, after a majority of the Ethereum network adopted the necessary software updates, the new, forked Ethereum Blockchain became active.[32] The Hard Fork had the effect of transferring all of the funds raised (including those held by the Attacker) from the DAO to a recovery address, where DAO Token holders could exchange their DAO Tokens for ETH.[33] All DAO Token holders who adopted the Hard Fork could exchange their DAO Tokens for ETH, and avoid any loss of the ETH they had invested.[34]

III. Discussion

The Commission is aware that virtual organizations and associated individuals and entities increasingly are using distributed ledger technology to offer and sell instruments such as DAO Tokens to raise capital. These offers and sales have been referred to, among other things, as "Initial Coin Offerings" or "Token Sales." Accordingly, the Commission deems it appropriate and in the public interest to issue this Report in order to stress that the U.S. federal securities law may apply to various activities, including distributed ledger technology, depending on the particular facts and circumstances, without regard to the form of the organization or technology

Security, a Proposal to guarantee the integrity of The DAO, SLOCK.IT BLOG (May 25, 2016), https ://blog.slock.it/dao-security-a-proposal-to- guarantee-the-integrity-of-the-dao-3473899ace9d.

29. See *TheDAO Proposal_ID 5*, ETHERSCAN, https://etherscan.io/token/thedao-proposal/5.

30. See Stephan Tual, *DAO Security Advisory: live updates*, SLOCK.IT BLOG (June 17, 2016), https://blog.slock.it/dao-security-advisory-live-updates-2a0a42a2d07b.

31. *Id.*

32. A minority group, however, elected not to adopt the new Ethereum Blockchain created by the Hard Fork because to do so would run counter to the concept that a blockchain is immutable. Instead they continued to use the former version of the blockchain, which is now known as "Ethereum Classic."

33. See Christoph Jentzsch, *What the 'Fork' Really Means*, SLOCK.IT BLOG (July 18, 2016), https://blog.slock.it/what-the-fork-really-means-6fe573ac31dd.

34. *Id.*

used to effectuate a particular offer or sale. In this Report, the Commission considers the particular facts and circumstances of the offer and sale of DAO Tokens to demonstrate the application of existing U.S. federal securities laws to this new paradigm.

A. Section 5 of the Securities Act

The registration provisions of the Securities Act contemplate that the offer or sale of securities to the public must be accompanied by the "full and fair disclosure" afforded by registration with the Commission and delivery of a statutory prospectus containing information necessary to enable prospective purchasers to make an informed investment decision. Registration entails disclosure of detailed "information about the issuer's financial condition, the identity and background of management, and the price and amount of securities to be offered...." *SEC v. Cavanagh*, 1 F. Supp. 2d 337, 360 (S.D.N.Y. 1998), *aff'd*, 155 F.3d 129 (2d Cir. 1998). "The registration statement is designed to assure public access to material facts bearing on the value of publicly traded securities and is central to the Act's comprehensive scheme for protecting public investors." *SEC v. Aaron*, 605 F.2d 612, 618 (2d Cir. 1979) (citing *SEC v. Ralston Purina Co.*, 346 U.S. 119, 124 (1953)), *vacated on other grounds*, 446 U.S. 680 (1980). Section 5(a) of the Securities Act provides that, unless a registration statement is in effect as to a security, it is unlawful for any person, directly or indirectly, to engage in the offer or sale of securities in interstate commerce. Section 5(c) of the Securities Act provides a similar prohibition against offers to sell, or offers to buy, unless a registration statement has been filed. Thus, both Sections 5(a) and 5(c) of the Securities Act prohibit the unregistered offer or sale of securities in interstate commerce. 15 U.S.C. § 77e(a) and (c). Violations of Section 5 do not require scienter. *SEC v. Universal Major Indus. Corp.*, 546 F.2d 1044, 1047 (2d Cir. 1976).

B. DAO Tokens Are Securities

1. Foundational Principles of the Securities Laws Apply to Virtual Organizations or Capital Raising Entities Making Use of Distributed Ledger Technology

Under Section 2(a)(1) of the Securities Act and Section 3(a)(10) of the Exchange Act, a security includes "an investment contract." *See* 15 U.S.C. §§ 77b-77c. An investment contract is an investment of money in a common enterprise with a reasonable expectation of profits to be derived from the entrepreneurial or managerial efforts of others. *See SEC v. Edwards*, 540 U.S. 389, 393 (2004); *SEC v. W.J. Howey Co.*, 328 U.S. 293, 301 (1946); *see also United Housing Found., Inc. v. Forman*, 421 U.S. 837, 852–53 (1975) (The "touchstone" of an investment contract "is the presence of an investment in a common venture premised on a reasonable expectation of profits to be derived from the entrepreneurial or managerial efforts of others."). This definition embodies a "*flexible rather than a static principle*, one that is capable of adaptation to meet the countless and variable schemes devised by those who seek the use of the money of others on the promise of profits." *Howey*, 328 U.S. at 299 (emphasis added). The test "permits the fulfillment of the statutory purpose of compelling full and fair disclosure relative to the issuance of 'the many types of instruments that in our commercial world fall within the ordinary concept of a security.'" *Id.* In analyzing whether something is a security, "form should be disregarded for substance," *Tcherepnin v. Knight*, 389 U.S. 332, 336 (1967), "and the emphasis should be on economic realities underlying a transaction, and not on the name appended thereto." *United Housing Found.*, 421 U.S. at 849.

2. Investors in The DAO Invested Money

In determining whether an investment contract exists, the investment of "money" need not take the form of cash. *See, e.g., Uselton v. Comm. Lovelace Motor Freight, Inc.*, 940 F.2d 564, 574 (10th Cir. 1991) ("[I]n spite of *Howey's* reference to an 'investment of money,' it is well established that cash is not the only form of contribution or investment that will create an investment contract.").

Investors in The DAO used ETH to make their investments, and DAO Tokens were received in exchange for ETH. Such investment is the type of contribution of value that can create an investment contract under *Howey*. *See SEC v. Shavers*, No. 4:13-CV-416, 2014 WL 4652121, at *1 (E.D. Tex. Sept. 18, 2014) (holding that an investment of Bitcoin, a virtual currency, meets the first prong of *Howey*); *Uselton*, 940 F.2d at 574 ("[T]he 'investment' may take the form of 'goods and services,' or some other 'exchange of value.'") (citations omitted).

3. With a Reasonable Expectation of Profits

Investors who purchased DAO Tokens were investing in a common enterprise and reasonably expected to earn profits through that enterprise when they sent ETH to The DAO's Ethereum Blockchain address in exchange for DAO Tokens. "[P]rofits" include "dividends, other periodic payments, or the increased value of the investment." *Edwards*, 540 U.S. at 394. As described above, the various promotional materials disseminated by Slock.it and its co-founders informed investors that The DAO was a for-profit entity whose objective was to fund projects in exchange for a return on investment.[35] The ETH was pooled and available to The DAO to fund projects. The projects (or "contracts") would be proposed by Contractors. If the proposed contracts were whitelisted by Curators, DAO Token holders could vote on whether The DAO should fund the proposed contracts. Depending on the terms of each particular contract, DAO Token holders stood to share in potential profits from the contracts. Thus, a reasonable investor would have been motivated, at least in part, by the prospect of profits on their investment of ETH in The DAO.

---

35. That the "projects" could encompass services and the creation of goods for use by DAO Token holders does not change the core analysis that investors purchased DAO Tokens with the expectation of earning profits from the efforts of others.

4. Derived from the Managerial Efforts of Others

a. The Efforts of Slock.it, Slock.it's Co-Founders, and The DAO's Curators Were Essential to the Enterprise

Investors' profits were to be derived from the managerial efforts of others—specifically, Slock.it and its co-founders, and The DAO's Curators. The central issue is "whether the efforts made by those other than the investor are the undeniably significant ones, those essential managerial efforts which affect the failure or success of the enterprise." *SEC v. Glenn W. Turner Enters., Inc.*, 474 F.2d 476, 482 (9th Cir. 1973). The DAO's investors relied on the managerial and entrepreneurial efforts of Slock.it and its co-founders, and The DAO's Curators, to manage The DAO and put forth project proposals that could generate profits for The DAO's investors.

Investors' expectations were primed by the marketing of The DAO and active engagement between Slock.it and its co-founders with The DAO and DAO Token holders. To market The DAO and DAO Tokens, Slock.it created The DAO Website on which it published the White Paper explaining how a DAO Entity would work and describing their vision for a DAO Entity. Slock.it also created and maintained other online forums that it used to provide information to DAO Token holders about how to vote and perform other tasks related to their investment. Slock.it appears to have closely monitored these forums, answering questions from DAO Token holders about a variety of topics, including the future of The DAO, security concerns, ground rules for how The DAO would work, and the anticipated role of DAO Token holders. The creators of The DAO held themselves out to investors as experts in Ethereum, the blockchain protocol on which The DAO operated, and told investors that they had selected persons to serve as Curators based on their expertise and credentials. Additionally, Slock.it told investors that it expected to put forth the first substantive profit-making contract proposal—a blockchain venture in its area of expertise. Through their conduct and marketing materials, Slock.it and its co-founders led investors to believe that they could be relied on to provide the significant managerial efforts required to make The DAO a success.

Investors in The DAO reasonably expected Slock.it and its co-founders, and The DAO's Curators, to provide significant managerial efforts after The DAO's launch. The expertise of The DAO's creators and Curators was critical in monitoring the operation of The DAO, safeguarding investor funds, and determining whether proposed contracts should be put for a vote. Investors had little choice but to rely on their expertise. At the time of the offering, The DAO's protocols had already been pre-determined by Slock.it and its co-founders, including the control that could be exercised by the Curators. Slock.it and its co-founders chose the Curators, whose function it was to: (1) vet Contractors; (2) determine whether and when to submit proposals for votes; (3) determine the order and frequency of proposals that were submitted for a vote; and (4) determine whether to halve the default quorum necessary for a successful vote on certain proposals. Thus, the Curators exercised significant control over the order and frequency of proposals, and could impose their own subjective criteria for whether the proposal should be whitelisted for a vote by DAO Token holders. DAO Token holders' votes were limited to proposals whitelisted by the Curators, and, although any DAO Token holder could put forth a proposal, each proposal would follow the same protocol, which included vetting and control by the current Curators. While DAO Token holders could put forth proposals to replace a Curator, such proposals were subject to control by the current Curators, including whitelisting and approval of the new address to which the tokens would be directed for such a proposal. In essence, Curators had the power to determine whether a proposal to remove a Curator was put to a vote.[36]

And, Slock.it and its co-founders did, in fact, actively oversee The DAO. They monitored The DAO closely and addressed issues as they arose, proposing a moratorium on all proposals until vulnerabilities in The DAO's code had been addressed and a security expert to monitor potential attacks on The DAO had been appointed. When the Attacker exploited a weakness in the code and removed investor funds, Slock.it and its co-founders stepped in to help resolve the situation.

b. DAO Token Holders' Voting Rights Were Limited

Although DAO Token holders were afforded voting rights, these voting rights were limited. DAO Token holders were substantially reliant on the managerial efforts of Slock.it, its co-founders, and the Curators.[37] Even if an investor's efforts help to make an enterprise profitable, those efforts do not necessarily equate with a promoter's significant managerial efforts or control over the enterprise. *See, e.g., Glenn W. Turner*, 474 F.2d at 482 (finding that a multi-level marketing scheme was an investment contract and that investors relied on the promoter's managerial efforts, despite the fact that investors put forth the majority of the labor that made the enterprise profitable, because the promoter dictated the terms and controlled the scheme itself); *Long v. Shultz*, 881 F.2d 129, 137 (5th Cir. 1989) ("An investor may authorize the assumption of particular risks that would create the possibility of greater profits or losses but still depend on a third party for all of the essential managerial efforts without which the risk could not pay off."). *See also generally SEC v. Merchant Capital, LLC*, 483 F.3d 747 (11th Cir. 2007) (finding an investment contract even where voting rights were provided to purported general partners, noting that the voting

---

36. DAO Token holders could put forth a proposal to split from The DAO, which would result in the creation of a new DAO Entity with a new Curator. Other DAO Token holders would be allowed to join the new DAO Entity as long as they voted yes to the original "split" proposal. Unlike all other contract proposals, a proposal to split did not require a deposit or a quorum, and it required a seven-day debating period instead of the minimum two-week debating period required for other proposals.

37. Because, as described above, DAO Token holders were incentivized either to vote yes or to abstain from voting, the results of DAO Token holder voting would not necessarily reflect the actual view of a majority of DAO Token holders.

process provided limited information for investors to make informed decisions, and the purported general partners lacked control over the information in the ballots).

The voting rights afforded DAO Token holders did not provide them with meaningful control over the enterprise, because (1) DAO Token holders' ability to vote for contracts was a largely perfunctory one; and (2) DAO Token holders were widely dispersed and limited in their ability to communicate with one another.

First, as discussed above, DAO Token holders could only vote on proposals that had been cleared by the Curators.[38] And that clearance process did not include any mechanism to provide DAO Token holders with sufficient information to permit them to make informed voting decisions. Indeed, based on the particular facts concerning The DAO and the few draft proposals discussed in online forums, there are indications that contract proposals would not have necessarily provide enough information for investors to make an informed voting decision, affording them less meaningful control. For example, the sample contract proposal attached to the White Paper included little information concerning the terms of the contract. Also, the Slock.it co-founders put forth a draft of their own contract proposal and, in response to questions and requests to negotiate the terms of the proposal (posted to a DAO forum), a Slock.it founder explained that the proposal was intentionally vague and that it was, in essence, a take it or leave it proposition not subject to negotiation or feedback. *See, e.g., SEC v. Shields*, 744 F.3d 633, 643–45 (10th Cir. 2014) (in assessing whether agreements were investment contracts, court looked to whether "the investors actually had the type of control reserved under the agreements to obtain access to information necessary to protect, manage, and control their investments at the time they purchased their interests.").

Second, the pseudonymity and dispersion of the DAO Token holders made it difficult for them to join together to effect change or to exercise meaningful control. Investments in The DAO were made pseudonymously (such that the real-world identities of investors are not apparent), and there was great dispersion among those individuals and/or entities who were invested in The DAO and thousands of individuals and/or entities that traded DAO Tokens in the secondary market—an arrangement that bears little resemblance to that of a genuine general partnership. *Cf. Williamson v. Tucker*, 645 F.2d 404, 422–24 (5th Cir. 1981) ("[O]ne would not expect partnership interests sold to large numbers of the general public to provide any real partnership control; at some point there would be so many [limited] partners that a partnership vote would be more like a corporate vote, each partner's role

---

38. Because, in part, The DAO never commenced its business operations funding projects, this Report does not analyze the question whether anyone associated with The DAO was an "[i]nvestment adviser" under Section 202(a)(11) of the Investment Advisers Act of 1940 ("Advisers Act"). *See* 15 U.S.C. § 80b-2(a)(11). Those who would use virtual organizations should consider their obligations under the Advisers Act.

having been diluted to the level of a single shareholder in a corporation.").[39] Slock.
it did create and maintain online forums on which investors could submit posts
regarding contract proposals, which were not limited to use by DAO Token holders
(anyone was permitted to post). However, DAO Token holders were pseudonymous,
as were their posts to the forums. Those facts, combined with the sheer number of
DAO Token holders, potentially made the forums of limited use if investors hoped
to consolidate their votes into blocs powerful enough to assert actual control. This
was later demonstrated through the fact that DAO Token holders were unable to
effectively address the Attack without the assistance of Slock.it and others. The DAO
Token holders' pseudonymity and dispersion diluted their control over The DAO.
See Merchant Capital, 483 F.3d at 758 (finding geographic dispersion of investors
weighing against investor control).

These facts diminished the ability of DAO Token holders to exercise meaningful
control over the enterprise through the voting process, rendering the voting rights
of DAO Token holders akin to those of a corporate shareholder. *Steinhardt Group,
Inc. v. Citicorp.*, 126 F.3d 144, 152 (3d Cir. 1997) ("It must be emphasized that the
assignment of nominal or limited responsibilities to the participant does not negate
the existence of an investment contract; where the duties assigned are so narrowly
circumscribed as to involve little real choice of action … a security may be found to
exist…. [The] emphasis must be placed on economic reality.") (citing *SEC v. Koscot
Interplanetary, Inc.*, 497 F.2d 473, 483 n. 14 (5th Cir. 1974)).

By contract and in reality, DAO Token holders relied on the significant managerial efforts provided by Slock.it and its co-founders, and The DAO's Curators, as described above. Their efforts, not those of DAO Token holders, were the "undeniably
significant" ones, essential to the overall success and profitability of any investment
into The DAO. *See Glenn W. Turner*, 474 F.2d at 482.

---

39. The Fifth Circuit in *Williamson* stated that:
    A general partnership or joint venture interest can be designated a security if the inves-
    tor can establish, for example, that (1) an agreement among the parties leaves so little
    power in the hands of the partner or venture that the arrangement in fact distributes
    power as would a limited partnership; or (2) the partner or venturer is so inexperienced
    and unknowledgeable in business affairs that he is incapable of intelligently exercising
    his partnership or venture powers; or (3) the partner or venturer is so dependent on
    some unique entrepreneurial or managerial ability of the promoter or manager that he
    cannot replace the manager of the enterprise or otherwise exercise meaningful part-
    nership or venture powers.
    Williamson, 645 F.2d at 424 & n.15 (court also noting that, "this is not to say that other factors
    could not also give rise to such a dependence on the promoter or manager that the exercise of part-
    nership powers would be effectively precluded.").

C. Issuers Must Register Offers and Sales of Securities Unless a Valid Exemption Applies

The definition of "issuer" is broadly defined to include "every person who issues or proposes to issue any security" and "person" includes "any unincorporated organization." 15 U.S.C. § 77b(a)(4). The term "issuer" is flexibly construed in the Section 5 context "as issuers devise new ways to issue their securities and the definition of a security itself expands." *Doran v. Petroleum Mgmt. Corp.*, 545 F.2d 893, 909 (5th Cir. 1977); *accord SEC v. Murphy*, 626 F.2d 633, 644 (9th Cir. 1980) ("[W]hen a person [or entity] organizes or sponsors the organization of limited partnerships and is primarily responsible for the success or failure of the venture for which the partnership is formed, he will be considered an issuer....").

The DAO, an unincorporated organization, was an issuer of securities, and information about The DAO was "crucial" to the DAO Token holders' investment decision. *See Murphy*, 626 F.2d at 643 ("Here there is no company issuing stock, but instead, a group of individuals investing funds in an enterprise for profit, and receiving in return an entitlement to a percentage of the proceeds of the enterprise.") (citation omitted). The DAO was "responsible for the success or failure of the enterprise," and accordingly was the entity about which the investors needed information material to their investment decision. *Id.* at 643–44.

During the Offering Period, The DAO offered and sold DAO Tokens in exchange for ETH through The DAO Website, which was publicly-accessible, including to individuals in the United States. During the Offering Period, The DAO sold approximately 1.15 billion DAO Tokens in exchange for a total of approximately 12 million ETH, which was valued in USD, at the time, at approximately $150 million. Because DAO Tokens were securities, The DAO was required to register the offer and sale of DAO Tokens, unless a valid exemption from such registration applied.

Moreover, those who participate in an unregistered offer and sale of securities not subject to a valid exemption are liable for violating Section 5. *See, e.g.*, *Murphy*, 626 F.2d at 650–51 ("[T]hose who ha[ve] a necessary role in the transaction are held liable as participants.") (citing *SEC v. North Am. Research & Dev. Corp.*, 424 F.2d 63, 81 (2d Cir. 1970); *SEC v. Culpepper*, 270 F.2d 241, 247 (2d Cir. 1959); *SEC v. International Chem. Dev. Corp.*, 469 F.2d 20, 28 (10th Cir. 1972); *Pennaluna & Co. v. SEC*, 410 F.2d 861, 864 n.1, 868 (9th Cir. 1969)); *SEC v. Softpoint, Inc.*, 958 F. Supp 846, 859–60 (S.D.N.Y. 1997) ("The prohibitions of Section 5 ... sweep[] broadly to encompass 'any person' who participates in the offer or sale of an unregistered, non-exempt security."); *SEC v. Chinese Consol. Benevolent Ass'n.*, 120 F.2d 738, 740–41 (2d Cir. 1941) (defendant violated Section 5(a) "because it engaged in selling unregistered securities" issued by a third party "when it solicited offers to buy the securities 'for value'").

D. A System that Meets the Definition of an Exchange Must Register as a National Securities Exchange or Operate Pursuant to an Exemption from Such Registration

Section 5 of the Exchange Act makes it unlawful for any broker, dealer, or exchange, directly or indirectly, to effect any transaction in a security, or to report any such transaction, in interstate commerce, unless the exchange is registered as a national securities exchange under Section 6 of the Exchange Act, or is exempted from such registration. *See* 15 U.S.C. §78e. Section 3(a)(1) of the Exchange Act defines an "exchange" as "any organization, association, or group of persons, whether incorporated or unincorporated, which constitutes, maintains, or provides a market place or facilities for bringing together purchasers and sellers of securities or for otherwise performing with respect to securities the functions commonly performed by a stock exchange as that term is generally understood...." 15 U.S.C. § 78c(a)(1).

Exchange Act Rule 3b-16(a) provides a functional test to assess whether a trading system meets the definition of exchange under Section 3(a)(1). Under Exchange Act Rule 3b-16(a), an organization, association, or group of persons shall be considered to constitute, maintain, or provide "a marketplace or facilities for bringing together purchasers and sellers of securities or for otherwise performing with respect to securities the functions commonly performed by a stock exchange," if such organization, association, or group of persons: (1) brings together the orders for securities of multiple buyers and sellers; and (2) uses established, non-discretionary methods (whether by providing a trading facility or by setting rules) under which such orders interact with each other, and the buyers and sellers entering such orders agree to the terms of the trade. [40]

A system that meets the criteria of Rule 3b-16(a), and is not excluded under Rule 3b- 16(b), must register as a national securities exchange pursuant to Sections 5 and 6 of the Exchange Act [41] or operate pursuant to an appropriate exemption. One frequently used exemption is for alternative trading systems ("ATS"). [42] Rule 3a1-1(a)(2)

---

40. *See* 17 C.F.R. § 240.3b-16(a). The Commission adopted Rule 3b-16(b) to exclude explicitly certain systems that the Commission believed did not meet the exchange definition. These systems include systems that merely route orders to other execution facilities and systems that allow persons to enter orders for execution against the bids and offers of a single dealer system. *See* Securities Exchange Act Rel. No. 40760 (Dec. 8, 1998), 63 FR 70844 (Dec. 22, 1998) (Regulation of Exchanges and Alternative Trading Systems) ("Regulation ATS"), 70852.

41. 15 U.S.C. § 78e. A "national securities exchange" is an exchange registered as such under Section 6 of the Exchange Act. 15 U.S.C. § 78f.

42. Rule 300(a) of Regulation ATS promulgated under the Exchange Act provides that an ATS is: any organization, association, person, group of persons, or system: (1) [t]hat constitutes, maintains, or provides a market place or facilities for bringing together purchasers and sellers of securities or for otherwise performing with respect to securities the functions commonly performed by a stock exchange within the meaning of [Exchange Act Rule 3b-16]; and (2) [t]hat does not: (i) [s]et rules governing the conduct of subscribers other than the conduct of subscribers' trading on such [ATS]; or (ii) [d]iscipline subscribers other than by exclusion from trading.
Regulation ATS, *supra* note 40, Rule 300(a).

exempts from the[43] definition of "exchange" under Section 3(a)(1) an ATS that complies with Regulation ATS, which includes, among other things, the requirement to register as a broker-dealer and file a Form ATS with the Commission to provide notice of the ATS's operations. Therefore, an ATS that operates pursuant to the Rule 3a1-1(a)(2) exemption and complies with Regulation ATS would not be subject to the registration requirement of Section 5 of the Exchange Act.

The Platforms that traded DAO Tokens appear to have satisfied the criteria of Rule 3b- 16(a) and do not appear to have been excluded from Rule 3b-16(b). As described above, the Platforms provided users with an electronic system that matched orders from multiple parties to buy and sell DAO Tokens for execution based on non-discretionary methods.

IV. Conclusion and References for Additional Guidance

Whether or not a particular transaction involves the offer and sale of a security—regardless of the terminology used—will depend on the facts and circumstances, including the economic realities of the transaction. Those who offer and sell securities in the United States must comply with the federal securities laws, including the requirement to register with the Commission or to qualify for an exemption from the registration requirements of the federal securities laws. The registration requirements are designed to provide investors with procedural protections and material information necessary to make informed investment decisions. These requirements apply to those who offer and sell securities in the United States, regardless whether the issuing entity is a traditional company or a decentralized autonomous organization, regardless whether those securities are purchased using U.S. dollars or virtual currencies, and regardless whether they are distributed in certificated form or through distributed ledger technology. In addition, any entity or person engaging in the activities of an exchange, such as bringing together the orders for securities of multiple buyers and sellers using established non- discretionary methods under which such orders interact with each other and buyers and sellers entering such orders agree upon the terms of the trade, must register as a national securities exchange or operate pursuant to an exemption from such registration.

To learn more about registration requirements under the Securities Act, please visit the Commission's website here. To learn more about the Commission's registration requirements for investment companies, please visit the Commission's website here. To learn more about the Commission's registration requirements for national securities exchanges, please visit the Commission's website here. To learn more

---

43. *See* 17 C.F.R. §240.3a1-1(a)(2). Rule 3a1-1 also provides two other exemptions from the definition of "exchange" for any ATS operated by a national securities association, and any ATS not required to comply with Regulation ATS pursuant to Rule 301(a) of Regulation ATS. *See* 17 C.F.R. §§240.3a1-1(a)(1) and (3).

about alternative trading systems, please see the Regulation ATS adopting release here.

For additional guidance, please see the following Commission enforcement actions involving virtual currencies:

- *SEC v. Trendon T. Shavers and Bitcoin Savings and Trust*, Civil Action No. 4:13- CV-416 (E.D. Tex., complaint filed July 23, 2013)
- *In re Erik T. Voorhees*, Rel. No. 33-9592 (June 3, 2014)
- *In re BTC Trading, Corp. and Ethan Burnside*, Rel. No. 33-9685 (Dec. 8, 2014)
- *SEC v. Homero Joshua Garza, Gaw Miners, LLC, and ZenMiner, LLC (d/b/a Zen Cloud)*, Civil Action No. 3:15-CV-01760 (D. Conn., complaint filed Dec. 1, 2015)
- *In re Bitcoin Investment Trust and SecondMarket, Inc.*, Rel. No. 34-78282 (July 11, 2016)
- *In re Sunshine Capital, Inc.*, File No. 500-1 (Apr. 11, 2017)

And please see the following investor alerts:

Bitcoin and Other Virtual Currency-Related Investments (May 7, 2014)

Ponzi Schemes Using Virtual Currencies (July 2013)

By the Commission.

Discussion Points

1. *Howey and the DAO report.* What were the key factors the SEC considered in determining whether DAO tokens constituted securities subject to federal securities laws? Discuss the Howey test and how it applies to DAO tokens. To what extent does the Howey test define the scope of securities regulations?

2. *Did the SEC get it right?* Was the DAO report overly broad? Could the report have been more specific on the issues of centralization and decentralization? Should it have included more definitions or a stronger advisory regarding how federal securities laws apply to the cryptocurrency space?

3. *Post-DAO and Initial Coin Offerings.* The DAO report was issued at a time when initial coin offerings were very popular. Why did the report fail to prevent future initial coin offerings? If the DAO report was issued in 2017, why did it take the SEC close to seven years before it began to take a hard stance on enforcement against tokens that existed before the report was issued?

4. Explain the legal significance of the Security and Exchange Commission's DAO report in the context of securities regulations and the usage of cryptocurrencies and blockchain technology.

5. Analyze the jurisdictional issues that arise in the SEC regulating the issuance of tokens and decentralized autonomous organizations.

6. Discuss the global impact of the DAO report and how other jurisdictions might respond to such guidance.

UNITED STATES OF AMERICA
Before the
SECURITIES AND EXCHANGE COMMISSION

SECURITIES EXCHANGE ACT OF 1934

Release No. 92607 / August 9, 2021

ADMINISTRATIVE PROCEEDING

File No. 3-20455

In the Matter of Poloniex, LLC, Respondent.	ORDER INSTITUTING CEASE-AND- DESIST PROCEEDINGS PURSUANT TO SECTION 21C OF THE SECURITIES EXCHANGE ACT OF 1934, MAKING FINDINGS, AND IMPOSING A CEASE- AND-DESIST ORDER

I.

The Securities and Exchange Commission ("Commission") deems it appropriate that cease-and-desist proceedings be, and hereby are, instituted pursuant to Section 21C of the Securities Exchange Act of 1934 ("Exchange Act") against Poloniex, LLC ("Poloniex" or "Respondent").

II.

In anticipation of the institution of these proceedings, Respondent has submitted an Offer of Settlement (the "Offer"), which the Commission has determined to accept. Solely for the purpose of these proceedings and any other proceedings brought by or on behalf of the Commission, or to which the Commission is a party, and without admitting or denying the findings herein, except as to the Commission's jurisdiction over it and the subject matter of these proceedings, which are admitted, Respondent consents to the entry of this Order Instituting Cease-and-Desist Proceedings Pursuant to Section 21C of the Securities Exchange Act of 1934, Making Findings, and Imposing a Cease-and-Desist Order ("Order"), as set forth below.

III.

On the basis of this Order and Respondent's Offer, the Commission finds[1] that:

Summary

1. Poloniex operated a digital asset trading platform (the "Poloniex Trading Platform") that meets the definition of an "exchange" under the federal securities laws. The Poloniex Trading Platform displayed a limit order book that matched the orders of multiple buyers and sellers in digital assets, including digital assets that were investment contracts under *SEC v. W.J. Howey Co.*, 328 U.S. 293 (1946), and therefore securities (hereinafter referred to as "Digital Asset Securities") based on established non-discretionary methods. Notwithstanding its operation of the Poloniex Trading Platform, Poloniex did not register as a national securities exchange nor did it operate pursuant to an exemption from registration at any time, and its failure to do so was a violation of Section 5 of the Exchange Act.

2. Poloniex began operations on January 18, 2014, and provided services to both U.S. and international users ("Users"). A User could utilize the Poloniex Trading Platform by registering for an account and funding the account with digital assets that the User deposited into a digital asset wallet maintained by the Poloniex Trading Platform.[2] The User could then trade these digital assets, which included Digital Asset Securities, through the Poloniex Trading Platform. A User could withdraw its digital asset balance from the Poloniex Trading Platform by providing the address of another digital asset wallet owned by the User, and by directing Poloniex to transfer all or part of the User's digital asset holdings to that wallet.

3. On July 25, 2017, the Commission issued its *Report of Investigation Pursuant to Section 21(a) of the Securities Exchange Act of 1934: The DAO* (Exchange Act Rel. No. 81207) (July 25, 2017) (the "DAO Report"). In the DAO Report, the Commission advised that a platform that offers trading of digital assets that are securities and operates as an "exchange," as defined by the federal securities laws, must register with the Commission as a national securities exchange or operate pursuant to an exemption from registration. Under Section 3(a)(10) of the Exchange Act, a security includes "an investment contract." *See* 15 U.S.C. § 78c(a)(10). An investment contract is an investment of money in a common enterprise with a reasonable expectation

---

1. The findings herein are made pursuant to Respondent's Offer of Settlement and are not binding on any other person or entity in this or any other proceeding.

2. A digital asset wallet is computer software that maintains public keys and addresses and is used to send and receive digital assets on a blockchain.

of profits to be derived from the entrepreneurial or managerial efforts of others. *See Howey*, 328 U.S. at 301. After the DAO Report was published and through November 2019, when Poloniex sold the Poloniex Trading Platform to a third party (the "Relevant Period"), Poloniex made available for trading, on the Poloniex Trading Platform, digital assets that were offered and sold as securities as defined by Section 3(a)(10) of the Exchange Act, generating millions of dollars in revenues from transaction fees charged to Users.

4. As discussed further below, during the Relevant Period, Poloniex met the criteria of an "exchange" as defined by Section 3(a)(1) of the Exchange Act and Rule 3b-16 thereunder. During the Relevant Period, Poloniex was not registered with the Commission as a national securities exchange nor did it operate pursuant to any exemption from registration. As a result, Poloniex violated Section 5 of the Exchange Act.

Respondent

5. Poloniex, LLC, is a Delaware limited liability company with its principal place of business in Boston, Massachusetts. Poloniex is a wholly-owned subsidiary of Pluto Holdings, Inc. ("Pluto"), a Delaware corporation, which is a wholly-owned subsidiary of Circle Internet Financial Limited ("Circle"), an Irish private company. Poloniex operated the Poloniex Trading Platform during the Relevant Period. In November 2019, Pluto sold the Poloniex Trading Platform to a third party.

Facts

The Poloniex Trading Platform: Users, Order Entry, and Display

6. During the Relevant Period, the Poloniex Trading Platform operated as a web- based trading platform that facilitated buying and selling certain digital assets, which included Digital Asset Securities, in the secondary market. The Poloniex Trading Platform was available to retail and institutional investors, including United States residents. Throughout the Relevant Period, the Poloniex Trading Platform was operated by individuals located in the United States and accessible to Users in the United States.

7. Prior to trading on the Poloniex Trading Platform, Poloniex required Users to create a Poloniex account. Beginning in early 2018, Poloniex required all potential account applicants to submit their full name, email address, proof of address, country of residence, and a record of their government-issued identification as part of the onboarding process.

8. When placing orders on the Poloniex Trading Platform, Poloniex required Users to have sufficient funds to cover the order at the time it was placed. Poloniex maintained custody of the digital assets deposited by Users and maintained a ledger that individually denominated the digital asset amounts belonging to each User. Once digital assets were sent to the Poloniex Trading Platform, Users were able to enter into trade agreements with other Users for purchases and sales of other dig-

ital assets. Once Users reached agreement, the Poloniex Trading Platform effected transfers to and from User accounts. Poloniex did not act as a principal to any of the transactions that took place on or through the Poloniex Trading Platform. Users could move their digital assets off the Poloniex Trading Platform by directing Poloniex to authenticate the transfer of digital assets to a blockchain address specified by the User.

9. The Poloniex Trading Platform's website provided a user-friendly interface for Users to enter and display orders on the Poloniex Trading Platform. Users entered buy or sell orders into the Poloniex Trading Platform, which included the digital asset trading pair (the assets being exchanged), size, price, and time-in-force. Users also had the ability to enter into the platform automated, algorithmic orders using Poloniex's API or using Poloniex's mobile trading application for certain handheld devices. As long as Poloniex's website was operational, Users could enter orders through the website 24 hours a day, seven days a week.

10. The Poloniex Trading Platform's website displayed to Users the current, top firm bids and offers for digital assets by symbol, price, and size. The website also displayed account information for Users and provided fields for Users to input orders in any available trading pair. Depending on the digital asset being traded, the digital asset could only be exchanged for (meaning one side of the digital asset trading pair had to be): Bitcoin, Ether, Monero, Tether, or USD Coin. Poloniex did not offer any fiat currency functionality or trading.

The Poloniex Order Types, Book of Orders, and Matching

11. Poloniex offered Users the ability to place three types of orders: a market order to buy or sell a digital asset at the best available price; a limit order to buy or sell a digital asset at a specific price or better; or a stop-limit order, which converts to a limit order when the best quote reaches or passes the stop price (i.e., the best bid is at or lower than the stop price for sell orders, or the best offer is at or higher than the stop price for buy orders).

12. A User could cancel an order if the cancellation instruction was received before the order matched with another order. Once Poloniex matched the orders, the orders could not be cancelled. If any order had only been partially filled, the User could cancel the unfilled portion of the order.

13. After the User entered an order, Poloniex included the order in its order book for matching with orders from other Users. After the User entered an order into the platform, Poloniex updated the User's account to reflect the open order and included it in the order book for matching with orders from other Users.

14. The Poloniex Trading Platform displayed and prioritized orders entered on the order book on the basis of price and time. Buy orders were prioritized in decreasing order of prices with the highest bid placed at the top of the order book and sell orders were prioritized in increasing order of prices with the lowest ask placed at the top of the order book.

15. Orders with same prices were aggregated in the order book and were filled in a first in, first out manner. Poloniex maintained internal ledgers to track Users' balances in digital assets and updated Users' balances after an order was matched.

Trading Fees

16. Poloniex employed a volume-tiered, maker-taker fee schedule. A maker's order existed on the order book prior to the trade; the taker's order matched or took the maker's order. Poloniex charged a per transaction percentage fee ranging from 0–0.25% based on the User's 30- day trading volume and maker/taker status of the trade. Poloniex deducted trading fees from each transaction and aggregated the fees in a Poloniex-owned address of the digital asset in question.

The Poloniex Trading Platform Allowed Users to Transact in Digital Asset Securities

17. Both before and after being acquired by Circle, Poloniex implemented a digital asset "listing process" that included an analysis of whether an applicant's digital asset was a security.

18. Prior to the issuance of the DAO Report, Poloniex regularly informed applicants that it monitored the digital asset community and selected digital assets for "listing" that it believed were part of unique and innovative projects. Poloniex also regularly informed applicants that, as a matter of company policy, Poloniex "cannot list any token that resembles a security" and Poloniex "suggest[ed] token dev[eloper]s familiarize themselves with the Howey Test."

19. If Poloniex determined there was risk associated with a particular digital asset, including risk that the digital asset was a security, Poloniex would request that the applicant provide a memorandum from a third-party law firm analyzing whether the digital asset could be considered a security under *Howey*.

20. Following the issuance of the DAO Report, Poloniex issued a blog post reiterating that Poloniex would not provide a trading market for Digital Assets Securities.

21. Nevertheless, in or around August 2017, Poloniex stated internally that it wanted to be "aggressive" in making available for trading new digital assets on the Poloniex Trading Platform, including digital assets that might be considered securities under *Howey*, in an effort to increase market share. This resulted in Poloniex making available for trading on the Poloniex Trading Platform digital assets that were investment contracts under *Howey*, and therefore, securities.

22. Upon Circle's acquisition of Poloniex in February 2018, Poloniex updated its process for reviewing digital assets to include (1) an initial screening and data collection; and (2) an evaluation for each digital asset applicant if it passed the initial screening. In 2018, Circle created an internal Executive Risk Committee to evaluate when it would be appropriate for the Poloniex Trading Platform to provide a trading market for a particular digital asset, and Circle formed an in-house "token" legal

team and engaged new outside counsel to provide additional legal advice on these decisions.

23. Nevertheless, in or around July 2018, Poloniex determined that it would continue to provide users of the Poloniex Trading Platform the ability to trade digital assets that were at "medium risk" of being considered securities under *Howey*. Poloniex made this determination to offer trading in "medium risk" Digital Asset Securities in light of the business rewards that would provide to Poloniex. This resulted in Poloniex continuing to make available to Users for trading on the Poloniex Trading Platform Digital Asset Securities, which resulted in the Poloniex Trading Platform operating as an unregistered exchange.

24. As a result of the above, during the Relevant Period, the Poloniex Trading Platform provided Users the ability to buy and sell digital assets that were offered and sold as investment contracts under *Howey*, and therefore, securities.

25. After conducting a re-review in 2018 of the 75 digital assets available to Users for trading, Poloniex determined to "delist" certain digital assets from the Poloniex Trading Platform. Poloniex ceased providing Users a trading market for these digital assets in two phases. In phase 1 in July 2018, Poloniex removed digital assets that traded in lower volumes and thus produced lower profits for Poloniex. In phase 2, occurring from September through November 2018, Poloniex undertook "to remove projects that are considered securities." But despite these "delistings," Poloniex continued to allow Users to trade certain Digital Asset Securities until it sold the Poloniex Trading Platform in November 2019.

Violations

26. As a result of the conduct described above, Poloniex violated Section 5 of the Exchange Act, which makes it unlawful for any broker, dealer, or exchange, directly or indirectly, to effect any transaction in a security, or to report any such transaction, in interstate commerce, unless the exchange is registered as a national securities exchange under Section 6 of the Exchange Act, or is exempted from such registration.

27. Section 3(a)(1) of the Exchange Act defines an "exchange" as

> any organization, association, or group of persons, whether incorporated or unincorporated, which constitutes, maintains, or provides a market place or facilities for bringing together purchasers and sellers of securities or for otherwise performing with respect to securities the functions commonly performed by a stock exchange as that term is generally understood, and includes the market place and the market facilities maintained by such exchange.

15 U.S.C. § 78c(a)(1). Exchange Act Rule 3b-16(a) provides a functional test to assess whether a trading system meets the definition of exchange under Section 3(a)(1) of the Exchange Act. Exchange Act Rule 3b-16(a) provides that an organization, association, or group of persons shall be considered to constitute, maintain,

or provide "a market place or facilities for bringing together purchasers and sellers of securities or for otherwise performing with respect to securities the functions commonly performed by an exchange" as those terms are used in Section 3(a)(1) of the Exchange Act if such an organization, association, or group of persons: (1) brings together the orders for securities of multiple buyers and sellers; and (2) uses established, non- discretionary methods (whether by providing a trading facility or by setting rules) under which such orders interact with each other, and the buyers and sellers entering such orders agree to the terms of the trade.[3]

28. A system that meets the criteria of Exchange Act Rule 3b-16(a), and is not excluded under Exchange Act Rule 3b-16(b), must register, pursuant to Section 5 of the Exchange Act, as a national securities exchange under Section 6 of the Exchange Act[4] or operate pursuant to an appropriate exemption. One of the available exemptions is for ATSs.[5] Exchange Act Rule 3a1-1(a)(2) exempts from the definition of "exchange" under Section 3(a)(1) an organization, association, or group of persons that complies with Regulation ATS.[6] Regulation ATS requires an ATS to, among other things, register as a broker-dealer, file a Form ATS with the Commission to notice its operations, and establish written safeguards and procedures to protect subscribers' confidential trading information. An ATS that complies with Regulation ATS and operates pursuant to the Rule 3a1-1(a)(2) exemption would not be required by Section 5 to register as a national securities exchange.

29. Poloniex satisfied the criteria of Exchange Act Rule 3b-16(a) and is not excluded under Rule 3b-16(b). As described above, Poloniex provided a limit order book for bringing together orders of multiple buyers and sellers. Poloniex received and stored orders from Users in digital assets, many of which were securities, on the Poloniex order book and displayed the top orders (including symbol, size, and price) as bids and offers on the Poloniex website. Poloniex provided the means for these

---

3. *See* 17 CFR § 240.3b-16(a). The Commission adopted Exchange Act Rule 3b-16(b) to explicitly exclude certain systems that the Commission believed did not meet the exchange definition. These systems include systems that merely route orders to other execution facilities and systems that allow persons to enter orders for execution against the bids and offers of a single dealer system. *See* Securities Exchange Act Rel. No. 40760 (Dec. 8, 1998), 63 FR 70844 (Dec. 22, 1998) (Regulation of Exchanges and Alternative Trading Systems, hereinafter "Regulation ATS Adopting Release"), at 70852.

4. *See* 15 U.S.C. §§ 78e-78f. A "national securities exchange" is an exchange registered as such under Section 6 of the Exchange Act.

5. Rule 300(a) of Regulation ATS provides that an ATS is "any organization, association, person, group of persons, or system: (1) [t]hat constitutes, maintains, or provides a market place or facilities for bringing together purchasers and sellers of securities or for otherwise performing with respect to securities the functions commonly performed by a stock exchange within the meaning of [Exchange Act Rule 3b-16]; and (2) [t]hat does not: (i) [s]et rules governing the conduct of subscribers other than the conduct of subscribers' trading on such [ATS]; or (ii) [d]iscipline subscribers other than by exclusion from trading."

6. *See* 17 CFR 240.3a1-1(a)(2). Rule 3a1-1 also provides exemptions from the definition of "exchange" for any ATS operated by a national securities association, and any ATS not required to comply with Regulation ATS pursuant to Rule 301(a) of Regulation ATS. *See* 17 CFR 240.3a1-1(a) (1) and (3). Neither of these exemptions are applicable in the present matter.

orders to interact and execute through the combined use of the Poloniex website, order book, and pre-programmed trading protocols defined in the Poloniex trading engine. These established non-discretionary methods allowed Users to agree upon the terms of their trades in Digital Asset Securities on Poloniex during the Relevant Period.

30. Despite operating as a Rule 3b-16(a) system, Poloniex did not register as a national securities exchange or operate pursuant to an exemption from such registration. Accordingly, Poloniex violated Section 5 of the Exchange Act.

Disgorgement and Civil Penalties

31. The disgorgement and prejudgment interest ordered in paragraph B is consistent with equitable principles and does not exceed Respondent's net profits from its violations, and will be distributed to harmed investors to the extent feasible. The Commission will hold funds paid pursuant to paragraph B in an account at the United States Treasury pending distribution. Upon approval of the distribution final accounting by the Commission, any amounts remaining that are infeasible to return to investors, and any amounts returned to the Commission in the future that are infeasible to return to investors, may be transferred to the general fund of the U.S. Treasury, subject to Section 21F(g)(3) of the Exchange Act.

IV.

In view of the foregoing, the Commission deems it appropriate and in the public interest to impose the sanctions agreed to in Respondent's Offer.

Accordingly, it is hereby ORDERED that:

A. Pursuant to Section 21C of the Exchange Act, Respondent Poloniex cease and desist from committing or causing any violations and any future violations of Section 5 of the Exchange Act.

B. Respondent Poloniex shall, within 10 days of the entry of this Order, pay disgorgement of $8,484,313.99, prejudgment interest of $403,995.12, and a civil money penalty of $1,500,000, for a total of $10,388,309.10, to the Securities and Exchange Commission. If timely payment of disgorgement and prejudgment interest is not made, additional interest shall accrue pursuant to SEC Rule of Practice 600. If timely payment of a civil money penalty is not made, additional interest shall accrue pursuant to 31 U.S.C. § 3717.

C. Payment must be made in one of the following ways:

1. Respondent may transmit payment electronically to the Commission, which will provide detailed ACH transfer/Fedwire instructions upon request;

2. Respondent may make direct payment from a bank account via Pay.gov through the SEC website at http://www.sec.gov/about/offices/ofm.htm; or

3. Respondent may pay by certified check, bank cashier's check, or United States postal money order, made payable to the Securities and Exchange Commission and hand-delivered or mailed to:

Enterprise Services Center Accounts Receivable Branch HQ Bldg., Room 181, AMZ-341 6500 South MacArthur Boulevard Oklahoma City, OK 73169

Payments by check or money order must be accompanied by a cover letter identifying Poloniex as Respondent in these proceedings, and the file number of these proceedings; a copy of the cover letter and check or money order must be sent to A. Kristina Littman, Chief, Cyber Unit, Division of Enforcement, Securities and Exchange Commission, 100 F Street, NE, Washington, DC 20549, or such other person or address as the Commission staff may provide.

D. Pursuant to Section 308(a) of the Sarbanes-Oxley Act of 2002, a Fair Fund is created for the disgorgement, prejudgment interest, and penalties referenced in paragraph B above. Amounts ordered to be paid as civil money penalties pursuant to this Order shall be treated as penalties paid to the government for all purposes, including all tax purposes. To preserve the deterrent effect of the civil penalty, Respondent agrees that in any Related Investor Action, it shall not argue that it is entitled to, nor shall it benefit by, offset or reduction of any award of compensatory damages by the amount of any part of Respondent's payment of a civil penalty in this action ("Penalty Offset"). If the court in any Related Investor Action grants such a Penalty Offset, Respondent agrees that it shall, within 30 days after entry of a final order granting the Penalty Offset, notify the Commission's counsel in this action and pay the amount of the Penalty Offset to the Securities and Exchange Commission. Such a payment shall not be deemed an additional civil penalty and shall not be deemed to change the amount of the civil penalty imposed in this proceeding. For purposes of this paragraph, a "Related Investor Action" means a private damages action brought against Respondent by or on behalf of one or more investors based on substantially the same facts as alleged in the Order instituted by the Commission in this proceeding.

By the Commission.

Vanessa A. Countryman
Secretary

Discussion Points

1. *Poloniex, LLC.* To what extent did the SEC clarify what activities constituted securities exchange operations? Was enough information provided for similarly-situated companies to determine whether they operate a securities exchange?

2. Discuss how the case interprets the definition of "digital asset" and the legal significance of the court's interpretation in the context of exchanging digital assets.

3. Should the SEC have determined which digital assets on the exchange constituted securities? Why or why not? What were the central issues addressed in the case in the context of exchanging digital assets?

4. Explain and analyze the legal factors that were considered in determining whether Poloniex, LLC violated any laws or regulations.

5. Identify and analyze any unresolved legal questions or ambiguities that stem from the case and might affect future exchanges of digital assets.

UNITED STATES OF AMERICA
Before the
SECURITIES AND EXCHANGE COMMISSION

SECURITIES ACT OF 1933

Release No. 11173 / March 22, 2023

ADMINISTRATIVE PROCEEDING

File No. 3-21349

In the Matter of Lindsay Dee Lohan Respondent.	ORDER INSTITUTING CEASE-AND- DESIST PROCEEDINGS PURSUANT TO SECTION 8A OF THE SECURITIES ACT OF 1933, MAKING FINDINGS, AND IMPOSING A CEASE- AND-DESIST ORDER

I.

The Securities and Exchange Commission ("Commission") deems it appropriate that cease- and-desist proceedings be, and hereby are, instituted pursuant to Section 8A of the Securities Act of 1933 ("Securities Act"), against Lindsay Dee Lohan ("Lohan" or "Respondent").

II.

In anticipation of the institution of these proceedings, Respondent has submitted an Offer of Settlement (the "Offer") which the Commission has determined to accept. Solely for the purpose of these proceedings and any other proceedings brought by or on behalf of the Commission, or to which the Commission is a party, and without admitting or denying the findings herein, except as to the Commission's jurisdiction over her and the subject matter of these proceedings, which are admitted, and except as provided herein in Section V, Respondent consents to the entry of this Order Instituting Cease-and-Desist Proceedings Pursuant to Section 8A of the Securities Act of 1933, Making Findings, and Imposing a Cease-and-Desist Order ("Order"), as set forth below.

III.

On the basis of this Order and Respondent's Offer, the Commission finds[1] that:

Summary

1. On February 11, 2021, Lohan—a well-known actress, singer, and internet personality—touted on social media a crypto asset security that was being offered and sold. Lohan did not disclose that she was being paid to give publicity to such security by the entity offering and selling it to the public. Lohan's failure to disclose this compensation violated Section 17(b) of the Securities Act, which makes it unlawful for any person to promote a security without fully disclosing the receipt and amount of such compensation from an issuer.

Respondent

2. Lohan, age 36, is a resident of Dubai, United Arab Emirates.

Facts

3. In February 2021, Lohan promoted a crypto asset security on Twitter in exchange for a payment of $10,000 from the issuer. Lohan, at the time of her promotion, had approximately 8.4 million Twitter followers.

4. Specifically, Lohan promoted a security being publicly offered by Tron Foundation Limited ("Tron"), and Tron's owner and control person Yuchen (Justin) Sun ("Sun"), called "Tronix" tokens ("TRX"). TRX tokens are offered and sold as investment contracts, and therefore constitute securities pursuant to Section 2(a)(1) of the Securities Act.

5. From August 2017 to the present, Tron and Sun have engaged in the continuous public offer and sale of TRX tokens. Based on Tron's and Sun's offering materials and public statements, purchasers of TRX tokens would have had a reasonable expectation of profits from their investment in the tokens. Tron and Sun explicitly promoted TRX as an investment and touted the potential for significant returns to investors through buying, holding, and trading TRX tokens. Tron and Sun worked to list TRX on numerous crypto asset trading platforms, including within the United

---

1. The findings herein are made pursuant to Respondent's Offer of Settlement and are not binding on any other person or entity in this or any other proceeding.

States, and publicly encouraged investors to purchase TRX through the new venues. Tron and Sun routinely touted the market capitalization, price, and trading volume of TRX, and published articles advising followers of purportedly opportunistic times to "invest" in TRX.

6. Based on Tron's and Sun's public statements, purchasers of the TRX tokens would have had a reasonable expectation that Tron and Sun would expend significant efforts to develop the Tron platform and a secondary trading market for TRX, which would increase the value of TRX tokens and drive investor profits. Tron's offering materials and marketing communications highlighted that the value of TRX depended entirely on Tron's efforts to develop and grow the Tron platform and drive demand for the token, thereby increasing its price on the secondary market. Tron's social media accounts and websites highlighted its profitability, accelerated growth, and the team's credentials and experience to demonstrate that the company would be able to implement its business plan effectively.

7. Lohan promoted the TRX offering on social media by posting the following to her Twitter account on February 11, 2021:

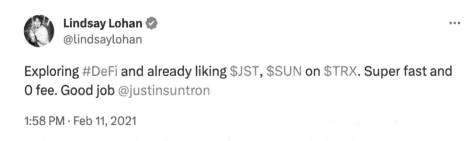

Lindsay Lohan ✔
@lindsaylohan

Exploring #DeFi and already liking $JST, $SUN on $TRX. Super fast and 0 fee. Good job @justinsuntron

1:58 PM · Feb 11, 2021

1,076 Reposts   **1,158** Quotes   **5,970** Likes   **110** Bookmarks

8. Tron, through an intermediary, paid Lohan $10,000 for this promotion and provided Lohan with the specific language to include in the Tweet. Lohan did not disclose that she had been paid by Tron, or the amount of compensation she received from Tron and Sun for promoting the TRX offering on Twitter.

9. Lohan's crypto asset security promotion occurred after the Commission warned in its July 25, 2017, DAO Report of Investigation that digital tokens or coins offered and sold may be securities, and those who offer and sell securities in the United States must comply with the federal securities laws. [2] The promotion also occurred nearly four years after the Commission's Division of Enforcement and Office

---

2. Report of Investigation Pursuant to Section 21(a) of the Securities Exchange Act of 1934: The DAO, Exchange Act Rel. No. 81207 (July 25, 2017).

of Compliance Inspections and Examinations issued a statement reminding market participants that "[a]ny celebrity or other individual who promotes a virtual token or coin that is a security must disclose the nature, scope, and amount of compensation received in exchange for the promotion. A failure to disclose this information is a violation of the anti-touting provisions of the federal securities laws."[3]

Lohan Violated Section 17(b) of the Securities Act

10. Section 17(b) of the Securities Act makes it unlawful for any person to: publish, give publicity to, or circulate any notice, circular, advertisement, newspaper, article, letter, investment service, or communication which, though not purporting to offer a security for sale, describes such security for a consideration received or to be received, directly or indirectly, from an issuer, underwriter, or dealer, without fully disclosing the receipt, whether past or prospective, of such consideration and the amount thereof.

11. Lohan violated Section 17(b) of the Securities Act by touting the TRX token offering on her Twitter account without disclosing that she received compensation from the issuer for doing so, and the amount of the consideration.

Disgorgement and Civil Penalties

12. The disgorgement and prejudgment interest ordered in paragraph IV.C is consistent with equitable principles and does not exceed Respondent's net profits from her violations and will be distributed to harmed investors, if feasible. The Commission will hold funds paid pursuant to paragraph IV.C in an account at the United States Treasury pending a decision whether the Commission in its discretion will seek to distribute funds. If a distribution is determined feasible and the Commission makes a distribution, upon approval of the distribution final accounting by the Commission, any amounts remaining that are infeasible to return to investors, and any amounts returned to the Commission in the future that are infeasible to return to investors, may be transferred to the general fund of the U.S. Treasury, subject to Section 21F(g)(3) of the Exchange Act. undertakings.

Undertakings

13. Respondent has undertaken to:

a. for a period of three (3) years from the date of this Order, forgo receiving or agreeing to receive any form of compensation or consideration, directly or indirectly, from any issuer, underwriter, or dealer, for directly or indirectly publishing, giving publicity to, or circulating any notice, circular, advertisement, newspaper, article, letter, investment service, or communication which,

---

3. *See* SEC Staff Statement Urging Caution Around Celebrity Backed ICOs (Nov. 1, 2017), *available at* https://www.sec.gov/news/public-statement/statement-potentially-unlawful-promotion-icos.

though not purporting to offer a crypto asset security for sale, describes such crypto asset security; and

b. continue to cooperate with the Commission's investigation in this matter.

14. In determining whether to accept the Offer, the Commission has considered these

IV.

In view of the foregoing, the Commission deems it appropriate to impose the sanctions agreed to in Respondent's Offer.

Accordingly, it is hereby ORDERED that:

A. Pursuant to Section 8A of the Securities Act, Respondent cease and desist from committing or causing any violations and any future violations of Section 17(b) of the Securities Act.

B. Respondent shall comply with the undertakings enumerated in Section III, paragraph 13(a) above.

C. Respondent shall pay disgorgement of $10,000, prejudgment interest of $670, and a civil money penalty in the amount of $30,000 to the Securities and Exchange Commission. Payment shall be made in the following installments: (i) $13,557 due within 14 days of the entry of the Order; (ii) $13,557 due within 120 days of the Order; (iii) $13,556 due within 240 days of the entry of the Order; and (iv) any remaining amount outstanding due within 360 days of the entry of the Order. Payments shall be applied first to post-order interest, which accrues pursuant to SEC Rule of Practice 600 and/or pursuant to 31 U.S.C. § 3717. Prior to making the final payment set forth herein, Respondent shall contact the staff of the Commission for the amount due. If Respondent fails to make any payment within 2 business days of the date agreed and/or in the amount agreed according to the schedule set forth above, all outstanding payments under this Order, including post- order interest, minus any payments made, shall become due and payable immediately at the discretion of the staff of the Commission without further application to the Commission. The Commission may distribute the funds paid pursuant to this paragraph if, in its discretion, the Commission orders the establishment of a Fair Fund pursuant to 15 U.S.C. § 7246, Section 308(a) of the Sarbanes-Oxley Act of 2002. The Commission will hold funds paid pursuant to this paragraph in an account at the United States Treasury pending a decision whether the Commission, in its discretion, will seek to distribute funds or, transfer them to the general fund of the United States Treasury, subject to Section 21F(g)(3). If timely payment is not made, additional interest shall accrue pursuant to SEC Rule of Practice 600.

D. Payment must be made in one of the following ways:

(1) Respondent may transmit payment electronically to the Commission, which will provide detailed ACH transfer/Fedwire instructions upon request;

(2) Respondent may make direct payment from a bank account via Pay.gov through the SEC website at http://www.sec.gov/about/offices/ofm.htm; or

(3) Respondent may pay by certified check, bank cashier's check, or United States postal money order, made payable to the Securities and Exchange Commission and hand-delivered or mailed to:

Enterprise Services Center Accounts Receivable Branch HQ Bldg., Room 181, AMZ-341 6500 South MacArthur Boulevard Oklahoma City, OK 73169

Payments by check or money order must be accompanied by a cover letter identifying Lindsay Dee Lohan as a Respondent in these proceedings, and the file number of these proceedings; a copy of the cover letter and check or money order must be sent to David Hirsch, Chief, Crypto Assets and Cyber Unit, Division of Enforcement, Securities and Exchange Commission, 100 F St., NE, Washington, DC 20549.

E. Amounts ordered to be paid as civil money penalties pursuant to this Order shall be treated as penalties paid to the government for all purposes, including all tax purposes. To preserve the deterrent effect of the civil penalty, Respondent agrees that in any Related Investor Action, she shall not argue that she is entitled to, nor shall she benefit by, offset or reduction of any award of compensatory damages by the amount of any part of Respondent's payment of a civil penalty in this action ("Penalty Offset"). If the court in any Related Investor Action grants such a Penalty Offset, Respondent agrees that she shall, within 30 days after entry of a final order granting the Penalty Offset, notify the Commission's counsel in this action and pay the amount of the Penalty Offset to the Securities and Exchange Commission. Such a payment shall not be deemed an additional civil penalty and shall not be deemed to change the amount of the civil penalty imposed in this proceeding. For purposes of this paragraph, a "Related Investor Action" means a private damages action brought against Respondent by or on behalf of one or more investors based on substantially the same facts as alleged in the Order instituted by the Commission in this proceeding.

V.

It is further Ordered that, solely for purposes of exceptions to discharge set forth in Section 523 of the Bankruptcy Code, 11 U.S.C. §523, the findings in this Order are true and admitted by Respondent, and further, any debt for disgorgement, prejudgment interest, civil penalty or other amounts due by Respondent under this Order or any other judgment, order, consent order, decree or settlement agreement entered in connection with this proceeding, is a debt for the violation by Respondent of the federal securities laws or any regulation or order issued under such laws, as set forth in Section 523(a)(19) of the Bankruptcy Code, 11 U.S.C. §523(a)(19).

By the Commission.

Vanessa A. Countryman
Secretary

Discussion Points

1. *TRX.* What was the purpose of TRX? What did the SEC consider in alleging that TRX was a security? Should we hold celebrities accountable for promoting investment schemes? Can you provide historical examples of celebrities being held accountable for promoting or advertising investment schemes before cryptocurrencies existed?

2. *Penalties.* Lindsay Lohan was ordered to pay $40,670 in penalties for her promotion of TRX. Are financial penalties against celebrities promoting digital assets justified or should the SEC have merely issued a warning instead? Should the SEC issue guidance about the promotion of digital assets to disincentivize promoters from financially benefitting from undisclosed investment schemes? Why or why not?

3. *Celebrity Endorsement.* Should celebrities and other promoters be required to disclose their digital asset investments? Should they be required to disclose any compensation they received in exchange for promoting an investment scheme?

4. Explain the main legal issues regarding Lohan's exchange of digital assets in the context of whether any laws or regulations were violated.

5. Discuss the legal impact that this case might have on the future of digital asset exchanges and potential privacy concerns that may arise.

6. Analyze and explain any counterarguments to the SEC's finding that Lohan violated Section 17(b) of the Securities Act.

II. Initial Coin Offerings

Initial Coin Offerings (ICOs) began to increase in prevalence between 2016 and 2018.[26] This growth was a result of the ability to use Ethereum blockchain and the use of smart contracts. A smart contract is a contract made in the blockchain that runs when pre-determined conditions are met. Prior to the 2016 development of Ethereum, the concept of cryptocurrency was limited to being a medium of exchange in peer-to-peer transfers. Ethereum blockchain provided tools for individuals to create their own digital token, including the flexibility and use of smart contracts. ICOs are used by start-up companies to raise funds in the offering of new cryptocurrencies. In return for capital to fund a new network's development, developers sell

---

26. *See* Chairman Jay Clayton, Chairman's Testimony on Virtual Currencies: The Roles of the SEC and CFTC, Testimony, U.S. Securities and Exchange Commission (Feb. 6, 2018) ("Coinciding with the substantial growth in cryptocurrencies, companies and individuals increasingly have been using so-called ICOs to raise capital for businesses and projects. Typically, these offerings involve the opportunity for individual investors to exchange currency, such as U.S. dollars or cryptocurrencies, in return for a digital asset labeled as a coin or token. The size of the ICO market has grown exponentially in the last year, and it is estimated that almost $4 billion was raised through ICOs in 2017.").

tokens of a new cryptocurrency that provide investors exclusive access to the future network. Whether the virtual coins being offered constitute securities depends on the circumstances surrounding the ICO.[27]

The SEC considers most ICO tokens to be securities. However, some ICO tokens may not be classified as securities. If ICO tokens are deemed securities, the offer and sale of the tokens will be subjected to federal securities laws.[28] As noted above, the Howey test includes four elements that must be met to determine if an asset is a security. When applying the Howey test, if a digital asset can be characterized "as an investment of money in a common enterprise with an expectation of profits derived from the efforts of others," it likely qualifies as a security.

Certain regulatory obligations are imposed when a digital asset can be classified as a security. A platform that brings purchasers and sellers together for the purpose of trading digital assets classified as securities is subject to SEC registration requirements.[29]

In the Matter of Munchee Inc.

Securities Act Release No. 10445

File No. 3-18304 (2017)

I.

The Securities and Exchange Commission ("Commission") deems it appropriate that cease-and-desist proceedings be, and hereby are, instituted pursuant to Section 8A of the Securities Act of 1933 ("Securities Act") against Munchee Inc. ("Munchee" or "Respondent").

II.

In anticipation of the institution of these proceedings, Respondent has submitted an Offer of Settlement (the "Offer") which the Commission has determined to accept. Solely for the purpose of these proceedings and any other proceedings brought by or on behalf of the Commission, or to which the Commission is a party, and without admitting or denying the findings herein, except as to the Commission's jurisdiction over it and the subject matter of these proceedings, which are admitted, Respondent consents to the entry of this Order Instituting Cease-and-Desist

---

27. *See* Investor Bulletin: Initial Coin Offerings, U.S. Securities and Exchange Commission (July 25, 2017); *see also* Chairman Jay Clayton, Statement on Cryptocurrencies and Initial Coin Offerings, U.S. Securities and Exchange Commission (Dec. 11, 2017) (noting that, "it is possible to conduct an ICO without triggering the SEC's registration requirements. For example, just as with a Regulation D exempt offering to raise capital for the manufacturing of a physical product, an initial coin offering that is a security can be structured so that it qualifies for an applicable exemption from the registration requirements.").

28. *See id.*

29. *Id.*

Proceedings Pursuant To Section 8A of the Securities Act, Making Findings, And Imposing A Cease-And-Desist Order ("Order"), as set forth below.

III.

On the basis of this Order and Respondent's Offer, the Commission finds that:

Summary

Munchee is a California business that created an iPhone application ("app") for people to review restaurant meals. In October and November 2017, Munchee offered and then sold digital tokens ("MUN" or "MUN token") to be issued on a blockchain or a distributed ledger. Munchee conducted the offering of MUN tokens to raise about $15 million in capital so that it could improve its existing app and recruit users to eventually buy advertisements, write reviews, sell food and conduct other transactions using MUN. In connection with the offering, Munchee described the way in which MUN tokens would increase in value as a result of Munchee's efforts and stated that MUN tokens would be traded on secondary markets.

Based on the facts and circumstances set forth below, MUN tokens were securities pursuant to Section 2(a)(1) of the Securities Act. MUN tokens are "investment contracts" under *SEC v. W.J. Howey Co.*, 328 U.S. 293 (1946), and its progeny, including the cases discussed by the Commission in its Report of Investigation Pursuant To Section 21(a) Of The Securities Exchange Act of 1934: The DAO (Exchange Act Rel. No. 81207) (July 25, 2017) (the "DAO Report"). Among other characteristics of an "investment contract," a purchaser of MUN tokens would have had a reasonable expectation of obtaining a future profit based upon Munchee's efforts, including Munchee revising its app and creating the MUN "ecosystem" using the proceeds from the sale of MUN tokens. Munchee violated Sections 5(a) and 5(c) of the Securities Act by offering and selling these securities without having a registration statement filed or in effect with the Commission or qualifying for exemption from registration with the Commission. On the second day of sales of MUN tokens, the company was contacted by Commission staff. The company determined within hours to shut down its offering, did not deliver any tokens to purchasers, and returned to purchasers the proceeds that it had received.

Respondent

Munchee is a privately-owned Delaware corporation based in San Francisco.

Facts

1. Munchee is a California business that created an app (the "Munchee App") for use with iPhones. The company began developing the app in late 2015 and launched the app in the second quarter of 2017.

2. The Munchee App allows users to post photographs and reviews of meals that they eat in restaurants. The Munchee App is available only in the United States.

3. Munchee and its agents control the content on multiple web pages, including but not limited to its website (the "Munchee Website"), an additional site where it posted Munchee's "white paper" (the "MUN White Paper"), a Twitter account, a Facebook page, and posts on various message boards (collectively, the "Munchee Web Pages").

Munchee Offers To Sell MUN To The General Public

4. By Fall 2017, Munchee had developed a plan to improve the Munchee App during 2018 and 2019 that included raising capital through the creation of the MUN token and incorporating the token into the Munchee App. The MUN is a token issued on the Ethereum blockchain. Munchee created 500 million MUN tokens and stated that no additional tokens could be created.

5. On or about October 1, 2017, Munchee announced it would be launching an "initial coin offering" or "ICO"[1] to offer MUN tokens to the general public. Munchee posted the MUN White Paper that described MUN tokens, the offering process, how Munchee would use the offering proceeds to develop its business, the way in which MUN tokens would increase in value, and the ability for MUN token holders to trade MUN tokens on secondary markets. Munchee posted information about the offering and the MUN White Paper through posts on the Munchee Web Pages, including on a blog, Facebook, Twitter, BitcoinTalk, and the Munchee Website.

6. MUN tokens were to be available for purchase by individuals in the United States and worldwide through websites and social media pages including, but not limited to, the Munchee Web Pages.

7. Pursuant to the MUN White Paper, Munchee sought to raise about $15 million in Ether by selling 225 million MUN tokens out of the 500 million total MUN tokens created by the company. Purchasers of MUN tokens in the earlier stages of the offering were offered discounts of 15% and 10% on the offering price. Munchee said it would keep the remaining 275 million MUN tokens and use those MUN tokens to support its business, including by paying rewards in the Munchee App with MUN tokens, paying its employees and advisors with MUN tokens, and "facilitating advertising transactions in the future." In the MUN White Paper and elsewhere, Munchee said that it would spend 75% of the offering proceeds to hire people for

---

1. An "initial coin offering" or "ICO" is a recently developed form of fundraising event in which an entity offers participants a unique digital "coin" or "token" in exchange for consideration (most commonly Bitcoin, Ether, or fiat currency). The tokens are issued and distributed on a "blockchain" or cryptographically-secured ledger. Tokens often are also listed and traded on online platforms, typically called virtual currency exchanges, and they usually trade for other digital assets or fiat currencies. Often, tokens are listed and tradable immediately after they are issued.

Issuers often release a "white paper" describing the particular project they seek to fund and the terms of the ICO. Issuers often pay others to promote the offering, including through social media channels such as message boards, online videos, blogs, Twitter, and Facebook. There are websites and social media feeds dedicated to discussions about ICOs and the offer, sale and trading of coins and tokens.

its development team and to market and promote the Munchee App, use 15% "for maintenance and to ensure the smooth operation of the MUN token ecosystem" and use 10% for "legals to make sure Munchee is compliant in all countries." Munchee described a timeline that provided for various development milestones in 2018 and 2019, including the development of a smart contract on the Ethereum blockchain to integrate "in-app" use of the MUN token and setting up in-app wallets for end-users.

8. The MUN White Paper referenced the DAO Report and stated that Munchee had done a "Howey analysis" and that "as currently designed, the sale of MUN utility tokens does not pose a significant risk of implicating federal securities laws." The MUN White Paper, however, did not set forth any such analysis.

Munchee's Plan To Create An "Ecosystem" And Take Other Steps To Increase The Value Of MUN

9. Munchee offered MUN tokens in order to raise capital to build a profitable enterprise. Munchee said that it would use the offering proceeds to run its business, including hiring people to develop its product, promoting the Munchee App, and ensuring "the smooth operation of the MUN token ecosystem."

10. While Munchee told potential purchasers that they would be able to use MUN tokens to buy goods or services in the future after Munchee created an "ecosystem," no one was able to buy any good or service with MUN throughout the relevant period.

11. On the Munchee Website, in the MUN White Paper and elsewhere, Munchee described the "ecosystem" that it would create, stating that it would pay users in MUN tokens for writing food reviews and would sell both advertising to restaurants and "in-app" purchases to app users in exchange for MUN tokens. Munchee also said it would work with restaurant owners so diners could buy food with MUN tokens and so that restaurant owners could reward app users—perhaps those who visited the restaurant or reviewed their meal—in MUN tokens. As a result, MUN tokens would increase in value. Below is an image of "Figure 1" from the MUN White Paper in which Munchee described how increased participation in the "ecosystem" would purportedly lead to increased value of MUN tokens:

Figure 1: Munchee Economic Model

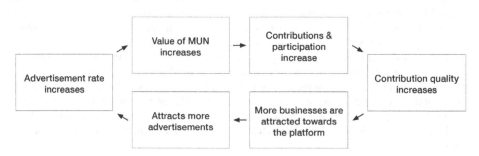

12. In the MUN White Paper, on the Munchee Website and elsewhere, Munchee and its agents further emphasized that the company would run its business in ways that would cause MUN tokens to rise in value. First, Munchee described a "tier" plan in which the amount it would pay for a Munchee App review would depend on the amount of the author's holdings of MUN tokens. For example, a "Diamond Level" holder having at least 300 MUN tokens would be paid more for a review than a "Gold Level" holder having only 200 MUN tokens. Also, Munchee said it could or would "burn" MUN tokens in the future when restaurants pay for advertising with MUN tokens, thereby taking MUN tokens out of circulation. Munchee emphasized to potential purchasers how they could profit from those efforts:

> Munchee could potentially choose to [sic] burn (take out of circulation) a small fraction of MUN tokens every time [sic] a restaurant pays Munchee as [sic] advertising fee. This, along with our tiered membership plan could potentially increase the appreciation of the remaining MUN tokens as the total supply in circulation reduces and as users would prefer holding their MUN tokens.

13. Munchee intended for MUN tokens to trade on a secondary market. In the MUN White Paper, Munchee stated that it would work to ensure that MUN holders would be able to sell their MUN tokens on secondary markets, saying that "Munchee will ensure that MUN token is available on a number of exchanges in varying jurisdictions to ensure that this is an option for all token-holders." Munchee represented that MUN tokens would be available for trading on at least one U.S.-based exchange within 30 days of the conclusion of the offering. It also stated that Munchee would buy or sell MUN tokens using its retained holdings in order to ensure there was a liquid secondary market in MUN tokens.

Munchee Promoted MUN Tokens And Purchasers Had A Reasonable Expectation Of Obtaining A Future Profit

14. Purchasers reasonably would have viewed the MUN token offering as an opportunity to profit. Purchasers had a reasonable expectation that they would obtain a future profit from buying MUN tokens if Munchee were successful in its entrepreneurial and managerial efforts to develop its business. Purchasers would reasonably believe they could profit by holding or trading MUN tokens, whether or not they ever used the Munchee App or otherwise participated in the MUN "ecosystem," based on Munchee's statements in its MUN White Paper and other materials. Munchee primed purchasers' reasonable expectations of profit through statements on blogs, podcasts, and Facebook that talked about profits.

15. For example, Munchee published a blog post on October 30, 2017 that was titled "7 Reasons You Need To Join The Munchee Token Generation Event." Reason 4 listed on the post was "As more users get on the platform, the more valuable your MUN tokens will become" and then went on to describe how MUN purchasers

could "watch[] their value increase over time" and could count on the "burning" of MUN tokens to raise the value of remaining MUN tokens.

16. Similarly, on or about October 23, 2017, one of Munchee's founders described the opportunity on a podcast about the MUN offering:

> So they [users] will create more quality content to attract more restaurants onto the platform. So the more restaurants we have, the more quality content Munchee has, the value of the MUN token will go up – it's like an underlying incentive for users to actually contribute and actually build the community.

17. In addition, Munchee made public statements or endorsed other people's public statements that touted the opportunity to profit. For example, on or about October 25, 2017, Munchee created a public posting on Facebook, linked to a third-party YouTube video, and wrote "199% GAINS on MUN token at ICO price! Sign up for PRE-SALE NOW!" The linked video featured a person who said "Today we are going to talk about Munchee. Munchee is a crazy ICO. If you don't know what an ICO is, it is called an initial coin offering. Pretty much, if you get into it early enough, you'll probably most likely get a return on it." This person went on to use his "ICO investing sheet" to compare the MUN token offering to what he called the "Top 15 ICOs of all time" and "speculate[d]" that a $1,000 investment could create a $94,000 return.

18. Munchee and its agents targeted the marketing of the MUN tokens offering to people with an interest in tokens or other digital assets that have in recent years created profits for early investors in ICOs. This marketing did not use the Munchee App or otherwise specifically target current users of the Munchee App to promote how purchasing MUN tokens might let them qualify for higher tiers and bigger payments on future reviews. Nor did Munchee advertise the offering of MUN tokens in restaurant industry media to reach restaurant owners and promote how MUN tokens might let them advertise in the future. Instead, Munchee and its agents promoted the MUN token offering in forums aimed at people interested in investing in Bitcoin and other digital assets, including on BitcoinTalk.org, a message board where people discuss investing in digital assets. These forums are available and attract viewers worldwide, even though the Munchee App was only available in the United States.

19. For example, one of Munchee's founders chose to appear and promote the MUN token offering on the podcast discussed above where the host talks with guests about blockchains and digital assets, emphasizing the financial value of "cryptocurrency." On that podcast, the Munchee founder talked about making money purchasing digital assets, including her own profits investing in Ether and other digital assets.

20. Similarly, Munchee offered to provide MUN tokens to people who published promotional videos, articles or blog posts in forums such as BitcoinTalk.org or otherwise helped Munchee promote the MUN token offering. More than 300 people

promoted the MUN token offering through social media and by translating MUN token offering documents into multiple languages so that Munchee could reach potential investors in South Korea, Russia, and other countries where the Munchee App was unavailable.

MUN Token Purchasers Reasonably Expected They Would Profit From The Efforts Of Munchee And Its Agents

21. Purchasers would reasonably have had the expectation that Munchee and its agents would expend significant efforts to develop an application and "ecosystem" that would increase the value of their MUN tokens.

22. Munchee highlighted the credentials, abilities and management skills of its agents and employees. For example, in the MUN White Paper and elsewhere, Munchee highlighted that its founders had worked at prominent technology companies and highlighted their skills running businesses and creating software.

23. As discussed above, Munchee said in the MUN White Paper that the value of MUN tokens would depend on the company's ability to change the Munchee App and create a valuable "ecosystem" that would inspire users to create new reviews, inspire restaurants to obtain MUN tokens to reward diners and pay Munchee for advertising, and inspire users to obtain MUN tokens to buy meals and to attain higher status within the Munchee App. Munchee said that it and its agents would undertake that work during 2018 and 2019.

24. Potential purchasers would have had a reasonable understanding that their future profit depended on Munchee creating a MUN "ecosystem." For example, on or about October 25, 2017, a person posted a video on YouTube to describe the MUN token offering. The person's YouTube channel has approximately 15,000 followers and was created by a self-proclaimed "[c]ryptocurrency enthusiast" who believed "[t]he early investor catches the bitcoin." In the video review, the person discussed that MUN token purchasers would profit only after Munchee did years of work:

> If you are investing in [MUN tokens] now, you do need to keep in mind that it will be awhile before the [Munchee] platform becomes active. So if you are looking at it as a speculative—I want to get it and flip it straight away—you really need to hold on to this one at least until it hits the app in 2018. Obviously, if you can hold this a bit longer until 2019, that is when I think the real value of Munchee is going to be delivered on once it, sort of, gets a lot of users on it.

Munchee Starts To Sell MUN On October 31, 2017

25. On or about October 31, 2017, Munchee started selling MUN tokens. Purchasers could pay one (1) Ether or one-twentieth (1/20) of a Bitcoin to buy 4,500 MUN. On or about November 1, 2017, Ether was trading on virtual currency exchanges for about $300 USD and Bitcoin was trading for about $6,500 USD.

Munchee Stopped Selling MUN When It Was
Contacted By Commission Staff

26. On November 1, 2017, Munchee stopped selling MUN tokens hours after being contacted by Commission staff. Munchee had not delivered any tokens to purchasers, and the company promptly returned to purchasers the proceeds that it had received. [2]

27. About 40 people purchased MUN tokens from Munchee. In aggregate, they paid about 200 Ether (or about $60,000 in USD at the time of the offering).

Legal Analysis

28. Under Section 2(a)(1) of the Securities Act, a security includes "an investment contract." See 15 U.S.C. § 77b. An investment contract is an investment of money in a common enterprise with a reasonable expectation of profits to be derived from the entrepreneurial or managerial efforts of others. See *SEC v. Edwards*, 540 U.S. 389, 393 (2004); *SEC v. W.J. Howey Co.*, 328 U.S. 293, 301 (1946); see also *United Housing Found., Inc. v. Forman*, 421 U.S. 837, 852–53 (1975) (The "touchstone" of an investment contract "is the presence of an investment in a common venture premised on a reasonable expectation of profits to be derived from the entrepreneurial or managerial efforts of others."). This definition embodies a *"flexible rather than a static principle*, one that is capable of adaptation to meet the countless and variable schemes devised by those who seek the use of the money of others on the promise of profits." *Howey*, 328 U.S. at 299 (emphasis added). The test "permits the fulfillment of the statutory purpose of compelling full and fair disclosure relative to the issuance of 'the many types of instruments that in our commercial world fall within the ordinary concept of a security.'" *Id.* In analyzing whether something is a security, "form should be disregarded for substance," *Tcherepnin v. Knight*, 389 U.S. 332, 336 (1967), "and the emphasis should be on economic realities underlying a transaction, and not on the name appended thereto." *Forman*, 421 U.S. at 849.

29. As the Commission discussed in the DAO Report, tokens, coins or other digital assets issued on a blockchain may be securities under the federal securities laws, and, if they are securities, issuers and others who offer or sell them in the United States must register the offering and sale with the Commission or qualify for an exemption from registration.

A. The MUN Tokens Were Securities

30. As described above, the MUN tokens were securities as defined by Section 2(a)(1) of the Securities Act because they were investment contracts.

---

2. Munchee and the investors entered into a contract of sale for MUN in which investors were irrevocably bound. On November 1, 2017, Munchee unilaterally terminated the contracts of sale, returning the money to investors. Any offer by Munchee to buy the investors' securities would have required registration of the transaction or an exemption from registration.

31. Munchee offered and sold MUN tokens in a general solicitation that included potential investors in the United States. Investors paid Ether or Bitcoin to purchase their MUN tokens. Such investment is the type of contribution of value that can create an investment contract.

32. MUN token purchasers had a reasonable expectation of profits from their investment in the Munchee enterprise. The proceeds of the MUN token offering were intended to be used by Munchee to build an "ecosystem" that would create demand for MUN tokens and make MUN tokens more valuable. Munchee was to revise the Munchee App so that people could buy and sell services using MUN tokens and was to recruit "partners" such as restaurants willing to sell meals for MUN tokens. The investors reasonably expected they would profit from any rise in the value of MUN tokens created by the revised Munchee App and by Munchee's ability to create an "ecosystem"—for example, the system described in the offering where restaurants would want to use MUN tokens to buy advertising from Munchee or to pay rewards to app users, and where app users would want to use MUN tokens to pay for restaurant meals and would want to write reviews to obtain MUN tokens. In addition, Munchee highlighted that it would ensure a secondary trading market for MUN tokens would be available shortly after the completion of the offering and prior to the creation of the ecosystem. Like many other instruments, the MUN token did not promise investors any dividend or other periodic payment. Rather, as indicated by Munchee and as would have reasonably been understood by investors, investors could expect to profit from the appreciation of value of MUN tokens resulting from Munchee's efforts.

33. Investors' profits were to be derived from the significant entrepreneurial and managerial efforts of others—specifically Munchee and its agents – who were to revise the Munchee App, create the "ecosystem" that would increase the value of MUN (through both an increased demand for MUN tokens by users and Munchee's specific efforts to cause appreciation in value, such as by burning MUN tokens), and support secondary markets. Investors had little choice but to rely on Munchee and its expertise. At the time of the offering and sale of MUN tokens, no other person could make changes to the Munchee App or was working to create an "ecosystem" to create demand for MUN tokens.

34. Investors' expectations were primed by Munchee's marketing of the MUN token offering. To market the MUN token offering, Munchee and its agents created the Munchee Website and the MUN White Paper and then posted on message boards, social media and other outlets. They described how Munchee would revise the Munchee App and how the new "ecosystem" would create demand for MUN tokens. They likened MUN to prior ICOs and digital assets that had created profits for investors, and they specifically marketed to people interested in those assets – and those profits—rather than to people who, for example, might have wanted MUN tokens to buy advertising or increase their "tier" as a reviewer on the Munchee App. Because of the conduct and marketing materials of Munchee and its agents, investors would have had a reasonable belief that Munchee and its agents could be

relied on to provide the significant entrepreneurial and managerial efforts required to make MUN tokens a success.

35. Even if MUN tokens had a practical use at the time of the offering, it would not preclude the token from being a security. Determining whether a transaction involves a security does not turn on labeling – such as characterizing an ICO as involving a "utility token"—but instead requires an assessment of "the economic realities underlying a transaction." *Forman*, 421 U.S. at 849. All of the relevant facts and circumstances are considered in making that determination. See *Forman*, 421 U.S. at 849 (purchases of "stock" solely for the purpose of obtaining housing not purchase of "investment contract"); see also *SEC v. C.M. Joiner Leasing Corp.*, 320 U.S. 344, 352–53 (1943) (indicating the "test... is what character the instrument is given in commerce by the terms of the offer, the plan of distribution, and the economic inducements held out to the prospect").

B. Munchee Offered And Sold MUN Tokens In Violation Of The Securities Act

36. As described above, Munchee offered and sold securities to the general public, including potential investors in the United States, and actually sold securities to about 40 investors. No registration statements were filed or in effect for the MUN token offers and sales and no exemptions from registration were available.

37. As a result of the conduct described above, Munchee violated Section 5(a) of the Securities Act, which states that unless a registration statement is in effect as to a security, it shall be unlawful for any person, directly or indirectly, to make use of any means or instruments of transportation or communication in interstate commerce or of the mails to sell such security through the use or medium of any prospectus or otherwise; or to carry or cause to be carried through the mails or in interstate commerce, by any means or instruments of transportation, any such security for the purpose of sale or for delivery after sale.

38. Also as a result of the conduct described above, Munchee violated Section 5(c) of the Securities Act, which states that it shall be unlawful for any person, directly or indirectly, to make use of any means or instruments of transportation or communication in interstate commerce or of the mails to offer to sell or offer to buy through the use or medium of any prospectus or otherwise any security, unless a registration statement has been filed as to such security.

Munchee's Remedial Actions

39. In determining to accept the Offer, and to not impose a civil penalty, the Commission considered remedial acts promptly undertaken by Respondent and cooperation afforded the Commission staff.

IV.

In view of the foregoing, the Commission deems it appropriate to impose the sanctions agreed to in Respondent's Offer.

Accordingly, it is hereby ORDERED that:

A. Pursuant to Section 8A of the Securities Act, Respondent Munchee cease and desist from committing or causing any violations and any future violations of Sections 5(a) and (c) of the Securities Act.

Discussion Points

1. *Repercussions of the Munchee Case.* The SEC cease-and-desist order to Munchee, Inc. proved that SEC was going to be regulating ICOs more closely and that the realm of utility tokens is much smaller than previously believed. Did the *Munchee* case reshape the ICO space?

2. *SEC commentary on ICOs.* Prior to the increase in prevalence of ICOs, the SEC had not issued any comment on cryptocurrency. Should they have?

3. *The SEC's focus.* Was the SEC focused on using ICOs for raising funds generally, or only for companies that are looking to build out future products?

4. *Implication of a closed loop system.* How would this case have been different, if at all, if MUN token was created at the time when it could have immediately been utilized within the Munchee platform? If there would have been a difference, would this token have been considered within the closed loop ecosystem, and not subject to securities laws?

5. *Should the SEC have taken more action?* The Munchee consent order was from 2017, yet the ICO continued to boom for the next few years. Could the SEC have done more to stop the continued rise in ICOs in 2018?

6. *The effect of Ethereum.* What ramifications, if any, did the development of Ethereum have on the characteristic of cryptocurrency as solely a medium of exchange?

In the Matter of Block.one

Securities Act of 1933 Release No. 10714

File No. 3-19568 (2019)

I.

The Securities and Exchange Commission ("Commission") deems it appropriate that cease- and-desist proceedings be, and hereby are, instituted pursuant to Section 8A of the Securities Act of 1933 ("Securities Act") against Block.one ("Block.one" or the "Respondent").

II.

In anticipation of the institution of these proceedings, Respondent has submitted an Offer of Settlement ("Offer") that the Commission has determined to accept. Solely for the purpose of these proceedings and any other proceedings brought by or on behalf of the Commission, or to which the Commission is a party, and without admitting or denying the findings herein, except as to the Commission's jurisdiction over it and the subject matter of these proceedings, which are admitted, Respondent consents to the entry of this Order Instituting Cease-and-Desist Proceedings Pursuant To Section 8A of the Securities Act of 1933, Making Findings, And Imposing a Cease-And-Desist Order ("Order"), as set forth below.

Summary

Block.one is a Cayman Islands-registered technology company that was established in 2016, and developed the EOSIO software, an operating system that would underlie one or more anticipated EOSIO-based blockchains. From June 26, 2017 through June 1, 2018 (the "Relevant Period"), Block.one conducted a "token distribution," or "initial coin offering" ("ICO"), in which it publicly offered and sold 900 million digital assets ("ERC-20 Tokens") in exchange for Ether, a digital asset, to raise capital to develop the EOSIO software and promote the launch of EOSIO-based blockchains.

Block.one raised Ether worth several billion dollars from the general public, including a portion from U.S. residents. Block.one did not register its offers and sales of the ERC-20 Tokens pursuant to the federal securities laws, nor did it qualify for an exemption to the registration requirements under the federal securities laws.

Based on the facts and circumstances set forth below, the ERC-20 Tokens were securities under the federal securities laws pursuant to *SEC v. W.J. Howey Co.*, 328 U.S. 293 (1946), and its progeny, including the cases discussed by the Commission in its Report of Investigation Pursuant To Section 21(a) Of The Securities Exchange Act of 1934: The DAO (Exchange Act Rel. No. 81207) (July 25, 2017) ("DAO Report"). A purchaser in the offering of ERC-20 Tokens would have had a reasonable expectation of obtaining a future profit based upon Block.one's efforts, including its development of the EOSIO software and its promotion of the adoption and success of EOSIO and the launch of the anticipated EOSIO blockchains. Block.one violated Sections 5(a) and 5(c) of the Securities Act by offering and selling these securities without having a registration statement filed or in effect with the Commission or qualifying for an exemption from registration.

IV.

Respondent

1. Block.one is a Cayman Islands-registered company and it currently has offices in Hong Kong and Blacksburg, Virginia. Neither Block.one nor its securities are registered with the Commission in any capacity.

Background

2. Block.one is a technology company that was established in 2016 to, among other things, develop the EOSIO software, an operating system designed to support public or private blockchains. The goal of the EOSIO software is to increase blockchain transaction speeds, reduce transaction costs, and improve scalability.

3. Block.one launched a website ("EOS.IO Website") and published a Technical White Paper ("White Paper") to market the EOSIO software and proposed EOSIO-based blockchains, and announced that it would be conducting an approximately year-long "initial coin offering," or "ICO" of tokens distributed on the Ethereum blockchain using the ERC-20 protocol.

4. Over the approximate one-year period from June 26, 2017, through June 1, 2018, Block.one offered and sold ERC-20 Tokens to the general public, selling and distributing 900 million ERC-20 Tokens in total. This was done through an automated and committed process, i.e., a "smart contract." When purchasing tokens, investors also entered into an electronic token purchase agreement ("Token Purchase Agreement"). Block.one also reserved 100 million tokens, referred to as "founders' tokens," for its own account. Block.one sold and distributed the ERC-20 Tokens in Dutch-style auctions on the following schedule: 200 million tokens were sold and distributed during the first five days of the ICO, and thereafter, 700 million tokens were split evenly into 350 consecutive 23-hour "distribution periods" of 2 million tokens each. On average, the ERC-20 Tokens sold for the equivalent of approximately $4.40 per token. In addition, the ERC-20 Tokens contained no restrictions on transfer following their initial sale and distribution, and the tokens began trading through online trading platforms as early as July 1, 2017.

5. Block.one ultimately raised several billion dollars' worth of Ether in the ICO, a portion of which was raised from U.S. persons notwithstanding certain measures, described below, undertaken by Block.one to prohibit U.S. persons from participating. At the close of the ICO, approximately 330,690 individual wallet addresses held the ERC-20 Tokens, with approximately 75% of all tokens held by 100 wallets.

6. The EOS.IO Website stated that the proceeds of the ICO would be "revenue" of Block.one, and it "intends to use certain of the proceeds for general administration and operating expenses, as well as to build a blockchain consulting business focusing on helping businesses re- imagine or build their businesses on the blockchain, developing more open source software that may be helpful to the community and building decentralized applications using EOS.IO Software."

7. As set forth in the Token Purchase Agreement, which was posted on the EOS.IO Website, and in other public statements, the ERC-20 Token was not the same token that eventually would be used on any anticipated EOSIO-based blockchains. Rather, the ERC-20 Token was designed to become fixed and non transferable on the Ethereum blockchain (a different blockchain platform) at the close of the ERC-20 Token sale, meaning that while a record of past transactions could be confirmed on the Ethereum blockchain, new transfers of the ERC-20 Token could not occur

on the Ethereum blockchain and the smart contract would have no further functionality at that point. Beginning in December 2017, Block.one began to release beta versions of the EOSIO software and explained that once the official version was published under an open source software license, anyone could view the software's code and use it to configure and launch blockchains (such as the EOS Blockchain, which would be a different blockchain than an Ethereum blockchain).

8. As anticipated, on June 1, 2018, Block.one's ICO closed, and the ERC-20 Token—which prior to this time had been transferrable in secondary market transactions—became fixed and non transferable. In addition to the EOSIO software, Block.one developed a "snapshot tool" that when used in conjunction with EOSIO, would allow any developer to launch a blockchain that, upon their election, could also contain the final ERC-20 Token register of accounts. Block.one advised that ERC-20 Token holders would need to register their token ownership through a smart contract on the Ethereum blockchain in order to be eligible to receive any native EOSIO-based blockchain tokens utilizing the snapshot tool, if and when those blockchains launched.

9. On June 14, 2018, the EOS Blockchain, the first EOSIO-based blockchain, was launched. The ERC-20 Tokens sold in the ICO remain fixed on the Ethereum blockchain, and the ERC-20 Tokens cannot be transferred.

Block.one Offered and Sold Securities Without Registration or an Applicable Exemption

10. Block.one launched the EOS.IO Website on May 11, 2017. Block.one subsequently sold and distributed the ERC-20 Tokens directly through the EOS.IO Website in exchange for Ether. The EOS.IO Website included certain measures intended to block U.S.-based purchasers from buying ERC-20 Tokens, including by blocking U.S.-based IP addresses from accessing the EOS.IO Website token sale page. In addition, Block.one required all ERC-20 Token purchasers to agree to the Token Purchase Agreement, which included provisions that U.S. persons were prohibited from purchasing ERC-20 Tokens, and that any purchase by a U.S. person was unlawful and rendered the purchase agreement null and void. Block.one did not, however, ascertain from purchasers whether they were in fact U.S.-based persons, and a number of U.S.-based persons purchased ERC-20 Tokens directly through the EOS.IO Website.

11. Block.one also undertook efforts for the purpose of, or that could reasonably be expected to have the effect of, conditioning the market in the U.S. for the ERC-20 Tokens, including by engaging in directed selling efforts. Among other things, Block.one participated in blockchain conferences in the U.S., including a prominent conference held in New York City in May 2017, to promote Block.one and which at times also promoted its ICO. In connection with the May 2017 Conference, Block.one advertised EOSIO on a large billboard in Times Square on May 22, 2017, pro-

moted EOSIO in informal informational sessions, and hosted a post-conference reception. Block.one also promoted its proposed business and ICO to U.S.-based persons on the EOS.IO Website and through various social media and forum posts. The EOS.IO Website, White Paper, and other promotional statements were accessible to purchasers and potential purchasers, and viewable by U.S. persons.

12. In addition, ERC-20 Tokens were traded and widely available for purchase on numerous online trading platforms open to U.S.-based purchasers throughout the duration of the ICO. Block.one did not take any steps to prevent the ERC-20 Tokens from being immediately resellable to U.S.-based purchasers in secondary market trades.

13. No registration statement concerning the offers and sales of ERC-20 Tokens was in effect at any time prior to or during the offering. The offers and sales did not qualify for any exemption from registration under the federal securities laws.

ERC-20 Token Purchasers Would Reasonably Have Expected That They Would Profit From the Efforts of Block.one

14. Block.one offered ERC-20 Tokens in order to raise capital and build a profitable enterprise, and ERC-20 Token purchasers would reasonably have understood that if Block.one was successful in doing so, their token purchase would be profitable.

15. At the time the ICO launched in June 2017, Block.one did not have any product in place, and its proposed software was largely conceptual. Purchasers would have understood that Block.one was a for-profit entity. Block.one stated that the ICO proceeds were "revenue" of the Company, and that it would use the proceeds to build a profitable enterprise by, among other things, developing the EOSIO software and promoting the widespread adoption of EOSIO and launch of anticipated EOSIO-based blockchains. Purchasers thus would have understood that Block.one's success in building and promoting the EOSIO software and promoting the launch of one or more EOSIO-based blockchains would make their token purchase profitable.

16. In January 2018, seven months into the 12-month ERC-20 Token offering, Block.one announced that it would invest $1 billion from the offering proceeds to "offer[] developers and entrepreneurs the funding they need to create community driven businesses leveraging EOSIO software."

17. In describing Block.one's plans to invest the proceeds of the ERC-20 Token sale to fund businesses that would use, directly or indirectly, an EOSIO-based blockchain, Block.one stated that "the money we spent on those initiatives will be returned value for the network" and that the money raised in the ICO would be spent wisely to fund development of EOSIO-based blockchains.

18. Over the approximately year-long ICO, ERC-20 Token purchasers' expectations were primed by Block.one's marketing of the ERC-20 Token and anticipated EOSIO blockchains. To market the ERC-20 Token, Block.one created the EOS.IO

Website and published an EOS White Paper and an "Introduction to EOS" technical paper. During the ICO, Block.one also was developing EOSIO software and released beta versions of the software to the public. Its founders also published articles and blog posts to promote the EOSIO software, and actively engaged U.S. purchasers and potential U.S. purchasers on social media, online message boards, and other outlets. In the course of marketing the EOSIO software, Block.one encouraged U.S. purchasers to rely on the founders' expertise and vision to secure the widespread adoption of the EOSIO software and anticipated launch of one or more EOSIO blockchains.

V.

Violations

19. As a result of the conduct described above regarding the offers and sales of ERC-20 Tokens in the ICO, Block.one violated Section 5(a) of the Securities Act, which states that unless a registration statement is in effect as to a security, it shall be unlawful for any person, directly or indirectly, to make use of any means or instruments of transportation or communication in interstate commerce or of the mails to sell such security through the use or medium of any prospectus or otherwise; or to carry or cause to be carried through the mails or in interstate commerce, by any means or instruments of transportation, any such security for the purpose of sale or for delivery after sale.

20. As a result of the conduct described above, Block.one violated Section 5(c) of the Securities Act, which states that it shall be unlawful for any person, directly or indirectly, to make use of any means or instruments of transportation or communication in interstate commerce or of the mails to offer to sell or offer to buy through the use or medium of any prospectus or otherwise any security, unless a registration statement has been filed as to such security.

VI.

In view of the foregoing, the Commission deems it appropriate to impose the sanctions agreed to in Respondent's Offer.

Accordingly, it is hereby ORDERED that:

A. Pursuant to Section 8A of the Securities Act, Respondent Block.one cease and desist from committing or causing any violations and any future violations of Sections 5(a) and 5(c) of the Securities Act.

B. Respondents shall, within 10 days of the entry of this Order, pay a civil money penalty in the amount of $24,000,000 to the Securities and Exchange Commission for transfer to the general fund of the United States Treasury, subject to Exchange Act Section 21F(g)(3). If timely payment is not made, additional interest shall accrue pursuant to 31 U.S.C. § 3717.

Payment must be made in one of the following ways:

1. Respondent may transmit payment electronically to the Commission, which will provide detailed ACH transfer/Fedwire instructions upon request;

2. Respondent may make direct payment from a bank account via Pay.gov through the SEC website at http://www.sec.gov/about/offices/ofm.htm; or

3. Respondent may pay by certified check, bank cashier's check, or United States postal money order, made payable to the Securities and Exchange Commission and hand-delivered or mailed to:

Enterprise Services Center Accounts Receivable Branch

HQ Bldg., Room 181, AMZ-341

6500 South MacArthur Boulevard

Oklahoma City, OK 73169

Payments by check or money order must be accompanied by a cover letter identifying Block.one as a Respondent in these proceedings, and the file number of these proceedings; a copy of the cover letter and check or money order must be sent to Lara Shalov Mehraban, Associate Regional Director, Division of Enforcement, Securities and Exchange Commission, New York Regional Office, 200 Vesey Street, Suite 400, New York, New York 10281.

C. Amounts ordered to be paid as civil money penalties pursuant to this Order shall be treated as penalties paid to the government for all purposes, including all tax purposes. To preserve the deterrent effect of the civil penalty, Respondent agrees that in any Related Investor Action, it shall not argue that it is entitled to, nor shall it benefit by, offset or reduction of any award of compensatory damages by the amount of any part of Respondent's payment of a civil penalty in this action ("Penalty Offset"). If the court in any Related Investor Action grants such a Penalty Offset, Respondent agrees that it shall, within 30 days after entry of a final order granting the Penalty Offset, notify the Commission's counsel in this action and pay the amount of the Penalty Offset to the Securities and Exchange Commission. Such a payment shall not be deemed an additional civil penalty and shall not be deemed to change the amount of the civil penalty imposed in this proceeding. For purposes of this paragraph, a "Related Investor Action" means a private damages action brought against Respondent by or on behalf of one or more investors based on substantially the same facts as alleged in the Order instituted by the Commission in this proceeding.

Discussion Points

1. *The outcome.* Was the amount of the SEC's penalty against Block.one appropriate? Why or why not?

2. *Distinguish Block.one and Munchee.* What were the main differences between the characteristics of *Block.one* and *Munchee*?

3. *Applying the Howey Test.* Apply the Howey test to Block.One's ERC-20 tokens. Is the ERC-20 token an investment contract? If no, which elements of the Howey test are not satisfied?

4. Explain the legal significance of the case in the context of token distribution and initial coin offerings.

5. How did the SEC characterize the violations committed by Block.one in relation to the Securities Act of 1933?

6. What factors did the SEC analyze in determining whether Block.one's tokens qualified as securities?

III. The Simple Agreement for Future Tokens (SAFT)

The Simple Agreement for Future Tokens ("SAFT") was developed in October 2017, during the ICO boom. It emerged in part to help companies issuing digital tokens raise funds. The SAFT is a contract that emerged as a possible mechanism of issuing digital assets without registration requirements. The purpose of the SAFT is to provide the organization that is issuing tokens the ability to raise funds to develop its network and tokens. Those tokens are later distributed, typically through an ICO.

The SAFT contract is commonly used when an organization sells an interest in tokens that have yet to be developed. Under the SAFT scheme, accredited investors receive the right to functional utility tokens at a discounted price, and token developers receive the funds to deliver those utility tokens upon development of the tokens. Thus, SAFTs are generally considered investment contracts. By utilizing the SAFT, an organization issues tokens under the belief that the issuance of the tokens would be subject to securities laws for accredited investors, but would not be subject to securities laws for the secondary, subsequent sale of the tokens.

The SAFT provides investors with the right to fully-functional utility tokens, delivered once the network is created and the tokens are functional.[30] Once the tokens have utility and are functional, SAFT investors' rights in the SAFT automatically

---

30. Juan Batiz-Benet, Marco Santori & Jesse Clayburgh, The SAFT Project: Toward a Compliant Token Sale Framework (2017), https://www.cooley.com/news/insight/2017/2017-10-24-saft-project -whitepaper.

convert into a right to delivery of the tokens.[31] The SAFT contract comprises a two-step configuration of issuing digital tokens: first, an initial registration-exempt securities offering to accredited investors. The securities the investors receive is actually a right to receive future tokens that will be developed using the funds raised in the private offering. Second, after the digital tokens can be utilized, the tokens will be distributed to the initial investors. The key to the ability of a SAFT to circumvent registration requirements is that once the tokens have utility and are issued, the tokens are not considered to be securities but rather commodities that may be freely traded on digital asset exchanges.

A SAFT transaction has four parts. The first part involves digital token developers securing commitments from accredited investors.[32] Second, token developers will enter into the SAFT with those accredited investors. Third, developers will use the funds raised from the SAFT to develop a token that has utility. Fourth, the token will be launched and delivered to investors, and secondary sales to the public may begin.[33]

Secondary sales of a SAFT may carry legal implications. For example, a SAFT contract may be subject to transfer restrictions. These restrictions may prohibit the assignment of the SAFT contract to certain persons, and may also prohibit the transfer of any rights contained in the SAFT contract to a third party without the issuer's written consent. The ability of a SAFT investor to engage with a secondary investor may depend on whether the tokens the SAFT holder has acquired through using the SAFT are characterized as securities or commodities.

SEC v. Telegram Grp. Inc.

448 F. Supp. 3d 352

United States District Court for the Southern District of New York (2020)

CASTEL, U.S.D.J.

The Securities and Exchange Commission ("SEC") seeks to enjoin Telegram Group Inc. and TON Issuer Inc. (collectively "Telegram") from engaging in a plan to distribute "Grams," a new cryptocurrency, in what it considers to be an unregistered offering of securities. In early 2018, Telegram received $1.7 billion from 175 sophisticated entities and high net-worth individuals in exchange for a promise to deliver 2.9 billion Grams. Telegram contends that the agreements to sell the 2.9 billion Grams are lawful private placements of securities covered by an exemption from the registration requirement. In Telegram's view, only the agreements with the individual purchasers are securities. Currently, the Grams will not be delivered

---

31. *Id.*
32. *See id.* at 16.
33. *Id.*

to these purchasers until the launch of Telegram's new blockchain, the Telegram Open Network ("TON") Blockchain. Telegram views the anticipated resales of Grams by the 175 purchasers into a secondary public market via the TON Blockchain as wholly-unrelated transactions and argues they would not be the offering of securities.

The SEC sees things differently. The 175 initial purchasers are, in its view, "underwriters" who, unless Telegram is enjoined from providing them Grams, will soon engage in a distribution of Grams in the public market, whose participants would have been deprived of the information that a registration statement would reveal.

Cryptocurrencies (sometimes called tokens or digital assets) are a lawful means of storing or transferring value and may fluctuate in value as any commodity would. In the abstract, an investment of money in a cryptocurrency utilized by members of a decentralized community connected via blockchain technology, which itself is administered by this community of users rather than by a common enterprise, is not likely to be deemed a security under the familiar test laid out in *S.E.C. v. W.J. Howey Co.*, 328 U.S. 293, 298–99 (1946). The SEC, for example, does not contend that Bitcoins transferred on the Bitcoin blockchain are securities. The record developed on the motion for a preliminary injunction presents a very different picture.

The Court finds that the SEC has shown a substantial likelihood of success in proving that the contracts and understandings at issue, including the sale of 2.9 billion Grams to 175 purchasers in exchange for $1.7 billion, are part of a larger scheme to distribute those Grams into a secondary public market, which would be supported by Telegram's ongoing efforts. Considering the economic realities under the Howey test, the Court finds that, in the context of that scheme, the resale of Grams into the secondary public market would be an integral part of the sale of securities without a required registration statement.

Telegram knew and understood that reasonable purchasers would not be willing to pay $1.7 billion to acquire Grams merely as a means of storing or transferring value. Instead, Telegram developed a scheme to maximize the amount initial purchasers would be willing to pay Telegram by creating a structure to allow these purchasers to maximize the value they receive upon resale in the public markets.

As part of its Howey analysis, the Court finds an implicit (though formally disclaimed) intention on the part of Telegram to remain committed to the success of the TON Blockchain post-launch. Indeed, Telegram, as a matter of fact rather than legal obligation, will be the guiding force behind the TON Blockchain for the immediate post-launch period while the 175 purchasers unload their Grams into the secondary market. As such, the initial 175 purchasers possess a reasonable expectation of profit based upon the efforts of Telegram because these purchasers expect to reap whopping gains from the resale of Grams in the immediate post-launch period. Under the Howey test, the series of contracts and understandings centered on Grams are a security within the meaning of the Securities Act of 1933 (the "Securities Act").

For reasons that will be more fully explained, the Court finds that the SEC has shown a substantial likelihood of success in proving that Telegram's present plan to distribute Grams is an offering of securities under the Howey test to which no exemption applies. The motion for a preliminary injunction will be granted.

At the preliminary injunction hearing, neither side offered live testimony, despite an opportunity to do so. (Doc. 58). The parties presented the Court with a fulsome Joint Stipulation of Facts ("Joint Stip."), (Doc. 72), and each side offered deposition testimony, exhibits, and declarations. The parties also filed cross-motions for summary judgment and the SEC filed a motion to strike an affirmative defense, motions which the Court finds unnecessary to reach at this juncture. Set forth below are the Court's findings of fact and conclusions of law on the motion for a preliminary injunction.[1]

FINDINGS OF FACT AND CONCLUSIONS OF LAW

A. Telegram.

In 2006, Pavel Durov founded VKontakte, a Russian version of Facebook. (Joint Stip. ¶ 9). With the help of Nikolai Durov, his brother and a skilled programmer, Pavel successfully built VKontakte into the largest Russian social media network. (Joint Stip. ¶¶ 11–13). Pavel accumulated a sizeable personal fortune before exiting VKontakte and leaving Russia over disputes with the Russian government. (Plaintiff's Exhibit ("PX") 18 at 2 (Doc. 122-18)); (Defs.' Resp. to Pls.' Counter-Statement at 51 (Doc. 120)).

In 2013, the Durov brothers founded Telegram and released Telegram Messenger, which remains Telegram's signature product. (Joint Stip. ¶¶ 16, 23); (Defs.' 56.1 Statement ¶¶ 42, 45 (Doc. 75)). Telegram is a private company, (Pl.'s 56.1 Statement ¶ 154 (Doc. 80)), and Pavel is its chief executive officer, (Joint Stip. ¶ 3). Messenger is a messaging app that offers end-to- end encryption and also contains a diverse ecosystem of groups, channels, and in-app commerce. (Joint Stip. ¶¶ 18–19, 22); (Doc. 80 at 1); (PX 18 at 7). Messenger is globally popular and currently has a monthly user base of approximately 300 million. (Doc. 75 ¶ 43). Messenger is also particularly popular among the cryptocurrency community and has been described as the "cryptocurrency world's preferred messaging app." (Joint Stip. ¶ 23); (Joint Exhibit ("JX") 8 at 12 (Doc. 72-8)). Telegram was founded with non-profit goals, (JX 8 at 5), and states that Messenger will never charge user fees or introduce advertising on the app, (Joint Stip. ¶ 21). As such, Messenger has never produced any revenues, (PX 18 at 1, 5), and, excluding the present offering of Grams, the Durov brothers have never received any income from their wildly successful creation. (Joint Stip. ¶¶ 14–15).

Messenger generates no revenues; nearly all of Messenger's expenses prior to 2018, including salaries and server costs, were paid for by Pavel out of his personal

---

1. Citations to evidence are illustrative only and are not intended to indicate that the cited evidence is the only evidence supporting the finding.

fortune. (Joint Stip. ¶ 17); (Doc. 80 ¶ 3). After receiving the $1.7 billion from the private offering of 2.9 billion Grams, Telegram used this newly raised capital to cover "way over 90 percent" of Telegram's expenses, which includes the costs of Messenger. (PX 12 at 53:2–3 (Doc. 122-12)); (Doc. 80 ¶ 12); (Malloy Decl., Ex. 4 at 1 (Doc. 167-4)). When describing its projected budgets for 2019 and 2020, which totaled $180 and $220 million respectively, Telegram stated that it still lacked plans to generate revenue from Messenger, so would continue to pay Messenger's way using funds from the offering of Grams and Pavel's personal wealth for the foreseeable future. (Doc. 80 ¶ 26); (PX 18 at 5, 8). Telegram subsequently reported that, from January 2018 to January 2020, it spent $405 million, about 24% of the proceeds from the offering of Grams, on the development of the TON Blockchain and the operations of Messenger. (Joint Stip. ¶¶ 144–45).

B. The TON Blockchain and Grams.

In 2017, Telegram began development of a proprietary blockchain and digital asset.[2] (Doc. 75 ¶ 49). The Durov brothers believed that Telegram could learn from the mistakes of existing blockchains and, by correcting their flaws, enable Telegram's new cryptocurrency to be the first to achieve truly widespread adoption. (Doc. 75 ¶¶ 46–48). Telegram's proposed blockchain would be named the "Telegram Open Network" ("TON") Blockchain and its native token would be called the "Gram."[3] (Doc. 75 ¶¶ 49, 52).

As part of the offering materials distributed in connection with the 2018 Sales discussed below, Telegram released a White Paper, authored by Nikolai and dated January 18, 2018, that discussed the unique features of the proposed TON Blockchain. (Joint Stip. ¶ 90); (JX 13 (Doc. 72-13)). The TON Blockchain would operate as a "Proof of Stake" system, which would rely on validator nodes (computers running full versions of the TON Blockchain software) to authenticate new blocks and to vote on rule changes. (Joint Stip. ¶¶ 122–23, 125); (JX 13 at 10); (McKeon Report ¶ 86, 190 (Doc. 102-1)). Validators would earn Grams for their services and would be required to stake at least 100,000 Grams as collateral. (Joint Stip. ¶¶ 125, 127); (JX 13 at 44). Due to the capital and technical resources required, acting as a validator would be beyond the ability of the hypothetical mass market user of the TON Blockchain. (Herlihy Report ¶ 19); (JX 13 at 45 ("[O]ne definitely cannot mine new TON coins on a home computer, let alone a smartphone.")).

---

2. A blockchain serves as the means of validating the authenticity of a transfer of a unit of cryptocurrency. It is a widely distributed but secure ledger or account of transactions. (Doc. 75 ¶¶ 1–3). Individual blockchain transactions are grouped together and then recorded in "blocks" that are linked to prior blocks creating a "chain." (Doc. 75 ¶¶ 7–8). No centralized master copy of the blockchain exists; instead current versions of the blockchain are kept by individual users connected across a network. (Doc. 75 ¶¶ 9–10); (Waxman Decl. at 1 n.1 (Doc. 16)).

3. A unit of a cryptocurrency can be used to store and transfer value, provide access to real-world services, offer voting or governance rights within the blockchain, or power applications and smart contracts built into the blockchain.

According to the White Paper, at least initially, the supply of Grams would be limited to five billion, which would be held by Telegram. (Joint Stip. ¶ 138); (JX 13 at 129). Each Gram subsequently sold by Telegram would be priced according to a formula that was based on the number of publicly outstanding Grams and priced each Gram slightly higher than the last one sold. (Joint Stip. ¶¶ 144–46); (JX 13 at 129–31). The price produced by this formula is called the "Reference Price." (Joint Stip. ¶ 144); (JX 13 at 129–30). If the market price of Grams fell below half of the Reference Price, Telegram (or the TON Foundation, discussed below), would have discretion to repurchase Grams and, by reducing the number of Grams in circulation, potentially prevent the market price from falling further. (Joint Stip. ¶ 122); (JX 13 at 131).

C. The 2018 Sales to Initial Purchasers.

In 2018, Telegram sold "interests in Grams" to 175 entities and high net worth individuals (the "Initial Purchasers") in exchange for dollars or euros. (Joint Stip. ¶ 40); (Doc. 75 ¶ 100); (JX 11 § 2.3 (Doc. 72-11)). The agreements (the "Gram Purchase Agreements") entitled the Initial Purchasers to receive an allotment of Grams upon the launch of the TON Blockchain. (Joint Stip. ¶ 140). Telegram sold to the Initial Purchasers in two rounds: the "Round One Sales" in January to February 2018 and the "Round Two Sales" in February to March 2018 (collectively, the "2018 Sales"). (Joint Stip. ¶¶ 41, 46, 54).

In the Round One Sales, Telegram sold approximately 2.25 billion Grams to 81 purchasers for $850 million, which included $385.5 million from 34 U.S. purchasers. (Joint Stip. ¶¶ 48–51); (JX 1 at 5 (Doc. 72-1)); (JX 9 at 17 (Doc. 72-9)). The Grams are to be delivered when, as, and if the TON Blockchain launches. The price per Gram was approximately $0.38. (Joint Stip. ¶ 87). The Gram Purchase Agreements for Round One Sales included a lockup provision, which bars resale of Grams after their delivery to the Initial Purchaser. (Joint Stip. ¶ 88). Three months after receiving the purchased and delivered Grams, the Round One Purchaser would be permitted to resell up to one quarter of its allotment of Grams. The remaining three quarters of the Grams would be free of restrictions in three equal tranches: 6, 12, and 18 months after the launch of the TON Blockchain. (Joint Stip. ¶ 88). By February 2, 2018, the SEC had contacted Telegram regarding the Round One Sales. (McGrath Decl., Ex. H (Doc. 83-8)); (McGrath Decl., Ex. K at 158:5–159:17 (Doc. 83-11)). On February 13, 2018, Telegram filed a Form D for the Round One Sales, claiming an exemption under Rule 506(c). (Joint Stip. ¶¶ 48, 52); (JX 1 at 6).

In the Round Two Sales, Telegram sold approximately 700 million Grams to 94 purchasers for $850 million, which included $39 million from five U.S. purchasers. (Joint Stip. ¶¶ 55–56); (JX 2 at 5 (Doc. 72-2)). The price per Gram was approximately $1.33. (Joint Stip. ¶ 94). Grams purchased in the Round Two Sales did not carry a lockup provision. (Joint Stip. ¶ 93). On March 29, 2018, Telegram filed a Form D for the Round Two Sales, claiming an exemption under Rule 506(c). (Joint Stip. ¶ 55);

(JX 2 at 6). Because of the claimed exemptions, Telegram did not register or file a registration statement for the Round One Sales or the Round Two Sales. (Joint Stip. ¶¶ 58–59). In total, the 2018 Sales raised $1.7 billion in exchange for approximately 2.9 billion Grams, which equates to 58% of all Grams. (Joint Stip. ¶ 43); (Doc. 75 ¶¶ 102–03); (Doc. 80 ¶ 37).

In advance of the 2018 Sales, Telegram circulated to all Initial Purchasers as well as other prospective purchasers a set of promotional materials, which included, among other things, primers, the Gram Purchase Agreements, the January 18, 2018 White Paper, and an explanation of certain risk factors. (Joint Stip. ¶¶ 60–64). These materials detailed the technical specifications of the TON Blockchain and the Gram, the terms of the Gram Purchase Agreements, Telegram's plans for distributing Grams and promoting Grams as a mass market cryptocurrency, as well as the financial opportunity presented by Grams. (Joint Stip. ¶¶ 60–104). In particular, the promotional materials specified that 4% of Grams would be reserved for the Telegram developers who were to build the TON Blockchain, including 1% for each Durov brother. (Joint Stip. ¶¶ 158–59); (JX 9 at 16). The developers' Grams would be subject to a four-year lockup period post-launch. (Joint Stip. ¶ 160); (JX 9 at 18).

The 1% of Grams given to each Durov brother is not the full extent of their ability to profit from the 2018 Sales. Indeed, the offering materials specifically noted that Telegram retained full discretion to allocate the funds raised between the TON Blockchain, Messenger, and Telegram generally. (JX 15 at 7–8). While a portion of the $1.7 billion has been used to develop the TON Blockchain, counsel for Telegram made plain at oral argument that Telegram still reserves the right to dividend any unspent portion of the proceeds of the 2018 Sales to Telegram's shareholders, i.e. the Durov brothers. As noted, Messenger charges no user fees and sells no advertising and, thus, the proceeds of the 2018 Sales stand to be a major source of the Durov brothers' profit for their years-long development of Telegram and Messenger.

The offering materials further detailed plans to integrate the TON Blockchain with Messenger in order to "leverag[e] Telegram's massive user base and developed ecosystem." (JX 9 at 11). Specifically, Telegram stated that 10% of Grams would be reserved for use in post-launch incentive programs, which would encourage the widespread adoption of Grams. (Joint Stip. ¶ 163); (JX 9 at 16). Half of this pool, 5% of all Grams, will be "distributed on a first-come, first- served basis to users of Telegram Messenger" who request Grams via a process within Messenger. (Defs.' Resp. Pl.'s 56.1 Statement ¶ 387 (Doc. 95)). Telegram also aimed to ensure that "[t]he Gram will serve as the principal currency for the in-app economy on [Messenger]" and that "Telegram's existing ecosystem will offer simple ways of buying the TON coins (Grams) and a range of services to spend them on, driving demand for the cryptocurrency." (JX 9 at 11, 13). The offering materials described Messenger-integrated applications to further mainstream adoption of the TON Blockchain. In particular, Telegram pitched that "[i]ntegrated into Telegram applications, the TON [W]allet is expected to become the world's most adopted cryptocurrency wallet."[4] (JX 9 at 11). Finally, the offering materials again emphasized that Telegram would use any proceeds raised to fund both the development of the TON Blockchain as well as the ongoing operations and expansion of Messenger. (JX 9 at 19).

Next, the promotional materials specified that Grams unallocated in the afore-mentioned plans and unsold in the 2018 Sales, an amount ultimately totaling 28% of Grams, would be allocated to a reserve pool, the TON Reserve. (Joint Stip. ¶ 162). Telegram stated its intention to create a non-profit foundation, the TON Foundation, to which it would transfer control of the TON Reserve as well as of governance functions for the TON Blockchain. (Joint Stip. ¶¶ 147, 151); (JX 15 at 8 (Doc. 72-15)); (JX 9 at 20). However, Telegram noted that there was no timetable for creating the TON Foundation and stated that it might not be created at all. (Joint Stip. ¶ 148); (JX 15 at 8). If the TON Foundation is not formed, then the TON Reserve would purportedly be "locked for perpetuity." (Doc. 75 ¶ 231). If created, the TON Foundation would be controlled by a board on which the Durov brothers would sit,[5] (Joint Stip. ¶ 153), and would have discretion to buy and sell Grams as needed to support the market price of Grams. (Joint Stip. ¶¶ 164–65). Though Telegram now disclaims the TON Foundation's power to buy Grams on the open market, the offering materials highlighted this power. (Joint Stip. ¶¶ 167–68); (JX 13 at 131).

Finally, the offering materials stated that participants in the 2018 Sales would receive a substantial discount on the price of Grams as compared to later sales. (JX 3 at 2 (Doc. 72-3) (describing a "private discount" of between 65.2% and 72% as compared to the price at an eventual public sale)). Based on the number of Grams sold, the Reference Price of Grams at the launch of the TON Blockchain would be approximately $3.62. (Joint Stip. ¶ 143).

D. Post-2018 Sales Actions.

Following receipt of funds from the 2018 Sales, Telegram began to develop theTON Blockchain and Grams. As discussed, Telegram also used funds from the 2018 Sales to maintain and expand Messenger. (Joint Stip. ¶¶ 144–45). In October

---

4. Digital wallets, pieces of software akin to a bank account for digital assets, store "private keys," which grant control over individual tokens, and permit users to easily send and receive tokens via the blockchain. (Doc. 75 ¶¶ 24–29).

5. The parties agree that, in its present formulation, the TON Foundation would be overseen by a board consisting of the Durov brothers and three other "independent" members, who would have "no connection to Telegram or its affiliates with experience in blockchain technology and/or TON." (Joint Stip. ¶ 154). However, Telegram has not consistently claimed that non-Durov board positions would be held by "independent" directors. (Drylewski Decl., Ex. 4 at 24 (Doc. 73-4) ("[T] he TON Foundation will have the following associated members or persons: (i) Pavel Durov; (ii) Nikolai Durov; and (iii) any other member or person selected by Pavel Durov and Nikolai Durov prior to the initial issuance of Grams or the incumbent members of the TON Foundation post-initial issuance.")).

2019, Telegram was prepared to launch the TON Blockchain and distribute Grams to the Initial Purchasers by the end of the month. (Doc. 75 ¶ 219); (McGrath Decl., Ex. J (Doc. 83-10)). If Telegram did not deliver Grams to the Initial Purchasers by October 31, 2019, the Gram Purchase Agreements would have obligated Telegram to refund any remaining funds from the 2018 Sales. (Joint Stip. ¶ 116). After this litigation commenced, the deadline was extended to April 30, 2020. (Joint Stip. ¶ 117). Since then Telegram has also continued efforts to further develop the TON Blockchain. (Joint Stip. ¶ 210). On January 6, 2020, Telegram posted a public statement to its website regarding the TON Blockchain, which stated that "Telegram will have no control over TON" and that "Grams won't help you get rich." (Drylewski Decl., Ex. 3 at 1, 2 (Doc. 73-3)).

E. Preliminary Injunction Standard in an SEC Action.

Section 20(b) of the Securities Act provides that:

> Whenever it shall appear to the Commission that any person is engaged or about to engage in any acts or practices which constitute or will constitute a violation of the provisions of this subchapter, or of any rule or regulation prescribed under authority thereof, the Commission may, in its discretion, bring an action in any district court of the United States...to enjoin such acts or practices, and upon a proper showing, a permanent or temporary injunction or restraining order shall be granted without bond.

15 U.S.C. § 77t(b) (2018).

The required "proper showing" depends on the nature of the relief sought. *S.E.C. v. Gonzalez de Castilla*, 145 F. Supp. 2d 402, 414–15 (S.D.N.Y. 2001). "A preliminary injunction enjoining violations of the securities laws is appropriate if the SEC makes a substantial showing of likelihood of success as to...a current violation...." *S.E.C. v. Cavanagh*, 155 F.3d 129, 132 (2d Cir. 1998) (quoting *S.E.C. v. Unifund SAL*, 910 F.2d 1028, 1041 (2d Cir. 1990)). If the SEC seeks to enjoin an ongoing violation of the securities laws, as is the case here, it must make a proper showing of a risk of future harm, but does not need to show a risk of repetition. *United States v. Or. St. Med. Soc'y*, 343 U.S. 326, 333 (1952) ("The sole function of an action for injunction is to forestall future violations.... All it takes to make the cause of action for relief by injunction is a real threat of future violation or a contemporary violation of a nature likely to continue or recur."); *S.E.C. v. Commonwealth Chem. Sec., Inc.*, 574 F.2d 90, 99 (2d Cir. 1978) ("Except for the case where the SEC steps in to prevent an ongoing violation, this language seems to require a finding of 'likelihood' or 'propensity' to engage in future violations."); see also *S.E.C. v. Gentile*, 939 F.3d 549, 556 (3d Cir. 2019) ("This principle is a corollary to the most basic rule of preventive injunctive relief—that the plaintiff must show a cognizable risk of future harm." (citing *Or. St. Med. Soc'y*, 343 U.S. at 333)). The SEC does not need "to show risk of irreparable injury or the unavailability of remedies at law" as required of private litigants. *Unifund SAL*, 910 F.2d at 1036. Therefore, for a preliminary injunction, the SEC must make a substantial showing of the likelihood of success in proving a current violation of the securities law as well as a substantial showing of a risk of future harm in the absence of such an injunction.

F. Section 5 Liability and the Howey Test.

Section 5 of the Securities Act prohibits the offer, sale, or delivery after sale of any security without an effective or filed registration statement. 15 U.S.C. § 77e(a), (c). As such, a prima facie case of a section 5 violation requires the SEC to show: (1) that no registration statement was in effect or filed; (2) defendant offered or sold a security; and (3) the offer or sale took place in interstate commerce. *S.E.C. v. Cavanagh*, 1 F. Supp. 2d 337, 361 (S.D.N.Y.), aff'd, 155 F.3d 129 (2d Cir. 1998). In this case, the foundational question is whether Telegram's contract, transaction, or scheme amounts to an offer or sale of a security.

"Congress' purpose in enacting the securities laws was to regulate investments, in whatever form they are made and by whatever name they are called." *S.E.C. v. Edwards*, 540 U.S. 389, 393 (2004) (quoting *Reves v. Ernst & Young*, 494 U.S. 56, 61 (1990)). As such, section 2(a)(1) of the Securities Act defines a "security" to include an "investment contract" as well as investment vehicles such as stocks and bonds.[6] 15 U.S.C. § 77b(a)(1). Known as the Howey test, the Supreme Court defined an "investment contract" as "a contract, transaction or scheme whereby a person invests his money in a common enterprise and is led to expect profits solely from the efforts of the promoter or a third party." *S.E.C. v. W.J. Howey Co.*, 328 U.S. 293, 298–99 (1946).

"The enterprise and the described materials, by the very nature of the operation of the securities laws, must be examined as of the time that the transaction took place, together with the knowledge and the objective intentions and expectations of the parties at that time." *S.E.C. v. Aqua-Sonic Prods. Corp.*, 524 F. Supp. 866, 876 (S.D.N.Y. 1981) (citing *United Hous. Found., Inc. v. Forman*, 421 U.S. 837, 852–53 (1975)), aff'd, 687 F.2d 577 (2d Cir. 1982); see also *Finkel v. Stratton Corp.*, 962 F.2d 169, 173 (2d Cir. 1992) ("[A] a sale occurs for [Securities Act] purposes when 'the parties obligate[] themselves to perform what they had agreed to perform even if the formal performance of their agreement is to be after a lapse of time.'" (quoting *Radiation Dynamics, Inc. v. Goldmuntz*, 464 F.2d 876, 891 (2d Cir. 1972))).

---

6. Section 3(a) of the Securities Exchange Act of 1934 contains a slightly different definition of "security." 15 U.S.C. § 78c(a)(10). However, "[a]lthough the precise wording of the two definitional sections differs, the Supreme Court has consistently held that the definitions are virtually identical and the coverage of the two Acts may be considered the same." *Gary Plastic Packaging Corp. v. Merrill Lynch, Pierce, Fenner & Smith, Inc.*, 756 F.2d 230, 238 (2d Cir. 1985) (citing *United Hous. Found., Inc. v. Forman*, 421 U.S. 837, 847 n.12 (1975)).

This definition of investment contract "embodies a flexible rather than a static principle, one that is capable of adaptation to meet the countless and variable schemes devised by those who seek the use of the money of others on the promise of profits." Howey, 328 U.S. at 299. In the analysis of purported investment contracts, "form should be disregarded for substance and the emphasis should be on economic reality." *Tcherepnin v. Knight*, 389 U.S. 332, 336 (1967); see also *Forman*, 421 U.S. at 849 (stating that "Congress intended the application of [the securities laws] to turn on the economic realities underlying a transaction, and not on the name appended thereto"); *Glen-Arden Commodities, Inc. v. Costantino*, 493 F.2d 1027, 1034 (2d Cir. 1974) (asking "whether, in light of the economic reality and the totality of circumstances," an instrument was an investment contract). Disclaimers, if contrary to the apparent economic reality of a transaction, may be considered by the Court but are not dispositive. *S.E.C. v. SG Ltd.*, 265 F.3d 42, 54 (1st Cir. 2001).

The Howey test provides the mode of analysis for an unconventional scheme or contract alleged to fall within the securities laws. Howey itself determined that a "scheme" involving the sale of small tracts of land, evidenced by contracts of sale and warranty deeds, together with service contracts for the growing of oranges on the land amounted to an "investment contract" that was a "security." *Howey*, 328 U.S. at 299–300. Courts have found other schemes and contracts governing a range of intangible and tangible assets to be securities. *Glen-Arden Commodities*, 493 F.2d 1027 (whiskey casks); *Miller v. Cent. Chinchilla Grp., Inc.*, 494 F.2d 414 (8th Cir. 1974) (chinchillas); *Balestra v. ATBCOIN LLC*, 380 F. Supp. 3d 340 (S.D.N.Y. 2019) (digital tokens).

G. Exemptions from the Registration Requirement.

If the relevant instruments are securities and a prima facie case of a section 5 violation is then established, "the burden shifts to the defendant to show that the securities were exempt from the registration requirement." *Cavanagh*, 155 F.3d at 133 (citing *S.E.C. v. Ralston Purina Co.*, 346 U.S. 119, 126 (1953)). "Registration exemptions are construed strictly to promote full disclosure of information for the protection of the investing public." *S.E.C. v. Cavanagh*, 445 F.3d 105, 115 (2d Cir. 2006). In this case, there are two relevant safe harbors from the registration requirement, section 4(a) of the Securities Act and Rule 506(c) of Regulation D.

Section 4(a)(1) exempts from the registration requirement of section 5 "transactions by any person other than an issuer, underwriter, or dealer," while section 4(a)(2) exempts "transactions by an issuer not involving a public offering." 15 U.S.C. § 77d(a)(1)–(2). Section 2(a)(11) of the Securities Act defines an "underwriter" as "any person who has purchased from an issuer with a view to...the distribution of any security." *Id.* § 77b(a)(11). A "'distribution,' as used in Section 2[(a)(11),] has been held to mean the equivalent of a 'public offering.'" *Neuwirth Inv. Fund Ltd. v. Swanton*, 422 F. Supp. 1187, 1194–95 (S.D.N.Y. 1975); see also *Gilligan, Will & Co.*

v. S.E.C., 267 F.2d 461, 466 (2d Cir. 1959) (stating that a "'distribution' requires a 'public offering'"); *Berckeley Inv. Grp., Ltd. v. Colkitt*, 455 F.3d 195, 215 (3d Cir. 2006) ("[T]hose courts interpreting [section 4(a)(1)] have uniformly concluded that the term 'distribution' is synonymous with 'public offering' as set forth under Section 4[a](2).").

In defining "public offering," the Supreme Court held that "it is essential to examine the circumstances under which the distinction [between public and private] is sought to be established and to consider the purposes sought to be achieved by such distinction." *Ralston Purina Co.*, 346 U.S. at 124 (quoting *S.E.C. v. Sunbeam Gold Mines Co.*, 95 F.2d 699, 701 (9th Cir. 1938)). As such, "the applicability of [section 4(a)(2)] should turn on whether the particular class of persons affected need the protection of the [Securities] Act. An offering to those who are shown to be able to fend for themselves is a transaction 'not involving any public offering.'" *Id.* at 125. The Second Circuit has also instructed that a "'[d]istribution' comprises 'the entire process by which in the course of a public offering the block of securities is dispersed and ultimately comes to rest in the hands of the investing public.'" *R.A. Holman & Co. v. S.E.C.*, 366 F.2d 446, 449 (2d Cir. 1966) (quoting *Lewisohn Copper Corp.*, 38 S.E.C. 226, 234 (1958)), aff'd on reh'g, 377 F.2d 665 (2d Cir. 1967). In claiming an exemption under section 4(a), the defendant is required to "establish[] that [its] sales do not constitute a disguised public distribution." *Cavanagh*, 1 F. Supp. 2d at 337.

Rule 506 of Regulation D states that "[o]ffers and sales of securities by an issuer that satisfy the conditions [of this Rule] shall be deemed to be transactions not involving any public offering within the meaning of section 4(a)(2) of the [Securities] Act." 17 C.F.R. § 230.506(a). To make use of this safe harbor, Rule 506(c) requires that the relevant securities are sold only to accredited investors and that the sales also satisfy Rule 502(d). *Id.* § 230.506(c). Rule 502(d) in turn bars the resale of securities sold under a Regulation D exemption without a registration statement. *Id.* § 230.502(d). Rule 502(d) further requires that the issuer "exercise reasonable care to assure that the purchasers of the securities are not underwriters within the meaning of section 2(a)(11) of the [Securities] Act." *Id.* Demonstrating reasonable care requires, among other things, "[r]easonable inquiry to determine if the purchaser is acquiring the securities for himself or for other persons." *Id.*

A defendant, who claims protection of an exemption from registration but fails to meet the requirements of that exemption, will be found to have violated the registration requirements of Securities Act.

H. The Gram Purchase Agreements and Associated Understandings and Undertakings, Including the Expected Resales into the Secondary Market, Are Viewed as One Scheme Under Howey.

Telegram argues that there are two distinct sets of transactions at issue in this case, one subject to the securities laws and one that is not. In Telegram's view, the first set of transactions was the offers and sales of the "interests in Grams," as embodied in the Gram Purchase Agreements, to the Initial Purchasers. While Telegram concedes that the Initial Purchasers' "interest in a Grams" are a security, it claims an exemption from registration under Regulation D. Telegram argues that a second and distinct set of transactions will be the delivery of the newly created Grams to the Initial Purchasers upon the launch of the TON Blockchain. Telegram stresses that, because, upon launch, Grams would have "functional consumptive uses" (i.e. could be used to store or transfer value), Grams would be a commodity and, therefore, not subject to the securities laws. Specifically, Telegram notes that, upon receipt of their Grams, Round Two Purchasers, who are not subject to a contractual lockup period, would then be free to use Grams as a currency to purchase goods or services on the TON Blockchain or to stake their Grams to become validators.

The economic reality of Telegram's course of conduct is straightforward and rather easily understood. Telegram entered into agreements and understandings with the Initial Purchasers who provided upfront capital in exchange for the future delivery of a discounted asset, Grams, which, upon receipt (and the expiration of the lockup periods for Round One Purchasers), would be resold in a public market with the expectation that the Initial Purchasers would earn a profit. A reasonable Initial Purchaser understands and expects that they will only profit if the reputation, skill, and involvement of Telegram and its founders remain behind the enterprise, including through the sale of Grams from the Initial Purchasers into the public market.

The Gram Purchase Agreements and the future delivery and resale of Grams are viewed in their totality for the purpose of the Howey analysis. In Howey, although the land purchase contracts and the service contracts were separate agreements that took effect at different points in time and a purchaser was not mandated to enter into both, the Court analyzed the entirety of the parties' interaction, finding that the whole scheme comprised a single investment contract and, therefore, a security. *Howey*, 328 U.S. at 297–98 (reversing the lower court's decision to "treat[] the contracts and deeds as separate transactions"). This Court finds as a fact that the economic reality is that the Gram Purchase Agreements and the anticipated distribution of Grams by the Initial Purchasers to the public via the TON Blockchain are part of a single scheme.

I. The Series of Understandings, Transactions, and Undertakings Between Telegram and the Initial Purchasers Is a Security.

As discussed, "a contract, transaction or scheme" is deemed an investment contract if it satisfies the four prongs of the Howey test, namely (1) an investment of money (2) in a common enterprise (3) with the expectation of profit (4) from the essential efforts of another. *Howey*, 328 U.S. at 298–99. The Court finds that the SEC has shown a substantial likelihood of success in proving that, at the time of the offers and sales to the Initial Purchasers, a reasonable investor expected to profit from Telegram's continued support for Grams and the underlying TON Blockchain through the distribution of Grams by the Initial Purchasers to the public. Therefore, the series of understandings, transactions, and undertakings between Telegram and the Initial Purchasers were investment contracts satisfying the Howey test and, therefore, are securities.

i. The Series of Understandings, Transactions, and Undertakings Should Be Evaluated as of the Time of the 2018 Sales.

Telegram argues that Grams should be evaluated under Howey at the time of their delivery to the Initial Purchasers, i.e. at the launch of the TON Blockchain. It asserts that it will not be part of a common enterprise and will not provide essential managerial efforts once the TON Blockchain is launched. The post-launch distribution of Grams by the Initial Purchasers, Telegram argues, is independent of any Telegram action. But Howey requires the Court to examine the series of understandings, transactions, and undertakings at the time they were made. The Court finds that the SEC has shown a substantial probability of success in proving that the series of understandings, transactions, and undertakings are investment contracts, and therefore are securities, under Howey.

Under the Securities Act, "[t]he term 'sale' or 'sell' shall include every contract of sale or disposition of a security or interest in a security, for value." 15 U.S.C. § 77b(a)(3). The Second Circuit has held that, for the purposes of the securities laws, a sale occurs when "the parties obligated themselves to perform what they had agreed to perform even if the formal performance of their agreement is to be after a lapse of time." *Radiation Dynamics*, 464 F.2d at 891; see also *Finkel*, 962 F.2d at 173. "[A] contract for the issuance or transfer of a security may qualify as a sale under the securities laws even if the contract is never fully performed." *Yoder v. Orthomolecular Nutrition Inst.*, 751 F.2d 555, 559 (2d Cir. 1985); *Vacold LLC v. Cerami*, 545 F.3d 114, 122 (2d Cir. 2008) (stating that a sale occurs "even if the later exchange of money and securities is contingent upon the occurrence of future events, such as the satisfaction of a financing condition, at least when the contingency is not so unlikely that it renders the stock transaction extremely speculative" (citing *Yoder*, 751 F.2d at 559 & n.4)); *Aqua-Sonic Prods. Corp.*, 524 F. Supp. at 876 (stating that a transaction "by the very nature of the operation of the securities laws, must be examined as of the time that the transaction took place" (citing *Forman*, 421 U.S. at 852– 53)), aff'd, 687 F.2d 577. Further, there can be little argument that an offer, as a unilateral act, occurs at the time it is made. 15 U.S.C. § 77b(a)(3) ("The term 'offer to sell', 'offer for sale', or 'offer' shall include every attempt or offer to dispose of, or solicitation of an offer to buy, a security or interest in a security, for value.").

Based on its filed Forms D, Telegram offered and sold Grams to the Initial Purchasers in the Round One and Round Two Sales by, at latest, February 13, 2018 and March 29, 2018, respectively. (JX 1 at 6); (JX 2 at 6). Whether the scheme, viewed as a whole, amounts to a security will be evaluated at this point in time.

ii. Investment of Money.

The first prong of Howey examines whether an investment of money was part of the relevant transaction. In this case, the Initial Purchasers invested money by providing dollars or euros in exchange for the future delivery of Grams. (JX 11 § 2.3); (JX 12 § 2.3 (Doc. 72-12)). In total, the Initial Purchasers provided Telegram with approximately $1.7 billion in exchange for the promised delivery of 2.9 billion Grams upon the launch of the TON Blockchain. (Joint Stip. ¶¶ 43, 48, 55); (Doc. 75 ¶¶ 102–03). Telegram does not dispute that there was an investment of money by the Initial Purchasers and the Court finds that this element has been established.

iii. Common Enterprise.

The second prong of Howey, the existence of a common enterprise, may be demonstrated through either horizontal commonality or vertical commonality. Horizontal commonality is established when investors' assets are pooled and the fortunes of each investor is tied to the fortunes of other investors as well as to the success of the overall enterprise. *Revak v. SEC Realty Corp.*, 18 F.3d 81, 87 (2d Cir. 1994); see also *SG Ltd.*, 265 F.3d at 49 (describing "horizontal commonality" as "a type of commonality that involves the pooling of assets from multiple investors so that all share in the profits and risks of the enterprise"); *ATBCOIN LLC*, 380 F. Supp. 3d at 353. In contrast, strict vertical commonality "requires that the fortunes of investors be tied to the fortunes of the promoter."[7] *Revak*, 18 F.3d at 88 (citing *Brodt v. Bache & Co., Inc.*, 595 F.2d 459, 461 (9th Cir. 1978)); see also *In re J.P. Jeanneret Assocs., Inc.*, 769 F. Supp. 2d 340, 360 (S.D.N.Y. 2011) (stating "that strict vertical commonality (like horizontal commonality) is sufficient to establish a common enterprise under Howey").

The SEC has shown horizontal commonality. After the 2018 Sales, Telegram pooled the money received from the Initial Purchasers and used it to develop the TON Blockchain as well as to maintain and expand Messenger. (Joint Stip. ¶¶ 44–45, 118). The ability of each Initial Purchaser to profit was entirely dependent on the successful launch of the TON Blockchain. If the TON Blockchain's development failed prior to launch, all Initial Purchasers would be equally affected as all would lose their opportunity to profit,[8] thereby establishing horizontal commonality at the time of 2018 Sales.

Further, horizontal commonality exists after the launch of the TON Blockchain. The plain economic reality is that, post-launch, the Grams themselves continue to

---

7. Strict vertical commonality is distinct from broad vertical commonality that merely requires that "the fortunes of the investors need be linked only to the efforts of the promoter." *Revak*, 18 F.3d at 87–88. In the Second Circuit, broad vertical commonality does not satisfy the common enterprise prong of the Howey test. *Id.* at 88.

8. While schemes with horizontal commonality often include a pro rata distribution of revenues or income, such a pro rata distribution is not required for horizontal commonality. *ATBCOIN LLC*, 380 F. Supp. 3d at 354.

represent the Initial Purchasers' pooled funds. *ATBCOIN LLC,* 380 F. Supp. 3d at 354 (finding a pooling of assets in a post-launch digital asset). Post-launch, the fortunes of the Initial Purchasers will also remain tied to each other's fortunes as well as to the fortunes of the TON Blockchain. Upon delivery of the Grams, Round Two Purchasers will possess an identical instrument, the value of which is entirely dependent on the success or failure of the TON Blockchain as well as on Telegram's enforcement of the lockup provisions on Round One Purchasers. All Initial Purchasers, Round One and Round Two, were dependent upon the success of the TON Blockchain software and, if it failed, all Initial Purchasers would suffer a diminution in the value of their Grams. The investors' fortunes are directly tied to the success of the TON Blockchain as a whole.[9] *Id.* (holding that "the value of [a post-launch digital asset] was dictated by the success of the [blockchain] enterprise as a whole, thereby establishing horizontal commonality"). The Court finds that the SEC has made the required showing of horizontal commonality because the record demonstrates that there was a pooling of assets and that the fortunes of investors were tied to the success of the enterprise as well as to the fortunes of other investors both before and after launch.

Alternatively, the SEC has made a substantial showing of strict vertical commonality. Each Initial Purchaser's anticipated profits were directly dependent on Telegram's success in developing and launching the TON Blockchain. Telegram's own fortunes were similarly dependent on the successful launch of the TON Blockchain as Telegram would suffer financial and reputational harm if the TON Blockchain failed prior to launch. Telegram was reliant on funds from the 2018 Sales to meet Messenger's $190 million and $220 million expenses for 2019 and 2020, respectively. (Doc. 80 ¶ 26); (PX 18 at 5, 8); (Joint Stip. ¶¶ 44–45). Failure to launch the TON Blockchain by the contractual deadline would require Telegram to return any unspent funds to the Initial Purchaser, depriving Telegram of its primary planned source of funding for Messenger's growing expenses. This loss of funding could potentially harm Telegram's ability to continue to expand or even maintain its signature product and, thereby, damage the fortunes of the company as a whole.

The offering materials accompanying the 2018 Sales further detail how Telegram's financial fortunes would continue to be inextricably linked to the fortunes of the TON Blockchain and, therefore, those of the Initial Purchasers, after launch. After launch, Telegram's most valuable asset would be the TON Reserve, consisting of 28% of all Grams. Telegram states that the TON Reserve would either be transferred to the TON Foundation, (Joint Stip. ¶ 162), or "locked for perpetuity," (Doc. 75 ¶ 231).

---

9. The Initial Purchasers' ability to time their potential sales of Grams or control other aspects of their ownership of Grams are insufficient to negate a finding that a common enterprise exists. *Aqua-Sonic Products Corp.,* 687 F.2d at 578–79 (finding a common enterprise existed though the relevant investment contract "was optional" and provided investors with control over aspects of the enterprise that affected their profits). The ability to sell their Grams, and thereby exit the common enterprise, does not mean that the Initial Purchasers are not part of a common enterprise while they continued to possess Grams.

However, Telegram is under no legal obligation to undertake either course of action and could instead choose to retain control over the TON Reserve.[10] In that case, the TON Reserve would be Telegram's largest asset, thereby linking the company's financial fortunes to the price of Grams and the success of the TON Blockchain.

Telegram would also suffer critical reputational damage if the TON Blockchain failed prior to or after launch. Telegram generated interest in Grams and the to-be-built TON Blockchain based on the reputation of Pavel and his team as the creators of Messenger, a fast growing and well-regarded app. See, e.g., (PX 3 ¶ 12 ("Telegram's founders had already created and launched a successful messenger application, which also gave us confidence that Telegram's ICO would be successful, as compared to unknown teams with no experience bringing a product to market.")). In raising $1.7 billion, Telegram emphasized its technical expertise, promoted its teams of "A-players," (JX 4 at 4 (Doc. 72-4)); (JX 8 at 21–24), and directly affixed its good name to the TON Blockchain (the "Telegram Open Network" Blockchain) and the Gram ("Telegram").

As such, the failure of Telegram's new signature cryptocurrency project soon after launch would tarnish the reputations of Telegram and the Durovs. The impairment of its goodwill, especially in light of its inability to generate revenue from Messenger, would significantly damage Telegram's ability to develop new products, attract needed technical talent, and potentially even to raise the capital needed to sustain Messenger. Conversely, the successful launch of the TON Blockchain would burnish Telegram's reputation, opening new and potentially financially lucrative doors for its next product idea. Based on the record presented, Telegram's fortunes are directly tied to the fortunes of the Initial Purchasers, which will rise and fall with the success or failure of the TON Blockchain. As such, the Court finds that the SEC has made a substantial showing of strict vertical commonality.

iv. Expectation of Profit.

Howey's third prong examines whether the investor entered the relevant transaction with the expectation of profit. Telegram disputes that Grams were purchased with an expectation of profit, arguing instead that the Initial Purchasers bought Grams with the expectation to use them as currency. The Court finds that the SEC has shown a substantial likelihood of success in proving that the Initial Purchasers purchased Grams in the 2018 Sales with an expectation of profit in the resale of those Grams to the public via the TON Blockchain, which would be developed by Telegram and the success of which would be implicitly guaranteed post-launch by Telegram.

---

10. Transferring the TON Reserve to the TON Foundation also might not restrict Telegram's control over this pool of Grams as Telegram is under no legal obligation to establish the TON Foundation with an actually independent board. See *supra* p. 10 n.5.

An investor possesses an expectation of profit when their motivation to partake in the relevant "contract, transaction or scheme" was "the prospects of a return on their investment." *Howey,* 328 U.S. at 301; see also *S.E.C. v. Hui Feng,* 935 F.3d 721, 730–31 (9th Cir. 2019) (finding the requisite expectation of profit even when this investment intent was secondary to a motive unrelated to profit). Profit means an "income or return, to include, for example, dividends, other periodic payments, or the increased value of the investment." *Edwards,* 540 U.S. at 394; see also *Forman,* 421 U.S. at 852 (stating that "[b]y profits, the Court has meant either capital appreciation resulting from the development of the initial investment").

In contrast to an investment intent, an individual may acquire an asset with "a desire to use or consume the item purchased." *Id.* at 852–53. A transaction does not fall within the scope of the securities laws when a reasonable purchaser is motivated to purchase by a consumptive intent. *Id.* The inquiry is an objective one focusing on the promises and offers made to investors; it is not a search for the precise motivation of each individual participant. *Warfield v. Alaniz,* 569 F.3d 1015, 1021 (9th Cir. 2009) ("Under *Howey,* courts conduct an objective inquiry into the character of the instrument or transaction offered based on what the purchasers were 'led to expect.'").

Based upon the totality of the evidence, the Court finds that, at the time of the 2018 Sales to the Initial Purchasers, a reasonable investor, situated in the position of the Initial Purchasers, would have purchased Grams with investment intent. The Court also finds that, without the expected ability to resell Grams into the secondary market, the $1.7 billion paid to Telegram would not have been raised. Several aspects of the 2018 Sales demonstrate this reasonable expectation of profit.

The sale price of Grams during the Round One and Round Two Sales, approximately $0.38 and $1.33 respectively, (JX 11 at 8); (JX 12 at 2), was set at a significant discount to the expected Reference Price post-launch and the expected market price in a post- launch public market, (JX 13 at 129–31). Upon the launch of the TON Blockchain, the only Grams available for public purchase would either be newly-released Grams from the TON Reserve or Grams resold by Round Two Purchasers, whose Gram Purchase Agreements did not contain a lockup clause. Under Telegram's pricing formula, the Reference Price of Grams held in the TON Reserve at launch would be approximately $3.62. (Joint Stip. ¶ 143). If the market price reached the Reference Price but no higher, it would offer Round One and Round Two Initial Purchasers an approximate 852% and 172% premium, respectively, over their cost of acquiring Grams. This would provide a substantial opportunity for the Initial Purchasers to profit on the resale of Grams, even if the market price of Grams fell below the Reference Price as the TON Reserve is not permitted to sell newly floated Grams for less than the Reference Price. (Joint Stip. ¶ 166); (JX 13 at 131); (Doody Report ¶ 38 (Doc. 122-10)).

Telegram also promoted the TON Foundation's power to support the market price of Grams. Specifically, the TON Foundation was authorized to repurchase Grams on the open market if their market price fell to half (or less) of the Reference

Price, which at launch would equate to approximately $1.81 per Gram. (Joint Stip. ¶ 167); (JX 13 at 131); (Doody Report ¶ 44). This provision created the reasonable expectation among Initial Purchasers that, even if the market price of Grams fell, the TON Foundation would support a market price that would enable the Initial Purchasers to sell their Grams at a considerable profit. (Doody Report ¶ 40). Further, this price floor mechanism was pitched as a means of arresting and reversing declines in Grams' market price, and thereby protecting the ability of the Initial Purchasers to profit from Gram resales, by reducing the supply of available Grams and presumably increasing the price per Gram. (Joint Stip. ¶ 122); (JX 13 at 131).

The size and concentration of their Gram purchases indicates that the Initial Purchasers purchased with investment, not consumptive, intent. The amount of capital raised ($1.7 billion), the large percentage of the total supply of Grams (58%), and the limited number of Initial Purchasers (175) support the finding that the Initial Purchasers did not intend to use their allotments of Grams as a substitute currency to store and transfer value.

The terms of the Gram Purchase Agreements also point to an investment intent on the part of the Initial Purchasers. In Round One, Grams were sold at $0.38 per Gram but were subject to a lockup agreement that prevented the Round One Purchasers from reselling their Grams until three months after launch. (Joint Stip. ¶ 88); (JX 11 § 10.1). After 3 months, a Round One Purchaser was then permitted to sell up to 25% of its allotment of Grams, with additional tranches of Grams unlocking 6 months, 12 months, and 18 months after launch. (Joint Stip. ¶ 88); (JX 11 § 10.1). In contrast, the Grams purchased by the Round Two Purchasers were not subject to such a lockup agreement. (Joint Stip. ¶ 93). This differential lockup granted an exclusive window for the Round Two Purchasers—who paid considerably more per Gram—to resell Grams and profit from their investment before Grams owned by Round One Purchasers could be sold into the market and thereby place downward pressure on the price of Grams. (PX 30 at 11 (Doc. 122-18)). This exclusive window creates a structural incentive for the Round Two Purchasers to resell their holdings of Grams quickly and indicates that the Round Two Purchasers bought Grams with an investment intent.

Further, the existence of the lockups tend to negate the likelihood that a reasonable Round One Purchaser purchased Grams for consumptive use. Simply put, a rational economic actor would not agree to freeze millions of dollars for up to 18 months (following a lengthy development period) if the purchaser's intent was to obtain a substitute for fiat currency. (Doody Report ¶ 5). The economic reality is that these lockups were part of the bargained-for-exchange with Round One Purchasers, who obtained their Grams at a much lower price than the Round Two Purchasers but with the expectation of a larger profit after the lockup period expired. The lockups supported the economic justification for Round Two Purchasers to pay a higher price for Grams because the Round Two Purchasers would have an exclusive window to sell without competition from Round One Purchasers.

The economic realities of the promised integration of Grams and the TON Block-chain with Messenger also support a finding of a reasonable expectation on the part of the Initial Purchasers that Grams would increase in value and return a profit. (Joint Stip. ¶ 9 ("Telegram informed the [I]nitial [P]urchasers that it hoped to inte-grate the TON Wallet into Telegram Messenger in part to encourage a wide adop-tion of Grams after launch.")); (JX 8 at 11–14 (primer section entitled "Telegram Messenger-TON Integration")); (JX 13 at 124). Integration of a TON Wallet into Messenger would quickly introduce Grams to Messenger's 300 million monthly user base. This anticipated integration fueled the Initial Purchasers' expectations of a spike in Gram demand upon launch.[11]

Telegram's offering materials targeted buyers who possessed investment intent. Promotional materials emphasizing opportunities for potential profit can demon-strate that purchasers possessed the required expectation of profits. See, e.g., *Forman*, 421 U.S. at 853–54; *Edwards*, 540 U.S. at 392. While the offering materials covered some potential consumptive uses, (JX 8 at 14), they also highlighted the opportunity for profit by capital appreciation and resale based on the discounted purchase price.[12] (JX 3 at 2); (JX 8 at 17). Specifically, the promotional materials highlighted the large discount, compared to the Reference Price, (Joint Stip. ¶ 143), as well as to the antic-ipated market price, (JX 3 at 2), at which Initial Purchasers could obtain Grams. The materials also discussed the TON Foundation's ability to provide a price floor for Grams in the case of market turmoil. (Joint Stip. ¶¶ 164–65); (JX 13 at 131). In toto, the offering materials fueled the expectation that, after launch, the Initial Purchasers would be able to resell their allotment of Grams for a profit.

Consumptive uses for Grams were not features that could reasonably be expect-ed to appeal to the Initial Purchasers targeted by Telegram. In seeking participants for the 2018 Sales, Telegram did not focus on cryptocurrency enthusiasts, specialty digital assets firms, or even mass market individuals who had a need for an alter-native to fiat currency. (Doc. 80 ¶ 142); (Doc. 95 ¶ 142). Instead, Telegram selected sophisticated venture capital firms (and other similar entities) as well as high net worth individuals with an inherent preference (i.e. their business model) toward an investment intent rather than a consumptive use. (Doc. 80 ¶¶ 139–42); (Doc. 95 ¶¶ 139–42); (PX 18 at 6).

The Court's finding that the Initial Purchasers had a reasonable expectation of profit is buttressed by Initial Purchasers' subjective views, as captured in internal memoranda and emails. The subjective intent of the Initial Purchasers does not necessarily establish the objective intent of a reasonable purchaser. However, the

---

11. The 2018 Sales also provided the opportunity for the Initial Purchasers to tap into the val-ue created by the growth of Messenger. (Doody Report ¶ 28 ("This integration provides avenues for Gram holders to profit from the growth of Telegram Messenger through their investment in Grams.")); (PX 7 ¶ 7 (Doc. 122-7)).

12. Information in promotional materials on consumptive uses can still create an expectation of profits if the materials "fuel[] expectations of profit." *SG Ltd.*, 265 F.3d at 54.

stated intent of prospective and actual purchasers, though not considered for the truth of their content, may be properly considered in the Court's evaluation of the motivations of the hypothetical reasonable purchaser. *S.E.C. v. Texas Gulf Sulphur Co.,* 446 F.2d 1301, 1305 (2d Cir. 1971) (finding that the testimony of individual investors "was relevant to whether [a document] was misleading to the 'reasonable investor'"); *Slevin v. Pedersen Assocs., Inc.,* 540 F. Supp. 437, 441 (S.D.N.Y. 1982). An actual Initial Purchaser declared that it "purchased Grams with the aim of making a profit when it ultimately sold the Grams" and "did not intend to use Grams for consumptive purposes." (PX 5 ¶¶ 21–22 (Doc. 122-5)). Another Initial Purchaser stated that they "hoped for an increase in the value of Grams and an opportunity to eventually sell Grams if the value increased" and did "not believe that [the investor entity] intended to use Grams as currency or for consumptive purposes." (PX 6 ¶ 6 (Doc. 122-6)). Other Initial Purchasers similarly viewed Grams as an investment, not a consumptive asset. (PX 1 ¶ 14 (Doc. 122-1)); (PX 2 ¶¶ 14, 18 (Doc. 122-2)); (PX 3 ¶¶ 7, 18, 20 (Doc. 122-3)); (PX 4 ¶¶ 6, 13 (Doc. 122-4)); (PX 7 ¶¶ 18, 19, 21); (PX 8 ¶ 11 (Doc. 122-11)); (PX 30 at 11); (PX 31 at 4 (Doc. 122-31)); see also (PX 1 ¶ 15 (stating that "[t]he pricing mechanism described by Telegram indicated that any future token offerings would sell Grams at a higher price")); (PX 7 ¶ 7 (stating that an investor "became interested in investing in the Telegram ICO because [it] did not think it was possible to invest into Telegram, the company, directly")). The subjective views of these Initial Purchasers, taken with the totality of the evidence, support the Court's finding that the SEC has shown a substantial likelihood of success in proving that a reasonable purchaser in the 2018 Sales had an expectation of profit.

Telegram argues that there can be no expectation of profit in light of its disclaimers and public statements emphasizing the consumptive use of Grams and rejecting any expectation of profit. (Drylewski Decl., Ex. 3 at 2 ("Third, you should NOT expect any profits based on your purchase or holding of Grams, and Telegram makes no promises that you will make any profits. Grams are intended to act as a medium of exchange between users in the TON ecosystem. Grams are NOT investment products and there should be NO expectation of future profit or gain from the purchase, sale or holding of Grams.")). However, such statements, including an internet post after the initiation of this action, are insufficient to negate the substantial evidence that a reasonable purchaser expected to profit from Grams upon their launch.

v. Efforts of Another.

The final Howey prong considers whether the expectation of profit stems from the efforts of another. Though *Howey* states that the expectation of profits should stem "solely from the efforts of the promoter or a third party," *Howey,* 328 U.S. at 299, subsequent decisions have focused on whether the "reasonable expectation of profits [were] derived from the entrepreneurial or managerial efforts of others." *For-*

man, 421 U.S. at 852; see also *Leonard,* 529 F.3d at 88 ("[W]e have held that the word 'solely' should not be construed as a literal limitation; rather, we 'consider whether, under all the circumstances, the scheme was being promoted primarily as an investment or as a means whereby participants could pool their own activities, their money and the promoter's contribution in a meaningful way.'" (quoting *S.E.C. v. Aqua-Sonic Prods. Corp.,* 687 F.2d 577, 582 (2d Cir. 1982)). The efforts of promotors, undertaken either before or after gaining control over investor funds, are relevant considerations due to Howey's focus on economic realities. *S.E.C. v. Mut. Benefits Corp.,* 408 F.3d 737, 743–44 (11th Cir. 2005) (stating that "[n]either *Howey* [n]or *Edwards* require such a clean distinction between a promoter's activities prior to his having use of an investor's money and his activities thereafter" and that "investment schemes may often involve a combination of both pre- and post-purchase managerial activities, both of which should be taken into consideration in determining whether *Howey*'s test is satisfied" (first citing *S.E.C. v. Eurobond Exch., Ltd.,* 13 F.3d 1334 (9th Cir. 1994); then citing *Gary Plastic Packaging Corp.,* 756 F.2d 230; and then citing *Glen-Arden Commodities,* 493 F.2d 1027)).

The Court finds that the SEC has shown a substantial likelihood of success in proving that, at the time of the 2018 Sales, a reasonable Initial Purchaser's expectation of profits from their purchase of Grams was based upon the essential entrepreneurial and managerial efforts of Telegram. As Telegram has noted, Grams do not exist and did not exist at the time of the 2018 Sales. (Doc. 71 at 7, 39). But the Initial Purchasers provided capital to fund the TON Blockchain's development in exchange for the future delivery of Grams, which they expect to resell for a profit. The offering materials recognize this economic reality and made Telegram's commitment to develop this project explicit. (JX 8 at 19 (stating that Telegram "intend[s] to use the proceeds raised from the offering for the development of the TON Blockchain")); see also (JX 11 at 7). Thus, to realize a return on their investment, the Initial Purchasers were entirely reliant on Telegram's efforts to develop, launch, and provide ongoing support for the TON Blockchain and Grams. The Court finds that if, after immediately after launch, Telegram and its team decamped to the British Virgin Islands, where Telegram is incorporated, and ceased all further efforts to support the TON Blockchain, the TON Blockchain and Grams would exist in some form but would likely lack the mass adoption, vibrancy, and utility that would enable the Initial Purchasers to earn their expected huge profits. See M. Todd Henderson & Max Raskin, *A Regulatory Classification of Digital Assets: Toward an Operational Howey Test for Cryptocurrencies, ICOs, and Other Digital Assets,* 2 Colum. Bus. L. Rev. 443, 461 (2019) (proposing a "Bahamas Test"). Initial Purchasers' dependence on Telegram to develop, launch, and support the TON Blockchain is sufficient to find that the Initial Purchasers' expectation of profits was reliant on the essential efforts of Telegram. See *ATBCOIN LLC,* 380 F. Supp. 3d at 357.

Telegram's advertised promotion of the TON Blockchain and Grams though integration with Messenger created a reasonable expectation in the minds of the Initial Purchasers that their anticipated profits were dependent on Telegram's essential post-launch efforts. Since announcing the TON Blockchain, Telegram's core message has been that Gram would be the first digital asset capable of true mass market adoption. (JX 4 at 1). Telegram highlighted the value proposition of participating in the launch of the first mainstream cryptocurrency in its offering materials for the 2018 Sales, (JX 8 at 5 (stating that "Telegram is uniquely positioned to establish the mass-market cryptocurrency")); see also (JX 9 at 5); (Joint Stip. ¶ 141), and has continue to emphasize the potential for Gram's mainstream adoption in its more recent public statements, (Drylewski Decl., Ex. 3 at 1 (stating its intention that "Grams will become a true complement to traditional currencies")). The Initial Purchasers recognized that an investment in Grams was a bet that Telegram could successfully encourage the mass adoption of Grams, thereby enabling a high potential return on the resales of Grams. See, e.g., (PX 7 at 8 (investment thesis stating that Grams "ha[ve] the potential to be the first truly mass market cryptocurrency")); (PX 31 at 4, 5 (investment thesis highlighting the chance to "ability to participate in what could be a category defining investment" and "[o]pportunity to invest in a token that could prevail as the leading store of value and smart-contract platform")).

At the time of the 2018 Sales, Telegram's stated goal of developing Grams into the first mass market cryptocurrency was plausible, to Telegram, the Initial Purchasers, and the wider market, because of Messenger and its enormous user base. If the plans for a technically identical blockchain were floated, stripped of Telegram's branding and support, it is unlikely that such an offering would have raised $1.7 billion in less than three months. Telegram's offering achieved its success because of its stated intention to integrate the TON Blockchain with Messenger in order to encourage the widespread use of Grams. Telegram knew that Messenger was the critical element for the TON Blockchain to become something more than a new competitor to other cryptocurrencies, bluntly stating that "Telegram will serve as a launch pad for TON, ensuring its technological superiority and widespread adoption at launch." (JX 9 at 20). A variety of planned integrations would introduce Grams to Messenger's 300 million current monthly users as well as to all future Messenger users, a category which appears set to grow quickly. (PX 17 at 2 (Doc. 122-17) (Pavel writing that he "see[s] both TON and Telegram as integral parts of the success of the project as Telegram provides the necessary user base and adoption to make the whole idea of mass market crypto-currency work")).

Investors also knew that Messenger represented the key to Grams' mass adoption and therefore expected Telegram to use Messenger to advance this goal. See, e.g., (PX 32 at 1 ("TON has an effective way to bootstrap the blockchain by leveraging Telegram's 200M active users.")); (PX 2 ¶ 14 ("Telegram already had a captive community of users, which made it less difficult to create a new network.")); (PX 1 ¶ 11 ("I felt that the Telegram Messenger's user base was a factor that was tied to how much demand there would be for Grams in the future.")); (PX 4 ¶¶ 14–15 (investor stating that it "felt that Telegram's Messenger application would continue to drive demand for Grams" and that "Grams would have a good synergy with Telegram's Messenger application")); (PX 5 ¶ 13 ("I viewed the Messenger platform and the to-be-developed TON platform to be connected.")); (PX 7 ¶ 19 ("Our belief was that with 180 million users, Telegram and its applications and uses would grow in popularity, and with increased use and demand the price of Grams would rise over time.")); (PX 33 at 2 ("The Telegram Messenger ecosystem provides a significant go to market advantage for TON.")); see also (PX 1 ¶¶ 11, 15); (PX 2 ¶ 7); (PX 5 ¶ 12); (PX 30 at 5); (PX 31 at 1). The Initial Purchasers reasonably expected that Telegram would continue to support the TON Blockchain in the post-launch period.

Telegram structured post-launch financial incentives to ensure that the link between Grams and Messenger was unmistakable to users. As part of its promotion of the 2018 Sales, Telegram stated it planned to reserve 10% of all Grams for post-launch incentive payments to encourage the growth of the TON ecosystem. (JX 8 at 18). Half of this pool, 5% of all Grams or nearly 250 million Grams, would be offered as incentives for Messenger users to try the TON Blockchain for the first time. (Drylewski Decl., Ex. 5 at 3–4 (Doc. 73-5)). Grams would be freely "distributed on a first-come, first-served basis to users of Telegram Messenger," who request them via Messenger. (Doc. 95 ¶ 387); (Drylewski Decl., Ex. 5 at 3–4). These incentives, which Telegram still plans to employ, are intended to entice Messenger users to interact with the TON Blockchain for a monetary reward, in hopes of generating a host of first time blockchain users. (Joint Stip. ¶ 163); (Doc. 95 ¶ 387).

The Gram Purchase Agreements anticipate a critical role for Telegram in the post- launch TON Blockchain. Section 5.2 of both the Round One and Round Two Purchase Agreements oblige Telegram to "use its reasonable endeavours to facilitate the use of [Grams] as the principal currency used on Telegram Messenger by building TON Wallets into Telegram Messenger." (JX 11 § 5.2); (JX 12 § 5.2). These still valid provisions created the reasonable expectation in the minds of the Initial Purchasers that, following launch, Telegram would integrate the TON Blockchain with Messenger and, thereby, continue to work to improve and advance the TON Blockchain. Further, the Gram Purchase Agreements' "Risk Factors" described a pertinent potential risk to the 2018 Sales as the "[r]isks [a]ssociated [w]ith [i]ntegrating the TON Blockchain and Telegram Messenger." (JX 14 at 5); see also (JX 15 at 5–6). It continued that "Telegram intends to integrate the TON Blockchain with Telegram Messenger as described in the 'Telegram Messenger-TON Integration' section of the Telegram [Round One] Primer," before warning that, due to any issues with this integration, "adoption of Grams as a form of currency within Telegram Messenger's existing ecosystem may be more limited than anticipated." (JX 14 at 5); see also (JX 15 at 5–6). The Gram Purchase Agreements' still enforceable terms set and continue to shape the Initial Purchasers' expectations and would lead a reasonable purchaser to believe that Telegram would work to integrate Messenger and the TON Blockchain in a manner to advance the TON Blockchain's success.

Indeed, as part of the 2018 Sales, Telegram explicitly promoted multiple ways in which the TON Blockchain and Grams would be directly integrated with Messenger. In the "Telegram Messenger-TON Integration" section of offering materials, Telegram stated that the official TON Wallet would be integrated into Messenger, thereby allowing Messenger users to control their Grams without leaving the app and permitting Grams to "serve as the principal currency for the in-app economy on Telegram." (JX 8 at 11, 13 ("Integrated into Telegram applications, the TON [W]allet is expected to become the world's most adopted cryptocurrency wallet.")); (JX 9 at 11); (Joint Stip. ¶ 140); see also (PX 31 at 2 (investor forecast that "[a]t launch, the Telegram TON [W]allet will become the world's most adopted cryptocurrency wallet"). Since the institution of this action, Telegram has purported to abandon of its promise to integrate the TON Wallet into Messenger. (Drylewski Decl., Ex. 3 at 2 ("At the time of the anticipated launch of the TON Blockchain, Telegram's TON Wallet application is expected to be made available solely on a stand-alone basis and will not be integrated with the Telegram Messenger service.")). However, such disclaimers are not dispositive and this disclaimer in particular is equivocal on its face. In the next breath, the disclaimer states that "Telegram may integrate the TON Wallet application with the Telegram Messenger service in the future." (*Id.*).

Telegram pledged to give Grams to its development team and the lockup provision governing those Grams fed reasonable expectations that this development team would continue to play an important role in the growth of the TON Blockchain. Specifically, Telegram has reserved 4% of all Grams for the TON Blockchain development team, including 1% for each Durov brother, and has stated that these Grams would be distributed subject to a four-year lockup period. (Joint Stip. ¶¶ 158–60); (JX 9 at 16, 18). A lockup period imposed on critical employees aligns their interests with the success of Grams and the TON Blockchain during the lockup period. These lockups have their most plausible and logical economic justification if the employees subject to the lockup will play a critical role in the ongoing success of the entity. In fact, one investor specifically discussed the developer lockup period with Pavel and then told him that, in terms of Pavel's own allocation of Grams, "more is better!" because it ensured that Pavel's interests were "fundamental[ly] aligned with the success of TON." (PX 25 at 2 (Doc. 122-25) (inquiring whether "the tokens issued to employees and developers pre launch being subject to the same lockup as the investors [as] [t]his is what typically happens for IPOs to ensure the people needed to deliver the core intellectual property have incentives to stay engaged through the lockup")); (Doc. 80 ¶ 148).

The cumulative effect of the advertised integration of the TON Blockchain with Messenger and the lockups placed on the developer's Grams created a reasonable expectation among the Initial Purchasers that Telegram would continue to provide essential support for the TON Blockchain after launch. See, e.g., (PX 2 ¶ 14 ("Based on Telegram's offering materials, we also believed that the Telegram team would continue to support and grow the TON network after launch and make it more useful, and the value of Grams would continue to go up.")); (PX 4 ¶ 14 ("Based on the due diligence I did, I expected Telegram to continue to work on the TON Blockchain platform it was building after launch, which would increase the value of Grams.")); (PX 6 ¶ 3 ("[Initial Purchaser] anticipated that Telegram would remain involved in the development of the TON network after it was launched.")). Based on the totality of the evidence, a reasonable Initial Purchaser would expect Telegram to continue to support and improve the TON Blockchain post-launch.

The Court finds that the SEC has shown a substantial likelihood of success in proving that the Initial Purchasers' investment was made with a reasonable expectation of Telegram's essential entrepreneurial and managerial efforts to develop and support the TON Blockchain and Grams.

* * *

Examining the totality of the evidence and considering the economic realities, the Court finds that the SEC has shown a substantial likelihood of success in proving that the 2018 Sales were part of a larger scheme, manifested by Telegram's actions, conduct, statements, and understandings, to offer Grams to the Initial Purchasers with the intent and purpose that these Grams be distributed in a secondary public market, which is the offering of securities under Howey.

J. Grams Are Not Evaluated Upon the Launch of the TON Blockchain.

Telegram argues that Grams, as distinct from the Gram Purchase Agreements, must be evaluated under Howey when the Grams come into existence with the launch of the TON Blockchain. Telegram then contends that, at launch, Grams would be commodities, not securities, because Grams would be used consumptively, would not be supported by Telegram's essential efforts, and would lack the requisite common enterprise. Telegram emphasizes that, even if the Court found Grams to be securities at the time of the 2018 Sales, Grams were then covered by a valid Rule 506(c) exemption. This exemption would extend until the launch of the TON Blockchain, at which point Grams would be commodities not covered by the securities laws.

The Court rejects Telegram's characterization of the purported security in this case. While helpful as a shorthand reference, the security in this case is not simply the Gram, which is little more than alphanumeric cryptographic sequence. Howey refers to an investment contract, i.e. a security, as "a contract, transaction or scheme," using the term "scheme" in a descriptive, not pejorative, sense. *Howey,* 328 U.S. at 298–99. This case presents a "scheme" to be evaluated under Howey that consists of the full set of contracts, expectations, and understandings centered on the sales and distribution of the Gram. *Howey* requires an examination of the entirety of the parties' understandings and expectations. *Howey*, 328 U.S. at 297–98 (declining to "treat[] the contracts and deeds as separate transactions"). Further, for the reasons discussed previously, the Court finds that the appropriate point at which to evaluate this scheme to sell and distribute Grams is at the point at which the scheme's participants had a meeting of the minds, i.e. at the time of the 2018 Sales, rather than the date of delivery.[13]

K. The Grams Sales to the Initial Purchasers Do Not Fall Within an Exemption and so Constitute a Violation of the Securities Laws.

Telegram admits it has filed no registration statements related to any offering of the Gram Purchase Agreements or Grams. (Joint Stip. ¶ 59). Instead, Telegram argues that the "offers and sales on interests in Grams" reflected in the Gram Purchase Agreements were made according to valid exemptions to the registration requirement under section 4(a)(2) and Rule 506(c). (Doc. 71 at 42). The Court finds that the SEC has shown a substantial likelihood of success in proving that Telegram sold Grams to the Initial Purchasers with the purpose and intent that those Grams then be distributed by the Initial Purchasers into a secondary public market. Telegram has failed to carry its burden of demonstrating a valid exemption either under section 4(a)(2) or Rule 506(c). The Court concludes that Telegram's offers and sales of the Grams represent an ongoing violation of section 5 and that the final step of this public distribution of a security without a registration statement must be enjoined.

On the evidence presented, the Court finds that the scheme is "a disguised public distribution." *Cavanagh*, 1 F. Supp. 2d at 337. Telegram's fundamental goal was to establish Grams as "the first mass market cryptocurrency." (JX 4 at 1). Telegram did not intend for Grams to come to rest with the 175 Initial Purchasers but to reach the public at large via post-launch resales by the Initial Purchasers. Therefore, Telegram's sale of Grams to the Initial Purchasers, who will function as statutory underwriters, is the first step in an ongoing public distribution of securities and, as such, Telegram cannot receive the benefit of an exemption from the registration requirement under either section 4(a) or Rule 506(c).

Section 4(a)(2) exempts "transactions by an issuer not involving a public offering" from section 5's registration requirement. 15 U.S.C. § 77d(a)(2). Telegram is the issuer of Grams.[14] A sale of securities is not a public offering when it is made "to those who are shown to be able to fend for themselves." *Ralston Purina Co.*, 346 U.S. at 125. Telegram argues that, because the Grams were offered to the Initial Purchasers, who were undoubtedly sophisticated investors capable of fending off themselves, there was no public offering and the section 4(a)(2) exemption applies

---

13. Even if the Court adopted Telegram's theory and evaluated Grams upon the launch of the TON Blockchain, it does not necessarily follow that Telegram's analysis of the Howey factors at launch is correct and, thereby, that Grams are not a security.

14. "The term 'issuer' means every person who issues or proposes to issue any security;...." 15 U.S.C. § 77b(a)(4).

to its sales of Grams. However, the ability of the Initial Purchasers to fend for themselves does not end the inquiry if the Grams were not intended to come to rest with the Initial Purchasers.

The Court finds that Telegram did not intend for the Grams to come to rest with the Initial Purchasers. Specifically, Telegram's goal of establishing Grams as "the first mass market cryptocurrency" required that the 58% of all Grams sold in the 2018 Sales reach a much wider pool than the 175 Initial Purchasers. As discussed previously, Telegram built economic incentives into the 2018 Sales, including large discounts and differential lockups, to ensure that the Initial Purchasers resold Grams soon after launch. Further, Telegram sought out participants for the 2018 Sales, such as major venture capital firms, that would purchase with an investment intent and so would sell their allocation of Grams quickly to earn a profit.

The Second Circuit has held that securities do not come to rest with investors who intend a further distribution. *Gilligan, Will & Co.*, 267 F.2d at 468 (stating that a security does not come to rest with an investor who purchased "speculatively" and with "a view to distribution"); see also *Geiger v. S.E.C.*, 363 F.3d 481, 487–88 (D.C. Cir. 2004) (stating that one "did not have to be involved in the final step of [a] distribution to have participated in it" and that the purchase of shares at "a substantial discount" followed by their quick resale supported a finding that the shares were not at rest). The Court finds that Telegram intended that Grams be distributed to the public through the Initial Purchasers. The Court further finds that the public "need[s] the protection of the [Securities] Act." *Ralston Purina Co.*, 346 U.S. at 125. The Court concludes that Telegram's offer and sale of Grams to the Initial Purchasers is a public offering and ineligible for a section 4(a)(2) exemption to the registration requirement.

Rule 506(c) exempts transactions that meet its conditions from section 5's registration requirement. 17 C.F.R. § 230.506(c). One requirement of Rule 506(c) exemption is that the issuer "exercise reasonable care to assure that the purchasers of the securities are not underwriters within the meaning of section 2(a)(11) of the [Securities] Act," which in turns requires a "[r]easonable inquiry to determine if the purchaser is acquiring the securities for himself or for other persons." *Id.* § 230.502(d). The Court finds that Telegram failed to use reasonable care to ensure that the Initial Purchasers were not underwriters, and therefore may not avail itself of a Rule 506(c) exemption.

Section 2(a)(11) defines an "underwriter" as "any person who has purchased from an issuer with a view to...the distribution of any security." 15 U.S.C. § 77b(a) (11). And, again, a distribution includes "the entire process by which in the course of a public offering the block of securities is dispersed and ultimately comes to rest in the hands of the investing public." *R.A. Holman & Co.*, 366 F.2d at 449. The Initial Purchasers bought Grams from Telegram, the issuer, with an intent to resell them for profit in the secondary market soon after launch of the TON Blockchain. The Grams would not and were not intended to come to rest with the Initial Purchasers but instead were intended to move from the Initial Purchasers to the general public. Therefore, this two-step process represents a public distribution and the Initial Purchasers, who acted as mere conduits to the general public, are underwriters.

Telegram argues that, even if Initial Purchasers are statutory underwriters, it complied with Rule 502(d) by taking reasonable care to ensure that the Initial Purchasers were purchasing for themselves and not to resell their Grams to others. Specifically, Telegram points to a representation and warranty in each Gram Purchase Agreement that required the Initial Purchasers to warrant that they were "purchasing the Tokens for [their] own account and not with a view towards, or for resale in connection with, the sale or distribution." (Doc. 75 ¶ 209); (JX 11 at 20). However, in evaluating the economic reality of this scheme, legal disclaimers do not control. The representation and warranty that the Initial Purchasers purchased without a view towards resale rings hollow in the face of the economic realities of the 2018 Sales. From Telegram's perspective, it was critical that the Initial Purchasers could flip their Grams in a post-launch secondary market because this feature would increase the amount of money it could raise. Based on these economic realities, Telegram's contrary representations will not be accorded controlling weight. Telegram did not take reasonable care to ensure that statutory underwriters were not participants in the 2018 Sales. As the 2018 Sales to the Initial Purchasers were merely a step in a public distribution of Grams and Telegram was aware that Initial Purchasers were statutory underwriters, Telegram's sales of Grams do not qualify for a Rule 506(c) exemption from the registration requirement.

The Court finds that the SEC has shown a substantial likelihood of success in proving that the Gram Purchase Agreements, Telegram's implied undertakings, and its understandings with the Initial Purchasers, including the intended and expected resale of Grams into a public market, amount to the distribution of securities, thereby requiring compliance with section 5. Telegram has failed to establish an exemption to the registration requirement under either section 4(a)(2) or Rule 506(c). Further, the Court concludes that the SEC has shown that the sale and imminent delivery of Grams represent a single ongoing violation of section 5. The Court also finds that the delivery of Grams to the Initial Purchasers, who would resell them into the public market, represents a near certain risk of a future harm, namely the completion of a public distribution of a security without a registration statement. An injunction, prohibiting the delivery of Grams to the Initial Purchasers and thereby preventing the culmination of this ongoing violation, is appropriate and will be granted.

CONCLUSION

Plaintiff's motion for a preliminary injunction, (Doc. 3), is GRANTED.

Discussion Points

1. *The outcome.* Telegram agreed to pay a civil penalty of $18.5 million and disgorge $1.224 billion to investors related to what the SEC claimed was an illegal unregistered public offering of securities. Do you think that imposing civil penalties is enough to encourage compliance with SEC regulations? Why or why not?

2. *The SEC's view of the SAFT.* Should the SEC have considered the SAFT model to allow non-accredited investors to participate in the purchase and sale of digital coins?

3. *Did the SEC go too far?* Should the SEC provide more flexibility in the secondary market to non-accredited investors.

In the Matter of BlockFi Lending LLC

Securities Act of 1933 Rel. No. 11029;

Investment Company Act of 1940Rel. No. 34503;

Administrative Proceeding File No. 3-20758 (2022)

I.

The Securities and Exchange Commission ("Commission") deems it appropriate that public cease-and-desist proceedings be, and hereby are, instituted pursuant to Section 8A of the Securities Act of 1933 ("Securities Act") and Section 9(f) of the Investment Company Act of 1940 ("Investment Company Act") against BlockFi Lending LLC ("BlockFi" or "Respondent").

II.

In anticipation of the institution of these proceedings, Respondent has submitted an Offer of Settlement (the "Offer") which the Commission has determined to accept. Solely for the purpose of these proceedings and any other proceedings brought by or on behalf of the Commission, or to which the Commission is a party, and without admitting or denying the findings herein, except as to the Commission's jurisdiction over it and the subject matter of these proceedings, which are admitted, Respondent consents to the entry of this Order Instituting Cease-and-Desist Proceedings Pursuant to Section 8A of the Securities Act of 1933 and Section 9(f) of the Investment Company Act of 1940, Making Findings, and Imposing a Cease-And-Desist Order ("Order"), as set forth below.

III.

On the basis of this Order and Respondent's Offer, the Commission finds[1] that:

Summary

1. From March 4, 2019 to the present, BlockFi, a New Jersey-based financial services company and wholly owned subsidiary of BlockFi, Inc., has offered and sold BlockFi Interest Accounts ("BIAs") to investors, through which investors lend crypto assets to BlockFi in exchange for BlockFi's promise to provide a variable monthly interest payment. BlockFi generated the interest paid out to BIA investors by deploying its assets in various ways, including loans of crypto assets made to institutional and corporate borrowers, lending U.S. dollars to retail investors, and by investing in equities and futures. As of March 31, 2021, BlockFi and its affiliates held approximately $14.7 billion in BIA investor assets. As of December 8, 2021, BlockFi and its affiliates held approximately $10.4 billion in BIA investor assets, and had approximately 572,160 BIA investors, including 391,105 investors in the United States.

2. Based on the facts and circumstances set forth below, the BIAs were securities because they were notes under *Reves v. Ernst & Young*, 494 U.S. 56, 64–66 (1990), and its progeny, and also because BlockFi offered and sold the BIAs as investment contracts, under *SEC v. W.J. Howey Co.*, 328 U.S. 293, 301 (1946), and its progeny, including the cases discussed by the Commission in its *Report of Investigation Pursuant To Section 21(a) Of The Securities Exchange Act of 1934: The DAO* (Exchange Act Rel. No. 81207) (July 25, 2017). BlockFi promised BIA investors a variable interest rate, determined by BlockFi on a periodic basis, in exchange for crypto assets loaned by the investors, who could demand that BlockFi return their loaned assets at any time. BlockFi thus borrowed the crypto assets in exchange for a promise to repay with interest. Investors in the BIAs had a reasonable expectation of obtaining a future profit from BlockFi's efforts in managing the BIAs based on BlockFi's statements about how it would generate the yield to pay BIA investors interest. Investors also had a reasonable expectation that BlockFi would use the invested crypto assets in BlockFi's lending and principal investing activity, and that investors would share profits in the form of interest payments resulting from BlockFi's efforts. BlockFi offered and sold the BIAs to the general public to obtain crypto assets for the general use of its business, namely to run its lending and investment activities to pay interest to BIA investors, and promoted the BIAs as an investment. BlockFi offered and sold securities without a registration statement filed or in effect with the Commission and without qualifying for an exemption from registration; as a result, BlockFi violated Sections 5(a) and 5(c) of the Securities Act.

3. BlockFi also made a materially false and misleading statement on its website from March 4, 2019 to August 31, 2021, concerning its collateral practices and, therefore, the risks associated with its lending activity. As a result, and as discussed

---

1. The findings herein are made pursuant to Respondent's Offer of Settlement and are not binding on any other person or entity in this or any other proceeding.

in more detail below, BlockFi violated Sections 17(a)(2) and 17(a)(3) of the Securities Act.

4. In addition, from at least December 31, 2019 to at least September 30, 2021, BlockFi operated as an unregistered investment company because it is an issuer of securities engaged in the business of investing, reinvesting, owning, holding, or trading in securities and owning investment securities, as defined by Section 3(a)(2) of the Investment Company Act, having a value exceeding 40% of its total assets (exclusive of Government securities and cash items). BlockFi violated Section 7(a) of the Investment Company Act by engaging in interstate commerce while failing to register as an investment company with the Commission.

Respondent

5. **BlockFi** is a Delaware limited liability company formed in 2018 and a wholly owned subsidiary of BlockFi Inc., with its principal place of business in Jersey City, New Jersey. On March 4, 2019, BlockFi began publicly offering and selling BIAs.

Other Relevant Entities

6. **BlockFi Inc.** is a Delaware corporation formed in 2017 with the same principal place of business as BlockFi.

7. **BlockFi Trading LLC ("BlockFi Trading")** is Delaware limited liability company formed in May 2019 and a wholly owned subsidiary of BlockFi Inc., with the same principal place of business as BlockFi.

Facts

BlockFi Offered and Sold BIAs as Investment Opportunities

8. On March 4, 2019, BlockFi publicly announced the launch of the BIA, through which investors could lend crypto assets to BlockFi and in exchange, receive interest, "paid monthly in cryptocurrency." Interest began accruing the day after assets were transmitted to BlockFi and compounded monthly, with interest payments made to accounts associated with each BIA investor, in crypto assets, on or about the first business day of each month.

9. BlockFi offered and sold BIAs to obtain crypto assets for the general use of its business, namely to use the assets in its lending and investment activities, which generated income both for BlockFi and to pay interest to BIA investors. BlockFi pooled the loaned assets, and exercised full discretion over how much to hold, lend, and invest. BlockFi had complete legal ownership and control over the loaned crypto assets, and advertised that it managed the risks involved.

10. Under BlockFi's terms for the BIA, investors:

grant BlockFi the right, without further notice to [the investor], to hold the cryptocurrency held in [the] account in BlockFi's name or in another name, and to pledge, repledge, hypothecate, rehypothecate, sell, lend, or otherwise transfer, invest or use any amount of such cryptocurrency, separately or together with other property, with all attendant rights of ownership, and for any period of time and without retaining in BlockFi's possession and/or control a like amount of cryptocurrency, and to use or invest such cryptocurrency at its own risk.

11. At all relevant times, BlockFi represented that it earned interest on the assets that it borrowed from BIA investors by lending those crypto assets to institutional borrowers. Beginning in September 2020, BlockFi disclosed on its website that it also purchased "SEC-regulated equities and predominantly CFTC-regulated futures" using BIA assets.

12. To begin investing in a BIA, an investor could transfer crypto assets to the digital wallet address assigned by BlockFi to the investor, or purchase crypto assets with fiat currency from BlockFi Trading for the purpose of investing in a BIA. BlockFi Trading accepted the crypto asset or fiat from the investor, and then transferred the asset or fiat to BlockFi. BlockFi did not hold private keys for the investors' wallet addresses; rather, investors' crypto assets were sent to BlockFi's wallet addresses at third-party custodians.

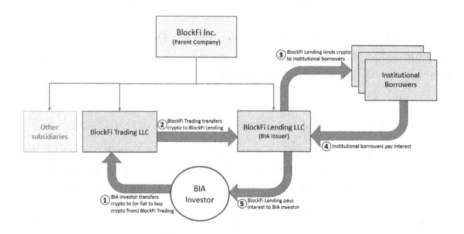

13. BIA investors were permitted to withdraw the equivalent to the crypto assets they loaned to BlockFi at any time, with some limitations, and could borrow money in U.S. dollars against the amount of crypto assets deposited in BIAs.

14. BlockFi adjusted the interest rates payable on BIAs for particular crypto assets periodically, and typically at the start of each month. BlockFi set the rates based, in part, on "the yield that [BlockFi] can generate from lending," to institutional borrowers, and thus it was correlated with the efforts that BlockFi put in to generate that yield. BlockFi periodically adjusted its interest rates payable on the BIAs in part after analysis of current yield on its investment and lending activity. BIA investors could demand that BlockFi repay the loaned crypto assets at any time.

15. BlockFi regularly touted the profits investors may earn by investing in a BIA. When announcing the BIA, BlockFi promoted the interest earned, promising "an industry-leading 6.2% [annual percentage yield]," compounded monthly. BlockFi described it as "an easy way for crypto investors to earn bitcoin as they HODL." [2]

16. Within the first few weeks of launching the BIA, BlockFi again touted investors' potential for profit. On March 20, 2019, BlockFi announced that BIAs experienced significant growth, including from large firms who participated in BIAs "as a way to bolster their returns." BlockFi asserted that it "provide[d] the average crypto investor with the tools to build their wealth," and that it "look[ed] forward to giving even more investors a chance to earn a yield on their crypto."

17. On April 1, 2019, BlockFi began to "tier" the interest rates that investors received, initially announcing that "BIA balances of up to and including 25 [Bitcoin] or 500 [Ether] (equivalent to roughly $100,000 and $70,000 respectively) will earn the 6.2% APY interest rate. All balances over that limit will earn a tiered rate of 2% interest." Even when changing the interest rates customers receive, BlockFi touted the yields to investors. On August 27, 2021, BlockFi stated that the adjustments to interest rates are done "with the goal of maintaining great rates for the maximum number of clients."

18. On January 1, 2021, BlockFi advertised that it had "distributed more than $50 million in monthly interest payments to [its] clients."

19. As of November 1, 2021, the interest rates BlockFi paid investors ranged from 0.1% to 9.5%, depending on the type of crypto asset and the size of the investment. For example, investors could receive 9.5% in interest for up to 40,000 Tether ("USDT") and 8.5% for anything over 40,000 USDT, as well as 4.5% interest for up to 0.1 Bitcoin ("BTC"), 1% for 0.1 to 0.35 BTC, and 0.1% for anything over 0.35 BTC.

20. BlockFi offered and sold the BIA securities to investors, including retail investors, through advertising and general solicitations on its website, www.blockfi. com. BlockFi also promoted distribution of the BIA offering through its social media accounts, including YouTube, Twitter, and Facebook. In addition, through its "Partner" program, an affiliate marketing program in which participants could "earn passive income by introducing your audience to financial tools for crypto investors," BlockFi extended its distribution of the BIA securities to retail investors through certain offers and promotions.

21. BlockFi did not have a Securities Act registration statement filed or in effect with the Commission for the offer and sale of the BIAs, nor did the offer and sale of BIAs qualify for an exemption from registration under the Securities Act.

----

2. "HODL" is a purposeful misspelling of "hold" and an acronym for "hold on for dear life," denoting buy-and-hold strategies in the context of crypto assets.

BlockFi Misrepresented the Level of Risk in the
BIA Investment Opportunity

22. BlockFi made a material misrepresentation to BIA investors concerning the level of risk in its loan portfolio. Beginning at the time of the BIA launch on March 4, 2019 and continuing to August 31, 2021, BlockFi made a statement in multiple website posts that its institutional loans were "typically" over-collateralized, when in fact, most institutional loans were not. When BlockFi began offering the BIA investment, it intended to require over-collateralization on a majority of its loans to institutional investors, but it quickly became apparent that large institutional investors were frequently not willing to post large amounts of collateral to secure their loans. Approximately 24% of institutional crypto asset loans made in 2019 were over- collateralized; in 2020 approximately 16% were over-collateralized; and in 2021 (through June 30, 2021) approximately 17% were over-collateralized. As a result, BlockFi's statement materially overstated the degree to which it secured protection from defaults by institutional borrowers through collateral. Through operational oversight, BlockFi's personnel failed to take steps to update the website statement to accurately reflect the fact that most institutional loans were not over-collateralized.

23. Although BlockFi made other disclosures on its website regarding its risk management practices, because of BlockFi's misrepresentation and omission about the level of risk in its loan portfolio, BIA investors did not have complete and accurate information with which to evaluate the risk that, in the event of defaults by its institutional borrowers, BlockFi would be unable to comply with its obligation to pay BIA investors the stated interest rates or return the loaned crypto assets to investors upon demand.

BlockFi Operated as an Unregistered Investment Company

24. As the issuer of the BIA, BlockFi is an "issuer" for purposes of the Investment Company Act.

25. After the launch of the BIA, BlockFi pooled the crypto assets it borrowed, and commingled and rehypothecated these crypto assets received from investors in the BIAs with BlockFi's other assets, including collateral received from institutional borrowers. As BlockFi took ownership of the loaned crypto assets from investors in the BIAs, BlockFi used the commingled assets to, among other things, make loans to institutional and retail borrowers, stake crypto assets, and purchase crypto asset trust shares and interests in private funds.

26. From at least December 31, 2019 to at least September 30, 2021, BlockFi owned certain investment securities, as defined by Section 3(a)(2) of the Investment Company Act—such as loans of crypto assets and U.S. dollars to counter parties, investments in crypto asset trusts and funds, and intercompany receivables—exceeding 40% of the value of its total assets (exclusive of Government securities and cash items) on an unconsolidated basis. For example, as of December 31, 2020, BlockFi

held loans to counter parties valued at over $1.9 billion, investments in crypto asset trusts and funds valued at approximately $1.5 billion, and intercompany receivables valued at approximately $847 million, which together constituted well over 40% of its approximately $4.8 billion in total assets.

27. Section 3(a)(1)(C) of the Investment Company Act defines "investment company" to mean any issuer that "is engaged or proposes to engage in the business of investing, reinvesting, owning, holding, or trading in securities, and owns or proposes to acquire investment securities having a value exceeding 40 per centum of the value of such issuer's total assets (exclusive of Government securities and cash items) on an unconsolidated basis." Section 3(a)(2) of the Investment Company Act defines "investment securities" to include all securities except government securities, securities issued by employees' securities companies, and securities issued by majority-owned subsidiaries of the owner which are not investment companies and not relying on exceptions set forth in Sections 3(c)(1) or 3(c)(7) of the Investment Company Act. Loans that BlockFi made to counter parties are considered investment securities under the Investment Company Act. As an issuer holding over 40% of the value of its total assets in investment securities from at least December 31, 2019 to at least September 30, 2021, BlockFi met the definition of an investment company during this time period.

28. Since at least December 31, 2019, BlockFi has engaged in interstate commerce by, among other things, making loans to institutional and retail investors, purchasing and selling other investment securities for its own account, and engaging in other business transactions in interstate commerce while an investment company within the meaning of Section 3(a)(1)(C) of the Investment Company Act.

29. Although BlockFi met the definition of "investment company" from at least December 31, 2019 to at least September 30, 2021, it did not register with the Commission as an investment company, meet any statutory exemptions or exclusions from the definition of an investment company, or seek an order from the Commission declaring that it was primarily engaged in a business other than that of investing, reinvesting, owning, holding, or trading in securities, or exempting it from complying with any provisions of the Investment Company Act or the rules thereunder. Although BlockFi has suggested that it was relying on the exclusion from the definition of "investment company" provided for "market intermediaries" by Section 3(c)(2) of the Investment Company Act during this period, it did not satisfy the terms of that exclusion. Thus, during the relevant period, BlockFi was required to have registered with the Commission as an investment company.

Legal Analysis

A. Violation of Section5(a) and 5(c) of the Securities Act

30. The Securities Act and the Exchange Act were designed to "eliminate serious abuses in a largely unregulated securities market." *United Housing Found., Inc. v. Forman*, 421 U.S. 837, 849 (1975). They are focused, among other things, "on the

capital market of the enterprise system: the sale of securities to raise capital for profit-making purposes...and the need for regulation to prevent fraud and to protect the interest of investors." *Id.* Under Section 2(a)(1) of the Securities Act and Section 3(a)(10) of the Exchange Act, a security includes any "note." See 15 U.S.C. §§ 77b & 78c. A note is presumed to be a security unless it falls into certain judicially- created categories of financial instruments that are not securities, or if the note in question bears a "family resemblance" to notes in those categories based on a four-part test. See *Reves v. Ernst & Young*, 494 U.S. 56, 64–66 (1990), and its progeny. Applying the *Reves* four-part analysis, the BIAs were notes and thus securities. First, BlockFi offered and sold BIAs to obtain crypto assets for the general use of its business, namely to run its lending and investment activities to pay interest to BIA investors, and purchasers bought BIAs to receive interest ranging from 0.1% to 9.5% on the loaned crypto assets. Second, BIAs were offered and sold to a broad segment of the general public. Third, BlockFi promoted BIAs as an investment, specifically as a way to earn a consistent return on crypto assets and for investors to "build their wealth." Fourth, no alternative regulatory scheme or other risk reducing factors exist with respect to BIAs.

31. Under Section 2(a)(1) of the Securities Act and Section 3(a)(10) of the Exchange Act, a security includes "an investment contract." *See* 15 U.S.C. §§ 77b, 78c. Based on the facts and circumstances set forth above, the BIAs were also offered and sold as "investment contracts," as they meet the elements for an investment contract under *SEC v. W.J. Howey Co.*, 328 U.S. 293, 301 (1946), and its progeny, including the cases discussed by the Commission in its *Report of Investigation Pursuant To Section 21(a) Of The Securities Exchange Act of 1934: The DAO* (Exchange Act Rel. No. 81207) (July 25, 2017), citing *Forman*, 421 U.S. at 852–53 (The "touchstone" of an investment contract "is the presence of an investment in a common venture premised on a reasonable expectation of profits to be derived from the entrepreneurial or managerial efforts of others."); *see also SEC v. R.G. Reynolds Enterprises, Inc.*, 952 F.2d 1125 1130–31 (9th Cir. 1991) (finding managed account product was an investment contract where investors provided funds in exchange for interest rate earned through the issuer's investment of the funds). BlockFi sold BIAs in exchange for the investment of money in the form of crypto assets. BlockFi pooled the BIA investors' crypto assets, and used those assets for lending and investment activity that would generate returns for both BlockFi and BIA investors. The returns earned by each BIA investor were a function of the pooling of the loaned crypto assets, and the ways in which BlockFi deployed those loaned assets. In this way, each investor's fortune was tied to the fortunes of the other investors. In addition, because BlockFi earned revenue for itself through its deployment of the loaned assets, the BIA investors' fortunes were also linked to those of the promoter, i.e., BlockFi. Through its public statements, BlockFi created a reasonable expectation that BIA investors would earn profits derived from BlockFi's efforts to manage the loaned crypto assets profitably enough to pay the stated interest rates to the investors. BlockFi had com-

plete ownership and control over the borrowed crypto assets, and determined how much to hold, lend, and invest. BlockFi's lending activities were at its own discretion, and BlockFi advertised that it managed the risks involved. Similarly, its investment activities were at its own discretion, and BlockFi could decide whether and how to invest the BIA assets in equities or futures.

32. BlockFi did not have a registration statement filed or in effect with the Commission for the offers and sales of BIAs, nor did it qualify for an exemption from registration under the Securities Act for those offers and sales.

33. As a result of the conduct described above, BlockFi violated Section 5(a) of the Securities Act, which prohibits, unless a registration statement is in effect as to a security, any person, directly or indirectly, from making use of any means or instruments of transportation or communication in interstate commerce or of the mails to sell such security through the use or medium of any prospectus or otherwise; or to carry or cause to be carried through the mails or in interstate commerce, by any means or instruments of transportation, any such security for the purpose of sale or for delivery after sale.

34. As a result of the conduct described above, BlockFi also violated Section 5(c) of the Securities Act, which prohibits any person, directly or indirectly, from making use of any means or instruments of transportation or communication in interstate commerce or of the mails to offer to sell or offer to buy through the use or medium of any prospectus or otherwise any security, unless a registration statement has been filed as to such security.

B. Violation of Section 17(a)(2) and 17(a)(3) of the Securities Act

35. As a result of the conduct described above, BlockFi violated Sections 17(a)(2) and 17(a)(3) of the Securities Act, which prohibit any person in the offer or sale of securities from obtaining money or property by means of any untrue statement of material fact or any omission to state a material fact necessary in order to make statements made not misleading, and from engaging in any practice or course of business which operates or would operate as a fraud or deceit upon the purchaser, respectively. From March 2019 through August 2021, BlockFi misrepresented on its website that its institutional loans were "typically" over-collateralized, when in fact, most institutional loans were not. Accordingly, although BlockFi made other disclosures on its website concerning its risk management practices, BIA investors did not have complete and accurate information with which to evaluate the risk that, in the event of defaults by BlockFi's institutional borrowers, BlockFi would be unable to comply with its obligation to pay BIA investors the stated interest rates or return the loaned crypto assets to investors upon demand. This false and misleading statement was in the offer and sale of BIAs, and as such was in the offer and sale of securities. A violation of these provisions does not require scienter and may rest on a finding of negligence. See *Aaron v. SEC*, 446 U.S. 685, 701–02 (1980).

C. Violation of Section 7(a) of the Investment Company Act

36. As a result of the conduct described above, BlockFi violated Section 7(a) of the Investment Company Act, which makes it unlawful for an unregistered investment company to, among other things, directly or indirectly "[o]ffer for sale, sell, or deliver after sale, by the use of the mails or any means or instrumentality of interstate commerce, any security or any interest in a security" or "engage in any business in interstate commerce."

37. From at least December 31, 2019 to at least September 30, 2021, BlockFi held assets meeting the definition of investment securities under Section 3(a)(2) of the Investment Company Act. These investment securities, which include the loans that BlockFi made to counter parties, had a value exceeding 40% of its total assets as set forth in Section 3(a)(1)(C) of the Investment Company Act. During these time periods, BlockFi was an issuer, was not registered as an investment company, and was not exempted or excluded from the Investment Company Act's definition of an investment company.

38. Section 3(c)(2) of the Investment Company Act excludes from the definition of investment company any person that is "primarily engaged in the business of…acting as a market intermediary…whose gross income normally is derived principally from such business and related activities." As defined in Section 3(c)(2)(B)(i), a "'market intermediary' is any person that regularly holds itself out as being willing contemporaneously to engage in, and that is regularly engaged in, the business of entering into transactions on both sides of the market for a financial contract or one or more such financial contracts," and whose "gross income normally is derived principally from such business and related activities." Under Section 3(c)(2)(B)(ii), "'financial contract' means any arrangement that (I) takes the form of an individually negotiated contract, agreement, or option to buy, sell, lend, swap, or repurchase, or other similar individually negotiated transaction commonly entered into by participants in the financial markets; (II) is in respect of securities, commodities, currencies, interest or other rates, other measures of value, or any other financial or economic interest similar in purpose or function to any of the foregoing; and (III) is entered into in response to a request from a counterparty for a quotation, or is otherwise entered into and structured to accommodate the objectives of the counterparty to such arrangement."

39. BlockFi did not satisfy the terms of the "market intermediary" exclusion under Section 3(c)(2) because it was not primarily engaged in the business of acting as a market intermediary; its principal source of gross income was not derived from intermediary business and related activities; and it did not regularly engage in the business of entering into transactions on both sides of the market for a financial contract. The BIAs, for example, were not "individually negotiated" financial contracts that were entered into in "response to a request from a counterparty for a quotation"

or structured to accommodate "the objectives of the counterparty." Moreover, Block-Fi only intermittently entered into individually negotiated transactions to borrow crypto assets, and initiated and did not structure those transactions for the counter parties' objectives. Consequently, neither the BIA nor BlockFi's individually negotiated borrowings met the definition of financial contract in Section 3(c)(2), and so BlockFi was not regularly engaged in the business of entering into transactions on both sides of the market for a financial contract. BlockFi's primary business was investing in investment securities, including institutional loans. Moreover, BlockFi did not meet any other statutory exemptions or exclusions from the definition of an investment company, or seek an order from the Commission declaring that it was primarily engaged in a business other than that of investing, reinvesting, owning, holding, or trading in securities, or exempting it from complying with any provisions of the Investment Company Act or the rules thereunder. For these reasons, and for the reasons set forth in paragraph 37 above, BlockFi was an investment company engaged in business in interstate commerce.

Subsequent Events, and Respondent's Cooperation and Remedial Efforts

40. On February 14, 2022, BlockFi Inc., Respondent's parent company, publicly announced that it intends to register under the Securities Act the offer and sale of a new investment product, BlockFi Yield, which will include the filing of an indenture and Form T-1 under the Trust Indenture Act of 1939. BlockFi has represented that the general structure of the BlockFi Yield investment product will be as follows:

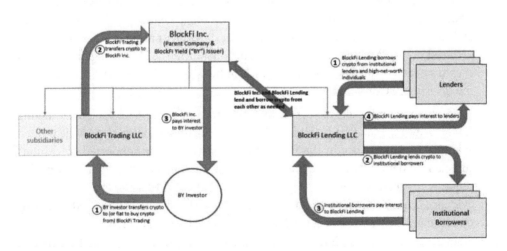

41. In determining to accept the Offer, the Commission considered remedial acts promptly undertaken by Respondent and cooperation afforded the Commission staff.

Undertakings

42. BlockFi has undertaken to, on the day of the institution of the Order, cease offering BIAs to new investors in the United States and cease accepting further investments or funds in the BIAs by current U.S. investors.

43. BlockFi has undertaken to, within 60 days of the institution of the Order, come into compliance with Section 7(a) of the Investment Company Act by either:

• Filing a notification of registration pursuant to Section 8(a) of the Investment Company Act, and then within 90 days of filing such notification of registration, filing a registration statement with the Commission, on the appropriate form; or

• Completing steps such that BlockFi is no longer required to be registered under Section 7(a) of the Investment Company Act and providing the Commission staff with sufficient credible evidence that it is no longer required to be registered under the Investment Company Act.

The Commission staff may grant a single 30-day extension for good cause shown.

44. A Form S-1 registration statement filed by BlockFi Inc. for BlockFi Yield (or any similar product) will not be declared effective if, among other things, BlockFi Inc., or any subsidiary or affiliate involved in the BlockFi Yield investment product or in the borrowing or lending of crypto assets to external parties, is not in compliance with Section 7(a) of the Investment Company Act. If a Form S-1 registration statement filed by BlockFi Inc. for BlockFi Yield is declared effective, BlockFi undertakes to, 180 days after the effectiveness date, provide the Commission staff with sufficient credible evidence to affirm that BlockFi, or any subsidiary or affiliate involved in the BlockFi Yield investment product or in the borrowing or lending of crypto assets to external parties, continues to be in compliance with Section 7(a) of the Investment Company Act.

45. BlockFi undertakes to certify, in writing, compliance with each undertaking set forth above. Each certification shall identify the undertaking(s), provide written evidence of compliance in the form of a narrative, and be supported by exhibits sufficient to demonstrate compliance. The Commission staff may make reasonable requests for further evidence of compliance, and BlockFi agrees to provide such evidence. Each certification and supporting material shall be submitted to Kristina Littman, Chief, Cyber Unit, Division of Enforcement, Securities and Exchange Commission, 100 F St., NE, Washington, DC 20549, with a copy to the Office of Chief Counsel of the Division of Enforcement, Securities and Exchange Commission, 100 F Street, NE, Washington, DC 20549, no later than 30 days from the date of the completion of each undertaking.

IV.

In view of the foregoing, the Commission deems it appropriate to impose the sanctions agreed to in Respondent's Offer.

Accordingly, it is hereby ORDERED that:

A. Pursuant to Section 8A of the Securities Act, Respondent cease and desist from committing or causing any violations and any future violations of Sections 5(a), 5(c), 17(a)(2) and 17(a)(3) of the Securities Act.

B. Pursuant to Section 9(f) of the Investment Company Act, Respondent shall cease and desist from committing or causing any violations and any future violations of Section 7(a) of the Investment Company Act, subject to Section III, paragraphs 43 through 44.

C. Respondent shall comply with the undertakings set forth in Section III, paragraphs 42 through 45 above.

D. Respondent shall pay a civil money penalty in the amount of $50,000,000.00 to the Securities and Exchange Commission for transfer to the general fund of the United States Treasury, subject to Exchange Act 21F(g)(3). Payment shall be made in the following installments:

1. Due within 14 days of the entry of this Order: $10,000,000 (the "Initial Payment")
2. Due 180 days of the entry of this Order: $10,000,000
3. Due 365 days of the entry of this Order: $10,000,000
4. Due 545 days of the entry of this Order: $10,000,000 Due 730 days of the entry of this Order: $10,000,000

Payments shall be applied first to post-order interest, which accrues pursuant to 31 U.S.C. 3717. Prior to making the final payment set forth herein, Respondent shall contact the staff of the Commission for the amount due. If Respondent fails to make any payment by the date agreed and/or in the amount agreed according to the schedule set forth above, all outstanding payments under this Order, including post-order interest, minus any payments made, shall become due and payable immediately at the discretion of the staff of the Commission without further application to the Commission.

Payment must be made in one of the following ways:

(1) Respondent may transmit payment electronically to the Commission, which will provide detailed ACH transfer/Fedwire instructions upon request;

(2) Respondent may make direct payment from a bank account via Pay.gov through the SEC website at http://www.sec.gov/about/offices/ofm.htm; or

(3) Respondent may pay by certified check, bank cashier's check, or United States postal money order, made payable to the Securities and Exchange Commission and hand-delivered or mailed to:

> Enterprise Services Center
>
> Accounts Receivable Branch
>
> HQ Bldg., Room 181, AMZ-341
>
> 6500 South MacArthur Boulevard
>
> Oklahoma City, OK 73169

Payments by check or money order must be accompanied by a cover letter identifying BlockFi Lending LLC as Respondent in these proceedings, and the file number of these proceedings; a copy of the cover letter and check or money order must be sent to Kristina Littman, Division of Enforcement, Securities and Exchange Commission, 100 F St., NE, Washington, DC 20549.

E. Amounts ordered to be paid as civil money penalties pursuant to this Order shall be treated as penalties paid to the government for all purposes, including all tax purposes. To preserve the deterrent effect of the civil penalty, Respondent agrees that in any Related Investor Action, they shall not argue that they are entitled to, nor shall they benefit by, offset or reduction of any award of compensatory damages by the amount of any part of Respondent's payment of a civil penalty in this action ("Penalty Offset"). If the court in any Related Investor Action grants such a Penalty Offset, Respondent agrees that it shall, within 30 days after entry of a final order granting the Penalty Offset, notify the Commission's counsel in this action and pay the amount of the Penalty Offset to the Securities and Exchange Commission. Such a payment shall not be deemed an additional civil penalty and shall not be deemed to change the amount of the civil penalty imposed in this proceeding. For purposes of this paragraph, a "Related Investor Action" means a private damages action brought against Respondent by or on behalf of one or more investors based on substantially the same facts as alleged in the Order instituted by the Commission in this proceeding.

Discussion Points

1. *The outcome.* Do you agree with the SEC's determination that the Blockfi Interest Accounts (BIAs), were unregistered securities? Do BIAs meet the definition of an investment contract under the Howey test?

2. *Compare.* What is the fundamental difference between the *Blockfi* and *Telegram* case? What is the difference between BIA and Grams? Is there any difference?

3. *What makes something an investment contract?* Why did the SEC determine that sharing of profits in the form of interest payments on cryptocurrency constitutes an investment contract?

The SEC's No-Action Letter Issued to TurnKey Jet, Inc.

On April 3, 2019, the SEC Division of Corporate Finance issued a No-Action letter to TurnKey Jet Inc. The no-action letter stemmed from TurnKey Jet's using utility tokens as prepaid jet cards. TurnKey jet was offering a private, centralized blockchain network and smart-contract using a utility token for clearing and payment. In the letter, the Division of Corporate Finance stated that it would not recommend enforcement action to the SEC if, in reliance on TurnKey Jet's opinion that TurnKey tokens are not securities, TurnKey Jet sold the tokens without registering under the Securities Act of 1933 and the Securities Exchange Act of 1934.

April 3, 2019

Response of the Division of Corporation Finance

Re: TurnKey Jet, Inc.

      Incoming letter dated April 2, 2019

Based on the facts presented, the Division will not recommend enforcement action to the Commission if, in reliance on your opinion as counsel that the Tokens are not securities, TKJ offers and sells the Tokens without registration under the Securities Act and the Exchange Act. Capitalized terms have the same meanings as defined in your letter.

In reaching this position, we particularly note that:

- TKJ will not use any funds from Token sales to develop the TKJ Platform, Network, or App, and each of these will be fully developed and operational at the time any Tokens are sold;
- the Tokens will be immediately usable for their intended functionality (purchasing air charter services) at the time they are sold;
- TKJ will restrict transfers of Tokens to TKJ Wallets only, and not to wallets external to the Platform;
- TKJ will sell Tokens at a price of one USD per Token throughout the life of the Program, and each Token will represent a TKJ obligation to supply air charter services at a value of one USD per Token;
- If TKJ offers to repurchase Tokens, it will only do so at a discount to the face value of the Tokens (one USD per Token) that the holder seeks to resell to TKJ, unless a court within the United States orders TKJ to liquidate the Tokens; and

- The Token is marketed in a manner that emphasizes the functionality of the Token, and not the potential for the increase in the market value of the Token.

This position is based on the representations made to the Division in your letter. Any different facts or conditions might require the Division to reach a different conclusion. Further, this response expresses the Division's position on enforcement action only and does not express any legal conclusion on the question presented.

Sincerely,

Jonathan A. Ingram

Chief Legal Advisor, FinHub

Division of Corporation Finance

Discussion Points

1. *Was the no action letter necessary?* Was it necessary for the SEC to issue this no-action letter? Should the SEC have issued this no-action letter when TurnKey Jet was operating in a closed-loop ecosystem?

2. *Apply the Howey test.* Apply the Howey test to TKJ tokens. Is it applicable? If not, which element or elements are not satisfied?

Three

Money Transmission Laws

I. Introduction

Money gains value when it moves from one person or place to another. The notion of exchange is fundamental to society. Exchanging goods and money has allowed for a transmission process to evolve. Money transmission has existed as long as money itself has existed, first in the form of bartering where people would transfer money or goods with one another in exchange for something they wanted, or as gift giving or lending of money, absent an exchange.

A. Background

Until 1871, greenbacks, notes, and the like were transferred by hand, sometimes involving third parties when the parties involved were not able to physically carry out the transfer. This changed when Western Union took advantage of their existing communications framework to leverage electronic transmissions of money. Western Union is seemingly the first modern-day technological innovation to allow fast and easy transmission of funds without requiring someone to physically go by horse or by car to transfer funds. Electronic transfers have evolved to include banks. Currently, wires leverage a network of banks and transfer service agencies around the world to transmit money in a relatively short amount of time. Regardless of where an individual is located in the world, they are able to receive a wire transfer if they can access a bank or an institution that handles wire transfers. The tradeoff for this global reach is the imposition of a wire transfer fee upon the transferor in connection with the wire service.

Technological innovations have made the transmission of money possible. At the helm of technological advancements is the goal of providing consumers ease of use. People simply want to do things easier, faster, and cheaper. Even one's own credit cards can act as a money transmitter when they initiate a balance transfer. One such innovation is automated clearing house ("ACH") transfers. ACH transfers have made wire transfers easier for banks. Banks aggregate and settle numerous transfers per day, instead of handling each transfer individually. This is referred to as a batch processing system. Batch processing results in transfers that are often free of charge, and are more convenient than using a negotiable instrument. However, one drawback to this system is that the amount of the transfer can be limited.

B. Comparing Money Transmitters with Banking Services

Money transmitters are different from the services offered by a bank. Money transmitters do not make loans or accept deposits the way a bank does. Instead, money transmitters simply provide a mechanism by which people can send or receive money. Western Union, MoneyGram, PayPal and Venmo are characteristic examples of money transmitters.

The number of services money transmitters provide consumers have greatly expanded through the years. PayPal is an online platform that allows authenticated users to make payments online for goods and services. Making payments online involves transferring money from one entity to another—from the person to the store. An inquiry into whether PayPal is a money transmitter quickly reveals their status in the industry and highlights the disjointed nature of money transmission laws. Fortunately, PayPal has listed all of its licenses in each state to make the query easier on the consumer.

In the United States, the virtual currency space is rapidly evolving, and the legal and regulatory approach to the virtual currency space is also evolving. This means that a business that meets the definition of a money transmitter or money services business (MSB) has to pay close attention to regulatory and statutory requirements to ensure compliance with federal and state laws. Currently, 49 states have enacted laws to control entities that engage in the business of money transmission. Montana is the only state that has yet to do so.

II. Money Transmitter Laws and Cryptocurrencies

Cryptocurrencies are transferred across networks and can be used to pay for goods and services. Notably, many statutes define "money" or "currency" as a legal tender. This begs the question: *if I am transferring cryptocurrency, am I really transferring money?* Furthermore, businesses that transmit money must obtain a money transmission license, so the question becomes: *if my business is engaged in transferring cryptocurrency, do I need a money transmission license?* Whether a business or person is engaged in money transmissions is necessarily dependent on whether they are transmitting money. The question then becomes: *is the transmission of cryptocurrency equivalent to the transfer of money?* Many states have a catch-all provision built into their money transmission statutes by including the phrase "medium of exchange" in the definition of money. One must exercise due care when interpreting a state's statute to determine whether a money transmitter license is required for a business or a person.

Fintech companies are defined as any business that uses technology and software to modify, improve, or automate traditional forms of financial services for businesses and consumers. Fintech companies are changing the traditional payment space with innovative financial and fintech solutions. In recent years, there has been an influx of global fintech companies entering the payment space. Before discussing how virtual currency fits in with the various current regulatory frameworks, there must be an understanding of the money transmission laws at the federal and state levels and how cryptocurrency fits into its definition, if at all.

III. Federal Money Transmitter Laws

A. FinCEN

The United States Department of Treasury established the Financial Crimes Enforcement Network (hereinafter "FinCEN") in April of 1990.[34] The Bank Secrecy Act (BSA) empowers the federal government to regulate money transmission. FinCEN's chief purpose is to safeguard the financial system and promote national security through the collection and analysis of financial data.

Another purpose of FinCEN is also to create a government-wide intelligence network to assist in the detection, investigation, and prosecution of money laundering, both domestically and internationally, and other financial activities relating to financial intelligence and financial criminal activities.[35] After September 11, 2001, FinCEN's purpose evolved when it was awarded official Treasury bureau status in accordance with the United States of America Patriot Act. It was evident that criminal activities were helping to finance terrorism, and FinCEN became the primary agency in overseeing, detecting, and preventing money laundering.

FinCEN describes a money services business (MSB) as a business that functions as a money transmitter, performing money transmission or fund transfer services. This view draws a distinction between a transmittor and a transmitter. The former initiates a transaction, while the latter executes a transaction. Money transmission services are the acceptance of currency or values that substitute for currency from one, and the transmission of it to another by any means.

The definition of a money transmitter varies slightly from state to state, but at their foundation, the state definitions connect back to the BSA definition of a money transmitter found at 31 C.F.R. § 103.11(uu)(5) which includes:

A. Any person, whether or not licensed or required to be licensed, who engages as a business in accepting currency, or funds denominated in currency, and transmits the currency or funds, or the value of the currency or funds, by any means through a financial agency or institution, a Federal Reserve Bank or other facility of one or more Federal Reserve Banks, the Board of Governors of the Federal Reserve System, or both, or an electronic funds transfer network; or

B. Any other person engaged as a business in the transfer of funds.

---

34. 1 Money Laundering, Asset Forfeiture and Compliance III (2022).
35. *Id.; see also* 1 Modern Privacy & Surveillance Law Sec. 361 (2021).

A person may be considered a money transmitter if their transactions meet Fin-CEN's definition of money transmission, regardless of whether the transaction is physical or virtual. Those who issue and sell securities and futures are generally outside the scope of the BSA, but may be subject to money transmission regulations depending on regulatory definitions of money transmitters, exemptions from certain definitions, and regulatory interpretations. For instance, according to FIN-2008-G008, the regulation will not consider one a money transmitter if they accept and transmit funds solely to effect a legitimate purchase, or sale of real currency or other commodities for or with a customer. However, one will be considered a money transmitter if funds are transferred to a third party that is not a part of the transaction.

B. Application of BSA Regulations to Money Transmission

Qualification as a an MSB under the BSA is dependent on the activities conducted, not business status. A person (individual, corporation or other) is a money transmitter if their activity includes receiving a form of value and transmitting, by any means, the same or different form of value to another person or location.

According to FinCEN, one is a money transmitter if they engage in accepting currency or funds, and later transmit the currency or funds, or the value of the currency or funds, through a financial institution. Additionally, FinCEN, also defines a money transmitter as a person engaged in the transfer of funds. Operating on a transactional or account basis also equates to being a money transmitter. Transactional basis is for one-off transactions without an ongoing transmitter relationship with the transmitter retaining funds only for the time needed to affect the transmission. On an account basis, there is an ongoing customer relationship with the transmitter, with the transmitter maintaining an account for the transactor to store funds. One can also be deemed a money transmitter if they accept value with the intent of transmitting it only under certain conditions. The following are strict FinCEN exemptions from being considered a money transmitter:

- providing network services to support money transmission
- acting as a payment processor
- only acting as an intermediary between BSA regulated institutions
- physically transporting currency, value that substitutes for currency, or similar, with no custodial interest
- providing prepaid access
- accepting and transmitting funds only central to selling goods or providing services, other than money transmission services, by one who is accepting and transmitting the funds

It is required by the BSA that MSBs have an effective, risk-based, anti-money laundering (AML) program. If a money transmitter's transactions equate to transmittal of funds (a series of transmittal orders), it must comply with FinCEN's Fund

Transfer Rule and the Funds Travel Rule. Convertible virtual currency (CVC) transactions also fall within the Funds Transfer Rule where transfers over $3,000 may trigger certain requirements on a money transmitter acting as either the financial institution for the transmitter or the recipient, or as an intermediary financial institution.

Accepting and transmitting value that substitutes for currency, i.e., virtual currency, is money transmission. Domestic and foreign CVC money transmitters must register with FinCEN as an MSB and comply with Anti-Money Laundering program record keeping, monitoring and reporting requirements.

C. FinCEN and the Cryptocurrency Space

With the emergence of cryptocurrency, FinCEN has issued several advisories about how financial laws and regulations apply to the business of virtual currencies. Virtual currencies, like real, tangible currencies, are vulnerable to being manipulated for money laundering or funding terrorism. For example, there are money laundering vulnerabilities in virtual currencies because some virtual currencies, like Bitcoin, are decentralized and do not have a resource serving as an intermediary. Illicit actors may also choose to use virtual currencies, because virtual currencies enable users to remain anonymous, are accepted around the world, and are relatively simple to navigate.

FinCEN sought to create "smart regulation" for virtual currencies that protect the United States financial system without being too hindering. One of FinCEN's first discussions of virtual currencies occurred in 2013, as they sought to understand the specific features that make virtual currencies susceptible to unlawful use. In 2013, FinCEN issued guidance to clarify the applicability of anti-money laundering (AML) laws and cryptocurrency compliance concerns for individuals involved in virtual currency transactions.

D. FinCEN's 2013 Guidance

Application of FinCEN's Regulations to Persons Administering, Exchanging, or Using Virtual Currencies

Guidance Fin-2013-G001 (Issued March 18, 2013)

The Financial Crimes Enforcement Network ("FinCEN") is issuing this interpretive guidance to clarify the applicability of the regulations implementing the Bank Secrecy Act ("BSA") to persons creating, obtaining, distributing, exchanging, accepting, or transmitting virtual currencies.[1] Such persons are referred to in this

---

1. FinCEN is issuing this guidance under its authority to administer the Bank Secrecy Act. *See* Treasury Order 180- 01 (March 24, 2003). This guidance explains only how FinCEN characterizes certain activities involving virtual currencies under the Bank Secrecy Act and FinCEN regulations.

guidance as "users," "administrators," and "exchangers," all as defined below.[2] A user of virtual currency is **not** an MSB under FinCEN's regulations and therefore is not subject to MSB registration, reporting, and recordkeeping regulations. However, an administrator or exchanger is an MSB under FinCEN's regulations, specifically, a money transmitter, unless a limitation to or exemption from the definition applies to the person. An administrator or exchanger is not a provider or seller of prepaid access, or a dealer in foreign exchange, under FinCEN's regulations.

Currency vs. Virtual Currency

FinCEN's regulations define currency (also referred to as "real" currency) as "the coin and paper money of the United States or of any other country that [i] is designated as legal tender and that [ii] circulates and [iii] is customarily used and accepted as a medium of exchange in the country of issuance."[3] In contrast to real currency, "virtual" currency is a medium of exchange that operates like a currency in some environments, but does not have all the attributes of real currency. In particular, virtual currency does not have legal tender status in any jurisdiction. This guidance addresses "convertible" virtual currency. This type of virtual currency either has an equivalent value in real currency, or acts as a substitute for real currency.

Background

On July 21, 2011, FinCEN published a Final Rule amending definitions and other regulations relating to money services businesses ("MSBs").[4] Among other things, the MSB Rule amends the definitions of dealers in foreign exchange (formerly referred to as "currency dealers and exchangers") and money transmitters. On July 29, 2011, FinCEN published a Final Rule on Definitions and Other Regulations Relating to Prepaid Access (the "Prepaid Access Rule").[5] This guidance explains the regulatory treatment under these definitions of persons engaged in virtual currency transactions.

It should not be interpreted as a statement by FinCEN about the extent to which those activities comport with other federal or state statutes, rules, regulations, or orders.

2. FinCEN's regulations define "person" as "an individual, a corporation, a partnership, a trust or estate, a joint stock company, an association, a syndicate, joint venture, or other unincorporated organization or group, an Indian Tribe (as that term is defined in the Indian Gaming Regulatory Act), and all entities cognizable as legal personalities." 31 CFR § 1010.100(mm).

3. 31 CFR § 1010.100(m).

4. *Bank Secrecy Act Regulations—Definitions and Other Regulations Relating to Money Services Businesses*, 76 FR 43585 (July 21, 2011) (the "MSB Rule"). This defines an MSB as "a person wherever located doing business, whether or not on a regular basis or as an organized or licensed business concern, wholly or in substantial part within the United States, in one or more of the capacities listed in paragraphs (ff)(1) through (ff)(7) of this section. This includes but is not limited to maintenance of any agent, agency, branch, or office within the United States."31 CFR § 1010.100(ff).

5. *Final Rule—Definitions and Other Regulations Relating to Prepaid Access*, 76 FR 45403 (July 29, 2011).

Definitions of User, Exchanger, and Administrator

This guidance refers to the participants in generic virtual currency arrangements, using the terms "user," "exchanger," and "administrator."[6] A *user* is a person that obtains virtual currency to purchase goods or services.[7] An *exchanger* is a person engaged as a business in the exchange of virtual currency for real currency, funds, or other virtual currency. An *administrator* is a person engaged as a business in issuing (putting into circulation) a virtual currency, and who has the authority to redeem (to withdraw from circulation) such virtual currency.

Users of Virtual Currency

A user who obtains convertible virtual currency and uses it to purchase real or virtual goods or services is **not** an MSB under FinCEN's regulations.[8] Such activity, in and of itself, does not fit within the definition of "money transmission services" and therefore is not subject to FinCEN's registration, reporting, and recordkeeping regulations for MSBs.[9]

Administrators and Exchangers of Virtual Currency

An administrator or exchanger that (1) accepts and transmits a convertible virtual currency or (2) buys or sells convertible virtual currency for any reason is a money transmitter under FinCEN's regulations, unless a limitation to or exemption from the definition applies to the person.[10] FinCEN's regulations define the term "money transmitter" as a person that provides money transmission services, or any other person engaged in the transfer of funds. The term "money transmission services" means "the acceptance of currency, funds, or other value that substitutes for cur-

---

6. These terms are used for the exclusive purpose of this regulatory guidance. Depending on the type and combination of a person's activities, one person may be acting in more than one of these capacities.

7. How a person engages in "obtaining" a virtual currency may be described using any number of other terms, such as "earning," "harvesting," "mining," "creating," "auto-generating," "manufacturing," or "purchasing," depending on the details of the specific virtual currency model involved. For purposes of this guidance, the label applied to a particular process of obtaining a virtual currency is not material to the legal characterization under the BSA of the process or of the person engaging in the process.

8. As noted above, this should not be interpreted as a statement about the extent to which the user's activities comport with other federal or state statutes, rules, regulations, or orders. For example, the activity may still be subject to abuse in the form of trade-based money laundering or terrorist financing. The activity may follow the same patterns of behavior observed in the "real" economy with respect to the purchase of "real" goods and services, such as systematic over- or under-invoicing or inflated transaction fees or commissions.

9. 31 CFR § 1010.100(ff)(1–7).

10. FinCEN's regulations provide that whether a person is a money transmitter is a matter of facts and circumstances. The regulations identify six circumstances under which a person is not a money transmitter, despite accepting and transmitting currency, funds, or value that substitutes for currency. 31 CFR § 1010.100(ff)(5)(ii)(A)–(F).

rency from one person *and* the transmission of currency, funds, or other value that substitutes for currency to another location or person by any means."[11]

The definition of a money transmitter does not differentiate between real currencies and convertible virtual currencies. Accepting and transmitting anything of value that substitutes for currency makes a person a money transmitter under the regulations implementing the BSA.[12] FinCEN has reviewed different activities involving virtual currency and has made determinations regarding the appropriate regulatory treatment of administrators and exchangers under three scenarios: brokers and dealers of e-currencies and e-precious metals; centralized convertible virtual currencies; and de-centralized convertible virtual currencies.

a. E-Currencies and E-Precious Metals

The first type of activity involves electronic trading in e-currencies or e-precious metals.[13] In 2008, FinCEN issued guidance stating that as long as a broker or dealer in real currency or other commodities accepts and transmits funds solely for the purpose of effecting a *bona fide* purchase or sale of the real currency or other commodities for or with a customer, such person is not acting as a money transmitter under the regulations.[14]

However, if the broker or dealer transfers funds between a customer and a third party that is not part of the currency or commodity transaction, such transmission of funds is no longer a fundamental element of the actual transaction necessary to execute the contract for the purchase or sale of the currency or the other commodity. This scenario is, therefore, money transmission.[15] Examples include, in part, (1) the transfer of funds between a customer and a third party by permitting a third party to fund a customer's account; (2) the transfer of value from a customer's currency

---

11. 31 CFR § 1010.100(ff)(5)(i)(A).

12. Ibid.

13. Typically, this involves the broker or dealer electronically distributing digital certificates of ownership of real currencies or precious metals, with the digital certificate being the virtual currency. However, the same conclusions would apply in the case of the broker or dealer issuing paper ownership certificates or manifesting customer ownership or control of real currencies or commodities in an account statement or any other form. These conclusions would also apply in the case of a broker or dealer in commodities other than real currencies or precious metals. A broker or dealer of e-currencies or e-precious metals that engages in money transmission could be either an administrator or exchanger depending on its business model.

14. *Application of the Definition of Money Transmitter to Brokers and Dealers in Currency and other Commodities*, FIN-2008-G008, Sept. 10, 2008. The guidance also notes that the definition of money transmitter excludes any person, such as a futures commission merchant, that is "registered with, and regulated or examined by … the Commodity Futures Trading Commission."

15. In 2011, FinCEN amended the definition of money transmitter. The 2008 guidance, however, was primarily concerned with the core elements of the definition—accepting and transmitting currency or value—and the exemption for acceptance and transmission integral to another transaction not involving money transmission. The 2011 amendments have not materially changed these aspects of the definition.

or commodity position to the account of another customer; or (3) the closing out of a customer's currency or commodity position, with a transfer of proceeds to a third party. Since the definition of a money transmitter does not differentiate between real currencies and convertible virtual currencies, the same rules apply to brokers and dealers of e-currency and e-precious metals.

b. Centralized Virtual Currencies

The second type of activity involves a convertible virtual currency that has a centralized repository. The administrator of that repository will be a money transmitter to the extent that it allows transfers of value between persons or from one location to another. This conclusion applies, whether the value is denominated in a real currency or a convertible virtual currency. In addition, any exchanger that uses its access to the convertible virtual currency services provided by the administrator to accept and transmit the convertible virtual currency on behalf of others, including transfers intended to pay a third party for virtual goods and services, is also a money transmitter.

FinCEN understands that the exchanger's activities may take one of two forms. The first form involves an exchanger (acting as a "seller" of the convertible virtual currency) that accepts real currency or its equivalent from a user (the "purchaser") and transmits the value of that real currency to fund the user's convertible virtual currency account with the administrator. Under FinCEN's regulations, sending "value that substitutes for currency" to another person or to another location constitutes money transmission, unless a limitation to or exemption from the definition applies.[16] This circumstance constitutes transmission **to another location**, namely from the user's account at one location (e.g., a user's real currency account at a bank) to the user's convertible virtual currency account with the administrator. It might be argued that the exchanger is entitled to the exemption from the definition of "money transmitter" for persons involved in the sale of goods or the provision of services. Under such an argument, one might assert that the exchanger is merely providing the service of connecting the user to the administrator and that the transmission of value is integral to this service. However, this exemption does not apply when the only services being provided are money transmission services.[17]

The second form involves a *de facto* sale of convertible virtual currency that is not completely transparent. The exchanger accepts currency or its equivalent from a user and privately credits the user with an appropriate portion of the exchanger's own convertible virtual currency held with the administrator of the repository. The exchanger then transmits that internally credited value to third parties at the user's direction. This constitutes transmission to **another person**, namely each third party to which transmissions are made at the user's direction. To the extent that the con-

---

16. See footnote 11 and adjacent text.
17. 31 CFR § 1010.100(ff)(5)(ii)(F).

vertible virtual currency is generally understood as a substitute for real currencies, transmitting the convertible virtual currency at the direction and for the benefit of the user constitutes money transmission on the part of the exchanger.

c. Decentralized Virtual Currencies

A final type of convertible virtual currency activity involves a decentralized convertible virtual currency (1) that has no central repository and no single administrator, and (2) that persons may obtain by their own computing or manufacturing effort.

A person that creates units of this convertible virtual currency and uses it to purchase real or virtual goods and services is a user of the convertible virtual currency and not subject to regulation as a money transmitter. By contrast, a person that creates units of convertible virtual currency and sells those units to another person for real currency or its equivalent is engaged in transmission to another location and is a money transmitter. In addition, a person is an exchanger and a money transmitter if the person accepts such de-centralized convertible virtual currency from one person and transmits it to another person as part of the acceptance and transfer of currency, funds, or other value that substitutes for currency.

Providers and Sellers of Prepaid Access

A person's acceptance and/or transmission of convertible virtual currency cannot be characterized as providing or selling prepaid access because prepaid access is limited to real currencies.[18]

Dealers in Foreign Exchange

A person must exchange the currency of two or more countries to be considered a dealer in foreign exchange.[19] Virtual currency does not meet the criteria to be con-

---

18. This is true even if the person holds the value accepted for a period of time before transmitting some or all of that value at the direction of the person from whom the value was originally accepted. FinCEN's regulations define "prepaid access" as "access to funds or the value of funds that have been paid in advance and can be retrieved or transferred at some point in the future through an electronic device or vehicle, such as a card, code, electronic serial number, mobile identification number, or personal identification number." 31 CFR § 1010.100(ww). Thus, "prepaid access" under FinCEN's regulations is limited to "access to funds or the value of funds." If FinCEN had intended prepaid access to cover funds denominated in a virtual currency or something else that substitutes for real currency, it would have used language in the definition of prepaid access like that in the definition of money transmission, which expressly includes the acceptance and transmission of "other value that substitutes for currency." 31 CFR § 1010.100(ff)(5)(i).

19. FinCEN defines a "dealer in foreign exchange" as a "person that accepts the currency, or other monetary instruments, funds, or other instruments denominated in the currency, of one or more countries in exchange for the currency, or other monetary instruments, funds, or other instruments denominated in the currency, of one or more other countries in an amount greater than $1,000 for any other person on any day in one or more transactions, whether or not for same-day delivery." 31 CFR § 1010.100(ff)(1).

sidered "currency" under the BSA, because it is not legal tender. Therefore, a person who accepts real currency in exchange for virtual currency, or vice versa, is not a dealer in foreign exchange under FinCEN's regulations.

Discussion Points

1. *FinCEN's definition of virtual currency.* Do you think FinCEN's definition of "virtual currency" too broad? Compare and contrast the characteristics of virtual currency and legal tender. How are they similar? How are they different?

2. *Two types of convertible virtual currencies.* What is the difference between centralized and decentralized virtual currencies? Do you think centralized or decentralized virtual currencies are more advantageous? Why?

3. *With whom should the power vest?* Do you think that states should promulgate their own AML laws or have concurrent jurisdiction with federal regulators such as the CFTC and FinCEN to enforce AML compliance among money transmitters? Why or why not? What would be the ramifications of state level AML laws? Would this hinder the proliferation of virtual currency transmission?

E. FinCEN's 2014 Administrative Rulings

The first guidance that FinCEN provided regarding virtual currency was considered too broad, and in need of clarification with respect to who exactly fell under these regulations. FinCEN needed to supply additional guidance. In 2014, FinCEN published two administrative rulings that provided further interpretation on whether a person's conduct within the convertible virtual currency market brings them within the definition of a money transmitter pursuant to the BSA.[36]

The first ruling established that "to the extent a user creates or 'mines' a convertible virtual currency solely for a user's own purposes, the user is not a money transmitter under the BSA."[37] The second ruling states that if a company purchases or sells convertible virtual currencies as an investment that is solely for the company's benefit, then they are not a money transmitter.[38]

---

36. Press Release, Financial Crimes Enforcement Network, FinCEN Publishes Two Rulings on Virtual Currency Miners and Investors (Jan. 30, 2014), https://www.fincen.gov/news/news-releases/fincen-publishes-two-rulings-virtual-currency-miners-and-investors.

37. *Id.*

38. *Id.*

Application of FinCEN's Regulations to Virtual Currency Software Development and Certain Investment Activity

FIN-2014-R002 (Jan. 30, 2014)

Dear []:

This responds to your letters of May 21, 2013 and July 10, 2013, seeking an administrative ruling from the Financial Crimes Enforcement Network ("FinCEN") regarding the status of [] (the "Company") as a money services business ("MSB") under the Bank Secrecy Act ("BSA"). Specifically, you ask whether the periodic investment of the Company in convertible virtual currency, and the production and distribution of software to facilitate the Company's purchase of virtual currency for purposes of its own investment, would make the Company a money transmitter under the BSA.

In your May 21, 2013 letter, you state that the Company intends to produce a piece of software that will facilitate the Company's purchase of virtual currency from sellers, by automating the collection of the virtual currency and the payment of the equivalent in currency of legal tender. The seller would initiate the process via the software's interface, offering its virtual currency to the Company, choosing among several options for a means of receiving the equivalent in currency of legal tender (check, credit to a designated credit, debit, or prepaid card, or payment processed through a third-party money transmitter), and paying a transaction fee. The software would not be sold or provided to any third party for resale, and it would be reserved for the sole use of the Company's counterparties.

Your addendum of July 10, 2013 clarifies that the Company intends to limit its activities to investing in convertible virtual currencies for its own account, purchasing virtual currency from sellers and reselling the currency at the Company's discretion, whenever such purchases and sales make investment sense according to the Company's business plan. The seller would offer its virtual currency to the Company via the software discussed above, and the Company would sell all or part of its virtual currency at a virtual currency exchange after receipt from the seller, at a time of the Company's choosing based on the Company's own investment decisions.

BSA Obligations of the Company as a Software Provider

On July 21, 2011, FinCEN published a Final Rule amending definitions and other regulations relating to MSBs (the "Rule").[1] The amended regulations define an MSB as "a person wherever located doing business, whether or not on a regular basis or as an organized business concern, wholly or in substantial part within the United States, in one or more of the capacities listed in paragraphs (ff)(1) through (ff)(6)

---

1. Bank Secrecy Act Regulations—Definitions and Other Regulations Relating to Money Services Businesses, 76 FR 43585 (July 21, 2011).

of this section. This includes but is not limited to maintenance of any agent, agency, branch, or office within the United States."[2]

BSA regulations, as amended, define the term "money transmitter" to include a person that provides money transmission services, or any other person engaged in the transfer of funds. The term "money transmission services" means the acceptance of currency, funds, or other value that substitutes for currency from one person *and* the transmission of currency, funds, or other value that substitutes for currency to another location or person by any means.[3] The regulations also stipulate that whether a person is a money transmitter is a matter of facts and circumstances, and identifies circumstances under which a person's activities would not make such person a money transmitter.[4]

The production and distribution of software, in and of itself, does not constitute acceptance and transmission of value, even if the purpose of the software is to facilitate the sale of virtual currency. As a result, the Company's production and distribution of its contemplated software would not make the Company a money transmitter subject to BSA regulation.[5]

BSA Obligations of the Company as an Investor in Virtual Currencies

On March 18, 2013, FinCEN issued guidance on the application of FinCEN's regulations to transactions in virtual currencies (the "guidance").[6] FinCEN's regulations define currency (also referred to as "real" currency) as "the coin and paper money of the United States or of any other country that [i] is designated as legal tender and that [ii] circulates and [iii] is customarily used and accepted as a medium of exchange in the country of issuance."[7] In contrast to real currency, "virtual" currency is a medium of exchange that operates like a currency in some environments, but does not have all the attributes of real currency. In particular, virtual currency does not have legal tender status in any jurisdiction.

The guidance addresses "convertible" virtual currency. This type of virtual currency either has an equivalent value in real currency, or acts as a substitute for real currency.

---

2. 31 CFR § 1010.100(ff).

3. 31 CFR § 1010.100(ff)(5)(i)(A) and (B).

4. 31 CFR § 1010.100(ff)(5)(ii).

5. A number of older FinCEN administrative rulings, although not directly on point because they interpret an older version of the regulatory definition of MSBs, explain the application of our definitions in comparable situations. *See, e.g.,* FIN-2009-R001, "Whether Certain Operations of a Service Provider to Prepaid Stored Value Program Participants is a Money Services Business," January 22, 2009, available at http://www.fincen.gov/statutes_regs/guidance/pdf/fin-2009-r001.pdf.

6. FIN-2013-G001, "Application of FinCEN's Regulations to Persons Administering, Exchanging, or Using Virtual Currencies," March 18, 2013.

7. 31 CFR § 1010.100(m).

For purposes of the guidance, FinCEN refers to the participants in generic virtual currency arrangements, using the terms "exchanger," "administrator," and "user." An *exchanger* is a person engaged as a business in the exchange of virtual currency for real currency, funds, or other virtual currency. An *administrator* is a person engaged as a business in issuing (putting into circulation) a virtual currency, and who has the authority to redeem (to withdraw from circulation) such virtual currency. A *user* is a person that obtains virtual currency to purchase goods or services on the user's own behalf.

The guidance makes clear that an administrator or exchanger of convertible virtual currencies that (1) accepts and transmits a convertible virtual currency or (2) buys or sells convertible virtual currency in exchange for currency of legal tender or another convertible virtual currency for any reason (including when intermediating between a user and a seller of goods or services the user is purchasing on the user's behalf) is a money transmitter under FinCEN's regulations, unless a limitation to or exemption from the definition applies to the person.[8] The guidance also makes clear that "a user who obtains convertible virtual currency and uses it to purchase real or virtual goods or services is **not** an MSB under FinCEN's regulations."

How a user engages in obtaining a virtual currency may be described using any number of other terms, such as "earning," "harvesting," "mining," "creating," "auto-generating," "manufacturing," or "purchasing," depending on the details of the specific virtual currency model involved. The label applied to a particular process of obtaining a virtual currency is not material to the legal characterization under the BSA of the process or of the person engaging in the process to send that virtual currency or its equivalent value to any other person or place. What is material to the conclusion that a person is not an MSB is not the mechanism by which person obtains the convertible virtual currency, but what the person uses the convertible virtual currency for, and for whose benefit. Activities that, in and of themselves, do not constitute accepting and transmitting currency, funds or the value of funds do not fit within the definition of "money transmission services" and therefore are not subject to FinCEN's registration, reporting, and recordkeeping regulations for MSBs.[9]

---

8. The definition of "money transmitter" in FinCEN's regulations defines six sets of circumstances—variously referred to as limitations or exemptions—under which a person is not a money transmitter, despite accepting and transmitting currency, funds, or value that substitute for currency. 31 CFR § 1010.100(ff)(5)(ii)(A)-(F).

9. However, a user wishing to purchase goods or services with a convertible virtual currency it has obtained, which pays the convertible virtual currency to a third party at the direction of a seller or creditor, may be engaged in money transmission. A number of older FinCEN administrative rulings, although not directly on point because they interpret an older version of the regulatory definition of MSBs, discuss situations involving persons that would have been exempted from MSB status, but for their payments to third parties not involved in the original transaction. *See* FIN-2008-R004 (Whether a Foreign Exchange Consultant is a Currency Dealer or Exchanger or Money Transmitter—05/09/2008); FIN-2008-R003 (Whether a Person That is Engaged in the Business

To the extent that the Company purchases and sells convertible virtual currency, paying and receiving the equivalent value in currency of legal tender to and from counterparties, all exclusively as investments for its own account, it is not engaged in the business of exchanging convertible virtual currency for currency of legal tender for other persons. In effect, when the Company invests in a convertible virtual currency for its own account, and when it realizes the value of its investment, it is acting as a user of that convertible virtual currency within the meaning of the guidance. As a result, to the extent that the Company limits its activities strictly to investing in virtual currency for its own account, it is not acting as a money transmitter and is not an MSB under FinCEN's regulations. However, any transfers to third parties at the behest of the Company's counterparties, creditors, or owners entitled to direct payments should be closely scrutinized, as they may constitute money transmission. (See footnote 10 to this ruling.)

If the Company were to provide services to others (including investment-related or brokerage services) that involved the accepting and transmitting of convertible virtual currency, or the exchange of convertible virtual currency for currency of legal tender or another convertible virtual currency, of course, additional analysis would be necessary to determine the Company's regulatory status and obligations with respect to such activity.[10] In addition, should the Company begin to engage as a business in the exchange of virtual currency against currency of legal tender (or even against other convertible virtual currency), the Company would become a money transmitter under FinCEN's regulations. Under such circumstances, the Company would have to register with FinCEN, implement an effective, risk-based anti-money laundering program, and comply with the recordkeeping, reporting, and transaction monitoring requirements applicable to money transmitters.

This ruling is provided in accordance with the procedures set forth at 31 CFR Part1010 Subpart G.[11] In arriving at the conclusions in this administrative ruling, we

---

of Foreign Exchange Risk Management is a Currency Dealer or Exchanger or Money Transmitter—05/09/2008); FIN-2008-R002 (Whether a Foreign Exchange Dealer is a Currency Dealer or Exchanger or Money Transmitter—05/09/2008).

10. For example, providing specific brokerage-related services might require the Company to be registered with the Securities and Exchange Commission (SEC) or the Commodities and Futures Trading Commission (CFTC), in which case the Company would be covered under the BSA as a securities broker-dealer or a commodities or futures trader. If the Company did not fall under SEC or CFTC supervision, then the extent to which its money transmission activities were integral to the non-money transmission services it provided would need to be considered in order to determine whether the Company could claim an exemption from the money transmitter definition under 31 CFR § 1010.100(ff)(5)(ii)(F), or would qualify as a money transmitter under FinCEN's regulations.

11. Your subsequent e-mail communication of September 24, 2013 has informed us that you received a subpoena from the New York State Department of Financial Services on August 9, 2013 regarding the Company's activities. Although you have not informed us, and we have not by other means become aware, of the substance of any investigation to which this subpoena may relate, we have waived the requirement in our regulations that you certify that the question at issue in this administrative ruling is not applicable to any ongoing investigation. See 31 CFR §§ 1010.711(a)(4).

have relied upon the accuracy and completeness of the representations you made in your communications with us. Nothing precludes FinCEN from arriving at a different conclusion or from taking other action should circumstances change or should any of the information you have provided prove inaccurate or incomplete. We reserve the right, after redacting your name and address, and similar identifying information for your clients, to publish this letter as guidance to financial institutions in accordance with our regulations.[12] You have fourteen days from the date of this letter to identify any other information you believe should be redacted and the legal basis for redaction.

If you have questions about this ruling, please contact FinCEN's regulatory helpline at (703) 905-3591.

Sincerely, //signed//

Jamal El-Hindi

Associate Director

Policy Division

Request for Administrative Ruling on the Application of FinCEN's Regulations to a Virtual Currency Payment System
Fin-2014-R012 (Issued: Oct. 27, 2014)

Dear []:

This responds to your letter of January 6, 2014, seeking an administrative ruling from the Financial Crimes Enforcement Network ("FinCEN") on behalf of [] (the "Company"), about the Company's possible status as a money services business ("MSB") under the Bank Secrecy Act ("BSA"). Specifically, you ask whether the convertible virtual currency payment system the Company intends to set up (the "System") would make the Company a money transmitter under the BSA. Based on the following analysis of the description of the System to provide payments to merchants who wish to receive customer payments in Bitcoin, FinCEN finds that, if the Company sets up the System, the Company would be a money transmitter and should comply with all risk management, risk mitigation, recordkeeping, reporting, and transaction monitoring requirements corresponding to such status.

You state in your letter that the Company wishes to set up a System that will provide virtual currency-based payments to merchants in the United States and (mostly) Latin America, who wish to receive payment for goods or services sold in a currency other than that of legal tender in their respective jurisdictions. The

---

12. 31 CFR §§ 1010.711–717.

Company would receive payment from the buyer or debtor in currency of legal tender ("real currency"), and transfer the equivalent in Bitcoin to the seller or creditor, minus a transaction fee. The current intended market for the System is the hotel industry in four Latin American countries where, because of currency controls and extreme inflation, merchants face substantial foreign exchange risks when dealing with overseas customers.

According to your letter, a merchant will sign up with the Company to use the System, and incorporate the Company's software into its website. Customers purchasing the merchant's goods or services (e.g., hotel reservations) will pay for the purchase using a credit card. Instead of the credit card payment going to the merchant, it will go to the Company, which will transfer the equivalent in Bitcoin to the merchant. The Company pays the merchant using the reserve of Bitcoin it has acquired from wholesale purchases from virtual currency exchangers at the Company's discretion (thus the Company assumes any exchange risk that occurs during the time between the Company's wholesale purchases and its payment to a merchant). The Company has no agreement with the customer and will only make payment to the merchant.

You maintain that the Company should not be regulated as a money transmitter because it does not conform to the definition of virtual currency exchanger, due to the fact that the Company makes payments from an inventory it maintains, rather than funding each individual transaction. You also maintain that, should the Company be considered an exchanger of convertible virtual currency, the Company's business should be covered under an exemption that applies to certain payment processing activities,[1] and/or the Company's transmissions should be deemed integral to the transaction and thereby covered under another exemption from money transmission.[2]

FinCEN's Virtual Currency Guidance

On March 18, 2013, FinCEN issued guidance on the application of FinCEN's regulations to transactions in virtual currencies (the "Guidance").[3] FinCEN's regulations define "currency" as "[t]he coin and paper money of the United States or of any other country that is designated as legal tender and that circulates and is customarily used and accepted as a medium of exchange in the country of issuance."[4] In contrast to real currency, "virtual" currency is a medium of exchange that operates like a currency in some environments, but does not have all the attributes of real currency. In particular, virtual currency does not have legal tender status in any jurisdiction. The

---

1. 31 CFR § 1010.100(ff)(5)(ii)(B).

2. 31 CFR § 1010.100(ff)(5)(ii)(F).

3. FIN-2013-G001("Application of FinCEN's Regulations to Persons Administering, Exchanging, or Using Virtual Currencies," March 18, 2013).

4. 31 CFR § 1010.100(m).

Guidance addresses "convertible" virtual currency. This type of virtual currency either has an equivalent value in real currency, or acts as a substitute for real currency.

For purposes of the Guidance, FinCEN refers to the participants in generic virtual currency arrangements, using the terms "exchanger," "administrator," and "user." An exchanger is a person engaged as a business in the exchange of virtual currency for real currency, funds, or other virtual currency. An administrator is a person engaged as a business in issuing (putting into circulation) a virtual currency, and who has the authority to redeem (to withdraw from circulation) such virtual currency. A user is a person that obtains virtual currency to purchase goods or services.[5] Under the Guidance, both exchangers and administrators are considered to be money transmitters unless a limitation or exemption from the definition of money transmitter applies to that person.[6]

FinCEN disagrees with your position that the Company does not convert the customer's real currency into virtual currency because the Company purchases and stores large quantities of Bitcoin that the Company then uses to pay the merchant. As described above, the Company is an exchanger under the Guidance because it engages as a business in accepting and converting the customer's real currency into virtual currency for transmission to the merchant. The fact that the Company uses its cache of Bitcoin to pay the merchant is not relevant to whether it fits within the definition of money transmitter. An exchanger will be subject to the same obligations under FinCEN regulations regardless of whether the exchanger acts as a broker (attempting to match two (mostly) simultaneous and offsetting transactions involving the acceptance of one type of currency and the transmission of another) or as a dealer (transacting from its own reserve in either convertible virtual currency or real currency).

FinCEN concludes that the Company would be a money transmitter, specifically because it is acting as an exchanger of convertible virtual currency, as that term was described in the Guidance. Additionally, you then ask, if FinCEN determines that the Company is an exchanger, whether either an exemption for certain payment processing activities or an exemption for transactions integral to the sale of other goods or services would apply.

FinCEN's definition of money transmission and existing exemptions

On July 21, 2011, FinCEN published a Final Rule amending definitions and other regulations relating to MSBs (the "Rule").[7] The amended regulations define an MSB as "a person wherever located doing business, whether or not on a regular basis or as an organized or licensed business concern, wholly or in substantial part within the

---

5. FIN-2014-R001 "Application of FinCEN's Regulations to Virtual Currency Mining Operations"—01/30/2014, clarified that a *user* is a person that obtains virtual currency to purchase goods or services *on the user's own behalf.* (emphasis added).

6. See FIN-2013-G001.

7. Bank Secrecy Act Regulations—Definitions and Other Regulations Relating to Money Services Businesses, 76 FR 43585 (July 21, 2011).

United States, in one or more of the capacities listed in paragraphs (ff)(1) through (ff)(7) of this section. This includes but is not limited to maintenance of any agent, agency, branch, or office within the United States."[8]

BSA regulations, as amended, define the term "money transmitter" to include a person that provides money transmission services, or any other person engaged in the transfer of funds. The term "money transmission services" means the acceptance of currency, funds, or other value that substitutes for currency from one person and the transmission of currency, funds, or other value that substitutes for currency to another location or person by any means.[9] The regulations also stipulate that whether a person is a money transmitter is a matter of facts and circumstances, and identifies circumstances under which a person's activities would not make such person a money transmitter.[10]

FinCEN stipulates four conditions for the payment processor exemption to apply to a particular business pattern:

a. the entity providing the service must facilitate the purchase of goods or services, or the payment of bills for goods or services (other than money transmission itself);

b. the entity must operate through clearance and settlement systems that admit only BSA-regulated financial institutions;

c. the entity must provide the service pursuant to a formal agreement; and

d. the entity's agreement must be at a minimum with the seller or creditor that provided the goods or services and receives the funds.[11]

The Company fails to satisfy one of these conditions. The Company is not operating through clearing and settlement systems that only admit BSA-regulated financial institutions as members. According to your letter the real currency payments from the consumer take place within a clearing and settlement system that only admits BSA-regulated financial institutions as members (specifically, a credit card network), however, the payment of the Bitcoin equivalent to the merchant, by definition, takes place outside such a clearing and settlement system, either to a merchant-owned virtual currency wallet or to a larger virtual currency exchange that admits both financial institution and non-financial institution members, for the account of the merchant.

---

8. 31 CFR § 1010.100(ff).

9. 31 CFR § 1010.100(ff)(5)(i)(A).

10. 31 CFR § 1010.100(ff)(5)(ii).

11. See 31 CFR § 1010.100(ff)(5)(ii)(B); see also FIN-2013-R002 ("Whether a Company that Offers a Payment Mechanism Based on Payable-Through Drafts to its Commercial Customers is a Money Transmitter"—11/13/2013). FIN-2013-R002 clarifies that for the payment processor exemption to apply, the entity must use a clearance and settlement system that intermediates solely between BSA regulated institutions.

With regard to whether the money transmission is integral to the provision of the Company's service, and thus potentially eligible for exemption, FinCEN has concluded that the money transmission that takes place within the System does not qualify for the exemption. There are three fundamental conditions that must be met for the exemption to apply:

a. The money transmission component must be part of the provision of goods or services distinct from money transmission itself;

b. The exemption can only be claimed by the person that is engaged in the provision of goods or services distinct from money transmission;

c. The money transmission component must be integral (that is, necessary) for the provision of the goods or services.

In FinCEN's view, the payment service that the Company intends to offer meets the definition of money transmission. Such money transmission is the sole purpose of the Company's System, and is not a necessary part of another, non-money transmission service being provided by the Company. Although rendered before the 2011 modifications to MSB definitions and in some cases involving a different type of MSB, FinCEN reached the same conclusion in several administrative rulings that apply to this particular point.[12]

For the above reasons, FinCEN has determined that the Company is engaged in money transmission, and such activity is not covered by either the payment processor or the integral exemption. Please note that FinCEN would reach the same conclusions if payments were made in virtual currencies other than Bitcoin. As a money transmitter, the Company will be required to (a) register with FinCEN, (b) conduct a comprehensive risk assessment of its exposure to money laundering,[13] (c) implement an Anti-Money Laundering Program based on such risk assessment, and (d) comply with the recordkeeping, reporting and transaction monitoring obligations set down in Parts 1010 and 1022 of 31 CFR Chapter X. Examples of such requirements include the filing of Currency Transaction Reports (31 CFR § 1022.310) and Suspicious Activity Reports (31 CFR § 1022.320), whenever applicable, gener-

---

12. See FIN-2008-R007 ("Whether a Certain Operation Protecting On-line Personal Financial Information is a Money Transmitter"—06/11/2008); FIN-2008-R004 ("Whether a Foreign Exchange Consultant is a Currency Dealer or Exchanger or Money Transmitter"—05/09/2008); FIN-2008-R003 ("Whether a Person That is Engaged in the Business of Foreign Exchange Risk Management is a Currency Dealer or Exchanger or Money Transmitter"—05/09/2008); and FIN-2008-R002 ("Whether a Foreign Exchange Dealer is a Currency Dealer or Exchanger or Money Transmitter"—05/09/2008).

13. We caution the Company about incorporating into its comprehensive risk assessment the delicate balance between helping merchants avoid losses due to the fluctuation of their currencies of legal tender because of inflationary trends or devaluation, on the one hand, and collaboration with their potential evasion of foreign exchange control regulations applicable in their jurisdictions, on the other.

al recordkeeping maintenance (31 CFR § 1010.410), and recordkeeping related to the sale of negotiable instruments (31 CFR § 1010.415). Furthermore, to the extent that any of the Company's transactions constitute a "transmittal of funds" (31 CFR § 1010.100(ddd)) under FinCEN's regulations, then the Company must also comply with the "Funds Transfer Rule" (31 CFR § 1010.410(e)) and the "Funds Travel Rule" (31 CFR § 1010.410(f)).

This ruling is provided in accordance with the procedures set forth at 31 CFR Part 1010 Subpart G. In arriving at the conclusions in this administrative ruling, we have relied upon the accuracy and completeness of the representations you made in your communications with us. Nothing precludes FinCEN from arriving at a different conclusion or from taking other action should circumstances change or should any of the information you have provided prove inaccurate or incomplete. We reserve the right, after redacting your name and address, and similar identifying information for your clients, to publish this letter as guidance to financial institutions in accordance with our regulations.[14] You have fourteen days from the date of this letter to identify any other information you believe should be redacted and the legal basis for redaction.

If you have questions about this ruling, please contact FinCEN's regulatory helpline at (703) 905-3591.

Sincerely, //signed//

Jamal El-Hindi

Associate Director

Policy Division

IV. FinCEN's 2019 Guidance

Six years after its initial guidance was released in 2013, on May 9, 2019, FinCEN issued *Application of FinCEN's Regulations to Certain Business Models Involving Convertible Virtual Currencies* (FIN-2019-G001).[39] The 2019 guidance did not provide new regulatory requirements, but provided businesses with further interpretation on how FinCEN regulations apply to business models in the convertible virtual currency space.[40] The 2019 guidance also clarifies which common business models involving the transmission of virtual currencies are subject to BSA regulations.

---

14. 31 CFR §§ 1010.711–717.

39. Press Release, Financial Crimes Enforcement Network, Application of FinCEN's Regulations to Persons Administering, Exchanging, or Using Virtual Currencies (May 9, 2019), https://www.fincen.gov/sites/default/files/2019-05/FinCEN%20Guidance%20CVC%20FINAL%20508.pdf.

40. *Id.*

Application of FinCEN's Regulations to Certain Business Models Involving Convertible Virtual Currencies Payment System

Fin-2019-G001 (May 9, 2019)

The Financial Crimes Enforcement Network (FinCEN) is issuing this interpretive guidance to remind persons subject to the Bank Secrecy Act (BSA) how FinCEN regulations relating to money services businesses (MSBs) apply to certain business models[1] involving money transmission denominated in value that substitutes for currency, specifically, convertible virtual currencies (CVCs).[2]

This guidance does not establish any new regulatory expectations or requirements. Rather, it consolidates current FinCEN regulations, and related administrative rulings and guidance issued since 2011, and then applies these rules and interpretations to other common business models involving CVC engaging in the same underlying patterns of activity.

This guidance is intended to help financial institutions comply with their existing obligations under the BSA as they relate to current and emerging business models involving CVC by describing FinCEN's existing regulatory approach to the issues most frequently raised by industry, law enforcement, and other regulatory bodies within this evolving financial environment. In this regard, it covers only certain business models and necessarily does not address every potential combination of facts and circumstances. Thus, a person working with a business model not specifically included in this guidance may still have BSA obligations.

The overall structure of this guidance is as follows:

Section 1 defines certain key concepts within the context of the guidance. Although the titles or names assigned to these key concepts may coincide with terms customarily used by industry and share similar attributes, for purposes of the guidance their meaning is limited to the definition provided in the guidance.

Section 2 consolidates and explains current FinCEN regulations, previous administrative rulings, and guidance involving the regulation of money transmission under the BSA. By consolidating and summarizing rules and interpretation in a single Section, this guidance provides a resource to help financial institutions comply with their existing obligations under the BSA as they relate to current and emerging activities involving CVC.

---

1. For a discussion of the concept of "business model" as used within this guidance, *see infra,* Section 1.1.

2. For a discussion of the concepts of "value that substitutes for currency" and "convertible virtual currency" as used within this guidance, *see infra,* Sections 1.2. and 1.3.

Section 3 summarizes the development and content of FinCEN's 2013 guidance on the application of money transmission regulations to transactions denominated in CVC.[3]

Sections 4 and 5 describe FinCEN's existing regulatory approach to current and emerging business models using patterns of activity involving CVC. This approach illustrates how FinCEN fits existing interpretations about certain activities to other activities that at first may seem unrelated, but conform to the same combination of key facts and circumstances.

Finally, Section 6 contains a list of resources to which interested parties may refer for further explanation about the content of the guidance, or to assist in evaluating facts and circumstances not expressly covered in this guidance.

1. Key Concepts

The following subsections describe how FinCEN frames certain key concepts for purposes of this guidance.

1.1. Business Model

Whether a person is a money transmitter under FinCEN's regulations is a matter of facts and circumstances.[4] Within the context of this guidance, "business model" refers to the subset of key facts and circumstances relevant to FinCEN's determination of (a) whether the specific person meets the definition of a particular type of financial institution and (b) what regulatory obligations are associated with the specific activities performed within the business model.

This guidance may refer to a pattern of activity as a business model using a title or name ("label") that may coincide with a label used by industry to designate a general type of product or service. The label, however, will not determine the regulatory application. Rather, this guidance applies to any business model that fits the same key facts and circumstances described in the guidance, regardless of its label. Conversely, the regulatory interpretations in this guidance will not apply to a business model using the same label, but involving different key facts and circumstances.

In addition, differences in similar business models may lead to different regulatory applications. The regulatory interpretations contained in this guidance may extend only to other business models consisting of the *same* key facts and circumstances as the business models described herein. Therefore, a particular regulatory interpretation may not apply to a person if their business model contains fewer, additional, or different features than those described in this guidance.

---

3. FIN-2013-G001, "Application of FinCEN's Regulations to Persons Administering, Exchanging, or Using Virtual Currencies," Mar. 18, 2013 ("2013 VC Guidance").

4. 31 CFR § 1010.100(ff)(5)(ii).

Lastly, a person who is engaged in more than one type of business model at the same time may be subject to more than one type of regulatory obligation or exemption. For example, a developer or seller of either a software application or a new CVC platform may be exempt from BSA obligations associated with *creating* or *selling* the application or CVC platform, but may still have BSA obligations as a money transmitter if the seller or developer also uses the new application to engage as a business in accepting and transmitting currency, funds, or value that substitutes for currency, or uses the new platform to engage as a business in accepting and transmitting the new CVC. Likewise, an exemption may apply to a person performing a certain role in the development or sale of a software application, while a different person using the same application to accept and transmit currency, funds, or value that substitutes for currency would be still subject to BSA obligations.

1.2. Value that Substitutes for Currency

1.2.1. Definitions

In 2011, FinCEN issued a final rule ("2011 MSB Final Rule")[5] defining a money services business as, "a person wherever located doing business, whether or not on a regular basis or as an organized or licensed business concern, wholly or in substantial part within the United States," operating directly, or through an agent, agency, branch, or office, who functions as, among other things, a "money transmitter."[6]

FinCEN's regulations define the term "money transmitter" to include a "person that provides money transmission services," or "any other person engaged in the transfer of funds."[7] A "transmittor," on the other hand, is "[t]he sender of the first transmittal order in a transmittal of funds. The term transmittor includes an originator, except where the transmittor's financial institution is a financial institution or foreign financial agency other than a bank or foreign bank."[8] In other words, a transmit*tor* initiates a transaction that the money transmit*ter* actually executes.

The term "money transmission services" is defined to mean *the acceptance of* currency, funds, or *other value that substitutes for currency* from one person *and the transmission of* currency, funds, or *other value that substitutes for currency* to another location or person by any means.[9] The term "other value that substitutes for currency" encompasses situations in which the transmission does not involve currency,[10]

---

5. Bank Secrecy Act Regulations—Definitions and Other Regulations Relating to Money Services Businesses, 76 FR 43585 (July 21, 2011).

6. 31 CFR § 1010.100(ff).

7. 31 CFR § 1010.100(ff)(5).

8. 31 CFR § 1010.100(fff).

9. 31 CFR § 1010.100(ff)(5)(i)(A) (emphasis added).

10. 31 CFR § 1010.100(m) (defining currency as "[t]he coin and paper money of the United States or of any other country that is designated as legal tender and that circulates and is customarily used and accepted as a medium of exchange in the country of issuance. Currency includes U.S. silver

or funds, but instead involves something that the parties to a transaction recognize has value that is equivalent to or can substitute for currency.

FinCEN's regulation does not limit or qualify the scope of the term "value that substitutes for currency." It can be created either (a) specifically for the purpose of being used as a currency substitute or (b) originally for another purpose but then repurposed to be used as a currency substitute by an administrator (in centralized payment systems) or an unincorporated organization, such as a software agency (in decentralized payment systems).[11] In either case, the persons involved in the creation and subsequent distribution of the value (either for the original purpose or for another purpose) may be subject to additional regulatory frameworks (other than the BSA) that govern licensing and chartering obligations, safety and soundness regulations, minimum capital and reserve requirements, general and financial consumer and investor protection, etc. When subject to these other regulatory frameworks, the person may be exempted from MSB status but be covered as a different type of financial institution under FinCEN regulations.

1.2.2. Application of BSA regulations to persons exempt from MSB status engaged in transactions denominated in any type of value that substitutes for currency

The term "money services business" does not include: (a) a bank or foreign bank; (b) a person registered with, and functionally regulated or examined by, the U.S. Securities and Exchange Commission (SEC) or the U.S. Commodity Futures Trading Commission (CFTC), or a foreign financial agency that engages in financial activities that, if conducted in the United States, would require the foreign financial agency to be registered with the SEC or CFTC; or, (c) a natural person who engages in certain identified MSB activity (i.e., dealing in foreign exchange, check cashing, issuing or selling traveler's checks or money orders, providing prepaid access, or money transmission) but does so on an infrequent basis and not for gain or profit.[12] Banks and persons registered with, and functionally regulated or examined by, the SEC or the CFTC, that engage in transactions denominated in value that substitutes for currency will be subject to BSA regulations according to the applicable section of 31 CFR Chapter X.[13]

---

certificates, U.S. notes and Federal Reserve notes. Currency also includes official foreign bank notes that are customarily used and accepted as a medium of exchange in a foreign country.")

11. *See* 2013 VC Guidance, at 4–5 (discussing centralized and decentralized payment systems).

12. 31 CFR § 1010.100(ff)(8). In the case of 1010.100(ff)(8)(ii), the exemption applies only if the person *itself* is registered with, and functionally regulated or examined by the SEC or CFTC; the exemption may not apply if it is, for example, the document instrumenting the offer or sale of an asset (and not the person offering or selling the asset) that which must be registered.

13. The appropriate definitions and specific regulations may be found as follows: banks (31 CFR §§ 1010.100(d) and 1020, respectively); brokers or dealers in securities (31 CFR §§ 1010.100(h) and 1023, respectively); futures commission merchants (31 CFR §§ 1010.100(x) and 1026, respectively); introducing brokers in commodities (31 CFR §§ 1010.100(bb) and 1026, respectively); and mutual funds (31 CFR §§ 1010.100(gg) and 1024, respectively).

1.2.3. Application of BSA regulations to persons not exempt from MSB status engaged in transactions denominated in any type of value that substitutes for currency

A person not exempt from MSB status under 31 CFR § 1010.100(ff)(8) may be a money transmitter when the person engages in transactions covered by FinCEN's definition of money transmission, regardless of the technology employed for the transmittal of value or the type of asset the person uses as value that substitutes for currency, or whether such asset is physical or virtual. In general, persons not covered by 1010.100(ff)(8)(ii) who issue securities and futures, or purchase and sell securities, commodities, and futures, are outside the scope of the BSA. However, such persons could be covered by BSA money transmission regulations under certain facts and circumstances, in accordance with (a) the regulatory definition of money transmitter, (b) any applicable exemption from the definition (*see* Section 2 below), and (c) regulatory interpretations such as those contained in FIN-2008-G008 and FIN- 2015-R001:

a. FIN-2008-G008, "Application of the Definition of Money Transmitter to Brokers and Dealers in Currency and other Commodities," September 10, 2008, states that as long as a broker or dealer in real currency or other commodities accepts and transmits funds solely for the purpose of effecting a *bona fide* purchase or sale of the real currency or other commodities for or with a customer, such person is not acting as a money transmitter under the regulations. However, if the broker or dealer transfers funds between a customer and a third party that is not part of the currency or commodity transaction, such transmission of funds is no longer a fundamental element of the actual transaction necessary to execute the contract for the purchase or sale of the currency or the other commodity, and the broker or dealer becomes a money transmitter. This regulatory interpretation extends to persons intermediating in the purchase and sale of securities or futures.[14]

b. FIN-2015-R001, "Application of FinCEN's Regulations to Persons Issuing Physical or Digital Negotiable Certificates of Ownership of Precious Metals," August 14, 2015, applies a similar interpretation to digital certificates evidencing the ownership of a certain amount of a commodity. This regu-

---

14. *See also* 2011 MSB Final Rule, 76 FR at 43594 (stating "[P]ersons that sell goods or provide services other than money transmission services, and only transmit funds as an integral part of that sale of goods or provision of services, are not money transmitters. For example, brokering the sale of securities, commodity contracts, or similar instruments is not money transmission notwithstanding the fact that the person brokering the sale may move funds back and forth between the buyer and seller to effect the transaction."). The 2011 MSB Final Rule updated, streamlined, and clarified MSB regulations based on FinCEN's large body of guidance and administrative rulings previously issued. 2011 MSB Final Rule, 76 FR at 43586. Such previous guidance or administrative rulings, which FinCEN has not withdrawn, remain instructive and are cited herein to assist in understanding FinCEN's current interpretation of its MSB regulations.

latory interpretation also extends to physical or digital certificates of ownership of securities or futures contracts.

In the regulatory interpretations above, money transmission could involve either (a) the movement of currency of legal tender to or from accounts originally set up to buy or sell commodities (or securities, or futures); or (b) the issuance and subsequent acceptance and transmission of a digital token that evidenced ownership of a certain amount of a commodity, security, or futures contract. At the time of the rulings mentioned above, the commodity, security, or futures contract *itself* was not used to engage in money transmission primarily because such contracts were fractioned in relatively large individual amounts not suitable for money transmission. However, if assets that other regulatory frameworks define as commodities, securities, or futures contracts were to be specifically issued or later repurposed to serve as a currency substitute, then the asset itself could be a type of value that substitutes for currency, the transfer of which could constitute money transmission.

Therefore, as explained above, money transmission may occur when a person (or an agent, or a mechanical or software agency owned or operated by such person) not exempt from MSB status:

a. uses any representation of currency of legal tender (paper money, coins, Federal Reserve Bank notes, United States notes, funds credited to an account) associated with the purchase or sale of commodities, securities, or futures contracts to engage in money transmission;

b. issues physical or digital tokens evidencing ownership of commodities, securities, or futures contracts that serve as value that substitutes for currency in money transmission transactions; or

c. issues or employs commodities, securities, or futures contracts by themselves as value that substitutes for currency in money transmission transactions.

1.3. Convertible Virtual Currency (CVC)

The term "virtual currency" refers to a medium of exchange that can operate like currency but does not have all the attributes of "real" currency, as defined in 31 CFR § 1010.100(m), including legal tender status.[15] CVC is a type of virtual currency that either has an equivalent value as currency, or acts as a substitute for currency, and is therefore a type of "value that substitutes for currency."

As mentioned above, the label applied to any particular type of CVC (such as "digital currency," "cryptocurrency," "cryptoasset," "digital asset," etc.) is not dispositive of its regulatory treatment under the BSA. Similarly, as money transmission

---

15. 2013 VC Guidance, at 1; *see also, infra,* section 3.

involves the acceptance and transmission of value that substitutes for currency *by any means*, transactions denominated in CVC will be subject to FinCEN regulations regardless of whether the CVC is represented by a physical or digital token, whether the type of ledger used to record the transactions is centralized or distributed, or the type of technology utilized for the transmission of value.

2. General Application of BSA Regulations to Money Transmission

Under the BSA, the term "person" means "[a]n individual, a corporation, a partnership, a trust or estate, a joint stock company, an association, a syndicate, joint venture, or other unincorporated organization or group, an Indian Tribe (as that term is defined in the Indian Gaming Regulatory Act), and all entities cognizable as legal personalities."[16]

In general, whether a person qualifies as an MSB subject to BSA regulation depends on the person's *activities* and not its formal business status. Thus, whether a person is an MSB will *not* depend on whether the person: (a) is a natural person or legal entity; (b) is licensed as a business by any state; (c) has employees or other natural persons acting as agents; (d) operates at a brick-and-mortar branch, or through mechanical or software agents or agencies; or (e) is a for profit or non-profit service.[17]

At the same time, a person still qualifies as a money transmitter if that person's activities include receiving one form of value (currency, funds, prepaid value, value that substitutes for currency – such as CVC, etc.) from one person and transmitting either the same or a different form of value to another person or location, by any means.[18] Similarly, a money transmitter may accept and transmit value in either order. That is, a person is still a money transmitter under FinCEN regulations if the person transmits value first, and only later accepts corresponding value for this transfer.[19]

Likewise, a person may be a money transmitter when operating either on a transactional basis or on an account basis.[20] A transactional basis includes one-off transactions where there is no expectation that the money transmitter will establish an

---

16. 31 CFR § 1010.100(mm).

17. FinCEN clarified these points in the Preamble to the 2011 MSB Final Rule, 76 FR, at 43587.

18. 2011 MSB Final Rule, 76 FR, at 43592.

19. *Ibid.*

20. Amendment to the Bank Secrecy Act Regulations Relating to Recordkeeping for Funds Transfers and Transmittals of Funds by Financial Institutions, 60 FR 220, Jan. 3, 1995 (stating "An established customer is defined as a person with an account with a financial institution or a person with respect to which the financial institution has obtained and maintains on file the name and address, as well as the customer's taxpayer identification number or, if none, alien identification number or passport number and country of issuance, and to which the financial institution provides financial services relying on that information.... Such relationships with nonbank financial institutions may include, but are not limited to, accounts with broker/dealers and ongoing contractual relationships between providers of money transmitting services and business customers.").

ongoing relationship with the transactor, and the money transmitter retains the currency, funds, or other value that substitutes for currency, only for the time required to effect the transmission. By contrast, an account basis includes circumstances where the transactor is an established customer of the money transmitter, as defined in 31 CFR § 1010.100(p), and the money transmitter may maintain an account for the transactor to store funds or value that substitutes for currency, from which the transactor can instruct the money transmitter to transfer them in whole or in part.

Finally, a person will qualify as a money transmitter if that person accepts value with the intent of transmitting it only under certain conditions. For example, if a person operates a platform that facilitates the conditional exchange of value between two parties—such as the exchange of CVC against currency only when an agreed upon exchange rate and amount is met—such person will be engaged in money transmission every time the conditions (such as the exchange rate and amount) are met and the person completes the reciprocal transfers.[21]

As discussed above, whether a person is a money transmitter depends on the facts and circumstances of a given case. FinCEN regulations, however, specify that certain activities are excluded from the definition of "money transmitter." Specifically, a person is not a money transmitter if that person only:

a. provides the delivery, communication, or network access services used by a money transmitter to support money transmission services;

b. acts as a payment processor to facilitate the purchase of, or payment of a bill for, a good or service through a clearance and settlement system by agreement with the creditor or seller;

c. operates a clearance and settlement system or otherwise acts as an intermediary solely between BSA regulated institutions;

d. physically transports currency, other monetary instruments, other commercial paper, or other value that substitutes for currency as a person primarily engaged in such business, such as an armored car, from one person to the same person at another location or to an account belonging to the same person at a financial institution, provided that the person engaged in physical transportation has no more than a custodial interest in the currency, other monetary instruments, other commercial paper, or other value at any time during the transportation;

e. provides prepaid access, as defined in 31 CFR § 1010.100(ff)(4); or

f. accepts and transmits funds only integral to the sale of goods or the provision of services, other than money transmission services, by the person who is accepting and transmitting the funds.[22]

---

21. *See* FIN-2014-R011, "Request for Administrative Ruling on the Application of FinCEN's Regulations to a Virtual Currency Trading Platform," Oct. 27, 2014.

22. 31 CFR § 1010.100(ff)(5)(ii)(A)-(F).

FinCEN interprets these exemptions strictly. Therefore, a person may not take advantage of a particular exemption if the activity it engages in does not conform fully to an exemption.[23]

2.1. BSA Obligations of Money Transmitters

The BSA regulatory framework begins with the expectation that financial institutions will operate under a culture of compliance supported by senior leadership, including owners, boards of directors, and senior executives. This culture of compliance will dictate the basic norms of behavior, knowledge, and transparency under which the management team, employees, and service providers will be held accountable.[24]

The BSA and its implementing regulations require MSBs to develop, implement, and maintain an effective written anti-money laundering program ("AML program") that is reasonably designed to prevent the MSB from being used to facilitate money laundering and the financing of terrorist activities. The AML program must, at a minimum: (a) incorporate policies, procedures and internal controls reasonably designed to assure ongoing compliance (including verifying customer identification, filing reports, creating and retaining records, and responding to law enforcement requests); (b) designate an individual responsible to assure day-to-day compliance with the program and BSA requirements; (c) provide training for appropriate personnel, including training in the detection of suspicious transactions; and, (d) provide for independent review to monitor and maintain an adequate program.[25] The AML program must be approved by the owner of the financial institution, or by the owner's representative (in the case of a corporation, such representative is the Board of Directors).

To assure that an AML compliance program is reasonably designed to meet the requirements of the BSA, MSBs should structure their programs to be risk-based. MSBs should assess their individual exposure to the risk of money laundering, terrorism finance, and financial crime based on the composition of customer base, the geographies served, and the financial products and services offered. MSBs must properly manage customer relationships and effectively mitigate risks by implementing controls commensurate with those risks.[26]

A well-developed risk assessment is part of sound risk management and assists MSBs in identifying and providing a comprehensive analysis of their individual risk profile. As part of its risk assessment, an MSB should determine both the identity

---

23. *See* FIN-2014-R010, "Administrative Ruling on the Application of FinCEN Regulations to Currency Transporters, Including Armored Car Services, and Exceptive Relief," Sept. 24, 2014.

24. *See* FIN-2014-A007, "Advisory to U.S. Financial institutions on Promoting a Culture of Compliance," Aug. 11, 2014.

25. 31 U.S.C. § 5318(g)(1); 31 CFR. § 1022.320(a)(2).

26. 31 CFR § 1022.210(b).

and the profile of its customers and MSBs must know enough about their customers to be able to determine the risk level they represent to the institution.

As an MSB, any non-exempt person engaged in money transmission must register with FinCEN within 180 days of starting to engage in money transmission.[27] Money transmitters must also comply with the recordkeeping, reporting, and transaction monitoring obligations set forth in Parts 1010 and 1022 of 31 CFR Chapter X.[28]

To the extent that any of the money transmitter's transactions constitute a "transmittal of funds"[29] under FinCEN's regulations, then the money transmitter must also comply with the "Funds Transfer Rule"[30] and the "Funds Travel Rule."[31] Additionally, as an MSB, the money transmitter must register with FinCEN within 180 days of starting to engage in money transmission.[32]

FinCEN regulations define a "transmittal of funds"[33] as a series of transmittal orders, and define a "transmittal order"[34] as an instruction to pay, among other things "a fixed or determinable amount of money...."[35] FinCEN has stated that transmittal of funds are not limited to wire transfers or electronic transfers. Examples provided in guidance are credits and debits to correspondent accounts, and using a check as a transmittal order within a transmittal of funds, in which case the check and any accompanying instructions are the transmittal order effecting the transmittal of funds.[36]

Because a transmittal order involving CVC is an instruction to pay "a determinable amount of money," transactions involving CVC qualify as transmittals of funds, and thus may fall within the Funds Travel Rule.[37] Under the Funds Travel Rule, a transmittal of funds of $3,000 or more (or its equivalent in CVC) may trigger certain requirements on a money transmitter acting as either the financial institution for the transmittor or recipient, or as an intermediary financial institution.

The money transmitter must obtain or provide the required regulatory information either before or at the time of the transmittal of value, regardless of how a mon-

---

27. 31 CFR § 1022.380.

28. Examples of such requirements include the filing of Currency Transaction Reports (31 CFR § 1022.310) and Suspicious Activity Reports (31 CFR § 1022.320), whenever applicable, general recordkeeping maintenance (31 CFR § 1010.410), and recordkeeping related to the sale of negotiable instruments (31 CFR § 1010.415).

29. 31 CFR § 1010.100(ddd).

30. *See* 31 CFR § 1010.410(e).

31. *See* 31 CFR § 1010.410(f).

32. 31 CFR § 1022.380.

33. 31 CFR § 1010.100(ddd).

34. 31 CFR § 1010.100(eee).

35. *Ibid.*

36. *See* FIN-1997-A007, "FinCEN FAQs on Funds "Travel" Regulations," January 1997; re-issued as FIN-2010-G004, "Funds "Travel" Regulations: Questions & Answers, Question 13," Nov. 9, 2010.

37. "Funds Travel Rule," *see* 31 CFR § 1010.410(f).

ey transmitter sets up their system for clearing and settling transactions, including those involving CVC.[38] In meeting this obligation, the parties to the transmittal of funds are not required to use the same system or protocol for both the actual transmission of value and the reception or transmission of the required regulatory information. As long as the obligated person provides the required regulatory information either before or at the time of the transmittal of value, if a given transmission protocol is unable to accommodate such information, the obligated person may provide such information in a message different from the transmittal order itself.[39]

Persons interested in determining whether a certain new activity or variation on an existing activity may subject them to FinCEN's regulatory requirements, or that find that FinCEN published regulation or guidance does not clearly reflect their business model, have several options for obtaining preliminary, general guidance, or definitive regulatory interpretation.[40]

3. Application of BSA Regulations to Money Transmission Involving CVC

The 2011 MSB Final Rule made clear that persons accepting and transmitting value that substitutes for currency, such as virtual currency, are money transmitters. Persons accepting and transmitting CVC are required (like any money transmitter) to register with FinCEN as an MSB and comply with AML program, recordkeeping, monitoring, and reporting requirements (including the filing of SARs and CTRs). These requirements apply equally to domestic and foreign-located CVC money transmitters doing business in whole or in substantial part within the United States, even if the foreign-located entity has no physical presence in the United States.

After the issuance of the 2011 MSB Final Rule, FinCEN received questions from industry on whether the new rule applied to transactions denominated in all types of virtual currency, including, for example, virtual currency that could only be used inside video games. Some persons involved in transactions denominated in CVC sought to register with FinCEN as either currency exchangers or prepaid access providers or sellers, rather than as money transmitters. FinCEN also received questions from persons purchasing CVCs to pay for goods or services, or planning to accept CVCs in payment of goods and services sold, concerned about their potential BSA obligations.

To address these and other issues, on March 18, 2013, FinCEN issued interpretive guidance on the application of FinCEN's regulations to transactions involving the acceptance of currency or funds and the transmission of CVC ("2013 VC Guid-

---

38. In general, a person that chooses to set up a transaction system that makes it difficult to comply with existing regulations may not invoke such difficulty as a justification for non-compliance or as a reason for preferential treatment.

39. *See* 31 CFR § 1010.410(f).

40. *See infra*, Section 6—Available Resources; *see also* MSB Examination Materials, available at https://www.fincen.gov/msb-examination-materials.

ance").[41] The 2013 VC Guidance described what CVC is for purposes of FinCEN regulations, and reminded the public that persons not exempted from MSB status that accept and transmit either real currency or anything of value that substitutes for currency, including virtual currency, are covered by the definition of money transmitter.[42]

The 2013 VC Guidance also identified the participants to generic CVC arrangements, including an "exchanger," "administrator," and "user," and further clarified that exchangers and administrators generally qualify as money transmitters under the BSA, while users do not. An *exchanger* is a person engaged as a business in the exchange of virtual currency for real currency, funds, or other virtual currency, while an *administrator* is a person engaged as a business in issuing (putting into circulation) a virtual currency, and who has the authority to redeem (to withdraw from circulation) such virtual currency.[43] A *user* is "a person that obtains virtual currency to purchase goods or services" on the user's own behalf.[44]

The 2013 VC Guidance explained that the method of obtaining virtual currency (e.g., "earning," "harvesting," "mining," "creating," "auto-generating," "manufacturing," or "purchasing") does not control whether a person qualifies as a "user," an "administrator" or an "exchanger."[45] In addition, it confirmed that exchangers are subject to the same obligations under FinCEN regulations regardless of whether the exchangers are directly brokering the transactions between two or more persons, or whether the exchangers are parties to the transactions using their own reserves, in either CVC or real currency.[46] The 2013 VC Guidance also discussed the appropriate regulatory treatment of administrators and exchangers under three common scenarios: brokers and dealers of e-currencies and e-precious metals; centralized CVCs; and decentralized CVCs.[47]

The 2013 VC Guidance also clarified that FinCEN interprets the term "another location" broadly. The definition of money transmitter includes a person that accepts and transmits value that substitutes for currency from one person to another person or to "another location." For example, transmission to another location occurs when an exchanger selling CVC accepts real currency or its equivalent from a

---

41. *See* FIN-2013-G001, "Application of FinCEN's Regulations to Persons Administering, Exchanging, or Using Virtual Currencies," Mar. 18, 2013.

42. *See, supra*, Section 1.3.

43. *See* 2013 VC Guidance, at 2.

44. *Ibid.*

45. *See also* FIN-2014-R001, "Application of FinCEN's Regulations to Virtual Currency Mining Operations," Jan. 30, 2014 (clarifying that a *user* is a person that obtains virtual currency to purchase goods or services on the user's own behalf).

46. *See* FIN-2014-R012, "Request for Administrative Ruling on the Application of FinCEN's Regulations to a Virtual Currency Payment System," Oct. 27, 2014. *See also*, FIN-2014-R011, "Request for Administrative Ruling on the Application of FinCEN's Regulations to a Virtual Currency Trading Platform," Oct. 27, 2014.

47. *See* 2013 VC Guidance, at 4–5 (discussing centralized and decentralized payment systems).

person and transmits the CVC equivalent of the real currency to the person's CVC account with the exchanger. This circumstance constitutes transmission to another location because it involves a transmission from the person's account at one location (e.g., a user's real currency account at a bank) to the person's CVC account with the exchanger.[48]

4. Guidance on Application of BSA Regulations to Common Business Models Involving the Transmission of CVC

This guidance sets forth examples of how FinCEN's money transmission regulations apply to several common business models involving transactions in CVC.[49] The description of each business model does not intend to reflect an industry standard or cover all varieties of products or services generally referred by the same label, but only highlight the key facts and circumstances of a specific product or service on which FinCEN based its regulatory interpretation.

4.1. Natural Persons Providing CVC Money Transmission (P2P Exchangers)

FinCEN's definition of an MSB includes both natural and legal persons engaged as a business in covered activities, "whether or not on a regular basis or as an organized business concern."[50] Peer-to-Peer (P2P) exchangers are (typically) natural persons engaged in the business of buying and selling CVCs. P2P exchangers generally advertise and market their services through classified advertisements, specifically designed platform websites, online forums, other social media, and word of mouth. P2P exchangers facilitate transfers from one type of CVC to a different type of CVC, as well as exchanges between CVC and other types of value (such as monetary instruments or payment products denominated in real currency). P2P exchangers may provide their services online or may arrange to meet prospective customers in person to purchase or sell CVC. Generally, once there is confirmation that the buyer has delivered or deposited the requested currency or CVC, the P2P exchanger will electronically provide the buyer with the requested CVC or other value.

A natural person operating as a P2P exchanger that engages in money transmission services involving real currency or CVCs must comply with BSA regulations as a money transmitter acting as principal. This is so regardless of the regularity or

---

48. *See* 2013 VC Guidance, at 4.

49. Although when describing a business model this guidance may use a label by which the general type of product or service may be commonly known, the interpretation provided herein applies only to the business model the guidance describes, and may not apply to any other variety or combination of factors that falls under the same generic label. For example, when in Section 4.4, FinCEN discusses how its regulations apply to certain money transmission in CVC executed within the context of ICOs, this interpretation applies exclusively to those transactions described in the guidance and may not apply to any other transactions may also be referred to as ICOs but follow a different business model.

50. 31 CFR § 1010.100(ff).

formality of such transactions or the location from which the person is operating. However, a natural person engaging in such activity on an infrequent basis *and* not for profit or gain would be exempt from the scope of money transmission.[51]

As a money transmitter, P2P exchangers are required to comply with the BSA obligations that apply to money transmitters, including registering with FinCEN as an MSB and complying with AML program, recordkeeping, and reporting requirements (including filing SARs and CTRs).[52]

4.2. CVC Wallets

CVC wallets are interfaces for storing and transferring CVCs. There are different wallet types that vary according to the technology employed, where and how the value is stored, and who controls access to the value. Current examples of different types of CVC wallets that vary by technology employed are mobile wallets, software wallets, and hardware wallets. Wallets may store value locally, or store a private key that will control access to value stored on an external server. Wallets may also use multiple private keys stored in multiple locations. Wallets where user funds are controlled by third parties are called "hosted wallets" whereas wallets where users control the funds are called "unhosted wallets."

The regulatory interpretation of the BSA obligations of persons that act as intermediaries between the owner of the value and the value itself is not technology- dependent. The regulatory treatment of such intermediaries depends on four criteria: (a) who owns the value; (b) where the value is stored; (c) whether the owner interacts directly with the payment system where the CVC runs; and, (d) whether the person acting as intermediary has total independent control over the value. The regulatory treatment of each type of CVC wallet based on these factors is described in the next subsection.

4.2.1. Hosted and Unhosted Wallet Providers

Hosted wallet providers are account-based money transmitters that receive, store, and transmit CVCs on behalf of their account holders, generally interacting with them through websites or mobile applications. In this business model, the money transmitter is the host, the account is the wallet, and the accountholder is the wallet owner. In addition, (a) the value belongs to the owner; (b) the value may be stored in a wallet or represented as an entry in the accounts of the host; (c) the owner interacts directly with the host, and not with the payment system; and (d) the host has total independent control over the value (although it is contractually obligated to access the value only on instructions from the owner).

---

51. 31 CFR § 1010.100(ff)(8)(iii).

52. For the regulatory treatment of those persons investing in CVCs, *see* FIN-2014-R002, "Application of FinCEN's Regulations to Virtual Currency Software Development and Certain Investment Activity," Jan. 30, 2014.

The regulatory framework applicable to the host, including the due diligence or enhanced due diligence procedures the host must follow regarding the wallet owner, varies depending on: (a) whether the wallet owner is a non-financial institution (in this context, a user, according to the 2013 VC Guidance), agent, or foreign or domestic counterparty; and (b) the type of transactions channeled through the hosted wallet, and their U.S. dollar equivalent.

When the wallet owner is a user, the host must follow the procedures for identifying, verifying and monitoring both the user's identity and profile, consistent with the host's AML program. When the wallet owner is an agent of the host, the host must comply with regulations and internal policies, procedures and controls governing a principal MSB's obligation to monitor the activities of its agent.[53] When the wallet owner is a financial institution other than an agent, the host must comply with the regulatory requirements applicable to correspondent accounts (or their MSB equivalents).[54]

Similarly, the regulatory requirements that apply to the transactions that host channels from or for the wallet owner will depend on the nature of the transaction. For example, where the transactions fall under the definition of "transmittal of funds," the host must comply with the Funds Travel Rule based on the host's position in the transmission chain (either as a transmittor's, intermediary, or recipient's financial institution), regardless of whether the regulatory information may be included in the transmittal order itself or must be transmitted separately.[55]

Unhosted wallets are software hosted on a person's computer, phone, or other device that allow the person to store and conduct transactions in CVC. Unhosted wallets do not require an additional third party to conduct transactions. In the case of unhosted, single-signature wallets, (a) the value (by definition) is the property of the owner and is stored in a wallet, while (b) the owner interacts with the payment system directly and has total independent control over the value. Insofar as the person conducting a transaction through the unhosted wallet is doing so to purchase goods or services on the user's own behalf, they are not a money transmitter.

4.2.2. Multiple-signature wallet providers

Multiple-signature wallet providers are entities that facilitate the creation of wallets specifically for CVC that, for enhanced security, require more than one private

---

53. *See* FIN-2016-G001, "Guidance on Existing AML Program Rule Compliance Obligations for MSB Principals with Respect to Agent Monitoring," Mar. 11, 2016.

54. *See* 31 CFR § 1010.610, "Due diligence programs for correspondent accounts for foreign financial institutions." *See also* "Guidance—(Interpretive Release 2004-1) Anti-Money Laundering Program—Requirements for Money Services Businesses with Respect to Foreign Agents or Foreign Counterparties," Dec. 14, 2004.

55. *See* 31 CFR § 1010.410(f).

key for the wallet owner(s) to effect transactions. Typically, multiple-signature wallet providers maintain in their possession one key for additional validation, while the wallet owner maintains the other private key locally. When a wallet owner wishes to effect a transaction from the owner's multiple-signature wallet, the wallet owner will generally submit to the provider a request signed with the wallet owner's private key, and once the provider verifies this request, the provider validates and executes the transaction using the second key it houses. With respect to an un-hosted multiple- signature wallet, (a) the value belongs to the owner and is stored in the wallet; (b) the owner interacts with the wallet software and/or payment system to initiate a transaction, supplying part of the credentials required to access the value; and (c) the person participating in the transaction to provide additional validation at the request of the owner does not have total independent control over the value.

If the multiple-signature wallet provider restricts its role to creating un-hosted wallets that require adding a second authorization key to the wallet owner's private key in order to validate and complete transactions, the provider is not a money transmitter because it does not accept and transmit value.[56] On the other hand, if the person combines the services of a multiple-signature wallet provider and a hosted wallet provider, that person will then qualify as a money transmitter. Likewise, if the value is represented as an entry in the accounts of the provider, the owner does not interact with the payment system directly, or the provider maintains total independent control of the value, the provider will also qualify as a money transmitter, regardless of the label the person applies to itself or its activities.

4.3. CVC Money Transmission Services Provided Through Electronic Terminals (CVC Kiosks)

CVC kiosks (commonly called "CVC automated teller machines (ATMs)" or "CVC vending machines") are electronic terminals that act as mechanical agencies of the owner-operator, to enable the owner-operator to facilitate the exchange of CVC for currency or other CVC. These kiosks may connect directly to a separate CVC exchanger, which performs the actual CVC transmission, or they may draw upon the CVC in the possession of the owner-operator of the electronic terminal.

An owner-operator of a CVC kiosk who uses an electronic terminal to accept currency from a customer and transmit the equivalent value in CVC (or vice versa) qualifies as a money transmitter both for transactions receiving and dispensing real currency or CVC. FinCEN issued guidance clarifying that owners/operators of ATMs that link an account holder with his or her account at a regulated depository institution solely to verify balances and dispense currency do not meet the defi-

---

56. 31 CFR § 1010.100(ff)(5)(ii)(A).

nition of a money transmitter.[57] The guidance addressing BSA coverage of private ATMs does not apply to the owner-operator of a CVC kiosk because CVC kiosks do not link account holders to their respective accounts at a regulated depository institution. Accordingly, owners-operators of CVC kiosks that accept and transmit value must comply with FinCEN regulations governing money transmitters.

4.4. CVC Money Transmission Services Provided Through Decentralized Applications (DApps)

Decentralized (distributed) application (DApp) is a term that refers to software programs that operate on a P2P network of computers running a blockchain platform (a type of distributed public ledger that allows the development of secondary blockchains), designed such that they are not controlled by a single person or group of persons (that is, they do not have an identifiable administrator). An owner/operator of a DApp may deploy it to perform a wide variety of functions, including acting as an unincorporated organization, such as a software agency to provide financial services.[58] Generally, a DApp user must pay a fee to the DApp (for the ultimate benefit of the owner/operator) in order to run the software. The fee is commonly paid in CVC.

The same regulatory interpretation that applies to mechanical agencies such as CVC kiosks applies to DApps that accept and transmit value, regardless of whether they operate for profit. Accordingly, when DApps perform money transmission, the definition of money transmitter will apply to the DApp, the owners/operators of the DApp, or both.

4.5. Anonymity-Enhanced CVC Transactions

Anonymity-enhanced CVC transactions are transactions either (a) denominated in regular types of CVC, but structured to conceal information otherwise generally available through the CVC's native distributed public ledger; or (b) denominated in types of CVC specifically engineered to prevent their tracing through distributed public ledgers (also called privacy coins).

A money transmitter that operates in anonymity-enhanced CVCs for its own account or for the accounts of others (regardless of the frequency) is subject to the same regulatory obligations as when operating in currency, funds, or non- anonymized CVCs. In other words, a money transmitter cannot avoid its regulatory obligations because it chooses to provide money transmission services using anonymity-enhanced CVC. The regulatory framework that applies to a person par-

---

57. *See* FIN-2007-G006, "Application of the Definitions of Money Services Business to Certain Owner-Operators of Automated Teller Machines Offering Limited Services," Dec. 3, 2007.

58. For an example of a DApp, *see* SEC's Release No. 81207 / July 25, 2017, "Report of Investigation Pursuant to Section 21(a) of the Securities Exchange Act of 1934: The DAO," available at https://www.sec.gov/litigation/investreport/34-81207.pdf.

ticipating in anonymity-enhanced CVC transactions depends on the specific role performed by the person, as set forth below in Section 4.5.1.

4.5.1. Providers of anonymizing services for CVCs

Providers of anonymizing services, commonly referred to as "mixers" or "tumblers," are either persons that accept CVCs and retransmit them in a manner designed to prevent others from tracing the transmission back to its source (anonymizing services provider), or suppliers of software a transmit*tor* would use for the same purpose (anonymizing software provider).

4.5.1(a) Anonymizing services provider

An anonymizing services provider is a money transmitter under FinCEN regulations. The added feature of concealing the source of the transaction does not change that person's status under the BSA.

FinCEN previously issued a regulatory interpretation that concluded that persons who accept and transmit value in a way ostensibly designed to protect the privacy of the transmit*tor* are providers of secure money transmission services and are not eligible for the integral exemption.[59] In order to be exempt from status as a money transmitter under the integral exemption, the person's business must be different from money transmission itself, and the money transmission activity must be necessary for the business to operate. The subject of this previous regulatory interpretation accepted and transmitted funds in a way designed to protect a consumer's personal and financial information from a merchant, when the consumer purchased goods or services through the Internet. FinCEN determined that the added feature of protecting consumers' information did not constitute an activity separate from the funds transmission itself, because the need to protect the consumers' personal and financial information only arose in connection with the transmission of funds. FinCEN concluded that the company was engaged in the business of offering secure money transmission, rather than security for which money transmission is integrally required. Accordingly, the company qualified as a money transmitter subject to BSA obligations.

The same analysis applies to anonymizing services providers: their business consists exclusively of providing secured money transmission. Therefore, a person (acting by itself, through employees or agents, or by using mechanical or software agencies) who provides anonymizing services by accepting value from a customer and transmitting the same or another type of value to the recipient, in a way de-

---

59. *See* FIN-2008-R007, "Whether a Certain Operation Protecting On-line Personal Financial Information is a Money Transmitter," Jun. 11, 2008. For a different business model, *see* FIN-2014-R006, "Whether a Company that Provides Online Real-Time Deposit, Settlement, and Payment Services for Banks, Businesses and Consumers is a Money Transmitter," Apr. 29, 2014.

signed to mask the identity of the transmitt*or*, is a money transmitter under FinCEN regulations.

4.5.1(b) Anonymizing software provider

An anonymizing software provider is not a money transmitter. FinCEN regulations exempt from the definition of money transmitter those persons providing "the delivery, communication, or network access services used by a money transmitter to support money transmission services."[60] This is because suppliers of tools (communications, hardware, or software) that may be utilized in money transmission, like anonymizing software, are engaged in trade and not money transmission.

By contrast, a person that utilizes the software to anonymize the person's own transactions will be either a user or a money transmitter, depending on the purpose of each transaction. For example, a user would employ the software when paying for goods or services on its own behalf, while a money transmitter would use it to engage as a business in the acceptance and transmission of value as a transmittor's or intermediary's financial institution.

Lastly, FinCEN issued guidance stating that originating or intermediary financial institutions that replace the proper identity of a transmittor or recipient in the transmittal order with a pseudonym or reference that may not be decoded by the receiving financial institution (i.e., substituting the full name of the transmittor with a numeric code) are not complying with their obligations under the Funds Travel Rule.[61]

4.5.2. Providers of anonymity-enhanced CVCs

A person that creates or sells anonymity-enhanced CVCs designed to prevent their tracing through publicly visible ledgers would be a money transmitter under FinCEN regulations depending on the type of payment system and the person's activity.[62] For example:

a. a person operating as the administrator of a *centralized* CVC payment system will become a money transmitter the moment that person issues anonymity- enhanced CVC against the receipt of another type of value;[63]

b. a person that uses anonymity-enhanced CVCs to pay for goods or services on his or her own behalf would not be a money transmitter under the BSA. However, if the person uses the CVC to accept and transmit value from one

---

60. 31 CFR § 1010.100(ff)(5)(ii).

61. *See* FIN-2010-G004, "Funds "Travel" Regulations: Questions & Answers," at Question 16, Nov. 09, 2010.

62. *See, supra*, Section 1.1.

63. A payment system may change from centralized to decentralized (*see* Section 5.2). This operational change does not alter the obligations of the person acting as administrator of the system, while the system worked on a centralized basis.

person to another person or location, the person will fall under the definition of money transmitter, if not otherwise exempted.

c. a person that develops a *decentralized* CVC payment system will become a money transmitter if that person also engages as a business in the acceptance and transmission of value denominated in the CVC it developed (even if the CVC value was mined at an earlier date). The person would not be a money transmitter if that person uses the CVC it mined to pay for goods and services on his or her own behalf.[64]

4.5.3. Money Transmitters that accept or transmit anonymity-enhanced CVCs

Many money transmitters involved in CVC transactions comply with their BSA obligations, in part, by incorporating procedures into their AML Programs that allow them to track and monitor the transaction history of a CVC through publicly visible ledgers.

As mentioned above, FinCEN has issued guidance stating that transmittor's or intermediary's financial institutions that replace the proper identity of a transmittor or recipient in the transmittal order with a pseudonym or reference that may not be decoded by the receiving financial institution (i.e., substituting the full name of the transmittor with a numeric code) are not complying with their obligations under the Funds Travel Rule.[65] A money transmitter must follow its AML risk assessment policies and procedures to determine under which circumstances the money transmitter will accept or transmit value already denominated in anonymity-enhanced CVCs. When knowingly accepting anonymity-enhanced CVCs (or regular CVC that has been anonymized), money transmitters engaged in CVC transactions subject to the Funds Travel Rule must not only track a CVC through the different transactions, but must also implement procedures to obtain the identity of the transmittor or recipient of the value.

4.6. Payment Processing Services Involving CVC Money Transmission

CVC payment processors are financial intermediaries that enable traditional merchants to accept CVC from customers in exchange for goods and services sold. CVC payment processors sometimes integrate with a merchant's point of sale or online shopping cart solution so that the value of goods being purchased is quoted in CVC. The CVC payment processor may collect the CVC from the customer and then transmit currency or funds to the merchant, or vice versa.

CVC payment processors fall within the definition of a money transmitter and are not eligible for the payment processor exemption because they do not satisfy all the required conditions for the exemption. Under the payment processor exemp-

---

64. *See* 2013 VC Guidance, at 4–5 (discussing centralized and decentralized payment systems).
65. *See, supra,* at 19 n. 59.

tion, a person is exempt from the definition of "money transmitter" when that person only "[a]cts as a payment processor to facilitate the purchase of, or payment of a bill for, a good or service through a clearance and settlement system by agreement with the creditor or seller."[66] To be eligible for the payment processor exemption, a person must:

a. facilitate the purchase of goods or services, or the payment of bills for goods or services (not just the money transmission itself);

b. operate through clearance and settlement systems that admit only BSA-regulated financial institutions;

c. provide its service pursuant to a formal agreement; and

d. enter a formal agreement with, at a minimum, the seller or creditor that provided the goods or services and also receives the funds.[67]

A person providing payment processing services through CVC money transmission generally is unable to satisfy the second condition because such money transmitters do not operate, either in whole or in part, through clearing and settlement systems that only admit BSA-regulated financial institutions as members. This condition is critical, because BSA-regulated financial institutions have greater visibility into the complete pattern of activities of the buyer or debtor, on the one hand, and the seller or creditor, on the other hand. Having BSA-regulated financial institutions at either end of the clearance and settlement of transactions reduces the need to impose additional obligations on the payment processor.[68] This same visibility simply does not exist when a CVC payment processor operates through a clearance and settlement system involving non-BSA regulated entities unless the CVC payment processor complies with the reporting obligations of a money transmitter.

Accordingly, in general, persons providing payment processing services in CVC will be money transmitters under the BSA, regardless of whether they accept and

---

66. 31 CFR § 1010.100(ff)(5)(ii)(B). For a discussion on the conditions applicable to the payment processor exemption from money transmission, *see, e.g.,* FIN-2013-R002, "Administrative Ruling on Whether a Company that Offers a Payment Mechanism Based on Payable-Through Drafts to its Commercial Customers is a Money Transmitter," Nov. 13, 2013. *See also,* FIN-2014-R009, "Application of Money Services Business Regulations to a Company Acting as an Independent Sales Organization and Payment Processor," Aug. 27, 2014.

67. *See* FIN-2014-R012, "Request for Administrative Ruling on the Application of FinCEN's Regulations to a Virtual Currency Payment System," Oct. 27, 2014.

68. *Id.* The CVC payment processor in that ruling received real currency payments from the buyer through a clearing and settlement system that only admits BSA-regulated financial institutions as members (specifically, a credit card network), but made payment of the Bitcoin equivalent to the merchant, to a merchant-owned virtual currency wallet or to a larger virtual currency exchange that admits both financial institution and non-financial institution members, for the account of the merchant.

transmit the same type of CVC, or they accept one type of value (such as currency or funds) and transmit another (such as CVC).[69]

4.7. CVC Money Transmission Performed by Internet Casinos

Internet casinos are virtual platforms created for betting on the possible outcome of events related to a number of gaming models (e.g., traditional casinos), but accepting deposits and bets and issuing payouts denominated in CVC. Internet casinos may also include entities known as predictive markets, information markets, decision markets, idea futures, and event derivatives.

FinCEN regulations define a casino, gambling casino or card club, as a person duly licensed or authorized to do business as such in the United States, whether under the laws of a State or a Territory or Insular Possession of the United States, or under the Indian Gaming Regulatory Act or other Federal, State, or tribal law or arrangement affecting tribal land, having gross annual gaming revenue in excess of $1 million, whether denominated in CVC or other value.[70] Any person engaged in the business of gambling that is not covered by the regulatory definition of casino, gambling casino, or card club, but accepts and transmits value denominated in CVC, may still be regulated under the BSA as a money transmitter. Indeed, even when the original transmission or the payout are done on a conditional basis (that is, only if a certain event occurs), money transmission under BSA regulations still occurs at the moment the condition is satisfied and the acceptance or transmission takes place.[71]

5. Specific Business Models Involving CVC Transactions that May be Exempt From the Definition of Money Transmission

5.1. CVC Trading Platforms and Decentralized Exchanges

CVC P2P trading platforms are websites that enable buyers and sellers of CVC to find each other. Sometimes, trading platforms also facilitate trades as an intermediary. Under FinCEN regulations, a person is exempt from money transmitter status if the person only provides the delivery, communication, or network access services used by a money transmitter to support money transmission services.[72] Consistent with this exemption, if a CVC trading platform only provides a forum where buyers and sellers of CVC post their bids and offers (with or without automatic matching of

---

69. A CVC payment processor will be eligible for the payment processor exemption only when it meets all criteria as described above. *See also, supra,* at 21 n. 64.

70. 31 CFR § 1010.100(t)(5) and (6).

71. Casinos, as defined above, have their own set of BSA/AML obligations (*see* 31 CFR Part 1010—General Provisions—and Part 1021—Rules for Casinos and Card Clubs). While not specifically exempted from MSB status, when a person falls under FinCEN's definitions for both casino and MSB, in general the regulatory obligations of a casino satisfy the obligations of an MSB, with the exception of registration.

72. 31 CFR § 1010.100(ff)(5)(ii)(A).

counterparties), and the parties themselves settle any matched transactions through an outside venue (either through individual wallets or other wallets not hosted by the trading platform), the trading platform does not qualify as a money transmitter under FinCEN regulations.[73] By contrast, if, when transactions are matched, a trading platform purchases the CVC from the seller and sells it to the buyer, then the trading platform is acting as a CVC exchanger, and thus falls within the definition of money transmitter and its accompanying BSA obligations.[74]

5.2. CVC Money Transmission Performed in the Context of Raising Funding for Development or Other Projects—Initial Coin Offerings

Initial coin offerings (ICOs) are generally a means to raise funds for new projects from early backers. Whether an ICO is subject to BSA obligations is a matter of facts and circumstances. This guidance will address, as an example, the BSA obligations of two common business models involving ICOs: (a) ICOs conducting a preferential sale of CVC to a select group of buyers (sometimes referred to as investors); and (b) ICOs raising funds by offering digital debt or equity instruments among a group of lenders or investors to finance a future project (which in turn may consist of the creation of a new CVC). This discussion does not attempt to address every possible ICO business model.[75]

In the first business model, the ICO consists of a group sale of CVC to a distinct set of preferred buyers. The exchange of CVC for another type of value may be instantaneous or deferred to a later date. The CVC and its application or platform may be already operational or it may be the seller's purpose to use the value received from the sale, in whole or in part, to develop such CVC, application, or platform. In some cases, after the initial centralized offering, any future creation of the CVC may occur through mining using a decentralized model. In any of these scenarios, the seller of the CVC is a money transmitter, acting in the role of administrator, because at the time of the initial offering the seller is the only person authorized to issue and redeem (permanently retire from circulation) the new units of CVC.[76] The

---

73. The obligations of the hosted wallet provider that utilizes the forum as a money transmitter under the BSA remain as described, *supra*, Section 3.2.

74. *See* FIN-2014-R011, "Request for Administrative Ruling on the Application of FinCEN's Regulations to a Virtual Currency Trading Platform," Oct. 27, 2014.

75. Nor does it affect the obligations of any of the participants described herein under other regulatory frameworks. For example, federal securities law may apply to the issuance of CVC as securities regardless of other intended purposes of the CVC. *See, e.g,* "Framework for 'Investment Contract' Analysis of Digital Assets," Securities and Exchange Commission, April 3, 2019, available at https://www.sec.gov/corpfin/framework-investment-contract-analysis-digital-assets. "Report of Investigation Pursuant to Section 21(a) of the Securities Exchange Act of 1934: The DAO," Securities and Exchange Commission, July 25, 2017, available at https://www.sec.gov/litigation/investreport/34-81207.pdf.

76. Whether by contractual agreement or business strategy an administrator declines to exercise such authorities is not relevant to the person's status as a money transmitter.

status of the seller as a money transmitter is not impacted by the coordinated or simultaneous sales; the timing of acceptance of one type of value and transmission of the other type (i.e., whether the exchange happens instantaneously or at a later date); or by the fact that the payment system may migrate from one operational status to another at any point in its lifetime (for example, changing from a central-ized, administrator-controlled system at origin to a decentralized, protocol-driven system after the initial sale).

In the second business model, the ICO raises funds for new projects by selling an equity stake or a debt instrument to early backers, or hedges a previous invest-ment in CVC through a derivative, such as a futures contract. The funded project generally involves the creation of DApps,[77] new CVCs (as well as the applications or platforms on which the CVCs will run), or new hedging instruments. ICOs are accomplished using distributed ledger platforms, in which investors receive a digital token as proof of investment. Depending on the purpose of the funded project and the seller's obligations to the investor, when the project is concluded the investor may: (a) receive new CVC in exchange for the token; (b) exchange the token for a DApp coin, which is a digital token that unlocks the use of DApps that provide various services; (c) use the original token itself as a new CVC or DApp coin; or (d) receive some other type of return on the original equity investment or debt instru-ment.[78] How BSA regulations apply to each of these scenarios will vary, as set forth below in Sections 5.2.1. to 5.2.3.

5.2.1. Status of Fundraising or Hedging Activity—Overview

Involvement of banks or persons registered with, and functionally regulated or ex-amined by the SEC or CFTC

The applicable AML regulations governing persons involved in an ICO through selling an equity stake or a debt instrument to early backers or through hedging a previous investment will depend on whether such persons are MSBs or exempt from MSB status under FinCEN regulations or rulings. Persons may be exempt from MSB status in two situations. First, FinCEN regulations expressly exempt from the definition of an MSB, among other things, (a) a bank or foreign bank; or (b) a person registered with, and functionally regulated or examined by, the SEC or CFTC, or a foreign financial agency that engages in financial activities that, if conducted in the United States, would require the foreign financial agency to

---

77. As discussed, *supra*, Section 4.4, DApps refer to software programs that run on distributed computing platforms—that is, platforms built across dispersed networks of computers designed to accomplish a shared objective.

78. A transaction where a person accepts currency, funds, or value that substitutes for currency in exchange for a new CVC at a preferential rate for a group of initial purchasers, before making the CVC available to the rest of the public, is simply engaging in money transmission, regardless of any specific label (such as "early investors") applied to the initial purchasers.

be registered with the SEC or CFTC.[79] Therefore, a person involved in ICO fund-raising activity as issuer, intermediary, or investor that is a bank, foreign bank, or a person registered with, and functionally regulated or examined by the SEC or CFTC will not be an MSB under FinCEN regulations. The person's AML obligations will flow from FinCEN regulations governing those types of financial institutions.[80]

Second, FinCEN regulations exempt persons from the definition of money transmitter under certain identified facts and circumstances, the most relevant of which is when the acceptance and transmission of value is only integral to the sale of goods or services different from money transmission.[81] Thus, if the person involved in the fundraising activity as an issuer, intermediary, or investor is not a bank, foreign bank, or a person registered with, and functionally regulated or examined by the SEC or CFTC, then any money transmission connected to the fundraising activity performed by the person generally will fall under the integral exemption,[82] unless the asset is issued to serve as value that substitutes for currency.[83]

Purchase and re-sale of digital tokens

The investor may hold the digital token or derivative until the underlying project is complete, or the investor may sell the digital token or derivative during the project's development. A re-sale can occur through a P2P transaction, or through a financial intermediary or secondary market. In general, the re-sale of the token or derivative does not create any BSA obligations for the initial investor. However, if a regulatory framework other than the BSA requires a person that either (a) purchases the token or derivative, or (b) intermediates in transactions in a primary or secondary market, to register as a broker or dealer in securities, futures commission merchant, or introducing broker in commodities, then the person will have the BSA obligations related to its status under these other regulatory frameworks.[84]

5.2.2. Status of a DApp Developer

The development of a DApp financed through ICO fundraising activity consists of the production of goods or services, and therefore is outside the definition of

---

79. 31 CFR § 1010.100(ff)(8). *See also, supra,* Section 1.2.2.

80. *See, supra,* at 5 n. 13.

81. *See, supra,* at 2 n. 4; 31 CFR § 1010.100(ff)(5)(F); FIN-2008-G008 "Application of the Definition of Money Transmitter to Brokers and Dealers in Currency and other Commodities," Sept. 10, 2008.

82. For additional discussion of the scope of the integral exemption, *see* FIN-2008-R004 "Whether a Foreign Exchange Consultant is a Currency Dealer or Exchanger or Money Transmitter," May 9, 2008, FIN-2008-R003 "Whether a Person that is Engaged in the Business of Foreign Exchange Risk Management is a Currency Dealer or Exchanger or Money Transmitter," May 9, 2008.

83. *See, supra,* Section 1.2.3.

84. *See, supra,* Section 1.2.2.

money transmission. Thus, the developer of a DApp is not a money transmitter for the mere act of creating the application, even if the purpose of the DApp is to issue a CVC or otherwise facilitate financial activities denominated in CVC.[85] However, if the developer of the DApp uses or deploys it to engage in money transmission, then the developer will qualify as a money transmitter under the BSA.

5.2.3. Status of a DApp User conducting financial activities

Once the DApp is finalized and in production, FinCEN regulations may apply to persons who use the DApp to conduct certain financial activities. For example, if an investor or an owner/operator uses or deploys the DApp to engage in money transmission denominated in CVC, then the investor or the owner/operator generally qualifies as a money transmitter under the BSA. Likewise, as mentioned above, if the developer of the DApp uses or deploys the DApp to engage in money transmission, then the developer will also qualify as a money transmitter.

5.3. Status of Creators of CVC and Distributed Applications Conducting CVC Transactions

The creators of a CVC sometimes issue (or "pre-mine") a certain number of CVC units in advance and then either distribute those units as payment for goods or services or repayment of obligations (such as amounts owed to project investors), or sell the units against currency, funds or another type of CVC once a market is established. To the extent that a person mines CVC and uses it solely to purchase goods or services on its own behalf, the person is not an MSB under FinCEN regulations, because these activities involve neither acceptance nor transmission of the CVC within the regulatory definition of money transmission services. However, if a person mines CVC and uses it to engage in money transmission, such person will be subject to FinCEN's registration, reporting, monitoring, and recordkeeping regulations for MSBs, as is the case with all money transmitters.[86]

5.4. CVC Money Transmission Performed by Mining Pools and Cloud Miners

In certain cases, persons (pool members) combine their computer processing resources to form a mining pool to enhance their chances of receiving a reward by being the first ones to verify the authenticity of a block of transactions denominated in CVC. A block reward would entitle them to receive consistent payouts, which are fees paid by the parties to a transaction for the service of authenticating its individual CVC transmission. Mining pools may be managed by a controlling person (centralized mining pools) or they may operate on a P2P basis (decentralized

---

85. *See* FIN-2014-R007, "Application of Money Services Business Regulations to the Rental of Computer Systems for Mining Virtual Currency," Apr. 29, 2014.

86. *See* FIN-2014-R001, "Application of FinCEN's Regulations to Virtual Currency Mining Operations," Jan. 30, 2014.

mining pools). In some centralized models, the person acting as the leader of the pool claims the total amount of CVC mined or received as fees from participants to the authenticated transactions. The leader then distributes this amount to the pool members in subsequent transfers, presumably in proportion to the computer processing provided, minus its own fee for managing the pool. In other centralized models, such as cloud mining, persons (contract purchasers) may purchase "mining contracts" from a seller of computer processing (the cloud miner) that grants these purchasers permission to use the cloud miner's computers to mine CVCs on the purchaser's behalf.

When the leader of the pool, the cloud miner, or the unincorporated organization or software agency acting on behalf of its owner/administrator transfer CVC to the pool members or contract purchasers to distribute the amount earned, this distribution does not qualify as money transmission under the BSA, as these transfers are integral to the provision of services (the authentication of blocks of transactions through the combined efforts of a group of providers, or through the equipment of the cloud miner). However, if the leader, the cloud miner, or the software agency combine their managing and renting services with the service of hosting CVC wallets on behalf of the pool members or contract purchasers, the leader, cloud miner, unincorporated organization or software agency, or the owner-administrator will fall under FinCEN's definition of money transmitter for engaging in account-based money transmission.

6. Available Resources

FinCEN expects that persons introducing innovative products or services to a highly regulated activity, such as money transmission, will ensure that the innovation complies with the regulatory framework applicable to such activity before the innovation is taken to market. Persons interested in determining whether a certain new activity or variation on an existing activity may subject them to FinCEN's regulatory requirements have several options for obtaining preliminary, general guidance or definitive regulatory interpretation.

Financial institutions with questions about this guidance, other guidance, administrative rulings or other matters related to compliance with the BSA and its implementing regulations may contact FinCEN's Resource Center Helpline at (800) 949-2732 or FRC@fincen.gov.

Persons requiring general information about the risk assessment, risk mitigation, recordkeeping, reporting, and transaction monitoring requirements applicable to money services businesses may consult the outreach material, including examiners' expectations about compliance contained in the Bank Secrecy Act / Anti- Money Laundering Examination Manual for Money Services Businesses (Dec. 2008).

For examples of previous interpretations on the application of FinCEN regulations to specific sets of facts and circumstances, interested persons may review the collection of guidance and administrative rulings.

Finally, in circumstances where neither the general and interpretive material available at FinCEN's public website, nor the information provided by FinCEN's Resource Center staff is sufficient to address the particulars of a situation, interested persons or their legal representatives may request FinCEN to provide individual guidance or an administrative ruling, by following the Requirements for Requesting an Administrative Ruling.[87]

Discussion Points

1. *Who can be a money transmitter?* Are developers who deploy the DApp money transmitters under the BSA? Why? Are peer to peer exchangers money transmitters? Why?

2. *Hosted vs. unhosted wallets.* Compare and contrast hosted and unhosted wallets. How does the intermediary's role in the case of a hosted wallet compare to an escrow agent? Is an intermediary an escrow agent with respect to a person's virtual currency? Why or why not?

3. *CVC kiosks.* CVC kiosks are CVC ATMs that enable the exchange of CVC for currency or other CVC. The owner-operator of a CVC kiosk which accepts and transmits CVC equivalent value is a money transmitter for receiving and dispensing real currency or CVC transactions. Should owners of CVC kiosks be required to follow FinCEN regulations? What are the benefits and what would be the drawbacks of requiring CVC kiosk owners to follow FinCEN regulations? How do these regulations protect consumers?

4. *Are DApp's safer for consumers?* Users of a DApp can interact through smart contracts without needing to reveal any personal identifiers. Do you think that DApps can increase the prevalence of fraud among CVCs? Should DApps be regulated? If so, by whom? Should DApps require the intervention of an intermediary?

---

87. *See also* 31 CFR §§ 1010.710–1010.717.

V. State Laws regarding Virtual Currencies

Every state's money transmitter law defines when an individual is a money transmitter. It is essential yet challenging for these virtual currency businesses to determine how these laws apply to virtual currency activities because almost all U.S. states have different approaches to money transmission licensing. Thus, a state-by-state analysis is necessary because some states may require that an individual get a license before they can engage in certain types of virtual currency activities. Many states provide additional clarity as to whether virtual currency is subject to regulation in their jurisdiction specifically. Below, there will be a discussion on the money transmitter laws in the states of Florida, New York, Pennsylvania, California, and others.

A. Florida

In August 2021, Florida's Office of Financial Regulation issued an industry alert stating that a person engaged in the business of selling virtual currency in Florida must obtain a license under its money transmission law. The Florida advisory is consistent with the holding in a Florida case, *State v. Espinoza*, which broadly interpreted its money transmitter statute. Florida maintains that selling virtual currency is subject to regulation.

However, on May 12, 2022, Governor Ron DeSantis signed bill CS/HB 273, which amends Florida's money services business laws to define virtual currency. The Bill takes effect in January 2023. Currently, "virtual currency" is not defined in Chapter 560. The Bill eases Florida's position on licensing requirements for virtual currency by stating that, "a money transmitter license is only required for persons acting as intermediaries between two parties if the intermediary has the unilateral ability to execute or prevent a transaction. Persons involved in a principal-to-principal, bilateral transaction are not subject to licensing."[41] This departs from Florida's current stance that requires money service business licensing for direct virtual currency sale and purchase transactions between two parties.

---

41. Carl A. Fornaris, *Florida Gov. Signs Bill that Defines 'Virtual Currency' and Eases Licensing Restrictions on Certain Virtual Currency Transactions in the State*, THE NATIONAL REVIEW, https://www.natlawreview.com/article/florida-gov-signs-bill-defines-virtual-currency-and-eases-licensing-restrictions (May 26, 2022).

Florida v. Espinoza
264 So. 3d 1055

District Court of Appeal of Florida, Third District (2019)

I. INTRODUCTION

The instant appeal concerns the application of Florida's statutes governing money services businesses and money laundering found in chapters 560 and 896 of the Florida Statutes, respectively, to alleged illicit transactions involving the virtual currency known as Bitcoin. At all times relevant, there was no mention of virtual currency nor of Bitcoin anywhere within the Florida Statutes. Both Espinoza and the State, as well as the amici, cite to various guidelines and regulations promulgated by the United States Department of the Treasury and other federal agencies to argue for or against the application of certain defined terms under section 560.103, Florida Statutes (2014), to virtual currency.

In 2014, the United States Department of the Treasury closely coordinated with the Financial Action Task Force ("FATF"), of which the United States is a leading member nation, to develop common definitions for virtual currency terms. The following definition for "virtual currency," which informs our decision, was proposed in a June 2014 report:

> Virtual currency is a digital representation of value that can be digitally traded and functions as (1) a medium of exchange; and/or (2) a unit of account; and/or (3) a store of value, but does not have legal tender status (i.e., when tendered to a creditor is a valid and legal offer of payment) in any jurisdiction.

See Financial Action Task Force, Virtual Currencies: Key Definitions and Potential AML/CFT Risks 4 (2014). The FATF Virtual Currencies Report identified and explained Bitcoin as follows:

> Bitcoin, launched in 2009, was the first decentralized convertible virtual currency, and the first cryptocurrency. Bitcoins are units of account composed of unique strings of numbers and letters that constitute units of the currency and have value only because individual users are willing to pay for them. Bitcoins are digitally traded between users with a high degree of anonymity and can be exchanged (purchased or cashed out) into US dollars and other fiat or virtual currencies. Anyone can download the free, open-source software from a website to send, receive, and store bitcoins and monitor Bitcoin transactions. Users can also obtain Bitcoin addresses, which function like accounts, at a Bitcoin exchanger or online wallet service. Transactions (fund flows) are publicly available in a shared transaction register and identified by the Bitcoin address, a string of letters and numbers that is not systematically linked to an individual. Bitcoin is capped at 21 million bitcoins (but each unit could be divided into smaller parts).

Id. This definition comports with that alleged in the arrest affidavit, which specifically stated that Bitcoin is:

> an electronic currency with no central authority and is not backed by any government. Bitcoins do not exist as discrete and unique single coins, but rather as balances of Bitcoins and Bitcoin portions. These balances exist as unique internet Bitcoin addresses contained in a public transportation ledger, called the "block chain." This ledger is maintained and verified by computers connected to the internet running the Bitcoin software. New Bitcoins are created at a predetermined rate and distributed to owners of those computers that are maintaining the ledger in a process referred to as "mining." The software is open source and can be installed by anyone who wishes to "mine" Bitcoins.

> To transfer some amount of Bitcoins, the spender directs that amount to be debited from the balance of his or her unique internet Bitcoin address and deposited to the balance of the receiver's unique Bitcoin address. This is frequently done through the use of wallet applications. The transaction is then verified by the miners to confirm that the correct keys were used and then it is added to the block chain. This prevents double spending because once the balance moves to a new unique address, a different private key becomes associated with it.

> Bitcoins can be transferred both in person and over the internet and are readily convertible to most world currencies. Exchanges exist that allow people to buy or sell Bitcoins with or for local currencies including United States dollars.

> …Bitcoins can also be used to purchase a variety of goods and services directly. Restaurants, coffee shops and cosmetic surgery clinics in Miami-Dade County accept Bitcoins for goods and services.

During the time leading up to the State's filing of the information, Espinoza was operating an unlicensed cash-for-bitcoins business. Espinoza came to the attention of law enforcement by way of an advertisement he posted on the internet for his services under the name "Michelhack." During four separate meetings with an undercover law enforcement agent, Espinoza agreed to trade bitcoins in exchange for cash. During their initial encounter, the undercover agent made clear to Espinoza his desire to remain anonymous. Espinoza agreed to engage in these transactions even though the agent intimated to Espinoza that this cash was derived from engaging in illegal activity and that he was planning to use the bitcoins to engage in further illegal activity. Against this backdrop, we apply the Florida Statutes and rules of procedure as they existed at the time of the alleged conduct to the facts of this case to determine whether the trial court erred in dismissing the information filed against Espinoza.

II. FACTUAL BACKGROUND AND PROCEDURAL HISTORY

On December 4, 2013, Detective Arias of the Miami Beach Police Department, working in conjunction with Special Agent Ponzi from the United States Secret Service's Miami Electronic Crimes Task Force ("Task Force"), accessed the Internet ebsite https://localbitcoins.com seeking to purchase Bitcoin. This website is a directory of buyers and sellers of bitcoins and lists the traders closest to the user's location. Users may search for sellers who will sell bitcoins online or in person for United States currency. Detective Arias discovered multiple individuals advertising the sale of bitcoins for United States currency in the Miami-Dade area including a user utilizing the username Michelhack, who was later identified as Espinoza. Michelhack's posting stated:

Contact Hours: anytime

Meeting preferences: Starbucks, internet café, restaurant, mall or bank

You will need to bring your wallet in your smartphone for the address the bitcoins will be deposited to

If you want to have local bitcoins escrow service I will have to add 1% to the final price

You will pay with cash in person

Call or text (XXX) XXX-8649 for further information

I will meet you in person for this transaction

Detective Arias, acting in an undercover capacity as an interested buyer, contacted the number listed in the advertisement for Michelhack via text message and requested a meeting in Miami Beach in order to exchange U.S. currency (cash) for bitcoins. The next day, Detective Arias met Espinoza at Nespresso Café located at 1105 Lincoln Road, Miami Beach, FL (the "first transaction"). At this meeting, which was observed and recorded by undercover supporting agents, Detective Arias paid Espinoza $500 in cash and received 0.40322580 bitcoins valued at $416.12. Espinoza earned a fee or profit of $83.67.

During the course of the first transaction, Detective Arias made clear his desire to remain anonymous and implied to Espinoza that he was involved in illicit activity. He made clear to Espinoza that he "did not want to have to provide a name or personal identification information to a bank or financial institution in order to conduct financial transactions." While not expressly representing to Espinoza that the $500 was the proceeds of an illegal transaction, Detective Arias certainly implied as much in that he told Espinoza, "since Liberty Reserve was shut down, I need a new way to 'pay for things.'" Espinoza "[a]cknowledged that he was familiar with Liberty Reserve," which "was a digital currency that was used for illicit transactions." Detective Arias further explained that "the people I do business with don't take credit cards" to which Espinoza replied "obviously." Based on their conversation, Detective Arias believed Espinoza was under the impression Detective Arias was himself involved in illicit criminal activity. In addition, Espinoza explained to Detective Arias how he makes money trading Bitcoin.

On January 10, 2014, Detective Arias contacted Espinoza and arranged to meet at an ice cream store in Miami Beach (the "second transaction"). During the course of the second transaction, Espinoza told Detective Arias he had multiple "Bitcoin wallets" that he used to store and transfer bitcoins. Detective Arias told Espinoza that he was in the business of buying stolen credit card numbers from Russian sellers, and that he needed the bitcoins to pay for those stolen credit card numbers. Detective Arias also told Espinoza he would be willing to trade stolen credit card numbers for bitcoins at their next transaction. Espinoza replied that he would "think about it." Espinoza then transferred one bitcoin to Detective Arias' Bitcoin address in exchange for $1000. Special Agent Ponzi calculated Espinoza's fee or profit for this second transaction to be approximately $167.56.

On January 27, 2014, Detective Arias searched databases for the Florida Office of Financial Regulation ("OFR") and the United States Department of the Treasury Financial Crimes Enforcement Network ("FinCEN") to determine whether Espinoza was registered as a "money services business." The search revealed that Espinoza was not registered in either database. Three days later, Detective Arias contacted Espinoza to arrange another transaction (the "third transaction"). Communicating exclusively through text messages, Detective Arias inquired of Espinoza how quickly the transaction could be completed stating, "How fast will u (sic) send me the [bitcoin] cuz (sic) my Russian buddies won't send me my [stuff] until they get the coin." Detective Arias then deposited $ 500 into Espinoza's Citibank bank account and provided Espinoza with Detective Arias' Bitcoin address. Espinoza then electronically transferred 0.54347826 bitcoins to Detective Arias' Bitcoin address.

After Detective Arias received the Bitcoin transfer, he texted Espinoza asking if he was able to "step it up next week." Espinoza replied, "OK. Sure. Let me know how many." Thereafter, Detective Arias negotiated the transfer of an additional $ 30,000 worth of bitcoins for a new batch of stolen credit card numbers Detective Arias represented to Espinoza to have been acquired from a recent data breach (the "fourth transaction"). On February 6, 2014, Detective Arias met Espinoza in the lobby of a Miami Beach hotel with the dual intent of conducting the fourth transaction and effectuating Espinoza's arrest. Detective Arias led Espinoza upstairs to a hotel room, which the Task Force had previously wired for audio and video surveillance to observe and record the transaction.

However, when Detective Arias produced a "flash roll" purportedly containing the $30,000 in $100 bills, Espinoza grew concerned the funds were counterfeit—which they, in fact, were. Espinoza inspected the bills and suggested either depositing a portion of the $30,000 into a bank or for Detective Arias to return with smaller denominations in order to verify the authenticity of the flash roll. Espinoza remained ready and willing to consummate the entire transaction, his only hesitation being with regard to the authenticity of the $30,000 in cash. Shortly thereafter, Detective Arias gave a signal and Espinoza was taken into custody without incident.

Just over a month following the fourth transaction, the State charged Espinoza, via information, with one count of unlawfully engaging "in the business of money transmitter while not being registered as a money transmitter or authorized vendor" in violation of sections 560.125(1) and (5)(a), Florida Statutes (2013) (Count 1) and two counts of money laundering, in violation of sections 896.101(3) and 896.101(5) (a) and (b), Florida Statutes (2014) (Counts 2 and 3). At the hearing below, the State orally amended the information to include a payment instrument seller. Espinoza moved to dismiss the information pursuant to Florida Rule of Criminal Procedure 3.190(c)(4) contending that the undisputed facts do not establish a prima facie case of guilt against him.

After Espinoza's arrest, the Legislature amended section 560.125(1) to include the following language: "A deferred presentment transaction conducted by a person not authorized to conduct such transaction under this chapter is void, and the unauthorized person has no right to collect, receive, or retain any principal, interest, or charges relating to such transaction." See § 560.125(1), Fla. Stat. (2014). Accordingly, the State charged Espinoza under the prior version of the statute.

More specifically, Espinoza argued as to Count 1 that Bitcoin does not qualify as "money transmitting" under section 560.125, because Bitcoin is not "money" under the statute. Espinoza argued as to Counts 2 and 3 that Bitcoin does not fall under the definition of a "financial transaction" or "monetary instrument" under Florida's Money Laundering Act. In response, the State filed a traverse as to Count 1 and moved to strike Espinoza's motion as to Counts 2 and 3. After a hearing, the trial court entered an order granting Espinoza's motion to dismiss the information in its entirety. The trial court agreed with Espinoza that neither Bitcoin nor his conduct with respect thereto fall within the ambit of chapter 560 requiring registration as a money services business. As to Counts 2 and 3, the trial court disagreed with Espinoza and found instead that the conduct at issue qualifies as a financial transaction but, nonetheless, granted the motion on the basis Espinoza lacked the requisite intent to be guilty of money laundering. This timely appeal followed.

Espinoza did not cross-appeal the trial court's finding that his conduct involving Detective Arias and Bitcoin constituted a financial transaction within the ambit of Chapter 896, Florida's Money Laundering Act.

III. JURISDICTION

Pursuant to section 924.07(1)(a), Florida Statutes (2016), and Florida Rule of Appellate Procedure 9.140(c)(1)(A), the State is permitted to appeal the trial court's order dismissing the information. See Fla. R. App. P. 9.140(c)(1)(A) ("The state may appeal an order [] dismissing an indictment or information or any count thereof ....."; see also § 924.07(1)(a) (using identical language as that found in Rule 9.140(c)(1)(A) to grant the State a right to appeal a trial court's order dismissing an information).

The State's appeal is timely because the notice of appeal was filed within "15 days of rendition of the order to be reviewed." Fla. R. App. P. 9.140(c)(3). Accordingly, this Court has jurisdiction to review the instant appeal under Florida Rule of Appellate Procedure 9.140(c)(1)(A). See *State v. Jiborn*, 135 So.3d 364, 365 n.2 (Fla. 5th DCA 2014) (explaining that "[a]ppellate review is authorized pursuant to Rule 9.140(c)(1)(A)" to consider the State's appeal of the trial court's order granting the motion to dismiss the amended information).

IV. STANDARD OF REVIEW

The standard of review for a trial court's order based on statutory interpretation is *de novo*. See *Mendenhall v. State*, 48 So.3d 740, 747 (Fla. 2010). Further, the standard of review for a trial court's order regarding a Rule 3.190(c)(4) motion to dismiss is *de novo*. See *Knipp v. State*, 67 So.3d 376, 378 (Fla. 4th DCA 2011) (citing *State v. Santiago*, 938 So.2d 603, 605 (Fla. 4th DCA 2006)); see also *State v. Walthour*, 876 So.2d 594, 595 (Fla. 5th DCA 2004) (citing *Bell v. State*, 835 So.2d 392 (Fla. 2d DCA 2003)).

V. ANALYSIS

Pursuant to Florida Rule of Criminal Procedure 3.190(c)(4), an individual is permitted to file a motion to dismiss an information or indictment on grounds that "[t]here are no material disputed facts and the undisputed facts do not establish a prima facie case of guilt against the defendant." A Rule 3.190(c)(4) motion to dismiss in criminal cases is treated like a summary judgment motion in civil cases and should be sparingly granted. See *State v. Nunez*, 881 So.2d 658, 660 (Fla. 3d DCA 2004) (citation omitted); see also *State v. Bonebright*, 742 So.2d 290, 291 (Fla. 1st DCA 1998) (explaining that a Rule 3.190(c)(4) motion to dismiss is "analogous to a motion for summary judgment in a civil case" and that "[b]oth should be granted sparingly" (citation omitted)).

A. Unlicensed Money Services Business (Count 1)

The issue for our determination under Count 1 is whether, based on the undisputed facts, Espinoza was acting as a payment instrument seller or engaging in the business of a money transmitter, either of which require registration as a money services business under Florida law. Given the plain language of the Florida statutes governing money service businesses and the nature of Bitcoin and how it functions, Espinoza was acting as both. Section 560.125, Florida Statutes (2013), provides, in pertinent part, as follows:

(1) A person may not engage in the *business of a money services business* or deferred presentment provider in this state unless the person is licensed or exempted from licensure under this chapter.

   . . . .

(5) A person who violates this section, if the violation involves:

> (a) Currency or payment instruments exceeding $ 300 but less than $ 20,000 in any 12-month period, commits a felony of the third degree, punishable as provided in s. 775.082, s. 775.083, or s. 775.084.

(emphasis added). A "money services business" is defined as "any person ... who acts as a *payment instrument seller*, foreign currency exchanger, check casher, or *money transmitter*." § 560.103(22), Fla. Stat. (2014) (emphasis added). The Florida Legislature has defined a "payment instrument seller" in this section as "a corporation, limited liability company, limited liability partnership, or foreign entity qualified to do business in this state which sells a payment instrument." § 560.103(30). Moreover, a "payment instrument" is "a check, draft, warrant, money order, travelers check, electronic instrument, *or other instrument, payment of money, or monetary value whether or not negotiable*." § 560.103(29) (emphasis added). "Monetary value" means *a medium of exchange, whether or not redeemable in currency.* § 560.103(21) (emphasis added). The Legislature has further defined a "money transmitter" as:

> [A] corporation, limited liability company, limited liability partnership, or foreign entity qualified to do business in this state which receives *currency, monetary value, or payment instruments* for the purpose of transmitting the same by any means, including transmission by wire, facsimile, electronic transfer, courier, the Internet, or through bill payment services or other businesses that facilitate such transfer within this country, or to or from this country.

§ 560.103(23) (emphasis added).

Espinoza does not dispute that he was not licensed to act as a money services business in the State of Florida. Rather, Espinoza contends his transactions with Detective Arias do not qualify as such on the grounds that (1) Bitcoin is not "money" or "monetary value" for purposes of the statutes governing money services businesses; (2) "money," "monetary value" and "funds" under chapter 560 should be interpreted to mean "currency" and neither Bitcoin nor bitcoins are currency; (3) because Espinoza was merely a seller of bitcoins, his conduct does not meet the statutory definition of being a money transmitter or payment instrument seller; (4) section 560.125 requires the transmission of money to a third-party or location and that did not occur here; and, (5) applying section 560.125 to Espinoza's conduct would violate his due process rights. These arguments ignore the plain meaning of the words used in the statutes. Inasmuch, Espinoza urges this court to apply the statutes as he wishes they were written instead of how they actually are written. We decline to do so.

Espinoza is charged in Count 1 with engaging "in the business of money transmitter while not being registered as a money transmitter" in violation of section 560.125 governing money services businesses. Pursuant to section 560.103(22), a "'money services business' means any person...who acts as a payment instrument seller ...." We need not look beyond the plain and unambiguous language of section 560.103 to conclude Espinoza acted as a "payment instrument seller" when he transferred bitcoins from one of his online bitcoin wallets to Detective Arias' online bitcoin address in exchange for cash in U.S. dollars.

There is no dispute that Bitcoin does not expressly fall under the definition of "currency" found in section 560.103(11). However, Bitcoin *does* fall under the definition of a "payment instrument." See § 560.103(29). Included in the definition of a payment instrument is "monetary value," which is defined as "a medium of exchange, whether or not redeemable in currency." §§ 560.103(21), (29). According to the arrest affidavit and the FATF Virtual Currency Report, referenced above, bitcoins are redeemable for currency. Espinoza does not argue to the contrary. Similarly, Bitcoin and bitcoins function as a "medium of exchange." See § 560.103(21).

Section 560.103(11) defines "currency" as:

[T]he coin and paper money of the United States or of any other country which is designated as legal tender and which circulates and is customarily used and accepted as a medium of exchange in the country of issuance. Currency includes United States silver certificates, United States notes, and Federal Reserve notes. Currency also includes official foreign bank notes that are customarily used and accepted as a medium of exchange in a foreign country.

The transactions at issue illustrate this point. Espinoza's own expert testified there were several restaurants in the Miami area that accept bitcoins as a form of payment, as well as a prominent Miami plastic surgeon, and conceded he was paid in bitcoins for his expert services in this case. Further, Espinoza was not merely selling his own personal bitcoins, he was marketing a business on https://localbitcoins.com. The service being marketed was the exchange of cash for bitcoins. Espinoza's posting expressly stated: "You will pay with cash in person" and "You will need to bring your wallet in your smartphone for the address the bitcoins will be deposited to."

Apart and aside from the plain language of the statute, the Florida OFR, the Florida state agency charged with regulation under chapter 560, has concluded a business offering a service "where a Coinbase user sends fiat currency to another Coinbase user to buy bitcoins" was subject to regulation thereunder. See In re Coinbase, Inc., Case No. 62670 (Fla. OFR November 13, 2015) (available from the agency clerk); see also § 560.105, Fla. Stat. (2014) (empowering the Office of Financial Regulation to regulate money services businesses). Like the Coinbase user, Detective

Arias paid cash to Espinoza to buy bitcoins. Like the Florida OFR with respect to the Coinbase user, we conclude Espinoza was required to register under chapter 560.

In addition to claiming he is not a payment instrument seller, Espinoza asserts Bitcoin does not qualify as "money" or "monetary value" for purposes of being a "money transmitter." He argues the Florida Legislature could not have contemplated the application of section 560.125 to virtual currencies when the statute was enacted. As such, Bitcoin cannot be considered currency because it is not legal tender on the basis that the terms "money" and "monetary value" are considered synonymous with the term "currency." They are not.

However, we need not consider legislative intent because section 560.103 is clear and unambiguous. Any assertion that "monetary value" is synonymous with "currency" overlooks the express language contained in section 560.103(21) which states that monetary value is "a medium of exchange, whether or not redeemable in currency." Espinoza's interpretation overlooks the "statutory tenet that courts should avoid readings that would render part of a statute meaningless." *Koile v. State*, 934 So.2d 1226, 1233 (Fla. 2006) (citing *Forsythe v. Longboat Key Beach Erosion Control Dist.*, 604 So.2d 452, 456 (Fla. 1992)). In addition, Espinoza's interpretation, which we decline to adopt, compelling that "monetary value" be synonymous with "currency" would render section 560.103(21) meaningless.

As a further grounds for dismissal, Espinoza argued, and the trial court concluded, that he did not qualify as a "money transmitter" because he did not receive currency, monetary value, or payment instruments for the purpose of transmitting the same to a third party. However, nothing contained within the definition of "money transmitter" under section 560.103(23) includes, explicitly or impliedly, the words "to a third party." The trial court reasoned that a "money transmitter" would necessarily operate like a middleman in a financial transaction, much like how Western Union accepts money from person A, and at the direction of person A, transmits it to person or entity B.

Chapter 560 defines a "money services business" as "any person" who "acts as a . . . money transmitter." § 560.103(22). "Money transmitter" is then defined as an entity "which receives currency, monetary value, or payment instruments for the purpose of *transmitting the same by any means*, including transmission by wire, facsimile, electronic transfer, courier, the Internet, or through bill payment services." § 560.103(23) (emphasis added). The statute's plain language clearly contains no third party transmission requirement in order for an individual's conduct to fall under the "money transmitter" definition. As such, we decline to add any third party or "middleman" requirement to the money transmitter definition found in section 560.103(23). See *Seagrave v. State*, 802 So.2d 281, 287 (Fla. 2001) ("[I]t is a basic principle of statutory construction that courts 'are not at liberty to add words to statutes that were not placed there by the Legislature.'" (quoting *Hayes v. State*, 750 So.2d 1, 4 (Fla. 1999))).

In contrast, the federal definition of "money transmitter" *does* include a third party transmission requirement. See 31 C.F.R. § 1010.100(ff)(5)(i)(A) (2014) (outlining that a "money transmitter" under federal law means a person engaged in the "acceptance of currency, funds, or other value that substitutes for currency from one person and the transmission of currency, funds, or other value that substitutes for currency to *another location or person* by any means" (emphasis added)). Thus, if our Legislature had intended the unambiguous language of section 560.103(23) to include the limiting words "to a third party," it would have included them. See *State v. Debaun*, 129 So.3d 1089, 1095 (Fla. 3d DCA 2013) ("[C]ourts may not invade the province of the legislature and add words which change the plain meaning of the statute." (citation omitted)).

Here, it is undisputed that Espinoza received currency (cash in U.S. dollars) for the purpose of transmitting monetary value or payment instruments (Bitcoin, which qualifies as both) by means of the Internet or other businesses that facilitate such transfer. However, the trial court imposed a bilateral limitation on the statutory definition of "money transmitter" not present in the statute. Under its reading, the phrase "transmitting the same by any means" would require Espinoza to both receive and transmit the same form of currency, monetary value or payment instrument for a transaction to fall within the ambit of section 560.103(23). In other words, if Espinoza received currency, he would have to transmit currency; if he received monetary value, he would have to transmit monetary value; and if he received a payment instrument, he would have to transmit a payment instrument. We disagree with this limitation.

The phrase "the same" modifies the list of payment methods or forms of value that includes "currency, monetary value, or payment instruments." The use of the word "or" is in the disjunctive and, as such, any of the three qualifies interchangeably on either side of the transaction. To hold otherwise, which would necessitate that the types of traditionally recognized money transmitting businesses, such as the trial court's Western Union example, receive only cash in order to transfer cash, would insert an additional requirement into the statute that is not presently there. Inasmuch, the ability of a customer to use a credit card, personal check, or cashier's check as a means of payment for the transfer of cash using the services of a Western Union-type money transmitting business would be impermissible under the trial court's reading of section 560.103(23). The difference between the trial court's Western Union example and the conduct at issue herein is that traditional Western Union-type money services businesses are registered as such with the Florida OFR. Espinoza's bitcoins-for-cash business is not.

In *United States v. Murgio*, 209 F.Supp.3d 698, 704–05 (S.D.N.Y. 2016), a case involving the Florida statutes applicable here, the United States Government alleged that the defendant, Murgio, operated and conspired to operate Coin.mx, a Bitcoin exchange, as an unlicensed money transmitting business in violation of federal and Florida law. The Government's allegations stemmed from an alleged scheme to bribe the chairman of the board of a federal credit union in order to hide the illegal nature of Coin.mx. *Id.* at 705. The Government alleged that "Murgio and his co-conspirators attempted to shield the true nature of his Bitcoin exchange business by operating through several front companies, including one known as 'Collectables Club,' to convince financial institutions that Coin.mx was just a members-only association of individuals interested in collectable items, like stamps and sports memorabilia." *Id.*

However, the district court rejected Murgio's argument that bitcoins are not covered by Florida's definition of "money transmitter" on the basis that they are not "currency, monetary value, or payment instruments" under Florida law. *Id.* at 712. In so doing, it reasoned that because bitcoins function as a "medium of exchange, whether or not redeemable in currency," they fall within Florida's express definitions of "monetary value" and "payment instruments." *Id.* (explaining that "[b]ecause bitcoins are 'monetary value,' they are also 'payment instruments'").

The district court further rejected Murgio's invocation of the rule of lenity, as do we, as a valid basis to decline application of chapter 560's definition of "monetary value" or "payment instrument" to bitcoins "because there is no statutory ambiguity here." *Id.* It reasoned that "the rule of lenity is particularly inapt in the context of Chapter 560, given that Bitcoin's raison d'être is to serve as a form of payment." *Murgio*, 209 F.Supp.3d at 712 (citing *Getting started with Bitcoin*, Bitcoin, https://bitcoin. org/en/getting-started (last visited Sept. 16, 2016)).

We agree with the district court's conclusion in *Murgio* that "there is no plausible interpretation of 'monetary value' or 'payment instruments,' as those terms are used in Chapter 560 that would place bitcoins outside of the statute's ambit." *Id.* at 713. See also *United States v. Faiella*, 39 F.Supp.3d 544, 545 (S.D.N.Y. 2014) (finding that Bitcoin clearly qualifies as "money" or "funds" for purposes of the federal money transmitter statute because "Bitcoin can be easily purchased in exchange for ordinary currency, acts as a denominator of value, and is used to conduct financial transactions" (citing *SEC v. Shavers*, No. 4:13-CV-416, 2013 WL 4028182, at *2 (E.D. Tex. Aug. 6, 2013))).

Murgio was decided after the trial court rendered its decision and during the pendency of this appeal and, as a result, the *Murgio* court was able to—and did—acknowledge and discuss the trial court's opinion. 209 F.Supp.3d at 713. It noted the trial court limited its discussion to "currency" and "payment instruments" and "did not contemplate the possibility that bitcoins qualify as "monetary value." *Id.* The district court further noted some factual differences between the conduct alleged in *Murgio* and in the instant case. *Id.* However, we do not find those differences dispositive given the standard applicable to the trial court's—and our—review of a Rule 3.190(c)(4) motion under the Florida Rules of Criminal Procedure. *Id.* at 714.

The defendant in *Faiella* was charged, in connection with the operation of an underground market in Bitcoin, with one count of operating an unlicensed money transmitting business in violation of 18 U.S.C. § 1960 (2012). *Faiella*, 39 F.Supp.3d at 545. The defendant argued that Bitcoin did not qualify as "money" under federal law. *Id.* at 545. The district court rejected that assertion and found that Bitcoin qualifies as "money" where the plain meaning of that term is "something generally accepted as a medium of exchange, a measure of value, or a means of payment." *Id.* (quoting *Money*, Merriam-Webster's Collegiate Dictionary (11th ed. 2009)). Similarly, because Bitcoin unambiguously serves as a "medium of exchange," it necessarily qualifies as "monetary value" for purposes of sections 560.125(1) and 560.125(5)(a).

In another recent case, the United States Supreme Court examined the definition of "money remuneration" in *Wisconsin Cent. Ltd. v. United States*, -- U.S. ---, 138 S.Ct. 2067, 201 L.Ed.2d 490 (2018). Specifically, *Wisconsin Cent. Ltd.* concerned whether stock options qualified as "money remuneration" under the Railroad Retirement Tax Act of 1937. *Id.* at 2070. Looking to the ordinary meaning of the words at the time Congress enacted the statute, the United States Supreme Court ultimately concluded that stock options did not fall under the definition of "money remuneration." *Id.* at 2074–75 ("The problem with the government's and the dissent's position today is not that stock and stock options weren't common in 1937, but that they were not then—and are not now—recognized as mediums of exchange."). However, the Court recognized that, although a statute's meaning is fixed at the time of enactment, "new applications may arise in light of changes in the world." *Id.* at 2074. Thus, the Court further held that "'money,' as used in this statute, must always mean a 'medium of exchange.' But what *qualifies* as a 'medium of exchange' may depend on the facts of the day." *Id.* Although Bitcoin did not exist at the time the registration requirements of chapter 560 were enacted, Bitcoin undoubtedly qualifies as a "medium of exchange" and Espinoza's bitcoins-for-cash business requires him to register as a payment instrument seller and money transmitter under chapter 560.

Finally, Espinoza argues that his conduct is even farther removed from what could be contemplated by the Florida money services statutes than the final order entered in *In re Petition for Declaratory Statement Moon, Inc.*, Case No. 59166 (Fla. OFR Apr. 6, 2015) (available from agency clerk). This is not the case. Moon, Inc., sought an opinion from the Florida OFR whether its business would require licensing under Florida law. *Id.* Moon's business plan contemplated the establishment of a Bitcoin kiosk utilizing an existing Florida licensed money services business that would process Bitcoin transactions. *Id.* A Moon customer would give U.S. dollars to the money services business in exchange for a PIN (personal identification number). *Id.* The customer would enter the PIN into one of Moon's kiosks. The kiosk would then initiate a transfer of bitcoins from an address owned by Moon. *Id.* Once the PIN is redeemed, the money services business would then pay Moon. *Id.*

In opining that Moon's proposed business activities did not fall within Florida's money transmitting licensing statutes, the Florida OFR found that Moon was not receiving currency, monetary value, or payment instruments for the purpose of transmitting same. *In re Petition for Declaratory Statement Moon, Inc.*, Case No. 59166 (Fla. OFR Apr. 6, 2015) (available from agency clerk). Rather, Moon merely facilitated the transfer of bitcoins through the use of a licensed money services business. *Id.* Here, no licensed money services business was utilized in the exchange of U.S. dollars for bitcoins that occurred between Espinoza and Detective Arias. As such, we find Moon's activities patently different from those engaged in by Espinoza.

First, Moon's customers' initial contact and deposit of U.S. dollars were with a licensed money services business. Second, the PIN provided by the licensed money services business to Moon's customers provided a mechanism by which the exchange of U.S. dollars for bitcoins could be identifiable and traceable to a specific customer and transaction, a scenario far different from the anonymity provided by the transactions conducted between Detective Arias and Espinoza.

The FATF Virtual Currency Report notes that:

[d]ecentralised systems are particularly vulnerable to anonymity risks. For example, by design, Bitcoin addresses, which function as accounts, have no names or other customer identification attached, and the system has no central server or service provider. The Bitcoin protocol does not require or provide identification and verification of participants or generate historical records of transactions that are necessarily associated with real world identity. There is no central oversight body and no AML [anti-money laundering] software currently available to monitor and identify suspicious transaction patterns. Law enforcement cannot target one central location or entity (administrator) for investigative or asset seizure purposes (although authorities can target individual exchangers for client information that the exchanger may collect). It thus offers a level of potential anonymity impossible with traditional credit and debit cards or older online payment systems, such as PayPal."

FATF, *supra*, at 9.

B. Money Laundering (Counts 2 and 3)

"As this court on more than one occasion has stated, the purpose of a Rule 3.190(c)(4) motion is to test the legal sufficiency of the charges brought by the State, it is not to require the State to demonstrate that it will secure a conviction at trial." *State v. Yaqubie*, 51 So.3d 474, 479 (Fla. 3d DCA 2010). Accordingly, this Court has consistently held that a Rule 3.190(c)(4)"motion to dismiss should be granted only where the most favorable construction to the State would not establish a prima facie case of guilt. And if there is any evidence upon which a reasonable jury could find guilt, such a motion must be denied." *State v. Terma*, 997 So.2d 1174, 1177 (Fla. 3d DCA 2008) (quoting *State v. McQuay*, 403 So.2d 566, 567–68 (Fla. 3d DCA 1981)).

Further, when considering a motion to dismiss pursuant to Rule 3.190(c)(4), the trial court may not make factual determinations, weigh conflicting evidence, or consider the credibility of witnesses. See *State v. Ortiz*, 766 So.2d 1137, 1142 (citing *State v. Fetherolf*, 388 So.2d 38, 39 (Fla. 5th DCA 1980)). "Even if the trial court doubts the sufficiency of the state's evidence, it cannot grant a motion to dismiss criminal charges simply because it concludes that the case will not survive a motion for a judgment of acquittal." *Id.* (quoting *State v. Paleveda*, 745 So.2d 1026, 1027 (Fla. 2d DCA 1999)).

On a Rule 3.190(c)(4) motion, the State is "entitled to the most favorable construction of the evidence with all inferences being resolved against the defendant." *Ortiz*, 766 So.2d at 1142. Rule 3.190(c)(4) levies no obligation on the State to pre-try its case; rather, the State is only required to provide sufficient facts to demonstrate that a reasonable jury could rule in its favor. See *State v. Arnal*, 941 So.2d 556, 558 (Fla. 3d DCA 2006). The State, in order to defeat a motion to dismiss, "need only specifically dispute a material fact alleged by the defendant or add additional material facts that meet the minimal requirement of a prima facie case." *State v. Kalogeropolous*, 758 So.2d 110, 112 (Fla. 2000). Thus, denial of the motion to dismiss is mandatory so long as a material fact is in dispute. *Id.* (citing *Boler v. State*, 678 So.2d 319, 323 (Fla. 1996)).

The State charged Espinoza with two counts of money laundering, in violation of sections 896.101(5)(b) and (5)(a), Florida Statutes (2014). The definition of "monetary instruments," which itself is used in the definition of "financial transaction," was amended by the Legislature to include the term "virtual currency" and became effective on July 1, 2017. See § 896.101(2)(f), Fla. Stat. (2017). However, the Legislature's subsequent amendment to this statute is irrelevant to our analysis as we are only considering the prior version that was in effect at the time of the transactions at issue here. Counts 2 and 3 state:

COUNT 2

And the aforesaid Assistant State Attorney, under oath, further information makes MICHELL ABNER ESPINOZA, on or about February 06, 2014, in the County and State aforesaid, did unlawfully conduct or attempt to conduct a financial transaction involving property or proceeds which an investigative or law enforcement officer, or someone acting under such officer's direction, represented as being derived from, or as being used to conduct or facilitate, specified unlawful activity, to wit: identity theft and/or credit card theft and/or violation of Chapter 817, when a person's conduct or attempted conduct was undertaken with the intent to promote the carrying on of said specified unlawful activity and/or avoid a transaction reporting requirement under state law, said financial transaction(s) totaling or exceeding $20,000 but less than $100,000 in the 12-month period ending February 6, 2014, in violation of s. 896.101(3) and s. 896.101(5)(b), Fla. Stat., contrary to the form of the Statute in such cases made and provided, and against the peace and dignity of the State of Florida.

COUNT 3

And the aforesaid Assistant State Attorney, under oath, further information makes MICHELL ABNER ESPINOZA, on or between December 05, 2013 and February 01, 2014, in the County and State aforesaid, did unlawfully, conduct or attempt to conduct a financial transaction involving property or proceeds which an investigative or law enforcement officer, or someone acting under such officer's direction, represented as being derived from, or as being used to conduct or facilitate, specified unlawful activity, to wit: identity theft and/or credit card theft and/or violation of Chapter 817, when a person's conduct or attempted conduct was undertaken with the intent to promote the carrying on of said specified unlawful activity and/or avoid a transaction reporting requirement under state law, said financial transaction(s) exceeding $300 but less than $20,000 in the 12 month period ending February 1, 2014, in violation of s. 896.101(3) and s. 896.101(5)(a), Fla. Stat., contrary to the form of the Statute in such cases made and provided, and against the peace and dignity of the State of Florida.

In response, Espinoza filed a sworn motion to dismiss wherein he incorporated his prior arguments as to Count 1 and further averred that the sale of bitcoins does not fall within the statutory definitions of "financial transactions" or "monetary instruments" under section 896.101. As such, Espinoza argued, his sale of bitcoins to Detective Arias does not constitute money laundering. The State moved to strike on the basis that a motion to dismiss a charge of money laundering is improper because money laundering requires "intent."

Section 896.101(3)(c) provides in part:

(3) It is unlawful for a person:

. . . .

(c) To conduct or attempt to conduct a financial transaction which involves property or proceeds which an investigative or law enforcement officer, or someone acting under such officer's direction, represents as being derived from, or as being used to conduct or facilitate, specified unlawful activity, *when the person's conduct or attempted conduct is undertaken with the intent*:

1. To promote the carrying on of specified unlawful activity;

(emphasis added). Clearly, the statute requires intent. Irrespective thereof, the trial court determined Espinoza lacked the necessary intent because, in its view, there was "no evidence that [Espinoza] did anything wrong, other than sell his Bitcoin to an investigator who wanted to make a case." However, "[k]nowledge is an ultimate question of fact and thus not subject to a motion to dismiss." See *Graves v. State*, 590 So.2d 1007, 1007 (Fla. 3d DCA 1991) (citations omitted); see also *Yaqubie*, 51 So.3d at 480 (explaining that intent and state of mind "is usually inferred from the circumstances surrounding the defendant's actions. Since the trier of fact has the opportunity to weigh the evidence and judge the credibility of the witnesses, it should determine intent or state of mind" (quoting *State v. Rogers*, 386 So.2d 278, 280 (Fla. 2d DCA 1980))). Accordingly, in dismissing the information, the trial court improperly decided a factual issue regarding Counts 2 and 3 in concluding Espinoza lacked the requisite intent under section 896.101(3)(c). See *State v. Book*, 523 So.2d 636, 638 (Fla. 3d DCA 1988) (holding that "intent or state of mind is not an issue to be decided on a motion to dismiss under Rule 3.190(c)(4)").

At the May 27, 2016 hearing, the testimony of Espinoza's own expert undercut defense counsel's reliance on FinCEN guidelines promulgated on March 18, 2013, when the expert testified that the FinCEN guidance meant "if somebody wanted to buy and sell Bitcoins as a business with the public that the person should register at the federal level as a money transmitter."

Further, the trial court made clear in its dismissal order that, among numerous other materials, it reviewed the arrest affidavit and depositions of Detective Arias in order to decide Espinoza's motion to dismiss. Detective Arias repeatedly told Espinoza about the illicit nature of his own activities, which formed the basis for his desire to trade the ill-gotten cash for bitcoins. This sworn testimony should have prompted the trial court to deny the motion to dismiss as to Counts 2 and 3. See *State v. Gutierrez*, 649 So.2d 926, 928 (Fla. 3d DCA 1995) ("On a motion to dismiss, if the affidavits and depositions filed in support of or in opposition to the motion create material disputed facts, it is improper for the trial court to determine factual issues and consider the weight of conflicting evidence or the credibility of witnesses." (citations omitted)).

Finally, while questioning—but stopping short of declaring unconstitutional on the basis of vagueness and/or overbreadth—Florida's money laundering statutes, the trial court concluded the State's case would not survive a motion for judgment of acquittal when it determined that there was "insufficient evidence as a matter of law that [Espinoza] committed any of the crimes as charged." However, the trial court is not permitted to grant a motion to dismiss based on serious doubts as to whether certain charges can survive a motion for judgment of acquittal. See *Ortiz*, 766 So.2d at 1142 ("Even if the trial court doubts the sufficiency of the state's evidence, it cannot grant a motion to dismiss criminal charges simply because it concludes that the case will not survive a motion for a judgment of acquittal." (quoting *Paleveda*, 745 So.2d at 1027)).

See *Williams v. State*, 154 So.3d 426, 428 (Fla. 4th DCA 2014) ("A motion for judgment of acquittal should be granted only when it is apparent that no legally sufficient evidence has been submitted under which a jury could find a verdict of guilty.").

VI. CONCLUSION

In conclusion, based on the foregoing, we reverse the trial court's order granting Espinoza's motion to dismiss the information and remand for further proceedings consistent with this opinion.

Reversed and remanded with instructions.

Discussion Points

1. *Did the court get it right?* Do you agree with the court's ruling? Why was Espinoza found to be a money transmitter? Did the court stretch the definition of "money transmitter" too far?

2. *Compare.* Compare the facts of *Espinoza* with those of *In re Petition for Declaratory Statement Moon, Inc.* How are they the same? How are they different?

3. *Should federal law predominate for money transmission?* Should federal money transmitter laws preempt state money transmitter laws and provide uniform definitions of "payment instruments" and "money transmitter"? Since one of the functions of money transmitter license requirements is to regulate interstate commerce, should Congress use its powers under the Commerce Clause of the federal Constitution to set uniform licensing requirements for individuals and businesses engaging in the transmission of cryptocurrency?

B. Pennsylvania

Pennsylvania has taken a different approach to regulating virtual currencies. The state issued guidance on what constitutes money under the Money Transmitter Act (MTA). The advisory states, "The MTA defines 'money' as 'currency or legal tender or any other product that is generally recognized as a medium of exchange.'"

Additionally, Pennsylvania law has defined money as "[l]awful money of the United States" and "[a] medium of exchange currently authorized or adopted by a domestic or foreign government."[42] Therefore, in Pennsylvania, only fiat currency or currency that is issued by the U.S. government is considered "money." Further, virtual currency has not been designated legal tender status, and in Pennsylvania, virtual currency is not considered money per the MTA.

---

42. Money Transmitter Act Guidance for Virtual Currency Business, https://www.dobs.pa.gov/Documents/Securities%20Resources/MTA%20Guidance%20for%20Virtual%20Currency%20Businesses.pdf.

Money Transmitter Act Guidance for
Virtual Currency Businesses

Pennsylvania Department of Banking and Securities (2019)

The Pennsylvania Department of Banking and Securities ("DoBS") has received multiple inquiries from entities engaged in various forms of virtual currency exchanges. As the DoBS will not be responding to these requests for guidance on a case-by-case basis, the DoBS is providing the following guidance on the applicability of the Money Transmission Business Licensing Law, otherwise known as the Money Transmitter Act ("MTA"), to virtual currency exchanges.

What Constitutes "Money" Under the MTA?

The MTA defines "money" as "currency or legal tender or any other product that is generally recognized as a medium of exchange." Additionally, Pennsylvania law has defined money as "[l]awful money of the United States" and "[a] medium of exchange currently authorized or adopted by a domestic or foreign government." See 1 Pa. C.S. §1991; see also 13 Pa. C.S. §1201(b)(24). Thus, only fiat currency, or currency issued by the United States government, is "money" in Pennsylvania. Virtual currency, including Bitcoin, is not considered "money" under the MTA. To date, no jurisdiction in the United States has designated virtual currency as legal tender.

When Is a Money Transmitter License Required
Under the MTA?

Section 2 of the MTA provides that "[n]o person shall engage in the business of transmitting money by means of a transmittal instrument for a fee or other consideration with or on behalf of an individual without first having obtained a license from the [DoBS]." 7 P.S.§6102. A "person" as defined in the MTA "includes an individual or an organization..." *Id.* at 6101(1). Although the "business of transmitting" is not defined in the MTA, the plain meaning of the word "transmit" is to "send or transfer from one person or place to another." See BLACK'S LAW DICTIONARY, 1499 (6th ed. 1990); 1 Pa. C.S. §1903(a). Thus, in order to "transmit" money under the MTA, fiat currency must be transferred with or on behalf of an individual to a 3rd party, and the money transmitter must charge a fee for the transmission.

Virtual Currency Trading Platforms

Several of the entities requesting guidance on the applicability of the MTA are web-based virtual currency exchange platforms ("Platforms"). Typically, these Platforms facilitate the purchase or sale of virtual currencies in exchange for fiat currency or other virtual currencies, and many Platforms permit buyers and sellers of virtual currencies to make offers to buy and/or sell virtual currencies from other users. These

Platforms never directly handle fiat currency; any fiat currency paid by or to a user is maintained in a bank account in the Platform's name at a depository institution.

Under the MTA, these Platforms are not money transmitters. The Platforms, while never directly handling fiat currency, transact virtual currency settlements for the users and facilitate the change in ownership of virtual currencies for the users. There is no transferring money from a user to another user or 3rd party, and the Platform is not engaged in the business of providing payment services or money transfer services.

Virtual Currency Kiosks, ATMs, and Vending Machines

Similarly, entities operating virtual currency kiosks, ATMs, and vending machines ("Kiosks") have also sought direction from the DoBS as to whether these entities would be "money transmitters" under the MTA. Some Kiosks are one-way systems which, for a transaction fee, dispense virtual currency in exchange for fiat currency, while others are two-way systems which, for a transaction fee, exchange both fiat currency for virtual currency and virtual currency for fiat currency. In both the one-way and two-way Kiosk systems, there is no transfer of money to any third party. The user of the Kiosk merely exchanges fiat currency for virtual currency and vice versa, and there is no money transmission. Thus, the entities operating the Kiosks would not be money transmitters under the MTA.

Discussion Points

1. *Money.* How does DoBS interpret the term "money"? Is a virtual currency trading platform considered to be a money transmitter? Why or why not?

2. *The presence of a third party.* Would the presence of a third party in the use of kiosks make an operating entity of a kiosk a money transmitter? Why or why not? What is significant about the presence of a third party in money transmission activities?

3. *Virtual currency as money.* Should virtual currency be considered money? What would be the regulatory and legal ramifications of considering virtual currency money?

C. Colorado

Interim Regulatory Guidance: Cryptocurrency and the
Colorado Money Transmitters Act

Colorado Department of Regulatory Agencies (September 20, 2018)

I. Purpose

This guidance outlines the Division of Banking's interpretation of the Colorado Money Transmitters Act (the "Act") as it relates to whether a person[1] or organization engaged in the business of buying, selling and/or facilitating the transfer of cryptocurrency within the state is required to be licensed as a money transmitter under Colorado law. Further, this document clarifies the definition of "money transmission" under the Act, and provides guidance as to the types of cryptocurrency transactions that fall within the scope of that definition.

This guidance does not amend the Act and is subject to change and/or withdrawal by the State Bank Commissioner or the State Banking Board. In addition, the Colorado guidance does not address applicable regulations, rules, or other guidance promulgated by the Financial Crimes Enforcement Network or other state regulators. Further, the Division cannot provide legal or business advice.

II. Background

A. Colorado Money Transmitters Act

The Act is a licensing statute, requiring persons engaged in the business of money transmission to obtain a license from the State Banking Board.[2]

The Act has been interpreted in accordance with the stated legislative directive, as follows:

> *It is declared to be the policy of this state that checks, drafts, money orders, or other instruments for the transmission or payment of credit or money are widely used by the people of this state as a process of settling accounts or debts and that sellers and issuers of the instruments receive, in the aggregate, large sums of money from the people of this state and it is therefore imperative that the integrity, experience, and financial responsibility and reliability of those engaged in the various types of businesses dealing in such instruments be above reproach. In order that the people of this state may be safeguarded from default in the*

---

1. A "person" means any natural person, firm, association, partnership, registered limited liability partnership, syndicate, joint stock company, unincorporated company or association, limited liability company, common law trust, or any corporation organized under the laws of the United States or of any state or territory of the United States or of any foreign country. § 11-110-103(14), C.R.S.

2. § 11-110-105, C.R.S.

payment of these instruments, it is necessary that proper regulatory authority be established through the banking board. Any person who sells or issues such instruments without complying with the provisions of Article 110 endangers the public interest.[3]

The Act seeks to protect consumers from defaults in the payments made through the transmission of money by requiring money transmitters to either post a surety bond or escrow securities.[4] The Act also sets forth application criteria for persons seeking licensure.[5] Further, the Act defines "money transmission" to mean:

The sale or issuance of exchange or engaging in the business of receiving money for transmission or transmitting money within the United States or to locations abroad by any and all means including but not limited to payment instrument, wire, facsimile, or electronic transfer.[6]

This definition identifies two actions that would constitute the practice of money transmission: (1) the sale or issuance of exchange, or (2) engaging in the business of receiving money for transmission or transmitting money within the United States or to locations abroad by any and all means. Thus, engaging in either of those actions would require a person to be licensed under the Act by the State Banking Board.

B. Cryptocurrencies

Cryptocurrencies, also referred to as virtual currencies, represent a means by which to electronically exchange value peer-to-peer. Cryptocurrency is a digital asset that is not recognized as legal tender; however, it may be used as a medium of exchange, a unit of account or a store of value, depending on its level of technological sophistication. Well-known cryptocurrencies such as Bitcoin, have been used as a medium of exchange based on widespread trading on secondary markets.

Markets for cryptocurrencies can be divided into two main categories: centralized and decentralized exchanges. Broadly speaking, the primary difference is that the former requires the user to surrender control of his or her cryptocurrency to a third party in order to place trades on the third party's platform, while the latter does not. At present, the exchanges with the highest average daily trading volume are centralized.

Generally, an exchange that offers fiat[7]-to crypto trading allows its users the ability to link their bank accounts in order to fund their exchange accounts with fiat

---

3. § 11-110-102, C.R.S.
4. § 11-110-108, C.R.S.
5. § 11-110-107, C.R.S.
6. § 11-110-103(11), C.R.S.
7. For purposes of this guidance, fiat currency references legal tender issued and backed by a government.

currency via automated clearing house or wire transfer, which they can then use to purchase cryptocurrencies. Likewise, a user wishing to liquidate his or her cryptocurrency holdings may sell them in exchange for fiat currency. In this way, these exchanges serve as digital on-ramps and off-ramps that allow users to move between fiat currency on the one hand and cryptocurrencies on the other.

Each of these exchanges allow for users to transfer cryptocurrency to any cryptocurrency wallet address within or outside of a particular trading exchange. Needing only the wallet address, a user can electronically transfer the cryptocurrency to another wallet.

III. Actions Requiring Licensure under the Act

A. Sale or Issuance of Exchange under the Act

The first action that would require licensure under the Act is the sale or issuance of "exchange."

The term "exchange" means any check, draft, money order, or other instrument for the transmission or payment of money or credit. It does not mean money or currency of any nation.[8] The terms check,[9] draft,[10] and money order[11] are well defined in statute, and constitute traditional instruments for the transmission or payment of money.

The term "other instrument for the transmission or payment of money or credit" is interpreted to include instruments with similar qualities as checks, drafts, and money orders. Those instruments would be limited to negotiable instruments ordering the payment of a fixed amount of money, payable to bearer or order on demand, or at a definite time.

With respect to a person in the business of buying, selling or facilitating the transfer of cryptocurrencies for transmission or payment, a license would not be required since the person is not engaged in the sale or issuance of a negotiable instrument, and therefore not engaged in money transmission.

---

8. §11-110-103(5), C.R.S.

9. A "check" means (i) a draft, other than a documentary draft, payable on demand and drawn on a bank, (ii) a cashier's check or teller's check, or (iii) a demand draft. An instrument may be a check even though it is described on its face by another term, such as "money order." §4-3-104((f), C.R.S.

10. A "draft" is a negotiable instrument that is an unconditional written order signed by the drawer directing another person to pay a certain sum of money on demand or at a definite time to a third person. §4-3-104(a) and (e), C.R.S.

11. A "money order" is a negotiable draft issued by an authorized entity to a purchaser, in lieu of a check, to be used to pay a debt or otherwise transmit funds upon the credit of the issuer. Black's Law Dictionary, 9th Ed. (2011).

B. Receiving Money for Transmission or Transmitting Money Within the United States or to Locations Abroad under the Act

The second action for which licensure under the Act would be required is:

engaging in the business of receiving money for transmission or transmitting money within the United States or to locations abroad by any and all means including but not limited to payment instrument, wire, facsimile, or electronic transfer.[12]

If a person is engaged in the business of transmitting money from one consumer to another within an exchange through the medium of cryptocurrency, that act would constitute money transmission and would be subject to licensure under the Colorado law.

IV. Conclusion

The Money Transmitters Act aims to regulate the transmission of money, meaning legal tender, and as noted, cryptocurrencies are not recognized as legal tender.

The direct transmission of cryptocurrency between two consumers is not subject to licensure under the Act.

With respect to transactions that involve a third party, the complete absence of fiat currency from a transmission from one consumer to another is not money transmission.

Conversely, the presence of fiat currency during a transmission may be subject to licensure under the Act.

State licensure would be required when:

- A person is engaged in the business of selling and buying cryptocurrencies for fiat currency; and
- A Colorado customer can transfer cryptocurrency to another customer within the exchange; and
- The exchange has the ability to transfer fiat currency through the medium of cryptocurrency.

If the person's business model has the ability to transfer fiat currency through the medium of cryptocurrency, the Division of Banking should be contacted at (303) 894-7575. The Division will individually analyze the entire course of a transmission to determine if licensure is required under the Money Transmitters Act, which is required before money transmission is conducted.

---

12. § 11-110-103(11), C.R.S.

D. Idaho

Series of No Action & Opinion Letters
Idaho Department of Finance (July 26, 2016)

July 26, 2016

Re: Money Transmitting—

Dear []:

The State of Idaho, Department of Finance (the "Department"), is in receipt of your letter dated July 21, 2016, responding to our inquiry of possible money transmission activities conducted by []. The Department would like to thank you for the quick response.

Based on the information you provided, it appears that [] is acting as a virtual currency "exchanger" that exchanges virtual currency for fiat currency. An exchanger that *sells its own inventory* virtual currency is generally not considered a virtual currency transmitter under the Idaho Money Transmitters Act. Alternatively, an exchanger that holds customer funds while arranging a satisfactory buy/sell order with a third party, and transmits virtual currency and fiat currency between buyer and seller, will typically be considered a virtual currency transmitter.

Given your representation that [] only transacted in limited amounts for Idaho consumers and those transactions were sourced from already-owned assets, the Department of Finance will take a no action position as to the licensing provisions of the Idaho Money Transmitters Act. The Department also fully understands your position of discontinuing bitcoin offerings to Idaho consumers, as of July 12, 2016. Should your business model change in the future to include currency transmission, do not hesitate to contact the Department for consultation on obtaining a money transmitter license to conduct business in Idaho.

Please feel free to contact me if you have questions. Sincerely,

Jeff Flora
Financial Examiner/Investigator
Idaho Department of Finance
800 Park Lane Suite 200
Boise, ID 83720
Jeff.flora@finance.idaho.gov
(208)332-8045

* * *

July 21, 2016

Via Email to Jeff.flora@finance.idaho.gov

Jeff Flora
Financial Examiner/Investigator
Idaho Department of Finance
800 Park Lane, Suite 200
Boise, ID 83720

Re:

Dear Mr. Flora,

This firm represents [] (the "**Company**"). We are in receipt of the Idaho Department of the Finance's (the "**Department**") letter dated July 7, 2016 inquiring about possible money transmission activities conducted by the Company.

The Company is a young start-up working in the virtual currency space. The Company offers its customers the ability to buy and sell virtual currency in exchange for USD. A customer is required to establish an account on the Company's website and provide certain identity information. Before the customer starts using the Company's buy/sell services, the customer must satisfactorily complete the Company's "know your customer" due diligence as required by its AML Program. The customer also provides their bank account or credit card information to the Company for the purpose of paying US' t" the Company for t"e purchase of digital currency. The Company then assists customers to either buy or sell virtual currency in return for USD.

The Company also provides hosted virtual currency wallets. The Company's digital wallets allow customers to store, send, receive, track and manage digital currency through the Company's website or mobile application. Wallet activity does not involve USD, and the Company does not otherwise maintain or transfer fiat currency balances for customers in or through their wallets. Consequently, there is no USD value attached to wallet activity.

The Company has reviewed its records and provides the following responses to your questions.

Are your cryptocurrency services offered or used by Idaho consumers and if so how long have your services been available?

The Company's services are not offered by Idaho consumers. However, the services have been used by Idaho consumers. The Company's first Idaho consumer account was created on June 11, 2015.

Do you currently have any Idaho consumers using your web site or mobile applications by buy, sell or transact cryptocurrency and if so how many customers and the total dollar amount of these transactions?

The Company has 30 Idaho consumer accounts, only two (2) of which have bought or sold virtual currency using the Company's services. A third Idaho consumer received a small amount of virtual currency (valued at US$2) through the Company as part of an awards program the consumer had with a separate entity. In each instance, the Company sourced the virtual currency from its already-owned assets. This means there was no third party involved in the transaction as would be expected where an exchange business is managing the transaction. The same is true of each instance where an Idaho consumer sold virtual currency. The Company paid the consumer USD and retained the purchased virtual currency as an asset. No third party was involved in the transaction. The total dollar value of all such transactions since June 11, 2015 is $386.23, which includes $13.31 in fees. The last transaction occurred on May 23, 2016.

Is your company relying on any exemptins from money transmitting regulations? If so please explain.

The regulatory landscape for virtual currencies has been in flux since its introduction. Virtual currency does not fit under the traditional definition of fiat currency, nor was it expressly included in most states' money transmission laws. This is beginning to change with the adoption of laws specific to bitcoin licensing or amendments to the existing money transmitter statutes that make clear a state's intent to regulate virtual currency exchanges.

The Company's belief that Ictivities in Idaho 'ere appropriate took several factors into consideration. The Company believed the definition of "payment instruments" under Idaho law was not broad enough to encompass virtual currencies. Also, it noted that "money" was not defined and believed it likely did not include virtual currency. This position would have been consistent with federal law which has not considered virtual currency to be legal tender. Additionally, the Company's transactions in Idaho were two party transactions, which the Company felt did not meet the typical meaning of money transmission. The Company believed it was akin to a sale of goods.

Nevertheless, given the uncertainty surrounding the laws, the Company elected, as of July 12, 2016, to no longer offer its Idaho consumers the opportunity to purchase or sell virtual currency through its website, mobile application or otherwise. The Company also elected on July 12, 2016 to terminate its provision of virtual currency wallets to Idaho consumers. The Company has stopped buy/sell transactions for Idaho consumers on its website and mobile application and has notified Idaho consumers of its decision to terminate their wallets. It will be assisting these consumers in transferring any virtual currency in their wallets to another provider. Importantly, these decisions were made independent of and prior to the Company's receipt of your letter on July 14, 2016.

The Company places a high degree of importance on regulatory compliance, exemplary performance and customer service. To our knowledge, all Idaho consumers have been satisfied with the services they received from the Company. The Company has not received any complaints from any Idaho consumer (verbal or written), or from any private consumer advocacy group, the Department, or any other regulatory agency on behalf of any Idaho consumer.

The information herein has been provided voluntarily to the Department. It does not constitute an admission of any wrongdoing or violation of Idaho law, and the Company reserves its rights in relation thereto.

If you have any questions, please feel free to call or email me at your convenience.

* * *

July 7, 2016

RE: Money Service Transmission

Dear []:

The Idaho Department of Finance ("Department") is charged with the administration and enforcement of several Idaho statutes, including the Idaho Money Transmitters Act. In this regard we regulate payment processors, money orders sellers, and other business models that constitute money transmission under the Act.

Your company has come to the attention of the Department as possibly offering a wide range of options related to the buying, selling and conversion of cryptocurrency (i.e. BitCoin, LiteCoin and Dogecoin) via your website [], and your mobile applications. Per Idaho Code §26-2902(11), this activity may fall under the definition of a money transmitter. In that regard, we request a response to the following questions.

- Are your cryptocurrency services offered or used by Idaho consumers and if so how long have your services been available?

- Do you currently have any Idaho consumers using your web site or mobile applications to buy, sell or transact cryptocurrency and if so how many customers and the total dollar amount of these transactions?

- Is your company relying on any exemptions from money transmitting regulations? If so, please explain.

This inquiry is made pursuant to Idaho Code §26-2914. This request should not be construed as a finding that any violation exists or has occurred, but that further information may be required to make an appropriate determination regarding your business processes. A favorable response is requested by July 29, 2016.

If you have any questions regarding this request, please contact the undersigned.

Sincerely,

Jeff Flora

Financial Examiner/Investigator

Idaho Department of Finance

800 Park Lane Suite 200

Boise, ID 83720

Jeff.flora@finance.idaho.gov

(208)332-8045

E. Illinois

Digital Currency Regulatory Guidance

The Illinois Department of Financial and Professional Regulation (2019)

Purpose

Digital currencies such as Bitcoin, Dogecoin, Ethereum, Litecoin, and ZCash have raised questions with respect to money transmission and exchange of currency. This guidance outlines the policy of the Illinois Department of Financial and Professional Regulation (the "Department") with regards to digital currencies. This guidance expresses the Department's interpretation of Illinois' Transmitters of Money Act,[1] ("TOMA") and its application to various activities involving digital currencies. This guidance seeks to establish the regulatory treatment of digital currencies under TOMA as it currently exists.

Types of Digital Currency

In short, a digital currency is an electronic medium of exchange used to purchase goods and services. A digital currency may also be exchanged for sovereign currency.[2] A digital currency, by nature of its properties detailed below, is distinct from other forms of sovereign currency.

---

1. Illinois Compiled Statutes (205 ILCS 657/1, *et seq.*)

2. In this guidance the term sovereign currency will be used to mean government-issued currencies with legal tender status in the country of issuance. In most literature pertaining to digital currency, the term fiat currency is used to refer to government-issued legal tender.

Legal Tender vs. Non-Legal Tender:

As of the date of this regulatory guidance, the Department is not aware of any jurisdiction in which digital currency has status as legal tender or of any digital currency issued by a government's central bank. As such, digital currencies exist outside the recognition of established financial institutions.

Centralized vs. Decentralized:

There are generally two basic types of digital currencies: *centralized* and *decentralized*. **Centralized digital currencies** are created and issued by a specified source. They rely on a person or entity with authority or control over the currency. Typically, the person or entity exercising authority or control over the centralized digital currency is also the creator of that currency.

In addition to the two types of centralized digital currency, there are numerous sub- classifications. Centralized digital currencies can be *non-convertible* meaning they can be purchased with sovereign currency, but cannot be exchanged back to sovereign currency. Centralized digital currencies can also be *convertible* meaning they can be converted back to sovereign currency. Additionally, some centralized digital currencies can be used only for purchase of goods and services from a closed universe of merchants, are specific to a particular virtual domain or world,[3] or have a theoretically open universe of merchants.

Decentralized digital currencies are not created or issued by a particular person or entity, have no administrator, and have no central repository. Although decentralized digital currency is not classified as a legal tender, it is convertible, meaning it has equivalent value in sovereign currency and can be exchanged to or for sovereign currency. Most, but not all, decentralized digital currencies are also cryptocurrencies. These include Bitcoin, Litecoin, Peercoin, Namecoin, Ether, etc. A cryptocurrency is based on a cryptographic protocol that manages the creation of new units of the currency on a shared ledger through a peer-to-peer network. Cryptocurrency is created through a process called mining performed by the "miner." Mining involves running an application on a computer that performs consensus algorithm calculations such as proof-work or proof-of-stake. When the computer performs a sufficient amount of these calculations, the cryptocurrency's underlying protocol generates a new unit of the currency which can be delivered to the miner's wallet. Because users' wallets act as the connection points of the digital currency's decentralized peer-to-peer network, transfers of digital currency are made directly from wallet to wallet, whereas transmissions of sovereign currencies must be made through one or more intermediaries such as a financial institution or money transmitter.

---

3. The term "virtual currency" commonly used by other governmental bodies can be used interchangeably with the term "digital currency" throughout this guidance document.

One differentiating characteristic of decentralized and centralized digital currency is that while centralized digital currency can have intrinsic value through backing by sovereign currency or precious metals, decentralized currency lacks intrinsic value. A unit of decentralized digital currency does not represent a claim on a commodity, and is not convertible by law. Its value is only what a buyer is willing to pay for it.

Most decentralized digital currencies are traded on third party exchange sites where the exchange rates with sovereign currencies are determined by averaging the transactions that occur. Decentralized digital currency can also be considered a new asset class that is neither currency nor commodity.

Application of Transmitters of Money Act

This guidance does not address money transmission activities involving the centralized digital currencies schemes in existence. As such, businesses engaging in activities that may be considered money transmission involving centralized digital currency schemes should seek an individual licensing determination from the Department.

This guidance is focused on money transmission activities involving decentralized digital currencies. Whether or not an Illinois money transmitter license is required for an entity to engage in the transmission of decentralized digital currencies turns on the question of whether decentralized digital currency is considered "money" as defined in TOMA. Accordingly, Section 5 of TOMA defines a "[m]oney transmitter" as:

> *[A] person who is located in or doing business in this State and who directly or through authorized sellers does any of the following in this State:*
>
> *1) Sells or issues payment instruments*
>
> *2) Engages in the business of receiving money for transmission or transmitting money.*
>
> *3) Engages in the business of exchanging, for compensation, money of the United States Government or a foreign government to or from money of another government.*

Furthermore, Section 5 of TOMA defines the action of "[t]ransmitting money" as:

> *[T]ransmission of money by any means, including transmissions to or from locations within the United States or to and from locations outside of the United States by payment instrument, facsimile or electronic transfer, or otherwise, and includes bill payment services.*

Section 5 of TOMA defines "[m]oney" as:

[A] medium of exchange that is authorized or adopted by a domestic or foreign government as a part of its currency and that is customarily used and accepted as a medium of exchange in the country of issuance.

Accordingly, although decentralized digital currencies are a representation of value that can function as a medium of exchange, they are not considered "money" for the purposes of TOMA as decentralized currencies have not been "authorized or adopted by a domestic or foreign government as a part of its currency." A person or entity engaged in the transmission of decentralized currencies, as they currently exist, would not be required to obtain a TOMA license. However, should transmission of decentralized digital currencies involve "money" in a transaction, that transaction may be considered money transmission depending on how the transaction is organized. Any person or entity engaging in a transaction involving both decentralized digital currencies and "money" should request a determination from the Department on whether or not such activity will require a TOMA license.

Regulatory Treatment of Digital Currencies:

In order to provide further guidance and clarity around how digital currencies are currently regulated, listed below are some examples of common types of digital currency transactions. Please note this is a non-exhaustive list.

Activities Generally Qualifying as Money Transmission

- Exchange involving both digital currency and sovereign currency through a third-party exchanger is generally considered to be money transmission. For example, some digital currency exchange sites facilitate exchanges by acting as an escrow-like intermediary. In a typical transaction, the buyer of digital currency sends "money" to the exchanger who holds the funds until it determines that the terms of the sale have been satisfied before transmitting the funds to the seller. Irrespective of its handling of the digital currency, the exchanger conducts money transmission by receiving the buyer's "money" in exchange for a promise to make it available to the seller.

- Exchange of digital currency for sovereign currency through an automated machine is generally considered to be money transmission. For example, several companies have begun selling automated machines commonly called "Bitcoin ATMs" that facilitate contemporaneous exchanges of digital currency for sovereign currency. Most such machines currently available, when operating in their default mode act as an intermediary between a buyer and seller, typically connecting through one of the established exchange sites. When a customer buys or sells bitcoins through a machine configured this way, the operator of the machine receives the buyer's money in exchange for the "business or receiving money for transmission or transmitting money."

Some digital currency ATMs, however, can be configured to conduct transactions only between the customer and the machine's operator, with no third parties involved. If the machine never involves a third party, and only facilitates a sale or purchase of digital currency by the machine's operator directly with the customer, there is no money transmission because at no time is money received in exchange for the "business or receiving money for transmission or transmitting money."

Activities Not Qualifying as Money Transmission

- Exchange of digital currency for money directly between two parties does not qualify as money transmission. This is essentially a sale of goods between two parties. The seller gives units of digital currency to the buyer, who pays the seller directly with "money." The seller does not receive "money" with the intent to transmit it to another entity or "engage in the business of exchanging, for compensation, money of the United States Government or a foreign government to or from money of another government."

- Transfer of digital currency by itself is not transmitting money. Because digital currency is not "money", the receipt of it with the intent to transmit it to another entity is not "transmitting money." This includes intermediaries who receive digital currency for transfer to a third party, and entities who, akin to depositories (commonly referred to as wallets), hold digital currency on behalf of customers.

- Exchange of one digital currency for another digital currency is not money transmission. Regardless of how many parties are involved, there is no receipt of "money" and therefore "transmitting money" does not occur.

- A merchant who accepts digital currency as payment for goods or services or an individual who pays for goods or services with digital currency are commonly referred to as "users" of digital currency. Regardless of how many parties are involved, no "money" is involved at any point in this transaction, so "transmitting money" does not occur.

- "Miners" or those who receive digital currency as payment for verifying transactions, typically by contributing software, connectivity, or computing power to process transactions. Although "miners" receive payment of digital currency for completing its work, "money" is not involved in the payment of this work, so "transmitting money" does not occur.

- Multi-signature software allows users to distribute authority over his or her digital currency among multiple different actors. This software requires multiple actors to authorize a digital currency transaction before the transaction can be consummated. Specifically, a multi-signature provider holds one of two or more private keys needed to authorize transactions. Regardless of how many parties are involved, no "money" is involved at any point in this transaction, so "transmitting money" does not occur.

- Blockchain 2.0 technologies refer to the use of a digital currency's decentralized or distributed ledger system for non-monetary purposes such as verifying ownership or authenticity in a digital capacity. This technology includes software innovations such as colored coins (i.e. coins that are marked specifically to represent a non-monetary asset), smart contracts (i.e. agreements implemented on a distributed ledger), and smart property (i.e. property that is titled using a decentralized distributed ledger). These uses for non- monetary purposes may use digital currency as a medium of exchange, but do not involve the exchange or transmission of "money" or the sale or issuance of a "payment instrument" and as a result "transmitting money" does not occur.

Licensing Considerations

- A digital currency business that conducts money transmission, as outlined above, must comply with all applicable licensing, reporting, net worth and other relevant requirements of the Transmitters of Money Act 205 ILCS 657/1 *et seq.*

- Any entity engaged in money transmission must comply with the permissible investment requirements as defined in 205 ILCS 657/50. No virtual currency has been approved by the Director as a permissible investment under this section. However, pursuant to 205 ILCS 657/50(b) at any time, the Director may approve or limit the extent to which other products may be considered a permissible investment.

F. Kansas

Regulatory Treatment of Virtual Currencies Under the Kansas Money Transmitter Act

Kansas Office of the State Commissioner (MT-2014-01) (June 6, 2014)

Purpose

The purpose of this guidance document is to clarify the applicability of the Kansas Money Transmitter Act (KMTA)[1] to persons or entities engaging in the use and/or transmission of virtual currencies.[2] This guidance document provides the policy of the Office of the State Bank Commissioner (OSBC) regarding the regulatory treatment of virtual currencies pursuant to the statutory definitions of the KMTA.

---

1. Kansas Statutes Annotated 9-508 *et seq.*
2. Much of this document is modeled after guidance issued by the Texas Department of Banking in Supervisory Memorandum 1037 and we thank them for allowing the OSBC to adapt it for use in Kansas.

Types of Virtual Currency

In broad terms, a virtual currency is an electronic medium of exchange typically used to purchase goods and services from certain merchants or to exchange for other currencies, either virtual or sovereign.[3] As of the date of this memorandum (2014), the OSBC is not aware of any virtual currency that has legal tender status in any jurisdiction, nor of any virtual currency issued by a governmental central bank. As such, virtual currencies exist outside established financial institution systems. There are many different virtual currency schemes, and it is not easy to classify all of them, but for purposes of this document, they can generally be divided into two basic types: centralized and decentralized.

Centralized virtual currencies are created and issued by a specified source. They rely on an entity with some form of authority or control over the currency. Typically, the authority behind a centralized virtual currency is also the creator. Centralized virtual currencies can be further divided into subclassifications that quickly become too complex to apply a universal policy. Some can be purchased with sovereign currency but cannot be exchanged back to sovereign currency; some can be converted back to sovereign currency; some are used only for purchase of goods and services from a closed universe of merchants, while others may have a theoretically open universe of merchants. Some centralized currencies are backed by the issuer with sovereign currency or precious metals, and therefore derive intrinsic value.

In contrast, decentralized virtual currencies are not created or issued by a particular person or entity, have no administrator, and have no central repository. Thus far, decentralized currencies are all cryptocurrencies such as Bitcoin, Litecoin, Peercoin, and Namecoin. A cryptocurrency is based on a cryptographic protocol that manages the creation of new units of the currency through a peer-to-peer network. The creation of cryptocurrency happens through a process called mining that basically involves running an application on a computer that performs proof-of-work calculations. When the computer performs a sufficient amount of these calculations, the cryptocurrency's underlying protocol essentially generates a new unit of the currency that can be delivered to the miner's wallet. Because users' wallets act as the connection points of the cryptocurrency's peer-to-peer network, transfers of cryptocurrency are made directly from wallet to wallet, without any intermediary, whereas transmissions of sovereign currencies must be made through one or more intermediaries such as a financial institution or money transmitter.

One important characteristic of cryptocurrency is its lack of intrinsic value. A unit of cryptocurrency does not represent a claim on a commodity and is not con-

---

3. As used in this document, sovereign currency refers to government-issued currency with legal tender status in the country of issuance, such as U.S. Dollars or Euros. This includes both government-issued fiat currency and commodity-backed currency that is designated as legal tender.

vertible by law. And unlike fiat currencies,[4] there is no governmental authority or central bank establishing its value through law or regulation. Its value is only what a buyer is willing to pay for it. Most cryptocurrencies are traded on third party exchange sites, where the exchange rates with sovereign currencies are determined by averaging the transactions that occur. Some experts consider cryptocurrency to be a new asset class that is neither currency nor commodity, but possessing characteristics of both, as well as characteristics of neither.

Application of Kansas Money Transmitter Act to Virtual Currency

Currency Exchange

The act of two-party currency exchange by itself is not covered by the KMTA regardless of whether it is sovereign currency being exchanged or virtual currency. Further, it is not regulated by the OSBC. However, the presence of a third party involved in a currency exchange transaction will likely subject the transaction to the KMTA as "money transmission" and is discussed further below.

Money Transmission

This guidance document does not address money transmission activities involving the various centralized virtual currencies in existence. Many of these types of virtual currency schemes are complicated and nuanced and general guidance cannot adequately cover all the possible types of these currencies. Thus, operators engaging in activities that may be considered money transmission involving a centralized virtual currency will have to seek an individual licensing determination from the OSBC.

This guidance is focused on money transmission activities involving decentralized cryptocurrencies, such as Bitcoin. Whether or not a Kansas money transmitter license is required for an entity to engage in the transmission of cryptocurrency turns on the question of whether cryptocurrency is considered "money" or "monetary value" under the KMTA. Money transmission is defined in statute and means "to engage in the business of receiving money or monetary value for transmission to a location within or outside the United States by... electronic means or any other means..."[5] Money is not defined in statute, but Black's Law Dictionary defines "money" as the "medium of exchange authorized or adopted by a government as part of its currency." Since no cryptocurrency is currently authorized or adopted by any governmental entity as part of its currency, it is clear that cryptocurrency is not considered "money" for the purposes of the KMTA.

---

4. Fiat currency is government-issued legal tender, such as the U.S. Dollar. It has no intrinsic value and does not represent a claim on a commodity; its value is established by law.

5. K.S.A. 9-508(g).

Monetary value, however, is defined in statute as "a medium of exchange, whether or not redeemable in money."[6] Medium of exchange is not defined by statute, but Black's Law Dictionary defines "medium of exchange" as "anything generally accepted as payment in a transaction and recognized as a standard of value." Cryptocurrencies are not generally accepted as payment in the current economy. While there may be a few retailers who are accepting Bitcoin or other cryptocurrencies, it is not generally accepted throughout the entire economy and does not even approach the extent to which U.S. Dollars (or other sovereign currencies) are accepted. Cryptocurrency also does not have a recognized standard of value. There is no set value for a single unit of a cryptocurrency. As stated above, the value of a unit of cryptocurrency is only what a buyer is willing to pay for it and what a seller is willing to accept in order to part with it. There is no intrinsic or set value for a unit of cryptocurrency.

Therefore, because cryptocurrencies as currently in existence are not considered "money" or "monetary value" by the OSBC, they are not covered by the KMTA. Since the KMTA does not apply to transmission of decentralized cryptocurrencies, an entity engaged solely in the transmission of such currency would not be required to obtain a license in the State of Kansas. However, should the transmission of virtual currency include the involvement of sovereign currency in a transaction, it may be considered money transmission depending on how such transaction is organized.

To provide further guidance, the regulatory treatments of some common types of transactions involving cryptocurrency are as follows:

- Exchange of cryptocurrency for sovereign currency between two parties is not money transmission under the KMTA. This is essentially a sale of goods between two parties. The seller gives units of cryptocurrency to the buyer, who pays the seller directly with sovereign currency. The seller does not receive the sovereign currency with the intent to transmit to another entity.

- Exchange of one cryptocurrency for another cryptocurrency is not money transmission. Regardless of how many parties are involved, since cryptocurrency is not considered "money" under the KMTA, no money transmission occurs.

- Transfer of cryptocurrency by itself is not money transmission. Because cryptocurrency is not money or monetary value, the receipt of it with the intent to transmit it to another entity is not money transmission. This includes intermediaries who receive cryptocurrency for transfer to a third party, and entities that, akin to depositories, hold cryptocurrencies on behalf of customers.

- Exchange of cryptocurrency for sovereign currency through a third-party exchanger is generally considered money transmission. For example, most

---

6. K.S.A. 9-508(f).

Bitcoin exchange sites facilitate exchanges by acting as an escrow-like intermediary. In a typical transaction, the buyer of cryptocurrency sends sovereign currency to the exchanger who holds the funds until it determines that the terms of the sale have been satisfied before remitting the funds to the seller. Irrespective of its handling of the cryptocurrency, the exchanger conducts money transmission by receiving the buyer's sovereign currency in exchange for a promise to make it available to the seller.

Exchange of cryptocurrency for sovereign currency through an automated machine may or may not be money transmission depending on the facts and circumstances of its operation and the flow of funds between the operator of the automated machine and the customer. For example, several companies have begun selling automated machines commonly called "Bitcoin ATMs" that facilitate contemporaneous exchanges of bitcoins for sovereign currency. Most such machines currently available, when operating in their default mode, act as an intermediary between a buyer and a seller, typically connecting through one of the established exchange sites. When a customer buys or sells bitcoins through a machine configured in this way, the operator of the machine receives the buyer's sovereign currency with the intent to transfer it to the seller. This would be considered money transmission under the KMTA and would require licensure. However, at least some Bitcoin ATMs can be configured to conduct transactions only between the customer and the operator or owner of the machine, with no third parties involved. If the machine never involves a third party, and only facilitates a sale or purchase of bitcoins by the machine's operator directly with the customer, there is no money transmission because at no time is sovereign money received by the owner or operator of the machine with the intent to transfer it to another entity.

Additional Issues with Virtual Currency

- A cryptocurrency business that conducts money transmission, as outlined above, must comply with all applicable licensing, reporting, net worth, and other relevant requirements of the Kansas Money Transmitter Act under K.S.A 9-508 *et seq.*

- Any entity engaged in money transmission must comply with the permissible investment requirements of K.S.A 9-513b and as defined in K.S.A. 9-508(j). For purposes of allowed permissible investments, no virtual currency has been approved for use under this section by the Commissioner. Therefore, if a licensed money transmitter is seeking to comply with the permissible investment requirement, it must have adequate U.S. currency or other approved investments to cover its outstanding payment instruments.

- For any entity intending to obtain licensing as a money transmitter, the OSBC will require any applicant who regularly handles virtual currencies in the course of its activities to submit a current third-party security audit of all relevant computer and information systems. Because of the increased risk that Kansas consumers may face when using the services of a money transmitter involved with virtual currencies, it is incumbent upon any license applicant to demonstrate that all of a customer's sovereign and virtual currency are secure while controlled by the transmitter.

This guidance document was originally issued on June 6, 2014 pursuant to K.S.A. 9-513 and K.S.A. 77-439. The Licensing Department has determined this guidance document has answered most virtual currency licensing questions since its issuance. However, this guidance document is only intended as general guidance. Any person engaged in virtual currency may request that the Licensing Department determine if their business model requires a license by submitting the following: a business plan, a diagram showing how fiat currency and/or virtual currency flows between persons, and a copy of any applicable contract.

The OSBC reserves the right to exercise its discretion in the application of this guidance document and it may edit, modify, or retract its interpretation at any time. Issued June 6, 2014; updated May 18, 2021.

G. North Carolina

Money Transmitter Frequently Asked Questions

North Carolina Office of the Commissioner of the Banks

https://nccob.nc.gov/financial-institutions/money-transmitters

General FAQs

Q. How do I apply for a money transmitter license?

A: Applications for a money transmitter license must be submitted via the Nationwide Multistate Licensing System & Registry (NMLS). The application fee is $1,500 plus fees assessed by NMLS.

Q. Is stored value or "prepaid access" regulated under the MTA?

A: Yes. Any business that issues stored value or prepaid access cards is defined as a money transmitter.

Q. May I operate through authorized delegates?

A: Yes. N.C. Gen. Stat. § 53-208.44(c) authorizes delegates. Licensees (not NCCOB) must issue a certificate of authority to each location where the licensee conducts business through an authorized delegate. The certificate must be posted in public view and read as follows: "Money transmission on behalf of (insert name of licensee) is conducted at this location pursuant to the North Carolina Money Transmitters Act N.C.G.S. § 53-208.41 et seq."

Q. My company only conducts business-to-business transactions, do I need a money transmitter license?

A: No. Money transmissions from a business to a business or from a business to a consumer do not require a money transmitter license. Per the MTA, money transmissions, including the sale or issuance of payment instruments or stored value, must be for personal, family, or household purposes. However, if you are acting on behalf of a business in taking money from a consumer, you **may** need a money transmitter license.

Q. Is the transmission of virtual currency regulated under the MTA?

A: Yes. The NC MTA requires all persons engaged in the business of money transmission to obtain a license. The NC MTA defines "money transmission" as the "act of engaging in the business of receiving money or monetary value for transmission within the United States or to locations abroad by any and all means, including payment instrument, wire, facsimile, or electronic transfer," and further defines "monetary value" as a "medium of exchange, whether or not redeemable in money." Virtual currency is a form of monetary value. See N.C. Gen. Stat. 53-208.3(a), 53-208.2(a)(11)(b), and 53-208.2(a)(12) (2015).

Q. Are virtual currency miners and users regulated under the MTA?

A: No. As noted above, the NC MTA regulates the transmission of virtual currency. It does not regulate the use of virtual currency. A "user" is someone who uses virtual currency to buy or sell goods and services. A merchant who accepts virtual currency as payment for goods or services is a user and does not require a license. A "miner" is someone who receives virtual currency as payment for verifying transactions, typically by providing computer resources to process data. Once the miner has completed its work, the miner generally becomes a "user" of virtual currency.

Q. Are virtual currency exchangers and administrators regulated under the MTA?

A: It depends. A virtual currency exchanger is a person that exchanges virtual currency for fiat currency or other virtual currencies, and vice versa. An exchanger that sells its own stock of virtual currency is generally not considered a virtual currency transmitter under the NC MTA. In contrast, an exchanger that holds customer funds while arranging a satisfactory buy/sell order with a third party, and transmits virtual currency and fiat currency between buyer and seller, will typically be considered a virtual currency transmitter.

A virtual currency administrator is a person that issues or redeems virtual currency. Although administrators must register with FinCEN and comply with the Bank Secrecy Act, merely acting as an administrator generally does not require a license under the NC MTA.

Q. Are there special licensing requirements applicable only to virtual currency transmitters?

A: No. The MTA applies to all transmitters of monetary value equally. It does not distinguish between virtual currency transmission and fiat transmission.

Q. Are Blockchain 2.0 technologies regulated by the NC MTA?

A: Generally, no. Blockchain 2.0 technologies refer to the use of the blockchain (or other similar virtual distributed ledger system) to verify ownership or authenticity in a digital capacity. This technology includes such software innovations as colored coins (i.e. coins that are marked specifically to represent a non-fiat-money asset), smart contracts (i.e. agreements implemented on a virtual distributed ledger), and smart property (i.e. property that is titled using a virtual distributed ledger). These uses of the blockchain generally do not involve the use of virtual currency as a medium of exchange. As a result, the NC MTA does not regulate these software innovations.

Q. Do providers of multi-signature software require a license under the NC MTA?

A: No. Multi-signature software allows a virtual currency user to distribute authority over his or her virtual currency among multiple different actors. This software requires multiple actors to authorize a virtual currency transaction before the transaction can be consummated. Specifically, a multi-signature provider holds one of two or more private keys needed to authorize transactions. Because the multi-signature provider cannot authorize a transaction alone, this provider is not holding virtual currency on behalf of another and does not engage in virtual currency transmission by signing transactions on behalf of the user.

Q. Are wallet providers regulated under the NC MTA?

A: Generally, yes. A hosted, custodial wallet provider is in the business of storing a user's virtual currency on a remote computer until such time as the user desires to spend or exchange the user's virtual currency. The hosted wallet provider typically agrees to safeguard the user's private keys and make them available at some later date. This custodial function is regulated under the NC MTA.

In contrast, a non-hosted, non-custodial wallet is typically outside the scope of the NC MTA. A non-hosted wallet is a piece of software deployed on the user's own computer or device that makes the user's private keys easier to use by the user. In a non-hosted, non-custodial model, the software provider never gains access to the user's private keys and does not agree to transmit the user's virtual currency later.

Q. What information is required to be reported quarterly?

A: All money transmitter licensees are required to complete the Money Services Businesses Call Report (MSBCR) in NMLS. The report includes national and state specific MSB information that is submitted on a quarterly and annual basis. Filing dates are as follows:

Filing	Reporting Period	Due Date
Q1	January 1–March 31	May 15
Q2	April 1–June 30	August 14
Q3	July 1–September 30	November 14
Q4	October 1–December 31	March 15

Q. Is there an annual renewal?

A: No. The money transmitter license is perpetual and not assignable. However, licensees will need to participate in NMLS' renewal process and pay the required fees to maintain its use of the system.

Q. Is a surety bond required?

A: Yes. The amount of the bond is based upon the aggregate volume of NC only transactions reported in the prior year's MSBCRs. For new licensees, the surety bond should be in the amount of $150,000. Subsequent to initial licensure, the surety bond amount should be adjusted annually by May 31, using the aggregate year's NC transaction volume. Use the table below to determine the bond amount:

NC Transmission Volume in U.S. Dollars	Required Assessment
Up to $1,000,000	$150,000
Greater than $1,000,000 but less than $5,000,000	$175,000
Greater than $5,000,000 but less than $10,000,000	$200,000
Greater than $10,000,000 but less than $50,000,000	$225,000
Greater than $50,000,000	$250,000

Licensees are required to submit an electronic surety bond through NMLS. Paper bonds are no longer accepted.

Q. Are there any fees required after obtaining a money transmission license?

A: Yes. Each licensee is required to pay an annual assessment. The assessment consists of a base amount of $5,000 for volumes up to $1,000,000.00, plus an additional sum, calculated using the prior year's NC transaction volume. The cumulative assessment is calculated as follows:

NC Transmission Volume in U.S. Dollars	Per U.S. Dollar
Greater than $1,000,000 but less than $5,000,000	$0.0008
Greater than $5,000,000 but less than $10,000,000	$0.0006
Greater than $10,000,000 but less than $50,000,000	$0.00004
Greater than $50,000,000	$0.0000006

Q. Are there annual reporting requirements?

A: Yes. No later than 90 days after the end of each calendar year, licensees shall file an annual report through NMLS, which shall include:

1. Annual financial statement, including balance sheet, statement of income or loss, statement of changes in shareholder's equity, if applicable, and statement of changes in financial position. In the case of a licensee that is a wholly owned subsidiary of another corporation, the consolidated audited annual financial statement of the parent corporation may be filed in lieu of the licensee's.

2. Any material changes to the information submitted by the licensee on its original application, which have not been previously reported through NMLS.

3. Copies of bank statements and other documentation related to the existence and quality of the licensee's permissible investments.

Q. Are virtual currency kiosks regulated under the MTA?

A: It depends. Virtual currency kiosks that allow consumers to purchase or sell virtual currency, from the kiosk operator's own supply of virtual currency, do not require a license under the MTA. Virtual currency kiosks that allow the transmission of virtual or fiat currency between consumers, or that hold virtual or fiat currency on behalf of consumers, require a license under the NC MTA.

Companies that operate virtual currency kiosks should verify ownership of the recipient's wallet to ensure funds are not sent to a third party. If a company will not or cannot verify ownership, it must seek licensure under the MTA. In verifying ownership, operators of virtual currency kiosks cannot rely on ownership requirements hidden in terms of service. Rather, virtual currency kiosks should include a separate screen or highlighted interface in which the consumer specifically affirms ownership of the recipient wallet.

Discussion Points

1. *Money Transmitter Laws.* What is the purpose behind money transmitter laws? Should money transmitters be regulated primarily on a state level, or would it be more efficient to have a federal-level regulatory license? Why?

2. *Colorado, Idaho, Illinois, Kansas.* Do you agree with the regulatory guidance issued in Colorado, Idaho, Illinois, and Kansas? What are their similarities and differences? How do these states view peer-to-peer transactions in cryptocurrencies? Do they distinguish between the different types of market participants, and their respective roles in the space? What would you do differently, if anything, if asked to rewrite the regulatory guidance in these states? Does the issued guidance in these states create a regulatory arbitrage? Should states provide their own view on centralized versus decentralized cryptocurrency networks? Are these states in a position to do this or should this be left to the federal government? How do these states differ from the federal government's position on regulating cryptocurrency exchanges and market participants?

3. *North Carolina.* How would North Carolina want to regulate cryptocurrency virtual wallets and digital stored value? Why are business-to-business transactions excluded from licensing? Should they be excluded? What are the potential regulatory pitfalls in excluding business-to-business transactions?

4. Analyze the legal significance of money transmitter licensing and state regulation in the context of safeguarding consumers and potentially preventing financial crimes.

H. New York and the BitLicense

In 2015, the New York Department of Financial Services ("NYDFS") made its first attempt at regulation in the Bitcoin and virtual currency industries with the establishment of the BitLicense. BitLicense is applicable to virtual currency exchanges in New York, and was created to combat unlawful activity involving virtual currencies such as cyber-attacks, fraud, and money laundering. By adopting the BitLicense,

NYDFS also sought to encourage virtual finance innovation. As of 2022, NYDFS has approved 25 entities to operate in the state of New York.

To conduct or engage in virtual currency business activity, an individual must obtain a license from the NYDFS. Registration is required of persons or businesses that engage in the following: "1) receive or transmit virtual currency, 2) store, hold or maintain virtual currency for customers, 3) buy and sell virtual currency as a customer business, 4) perform currency exchange services, or 5) control, administer or issue virtual currencies...."[43] Once an applicant applies for a BitLicense, the NYDFS Superintendent then approves or denies the application within ninety days from the filing. If an application is denied, an applicant must immediately cease operation in New York. If an applicant does not satisfy all of the regulatory requirements, the Superintendent can give that applicant a conditional license, allowing them to conduct business with a more flexible regulatory framework for no more than two years.

BitLicense encourages consumer protection in a variety of ways. Businesses that have a BitLicense must disclose all material risks associated with their products and services to their consumers. They are also required to create written policies and procedures for the NYDFS in an effort to resolve consumer complaints.[44] Additionally, licensed businesses have to create written anti-fraud policies and an anti-fraud program to ensure compliance with current anti-money laundering laws. The Superintendent examines a licensed business every two years to ensure they are in compliance with all procedures.

Applying for a BitLicense is expensive. It costs approximately $5,000 for a license application, and there are additional fees for completion of the application. The application process and fees can be a deterrent for companies, especially for those that do not have sufficient cash flow.

It is argued that BitLicense prevents the evolution of virtual currency by drawing it back to traditional centralized systems.[45] This is because it requires the virtual currency to be backed by a fiat currency, which does not foster a decentralized banking system. Further, BitLicense requires that licensees disclose personal and identifiable information, which contradicts the feature that individuals' information is kept anonymous. In New York, the size of the virtual currency industry is dwindling because many Bitcoin businesses left the state of New York. Because many companies left the state of New York, there are fewer businesses to transact with, which could become an issue for someone who is looking to grow their business.

---

43. Samantha J. Syska, *Eight-Years-Young: How the New York Bitlicense Stifles Bitcoin Innovation and Expansion with Its Premature Attempt to Regulate the Virtual Currency Industry*, 17 J. High Tech. L. 313, 329 (2017).

44. *Id.* at 331.

45. *Id.* at 336.

New York Codes, Rules and Regulations
Title 23 — Financial Services
Chapter I - Regulations of the Superintendent of Financial Services

The text of the New York Bit License rules appears in the Appendix. Review those provisions and consider the following Discussion Points.

Discussion Points

1. *Too restrictive?* Do you think that NYDFS needs to revise its BitLicense regulations? Are they too restrictive? Do you think that the current BitLicense requirements prevent small and mid-sized virtual currency businesses from operating in New York?

2. *Limiting the playing field.* Licensed businesses are only able to transact with consumers and businesses that are also licensed. Does this promote consumer protection or hinder interstate commerce?

3. *Enforcement actions.* As of November 2022, there are less than five enforcement actions that have been filed against businesses for failing to comply with BitLicense requirements. What does this suggest? Do you think this means all businesses are following BitLicense regulations or do you think this means NYDFS is not really concerned about enforcing the regulations?

4. *Is this really meant to protect consumers?* Do you think that BitLicense requirements are meant to protect consumers from unlawful activity? Why or why not?

Four

Commodities

I. The Commodity Futures Trading Commission

The Commodity Futures Trading Commission ("CTFC" or the "Commission") is a federal agency that regulates the U.S. derivatives market, including futures, options and swaps. Congress passed the Commodity Futures Trading Commission Act in 1974. This Act granted the CFTC exclusive jurisdiction over future trading in different commodities. Pursuant to the Act's predecessor, the Commodity Exchange Act (CEA), the CFTC can regulate agricultural commodities.

The CFTC maintains general anti-fraud and manipulation enforcement authority over virtual currency cash markets as a commodity in interstate commerce. As a result, under the CEA, the CFTC has authority to promulgate regulations with respect to virtual currency.

The Commodity Exchange Act: Definition of "Commodity"

1. *Commodity.* The term "commodity" means wheat, cotton, rice, corn, oats, barley, rye, flaxseed, grain sorghums, mill feeds, butter, eggs, Irish potatoes, wool, wool tops, fats and oils (including lard, tallow, cottonseed oil, peanut oil, soybean oil, and all other fats and oils), cottonseed meal, cottonseed, peanuts, soybeans, soybean meal, livestock, livestock products, and frozen concentrated orange juice, and all other goods and articles, except onions (as provided by section 13-1) and motion picture box office receipts (or any index, measure, value, or data related to such receipts), and all services, rights, and interests (except motion picture box office receipts, or any index, measure, value or data related to such receipts) in which contracts for future delivery are presently or in the future dealt in.[46]

2. *Key Sections of the Commodity Exchange Act.*

   a. *Section 6c(b)*— Makes it unlawful for any person to "offer to enter into, enter into or confirm the execution of, any transaction involving any commodity...which is of the character of, or is commonly known to the trade as, an 'option'..., 'bid', 'offer', 'put', [or] 'call'...contrary to any

---

46. 7 U.S.C. § 1a(9).

rule, regulation, or order of the Commission prohibiting any such transaction."[47]

b. *Section 7b-3(a)(1)*—Forbids any person from operating "a facility for the trading or processing of swaps unless the facility is registered as a sweep execution facility or as a designated contract market...."[48]

c. *Section 32.2 Commodity option transactions; general authorization.* Subject to §§ 32.1, 32.4, and 32.5, which shall in any event apply to all commodity option transactions, it shall be unlawful for any person or group of persons to offer to enter into, enter into, confirm the execution of, maintain a position in, or otherwise conduct activity related to any transaction in interstate commerce that is a commodity option transaction, unless: (a) Such transaction is conducted in compliance with and subject to the provisions of the Act, including any Commission rule, regulation, or order thereunder, otherwise applicable to any other swap, or (b) Such transaction is conducted pursuant to § 32.3.[49]

d. *Section 37.3(a)(1) Requirements and procedures for registration.* Any person operating a facility that offers a trading system or platform in which more than one market participant has the ability to execute or trade swaps with more than one other market participant on the system or platform shall register the facility as a swap execution facility under this part or as a designated contract market under part 38.[50]

e. *Futures Commission Merchant.* Any person registered or required to be registered as a futures commission merchant with the CFTC under the Commodity Exchange Act, except persons who register pursuant to Section 4f(a)(2) of the Commodity Exchange Act.[51]

3. *Designated Contract Market.* Designated Contract Markets (DCMs) are boards of trade (or exchanges) that operate under the regulatory oversight of the CFTC, pursuant to Section 5 of the Commodity Exchange Act.[52] DCMs are most like traditional futures exchanges, which may allow access to their facilities by all types of traders, including retail customers. DCMs may list for trading futures or option contracts based on any underlying commodity, index or instrument.

4. *Contract for Differences.* A Contract for Differences (CFD) generally is an agreement to exchange the difference in value of an underlying asset between the time at which a CFD position is established and the time at

---

47. 7 U.S.C. § 6c(b).
48. 7 U.S.C. § 7b-3(a)(1).
49. 17 CFR § 32.2.
50. 17 CFR § 37.3(a)(1).
51. 75 FR 65812 § 1026.100(f).
52. Designated Contract Markets, CFTC, https://www.cftc.gov/IndustryOversight/Trading Organizations/index.htm.

which it is terminated.[53] If the value increases, the seller pays the buyer the difference; if the value decreases, the buyer pays the seller the difference. CFDs can be traded on a number of products, including treasuries, foreign exchange rates, commodities, equities, and stock indexes.

5. *Derivatives Clearing Organization.* A derivatives clearing organization (DCO) is an entity that enables each party to an agreement, contract, or transaction to substitute, through novation or otherwise, the credit of the DCO for the credit of the parties; arranges or provides, on a multilateral basis, for the settlement or netting of obligations; or otherwise provides clearing services or arrangements that mutualize or transfer credit risk among participants.[54]

In the Matter of Coinflip, Inc., d/b/a Derivabit, and Francisco Riordan

CFTC Docket. No. 15-29 (2015)

I.

The Commodity Futures Trading Commission ("Commission") has reason to believe that from in or about March 2014 to at least August 2014 (the "Relevant Period"), Coinflip, Inc., d/b/a Derivabit ("Coinflip") and Francisco Riordan ("Riordan") (the "Respondents") violated Sections 4c(b) and 5h(a)(1) of the Commodity Exchange Act, as amended (the "Act"), 7 U.S.C. §§ 6c(b) and 7b-3(a)(1) (2012), and Commission Regulations 32.2 and 37.3(a)(1), 17 C.F.R. § 32.2 and 37.3(a)(1) (2014). Therefore, the Commission deems it appropriate and in the public interest that public administrative proceedings be, and hereby are, instituted to determine whether the Respondents engaged in the violations set forth herein and to determine whether any order should be issued imposing remedial sanctions.

II.

In anticipation of the institution of an administrative proceeding, the Respondents have submitted an Offer of Settlement ("Offer"), which the Commission has determined to accept. Without admitting or denying any of the findings or conclusions herein, Respondents consent to the entry of this Order Instituting Proceedings Pursuant to Sections 6(c) and 6(d) of the Commodity Exchange Act, Making Findings and Imposing Remedial Sanctions ("Order") and acknowledge service of this Order.[1]

---

53. 77 FR 482059 (Aug. 13, 2012).

54. 7 U.S.C. § 1a(15).

1. Respondents consent to the entry of this Order and to the use of these findings in this proceeding and in any other proceeding brought by the Commission or to which the Commission is a party; provided, however, that Respondents do not consent to the use of the Offer, or the findings or conclusions in the Order consented to in the Offer, as the sole basis for any other proceeding brought

III.

The Commission finds the following:

A. Summary

During the Relevant Period, Respondents violated Sections 4c(b) and 5h(a)(l) of the Act and Commission Regulations 32.2 and 37.3(a)(l) by conducting activity related to commodity options contrary to Commission Regulations and by operating a facility for the trading or processing of swaps without being registered as a swap execution facility or designated contract market. Specifically, during the Relevant Period, Respondents operated an online facility named Derivabit, offering to connect buyers and sellers of Bitcoin option contracts.[2]

B. Respondents

Coinflip, Inc. is a Delaware corporation with a principal place of business in San Francisco, California. During the Relevant period, Coinflip operated Derivabit and its website derivabit.com. Coinflip has never been registered with the Commission.

Francisco Riordan is an individual residing in San Francisco, California. Riordan is a founder, the chief executive officer, and controlling person of Coinflip. Riordan has never been registered with the Commission.

C. Facts

Coinflip Conducted Activity Related to Illegal Commodity Options

Beginning in March 2014, Coinflip advertised Derivabit as a "risk management platform…that connects buyers and sellers of standardized Bitcoin options and futures contracts." During this period, Coinflip designated numerous put and call options contracts as eligible for trading on the Derivabit platform. For these contracts, Coinflip listed Bitcoin as the asset underlying the option and denominated the strike and delivery prices in US Dollars. According to the derivabit.com website, a customer could place orders by registering as a user and depositing Bitcoin into an account in the user's name. Premiums and payments of settlement of the option contracts were to be paid using Bitcoin at a spot rate determined by a designated thirdparty Bitcoin currency exchange. Users had the ability to, and in fact did, post

---

by the Commission, other than in a proceeding in bankruptcy or to enforce the terms of this Order. Nor do Respondents consent to the use of the Offer or the Order, or the findings or conclusions in this Order consented to in the Offer, by any other party in any other proceeding.

2. Bitcoin is a "virtual currency," defined here as a digital representation of value that functions as a medium of exchange, a unit of account, and/or a store of value, but does not have legal tender status in any jurisdiction. Bitcoin and other virtual currencies are distinct from "real" currencies, which are the coin and paper money of the United States or another country that are designated as legal tender, circulate, and are customarily used and accepted as a medium of exchange in the country of issuance.

bids or offers for the designated options contracts. Coinflip confirmed the bid or offer by communicating it to all users through its website.[4]

During the Relevant Period, Derivabit had approximately 400 users.

Riordan Controlled Coinflip and Directed Its Operations

Riordan was the founder, engineer and Chief Executive Officer of Coinflip. He exercised control over Coinflip's daily operations and possessed the power or ability to control all aspects of the Derivabit platform. Riordan participated in key aspects of Coinflip's illegal activity, including designing and implementing the Derivabit trading platform. Riordan's control enabled him to make design and substantive changes to Coinflip's operations, including the transition from offering Bitcoin options to OTC Bitcoin Forward Contracts. Ultimately, Riordan possessed the power and ability to direct Coinflip to cease operating the Derivabit platform.

LEGAL DISCUSSION

A. Virtual Currencies Such as Bitcoin are Commodities

Section 1a(9) of the Act defines "commodity" to include, among other things, "all services, rights, and interests in which contracts for future delivery are presently or in the future dealt in." 7 U.S.C. § 1a(9). The definition of a "commodity" is broad. *See, e.g., Board of Trade of City of Chicago v. SEC*, 677 F. 2d 1137, 1142 (7th Cir. 1982). Bitcoin and other virtual currencies are encompassed in the definition and properly defined as commodities.

B. Coinflip Violated Sections 4c(b) Act and Commission Regulation 32.2

Section 4c(b) of the Act makes it unlawful for any person to "offer to enter into, enter into or confirm the execution of, any transaction involving any commodity…which is of the character of, or is commonly known to the trade as, an 'option'…, 'bid', 'offer', 'put', [or] 'call'…contrary to any rule, regulation, or order of the Commission prohibiting any such transaction." Section 1.3(hh) defines a "commodity option transaction" and "commodity option" to "mean any transaction or agreement in interstate commerce which is or is held out to be of the character of,

---

4. In July 2014, Coinflip began to offer what it characterized as "OTC Bitcoin Forward Contracts" for trading. Under this model, a Derivabit user would be matched through competitive bidding with a counterparty to execute a contract to exchange US Dollars for Bitcoins at a predetermined price and date. As part of its services, Coinflip would calculate and hold initial and maintenance margin payments and would also calculate and facilitate the transfer of final settlements at maturity or early termination. Coinflip advertised that the users could choose to institute an early termination at any time if its position was "in the money." Although the price would be expressed as an exchange rate between US Dollars and Bitcoins, Coinflip required all settlements and margin payments to be transacted in Bitcoins. No bids or offers were posted by Derivabit users for these contracts. Although these activities may have violated, or led to violations of, the Commodity Exchange Act, the Commission does not address this conduct here.

or is commonly known to the trade as, an 'option,' 'privilege,' 'indemnity,' 'bid,' 'offer,' 'call,' 'put,' 'advance guaranty,' or 'decline guaranty,' and which is subject to regulation under the Act and these regulations." Section 32.2 of the Commission's Regulations, in turn, provides that it shall be unlawful for any person to "offer to enter into, enter into, confirm the execution of, maintain a position in, or otherwise conduct activity related to any transaction in interstate commerce that is a commodity option transaction unless: (a) [s]uch transaction is conducted in compliance with and subject to the provisions of the Act, including any Commission rule, regulation, or order thereunder, otherwise applicable to any other swap, or (b) [s]uch transaction is conducted pursuant to [Regulation] 32.3."

Between at least March 2014 and July 2014, Respondents conducted activity related to commodity option transactions, offered to enter into commodity option transactions and/or confirmed the existence of commodity option transactions. The options transactions were not conducted in compliance with Section 5h(a)(1) of the Act or Regulation 37.3(a)(l), a section of the Act and a Commission regulation otherwise applicable to swaps *(see infra* Section C) and were not conducted pursuant to Regulation 32.3.[5] Accordingly, Coinflip violated Section 4c(b) of the Act and Commission Regulation 32.2.

C. Coinflip Violated Section 5h(a)(l) of the Act

Section 5h(a)(1) of the Act forbids any person from operating "a facility for the trading or processing of swaps unless the facility is registered as a swap execution facility or as a designated contract market...." 7 U.S.C. § 7b-3(a)(1). Section 1(a)(47) of the Act's definition of "swap" includes option contracts. 7 U.S.C. § 1a(47)(A)(i). Regulation 37.3(a)(1) similarly requires that any "person operating a facility that offers a trading system or platform in which more than one market participant has the ability to execute or trade swaps with more than one other market participant on the system or platform shall register the facility as a swap execution facility under this part or as a designated contract market under part 38 of this chapter." 17 C.F.R. § 37.3(a)(l) (2014).

During the Relevant Period, Coinflip operated a facility for the trading of swaps. However, Coinflip did not register the facility as a swap execution facility or designated contract market. Accordingly, Coinflip violated Section 5h(a)(l) of the Act and Regulation 37.3(a)(1).

---

5. To take advantage of the "trade option" exemptions set forth in Regulation 32.3, the offeror of the option must be an eligible contract participant as defined in Section 1a(18) of the Act or "producer, processor, or commercial user of, or a merchant handling the commodity," and have a reasonable basis to believe that the offeree was a "producer, processor, or commercial user of, or a merchant handling the commodity that is the subject of the commodity option transaction, or the products or by-products thereof, and such offeree is offered or entering into the commodity option transaction solely for purposes related to its business as such." 17 C.F.R. §§ 32.3(a)(1)(i)-(ii) and 32.3(a)(2).

D. Riordan Is Liable for Coinflip's Violations as Its Controlling Person Under Section 13(b) of the Act

Riordan controlled Coinflip, directly or indirectly, and did not act in good faith or knowingly induced, directly or indirectly, Coinflip's acts in violation of the Act and Regulations; therefore, pursuant to Section 13(b) of the Act, 7 U.S.C. § 13c(b) (2012), Riordan is liable for Coinflip's violations of Sections 4c(b) and 5h(a)(1) of the Act, 7 U.S.C. §§ 6c(b) and 7b-3(a)(l) (2012) and Regulations 32.2 and 37.3(a)(1), 17 C.F.R. §§ 32.2 and 37.3(a)(1) (2014).

IV.

FINDINGS OF VIOLATIONS

Based on the foregoing, the Commission finds that, during the Relevant Period, Respondents violated Sections 4c(b) and 5h(a)(1) of the Act, 7 U.S.C. §§ 4c(b) and 7b-3(a)(l) (2012), and Commission Regulations 32.2 and 37.3(a)(l), 17 C.F.R. §§ 32.2 and 37.3(a)(1) (2014).

Discussion Points

1. *The CFTC's regulatory authority over swaps.* Should the SEC and CFTC have concurrent authority to regulate swaps? If one regulatory agency, such as the CFTC, gains complete regulatory authority over virtual currencies, should that agency also have complete authority to regulate swaps involving virtual currencies?

2. *The timing of CoinFlip.* The *CoinFlip* case was litigated in 2015, a couple of years before the ICO boom in 2017. Should the CFTC have been focused on regulating swap facilities like CoinFlip? Why or why not?

3. *Virtual currencies as commodities.* Do you agree with the CFTC that virtual currencies are commodities? Why or why not?

4. *Who should regulate virtual currencies?* Should the CFTC have regulatory authority over virtual currencies? What would be the benefits and what would be the drawbacks?

II. Key CFTC Cases Regarding Cryptocurrencies

Blockchain transactions, such as those including Bitcoin, Ethereum, and Litecoin, have increased in frequency. The rising popularity of cryptocurrencies requires the CFTC to regulate the cryptocurrency market.

CFTC v. Patrick K. McDonnell, and Cabbagetech, Corp. d/b/a Coin Drop Markets

287 F. Supp. 3d 213 (E.D.N.Y. 2018)

I. Introduction

The Commodity Futures Trading Commission ("CFTC") sues Patrick McDonnell and his company Coin Drop Markets. CFTC alleges defendants "operated a deceptive and fraudulent virtual currency scheme... for purported virtual currency trading advice" and "for virtual currency purchases and trading... and simply misappropriated [investor] funds." See CFTC Complaint, ECF No. 1, Jan. 18, 2018, at 1 ("CFTC Compl.").

CFTC seeks injunctive relief, monetary penalties, and restitution of funds received in violation of the Commodity Exchange Act ("CEA"). *Id.* at 11.

Until Congress clarifies the matter, the CFTC has concurrent authority, along with other state and federal administrative agencies, and civil and criminal courts, over dealings in virtual currency. An important nationally and internationally traded commodity, virtual currency is tendered for payment for debts, although, unlike United States currency, it is not legal tender that must be accepted. Title 31 U.S.C. § 5103 ("United States coins and currency... are legal tender for all debts...").

A. Commodity Futures Trading Commission ("CFTC") Standing

The primary issue raised at the outset of this litigation is whether CFTC has standing to sue defendants on the theory that they have violated the CEA. Title 7 U.S.C. § 1. Presented are two questions that determine the plaintiff's standing: (1) whether virtual currency may be regulated by the CFTC as a commodity; and (2) whether the amendments to the CEA under the Dodd-Frank Act permit the CFTC to exercise its jurisdiction over fraud that does not directly involve the sale of futures or derivative contracts.

Both questions are answered in the affirmative. A "commodity" encompasses virtual currency both in economic function and in the language of the statute. Title 7 U.S.C. § 1(a)(9) (The CEA defines "commodity" as agricultural products and "all other goods and articles... and all services, rights, and interests... in which contracts for future delivery are presently or in the future dealt in.").

CFTC's broad authority extends to fraud or manipulation in derivatives markets and underlying spot markets. See Title 7 U.S.C. § 9(1). CFTC may exercise its enforcement power over fraud related to virtual currencies sold in interstate commerce. See Title 17 C.F.R. § 180.1.

B. Injunctive Relief

After hearing testimony from an Investigator in the Division of Enforcement for the CFTC, the court finds the plaintiff has made a preliminary prima facie showing that the defendants committed fraud by misappropriation of investors' funds and misrepresentation through false trading advice and promised future profits.

A preliminary injunction is granted in favor of the CFTC. The court finds a reasonable likelihood that without an injunction the defendants will continue to violate the CEA. An order outlining the terms of relief is issued and attached. *See* Appendix A, Order of Preliminary Injunction and Other Relief ("App. A, Prelim. Injunction").

II. Facts

Patrick McDonnell and his company CabbageTech, Corp., doing business as Coin Drop Markets ("defendants"), offered fraudulent trading and investment services related to virtual currency. *See* Description of "Virtual Currencies" *infra* Part III, in the spring and summer of 2017. Christopher Giglio Declaration, ECF No. 21, Feb. 26, 2018, Ex. 2 ("Giglio Decl.") ¶¶ 13,14.

Customers from the United States and abroad paid defendants for "membership" in virtual currency trading groups purported to provide exit prices and profits of up to "300%" per week. *Id.* ¶¶ 17–20. Defendants advertised their services through "at least two websites, www.coindropmarkets.com and www.coindrops.club," as well as on the social media platform Twitter. *Id.* ¶¶ 15–17.

"Investors" transferred virtual currency to the defendants for "day" trading. *Id.* ¶ 21 ("McDonnell claimed that he could generate profits of 2 to 300% each day for [an] Investor…and that $1,000 in Litecoin [a type of virtual currency] should be earning $200 to $250 per day through trading.").

After receiving membership payment or virtual currency investments, defendants deleted their "social media accounts" and "websites and ceased communicating with…customers around July, 2017." *Id.* ¶ 26. Defendants provided minimal, if any, virtual currency trading advice and never achieved the promised return on investment. *Id.* ¶ 27. When customers asked for a return of their membership fee, or virtual currency investment, the defendants refused and misappropriated the funds. *Id.* ¶¶ 27–32.

Discussion Points

1. *What is the proper standard?* In its reasoning, the court stated it "found a reasonable likelihood that without an injunction the defendants will continue to violate the CEA." Does the court adequately define what a "reasonable likelihood" is? Is this lower than the civil "preponderance of the evidence" standard? Is this higher than the criminal standard of "beyond a reasonable doubt"? Should the standard for culpability be elevated in cases such as *McDonnell*?

2. *Combatting deceptive and fraudulent schemes.* McDonnell was found to have fully owned and operated a "deceptive and fraudulent virtual currency scheme." Do you think the CFTC is becoming more concerned about consumer protection from fraud and deceptive practices? Do you think the penalty imposed on McDonnell is enough to deter deceptive and fraudulent practices in the virtual currency space? Why or why not?

3. *Scienter.* What degree of scienter is needed for the court to find fraud? Which of the following five standards did the court apply: knowingly, purposely, willfully, recklessly, or intentionally? Which standard do you think the court should have applied? Can you be held liable without the intent to defraud? Why or why not? Does the court discuss this?

Commodity Futures Trading Commission v. My Big Coin Pay, Inc.
334 F. Supp. 3d 492 (D. Mass. 2018)

Defendant Randall Crater and all Relief Defendants[1] move to dismiss this case brought by plaintiff Commodity Future Trading Commission ("CFTC"). The amended complaint alleges a fraudulent "virtual currency scheme" in violation of the Commodity Exchange Act ("CEA" or "the Act") and a CFTC implementing regulation banning fraud and/or manipulation in connection with the sale of a commodity. See 7 U.S.C. § 9(1); 17 C.F.R. § 180.1(a). Defendants' principal argument is that CFTC fails to state a claim because My Big Coin ("MBC" or "My Big Coin"), the allegedly fraudulent virtual currency involved in the scheme, is not a "commodity" within the meaning of the Act. They also argue that the CEA provision and CFTC regulation are restricted to cases involving market manipulation and do not reach the fraud alleged here. Finally, they assert that plaintiff's amended complaint fails to support its allegations of misappropriation. The motion is denied.

I. Factual Background

For purposes of resolving this motion I accept as true the following well-pleaded facts, recited as alleged in the amended complaint. See *Ocasio-Hernández v. Fortuño-Burset*, 640 F.3d 1, 5 (1st Cir. 2011).

Mr. Crater and the non-moving codefendants[2] "operated a virtual currency scheme in which they fraudulently offered the sale of a fully-functioning virtual cur-

---

1. The Relief Defendants are Kimberly Renee Benge; Kimberly Renee Benge d/b/a Greyshore Advertisement a/k/a Greyshore Advertiset; Barbara Crater Meeks; Erica Crater; Greyshore, LLC; and Greyshore Technology, LLC.

2. In addition to Mr. Crater, the amended complaint names as defendants other individuals (Mark Gillespie, John Roche, Michael Kruger) and now-defunct corporate entities (My Big Coin Pay, Inc.; My Big Coin, Inc.). All these defendants have defaulted, see Docket ## 85–88, except for

rency" called "My Big Coin".[3] Docket # 63 (hereinafter "Am. Compl.") ¶ 1. In short, defendants enticed customers to buy My Big Coin by making various untrue and/ or misleading statements and omitting material facts. The falsities included that My Big Coin was "backed by gold," could be used anywhere Mastercard was accepted, and was being "actively traded" on several currency exchanges. See, *e.g., id.* ¶ 39. Defendants also made up and arbitrarily changed the price of My Big Coin to mimic the fluctuations of a legitimate, actively-traded virtual currency. When victims of the fraud purchased My Big Coin, they could view their accounts on a website but "could not trade their MBC or withdraw funds...." *Id.* ¶ 37. Defendants obtained more than $6 million from the scheme, some of which is currently held by the several Relief Defendants.

Plaintiff brought suit on January 16, 2018, alleging violations of Section 6(c)(1) of the Commodities Exchange Act, 7 U.S.C. § 9(1), and CFTC Regulation 180.1(a), 17 C.F.R. § 180.1(a). It also moved for a temporary restraining order and a preliminary injunction. The court granted the temporary restraining order and defendants subsequently consented to a preliminary injunction. Thereafter, plaintiff amended its complaint and defendants filed the pending motion to dismiss, which both parties extensively briefed and argued.

II. Legal Principles

"To survive a motion to dismiss, a complaint must contain sufficient factual matter, accepted as true, to 'state a claim to relief that is plausible on its face.'" *Ashcroft v. Iqbal*, 556 U.S. 662, 678 (2009) (quoting *Bell Atl. Corp. v. Twombly*, 550 U.S. 544, 570 (2007)). "A claim has facial plausibility when the plaintiff pleads factual content that allows the court to draw the reasonable inference that the defendant is liable for the misconduct alleged." Id. For purposes of a motion to dismiss, the court accepts all well-pleaded factual allegations as true and draws all reasonable inferences in the plaintiff's favor. See *Rodríguez-Reyes v. Molina-Rodríguez*, 711 F.3d 49, 52–53 (1st Cir. 2013).

III. Application

A. Jurisdiction

As an initial matter, although defendants suggest that this court does not have subject matter jurisdiction for lack of a federal question, their underlying argument

---

Mr. Kruger who was served on September 3, 2018 in accordance with the court's alternative service Order. See Docket ## 96, 102.

3. According to the amended complaint, a virtual currency is "a digital representation of value that functions as a medium of exchange, a unit of account, and/or a store of value, but does not have legal tender status in any jurisdiction." Am. Compl. ¶ 25. Unlike United States dollars or other "'real' currencies," virtual currencies "use decentralized networks to track transactions between persons," and transfers are recorded in a "decentralized ledger" that functions without any "central intermediary in which both users need to trust." *Id.*

that the alleged conduct did not involve a "commodity" goes to the merits of plaintiff's claim, not jurisdiction. This court has subject matter jurisdiction because the case presents a federal question, see 28 U.S.C. § 1331, and because federal law expressly authorizes CFTC to sue and the court to grant appropriate relief, see 7 U.S.C. §13a-1(a); 28 U.S.C. § 1345. See, *e.g.*, *CFTC v. Hunter Wise Commodities, LLC*, 749 F.3d 967, 974 (11th Cir. 2014) ("[Defendant-Appellants] argue the Commission's statutory authority, its 'jurisdiction,' does not reach the transactions at issue, but we note at the outset that this is not a matter of the court's jurisdiction to hear this case.").

B. Whether Plaintiff Has Adequately Alleged the Sale of a "Commodity" Under the CEA

"The Commodity Exchange Act (CEA) has been aptly characterized as a 'comprehensive regulatory structure to oversee the volatile and esoteric futures trading complex.'" *Merrill Lynch, Pierce, Fenner & Smith, Inc. v. Curran*, 456 U.S. 353, 356 (1982) (internal citation omitted) (quoting H.R.Rep. No. 93–975, at 1 (1974) (hereinafter "House Report")). Accordingly, the present Act generally grants CFTC exclusive jurisdiction over futures contracts and the exchanges where they are traded. See 7 U.S.C. § 2(a)(1)(A).[4] CFTC has additional powers under the statute, including the general anti-fraud and anti-manipulation authority over "any…contract of sale of any commodity in interstate commerce" pursuant to which it brings the claims in this case. See 7 U.S.C. § 9(1).

As noted above, plaintiff alleges violations of CEA Section 6(c)(1) and CFTC regulation 180.1(a). Both provisions apply to the fraud alleged in this case if the conduct involved a "commodity" under the CEA. See 7 U.S.C. § 9(1) (banning, inter alia, the use of "any manipulative or deceptive device or contrivance" "in connection with any…contract of sale of any commodity in interstate commerce"); 17 C.F.R. §180.1(a) (banning, inter alia, the use of "any manipulative device, scheme, or artifice to defraud" "in connection with any…contract of sale of any commodity in interstate commerce"). Therefore, to state a viable claim, plaintiff must adequately plead that My Big Coin is a commodity.

"Commodity" is a defined term in the CEA. See 7 U.S.C. § 1a(9). It includes a host of specifically enumerated agricultural products as well as "all other goods and articles…and all services rights and interests…in which contracts for future delivery are presently or in the future dealt in." *Id.* The full definition reads:

> The term "commodity" means wheat, cotton, rice, corn, oats, barley, rye, flaxseed, grain sorghums, mill feeds, butter, eggs, Solanum tuberosum (Irish potatoes), wool, wool tops, fats and oils (including lard, tallow, cottonseed oil,

---

4. Simply put, a "futures contract" is an agreement to buy or sell a certain quantity of a commodity at a certain price at a certain time in the future. See *CFTC v. Erskine*, 512 F.3d 309, 323 (6th Cir. 2008). Such contracts are standardized so they may be traded on exchanges. See *id.*

peanut oil, soybean oil, and all other fats and oils), cottonseed meal, cotton-seed, peanuts, soybeans, soybean meal, livestock, livestock products, and frozen concentrated orange juice, and all other goods and articles, except onions (as provided by section 13-1 of this title) and motion picture box office receipts (or any index, measure, value, or data related to such receipts), and all services, rights, and interests (except motion picture box office receipts, or any index, measure, value or data related to such receipts) in which contracts for future delivery are presently or in the future dealt in.

Defendants contend that because "contracts for future delivery" are indisputably not "dealt in" My Big Coin, it cannot be a commodity under the CEA. They take the position that in order to satisfy the CEA's "commodity" definition, the specific item in question must itself underlie a futures contract. Plaintiff responds that "a 'commodity' for purposes of [the CEA definition] is broader than any particular type or brand of that commodity." Docket # 70 at 10.[5] Pointing to the existence of Bitcoin futures contracts, it argues that contracts for future delivery of virtual currencies are "dealt in" and that My Big Coin, as a virtual currency, is therefore a commodity.[6]

The text of the statute supports plaintiff's argument. The Act defines "commodity" generally and categorically, "not by type, grade, quality, brand, producer, manufacturer, or form." Docket # 70 at 11. For example, the Act classifies "livestock" as a commodity without enumerating which particular species are the subject of futures

---

5. Plaintiff also attempts to sidestep the issue of futures contracts by arguing that My Big Coin is a "good" or an "article" and that items in these categories are commodities under the CEA even in the absence of contracts for future delivery. That argument is unavailing. The "dealt in" clause applies to both "goods and articles" as well as "services, rights, and interests." See *United States v. Brooks*, 681 F.3d 678, 694 (5th Cir. 2012) ("Natural gas is plainly a 'good' or 'article.' The question thus turns on whether it is a good 'in which contracts for future delivery are presently or in the future dealt with.'"); *Bd. of Trade of City of Chicago v. S.E.C.*, 677 F.2d 1137, 1142 (7th Cir. 1982) ("literally anything other than onions [can] become a 'commodity' and thereby subject to CFTC regulation simply by its futures being traded on some exchange"), judgment vacated as moot *SEC v. Bd. of Trade of City of Chicago*, 459 U.S. 1026 (1982); *CFTC v. McDonnell*, 287 F. Supp. 3d 213, 228 (E.D.N.Y. 2018) ("Where a futures market exists for a good, service, right, or interest, it may be regulated by CFTC, as a commodity."); *CFTC v. Reed*, 481 F. Supp. 2d 1190, 1194 (D. Colo. 2007) ("In 1974 the CEA was amended to expand its jurisdiction from a statutory list of enumerated commodities to include all goods and articles in which a futures contract is traded."); see also *Dunn v. CFTC*, 519 U.S. 465, 469 (1997) ("the 1974 amendments that created the CFTC [] dramatically expanded the coverage of the statute to include nonagricultural commodities 'in which contracts for future delivery are presently or in the future dealt in' ....").

6. The court takes judicial notice of the undisputed facts that (a) Bitcoin futures are presently traded; and (b) no futures contracts exist for My Big Coin. See *In re Colonial Mortg. Bankers Corp.*, 324 F.3d 12, 15 (1st Cir. 2003) (court should consider matters susceptible to judicial notice in ruling on a motion to dismiss, including matters of public record); Bitcoin Futures Contract Specs, CME GROUP, https://www.cmegroup.com/trading/equity-index/us-index/bitcoin_contract_specifications.html (last visited September 25, 2018); Summary Product Specifications Chart for Cboe Bitcoin (USD) Futures, CBOE FUTURES EXCHANGE, http://cfe.cboe.com/cfe-products/xbt-cboe-bitcoin-futures/contract-specifications (last visited September 25, 2018).

trading. Thus, as plaintiff urges, Congress' approach to defining "commodity" signals an intent that courts focus on categories—not specific items—when determining whether the "dealt in" requirement is met.

This broad approach also accords with Congress's goal of "strengthening the federal regulation of the...commodity futures trading industry," House Report at 1, since an expansive definition of "commodity" reasonably assures that the CEA's regulatory scheme and enforcement provisions will comprehensively protect and police the markets. That goal is particularly relevant here, given that the court is construing the term "commodity" not in a vacuum, but rather as it functions within the CEA's anti- fraud enforcement provision of Section 6(c)(1). As the Supreme Court has instructed in an analogous context, such statutes are to be "construed 'not technically and restrictively, but flexibly to effectuate [their] remedial purposes." *SEC v. Zandford*, 535 U.S. 813, 819 (2002) (analyzing Section 10(b) of the Securities Exchange Act) (quoting *SEC v. Capital Gains Research Bureau, Inc.*, 375 U.S. 180, 195 (1963)).

Finally, the scant case law on this issue also supports plaintiff's approach. In a series of cases involving natural gas, courts have repeatedly rejected arguments that a particular type of natural gas was not a commodity because that specific type was not the subject of a futures contract. See *United States v. Brooks*, 681 F.3d 678 (5th Cir. 2012); *United States v. Futch*, 278 F. App'x 387, 395 (5th Cir. 2008); *United States v. Valencia*, No. CR.A. H-03-024, 2003 WL 23174749, at *8 (S.D. Tex. Aug. 25, 2003), order vacated in part on reconsideration, No. CRIM.A. H-03-024, 2003 WL 23675402 (S.D. Tex. Nov. 13, 2003), rev'd and remanded on other grounds, 394 F.3d 352 (5th Cir. 2004). Rather, the courts held that because futures contracts in natural gas underlaid by gas at Henry Hub, Louisiana were dealt in, and because natural gas is "fungible" and may move freely throughout a national pipeline system, this was sufficient to show that natural gas, including the types at issue in these cases, was a commodity. See *Brooks*, 681 F.3d at 694–95 (observing that "it would be peculiar that natural gas at another hub is not a commodity, but suddenly becomes a commodity solely on the basis that it passes through Henry Hub, and ceases to be a commodity once it moves onto some other locale"); *Futch*, 278 F. App'x at 395 (noting that "Henry Hub is the nexus of several major natural gas pipelines" and focusing on "the type of commodity in question, natural gas"); *Valencia*, 2003 WL 23174749 at *8 (noting that "natural gas is fungible" and finding that "natural gas for delivery on the West Coast or otherwise, is a commodity."). [7] Taken together, these decisions align with plaintiff's argument that the CEA only requires the existence of futures trading within a certain class (e.g. "natural gas") in order for all items within that class (e.g. "West Coast" natural gas) to be considered commodities.

---

7. The *Valencia* court somewhat hedged this ruling, stating that "the issue...of whether 'West Coast gas' is a commodity 'in which contracts for future delivery are presently or in the future dealt in' is a fact question." *Valencia*, 2003 WL 23174749 at *8.

Here, the amended complaint alleges that My Big Coin is a virtual currency and it is undisputed that there is futures trading in virtual currencies (specifically involving Bitcoin). That is sufficient, especially at the pleading stage, for plaintiff to allege that My Big Coin is a "commodity" under the Act.[8] See *CFTC v. McDonnell*, 287 F. Supp. 3d 213, 228 (E.D.N.Y. 2018) ("Virtual currencies can be regulated by CFTC as a commodity."); *In re BFXNA Inc.*, CFTC Docket 16-19, at 5–6 (June 2, 2016) ("[V]irtual currencies are encompassed in the [CEA] definition and properly defined as commodities."); *In re Coinflip, Inc.*, CFTC Docket No. 15-29, at 3 (Sept. 17, 2015) (same).[9] Accordingly, defendants' first ground for dismissal fails.

C. Whether Section 6(c)(1) and Regulation 180.1(a) Reach the Fraud Alleged

Defendants argue, second, that even if My Big Coin is a commodity, the complaint is still deficient because the laws under which the claims are brought "were meant to combat fraudulent market manipulation—not the kind of garden variety sales puffery that the Amended Complaint alleges." Docket # 69 at 15. That argument fails because both Section 6(c)(1) and Regulation 180.1 explicitly prohibit fraud even in the absence of market manipulation. See 7 U.S.C. § 9 (banning the use of any "manipulative **or** deceptive device or contrivance" in connection with the sale of a commodity) (emphasis added); 17 C.F.R. § 180.1(a) (banning the use of "any manipulative device, scheme, or artifice to defraud," the making of "any untrue or misleading statement of a material fact," or the use of "any act, practice, or course of business, which operates…as a fraud or deceit …." in connection with the sale of a commodity). Courts have accordingly recognized CFTC's power to prosecute fraud under these provisions. See *CFTC v. S. Tr. Metals, Inc.*, No. 16-16544, 2018 WL 3384266, at *1, 6, 15 (11th Cir. July 12, 2018) (affirming judgment for CFTC in "commodities-fraud case" alleging violations of Regulation 180.1 that "involve[d] no allegation…that the Defendants manipulated the price of a commodity"); *McDonnell*, 287 F. Supp. 3d at 229 ("Language in 7 U.S.C. § 9(1), and 17 C.F.R. § 180.1, establish the CFTC's regulatory authority over the manipulative schemes, fraud, and misleading statements alleged in the complaint."), aff'd on reconsideration, No. 18-CV-361, 2018 WL 3435047, at *2 (E.D.N.Y. July 16, 2018) ("Title 7 U.S.C. § 9(1) gives the CFTC standing to exercise its enforcement power over the fraudulent schemes alleged in the complaint."); *CFTC v. Hunter Wise Commodities, LLC*, 21 F. Supp. 3d

---

8. Contrary to defendants' argument, the amended complaint alleges that My Big Coin and Bitcoin are sufficiently related so as to justify this categorical treatment. Plaintiffs have alleged that My Big Coin and Bitcoin are both virtual currencies, see Am. Compl. ¶ 26, and have alleged various characteristics common to virtual currencies, see Am. Compl. ¶ 25. That is enough under the court's reading of the statute and the principles discussed herein.

9. While *McDonnell*, *In re Coinflip*, and *In re BFXNA* can be distinguished on their facts since each case involved the virtual currency Bitcoin, these orders are nevertheless useful data points. Each supports the court's view that the appropriate inquiry under the CEA is whether contracts for future delivery of virtual currencies are dealt in, not whether a particular type of virtual currency underlies a futures contract.

1317, 1348 (S.D. Fla. 2014) (finding defendants liable for violating Section 6(c)(1) and Regulation 180.1 in fraud case not involving allegations of market manipulation). But see *CFTC v. Monex Credit Co.*, No. SACV 17–01868 JVS (DFMx), 2018 WL 2306863, at *7–10 (C.D. Cal. May 1, 2018) (finding that Section 6(c)(1) prohibits only fraud-based market manipulation). Though some isolated statements in the legislative history surrounding Section 6(c)(1) suggest Congress was, perhaps, principally concerned with combating manipulation, see Docket # 69 at 15, these statements are insufficient to overcome the broad language in the statute as it was passed.

D. Whether the Amended Complaint Fails to Support its Misappropriation Theory

Finally, though the amended complaint references misappropriation, the relevant count is "fraud by deceptive device or contrivance" in violation of Section 6(c)(1) and Regulation 180.1(a). The amended complaint sets forth in detail the allegations supporting this charge. As such, any failure to allege that defendants had an obligation to use customer funds in a certain way has no bearing on whether plaintiff has adequately pleaded this claim.

IV. Conclusion

Defendants' motion to dismiss (Docket # 68) is denied.

In the Matter of iFinex Inc., BFXNA Inc., and BFXWW Inc.
CFTC Docket No. 22-05 (2021)

I. INTRODUCTION

The Commodity Futures Trading Commission ("Commission") has reason to believe that from at least March 1, 2016 through at least December 31, 2018 (the "Relevant Period") Respondents iFinex Inc. ("iFinex"), BFXNA Inc. ("BFXNA"), and BFXWW Inc. ("BFXWW") all doing business as "Bitfinex" (collectively, "Respondents" or "Bitfinex"), violated Sections 4(a) and 4d of the Act, 7 U.S.C. §§ 6(a) and 6d (2018); and that BFXNA further violated Part VII. A of the Commission's 2016 Order in *In re BFXNA Inc. d/b/a Bitfinex*, CFTC No. 16-19, 2016 WL 3137612 (June 2, 2016) ("2016 Order"), which directed BFXNA to cease and desist from violating Sections 4(a) and 4d, as Bitfinex has continued to offer, confirm the execution of, and receive funds for financed retail commodity transactions that were not made on or subject to the rules of a board of a trade that has been designated or registered by the CFTC. Therefore, the Commission deems it appropriate and in the public interest that public administrative proceedings be, and hereby are, instituted to determine whether Bitfinex engaged in the violations set forth herein and to determine whether any order should be issued imposing remedial sanctions.

In anticipation of the institution of an administrative proceeding, Respondents have submitted an Offer of Settlement ("Offer"), which the Commission has determined to accept. Without admitting or denying any of the findings or conclusions herein, Respondents consent to the entry of this Order Instituting Proceedings Pursuant to Section 6(c) and (d) of the Commodity Exchange Act, Making Findings, and Imposing Remedial Sanctions ("Order"), and acknowledges service of this Order.[1]

II. FINDINGS

The Commission finds the following:

A. SUMMARY

During the Relevant Period and continuing to the present day, Respondents have offered spot and leveraged, margined, or financed trading in various digital assets including bitcoin, ether, and tether tokens.[2] Throughout the Relevant Period, Respondents have offered, executed, and/or confirmed the execution of off-exchange leveraged, margined, or financed transactions with U.S. customers who were not eligible contract participants or eligible commercial entities[3] (collectively, "non-ECPs" or "retail customers"), in violation of Section 4(a) of the Act, 7 U.S.C. § 6(a) (2018). Respondents have also accepted fiat currency, bitcoin, U.S. dollar tether tokens ("USDt"), and other cryptocurrencies in connection with the aforementioned retail commodity transactions. By accepting funds and orders for retail commodity transactions, Respondents also operated as a futures commission merchant ("FCM") without obtaining the required registration in violation of Section 4d(a)(1) of the Act, 7 U.S.C. § 6d(a)(1) (2018).

On June 2, 2016, the Commission entered an administrative order finding that from in or about April 2013 to at least February 2016, BFXNA had violated the then-effective Sections 4(a) and 4d of the CEA, and ordering BFXNA to cease and desist from the violations as charged. *See* 2016 Order. By continuing to offer, execute,

---

1. Respondents consent to the use of the findings of fact and conclusions of law in this Order in this proceeding and in any other proceeding brought by the Commission or to which the Commission is a party or claimant, and agrees that they shall be taken as true and correct and be given preclusive effect therein, without further proof. Respondents do not consent, however, to the use of this Order, or the findings or conclusions herein, as the sole basis for any other proceeding brought by the Commission or to which the Commission is a party or claimant, other than: a proceeding in bankruptcy or receivership; or a proceeding to enforce the terms of this Order. Respondents do not consent to the use of the Offer or this Order, or the findings or conclusions in this Order, by any other party in any other proceeding.

2. Bitcoin, ether, litecoin, and tether tokens, along with other digital assets, are encompassed within the broad definition of "commodity" under Section 1a(9) of the Act, 7 U.S.C. § 1a(9) (2018), and are therefore subject to applicable provisions of the Act and Regulations, which include Section 6(c)(1) of the Act and Regulation 180.1(a). *See, e.g., CFTC v. McDonnell*, 287 F. Supp. 3d 213, 226 (E.D.N.Y 2018) ("Virtual currencies can be regulated by CFTC as a commodity."), *mot. for reconsideration denied*, 321 F. Supp. 3d 366 (E.D.N.Y. 2018).

3. Eligible contract participants and eligible commercial entities are defined in Sections 1a(18) and 1a(17) of the Act, 7 U.S.C. §§ 1a(17), (18) (2018), respectively.

and/or confirm the execution of retail leveraged, margined, or financed commodity transactions that were not made on or subject to the rules of a board of trade that has been designated or registered by the CFTC as a contract market for the specific commodity, and by accepting funds and orders for those transactions, throughout the Relevant Period, BFXNA, has also violated Part VII. A of the 2016 Order.

B. RESPONDENTS

iFinex Inc. was incorporated in the British Virgin Islands on May 21, 2013. iFinex operates the Bitfinex trading platform. iFinex has never been registered with the Commission in any capacity.

BFXNA Inc. was incorporated in the British Virgin Islands on November 4, 2014. BFXNA is a wholly-owned subsidiary of iFinex. According to Bitfinex's Terms of Service ("TOS"), U.S. persons and individuals who make deposits, withdrawals, or transfers through U.S. financial institutions are BFXNA's customers. BFXNA has been registered as a money service business ("MSB") with the Financial Crimes Enforcement Network ("FinCEN") of the U.S. Department of the Treasury since January 30, 2015. BFXNA has never been registered with the Commission in any capacity.

BFXWW Inc. was incorporated in the British Virgin Islands on April 28, 2015. BFXWW is a wholly-owned subsidiary of iFinex. According to Bitfinex's TOS, BFX-WW contracts with non-U.S. customers. BFXWW has never been registered with the Commission in any capacity.

C. FACTS

Bitfinex offers trading of cryptocurrency products,[4] including bitcoin, ether, lite-coin, and tether tokens, to customers on its website, www.bitfinex.com, the Bitfinex mobile application, and by direct connection to its trading engine servers via the Bitfinex application programming interface.

Bitfinex offers trading on a leveraged or margined basis on both long and short positions. The amount of initial equity Bitfinex requires that a customer have in order to trade on margin varies by product. For example, for the BTC/USD pair, the maximum leverage for margin trading is 10x, meaning that the customer must have 10% of the value of that position, subject to certain haircuts. During the Relevant Period, the substantial majority of margin trading was financed through Bifinex's peer-to-peer ("P2P") funding program. Through P2P, Bitfinex customers who held fiat or cryptocurrency in their Bitfinex account would "lend" those funds to other Bitfinex customers.

---

4. Beginning in or around September 2019, certain customers could trade cryptocurrency swaps products or "perpetual contracts" on the Bitfinex platform. Respondents represent that these products are offered by iFinex Financial Technologies Limited, a subsidiary of iFinex, Inc.

To provide margin funding, Bitfinex customers had to create a funding order that included the amount of funds available, interest rate, and period of funding. Bitfinex set the minimum financing duration at two days, and the maximum duration at 120 days. Once an offer to borrow was accepted, the financing recipient would then use those funds to buy, sell, and trade on the Bitfinex platform.

To trade with margin, Bitfinex customers are required to hold a percentage of the value of their open positions in a "Margin Wallet" on the exchange. Margin Wallets can hold fiat or cryptocurrencies such as tether tokens or bitcoin. A customer's margined positions will remain open until the customer submits a closing trade, or Bitfinex initiates a forced liquidation. Typically, Bitfinex customers receive a margin call when the net value of their account equity held in the Margin Wallet drops below the required amount of margin for their open positions. If the equity falls below the required maintenance margin, Bitfinex will force-liquidate the customer's positions and will act as the counterparty to that transaction.

During the Relevant Period, Bitfinex's TOS required that, to engage in margin trading, customers:…irrevocably appoint Bitfinex to act as your exclusive agent in respect of any contract on the Site in which you are a Financing Recipient. Specifically, you hereby grant Bitfinex agency, and you authorize and instruct Bitfinex: to implement, levy, monitor, and maintain a lien on all Fiat amounts and Digital Tokens in your name or control in any Account (including any subaccount or any Digital Tokens Wallet) on the Site in favor of one or more Financing Providers (a "Lien"); and, to liquidate any Digital Tokens or Fiat in your name or control in any Account (including any subaccount or any Digital Tokens Wallet) if necessary to ensure that any Financing Provider on the Site from whom you have obtained financing is repaid in full.

Bitfinex force-liquidated certain positions and/or acted as a counterparty to certain transactions with non-ECP U.S. persons during the Relevant Period.

In the 2016 CFTC Order, the Commission ordered Bitfinex to cease and desist from offering, entering into, executing, or confirming the execution of financed retail commodity transactions to U.S. non-ECP customers unless such transactions are made on or subject to the rules of a board of a trade that has been designated or registered by the CFTC as a contract market or derivatives transaction execution facility in violation of Section 4(a) of the Act, and from accepting orders for retail commodity transactions and receiving funds from those customers in connection with those transactions in violation of Section 4d(a) of the Act, and order.

Bitfinex's TOS stated that U.S. persons, subject to certain exceptions for ECPs as determined by Bitfinex in its sole discretion, could not access the platform's services as of October 5, 2017, and U.S. entities could not access the platform's services as of August 15, 2018. During the Relevant Period, customers, including those in the U.S., needed to provide only their name and a valid email address to open a "basic account" with Bitfinex. Throughout the Relevant Period, a basic account holder could deposit and withdraw cryptocurrencies, engage in exchange and margin trading, and provide margin funding, among other activities.

Respondents represent that Bitfinex has performed its own IP/location checks for customers for all accounts, including basic accounts, throughout the Relevant Period, including whenever a customer accessed their account; and further represent that since at least in or about November 2017, identified non-ECP U.S. persons were not permitted to withdraw fiat or stablecoin.[5] Respondents also represent, that in or around November 2017, they expanded user verification procedures, previously in place for New York residents and others, to include U.S. individual customers.

However, during the Relevant Period, Bitfinex's actions were not adequate to prohibit non-ECP U.S. persons from engaging in retail commodity transactions. Bitfinex was aware that some non-ECP U.S. customers continued to access the platform after the changes to the TOS. For example, on March 12, 2018, a Bitfinex manager reminded the entire customer support team that customers "can deposit/withdraw cryptocurrencies and trade fully (including USD pairs) without being verified on our site, there are no limits to this.... As background—it['s] not that hard to buy/ sell BTC or whatever from another site and transfer it here, so anyone who is that motivated to use our site will have done so already. . ." Bitfinex customers, including those in the U.S., could click through and simply ignore the TOS and continue to access the Bitfinex platform.

In November 2018 Bitfinex developed an "Individual On-boarding Procedure" that outlined the "Know-Your-Customer" ("KYC")[6] program developed to "mitigate against Bitfinex, its customers and the products and services Bitfinex provides being used to facilitate money laundering, terrorist financing, sanctions violations, or other illicit activity." This procedure allowed U.S. citizens that were "Bitfinex Personnel" (i.e., current employees or contractors) to trade on the Bitfinex Platform. In internal documents dated November 26, 2018, Bitfinex Personnel were advised that the platform "can no longer accept US residents (as of 4 Aug. 2017) if encountered" and instructed to not include U.S. persons on the "worksheet" used to track customer verification requests.

Throughout the Relevant Period, Bitfinex accepted deposits and withdrawals in fiat currency and other cryptocurrencies including bitcoin and USDt. Bitfinex's systems and TOS required that customers needed to be "verified" in order to deposit fiat assets and USDt tokens, but need not be verified to deposit bitcoin or certain other cryptocurrencies. Respondents have represented that a customer cannot withdraw fiat or cryptocurrency assets, including USDt tokens, bitcoin, and other digital assets, without Bitfinex confirming that the customer is not a U.S. person. However, Bitfinex customers have been able to deposit cryptocurrencies and enter into retail

---

5. Bitfinex also represents that its Onboarding Team rejected new applications submitted by self-identified U.S. citizens or residents and proactively screened certain customers onboarded before the prohibition on U.S. persons went into effect.

6. Bitfinex had a KYC program in place throughout the Relevant Period. Bitfinex represents that the Individual On-boarding Procedure updated and enhanced prior customer verification procedures.

commodity transactions on the Bitfinex platform without providing documentary proof of residence.

At various times during the Relevant Period, Bitfinex's customer service representatives communicated with U.S.-based customers regarding various issues related to their accounts, including address changes that clearly identified the customers' geographic location. On various occasions, customer service representatives encouraged customers based in the U.S. to use a VPN to create a private network from a public internet connection and mask the customer's internet protocol (IP) address. For example, on or around April 3, 2018, a Bitfinex customer service representative informed a U.S. based customer that the platform is "not against VPNs...by any means—quite the opposite actually" and further stated that "Most users who simply use our platform to trade or offer margin funding will not need to provide KYC information"; however, if "AML-CTF flags are triggered...we may require our users to provide KYC information."[7]

III. LEGAL DISCUSSION

A. Bitfinex Engaged in Illegal, Off-Exchange Retail Commodity Transactions in Violation of Section 4(a) of the Act

Pursuant to Section 2(c)(2)(D) of the Act, 7 U.S.C. § 2(c)(2)(D) (2018), any agreement, contract, or transaction in any commodity that is entered into with or offered to (even if not entered into with) non-ECPs on a leveraged or margined basis or financed by the offeror, counterparty, or a person acting in concert with the offeror or counterparty is, subject to certain exceptions, subject to Section 4(a) of the Act, 7 U.S.C. § 6(a) (2018), "as if the agreement, contract, or transaction was a contract of sale of a commodity for future delivery."

Section 4(a) of the Act makes it unlawful for any person to offer to enter into, enter into, execute, confirm the execution of, or conduct an office or business in the United States for the purpose of soliciting, or accepting any order for, or otherwise dealing in any transaction in, or in connection with, a commodity futures contract, unless such transaction is made on or subject to the rules of a board of trade that has been designated or registered by the CFTC as a contract market for the specific commodity.

During the Relevant Period, Respondents offered to enter into, entered into, executed, and/or confirmed the execution of margined or leveraged retail commodity transactions with non-ECP U.S. persons on the Bitfinex platform. These retail commodity transactions were not conducted on or subject to the rules of a board of trade that has been designated or registered by the CFTC as a contract market and therefore violated Section 4(a) of the Act.

---

7. Respondents represented that after the Relevant Period, there may have been some U.S. customers that its systems did not identify and that they closed accounts for customers identified as being non-ECP U.S. persons.

B. Bitfinex Operated as an Unregistered Futures Commission Merchant in Violation of Section 4d(a)(1) of the Act.

Section 1a(28) of the Act, 7 U.S.C. § 1a(28) (2018), in relevant part, defines an FCM as any individual, association, partnership, corporation or trust that engages in soliciting or in accepting orders for or acting as a counterparty in "any agreement, contract, or transaction described in … section (2)(c)(2)(D)(i)" and, in connection therewith, "accepts any money … or property (or extends credit in lieu thereof) to margin … trades or contracts that result or may result therefrom." Section 4d(a)(1) of the Act, 7 U.S.C. § 6d(a)(1) (2018), in pertinent part, makes it unlawful for any person to act as an FCM unless registered with the Commission as an FCM.

As described above, Bitfinex, while not registered as an FCM, acted during the Relevant Period as an FCM as defined in Section 1a(28) of the Act by accepting orders for and acting as a counterparty to retail commodity transactions with customers, and accepting money or property, including bitcoin and other cryptocurrencies, to margin these transactions. Therefore, Respondents violated Section 4d(a)(1) of the Act.

C. BFXNA Violated the Prior Commission Order

The Commission issued its 2016 Order in *In re BFXNA Inc. d/b/a Bitfinex*, CFTC No. 16-19, 2016 WL 3137612 (June 2, 2016), and found that Respondent BFXNA had violated Sections 4(a) and 4d of the CEA, 7 U.S.C. §§ 6(a), 6d (2012). Part VII. A of the 2016 Order directs Respondent BFXNA Inc. to cease and desist from violating Sections 4(a) and 4d.

During the Relevant Period, BFXNA repeatedly violated the CEA, Regulations, and the 2016 Order because it offered to enter into, executed, and/or confirmed the execution of leveraged, margined, or financed retail commodity transactions, and none of the financed retail commodity transactions were conducted on or subject to the rules of a board of trade that has been designated or registered by the CFTC as a contract market in violation of Section 4(a) of the Act. BFXNA also repeatedly violated the CEA, Regulations, and the 2016 Order because it accepted orders for retail commodity transactions and received funds from those customers in connection with retail commodity transactions while not registered with the Commission in any capacity in violation of Section 4d of the Act. Respondent BFXNA thus violated Part VII.A of the 2016 Order.

III. FINDINGS OF VIOLATIONS

Based on the foregoing, the Commission finds that, during the Relevant Period, Respondents iFinex Inc., BFXNA Inc., and BFXWW Inc. violated Sections 4(a) and 4d(a)(1) of the Act, 7 U.S.C. §§ 6(a), 6d(a)(1) (2018) and Respondent BFXNA Inc. further violated Part VII.A of the 2016 Order.

Discussion Points

1. *Compare.* What are the differences between this case and *McDonnell*? How are the rulings similar and how are they different? Do the rulings of these cases suggest a trend the courts are taking in regulating swaps?

2. *P2P exchange.* Was Bitfinex a peer to peer exchange? Do you think platforms that offer peer to peer exchanges should be regulated differently than regular, non-decentralized exchanges?

3. *Swap execution facilities.* The CFTC has regulatory authority over commodity and currency swaps. Should swap execution facilities be required to register with the CFTC? Why or why not? Should the CFTC impose more regulations over swap execution facilities?

In the Matter of Tether Holdings Limited, Tether Operations Limited, Tether Limited and Tether International Limited

CFTC Docket No. 22-04 (2021)

I. INTRODUCTION

The Commodity Futures Trading Commission ("Commission") has reason to believe that from at least June 1, 2016 to February 25, 2019 (the "Relevant Period"), Respondents Tether Holdings Limited, Tether Operations Limited, Tether Limited, and Tether International Limited, all doing business as "Tether" (collectively, "Respondents" or "Tether"), violated Section 6(c)(1) of the Commodity Exchange Act ("Act"), 7 U.S.C. § 9(1) (2018), and Commission Regulation ("Regulation") 180.1(a)(2), 17 C.F.R. § 180.1(a)(2) (2020). Therefore, the Commission deems it appropriate and in the public interest that public administrative proceedings be, and hereby are, instituted to determine whether Respondents engaged in the violations set forth herein and to determine whether any order should be issued imposing remedial sanctions.

In anticipation of the institution of an administrative proceeding, Respondents have submitted an Offer of Settlement ("Offer"), which the Commission has determined to accept. Without admitting or denying any of the findings or conclusions herein, Respondents consent to the entry of this Order Instituting Proceedings Pursuant to Section 6(c) and (d) of the Commodity Exchange Act, Making Findings, and Imposing Remedial Sanctions ("Order"), and acknowledges service of this Order.[1]

---

1. Respondents consent to the use of the findings of fact and conclusions of law in this Order in this proceeding and in any other proceeding brought by the Commission or to which the Commission is a party or claimant, and agrees that they shall be taken as true and correct and be given

II. FINDINGS

The Commission finds the following:

A. SUMMARY

Tether introduced the U.S. dollar tether token ("USDt" or "tether token") as a stablecoin in 2014. The USDt is a commodity as defined by the Act. At various times during the Relevant Period, Tether misrepresented to customers and the market that Tether maintained sufficient fiat reserves to back every USDt in circulation "one-to-one" with the "equivalent amount of corresponding fiat currency" held in reserves by Tether (the "Tether Reserves"), and that Tether would undergo routine, professional audits to demonstrate that it maintained "100% reserves at all times." In fact, during the majority of the Relevant Period, Tether failed to maintain fiat currency reserves in accounts in Tether's own name or in an account titled and held "in trust" for Tether (collectively the "Tether Bank Accounts") to back every USDt in circulation. While Tether represents that it maintained adequate reserves, some of the Tether Reserves were in accounts other than the Tether Bank Accounts, and at times included receivables and non-fiat assets among its counted reserves. In addition, at least until 2018, Tether utilized a manual process to track the Tether Reserves, which did not capture the real-time status of the Tether Reserves. Further, from at least 2018 through February 25, 2019, Tether failed to disclose that the Tether Reserves included unsecured receivables, commercial papers, funds held by third- parties, and other non-fiat assets. Finally, Tether Reserves were not routinely audited.

B. RESPONDENTS

Tether Holdings Limited was incorporated in the British Virgin Islands on September 5, 2014. Tether Holdings Limited owns 100% of Tether Operations Limited, Tether Limited, and Tether International Limited. Tether Holdings Limited has never been registered with the Commission in any capacity.

Tether Limited was incorporated in Hong Kong on September 8, 2014. Tether Limited operated Tether's website and token platform, tether.to from September 8, 2014 through March 15, 2017. Throughout the Relevant Period, Tether Limited was and continues to be registered with FinCEN as a non-bank financial institution known as a Money Services Business ("MSB"). Tether Limited has never been registered with the Commission in any capacity.

---

preclusive effect therein, without further proof. Respondents do not consent, however, to the use of this Order, or the findings or conclusions herein, as the sole basis for any other proceeding brought by the Commission or to which the Commission is a party or claimant, other than: a proceeding in bankruptcy or receivership; or a proceeding to enforce the terms of this Order. Respondents do not consent to the use of the Offer or this Order, or the findings or conclusions in this Order, by any other party in any other proceeding.

Tether Operations Limited was incorporated in the British Virgin Islands on March 15, 2017. Tether Operations Limited operates Tether's website and token platform, tether.to. Tether Operations Limited has never been registered with the Commission in any capacity.

Tether International Limited was incorporated in the British Virgin Islands on March 15, 2017. Tether International Limited has never been registered with the Commission in any capacity.

C. OTHER RELEVANT ENTITIES[2]

iFinex Inc. ("iFinex") is a privately-held financial technology company incorporated in the British Virgin Islands on May 21, 2013. iFinex operates the Bitfinex trading platform.

BFXNA Inc. ("BFXNA") was incorporated in the British Virgin Islands on November 4, 2014. BFXNA is a wholly-owned subsidiary of iFinex.

BFXWW Inc. ("BFXWW") was incorporated in the British Virgin Islands on April 28, 2015. BFXWW is a wholly-owned subsidiary of iFinex.

D. FACTS

1. The Tether Token

Since its launch in 2014, Respondents have represented that the tether token is a "stablecoin," a type of virtual currency whose value is pegged to fiat currency. At launch, Respondents announced, through their Facebook account, that: "Tether means a digital tie between a real-world asset and the digital assets backed by currencies." Although Respondents offer tether tokens in several national currencies, the dominant tether token is the U.S. dollar tether token, commonly referred to as "USDt." Throughout the Relevant Period, Respondents repeatedly represented that one USDt may always be redeemed for one U.S. dollar. Respondents' website represents the purpose and value of the USDt token as:

> Tether is a token backed by actual assets, including USD and Euros. One Tether equals one underlying unit of the currency backing it, e.g., the U.S. Dollar, and is backed 100% by actual assets in the Tether platform's reserve account. Being anchored or "tethered" to real world currency, Tether provides protection from the volatility of cryptocurrencies.

Beginning in January 2015, tether tokens have been used to deposit and withdraw funds on the Bitfinex platform. Tether tokens provide a medium of exchange across

---

2. iFinex, BFXNA and BFXWW collectively did business as "Bitfinex" throughout the Relevant Period. Concurrently with this Order, the Commission is issuing an order against Bitfinex settling separate and distinct violations of Sections 4(a) and 4d(a)(1) of the Act, 7 U.S.C. §§ 6(a), 6d(a)(1) (2018), as well as BFXNA's violation of Part VII. A of the Commission's 2016 Order in *In re BFXNA Inc. d/b/a Bitfinex*, CFTC No. 16-19, 2016 WL 3137612 (June 2, 2016).

cryptocurrency trading platforms. For example, a trader may transfer USDt to Bitfinex or another cryptocurrency exchange and use the tether tokens to purchase or trade digital assets such as bitcoin. BTC/USDT is a frequently traded pair.

Before November 2017, customers could only acquire and redeem tether tokens directly from Respondents. To do so, typically, customers transferred the corresponding amount of U.S. dollars in order to acquire USDt from Respondents and received the corresponding amount of U.S. dollars in exchange for redeemed USDt, less any applicable fees. On or around

November 19, 2017, Respondents experienced a cyber-attack during which the attackers caused the unauthorized transfer of nearly 31 million USDt tokens that had been authorized but not issued (the "2017 Tether Hack"). No reserve funds were at risk or stolen during the 2017 Tether Hack. Following the 2017 Tether Hack, and continuing until on or about November 27, 2018, Respondents ceased directly issuing and redeeming tether tokens, and tether tokens could only be issued or redeemed through Bitfinex. Thereafter, beginning in or around November 27, 2018, customers could obtain USDt tokens from Bitfinex or Tether. Today, tether tokens can be obtained from dozens of cryptocurrency exchanges, including several operating in the U.S.

2. Respondents' Untrue or Misleading Statements and Omissions: USDt Would Be Fully Backed by US Dollars Held In the Tether Bank Accounts

Throughout the Relevant Period, Respondents represented that Tether backed every tether token in circulation 1:1 with corresponding fiat currency reserves held by Tether. Prior to February 25, 2019, Respondents' website consistently represented that tether tokens are "100% Backed: Every tether [token] is always backed 1-to-1 by traditional currency held in our reserves. So 1 USDT is always equivalent to 1 USD."

Until February 25, 2019, Respondents' Terms of Service similarly represented that:

> Tether Tokens are fully backed by the currency or property used to purchase them at issuance. Tether Tokens are denominated in a range of currencies. For example, if you purchase EURT, your Tethers are fully backed by Euros. If you cause to be issued EURT 100.00, Tether holds €100.00 to back those Tether Tokens. [...] Tether Tokens are backed by money, but they are not money themselves. Tether will not issue Tether Tokens for consideration that is other Digital Tokens (for example, bitcoin), and will not redeem Tether Tokens for other Digital Tokens; only money will be accepted upon issuance, and only money will be provided upon redemption.

Respondents' website includes a page entitled 'Transparency Page,' (the "Tether Transparency Page"). A June 20, 2018 announcement on the Tether Transparency Page stated "All Tethers in circulation are fully backed by USD reserves. Full stop.... Reserves have always, and will always, match the number of Tethers in circulation."

Beginning on April 16, 2015 and continuing throughout the Relevant Period, a whitepaper entitled "Tether: Fiat Currencies on the Bitcoin blockchain" (the "Tether Whitepaper") has been available on Tether's website. Respondents' representations in the Tether Whitepaper include:

> Tethers are fully reserved in a one-to-one ratio, completely independent of market forces, pricing, or liquidity constraints. Tether has a simple and reliable Proof of Reserves implementation and undergoes regular professional audits. Our underlying banking relationships, compliance, and legal structure provide a secure foundation for us to be the custodian of reserve assets and issuer of tethers.... Each Tether issued into circulation will be backed in a one-to-one ratio with the equivalent amount of corresponding fiat currency held in reserves by Hong Kong based Tether Limited. As the custodian of the backing asset we are acting as a trusted third party responsible for that asset.... Tether Limited has a bank account which will receive and send fiat currency to users who purchase/redeem tethers directly with us.

Similarly, in announcing a new banking relationship on November 1, 2018, Tether again represented that "USDT in the market are fully backed by US dollars that are safely deposited in our bank accounts."

Respondents also made similar representations in blog posts, interviews, and even public court filings. For example, in April 2017, in a federal lawsuit filed by Tether Limited, iFinex and Bitfinex, the companies alleged that "Tether is a digital token and each tether unit issued into circulation is backed one-to-one by the U.S. Dollar, i.e., customer dollars held by Tether." *iFinex v. Wells Fargo*, Case No. 3:17-cv-01882 (N.D. Cal. Apr. 5, 2017).

3. The Tether Reserves: USDt Was Not At All Times Fully Backed by U.S. Dollars Held In the Tether Bank Accounts

In contrast to Respondents' statements, Respondents did not at all times hold sufficient fiat reserves in the Tether Bank Accounts to back USDt tokens in circulation for the substantial majority of the Relevant Period. Indeed, for the time period of September 2, 2016 through November 1, 2018, the aggregate amount of fiat currency held by Tether in the Tether Bank Accounts was less than the corresponding USDt tokens in circulation on 573 of 791 days, meaning that, contrary to Respondents' representations, the Tether Reserves were "fully-backed" by fiat currency reserves held in the Tether Bank Accounts only 27.6% of the time. Instead, at various times, Tether maintained some of the Tether Reserves in bank accounts other than the Tether Bank Accounts. Tether represents that, at times, it also included receivables and non-fiat assets among its counted reserves; and further represents that Tether has not failed to satisfy a redemption request for tether tokens.

Beginning on or around May 5, 2017, Respondents began depositing some of their cash holdings, including funds comprising the Tether Reserves, in an account at Bank 1 titled in the name of the individual serving as Tether's General Counsel, In Trust for Tether Limited (the "GC Trust Account"). Beginning on or around June 2, 2017, some of the Tether Reserves were held in Bitfinex's bank accounts and commingling with Bitfinex operational and customer funds, amounting to approximately $382 million by September 14, 2017. On September 15, 2017, Respondent Tether International opened an account in its name. On that same day, Bitfinex transferred $382,064,782 in reserve funds from one of its bank accounts to Tether International's newly-opened bank account.

During this same period, the number of tether tokens in circulation grew by at least a hundred million month-to-month: on June 1, 2017, there were at least 109,844,263 tether tokens in circulation; by July 1, 2017, there were at least 214,852,881 tethers in circulation; by August 1, 2017, there were at least 319,398,873 tether tokens in circulation; and, by September 15, 2017, there were at least 442,481,760 tether tokens in circulation. During this same time, the amount held in the GC Trust Account never exceeded $61.5 million.

At various times during the Relevant Period, Respondents relied upon unregulated entities and certain third-parties to hold some of their funds, including Tether Reserves, and for a period of time commingled Tether Reserves with funds belonging to Bitfinex and/or Bitfinex customers. In aggregate, during the Relevant Period Tether and Bitfinex's assets included funds held by or received from third-parties pursuant to at least 51 different arrangements, only 22 of which were documented through loan agreements, trust agreements, or other formal contracts.

On or about October 2017, Respondents opened an account with an unlicensed money transmitting business (the "Payment Processor") registered in Panama. Bitfinex had opened accounts with the same Payment Processor beginning in or around 2014.

In aggregate, Respondents and Bitfinex had at least twelve accounts with Payment Processor (the "PP Accounts"). The PP Accounts held funds received from customers, including those in the U.S., in connection with tether tokens issuances and funds related to Bitfinex customer transactions. Beginning in August 2018, the PP Accounts also held funds comprising part of the Tether Reserves. Respondents had no written agreements governing the Payment Processor's handling of the PP Accounts, and Respondents did not receive or have access to all periodic account statements issued by the Payment Processor, but instead maintained an internal ledger of the funds they believed were being held in those accounts.

From at least October 2017 through November 1, 2018, Respondents and Bitfinex directed customers to deposit funds by wiring them to the Payment Processor. In the first quarter of 2018, for example, customers deposited more than $480 million into the PP Accounts. By April 2018, media reports began to emerge that authorities seized approximately $371 million in funds held by Payment Processor. At or around the same time, Bitfinex encountered increasing difficulties withdrawing

funds from the PP Accounts. Internally, Respondent and Bitfinex's CFO characterized the situation as a "liquidity crisis." Nevertheless, Bitfinex continued to rely upon
the Payment Processor to hold funds, and by July 2018, the CFO told PP "over 80%
of our money is now with you." At that time, the PP Accounts held in excess of one
billion dollars. In August 2018, the CFO informed the Payment Processor "we have
too much money with you and almost nothing elsewhere."

Respondents transferred funds between Tether and Bitfinex to assist Bitfinex in
responding to this "liquidity crisis." For example, in November 2018, Respondents
transferred $625 million from Respondents' bank accounts—funds comprising the
Tether Reserves—to Bitfinex to provide Bitfinex with liquidity it needed, unrelated
to USDt.[3] To "offset" this transfer, Bitfinex directed PSP to make a ledger entry reflecting a transfer of $625 million from Bitfinex to Tether. On November 2, 2018, a
similar set of transactions occurred. At this time, Respondents' and Bitfinex's funds
held by the Payment Processor were at least encumbered, but more likely wholly
unavailable. Subsequently, Tether Limited and iFinex entered into a Credit Facility
Agreement, finalized in March 2019, that retroactively formalized the November
2018 transfer of $625 million, among others. Respondents represent that in January
2021, iFinex repaid the loan in full.

Beginning in or before August 2018, Tether Reserves were held in non-fiat financial products and other less-liquid assets including commercial paper, and bank
repurchase agreements. At various times during the Relevant Period, Respondents
also considered anticipated receivables and anticipated wire transfers as assets for
purposes of calculating the Tether Reserves.

On February 25, 2019, Respondents amended their disclosures to state that
"Tether Tokens are 100% backed by Tether's Reserves," defined as "traditional currency and cash equivalents and, from time to time, may include other assets and
receivables from loans made by Tether to third parties, which may include affiliated
entities."

4. The Tether Reserves Were Not Audited

No audit of the Tether Reserves occurred during or prior to the Relevant Period.
Respondents retained independent third-parties to conduct reviews of the Tether
Reserves twice during the Relevant Period. First, in 2017, Respondents retained
an accounting firm to perform a review of the Tether Reserves, as reported on the
Tether Transparency Page, against fiat currency held in Tether's name on a single
date, September 15, 2017, a date selected by Respondents and known to their principals ahead of the accounting firm's review. On that date, with the full knowledge

---

3. Respondents and Bitfinex shared common ownership, leadership, management, employees
and operational resources. For example, the same individuals at Tether and Bitfinex serve as Chief
Executive Office, Chief Financial Officer, Chief Technology Officer and General Counsel, respectively. They have also shared common business functions including marketing, audit, legal, compliance,
finance, tech and support resources.

of Respondents, Bitfinex transferred $382,064,782 from Bitfinex's bank accounts to Tether's newly-opened bank account. Second, in 2018, Respondents retained a law firm to compare Tether's holdings in two bank accounts to the USDt in circulation as of June 1, 2018, based on the information provided by Respondents or publicly available on the blockchain. Thereafter, on October 15, 2018, Respondents released a statement claiming that the firm "based on a random date balance inspection and a full review of relevant documentation of bank accounts, confirmed that all tether tokens in circulation as of that date were indeed fully backed by USD reserves." In 2018, Tether stated publicly that professional audits were not obtainable at that time. To date, Respondents have not completed an audit of the Tether Reserves.

5. Respondents Failed to Employ an Automated Process to Track Reserves

Tether did not accurately track reserves at all times during the Relevant Period. In particular, at least until 2018, Respondents did not employ an automated method for tracking Tether Reserves against tether tokens in circulation in real time. Respondents developed an additional internal, proprietary database (the "Tether Database") after the 2017 Tether Hack. The Tether Database stores data regarding tether token issuances and redemptions, as well as transaction information for customers' deposits and withdrawals. For much of the Relevant Period, there was no automated process for incorporating bank statements and balances into the Tether Database, and information regarding the amount of fiat currency held in Respondents' accounts as Tether Reserves had to be manually inputted into the Tether Database. Further, at least until 2018, Respondent's internal accounting system for tracking fiat balances, including bank balances for USDt reserves, primarily consisted of a spreadsheet (the "Reserve Spreadsheet"). The Tether executive team was ultimately responsible for the Reserve Spreadsheet. The Reserve Spreadsheet required manual updates and was not always kept up to date in real time. Respondents were aware of the limitations of the Reserve Spreadsheet. For example, in an internal chat on June 15, 2016, Tether's then-Chief Strategy Officer informed Respondents' CFO and other employees stated that the: "transparency page needs to be dealt with ASAP...I am surprised the issuance address is not updated dynamically, btw...and how often does the bank balance get updated?" Following the Relevant Period, Respondents have implemented more automated processes for tracking and updating bank balances and reporting information about the Tether Reserves on the Tether Transparency Page.

III. LEGAL DISCUSSION

A. USDt is a Commodity in Interstate Commerce

Digital assets such as bitcoin, ether, litecoin, and tether tokens are commodities. As defined under Section 1a(9) of the Act, 7 U.S.C. § 1a(9) (2018), commodities, with limited exceptions, includes all manner of "other goods and articles...and all services, rights and interests...in which contracts for future delivery are presently or in the future dealt in." See *Bd. of Trade of City of Chicago v. SEC*, 677 F. 2d 1137, 1142 (7th Cir. 1982) ("This language was also meant to encompass futures markets that were expected to be expanded to cover non-traditional goods and services...") *vacated on other grounds*, 459 U.S. 1026 (1982). Digital assets are commodities and subject to applicable provisions of the Act and Regulations, including Section 6(c)(1) of the Act and Regulation 180.1(a). *See, e.g., CFTC v. McDonnell*, 287 F. Supp. 3d 213, 217 (E.D.N.Y. 2018) ("Virtual currencies can be regulated by CFTC as a commodity.... They fall well-within the common definition of 'commodity' as well as the [Act's] definition of 'commodities' as 'all other goods and articles...in which contracts for future delivery are presently or in the future dealt in.'"); *CFTC v. My Big Coin Pay, Inc.*, 334 F. Supp. 3d 492, 495– 98 (D. Mass. 2018) (denying motion to dismiss; determining that a non-bitcoin virtual currency is a "commodity" under the Act); *In re Coinflip, Inc.*, CFTC No. 15-29, 2015 WL 5535736, at *2 (Sept. 17, 2015) (consent order) ("bitcoin and other virtual currencies are encompassed in the definition [of Section 1a(9) of the Act] and properly defined as commodities."). The USDt token, a virtual currency stablecoin, is a commodity and subject to applicable provisions of the Act and Regulations.

The Act broadly defines the terms "interstate commerce" and "in interstate commerce." *See* Sections 1a(30) of the Act (defining "interstate commerce") and 2(b) of the Act (providing that, for purposes of the Act, a transaction is "in interstate commerce" if the traded item is part of the current of commerce "from one State" to another), 7 U.S.C. §§ 1a(30), 2(b) (2018). Section 1a(13) of Act defines the term "contract of sale" to include sales, agreements of sale, and agreements to sell. 7 U.S.C. § 1a(13) (2018). Digital assets, like USDt tokens, constitute a commodity in interstate commerce under Section 6(c)(1) of the Act. *McDonnell*, 332 F.Supp.3d at 717, 723 (holding Section 6(c)(1) and Regulation 180.1(a) were violated by fraudulent misrepresentations in connection with digital asset transactions, as those digital assets were commodities in interstate commerce).

B. By Intentionally or Recklessly Making Untrue or Misleading Statements and Omissions of Material Facts, Tether Violated Section 6(c)(1) of the Act and Regulation 180.1(a)(2)

Taken together, Section 6(c)(1) of the Act, 7 U.S.C. § 9(1) (2018), and Regulation 180.1(a)(2), 17 C.F.R. § 180.1(a)(2) (2020), prohibit "intentionally or recklessly...mak[ing] any untrue or misleading statement of a material fact or to omit to state a material fact necessary in order to make the statements made not untrue or misleading" in connection with any swap, or contract of sale of any commodity in interstate commerce, or for future delivery on or subject to the rules of any registered entity. Respondents violated Section 6(c)(1) and Regulation 180.1(a)(2) by intentionally or recklessly making untrue or misleading statements of material facts and by omitting to state material facts necessary in order to make statements made not untrue or misleading. Those untrue or misleading statements and omissions included: repeated representations that Tether would fully back the USDt token with fiat currency, specifically, the US Dollar, in accounts held in Tether's own name; omissions regarding the actual backing of USDt including non-fiat assets, such as commercial paper; representations that Tether would undergo regular professional audits; and omissions regarding the pre- disclosed timing of one of the two reviews that Tether did undertake.

IV. FINDINGS OF VIOLATIONS

Based on the foregoing, the Commission finds that, during the Relevant Period, Tether violated Section 6(c)(1) of the Act, 7 U.S.C. §9(1) (2018), and Regulation §180.1(a)(2), 17 C.F.R. §180.1(a)(2) (2020).

Discussion Points

1. *Stablecoins.* What is a stablecoin? What are the advantages and disadvantages of stablecoins?

2. *Centralized or decentralized?* Are Tether tokens centralized or decentralized? Are stablecoins centralized or decentralized? What is the difference between a centralized cryptocurrency and a decentralized cryptocurrency? What do you think are the pros and cons of each?

3. *Fiat currency.* What is fiat currency? Does it have intrinsic value? If fiat currency derives its value from being adopted as a common medium of exchange, should cryptocurrency be considered fiat currency? Can cryptocurrency be considered fiat currency? What prevents cryptocurrency from being considered fiat?

4. *Findings.* Tether was required to pay a civil monetary penalty of $41 million and cease and desist from any further violations of the Commodity Exchange Act and CFTC regulations. Do you think this is an appropriate remedy? Does this kind of penalty help achieve compliance with CFTC regulations? What do you think would be the best deterrent from the kind of violations we've seen in the cases in this chapter?

Consent Order for Permanent Injunction, Civil Monetary Penalty and Other Equitable Relief Against Defendant Jimmy Gale Watson
CFTC v. McAfee, Case 1:21-cv-01919-JGK (S.D.N.Y July 14, 2022)

I. INTRODUCTION

On March 5, 2021, Plaintiff Commodity Futures Trading Commission ("Commission" or "CFTC") filed a Complaint against Defendants John David McAfee

("McAfee") and Jimmy Gale Watson ("Watson") seeking injunctive and other equitable relief, as well as the imposition of civil penalties, for violations of the Commodity Exchange Act ("Act"), 7 U.S.C. §§ 1–26, and the Commission's Regulations ("Regulations") promulgated thereunder, 17 C.F.R. pts. 1–190 (2021).

II. CONSENTS AND AGREEMENTS

To effect settlement of all charges alleged in the Complaint against Watson without a trial on the merits or any further judicial proceedings, Watson:

1. Consents to the entry of this Consent Order for Permanent Injunction, Civil Monetary Penalty, and Other Equitable Relief Against Defendant Jimmy Gale Watson ("Consent Order");

2. Affirms that he has read and agreed to this Consent Order voluntarily, and that no promise, other than as specifically contained herein, or threat, has been made by the CFTC or any member, officer, agent, or representative thereof, or by any other person, to induce consent to this Consent Order;

3. Acknowledges service of the summons and Complaint;

4. Admits the jurisdiction of this Court over him and the subject matter of this action pursuant to Section 6c of the Act, 7 U.S.C. § 13a-1;

5. Admits the jurisdiction of the CFTC over the conduct and transactions at issue in this action pursuant to the Act;

6. Admits that venue properly lies with this Court pursuant to 7 U.S.C. § 13a-l(e);

7. Waives:

   a. Any and all claims that he may possess under the Equal Access to Justice Act, 5 U.S.C. § 504 and 28 U.S.C. § 2412, and/or the rules promulgated by the Commission in conformity therewith, Part 148 of the Regulations, 17 C.F.R. pt. 148 (2021), relating to, or arising from, this action;

   b. Any and all claims that he may possess under the Small Business Regulatory Enforcement Fairness Act of 1996, Pub. L. No. 104-121, tit. II, §§ 201–53, 110 Stat. 847, 857-74 (codified as amended at 28 U.S.C. § 2412 and in scattered sections of 5 U.S.C. and 15 U.S.C.), relating to, or arising from, this action;

   c. Any claim of Double Jeopardy based upon the institution of this action or the entry in this action of any order imposing a civil monetary penalty or any other relief, including this Consent Order; and

   d. Any and all rights of appeal from this action;

8. Consents to the continued jurisdiction of this Court over him for the purpose of implementing and enforcing the terms and conditions of this Consent Order and for any other purpose relevant to this action, even if Watson now or in the future resides outside the jurisdiction of this Court;

9. Agrees that he will not oppose enforcement of this Consent Order on the ground, if any exists, that it fails to comply with Rule 65(d) of the Federal Rules of Civil Procedure and hereby waives any objection based thereon;

10. Agrees that neither he nor any of his agents or employees under his authority or control shall take any action or make any public statement denying, directly or indirectly, any allegation in the Complaint or the Findings of Fact or Conclusions of Law in this Consent Order, or creating or tending to create the impression that the Complaint and/or this Consent Order is without a factual basis; provided, however, that nothing in this provision shall affect his: (a) testimonial obligations, or (b) right to take legal positions in other proceedings to which the CFTC is not a party. Watson shall comply with this agreement, and shall undertake all steps necessary to ensure that all of his agents and/or employees under his authority or control understand and comply with this agreement;

11. Consents to the entry of this Consent Order without admitting or denying the allegations of the Complaint or any findings or conclusions in this Consent Order, except as to jurisdiction and venue, which he admits;

12. Consents to the use of the findings and conclusions in this Consent Order in this proceeding and in any other proceeding brought by the Commission or to which the Commission is a party or claimant, and agrees that they shall be taken as true and correct and be given preclusive effect therein, without further proof;

13. Does not consent, however, to the use of this Consent Order, or the findings and conclusions herein, as the sole basis for any other proceeding brought by the Commission or to which the Commission is a party, other than a: statutory disqualification proceeding; proceeding in bankruptcy, or receivership; or proceeding to enforce the terms of this Order;

14. Agrees to provide immediate notice to this Court and the CFTC by certified mail, in the manner required by paragraph 44 of Part VI of this Consent Order, of any bankruptcy proceeding filed by, on behalf of, or against him, whether inside or outside the United States; and

15. Agrees that no provision of this Consent Order shall in any way limit or impair the ability of any other person or entity to seek any legal or equitable remedy against Watson in any other proceeding.

III. FINDINGS OF FACT AND CONCLUSIONS OF LAW

The Court, being fully advised in the premises, finds that there is good cause for the entry of this Consent Order and that there is no just reason for delay. The Court therefore directs the entry of the following Findings of Fact, Conclusions of Law, permanent injunction and equitable relief pursuant to Section 6c of the Act, 7 U.S.C. § 13a-1, as set forth herein. The findings and conclusions in this Consent Order are not binding on any other party to this action.

THE PARTIES AGREE AND THE COURT HEREBY FINDS:

A. Findings of Fact

The Parties to this Consent Order

16. Plaintiff Commodity Futures Trading Commission is an independent federal regulatory agency that is charged by Congress with administering and enforcing the Act and the Regulations.

17. Defendant **Jimmy Gale Watson Jr.** is a natural person who currently resides in Texas. Watson has never been registered with the Commission.

Overview of Virtual Currencies

18. A virtual currency is a type of digital asset defined here as a digital representation of value that functions as a medium of exchange, a unit of account, and/or a store of value, but does not have legal tender status in any jurisdiction. Bitcoin, ether, verge, dogecoin, reddcoin, and other virtual currencies are distinct from "real" currencies, which are the coin and paper money of the United States or another country that are designated as legal tender, circulate, and are customarily used and accepted as a medium of exchange in the country of issuance.

19. Digital assets, such as bitcoin, ether, and other virtual currencies such as verge, dogecoin, and reddcoin, identified in the Complaint are encompassed by the definition of "commodity" under Section la(9) of the Act, 7 U.S.C. §la(9).

Defendants' Scheme to Manipulate

20. From at least in or around December 2017 through at least in or around February 2018 (the "Relevant Period"), Watson was employed by and acted in concert with co-Defendant John David McAfee ("McAfee") and others while engaged in a digital asset "pump and dump" manipulative and deceptive scheme in which Defendants endorsed several digital assets through social media distributed nation- and worldwide, for the purpose of inducing investors, including those in New York, New York, into entering into contracts of sale of virtual currency, including bitcoin, verge, dogecoin, and reddcoin, among others, through electronic web-based virtual currency trading platforms based in various states and countries, thereby increasing short-term demand and higher prices for the digital assets that Defendants had secretly purchased shortly before.

21. As part of the scheme, Watson assisted McAfee with strategically selecting digital assets that would be suitable for the pump-and-dump scheme.

22. *Dogecoin Strategy.* For example, on or around January 3, 2018, Watson assisted McAfee by strategizing as to the next digital asset to be the vehicle of the pump-and-dump scheme. Watson recommended dogecoin. Watson also recommended that McAfee wait for dogecoin to increase in price after their building of a position

before tweeting out the promotion. Watson predicted to McAfee that the market price of dogecoin would likely "skyrocket" almost immediately after McAfee's tweet, just as other digital assets touted by McAfee had done.

23. *Dogecoin Build.* Watson built a position in dogecoin, spending approximately 4.1 btc to purchase approximately 6.7 million dogecoin.

24. *Dogecoin Pump.* On or around January 8, 2018, or about five days after Watson recommended to McAfee dogecoin as the next coin to promote, McAfee's Twitter account issued a tweet endorsing dogecoin as his "Coin of the Week." The tout did not disclose Defendants' financial interest in dogecoin, their intent to dump dogecoin as the price spiked after being touted, or the fact that McAfee was not endorsing dogecoin without bias as a long-term value for investors.

25. *Dogecoin Dump.* Almost immediately after McAfee's tout by tweet of dogecoin, Watson sold his dogecoin position for a net profit of more than 2.9 btc.

26. During the Relevant Period, McAfee and Watson, directly and through others, engaged in similar iterations of the pump-and-dump scheme with respect to other digital assets as well.

B. Conclusions of Law

Jurisdiction and Venue

27. This Court possesses jurisdiction over this action pursuant to 28 U.S.C. § 1331 (codifying federal question jurisdiction) and 28 U.S.C. § 1345 (providing that U.S. district courts have original jurisdiction over civil actions commenced by the United States or by any agency expressly authorized to sue by Act of Congress). Section 6c(a)of the Act,7U.S.C.§13a-l(a), provides that the Commission may bring actions for injunctive relief or to enforce compliance with the Act or any rule, regulation, or order thereunder in the proper district court of the United States whenever it shall appear to the Commission that any person has engaged, is engaging, or is about to engage in any act or practice constituting a violation of any provision of the Act or any rule, regulation, or order thereunder.

28. Venue properly lies with this Court pursuant to 7 U.S.C. § 13a-l(e), because the acts and practices in violation of the Act occurred within this District.

Fraud and Manipulation by Deceptive Device or Contrivance Violations of Section 6(c)(l) of the Act, 7 U.S.C. § 9(1), and Regulation 180.l(a), 17 C.F.R. § 180.l(a) (2021)

29. Section 6(c)(l) of the Act, 7 U.S.C. § 9(1), makes it unlawful for any person, directly or indirectly, to:

> use or employ, or attempt to use or employ, in connection with any swap, or a contract of sale of any commodity in interstate commerce, or for future delivery on or subject to the rules of any registered entity, any manipulative or deceptive device or contrivance, in contravention of such rules and regula-

tions as the Commission shall promulgate by not later than 1 year after [July 21, 2010, the date of enactment of the Dodd-Frank Wall Street Reform and Consumer Protection Act]....

30. Commission Regulation 180.l(a), 17 C.F.R. § 180.l(a), provides in part:

It shall be unlawful for any person, directly or indirectly, in connection with any swap, or contract of sale of any commodity in interstate commerce, or contract for future delivery on or subject to the rules of any registered entity, to intentionally or recklessly:

1. Use or employ, or attempt to use or employ, any manipulative device, scheme, or artifice to defraud;

2. Make, or attempt to make, any untrue or misleading statement of a material fact or to omit to state a material fact necessary in order to make the statements made not untrue or misleading;

3. Engage, or attempt to engage, in any act, practice, or course of business, which operates or would operate as a fraud or deceit upon any person....

31. Watson willfully aided, abetted, counseled and worked in combination and in concert with McAfee in making or attempting to make untrue or misleading statements of material fact or omitting to state or attempting to omit material facts necessary in order to make statements made not untrue or misleading. Therefore, pursuant to Section 13(a) of the Act, 7 U.S.C. § 13c(a), Watson is liable as a principal for violations of Section 6(c)(l) of the Act and Regulation 180.1.

Price Manipulation

Violations of Sections 6(c)(3) and 9(a)(2) of the Act, 7 U.S.C. §§ 9(3), 13(a)(2), and Regulation 180.2, 17 C.F.R. § 180.2 (2021)

32. Section 6(c)(3) of the Act, 7 U.S.C. § 9(3) makes it unlawful for "any person, directly or indirectly, to manipulate or attempt to manipulate the price of any swap, or of any commodity in interstate commerce, or for future delivery on or subject to the rules of any registered entity."

33. Section 9(a)(2) of the Act, 7 U.S.C. § 13(a)(2), makes it unlawful for "[a]ny person to manipulate or attempt to manipulate the price of any commodity in interstate commerce, or for future delivery on or subject to the rules of any registered entity, or any swap...."

34. Commission Regulation 180.2, 17 C.F.R. § 180.2, makes it "unlawful for any person, directly or indirectly, to manipulate or attempt to manipulate the price of any swap, or of any commodity in interstate commerce, or for future delivery on or subject to the rules of any registered entity."

35. Watson willfully aided, abetted, counseled and worked in combination and in concert with McAfee in attempting to manipulate the price of a commodity in interstate commerce or for future delivery on or subject to the rules of any registered entity. Therefore, pursuant to Section 13(a) of the Act, 7 U.S.C. § 13c(a), Watson is liable as a principal for violations of Section 6(c)(l) of the Act and Regulation 180.1.

36. Unless restrained and enjoined by this Court, there is a reasonable likelihood that Watson will continue to engage in the acts and practices alleged in the Complaint and in similar acts and practices in violation of the Act and Regulations.

IV. PERMANENT INJUNCTION IT IS HEREBY ORDERED THAT:

37. Based upon and in connection with the foregoing conduct, pursuant to Section 6c of the Act, 7 U.S.C. § 13a-l, Watson is permanently restrained, enjoined and prohibited from directly or indirectly:

- in connection with contracts of sale of commodities in interstate commerce, making or attempting to make untrue or misleading statements of material fact or omitting to state or attempting to omit material facts necessary in order to make statements made not untrue or misleading, such as misleadingly characterizing digital asset recommendations as based on substantial research into long-term value, rather than simply digital assets susceptible to the pump-and-dump scheme; misleadingly issuing purportedly unbiased digital asset touts by tweet while disclaiming financial interest in a short-term price rise; and misrepresenting or concealing the true motive of Defendants' digital asset touts by tweet, namely, to contribute to a short-term price rise and secretly trade out of the position into that price rise, in violation of Section 6(c)(1) of the Act, 7 U.S.C. § 9(1), and Regulation 180.l(a), 17 C.F.R. § 180.l(a);

- manipulating or attempting to manipulate the price of a commodity in interstate commerce or for future delivery on or subject to the rules of any registered entity in violation of Sections 6(c)(3) and 9(a)(2) of the Act and Regulation 180.2.

38. Watson is also permanently restrained, enjoined and prohibited from directly or indirectly:

- Trading on or subject to the rules of any registered entity (as that term is defined in Section la(40) of the Act, 7 U.S.C. § la(40));

- Entering into any transactions involving "commodity interests" (as that term is defined in Regulation 1.3, 17 C.F.R. § 1.3 (2021)), for his own personal account or for any account in which he has a direct or indirect interest;

Having any commodity interests traded on his behalf;

Controlling or directing the trading for or on behalf of any other person or entity, whether by power of attorney or otherwise, in any account involving commodity interests;

Soliciting, receiving or accepting any funds from any person for the purpose of purchasing or selling any commodity interests;

Applying for registration or claiming exemption from registration with the Commission in any capacity, and engaging in any activity requiring such registration or exemption from registration with the Commission, except as provided for in Regulation 4.14(a)(9), 17 C.F.R § 4.14(a)(9) (2021); and/or

Acting as a principal (as that term is defined in Regulation 3.l(a), 17 C.F.R. § 3.l(a) (2021)), agent or any other officer or employee of any person (as that term is defined in 7 U.S.C. § la(38)), registered, exempted from registration or required to be registered with the Commission except as provided for in 17 C.F.R § 4.14(a)(9).

DISGORGEMENT AND CIVIL MONETARY PENALTY

39. Watson shall pay disgorgement in the amount of One Hundred Forty Four Thousand Seven Hundred Thirty Six Dollars ($144,736) ("Disgorgement Obligation"), representing the gains received in connection with such violations, within thirty days of the date of the entry of this Consent Order. If the Disgorgement Obligation is not paid in full within thirty days of the date of entry of this Consent Order, then post-judgment interest shall accrue on the Disgorgement Obligation beginning on the date of entry of this Consent Order and shall be determined by using the Treasury Bill rate prevailing on the date of entry of this Consent Order pursuant to 28 U.S.C. § 1961.

40. Watson shall pay his Disgorgement Obligation and any post-judgment interest by electronic funds transfer, U.S. postal money order, certified check, bank cashier's check, or bank money order. If payment is to be made other than by electronic funds transfer, then the payment shall be made payable to the Commodity Futures Trading Commission and sent to the address below:

Commodity Futures Trading Commission Division of Enforcement

6500 S. MacArthur Blvd.

HQ Room 181

Oklahoma City, OK 73169

(405) 954-6569 office

(405) 954-1620 fax

Tonia.King@faa.gov

If payment by electronic funds transfer is chosen, Watson shall contact Tonia King or her successor at the address above to receive payment instructions and shall fully comply with those instructions. Watson shall accompany payment of the Disgorgement Obligation with a cover letter that identifies Watson and the name and docket number of this proceeding. Watson shall simultaneously transmit copies of the cover letter and the form of payment to the Chief Financial Officer, Commodity Futures Trading Commission, Three Lafayette Centre, 1155 21st Street, NW, Washington, D.C. 20581.

B. Civil Monetary Penalty

41. Watson shall pay a civil monetary penalty in the amount of One Hundred Forty Four Thousand Seven Hundred Thirty Six Dollars ($144,736) ("CMP Obligation"), within thirty days of the date of the entry of this Consent Order. If the CMP Obligation is not paid in full within thirty days of the date of entry of this Consent Order, then post-judgment interest shall accrue on the CMP Obligation beginning on the date of entry of this Consent Order and shall be determined by using the Treasury Bill rate prevailing on the date of entry of this Consent Order pursuant to 28 U.S.C. § 1961.

42. Watson shall pay his CMP Obligation and any post-judgment interest, by electronic funds transfer, U.S. postal money order, certified check, bank cashier's check, or bank money order. If payment is to be made other than by electronic funds transfer, then the payment shall be made payable to the Commodity Futures Trading Commission and sent to the address below:

Commodity Futures Trading Commission Division of Enforcement

6500 S. MacArthur Blvd.

HQ Room 181

Oklahoma City, OK 73169

(405) 954-6569 office

(405) 954-1620 fax

Tonia.King@faa.gov

If payment by electronic funds transfer is chosen, Watson shall contact Tonia King or her successor at the address above to receive payment instructions and shall fully comply with those instructions. Watson shall accompany payment of the CMP Obligation with a cover letter that identifies Watson and the name and docket number of this proceeding. Watson shall simultaneously transmit copies of the cover letter and the form of payment to the Chief Financial Officer, Commodity Futures Trading Commission, Three Lafayette Centre, 1155 21st Street, NW, Washington, D.C. 20581.

C. Provisions Related to Monetary Sanctions

43. Partial Satisfaction: Acceptance by the Commission of any partial payment of Watson's Disgorgement Obligation, or CMP Obligation shall not be deemed a waiver his obligation to make further payments pursuant to this Consent Order, or a waiver of the Commission's right to seek to compel payment of any remaining balance.

VI. MISCELLANEOUS PROVISIONS

44. Until such time as Watson satisfies in full his Disgorgement Obligation and CMP Obligation under this Consent Order, upon the commencement by or against Watson of insolvency, receivership or bankruptcy proceedings or any other proceedings for the settlement of Watson's debts, all notices to creditors required to be furnished to the Commission under Title 11 of the United States Code or other applicable law with respect to such insolvency, receivership bankruptcy or other proceedings, shall be sent to the address below:

Secretary of the Commission

Legal Division

Commodity Futures Trading Commission Three Lafayette Centre

1155 21st Street N.W.

Washington, DC 20581

45. Notice: All notices required to be given by any provision in this Consent Order, except as set forth in paragraph 44, above shall be sent certified mail, return receipt requested, as follows:

Notice to Commission:

Manal M. Sultan, Deputy Director Division of Enforcement

Commodity Futures Trading Commission Ted Weiss Federal Building

290 Broadway, Suite 600

New York, NY 10007

Notice to Defendant Watson:

Jimmy Gale Watson

c/o Arnold Spencer, Esq. Spencer & Associates

5956 Sherry Lane, Suite 2000 Dallas, Texas 75225

All such notices to the Commission shall reference the name and docket number of this action.

46. Change of Address/Phone: Until such time as Watson satisfies in full his Disgorgement Obligation, and CMP Obligation as set forth in this Consent Order, Watson shall provide written notice to the Commission by certified mail of any change to his telephone number and mailing address within ten calendar days of the change.

47. Entire Agreement and Amendments: This Consent Order incorporates all of the terms and conditions of the settlement among the parties hereto to date. Nothing shall serve to amend or modify this Consent Order in any respect whatsoever, unless: (a)reduced to writing; (b) signed by all parties hereto; and (c) approved by order of this Court.

48. Invalidation: If any provision of this Consent Order or if the application of any provision or circumstance is held invalid, then the remainder of this Consent Order and the application of the provision to any other person or circumstance shall not be affected by the holding.

49. Waiver: The failure of any party to this Consent Order at any time to require performance of any provision of this Consent Order shall in no manner affect the right of the party at a later time to enforce the same or any other provision of this Consent Order. No waiver in one or more instances of the breach of any provision contained in this Consent Order shall be deemed to be or construed as a further or continuing waiver of such breach or waiver of the breach of any other provision of this Consent Order.

50. Continuing Jurisdiction of this Court: This Court shall retain jurisdiction of this action to ensure compliance with this Consent Order and for all other purposes related to this action, including any motion by Watson to modify or for relief from the terms of this Consent Order.

51. Injunctive and Equitable Relief Provisions: The injunctive and equitable relief provisions of this Consent Order shall be binding upon Watson, upon any person under his authority or control, and upon any person who receives actual notice of this Consent Order, by personal service, e-mail, facsimile or otherwise insofar as he or she is acting in active concert or participation with Watson.

52. Counterparts and Facsimile Execution: This Consent Order may be executed in two or more counterparts, all of which shall be considered one and the same agreement and shall become effective when one or more counterparts have been signed by each of the parties hereto and delivered (by facsimile, e-mail, or otherwise) to the other party, it being understood that all parties need not sign the same counterpart. Any counterpart or other signature to this Consent Order that is delivered by any means shall be deemed for all purposes as constituting good and valid execution and delivery by such party of this Consent Order.

53. Contempt: Watson understands that the terms of the Consent Order are enforceable through contempt proceedings, and that, in any such proceedings he may not challenge the validity of this Consent Order.

54. Agreements and Undertakings: Watson shall comply with all of the undertakings and agreements set forth in this Consent Order.

There being no just reason for delay, the Clerk of the Court is hereby ordered to enter this *Consent Order for Permanent Injunction, Civil Monetary Penalty and Other Equitable Relief Against Defendant Jimmy Gale Watson* forthwith and without further notice.

Notes

1. *Do you agree with the outcome?* Do you think the CFTC is taking enough action to deter bad actors like McAfee from engaging in illicit activities such as price manipulation and making misrepresentations to consumers? Do you think that a permanent injunction was the proper remedy? Do you think this Consent Order sets good precedent for regulators to deal with similar issues in the future?

2. *The role of the SEC.* Should the SEC be more proactive in taking preventative measures against these kinds of schemes from occurring in the cryptocurrency space? Why or why shouldn't the SEC be more heavily involved in regulating cryptocurrency markets? Is the CFTC better positioned to respond to issues like those present in the above Consent Order?

3. *The impact of McAfee and Watson's actions on consumers.* How were consumers adversely impacted by McAfee and Watson's activities? What legal protections should be in place for consumers who are victims of fraudulent practices in the cryptocurrency market? Are regulators doing enough to respond to these issues?

In the Matter of bZeroX, LLC; Tom Bean; and Kyle Kistner

CFTC Docket No. 22-31, (September 2022)

UNITED STATES OF AMERICA
Before the
COMMODITY FUTURES TRADING COMMISSION

In the Matter of: bZeroX, LLC; Tom Bean; and Kyle Kistner, Respondents.	CFTC Docket No. 22-31

ORDER INSTITUTING PROCEEDINGS PURSUANT TO SECTION 6(c)
AND (d) OF THE COMMODITY EXCHANGE ACT, MAKING FINDINGS,
AND IMPOSING REMEDIAL SANCTIONS

I. INTRODUCTION

The Commodity Futures Trading Commission ("Commission") has reason to believe that, from at least approximately June 1, 2019 to approximately August 23, 2021 (the "bZx Relevant Period"), bZeroX, LLC ("bZeroX"); Tom Bean ("Bean"); and Kyle Kistner ("Kistner") (collectively, "Respondents") violated Sections 4(a) and 4d(a)(1) of the Commodity Exchange Act ("Act"), 7 U.S.C. §§ 6(a), 6d(a)(1), and Commission Regulation ("Regulation") 42.2, 17 C.F.R. § 42.2 (2021); and that, from approximately August 23, 2021 to the present (the "DAO Relevant Period," and together with the bZx Relevant Period, the "Relevant Period"), Bean and Kistner violated Sections 4(a) and 4d(a)(1) of the Act and Regulation 42.2. Therefore, the Commission deems it appropriate and in the public interest that public administrative proceedings be, and hereby are, instituted to determine whether Respondents engaged in the violations set forth herein and to determine whether any order should be issued imposing remedial sanctions.

In anticipation of the institution of an administrative proceeding, Respondents have submitted an Offer of Settlement ("Offer"), which the Commission has determined to accept. Without admitting or denying any of the findings or conclusions herein, Respondents consent to the entry of this Order Instituting Proceedings Pursuant to Section 6(c) and (d) of the Commodity Exchange Act, Making Findings, and Imposing Remedial Sanctions ("Order"), and acknowledge service of this Order.[1]

II. FINDINGS

The Commission finds the following:

A. SUMMARY

During the Relevant Period, Respondents designed, deployed, marketed, and made solicitations concerning a blockchain-based software protocol that accepted orders for and facilitated margined and leveraged retail commodity transactions (functioning similarly to a trading platform). This protocol (the "bZx Protocol") permitted users to contribute margin (collateral) to open leveraged positions whose ultimate value was determined by the price difference between two digital assets from the time the position was established to the time it was closed. The bZx Protocol purported to offer users the ability to engage in these transactions in a decentralized environment—i.e., without third-party intermediaries taking custody of user assets.

In so doing, Respondents—who have never registered with the Commission—unlawfully engaged in activities that could only lawfully be performed by a registered designated contract market ("DCM") and other activities that could only lawfully be performed by a registered futures commission merchant ("FCM"). In addition, Respondents did not conduct know-your- customer ("KYC") diligence on their customers as part of a customer identification program ("CIP"), as required of FCMs.

B. RESPONDENTS

bZeroX, LLC is a Delaware limited liability company ("LLC") with its registered agent in Delaware. bZeroX was founded and was co-owned and controlled during the bZx Relevant Period by Bean and Kistner. During the bZx Relevant Period, bZeroX created and operated the bZx Protocol that facilitated the unlawful transactions described herein. On approximately August 23, 2021, bZeroX transferred control of the bZx Protocol to the bZx DAO, a decentralized autonomous organiza-

---

1. Respondents consent to the use of the findings of fact and conclusions of law in this Order in this proceeding and in any other proceeding brought by the Commission or to which the Commission is a party or claimant, and agrees that they shall be taken as true and correct and be given preclusive effect therein, without further proof. Respondents do not consent, however, to the use of this Order, or the findings or conclusions herein, as the sole basis for any other proceeding brought by the Commission or to which the Commission is a party or claimant, other than: a proceeding in bankruptcy or receivership; or a proceeding to enforce the terms of this Order. Respondents do not consent to the use of the Offer or this Order, or the findings or conclusions in this Order, by any other party in any other proceeding.

tion ("DAO"), which subsequently, on approximately December 18, 2021, renamed itself and is now doing business as the Ooki DAO.[2] bZeroX has never been registered with the Commission in any capacity.

Tom Bean is a Georgia resident who, with Kistner, founded, co-owned, and controlled bZeroX during the bZx Relevant Period. Bean is also a member of the Ooki DAO (formerly doing business as the bZx DAO) and has performed certain work (such as protocol development and marketing work) on the Ooki DAO's behalf during the DAO Relevant Period. Bean has never been registered with the Commission in any capacity.

Kyle Kistner is a Georgia resident who, with Bean, founded, co-owned, and controlled bZeroX during the bZx Relevant Period. Kistner is also a member of the Ooki DAO (formerly doing business as the bZx DAO) and has performed certain work (such as business and budget planning and marketing work) on the Ooki DAO's behalf during the DAO Relevant Period. Kistner has never been registered with the Commission in any capacity.

C. FACTS

1. Respondents Designed, Deployed, Operated, Marketed, and Controlled the bZx Protocol During the bZx Relevant Period.

During the bZx Relevant Period, the bZx Protocol was a collection of smart contracts on the Ethereum blockchain that purported to facilitate transactions without intermediaries.[3] The bZx Protocol enabled any person with an Ethereum wallet to contribute margin (collateral) to open leveraged positions whose value was determined by the price difference between two digital assets from the time the position was established to the time it was closed.[4] For example, if a trader believed that the

---

2. As set forth below, the Ooki DAO is an unincorporated association comprised of holders of Ooki DAO Tokens ("Ooki Tokens") who vote those tokens to govern (e.g., to modify, operate, market, and take other actions with respect to) the bZx Protocol (which the Ooki DAO has renamed the "Ooki Protocol"). The Ooki DAO (formerly doing business as the bZx DAO) has never been registered with the Commission in any capacity. By this Order, the Commission is resolving charges with bZeroX relating to its conduct during the bZx Relevant Period; with Bean and Kistner as control persons of bZeroX during the bZx Relevant Period, as well as for their active participation in the Ooki DAO (i.e., voting their BZRX or Ooki Tokens to govern the BZX DAO (later the Ooki DAO) by, for example, directing the operation of the bZx Protocol (later the Ooki Protocol)) during the DAO Relevant Period. This Order does not resolve charges with the Ooki DAO itself.

3. A blockchain is a distributed, shared, immutable ledger that facilitates the process of recording transactions and tracking digital assets in a consensus-based network. A "smart contract" is a self-enforcing piece of computer code containing all terms of a contract—meaning the software can execute the agreement contained in the contract without additional input from the parties.

4. A digital asset is anything that can be stored and transmitted electronically and has associated ownership or use rights. Digital assets include virtual currencies, which are digital representations of value that function as mediums of exchange, units of account, and/or stores of value. Ether ("ETH") is the Ethereum blockchain's native virtual currency. In addition, Ethereum's ERC-20 token standard permits the conversion of non-ETH virtual currencies into tokens that can be traded on Ethereum.

price of ETH would rise relative to the price of DAI, the trader might open a 5x long position in ETH versus DAI (i.e., a position worth five times the increase in the price of ETH relative to DAI from the time the position was established to the time it was closed). To do so, the trader would proceed as follows:

1. The trader would post collateral (e.g., ETH) to a bZx Protocol smart contract as margin to open the leveraged position.[5]

2. The smart contract would borrow DAI from a bZx Protocol liquidity pool, whose assets were supplied by liquidity providers who, in exchange, had received interest-generating tokens, as well as BZRX Protocol Tokens ("BZRX Tokens") conferring voting rights on certain matters relevant to bZx Protocol governance.[6]

3. The smart contract would exchange the borrowed DAI for ETH on a separate, on-chain decentralized exchange.

4. The smart contract would lock (i.e., prevent from being withdrawn absent conditions expressly written in to the smart contract) the newly received ETH and create a token representing the newly established 5x long position.

5. The smart contract would send that token to the trader.

If the trader was correct (i.e., that the price of ETH would rise relative to the price of DAI), the trader could redeem the token reflecting the position for a profit (i.e., the smart contract would transfer the resulting profit to the trader). If the trader was incorrect (i.e., the price of ETH did not rise relative to the price of DAI), the trader could still redeem the token, except instead of paying profits, the smart contract would retain however much of the collateral was needed to cover the loss. If the trader wished to open a short position, the trading mechanics would be similar, except the trader would borrow ETH and swap it into DAI. Traders could open similar positions involving various additional virtual currencies.

The transactions on the bZx Protocol did not involve contracts of sale of digital assets; rather, they involved leveraged positions whose value was determined by the price difference between two digital assets. Positions on the bZx Protocol automatically rolled over every 28 days (and could thus exist perpetually) and could be liquidated at any time.

For example, DAI is an ERC-20 token that can be transacted with on the Ethereum blockchain and whose value is pegged one-to-one to the price of the U.S. dollar.

5. Notably, positions on the bZx Protocol were required to be overcollateralized—i.e., the value of the collateral was required to exceed the value of the borrowed asset. This was to ensure repayment of the borrowed asset. Prior to a trader closing an open position, if the position had lost too much value, the bZx Protocol was designed to facilitate the automatic liquidation of the position and retention and sale of the posted collateral to cover the loss.

6. The BZRX Tokens conferred voting rights in proportion to the holder's percentage of total BZRX Tokens issued. Additional BZRX Tokens were otherwise minted and allocated to certain individuals, including Bean and Kistner.

bZeroX, through Bean and Kistner, among others, developed a website to market, solicit orders for, and facilitate access to the bZx Protocol. For example, bZeroX's website claimed that it offered a superior margin trading experience because "[t]here is no need for any verification, KYC or AML." The website further claimed that bZeroX did not take custody of users' assets, and there were minimal liquidation penalties. Bean and Kistner also made public statements, appeared in interviews, wrote articles, led calls with community members that are publicly available on YouTube, and otherwise publicly marketed and solicited members of the public to utilize the bZx Protocol. The bZeroX website enabled users, through the click of a few buttons, to transfer assets and open positions on the bZx Protocol using the mechanics described above. bZeroX collected fees from users, including origination fees, trading fees, and a percentage of interest paid to lenders. bZeroX purports to have collected approximately $50,000 in fees prior to June 2020 (all of which was paid to auditors) and, between June 2020 and August 2021, approximately $500,000 in fees (approximately $350,000 of which was paid to employees, service providers, contractors, and other third parties for similar expenses).[7]

Prior to August 23, 2021 (at which time bZeroX transferred control of the bZx Protocol to the bZx DAO), bZeroX (through Bean and Kistner exclusively) retained "administrator keys" ("Keys") permitting bZeroX to access and control the operation of, and the funds held in, the smart contracts involved in the above processes. The Keys enabled bZeroX, for example, to update relevant smart contract code to adjust how the smart contracts operated; pause or suspend trading; pause or suspend contributions or withdrawals of assets and redemptions of tokens to close positions; and otherwise direct disposition of the funds held in the bZx Protocol smart contracts.[8]

During the bZx Relevant Period, bZeroX did not maintain a CIP and explicitly advertised the lack of KYC or AML compliance as a positive feature of the bZx Protocol. bZeroX offered any user anywhere in the world, including in the United States, the ability to trade on the bZx Protocol and, specifically, did not take any steps to exclude U.S. and/or non-eligible contract participants ("non-ECPs") (as defined in Section 1a(18) of the Act, 7 U.S.C. § 1a(18)) from the bZx Protocol.

Bean and Kistner controlled bZeroX during the bZx Relevant Period. For example, Bean and Kistner were the only members of bZeroX and were exclusively responsible for approving bZeroX's business conduct, regulatory decisions, and the technical development of the bZx Protocol.

---

7. Fees are held in BZRX Tokens or 3CRV (a stablecoin that is redeemable for DAI, USDT, or USDC on Curve.Finance). The listed figures reflect approximate conversions to U.S. Dollars as of approximately September 14, 2021.

8. During the bZx Relevant Period, bZeroX did, in fact, utilize the Keys several times to pause trading and suspend users' ability to withdraw funds following several alleged incidents on the bZx Protocol involving alleged third-party exploitation of deficiencies in the bZx Protocol's code and theft of users' assets.

2. During the DAO Relevant Period, Bean and Kistner Were Members of the bZx DAO (Eventually Renamed the Ooki DAO During the DAO Relevant Period), Which Controlled and Operated the bZx Protocol (Eventually Renamed the Ooki Protocol During the DAO Relevant Period).

On approximately August 23, 2021, bZeroX transferred control of the bZx Protocol (including relevant Keys) to the bZx DAO. From that point forward, the bZx DAO could act with respect to the bZx Protocol only through a vote of BZRX Token holders. Bean and Kistner determined that transitioning to a DAO would insulate the bZx Protocol from regulatory oversight and accountability for compliance with U.S. law. As Kistner stated in a public call with the bZx community regarding the transition to the bZx DAO:

> It's really exciting. We're going to be really preparing for the new regulatory environment by ensuring bZx is future-proof. So many people across the industry right now are getting legal notices and lawmakers are trying to decide whether they want DeFi companies to register as virtual asset service providers or not – and really what we're going to do is take all the steps possible to make sure that when regulators ask us to comply, that we have nothing we can really do because we've given it all to the community.

In practice, however, the bZx DAO controlled and operated the bZx Protocol just as bZeroX before it had done. Just as bZeroX (like any LLC) governed the bZx Protocol through the votes of its members (i.e., Bean and Kistner), the bZx DAO governed the bZx Protocol through the votes of BZRX Token holders. Specifically, any BZRX Token holder had the right to propose, and to vote his or her BZRX Tokens to effect, changes to the bZx Protocol or otherwise shape the direction of the bZx DAO's business. The general process was that any new proposals were first discussed on the bZx Community Forum ("bZx Forum"). Proposals that were not widely supported typically ended there. If there was sufficient support, a non-binding "snapshot vote" could be conducted to gauge support for a particular proposal. If a proponent believed there was sufficient support, a binding vote could be held directly on the bZx Protocol through a fork of the Compound Bravo Governance Module smart contract that enabled BZRX Token holders to vote those tokens for or against a proposal. Approved proposals were implemented by individuals as authorized by the bZx DAO.

For example, on approximately August 24, 2021, Bean and Kistner proposed in the bZx Forum that the bZx DAO approve an omnibus funding plan for going-forward bZx DAO operations—including release of funds for marketing, operations, development, community management, and legal expenses. The proposal passed a snapshot vote unanimously, and BZRX Token holders voted to approve the proposal in September 2021. Funds were subsequently released from the bZx DAO Treasury (which contained bZx Protocol revenue) to pay certain of the approved expenses. Similarly, in approximately December 2021, the bZx DAO voted to utilize funds from the bZx DAO Treasury to compensate certain bZx DAO members who lost funds in connection with an alleged security breach and theft of funds on the bZx Protocol.

More generally, Bean and Kistner possess BZRX Tokens and have participated in bZx DAO governance, including by participating in many discussions in online governance forums, making other governance proposals, and voting their BZRX Tokens in favor of such proposals.

During the DAO Relevant Period, the bZx Protocol otherwise operated as described in Section II.C.1 *supra*, through the votes and acquiescence of the bZx DAO. With the bZx DAO's support, Bean and Kistner continued to market and publicly solicit members of the public to trade on the bZx Protocol. The bZx DAO controlled all Keys previously controlled by bZeroX. Like bZeroX, the bZx DAO did not maintain a CIP, explicitly advertised the lack of KYC or AML compliance as a positive feature of the bZx Protocol, and did not take any steps to exclude U.S. and/or non-ECPs from the bZx Protocol.

On approximately December 18, 2021, through a vote of BZRX Token holders, the bZx DAO renamed itself the Ooki DAO. The bZx DAO repeatedly publicly described this process as merely a "rebrand." This process did not result in legal changes to the DAO's business or material changes to its operations.[9] The Ooki DAO now operates the bZx Protocol (which the Ooki DAO has renamed the Ooki Protocol) in the exact same manner that the bZx DAO operated the bZx Protocol (i.e., through the votes of Ooki Token holders). The Ooki DAO website describes specific Ooki DAO procedures for proposing and voting on Ooki DAO governance proposals, which are consistent with the procedures utilized when the Ooki DAO was doing business as the bZx DAO, as summarized above.

III. LEGAL DISCUSSION

A. During the bZx Relevant Period, Respondents Violated Sections 4(a) and 4d(a)(1) of the Act and Regulation 42.2.

1. Respondents Engaged in Unlawful Off-Exchange Leveraged and Margined Retail Commodity Transactions in Violation of Section 4(a) of the Act.

---

9. Respondents represent that, at this time, bZeroX (which, as described above, was the predecessor to the bZx DAO and had not operated the bZx Protocol since it transferred control over the bZx Protocol to the bZx DAO on or about August 23, 2021) ceased engaging in any business activities; and, from this point forward, that certain members of the bZx DAO did not engage in additional activities relating to the newly renamed Ooki Protocol. In addition, Respondents represent that, in connection with this rebrand, the Ooki DAO deployed additional smart contracts that controlled staking and governance for the Ooki DAO, just as previous smart contracts controlled staking and governance for the bZx DAO. These additional smart contracts were largely necessitated by the fact that the renamed Ooki DAO now offered Ooki Tokens (instead of BZRX Tokens) to govern the renamed Ooki Protocol, and BZRX Token holders needed the ability to convert those tokens into Ooki Tokens (as they were permitted to do), and votes by holders of those Ooki Tokens (instead of holders of BZRX Tokens) would now be used to govern the Ooki Protocol.

Virtual currencies such as ETH, DAI, and others traded on the bZx Protocol are "commodities" under the Act. *See, e.g., United States v. Reed*, No. 20-cr-500 (JGK), 2022 WL 597180, at *3–5 (S.D.N.Y. Feb. 28, 2022); *CFTC v. McDonnell*, 287 F. Supp. 3d 13, 228–29 (E.D.N.Y. 2018); *In re Coinflip, Inc.*, CFTC No. 15-29, 2015 WL 5535736, at *2 (Sept. 17, 2015).

Section 2(c)(2)(D) of the Act, 7 U.S.C. § 2(c)(2)(D), applies to "any agreement, contract, or transaction in any commodity that is…entered into with, or offered to (even if not entered into with), a [non-ECP]…on a leveraged or margined basis…." and which does not result in actual delivery within 28 days (hereafter, "leveraged or margined retail commodity transactions"). Act § 2(c)(2)(D) (i), (ii)(III)(aa), 7 U.S.C § 2(c)(2)(D)(i), (ii)(III)(aa). Section 4(a) of the Act, 7 U.S.C. § 6(a), applies to leveraged or margined retail commodity transactions as if those transactions were contracts of sale of a commodity for future delivery. Act § 2(c)(2)(D)(iii), 7 U.S.C § 2(c)(2)(D)(iii).

Section 4(a) of the Act, 7 U.S.C. § 4(a), in relevant part, makes it unlawful for any person to offer to enter into, enter into, execute, confirm the execution of, or conduct an office or business in the United States for the purpose of soliciting or accepting any order for, or otherwise dealing in, any transaction in, or in connection with, a contract for the purchase or sale of a commodity for future delivery, unless such transaction is made on or subject to the rules of a board of trade that has been designated or registered by the CFTC as a contract market for the specific commodity (i.e., a DCM).

During the bZx Relevant Period, utilizing the bZx Protocol, bZeroX offered to enter into, entered into, executed, confirmed the execution of, and/or conducted business in the United States for the purpose of soliciting and/or accepting orders for, and/or otherwise dealing in, leveraged or margined retail commodity transactions with non-ECP U.S. residents that did not result in actual delivery within 28 days. These leveraged or margined retail commodity transactions were not conducted on or subject to the rules of a board of trade that has been designated or registered by the CFTC as a contract market. Thus, Respondents violated Section 4(a) of the Act.

2. Respondents Unlawfully Engaged in Activities That Could Only Lawfully Be Performed by Registered FCMs in Violation of Section 4d(a)(1) of the Act.

Section 1a(28) of the Act, 7 U.S.C. § 1a(28), in relevant part, defines an FCM as any individual, association, partnership, corporation or trust that engages in soliciting or in accepting orders for "any agreement, contract, or transaction described in…section (2)(c)(2)(D)(i)" and, in connection therewith, "accepts any money…or property (or extends credit in lieu thereof) to margin…trades or contracts that result or may result therefrom." Section 4d(a)(1) of the Act, 7 U.S.C. § 6d(a)(1), in pertinent part, makes it unlawful for any person to act as an FCM unless registered with the Commission as an FCM. *See, e.g., Reed*, 2022 WL 597180, at *2–3 (holding indictment sufficiently alleged that entity operated as an unregistered FCM where entity solicited and accepted orders for trades in futures contracts and other derivative products tied to the value of virtual currencies, accepted virtual currency to margin and guarantee its derivative products, and offered leverage to customers on certain products).

As described above, during the bZx Relevant Period, bZeroX, utilizing the bZx Protocol, while not registered as an FCM, acted as an FCM as defined in Section 1a(28) of the Act by soliciting and accepting orders for leveraged or margined retail commodity transactions with customers; and accepting money or property to margin those transactions. Thus, Respondents violated Section 4d(a)(1) of the Act.[10]

3. Respondents Failed to Adopt a CIP in Violation of Regulation 42.2.

Regulation 42.2, 17 C.F.R. § 42.2 (2021), provides that every FCM shall comply with the Bank Secrecy Act and related regulations, which require the FCM to adopt a CIP to facilitate KYC diligence on the FCM's customers. Regulation 42.2 applies to individuals and entities acting as unregistered FCMs. *See, e.g., CFTC v. HDR Global Trading Limited*, No. 1:20-cv-08132, 2021 WL 3722183 at ¶ 39 (S.D.N.Y. Aug. 10, 2021) (consent order) (finding defendant who acted as an unregistered FCM liable for failing to adopt a CIP as required by Regulation 42.2).

During the bZx Relevant Period, by acting as an unregistered FCM, bZeroX was required to adopt a CIP but failed to do so, and in fact explicitly marketed the lack of KYC diligence as a positive feature of the bZx Protocol. In so doing, Respondents violated Regulation 42.2.

4. Respondents Bean and Kistner Are Liable as Controlling Persons for bZx's Violations of the Act and Regulation 42.2.

Controlling persons are liable for violations of the entities they control under certain circumstances. Section 13(b) of the Act, 7 U.S.C. § 13c(b), states that a controlling person of an entity is liable for the violations of that entity if the controlling person knowingly induced the violations, directly or indirectly, or did not act in good faith. "A fundamental purpose of Section 13[(b)] is to allow the Commission to reach behind the corporate entity to the controlling individuals of the corporation

---

10. The Commission issues this Order because Respondents, who were not registered with the Commission, engaged in certain activities that could only lawfully be performed by a registered DCM, and other activities that could only lawfully be performed by a registered FCM. It was (and remains) Respondents' responsibility to avoid unlawfully engaging in activities that could only be performed by registered entities and, should they ever wish to register, to structure their business in a manner that is consistent with Commission registration requirements. *See, e.g., Reed*, 2022 WL 597180, at *3 (holding that even if an entity might have fallen within multiple of the Act's registration categories, "the [Act's] registration categories are not exclusive of one another," and whether an entity unlawfully acted as an unregistered FCM should be determined simply by whether the entity "fall[s] ... within the definition of an FCM").

and to impose liability for violations of the Act directly on such individuals as well as the corporation itself." *R.J. Fitzgerald*, 310 F.3d at 1334 (citation omitted) (holding defendant was a controlling person when the defendant was the company's principal and "exercised the ultimate choice-making power with the firm regarding its business decisions," "reviewed and approved the activities that…violated the Act," and "was ultimately responsible for compliance with all applicable rules on commodities solicitations").

During the bZx Relevant Period, Bean and Kistner controlled bZeroX, directly or indirectly, and did not act in good faith or knowingly induced, directly or indirectly, bZeroX's act or acts in violation of the Act and Regulations; therefore, pursuant to Section 13(b) of the Act, Bean and Kistner are liable for bZeroX's violations of Sections 4(a) and 4d(a)(1) of the Act and Regulation 42.2.

B. During the DAO Relevant Period, the Ooki DAO (formerly d/b/a the bZx DAO) Violated Sections 4(a) and 4d(a)(1) of the Act and Regulation 42.2, and Bean and Kistner, as Members of the Ooki DAO, Are Personally Liable for the Ooki DAO's Violations.[11]

1. The Ooki DAO Is an Unincorporated Association.

An unincorporated association is "a voluntary group of persons, without a charter, formed by mutual consent for the purpose of promoting a common objective." *See, e.g., So. Cal. Darts Ass'n v. Zaffina*, 762 F.3d 921, 927 (9th Cir. 2014) (holding that former incorporated entity promoting competitive play of darts whose corporate powers had been suspended was an unincorporated association under federal law); *Heinold Hog Market, Inc. v. McCoy*, 700 F.2d 611, 613–14 (10th Cir. 1983) (holding that the "National Commodity Exchange" ("NCE"), an affiliate of an organization devoted to tax reform that converted customers' federal reserve notes to gold and silver and then back to federal reserve notes to pay customer creditors, was an unincorporated association where multiple individuals operated the NCE with the purpose of allowing customers to pay creditors without generating a paper trail in the Federal Reserve System); *Seattle Affiliate of October 22nd Coalition to Stop Police Brutality, Repression and the Criminalization of a Generation v. City of Seattle*, No. C04 0860L, 2005 WL 3418415, at *2 (W.D. Wash. Dec. 12, 2005) (holding that local advocacy group was an unincorporated association despite that group did not have an official "membership" list where group had existed in city for years; operated as a local affiliate of a national group; participated in publications, events, and rallies; and utilized an egalitarian, volunteer-oriented structure to meet its objectives).

---

11. In this section, the Commission uses the term "Ooki DAO" as shorthand for the "Ooki DAO (formerly d/b/a the bZx DAO)." Likewise, in this section, the Commission uses the term "Ooki Protocol" as shorthand for the "Ooki Protocol (formerly branded as the bZx Protocol)."

The Ooki DAO meets the federal definition of an unincorporated association. It is a "voluntary group of persons" (Ooki Token holders who voluntarily vote their Ooki Tokens), "without a charter" (no Ooki DAO corporate charter exists), "formed by mutual consent for the purpose of promoting a common objective" (Ooki Token holders who voluntarily vote for the purpose of promoting the common objective of governing the Ooki Protocol). Notably, the Ooki DAO exists for exactly the same purpose as bZeroX before it—to run a business (i.e., to govern and operate the Ooki Protocol). The Ooki DAO is thus an unincorporated association.

While the Ooki DAO does not explicitly define its own membership, the federal definition of an unincorporated association makes clear that the Ooki DAO is comprised of individuals who voluntarily join together to pursue the common objective of participating in the governance of the Ooki Protocol. An unambiguous way that individuals join together to govern the Ooki Protocol is by voting their Ooki Tokens. Once an Ooki Token holder votes his or her Ooki Tokens to affect the outcome of an Ooki DAO governance vote, that person has voluntarily participated in the group formed to promote the common objective of governing the Ooki Protocol and is thus a member of the Ooki DAO unincorporated association.

2. The Ooki DAO Violated Sections 4(a) and 4d(a)(1) of the Act and Regulation 42.2 During the DAO Relevant Period.

The Ooki DAO controlled and operated the Ooki Protocol (including the Keys to the Ooki Protocol) during the entirety of the DAO Relevant Period in the same manner that bZeroX controlled and operated the bZx Protocol during the bZx Relevant Period.

Thus, during the DAO Relevant Period, utilizing the Ooki Protocol, the Ooki DAO offered to enter into, entered into, executed, confirmed the execution of, and/or conducted business in the United States for the purpose of soliciting and/ or accepting orders for, and/or otherwise dealing in, leveraged or margined retail commodity transactions with non-ECP U.S. residents that did not result in actual delivery within 28 days. These leveraged or margined retail commodity transactions were not conducted on or subject to the rules of a board of trade that has been designated or registered by the CFTC as a contract market. Thus, the Ooki DAO violated Section 4(a) of the Act.

Similarly, during the DAO Relevant Period, the Ooki DAO, while not registered as an FCM, acted as an FCM as defined in Section 1a(28) of the Act by soliciting and accepting orders for leveraged or margined retail commodity transactions with customers; and accepting money or property to margin those transactions. Thus, the Ooki DAO violated Section 4d(a)(1) of the Act.

Finally, during the DAO Relevant Period, by acting as an unregistered FCM, the Ooki DAO was required to adopt a CIP but failed to do so, and in fact explicitly marketed the lack of KYC diligence as a feature of the Ooki Protocol. In so doing, the Ooki DAO violated Regulation 42.2.

3. As Members of the Ooki DAO, Bean and Kistner Are Personally Liable for the Ooki DAO's Violations of the Act and Regulation 42.2.

Individual members of an unincorporated association organized for profit are personally liable for the debts of the association under principles of partnership law. *See, e.g., Karl Rove & Co. v. Thornburgh*, 39 F.3d 1273, 125 (5th Cir. 1994) (citations omitted) (distinguishing liability of individual members of for-profit unincorporated associations, which is determined by partnership law, with liability of individual members of non-profit unincorporated associations, which is determined by the law of agency); *Shortlidge v. Gutoski*, 484 A.2d 1083, 1086 (N.H. 1984) (citations omitted) (noting that each member of an unincorporated association organized for profit is treated as a partner of the association, is jointly liable with other members for the association's debts, and can have his or her personal assets reached by creditors of the association; and noting that membership in unincorporated associations often "results from sheer ignorance of the possible degree of personal liability of its members"); *Libby v. Perry*, 311 A.2d 527, 533 (Me. 1973) (citation omitted) (noting established rule that in for-profit voluntary unincorporated associations, "members are mere partners and as such are personally liable for all its debts").

The Ooki DAO is a for-profit unincorporated association. It charges fees for its products and services, generates revenue, has distributed revenue to its members in various forms, offers ownership rights in the Ooki DAO in the form of Ooki Tokens, collects and liquidates collateral from users, and has never sought to be characterized as a non-profit organization in any federal or state registration or tax filing. *See, e.g., Heinold Hog Market*, 700 F.2d at 615–16 (noting that unincorporated association NCE appeared to operate for profit where it charged for its services, bought and sold commodities, assumed the risk of commodity market price declines, and recouped losses from account holders when prices increased).

As members of the for-profit Ooki DAO unincorporated association (i.e., as Ooki Token holders who voted their Ooki Tokens to govern the Ooki DAO by, for example, directing the operation of the Ooki Protocol), Bean and Kistner are personally liable for the Ooki DAO's debts. Accordingly, they are personally liable for the Ooki DAO's violations of the Act and Regulations set forth in Section III.B.2 *supra*.[12]

IV. FINDINGS OF VIOLATIONS

Based on the foregoing, the Commission finds that, during the Relevant Period, Respondents violated Sections 4(a) and 4d(a)(1) of the Act, 7 U.S.C. §§ 6(a) and 6d(a)(1), and Regulation 42.2, 17 C.F.R. § 42.2 (2021).

---

12. As set forth in Note 2 *supra*, by this Order, the Commission is resolving charges against Bean and Kistner for their actions as members of the Ooki DAO, but is not resolving charges against the Ooki DAO itself. As such, the Commission does not take a position in this Order as to the appropriate monetary sanctions against the Ooki DAO for the violations of law described herein.

V. OFFER OF SETTLEMENT

Respondents have submitted the Offer in which they, without admitting or denying the findings and conclusions herein:

1. Acknowledge service of this Order;

2. Admit the jurisdiction of the Commission with respect to all matters set forth in this Order and for any action or proceeding brought or authorized by the Commission based on violation of or enforcement of this Order;

3. Waive:

   1. The filing and service of a complaint and notice of hearing;

   2. A hearing;

   3. All post-hearing procedures;

   4. Judicial review by any court;

   5. Any and all objections to the participation by any member of the Commission's staff in the Commission's consideration of the Offer;

   6. Any and all claims that they may possess under the Equal Access to Justice Act, 5 U.S.C. § 504, and 28 U.S.C. § 2412, and/or the rules promulgated by the Commission in conformity therewith, Part 148 of the Regulations, 17 C.F.R. pt. 148, relating to, or arising from, this proceeding;

   7. Any and all claims that they may possess under the Small Business Regulatory Enforcement Fairness Act of 1996, Pub. L. No. 104-121, tit. II, §§ 201–253, 110 Stat. 847, 857–74 (codified as amended at 28 U.S.C. § 2412 and in scattered sections of 5 U.S.C. and 15 U.S.C.), relating to, or arising from, this proceeding; and

   8. Any claims of Double Jeopardy based on the institution of this proceeding or the entry in this proceeding of any order imposing a civil monetary penalty or any other relief, including this Order;

4. Stipulate that the record basis on which this Order is entered shall consist solely of the findings contained in this Order to which Respondents have consented in the Offer;

E. Consent, solely on the basis of the Offer, to the Commission's entry of this Order that:

1. Makes findings by the Commission that Respondents violated Sections 4(a) and 4d(a)(1) of the Act, 7 U.S.C. §§ 6(a) and 6d(a)(1), and Regulation 42.2, 17 C.F.R. § 42.2 (2021);

2. Orders Respondents to cease and desist from violating Sections 4(a) and 4d(a)(1) of the Act and Regulation 42.2;

3. Orders Respondents to pay, jointly and severally, a civil monetary penalty in the amount of two hundred and fifty thousand dollars ($250,000) within ten (10) days of the date of entry of this Order, plus post-judgment interest in the event such civil monetary penalty is not paid within ten days of the date of entry of this Order;

4. Orders Respondents and any of bZeroX's successors and assigns to comply with the conditions and undertakings consented to in the Offer and as set forth in Part VI of this Order.

Upon consideration, the Commission has determined to accept the Offer.

VI. ORDER

Accordingly, IT IS HEREBY ORDERED THAT:

1. Respondents and any of bZeroX's successors and assigns shall cease and desist from violating Sections 4(a) and 4d(a)(1) of the Act, 7 U.S.C. §§ 6(a) and 6d(a)(1), and Regulation 42.2, 17 C.F.R. § 42.2 (2021).

2. Respondents shall pay, jointly and severally, a civil monetary penalty in the amount of two hundred and fifty thousand dollars ($250,000) ("CMP Obligation"), within ten (10) days of the date of the entry of this Order. If the CMP Obligation is not paid in full within ten days of the date of entry of this Order, then post-judgment interest shall accrue on the CMP Obligation beginning on the date of entry of this Order and shall be determined by using the Treasury Bill rate prevailing on the date of entry of this Order pursuant to 28 U.S.C. § 1961.

   Respondents shall pay the CMP Obligation and any post-judgment interest by electronic funds transfer, U.S. postal money order, certified check, bank cashier's check, or bank money order. If payment is to be made other than by electronic funds transfer, then the payment shall be made payable to the Commodity Futures Trading Commission and sent to the address below:

MMAC/ESC/AMK326

Commodity Futures Trading Commission Division of Enforcement

6500 S. MacArthur Blvd.

HQ Room 181

Oklahoma City, OK 73169

(405) 954-6569 office

(405) 954-1620 fax Tonia.King@faa.gov

If payment is to be made by electronic funds transfer, Respondents shall contact Tonia King or her successor at the above address to receive payment instructions and shall fully comply with those instructions. Respondents shall accompany payment of the CMP Obligation with a cover letter that identifies the paying Respondent and the name and docket number of this proceeding. The paying Respondent shall simultaneously transmit copies of the cover letter and the form of payment to the Chief Financial Officer, Commodity Futures Trading Commission, Three Lafayette Centre, 1155 21st Street, NW, Washington, D.C. 20581, and to Charles Marvine, Deputy Director, Commodity Futures Trading Commission, 2600 Grand Boulevard, Suite 210, Kansas City, MO 64108.

3. Respondents and any of bZeroX's successors and assigns shall comply with the following conditions and undertakings set forth in the Offer:

1. Public Statements: Respondents agree that neither they nor any of bZeroX's successors and assigns, agents or employees under their authority or control shall take any action or make any public statement denying, directly or indirectly, any findings or conclusions in this Order or creating, or tending to create, the impression that this Order is without a factual basis; provided, however, that nothing in this provision shall affect Respondents': (i) testimonial obligations; or (ii) right to take legal positions in other proceedings to which the Commission is not a party. Respondents and any of bZeroX's successors and assigns shall comply with this agreement and shall undertake all steps necessary to ensure that all of their agents and/or employees under their authority or control understand and comply with this agreement.

2. Cooperation, in General: Respondents shall cooperate fully and expeditiously with the Commission, including the Commission's Division of Enforcement and any other governmental agency or any self-regulatory organization, in this action, and in any current or future Commission investigation, civil litigation, or administrative matter relating to, or arising from, this action, including but not limited to any Commission lawsuit against the Ooki DAO. As part of such cooperation, Respondents agree to voluntarily, for example, produce documents, things, and information as requested, provide declarations, respond to written discovery, and give testimony.

3. Participation in the Ooki DAO: Respondents shall cease all participation in the governance, operation, or any other activities of the Ooki DAO. Without limitation, Respondents shall not make proposals, directly or indirectly through others, related to Ooki DAO governance; or vote any Ooki Tokens they own or control.

4. Partial Satisfaction: Respondents understand and agree that any acceptance by the Commission of any partial payment of Respondents' CMP Obligation shall not be deemed a waiver of their obligation to make further payments pursuant to this Order, or a waiver of the Commission's right to seek to compel payment of any remaining balance.

5. Change of address/ phone: Until such time as Respondents satisfy in full their CMP Obligation as set forth in this Order, Respondents shall provide written notice to the Commission by certified mail of any change to their telephone number and mailing address within ten calendar days of the change. Notice should be provided to the Chief Financial Officer, Commodity Futures Trading Commission, Three Lafayette Centre, 1155 21st Street, NW, Washington, D.C., 20581, and to Charles Marvine, Deputy Director, Commodity Futures Trading Commission, 2600 Grand Boulevard, Suite 210, Kansas City, MO 64108.

6. Until such time as Respondents satisfy in full their CMP Obligation, upon the commencement by or against Respondents of insolvency, receivership, or bankruptcy proceedings or any other proceedings for the settlement of Respondents' debts, all notices to creditors required to be furnished to the Commission under Title 11 of the United States Code or other applicable law with respect to such insolvency, receivership bankruptcy or other proceedings, shall be sent to the address below:

Secretary of the Commission
Office of the General Counsel
Commodity Futures Trading Commission
Three Lafayette Centre
1155 21st Street N.W.
Washington, DC 20581

The provisions of this order shall be effective as of this date

By the Commission.
Christopher J. Kirkpatrick
Secretary of the Commission
Commodity Futures Trading Commission
Dated: September 22, 2022

Discussion Points

1. *bZeroX, LLC.* How is this case similar or different from the Coinflip case?
2. *Penalty.* bZeroX and its founders were fined $250,000 by the CFTC. Is this the CFTC's first-of-its-kind case against a DAO? Was this penalty sufficient, in your opinion? Why or why not?
3. Explain the legal significance of registering for both designated contract markets (DCMs) and futures commission merchants (FCMs) in the context of maintaining market integrity and protecting investors.

4. Discuss the potential legal implications, both negative and positive, of the regulatory measures and safeguards established by the CFTC to ensure transparency and fair practices in registered DCMs and FCMs.

5. What key measures would an entity's compliance program have in place to maintain regulatory compliance for registered DCMs and FCMs? Why?

6. Discuss the broader significance of this case in terms of the CFTC's purported mission to foster open, transparent, and competitive markets while safeguarding market participants' interests.

Five

Custody of Digital Assets

I. Introduction

A variety of custody options to manage the use of digital assets are emerging as the virtual currency market evolves. Digital assets are assets that exist virtually, and there are five categories of digital assets. These five categories include security tokens, utility tokens, cryptocurrencies, e-money and stablecoins.

Before discussing the regulatory considerations in this space, it is imperative to understand the role of custodians in the financial market. Generally, custodians are institutions that provide customers with an array of financial services. Think of custodians as vaults that hold investors' assets in both electronic and physical form, and maintain the assets in a secure manner. Similarly, custodians safekeep customer's digital assets.

Digital wallets provide places for consumers to store and access their cryptocurrency. There are two forms of digital wallets: hot and cold. Similar to the functions of a traditional bank account, consumers can make deposits, transfers, and withdrawals from their digital wallet. However, regulatory agencies do not provide any safeguards over digital wallets as they do over FDIC insured banks. Consequently, consumers can become victims of fraud, and custodial digital wallets can be hacked, leaving consumers with no recourse or remedy.

II. Office of the Comptroller of the Currency

The Office of the Comptroller of the Currency (OCC) is an independent bureau of the U.S. Department of Treasury. The OCC charters, regulates, and supervises all national banks, federal savings associations, and federal branches and agencies of foreign banks. The business of banking is rapidly changing as digital technologies continue to proliferate. As mentioned in previous chapters, digital technological innovations provide consumers convenience and accessibility, but they also pose risks.

The OCC provides policies, guidance, advisories, and information regarding the use of digital assets in the federal banking system. For instance, the OCC has released various Interpretive Letters that clarify the OCC's stance on digital assets. Particularly, in Interpretive Letters 1170, 1172, and 1174, the OCC noted that banks should only engage in cryptocurrency activities if they could do so in a way that was consistent with safe banking practices.

Until summer 2020, guidance had not yet been issued regarding the treatment of digital wallets. This changed when the OCC issued Interpretive Letter 1170 in July 2020.[55] This Letter describes that banks have been safekeeping digital assets since 1998, and as such, it is important for banks to have the ability to safekeep cryptocurrency. The Letter also regards how banks have long safekept a consumer's assets, have had the authority to perform functions electronically, can conduct both fiduciary and non-fiduciary actions, and escrow encryption keys.[56] The Letter further states that banks should update their procedures to accommodate new technologies and innovations, and points to three three indicators that demonstrate a growing demand for bank safekeeping of digital assets: (1) that private keys are essential for consumers to retain their cryptocurrency; (2) banks can offer secure storage; and (3) some investment advisors want to manage their clients' cryptocurrencies through national banks.[57]

Also discussed in Interpretative Letter 1170 is compliance. For a nationally chartered bank to successfully provide custodial services for digital assets, it must comply with 12 CFR Part 9, relevant state laws, and any other applicable rules and regulations.[58] The same principles apply to federal savings associations that must comply with 12 CFR Part 150 as well as the relevant state and local laws and other applicable rules and regulations.[59]

The OCC strongly urges that when deciding to move forward with providing custodial services, a bank or savings association should develop such activities with "sound risk management practices" that align with the bank's business plan as well as an appropriate review of the consumer's needs and wants.[60]

---

55. OCC Guidance 1170 (July 22, 2020), https://www.occ.gov/topics/charters-and-licensing /interpretations-and-actions/2020/int1170.pdf. Notably, the guidance states that cryptocurrency is designed to work as a medium of exchange.

56. "[T]he OCC has found that the authority to provide safekeeping services extends to digital activities and, specifically, that national banks may escrow encryption keys used in connection with digital certificates because a key escrow service is a functional equivalent to physical safekeeping." *Id.* at 8. The OCC first authorized the storage of encryption keys in escrow in 1998 and reaffirmed its position in 2001. OCC Conditional Approval 479 (July 27, 2001); Ria Bhutoria, *The OCC Authorizes Cryptocurrency Custody*, FIDELITY DIGITAL ASSETS (Aug. 25, 2020), https://www.fidelitydigitalassets .com/articles/occ-authorizes-cryptocurrency-custody.

57. *Id.*

58. 12 CFR Part 9 implemented 12 U.S.C. § 92a, which gives the OCC express authority to grant fiduciary powers to national banks. *Id.* at 9.

59. *Id.*

60. *Id.* at 9–10.

Authority of a National Bank to Provide Cryptocurrency Custody Services for Customers

Office of the Comptroller of the Currency, Interpretive Letter 1170 (July 22, 2020)

Introduction and Summary Conclusion I.

This letter responds to your request regarding the authority of a national bank to provide cryptocurrency custody services for customers. For the reasons discussed below, we conclude a national bank may provide these cryptocurrency custody services on behalf of customers, including by holding the unique cryptographic keys associated with cryptocurrency.[1] This letter also reaffirms the OCC's position that national banks may provide permissible banking services to any lawful business they choose, including cryptocurrency businesses, so long as they effectively manage the risks and comply with applicable law.[2]

II. Background

Cryptocurrencies—also known as "digital currencies" or "virtual currencies"—are designed to work as a medium of exchange and are created and stored electronically.[3] Depending on the type of cryptocurrency, it may have characteristics of either fiat money or money backed by some underlying asset(s) or claim(s). Fiat money refers to instruments that do not have intrinsic value but that individuals and institutions are willing to use for purposes of purchase and investment because they are issued by a government. Government-issued currencies, including the U.S. dollar following abandonment of the gold standard, are traditional fiat money. Some types of cryptocurrencies may have similar characteristics as fiat money because they are not backed by any other assets. Other types of money may be backed by assets (such as a commodity). The U.S. dollar was a type of asset-backed money prior to abandonment of the gold standard. Some types of cryptocurrencies may have similar characteristics to this type of money. For example, stablecoin is a type of cryptocurrency that is backed by an asset, such as a fiat currency or a commodity.

While cryptocurrency shares certain characteristics of these traditional types of money, the exchange mechanism is novel. The exchange mechanism for most cryp-

---

1. As discussed further below, this conclusion also applies to Federal savings associations (FSAs).

2. Banks determine the levels and types of risks that they will assume. Banks that operate in compliance with applicable law, properly manage customer relationships and effectively mitigate risks by implementing controls commensurate with those risks are neither prohibited nor discouraged from providing banking services. As the federal banking agencies have previously stated, banks are encouraged to manage customer relationships and mitigate risks based on customer relationships rather than declining to provide banking services to entire categories of customers. See Joint Statement on Risk-Focused Bank Secrecy Act/Anti-Money Laundering Supervision, at 2 (July 22, 2019), available at https://www.occ.gov/news-issuances/news-releases/2019/nr-ia-2019-81a.pdf.

3. The term "cryptocurrency" as used in this letter also encompasses digital assets that are not broadly used as currencies.

tocurrencies is based on two separate underlying technologies. The first is advanced cryptography, which is used to protect information related to the cryptocurrency. Cryptography allows the creation of digital code that generally cannot be altered without the permission of the creator.

The second type of technology underlying cryptocurrencies' exchange mechanism is known as "distributed ledger technology," and consists of a shared electronic database where copies of the same information are stored on multiple computers. This shared database functions as both a mechanism to prevent tampering and as a way to add new information to the database. Information will not be added to the distributed ledger until consensus is reached that the information is valid. Furthermore, attempts to change the information on one computer will not impact the information on the other computers. Some distributed ledgers are known as "blockchains" because the transactions stored on the ledger are sequentially grouped together in blocks, thus creating a chronological record of all transactions to that point.[4]

Cryptocurrencies do not exist in any physical form. They exist only on the distributed ledger on which they are recorded. A particular unit of cryptocurrency is assigned to a party through the use of a set of unique cryptographic keys. Those keys allow that party to transfer the cryptocurrency to another party.[5] If those keys are lost, a party will generally be unable to access its cryptocurrency. Furthermore, if a third party gains access to those keys, that third party can use the keys to transfer the cryptocurrency to themselves.

The first widely-adopted cryptocurrency, Bitcoin, was introduced in 2008.[6] Since the creation of Bitcoin, hundreds of additional virtual currencies have been created, all of which have different characteristics and potential uses. Some cryptocurrencies may have characteristics of currency or cash, including as a medium of exchange, but with a new exchange mechanism (i.e., electronic transfer without an intermediary). This letter expresses no opinion on whether cryptocurrencies may be exchanged for purposes of 12 U.S.C. 24 (Seventh).

Cryptocurrencies have been used for a variety of payment and investment activities. Bitcoin remains the most widely used and valuable cryptocurrency, with a

---

4. See, e.g., How does Bitcoin work?, bitcoin.org (last visited July 20, 2020), https://bitcoin.org /en/how-it-works (describing Bitcoin's shared public ledger as a blockchain).

5. See, e.g., FAQs, How does Bitcoin work?, bitcoin.org (last visited July 20, 2020), https://bitcoin .org/en/faq#how- does-bitcoin-work (from a user perspective, Bitcoin is nothing more than an application that provides a digital wallet); How does Bitcoin work?, bitcoin.org (last visited July 20, 2020), https://bitcoin.org/en/how-it-works (describing use of keys to sign transactions); How do Bitcoin Transactions Work?, Coindesk.com (last visited July 20, 2020), https://www.coindesk.com/ information/how-do-bitcoin-transactions-work/.

6. See Satoshi Nakamoto, Bitcoin: A Peer-to-Peer Electronic Cash System, available at https ://bitcoin.org/bitcoin.pdf (Bitcoin Whitepaper).

current market capitalization approximately \$170 billion.[7] Bitcoin is now accepted as payment by thousands of merchants worldwide; customers may even purchase Bitcoin for cash at various retail locations.[8] Contracts on Bitcoin futures have been established and options on Bitcoin futures are now trading.[9] The SEC recently approved a Bitcoin futures fund.[10] Although transactions in cryptocurrencies can occur directly between parties via decentralized, peer-to-peer cryptocurrency transactions, many cryptocurrencies may also be traded through centralized, online cryptocurrency exchanges where parties trade one cryptocurrency for another or trade for fiat currencies such as the U.S. dollar through a financial intermediary.[11] Some centralized cryptocurrency exchanges have obtained state banking licenses as trust banks.[12]

As of June 2020, a majority of states have adopted laws and regulations pertaining to cryptocurrencies.[13] Recent survey evidence suggests that almost 40 million Amer-

---

7. See Top 100 Cryptocurrencies by Market Capitalization, Coinmarketcap.com, (last visited July 20, 2020), https://coinmarketcap.com/.

8. See Maddie Shepherd, How Many Businesses Accept Bitcoin? (last visited July 20, 2020), https://www.fundera.com/resources/how-many-businesses-accept-bitcoin (reporting that nearly 15,174 merchants worldwide accept bitcoin as of December 31, 2019). See also Turner Wright, LibertyX Allows BTC Purchases in Cash at 7-Eleven, CVS, and Rite Aid, Cointelegraph.com (June 23, 2020), https://cointelegraph.com/news/libertyx- allows-btc-purchases-in-cash-at-7-eleven-cvs -and-rite-aid.

9. See CME Group, Bitcoin futures and options on futures (last visited July 20, 2020), https ://www.cmegroup.com/trading/bitcoin-futures.html.

10. In December of 2019, the SEC approved an investment fund that invests in bitcoin futures contracts. See Kevin Helms, SEC Approves Bitcoin Futures Fund, Bitcoin.com (Dec. 7, 2019), https ://news.bitcoin.com/sec-approves- bitcoin-futures-fund/.

11. See Top Cryptocurrency Spot Exchanges, Coinmarketcap.com (last visited July 20, 2020), https://coinmarketcap.com/rankings/exchanges/ (listing over 300 separate cryptocurrency exchanges). "Decentralized" in this context refers to the lack of a third-party intermediary; instead, buyers and sellers exchange cryptocurrency directly. "Centralized" refers to a third-party intermediary (such as a banking organization) that facilitates trades between buyers and sellers. See Dylan Dedi, Centralized Cryptocurrency Exchanges, Explained, Cointelegraph.com (March 10, 2018), https ://cointelegraph.com/explained/centralized-cryptocurrency-exchanges- explained.

12. See, e.g., New York Department of Financial Services, Financial Services Superintended Linda A. Lacewell Announces Grant of DFS Trust Charter to Enable Fidelity to Engage in New York's Growing Virtual Currency Marketplace (Nov. 19, 2019), https://www.dfs.ny.gov/reports_and_publications/press_releases/pr1911191; New York Department of Financial Services, NYDFS Grants Charter to "Gemini" Bitcoin Exchange founded by Cameron and Tyler Winklevoss (Oct. 5, 2015), https://www.dfs.ny.gov/reports_and_publications/press_releases/pr1510051.

13. Numerous states have adopted or proposed legislation that relates to cryptocurrency, usually exempting digital currencies from money transmitter licensing requirements and securities laws or recognizing that records secured through blockchain technology have the same legal status as written records. See Dale Werts, Blockchain & Cryptocurrency: State Law Roundup 2019 (July 18, 2019), https://www.jdsupra.com/legalnews/blockchain- cryptocurrency-state-law-59816/.

icans own cryptocurrencies.[14] Institutional investors also have invested in crypto-currencies.[15]

III. The Proposed Activities

The bank has proposed to offer cryptocurrency custody services to its customers as part of its existing custody business. We understand that there is a growing demand for safe places, such as banks,[16] to hold unique cryptographic keys associated with cryptocurrencies on behalf of customers and to provide related custody services.[17] These services are in demand for several reasons. First, because the underlying keys to a unit of cryptocurrency are essentially irreplaceable if lost, owners may lose access to their cryptocurrencies as a result of misplacing their keys, resulting in significant losses of value.[18] Second, banks may offer more secure storage services

---

14. See Helen Partz, 11% of Americans Own Bitcoin, Major Awareness Increased Since 2017, Yahoo! Finance (Apr. 30, 2019), https://finance.yahoo.com/news/11-americans-own-bitcoin-major-164400483.html.

15. See, e.g., Olga Kharif, Fidelity Says a Third of Big Institutions Own Crypto Assets (June 9, 2020), BNN Bloomberg, https://www.bnnbloomberg.ca/fidelity-says-a-third-of-big-institutions-own-crypto-assets-1.1447708 (reporting that, according to a survey by Fidelity Investments, 36 percent of institutional investors in the U.S. and Europe report holding crypto assets); Luke W. Vrotsos and Cindy H. Zhang, Harvard Invests Millions in New Cryptocurrency, The Harvard Crimson, April 12, 2019, available at https://www.thecrimson.com/article/2019/4/12/hmc-crypto-investment/; Jonathan Watkins, The Institutional Crypto Backers: How Endowments are Allocating to Cryptocurrency Investments (Apr. 2019), available at https://www.globalcustodian.com/wp-content/uploads/2019/04/The-institutional-crypto-backers-How-endowments- are-allocating-to-crypto currency-investments.pdf.

16. States are beginning to recognize the growing demand for safe locations to hold cryptocurrencies. At least one state has passed legislation and promulgated regulations allowing state-chartered banks to opt-in to providing custody services for digital assets. See, e.g., Wyo. Admin. Code 021.0002.19. These regulations were promulgated pursuant to Wyoming Statute ("W.S.") 34-29-104, Digital asset custodial services. Under W.S. 34-29-104, banks that elect to provide digital asset custodial services must comply with all provision of W.S. 34-29-104 and the new regulations (known as the enhanced digital custody opt-in regime). The states of Hawaii and Rhode Island have also recently proposed legislation on digital asset custody. See Hawaii SB2594 (introduced Jan. 17, 2020), available at https://www.capitol.hawaii.gov/measure_indiv.aspx?billtype=SB&billnumber=2594&year=2020; Rhode Island HB7989, available at https://legiscan.com/RI/bill/H7989/2020 (introduced Mar. 11, 2020).

17. See, e.g., Melanie Kramer, Will Cryptocurrency Custody Services Fuel Institutional Demand?, Bitcoinist.com (July 22, 2018), https://bitcoinist.com/crypto-custody-services-fuel-institutional-demand/ (describing how institutional investors may feel more comfortable maintaining cryptocurrencies in the custody of banks than exchanges).

18. One empirical analysis of the bitcoin blockchain calculated that roughly 20% of all currently outstanding bitcoin have been lost. See Jeff John Roberts and Nicolas Rapp, Nearly 4 Million Bitcoins Lost Forever, New Study Says, Fortune (Nov. 25, 2017), available at http://fortune.com/2017/11/25/lost-bitcoins/; see also, Alison Sider and Stephanie Young, Good News! You Are a Bitcoin Millionaire. Bad News! You Forgot Your Password, The Wall Street Journal (Dec. 19, 2017), available at https://www.wsj.com/articles/good-news-you-are-a-bitcoin-millionaire-.

compared to existing options.[19] Third, some investment advisers may wish to manage cryptocurrencies on behalf of customers and may wish to utilize national banks as custodians for the managed assets.

Providing custody for cryptocurrencies would differ in several respects from other custody activities. Cryptocurrencies are generally held in "wallets," which are programs that store the cryptographic keys associated with a particular unit of digital currency. Because digital currencies exist only on the blockchain or distributed ledger on which they are stored, there is no physical possession of the instrument. Instead, the right to a particular unit of digital currency is transferred from party to party by the use of unique cryptographic keys. Therefore, a bank "holding" digital currencies on behalf of a customer is actually taking possession of the cryptographic access keys to that unit of cryptocurrency. Those keys are held in a "wallet" that protects the keys from discovery by a third party.[20] Keys can be stored in "hot" wallets or "cold" wallets. Hot wallets are connected to the internet, which makes them convenient to access but more susceptible to hacking. Cold wallets are physical devices that are completely offline (for example, paper or hardware wallets that can be stored in a physical vault). Currently, cold storage is considered the most secure method of storing cryptographic keys.[21]

The OCC recognizes that, as the financial markets become increasingly technological, there will likely be an increasing need for banks and other service providers to leverage new technology and innovative ways to provide traditional services on behalf of customers. By providing such services, banks can continue to fulfill the financial intermediation function they have historically played in providing payment, loan and deposit services. Through intermediated exchanges of payments, banks facilitate the flow of funds within our economy and serve important financial risk management and other financial needs of bank customers.[22]

IV. Discussion

National banks have long provided safekeeping and custody services for a wide variety of customer assets, including both physical objects and electronic assets. These functions of national banks are well established and extensively recognized

---

19. Some cryptocurrency exchanges that store access to cryptocurrency on behalf of customers have proven vulnerable to hacking and theft. See Steven Russolillo and Eun-Young Jeong, Cryptocurrency Exchanges Are Getting Hacked Because It's Easy, The Wall Street Journal (July 16, 2018), available at https://www.wsj.com/articles/why-cryptocurrency-exchange-hacks-keep-happening -1531656000 (detailing light security and regulatory gaps at some cryptocurrency exchanges).

20. See, e.g., Aziz, Guide to Cryptocurrency Wallets: Why Do You Need Wallets? (last visited July 20, 2020) https://masterthecrypto.com/guide-to-cryptocurrency-wallets/ (holding cryptocurrency at an exchange means having the exchange host the wallet).

21. See, e.g., Hot wallet vs cold wallet in cryptocurrency storage, Coin Insider, https://www .coininsider.com/hot-vs- cold-wallets-cryptocurrency/ (last visited July 16, 2020).

22. See, e.g., OCC Interpretive Letter No. 1110 (Jan. 30, 2009); OCC Interpretive Letter No. 1101 (July 7, 2008); OCC Interpretive Letter No. 1079 (April 19, 2007).

as permissible activities for national banks.[23] The OCC concludes, for the reasons discussed below, that providing cryptocurrency custody services, including holding the unique cryptographic keys associated with cryptocurrency, is a modern form of these traditional bank activities.

Safekeeping services are among the most fundamental and basic services provided by banks.[24] Bank customers traditionally used special deposit and safe deposit boxes for the storage and safekeeping of a variety of physical objects, such as valuable papers, rare coins, and jewelry.[25] As the banking industry entered the digital age, the OCC recognized the permissibility of electronic safekeeping activities. Specifically, the OCC has concluded that a national bank may escrow encryption keys used in connection with digital certificates,[26] finding that the key escrow service is a functional equivalent to physical safekeeping, except it uses electronic technology suitable to the digital nature of the item to be kept safe. The OCC has also concluded that a national bank may provide secure web-based document storage, retrieval and collaboration of documents and files containing personal information or valuable confidential trade or business information because these services are the electronic expression of traditional safekeeping services provided by banks.[27] The OCC codified these interpretive rulings in 12 CFR Part 7.[28]

Traditional bank custodians frequently offer a range of services in addition to simple safekeeping of assets. For example, a custodian providing core domestic custody services for securities typically settles trades, invests cash balances as directed, collects income, processes corporate actions, prices securities positions, and provides recordkeeping and reporting services.[29] It is well-established that nation-

---

23. See OCC Conditional Approval 479 (July 27, 2001) (Conditional Approval 479). "Safekeeping" implies the basic service of a bank holding on to an asset for a customer (e.g., gold or securities). "Custody" is a broader term that may involve all aspects of bank services performed for customers in relation to items they are holding for them (i.e., processing, settlement, fund administration). Historically, banks only offered safekeeping services, which then evolved into banks providing custodial services to their customers. See Comptroller's Handbooks on Custody Services (Jan. 2002) (Custody Handbook).

24. Colorado Nat. Bank of Denver v. Bedford, 310 U.S. 41, 50 (1940) (finding that providing safe deposit boxes is "such a generally adopted method of safeguarding valuables [that it] must be considered a banking function authorized by Congress" under the National Bank Act). The safekeeping of valuable personal property is a traditional function that banks have performed since the earliest times. "Originally the business of banking consisted only in receiving deposits, such as bullion, plate and the like for safe-keeping until the depositor should see fit to draw it out for use...." Oulton v. German Savings and Loan Soc'y, 84 U.S. 109, 118 (1872); see also Bank of California v. City of Portland, 157 Ore. 203, 69 P.2d 273 (1937).

25. See Conditional Approval 479; Comptroller's Handbook on Custody Services (Custody Handbook) (Jan. 2002) at page 15 (jewelry listed as one of the miscellaneous assets that banks hold via on-premises custody).

26. See OCC Conditional Approval 267 (Jan. 12, 1998) (Conditional Approval 267).

27. See Conditional Approval 479.

28. See 12 CFR §§ 7.5002(a)(4) and 7.5005(a).

29. See Custody Handbook at 2.

al banks may provide custody services to their customers in either a fiduciary or non-fiduciary capacity. 12 U.S.C. 92a expressly authorizes the OCC to grant fiduciary powers to national banks.[30] National banks may also provide non- fiduciary custody services to their customers.[31] The OCC has determined national banks may act as non-fiduciary custodians pursuant to the business of banking and their incidental powers.[32] OCC guidance has recognized that banks may hold a wide variety of assets as custodians, including assets that are unique and hard to value.[33] These custody activities often include assets that transfer electronically.[34] The OCC generally has not prohibited banks from providing custody services for any particular type of asset, as long as the bank has the capability to hold the asset and the assets are not illegal in the jurisdiction where they will be held.[35]

Providing custody services for cryptocurrency falls within these longstanding authorities to engage in safekeeping and custody activities. As discussed below, this is a permissible form of a traditional banking activity that national banks are authorized to perform via electronic means.[36] Providing such services is permissible

---

30. "The Comptroller of the Currency shall be authorized and empowered to grant by special permit to national banks applying therefor, when not in contravention of State or local law, the right to act as trustee, executor, administrator, registrar of stocks and bonds, guardian of estates, assignee, receiver, or in any other fiduciary capacity in which State banks, trust companies, or other corporations which come into competition with national banks are permitted to act under the laws of the State in which the national bank is located." 12 U.S.C. 92a(a). 12 CFR Part 9 implements 12 U.S.C. 92a. The fiduciary capacities defined under Part 9 are "trustee, executor, administrator, registrar of stocks and bonds, transfer agent, guardian, assignee, receiver, or custodian under a uniform gifts to minors act; investment adviser, if the bank receives a fee for its investment advice; any capacity in which the bank possesses investment discretion on behalf of another; or any other similar capacity that the OCC authorizes pursuant to 12 USC 92a." See 12 CFR 9.2(e).

31. National banks do not need the trust or fiduciary powers found in sections 92a to offer these custodial services. Thus, no trust powers are necessary in order to conduct these activities. See Conditional Approval 267.

32. See, e.g., Conditional Approval 267 (agency services such as custody that do not involve fiduciary powers are performed by banks as part of their incidental powers); OCC Interpretive Letter 1078 (April 19, 2007) (authority of national banks to engage in custody activities derives from general business of banking, and from incidental powers language in 12 U.S.C. § 24(Seventh)).

33. See, generally, Comptroller's Handbook, Unique and Hard-to-Value Assets (August 2012) (providing guidance on bank management of unique assets and listing examples of such assets, including real estate, closely held businesses, mineral interests, loans and notes, life insurance, tangible assets, and collectibles). See also Comptroller's Handbooks on Custody Services (Jan. 2002) (Custody Handbook), Asset Management (Dec. 2000), Asset Management Operations and Controls (Jan. 2011), Retirement Plan Products and Services (Feb. 2014), Conflicts of Interest (Jan. 2015); OCC Bulletin 2013-29, "Third-Party Relationships—Risk Management Guidance" (Oct. 30, 2013).

34. See Custody Handbook at 19, 70 (describing book-entry securities as securities that transfer electronically and stating that banks should assess their technological readiness to maintain a competitive position).

35. See Custody Handbook at 7.

36. 12 CFR 7.5002(a) provides that a national bank may perform, provide, or deliver through electronic means and facilities any activity, function, product, or service that it is otherwise authorized to perform, provide, or deliver. This regulatory provision is based on the longstanding

in both non-fiduciary and fiduciary capacities. A bank that provides custody for cryptocurrency in a non-fiduciary capacity would essentially provide safekeeping for the cryptographic key that allows for control and transfer of the customer's cryptocurrency. In most, if not all, circumstances, providing custody for cryptocurrency will not entail any physical possession of the cryptocurrency. Rather, a bank "holding" digital currencies on behalf of a customer is actually taking possession of the cryptographic access keys to that unit of cryptocurrency.[37] As described above, the OCC has found that the authority to provide safekeeping services extends to digital activities and, specifically, that national banks may escrow encryption keys used in connection with digital certificates because a key escrow service is a functional equivalent to physical safekeeping. Holding the cryptographic access key to a unit of cryptocurrency is an electronic corollary of these traditional safekeeping activities. The OCC's regulations in Subpart E of Part 7 explicitly authorize national banks to perform, provide or deliver through electronic means and facilities any activities that they are otherwise authorized to perform.[38] Because national banks are authorized to perform safekeeping and custody services for physical assets, national banks are likewise permitted to provide those same services via electronic means (i.e., custody of cryptocurrency).[39]

"transparency doctrine," under which the OCC looks through the means by which a product is delivered and focuses instead on the authority of the national bank to offer the underlying product or service. See 67 FR 34992, 34996 (May 17, 2002). See also OCC Conditional Approval 369 (Feb. 25, 2000) (national bank may host a virtual mall consisting of a web page with links to third-party merchants arranged according to product or service offered); OCC Conditional Approval 304 (Mar. 5, 1999) (electronic bill presentment is part of the business of banking); Conditional Approval 267 (a national bank may store electronic encryption keys as an expression of the established safekeeping function of banks); OCC Conditional Approval 220 (Dec. 2, 1996) (the creation, sale, and redemption of electronic stored value in exchange for dollars is part of the business of banking because it is the electronic equivalent of issuing circulating notes or other paper-based payment devices like travelers checks).

37. Banks may offer different methods of providing cryptocurrency custody services, depending on their expertise, risk appetite, and business models. Some banks may offer to store copies of their customers' private keys while permitting the customer to retain their own copy. Such services may be more akin to traditional safekeeping and would permit the customer to retain direct control over their own cryptocurrencies. Other banks may permit customers to transfer their cryptocurrencies directly to control of the bank, thereby generating new private keys which would be held by the institution on behalf of the customer. Such services may be more akin to traditional custody services, but as with traditional custody, would not permit the customer to maintain direct control of the cryptocurrency. Banks may also offer other custody models that may be appropriate. Banks acting as fiduciaries for cryptocurrency should consider how to ensure their custody models comply with requirements of 12 CFR 9.13 and 12 CFR 150.230–250.

38. See 12 CFR 7.5002(a).

39. The services national banks may provide in relation to the cryptocurrency they are custodying may include services such as facilitating the customer's cryptocurrency and fiat currency exchange transactions, transaction settlement, trade execution, recording keeping, valuation, tax services, reporting, or other appropriate services. A bank acting as custodian may engage a sub-custodian for cryptocurrency it holds on behalf of customers and should develop processes to ensure that the sub-custodian's operations have proper internal controls to protect the customer's cryp-

To the extent that a national bank with trust powers conducts cryptocurrency custody activities in a fiduciary capacity, such activities would be permissible if conducted in compliance with 12 CFR Part 9, applicable state law, and any other applicable law, such as the instrument that created the fiduciary relationship. A national bank holding cryptocurrencies in a fiduciary capacity—such as a trustee, an executor of a will, an administrator of an estate, a receiver, or as an investment advisor—would have the authority to manage them in the same way banks can manage other assets they hold as fiduciaries.[40]

These conclusions apply equally to federal savings associations (FSAs). Like national banks, FSAs may provide custody services in either a fiduciary or non-fiduciary capacity. The OCC may grant fiduciary powers to an FSA under 12 U.S.C. 1464(n).[41] These fiduciary activities of an FSA must be conducted in compliance with 12 CFR Part 150. In addition, FSAs have authority to act as a non-fiduciary custodian under 12 U.S.C. 1464.[42] Similar to national banks, FSAs are authorized to "use, or participate with others to use, electronic means or facilities to perform any function, or provide any product or service, as part of an authorized activity."[43] Accordingly, for the same reasons described above with respect to national banks, providing custody services for cryptocurrency falls within an FSA's established authority to provide custody services.

A national bank or FSA engaging in new activities should develop and implement those activities consistent with sound risk management practices and align them with the bank's overall business plans and strategies as set forth in OCC guidance.[44] There may be services that banks may provide in connection with cryptocurrencies that are unique to cryptocurrency.[45] As with all other activities performed by national banks and FSAs, a national bank or FSA that provides cryptocurrency custody

---

tocurrency. See, e.g., Custody Handbook at 15–16. As set forth below, banks should develop and implement new activities in accordance with OCC guidance.

40. National banks acting as fiduciaries are usually subject to heightened standards of care under applicable law in comparison to non-fiduciaries. Given the continued evolution of the cryptocurrency sector, banks managing cryptocurrency as fiduciaries should ensure they keep abreast of best practices to ensure they continue to meet these heightened standards.

41. 12 U.S.C. 1464(n)(1) states, "The Comptroller may grant by special permit to a Federal savings association applying therefor the right to act as trustee, executor, administrator, guardian, or in any other fiduciary capacity in which State banks, trust companies, or other corporations which compete with Federal savings associations are permitted to act under the laws of the State in which the Federal savings association is located."

42. See Testimony of John Bowman, Chief Counsel, Office of Thrift Supervision, before the Senate Committee on Banking, Housing, and Urban Affairs (June 22, 2004) (HOLA allows thrifts to provide trust and custody services on the same basis as national banks).

43. See 12 CFR 155.200(a).

44. See OCC Bulletin 2017-43, "New, Modified, or Expanded Bank Products and Services: Risk Management Principles" (Oct. 20, 2017).

45. Custody agreements are an important risk management tool and should clearly establish the custodian's duties and responsibilities. See Custody Handbook at 8. The handling, treatment, and servicing of cryptocurrencies held in custody may raise unique issues that should be addressed in

services must conduct these activities in a safe and sound manner, including having adequate systems in place to identify, measure, monitor, and control the risks of its custody services. Such systems should include policies, procedures, internal controls, and management information systems governing custody services. Effective internal controls include safeguarding assets under custody, producing reliable financial reports, and complying with laws and regulations. The OCC has previously described that custody activities should include dual controls, segregation of duties and accounting controls.[46] A custodian's accounting records and internal controls should ensure that assets of each custody account are kept separate from the assets of the custodian and maintained under joint control to ensure that that an asset is not lost, destroyed or misappropriated by internal or external parties. Other considerations include settlement of transactions, physical access controls, and security servicing. Such controls may need to be tailored in the context of digital custody. Specialized audit procedures may be necessary to ensure the bank's controls are effective for digital custody activities. For example, procedures for verifying that a bank maintains access controls for a cryptographic key will differ from the procedures used for physical assets. Banks seeking to engage in these activities should also conduct legal analysis to ensure the activities are conducted consistent with all applicable laws.

Consistent with OCC regulations and guidance on custody activities, the risks associated with an individual account should be addressed prior to acceptance.[47] A custodian's acceptance process should provide an adequate review of the customer's needs and wants, as well as the operational needs of the account. During the acceptance process, the custodian should also assess whether the contemplated duties are within its capabilities and are consistent with all applicable law. Understanding the risks of cryptocurrency, the due diligence process should include a review for compliance with anti-money laundering rules. Banks should also have effective information security infrastructure and controls in place to mitigate hacking, theft, and fraud. Banks should also be aware that different cryptocurrencies may have different technical characteristics and may therefore require risk management procedures specific to that particular currency. Different cryptocurrencies may also be subject to different OCC regulations and guidance outside of the custody context, as well

---

the agreement, such as (for example) the treatment of "forks" or splits in the code underlying the cryptocurrency being held.

46. See Custody Handbook at 6–8. Banks with fiduciary powers that hold assets as fiduciaries are subject to the requirements of 12 CFR Part 9 (for national banks) and Part 150 (for FSAs). These regulations include specific provisions governing the custody of fiduciary assets. See 12 CFR 9.13 (national banks); 12 CFR 150.230–250 (FSAs).

47. See 12 CFR 9.6(a) (requiring bank fiduciaries to perform a pre-acceptance review before accepting a fiduciary account to determine whether the bank can properly administer it); Custody Handbook at 7–8.

as non-OCC regulations.[48] A national bank should consult with OCC supervisors as appropriate prior to engaging in cryptocurrency custody activities. The OCC will review these activities as part of its ordinary supervisory processes.

I trust this is responsive to your inquiry.

Discussion Points

1. *Crypto-custodial services.* The July 2020 interpretation affirms that national banks, including federally chartered banks and thrifts, may provide crypto-custodial services for crypto assets. This interpretation provides national banks with the opportunity to generate new revenue systems, a new client base, and develop new digital payment and asset protection solutions.

2. *Who should take control?* Who should regulate the custody of crypto assets? Should federal or state regulators be in charge of its regulation? Should there be concurrent authority among federal and state regulators to do so? Should states have the power to regulate the custody of crypto assets in state-chartered banks and credit unions?

3. *The reach of the FDIC.* Should the FDIC provide insurance on the custody of crypto assets? Why or why not? If the FDIC was to ensure the custody of crypto assets in federally chartered banks, how would this affect customers who have crypto assets in state-chartered banks and credit unions that are not under the FDIC's purview?

OCC Chief Counsel's Interpretation on National Bank and Federal Savings Association Authority to Hold Stablecoin Reserves

Office of the Comptroller of the Currency, Interpretive Letter 1172

(September 2020)

I. Introduction and Summary Conclusion

This letter addresses the authority of a national bank to hold deposits that serve as reserves for certain "stablecoins." Generally, a stablecoin is a type of cryptocurrency designed to have a stable value as compared with other types of cryptocur-

---

48. For example, cryptocurrencies that are considered "securities" for purposes of the Federal securities laws may be subject to the OCC's regulations on recordkeeping and confirmation requirements for securities transactions, 12 CFR Part 12, as well as the Federal securities laws administered by the SEC.

rency, which frequently experience significant volatility. One type of stablecoin is backed by an asset such as a fiat currency. Reports suggest stablecoins have various applications, including the potential to enhance payments on a broad scale,[1] and are increasingly in demand.[2] As described further below, stablecoin issuers may desire to place assets in a reserve account with a national bank to provide assurance that the issuer has sufficient assets backing the stablecoin in situations where there is a hosted wallet.[3] For the reasons discussed below, we conclude that a national bank may hold such stablecoin "reserves" as a service to bank customers.[4] We are not presently addressing the authority to support stablecoin transactions involving un-hosted wallets. In addition, this letter only addresses the use of stablecoin backed on a 1:1 basis by a single fiat currency where the bank verifies at least daily that reserve account balances are always equal to or greater than the number of the issuer's outstanding stablecoins.[5]

A bank providing services in support of a stablecoin project must comply with all applicable laws and regulations and ensure that it has instituted appropriate controls and conducted sufficient due diligence commensurate with the risks associated with maintaining a relationship with a stablecoin issuer. The due diligence process should facilitate an understanding of the risks of cryptocurrency and include a review for compliance with applicable laws and regulations, including those related to the Bank Secrecy Act (BSA) and anti-money laundering. In this regard, the review should include, but not be limited to, customer due diligence requirements under the BSA[6]

---

1. See, e.g., Marc Di Maggio and Nicholas Platias, Is Stablecoin the Next Big Thing in E-Commerce?, Harv. Bus. Rev. (May 21, 2020), available at https://hbr.org/2020/05/is-stablecoin-the-next-big-thing-in-e-commerce.

2. See, e.g., Antonio Madeira, On Solid Ground: Stablecoins Thriving Amid Financial Uncertainty, Cointelegraph.com (Aug. 2, 2020), available at https://cointelegraph.com/news/on-solid-ground-stablecoins- thriving-amid-financial-uncertainty.

3. "Cryptocurrencies are generally held in 'wallets,' which are programs that store the cryptographic keys associated with a particular unit of digital currency." OCC Interpretive Letter No. 1170, at 5 (July 22, 2020), available at https://www.occ.gov/topics/charters-and-licensing/interpretations-and-actions/2020/int1170.pdf (IL 1170). A hosted wallet is an account-based software program for storing cryptographic keys controlled by an identifiable third party. These parties receive, store, and transmit cryptocurrency transactions on behalf of their account holders; the account holder generally does not have access to the cryptographic keys themselves. In contrast, an un- hosted or personal wallet is one where an individual owner of a cryptocurrency maintains control of the cryptographic keys for accessing the underlying cryptocurrency.

4. These conclusions apply only to the deposit activities of national banks and Federal savings associations (FSAs). This letter expresses no conclusion on the application of any other laws to the stablecoin activities discussed in this letter or on the permissibility of these activities for any institutions other than those supervised by the OCC.

5. The current stablecoin activities discussed in this letter would not contribute to the global and systemic risks noted by the Financial Stability Board in its recent consultation. See Fin. Stability Board, Addressing the Regulatory, Supervisory and Oversight Challenges Raised by "Global Stablecoin" Arrangements (Apr. 14, 2020), available at https://www.fsb.org/wp-content/uploads/P140420-1.pdf.

6. 31 C.F.R. § 1020.210(b)(5).

and the customer identification requirements under section 326 of the USA PA-TRIOT Act.[7] A national bank or FSA must also identify and verify the beneficial owners of legal entity customers opening accounts.[8] A national bank or FSA must also comply with applicable federal securities laws.[9]

II. Stablecoin Reserves

Cryptocurrencies—also known as "digital currencies" or "virtual currencies"—are often designed to work as a medium of exchange and are created and stored electronically.[10] As we previously described, cryptocurrencies are enabled by two technologies: cryptography and distributed ledger technology.[11] Cryptography and distributed ledger technology are both rapidly evolving technologies. As described above, "stablecoin" often refers to a particular type of digital coin that is backed by another asset, such as a fiat currency.

Like cryptocurrencies more broadly, stablecoins are an evolving technology. Different types of stablecoins may share certain characteristics, but there are variations in the way various cryptocurrencies described as "stablecoins" work. Cryptocurrencies referred to as "stablecoins" may be backed by a fiat currency, a commodity, or another cryptocurrency. Fiat-backed stablecoins are typically redeemable for the underlying fiat currency, where one unit of the stablecoin can be exchanged for one unit of the underlying fiat currency. Other types of cryptocurrencies described as "stablecoins" may be more complex, backed by commodities, cryptocurrencies, or other assets but with values that are pegged to a fiat currency or managed by algorithm. For purposes of this letter, we consider a "stablecoin" to be a unit of cryptocurrency associated with hosted wallets that is backed by a single fiat currency and redeemable by the holder of the stablecoin on a 1:1 basis for the underlying fiat currency upon submission of a redemption request to the issuer. We are only opining on those facts and circumstances at this time.

---

7. 12 C.F.R. § 21.21(c)(2); 31 C.F.R. § 1020.220. See also OCC Bulletin 2016-10, Prepaid Cards: Interagency Guidance to Issuing Banks on Applying Customer Identification Program Requirements to Holders of Prepaid Cards (Mar. 21, 2016), available at https://occ.gov/news-issuances/bulletins/2016/bulletin-2016-10.html.

8. 31 C.F.R. § 1010.230.

9. We note that staff of the Securities and Exchange Commission (SEC) has issued a statement encouraging issuers of stablecoins of the type described herein to contact the staff with any questions they may have to help ensure that such stablecoins are structured, marketed, and operated in compliance with the federal securities laws. The statement notes that the staff stands ready to engage with market participants, and, depending on the particular facts and circumstances, to assist them and consider providing, if appropriate, a "no-action" position regarding whether activities with respect to a specific stablecoin may invoke the application of the federal securities laws. See SEC FinHub Staff Statement on OCC Interpretation (Sept. 21, 2020).

10. The OCC recently described many features of cryptocurrency. See IL 1170.

11. IL 1170, at 2.

Companies that issue stablecoins often desire to place the funds backing the stablecoin, or reserve funds, with a U.S. bank. Public independent auditors' statements
of several stablecoin issuers indicate reserve funds are placed as deposits with U.S.
banks. Several of these issuers promote these reserves—and the fact that they are
held by banks—to support the trustworthiness of their stablecoin. In light of the
public interest in these reserve accounts, this letter addresses the legal authority of
national banks to hold stablecoin reserves on behalf of customers.

III. Discussion

We understand that some stablecoin issuers may desire to place the cash reserves
backing their issued stablecoin with a national bank. In the most basic example, a
stablecoin issuer may seek to place its reserve funds in a deposit account with a national bank. National banks are expressly authorized to receive deposits.[12] Receiving
deposits is recognized as a core banking activity.[13] As the OCC recently reaffirmed,
national banks may provide permissible banking services to any lawful business
they choose, including cryptocurrency businesses, so long as they effectively manage the risks and comply with applicable law, including those relating to the BSA and
anti-money laundering.[14] Accordingly, national banks may receive deposits from
stablecoin issuers, including deposits that constitute reserves for a stablecoin associated with hosted wallets. In connection with these activities, a national bank may
also engage in any activity incidental to receiving deposits from stablecoin issuers.[15]
Likewise, an FSA is authorized to take deposits,[16] including from an issuer of stablecoin associated with hosted wallets.

As with any deposit product, a national bank or FSA that accepts reserve accounts should be aware of the laws and regulations relating to deposit insurance
coverage, including deposit insurance limits,[17] and the requirements for deposit

---

12. 12 U.S.C. 24 (Seventh).

13. See, e.g., 12 C.F.R. § 5.20(e).

14. See IL 1170, at 1. In IL 1170, the OCC reaffirmed its view that banks determine the levels and
types of risks that they will assume. Banks that operate in compliance with applicable law, properly
manage customer relationships and effectively mitigate risks by implementing controls commensurate with those risks are neither prohibited nor discouraged from providing banking services. As the
federal banking agencies have previously stated, banks are encouraged to manage customer relationships and mitigate risks based on customer relationships rather than declining to provide banking
services to entire categories of customers. See Joint Statement on Risk-Focused Bank Secrecy Act/
Anti-Money Laundering Supervision, at 2 (July 22, 2019), available at https://www.occ.gov/news
- issuances/news-releases/2019/nr-ia-2019-81a.pdf.

15. 12 C.F.R. § 7.4007 (permitting "any activity incidental to receiving deposits, including issuing
evidence of accounts, subject to such terms, conditions, and limitations prescribed by the Comptroller of the Currency and any other applicable Federal law").

16. See 12 U.S.C. 1464(b).

17. See generally 12 U.S.C. 1821; 12 C.F.R. Part 330.

insurance to "pass through" to an underlying depositor, if applicable.[18] Stablecoin reserve accounts could be structured as either deposits of the stablecoin issuer or as deposits of the individual stablecoin holder if the requirements for pass through insurance are met.[19] Accordingly, a national bank or FSA should provide accurate and appropriate disclosures regarding deposit insurance coverage. A national bank or FSA must ensure that its deposit activities comply with applicable laws and regulations, including those relating to the BSA and anti-money laundering. Specifically, a national bank or FSA must ensure that it establishes and maintains procedures reasonably designed to assure and monitor its compliance with the BSA and its implementing regulations, including but not limited to customer due diligence requirements under the BSA[20] and the customer identification requirements under section 326 of the USA PATRIOT Act.[21] A national bank or FSA must also identify and verify the beneficial owners of legal entity customers opening accounts.[22] A national bank or FSA must also comply with applicable federal securities laws.

New bank activities should be developed and implemented consistently with sound risk management principles and should align with banks' overall business plans and strategies.[23] Bank management should establish appropriate risk management processes for new activity development and effectively identify, measure, monitor, and control the risks associated with new activities. In particular, reserves associated with stablecoins could entail significant liquidity risks. The OCC expects all banks to manage liquidity risk with sophistication equal to the risks undertaken

---

18. 12 C.F.R. Part 330; FDIC General Counsel's Op. No. 8 (Nov. 13, 2008), available at https ://www.govinfo.gov/content/pkg/FR-2008-11-13/pdf/E8-26867.pdf. For example, in the context of prepaid cards, OCC guidance has explained that, according to FDIC General Counsel's Opinion No. 8, "stored value (electronic cash) issued by banks will be insured if the funds underlying the electronic cash remain in a customer's account until it is transferred to a merchant or other third party, who in turn collects the funds from the customer's bank. However, bank-issued electronic cash does not result in an insured deposit when the underlying funds are placed in a reserve or general liability account held by the issuing bank to pay merchants and other payees as they make claims for payments." OCC Bulletin 1996-48 (Sept. 3, 1996), https://www.occ.gov/news- issuances/ bulletins/1996/bulletin-1996-48.html.

19. 12 C.F.R. Part 330; FDIC General Counsel's Op. No. 8 (Nov. 13, 2008). The general requirements for pass- through deposit insurance coverage are: (1) the account records at the bank must disclose the existence of the third- party custodial relationship; (2) the bank's records or records maintained by the custodian or other party must disclose the identities of the actual owners of the funds and the amount owned by each such owner; and (3) the deposits actually must be owned (under the agreements among the parties) by the named owners.

20. 31 C.F.R. § 1020.210(b)(5).

21. 12 C.F.R. § 21.21(c)(2); 31 C.F.R. § 1020.220. See also OCC Bulletin 2016-10, Prepaid Cards: Interagency Guidance to Issuing Banks on Applying Customer Identification Program Requirements to Holders of Prepaid Cards (Mar. 21, 2016).

22. 31 C.F.R. § 1010.230.

23. See OCC Bulletin 2017-43, New, Modified, or Expanded Bank Products and Services: Risk Management Principles, available at https://www.occ.gov/news-issuances/bulletins/2017/bulletin -2017-43.html.

and complexity of exposures. [24] A bank may also enter into appropriate contractual agreements with a stablecoin issuer governing the terms and conditions of the services that the bank provides to the issuer. [25] Such agreements may include contractual restrictions or requirements with respect to the assets held in the reserve account. The agreement may also specify the respective responsibilities of the parties, such as the steps the parties will take to ensure the appropriate party will be deemed the issuer or obligor of the stablecoin. For example, the bank should have appropriate agreements in place with an issuer to verify and ensure that the deposit balances held by the bank for the issuer are always equal to or greater than the number of outstanding stablecoins issued by the issuer. Such agreements should include mechanisms to allow the bank to verify the number of outstanding stablecoins on a regular basis. [26] In the analogous context of prepaid cards distributed and sold by third-party program managers, interagency guidance specifically contemplates that banks would enter into contracts with third-party program managers permitting banks to audit the third-party program managers. [27]

A bank should consider all relevant risk factors, including liquidity risk and compliance risk, before entering any agreement or relationship with a stablecoin issuer.

/s/

Jonathan V. Gould
Senior Deputy Comptroller and Chief Counsel

---

24. See Comptroller's Handbook on Liquidity (June 2012), at 4, available at https://occ.gov/publications-and- resources/publications/comptrollers-handbook/files/liquidity/pub-ch-liquidity.pdf. For example, a critical component of an institution's ability to effectively respond to potential liquidity stress is the availability of a cushion of unencumbered highly liquid assets without legal, regulatory, or operational impediments that can be sold or pledged to obtain funds in a range of stress scenarios. Id. at 30.

25. OCC guidance has previously recognized the importance of contracts in establishing responsibilities and liability in the context of prepaid cards. In describing the responsibilities of national banks participating in then-emergent prepaid card systems, the OCC said: "A bank should be clear as to who bears the responsibility at each stage of an electronic cash transaction. Thus far, transactional rules for some electronic cash systems are not well established by current law. Accordingly, in many important respects, the transactional rules for such systems must be established by contract." OCC Bulletin 1996-48 (Sept. 3, 1996). See also OCC Bulletin 2016-10, Prepaid Cards: Interagency Guidance to Issuing Banks on Applying Customer Identification Program Requirements to Holders of Prepaid Cards (Mar. 21, 2016). Similarly, a bank that receives deposits from a stablecoin issuer should enter into appropriate contracts to define the responsibilities of the parties.

26. Banks are subject to capital and reserve requirements intended to ensure that banks have sufficient liquidity and are able to meet the needs of customers, including by satisfying withdrawals and cashing checks. See generally, 12 C.F.R. Part 204 (reserve requirements); 12 C.F.R. Part 3 (capital requirements). See also Comptroller's Handbook on Cash Accounts (Mar. 1998), available at https://www.occ.treas.gov/publications-and-resources/publications/comptrollers-handbook/files/cash-accounts/pub-ch-cash-accounts.pdf; Comptroller's Handbook on Depository Services (Aug. 2010), available at https://www.occ.gov/publications-and- resources/publications/comptrollers-handbook/files/depository-services/pub-ch-depository-services.pdf.

27. See OCC Bulletin 2016-10, Prepaid Cards: Interagency Guidance to Issuing Banks on Applying Customer Identification Program Requirements to Holders of Prepaid Cards (Mar. 21, 2016).

Discussion Points

1. *Stablecoins and banks.* This interpretive letter concluded that under the banks' existing authority to receive deposits, banks may hold deposits serving as stablecoin reserves that are backed on a 1:1 basis by a single fiat currency and held in hosted wallets.

2. *Is the OCC doing enough?* In your opinion, is the OCC taking a proactive approach toward safeguarding the crypto assets of consumers? Should the OCC be doing more?

OCC Chief Counsel's Interpretation on National Bank and Federal Savings Association Authority to Use Independent Node Verification Networks and Stablecoins for Payment Activities

Office of the Controller of the Currency, Interpretive Letter 1174 (January 4, 2021)

I. Introduction and Summary Conclusion

This letter addresses the legal permissibility of certain payment-related activities that involve the use of new technologies, including the use of independent node verification networks (INVNs or networks) and stablecoins, to engage in and facilitate payment activities. National banks and Federal savings associations (collectively referred to as "banks") may use new technologies, including INVNs and related stablecoins, to perform bank-permissible functions, such as payment activities.

An INVN consists of a shared electronic database where copies of the same information are stored on multiple computers. One common form of an INVN is a distributed ledger.[1] Cryptocurrency transactions are recorded on these ledgers.[2] An INVN's participants, known as nodes, typically validate transactions, store transaction history, and broadcast data to other nodes.[3]

---

1. See OCC Interpretive Letter 1170 (Jul. 22, 2020) (IL 1170) (describing distributed ledger technology as a shared electronic database where copies of the same information are stored on multiple computers. This shared database functions as both a mechanism to prevent tampering and as a way to add new information to the database. Information will not be added to the distributed ledger until consensus is reached that the information is valid. INVNs represent one of the key technologies that support the novel exchange mechanism underlying cryptocurrency. The other key technology is advanced cryptography.).

2. The OCC described many features of cryptocurrency in IL 1170. In addition, the OCC recently addressed the permissibility of a national bank holding reserves for stablecoins that are backed by fiat currency on at least a 1:1 basis in situations where there is a hosted wallet. See OCC Interpretive Letter 1172 (Sept. 21, 2020) (IL 1172).

3. Nodes are generally either full nodes or light nodes. Full nodes verify transactions, maintain consensus between other nodes, and contain a full copy of the ledger's entire history. Light nodes generally consist of wallets that download only the headers of blocks to validate their authenticity and save hard drive space for users by not storing a full copy of the ledger's history. One example of

A stablecoin is a type of cryptocurrency that is designed to have a stable value as compared with other types of cryptocurrency. [4] Some stablecoins are backed by a fiat currency, such as the U.S. dollar. Fiat-backed stablecoins can typically be exchanged for the underlying fiat currency, where one unit of the stablecoin can be exchanged for one unit of the underlying fiat currency. [5] In this regard, the stablecoin represents a mechanism for storing, transferring, transmitting, and exchanging the underlying fiat currency value, all of which are key to facilitate payment activities. One example of stablecoin as a mechanism to facilitate payment activities is the payment of remittances, which often involve cross-border transfers of money. [6]

Courts and the OCC have long recognized that the primary role of banks is to act as financial intermediaries, facilitating the flow of money and credit among different parts of the economy. [7] "The very object of banking is to aid the operation of the laws of commerce by serving as a channel for carrying money from place to place, as the rise and fall of supply and demand require, and it may be done by rediscounting the bank's paper or by some other form of borrowing." [8] The precedents and history [9]

---

a light node may be a customer's digital wallet on the customer's mobile phone. See, e.g., Josh Evans, Blockchain Nodes: An In-Depth Guide, Nodes.com (Sept. 22, 2020), available at https://nodes .com/; Blockchain: What are nodes and masternodes?, Medium.com (Sept. 22, 2020), available at https://medium.com/coinmonks/blockchain-what-is-a-node-or-masternode-and-what-does-it-do-4d9a4200938f. A bank may want to serve as a full node on an INVN due to the wider range of capabilities on a full node as compared to a light node, as described above.

4. See IL 1172. See also *President's Working Grp. on Fin. Markets Releases Statement on Key Regulatory & Supervisory Issues Relevant to Certain Stablecoins*, Treas. SM-1223 (Dec. 23, 2020) (providing an initial assessment of regulatory and supervisory considerations for participants in certain stablecoin arrangements and clarifying expectations for the retail payment application of stablecoins), available at https://home.treasury.gov/news/press-releases/sm1223.

5. IL 1172 noted that other types of cryptocurrencies described as "stablecoins" may be more complex, backed by commodities, cryptocurrencies, or other assets but with values that are pegged to a fiat currency or managed by algorithm.

6. Facilitating cross-border payments in stablecoin may improve the speed and cost of transferring funds anywhere in the world; traditional remittances often come with high fees and may take several days to complete. See Hugo Renaudin, Driven by Financial Institutions, Stablecoin Acceptance Turns a Corner, Cointelegraph.com (June 14, 2020), available at https://cointelegraph.com/ news/driven-by-financial-institutions-stablecoin-acceptance-turns-a- corner.

7. See, e.g., OCC Interpretive Letter 1102 (Nov. 2008) (IL 1102); see also NationsBank of North Carolina, N.A. v. Variable Life Annuity Co., 513 U.S. 251, 252 (1995) ("VALIC"); OCC Interpretive Letter 499 (Feb. 12, 1990).

8. Auten v. U.S. Nat'l Bank of New York, 174 U.S. 125, 143 (1899).

9. See IL 1102; OCC Interpretive Letter 892 (Sept. 8, 2000). The OCC's view of banks as financial intermediaries comports with the historical role of banks in the economy. See Peter Olson, Regulation's Role in Bank Changes, 18 ECON. POL'Y REV. 13, Federal Reserve Bank of New York (2012), available at https://www.newyorkfed.org/medialibrary/media/research/epr/2012/EPRvol18n2.pdf. As early as the Roman Empire, banks served as intermediaries that mediated between borrowers and lenders, obviating direct contact between them. These banks dealt with the day to day needs of their clients for cash. See Peter Termin, Financial Intermediation in the Early Roman Empire, 64 J. ECON. HIST. 705 (2004). In the 17th century, Dutch merchant banks, such as the Bank of Amsterdam, held deposits and transferred money between accounts; in 18th century England, merchant

reflect that a bank's role as financial intermediary can take many forms: providing payments transmission services, borrowing from savers and lending to users, and participating in the capital markets. As the recognized intermediaries between other, non-bank participants in the financial markets and the payment systems, banks possess the expertise to facilitate the exchange of payments and securities between, and settle transactions for, parties and to manage their own intermediation position.

Over time, banks' financial intermediation activities have evolved and adapted in response to changing economic conditions and customer needs. Banks have adopted new technologies to carry out bank-permissible activities, including payment activities.[10] The emergence of new technologies to facilitate payments, support financial transactions, and meet the evolving financial needs of the economy has led to a demand for banks to use INVNs to carry out their traditional functions. The changing financial needs of the economy are well-illustrated by the increasing demand in the market for faster and more efficient payments through the use of decentralized technologies, such as INVNs, which validate and record financial transactions, including stablecoin transactions.[11]

---

banks accepted deposits and loaned money to landowners and merchants. Id. Besides deposit taking and lending, another crucial component of financial intermediation is connecting participants in the financial system through the processing of payments. As financial intermediaries, banks have processed payments on behalf of their customers for centuries. For example, in ancient Mesopotamia and Egypt, customers would deposit goods (such as grains) in palaces, temples, and private houses that served as banks. Deposit receipts for these goods were transferable and facilitated transactions and payments between customers. See Chao Gu, Fabrizio Mattesini, Cyril Monnet, & Randall Wright, Banking: A New Monetarist Approach, 80 REV. ECON. STUD. 636 (2013). During the era of Medici banking in the 15th century, Italian bankers facilitated payments by book transfer on the instruction of oral or written orders. See Raymond de Roover, The Rise and Decline of the Medici Bank, Harvard University Press, at 2 (1963). In medieval times, Venetian bankers accepted commodities on deposit that were used to facilitate transactions, and deposit receipts began circulating in place of cash for payments in the early 17th century. See Gu, Mattesini, Monnet, & Wright, supra. During the second half of the 17th century, goldsmith bankers in London operated a system of payments through mutual debt acceptance and interbanker clearing. See Stephen Quinn, Goldsmith-Banking: Mutual Acceptance and Interbanker Clearing in Restoration London, 34 EXPLO-RATIONS IN ECON. HIS. 411 (1997).

10. For example, and as discussed below, banks have adopted new technologies in their development and operation of electronic funds transfer systems, real-time settlement systems, and stored value systems. See OCC Interpretive Letter 890 (May 15, 2000) (IL 890): OCC Interpretive Letter 854 (Feb. 25, 1999) (IL 854); OCC Interpretive Letter 1157 (Nov. 12, 2017) (IL 1157); OCC Interpretive Letter 1140 (Jan. 13, 2014) (IL 1140); OCC Conditional Approval Letter 220 (Dec. 2, 1996); OCC Conditional Approval Letter 568 (Dec. 31, 2002); OCC Interpretive Letter 737 (Aug. 19, 1996) (IL 737)

11. See, e.g., Michael del Castillo, Visa Partners with Ethereum Digital-Dollar Startup that Raised $271 Million (Dec. 2. 2020), available at https://www.forbes.com/sites/michaeldelcastillo/2020/12/02/visa-partners-with- ethereum-digital-dollar-startup-that-raised-271-million/?sh=30afc9ac4b1f; Advancing Our Approach to Digital Currency: Visa's Outlook on New Digital Currency Payment Flows (July 22, 2020), available at https://usa.visa.com/visa-everywhere/blog/bdp/2020/07/21/advancing-our-approach-1595302085970.html; Helen Partz, Japanese Banking Giant to Issue Its Own Stablecoin in Late 2020, Cointelegraph.com (July 14, 2020), available at https://cointelegraph.

Industry participants recognize that using stablecoins to facilitate payments may combine the efficiency and speed of digital currencies with the stability of existing currencies.[12] As discussed below, stablecoins can provide a means of transmitting value denominated in an existing currency using INVN technology. Stablecoins thus provide a means by which participants in the payment system may avail themselves of the potential advantages associated with INVNs. Billions of dollars' worth of stablecoin trade globally, and demand for stablecoin continues to grow.[13]

As discussed below, INVNs and related stablecoins represent new technological means of carrying out bank-permissible payment activities. We therefore conclude that a bank may validate, store, and record payments transactions by serving as a node on an INVN. Likewise, a bank may use INVNs and related stablecoins to carry out other permissible payment activities. A bank must conduct these activities consistent with applicable law and safe and sound banking practices.

As noted in a recent statement of the President's Working Group on Financial Markets, stablecoin arrangements "should have the capability to obtain and verify the identity of all transacting parties, including for those using unhosted wallets."[14] "The stablecoin arrangement should have appropriate systems, controls, and practices in place to manage these risks, including to safeguard reserve assets. Strong reserve management practices include ensuring a 1:1 reserve ratio and adequate financial resources to absorb losses and meet liquidity needs."[15]

II. Discussion

The OCC has recognized that bank-permissible activities may be conducted with new and evolving technologies. Banks may use electronic means or facilities to perform any function, or provide any product or service, as part of an authorized activ-

---

com/news/japanese-banking-giant-mufg-to-issue-its-own-stablecoin-in-h2-2020; Marie Huillet, Japanese Banking Giant Mizuho to Launch Its Yen-Pegged Stablecoin in March (Feb. 21, 2019), available at https://cointelegraph.com/news/japanese-banking-giant-mizuho-to-launch-its-yen -pegged-stablecoin-in- march; Press Release, Wells Fargo & Co., Wells Fargo to Pilot Internal Settlement Service Using Distributed Ledger Technology (Sept. 17, 2019), available at https://newsroom. wf.com/press-release/innovation-and-technology/wells-   fargo-pilot-internal-settlement-service -using; Press Release, JP Morgan Chase & Co., J.P. Morgan Creates Digital Coin for Payments (Feb. 14, 2019), available at https://www.jpmorgan.com/global/news/digital-coin-payments. These examples are descriptive only. This letter expresses no view on the permissibility of, or other considerations related to, the activities described therein.

12. See, e.g., Advancing Our Approach to Digital Currency: Visa's Outlook on New Digital Currency Payment Flows (July 22, 2020).

13. See, e.g., Zack Voell, Stablecoin Supply Breaks $10B as Traders Demand Dollars Over Bitcoin, Coindesk.com (May 12, 2020) available at https://www.coindesk.com/stablecoin-supply -breaks-10b-as-traders-demand-dollars- over-bitcoin; USD Coin, Coinmarketcap.com (last accessed Jan. 4, 2021), available at https://coinmarketcap.com/currencies/usd-coin.

14. *President's Working Grp. on Fin. Markets Releases Statement on Key Regulatory & Supervisory Issues Relevant to Certain Stablecoins*, Treas. SM-1223 (Dec. 23, 2020).

15. *Id.*

ity.[16] Consistent with this precedent, banks may serve as a node on an INVN and use INVNs and related stablecoins to conduct permissible banking activities, including authorized payment activities.

National banks may engage in payment-related activities as activities within the business of banking.[17] The OCC has found that "[p]ayment system activities (e.g., electronic payments message transmission, electronic payments processing, and payments settlement among members) are clearly within the business of banking and are functionally consistent with the primary role of banks as financial intermediaries."[18] Similarly, FSAs may engage in payment- related activities and may transfer customer funds "by any mechanism or device," including through electronic means.[19]

The OCC has repeatedly recognized that banks may conduct permissible payment activities using new and evolving technologies. As discussed above, banks may use electronic means or facilities to perform any function, or provide any product or service, as part of an authorized activity.[20] Moreover, the OCC has explicitly permitted national banks to adopt new technologies as a means of executing payment services, consistent with safe and sound banking practices and applicable law. For example, the OCC has concluded that national banks may engage in activities related to electronic funds transfer systems,[21] real-time settlement systems,[22] and stored value systems as part of their permissible payments-related activities.[23] Courts have similarly recognized that banks' authority to engage in payment activities encompasses new and evolving payment technologies.[24] These precedents are consistent

---

16. See 12 C.F.R. § 7.5000 et seq.; 12 C.F.R. § 155.200.

17. See, e.g., IL 1157; IL 1140; OCC Interpretive Letter 1014 (Jan. 10, 2005); OCC Interpretive Letter 929 (Feb. 11, 2002); OCC Interpretive Letter 993 (May 16, 1997) (IL 993); IL 737; OCC Conditional Approval Letter 220.

18. IL 1140, at 3 n. 12.

19. See 12 C.F.R. § 145.17. As discussed above, FSAs are also permitted to use, or participate with others to use, electronic means or facilities to perform any function, or provide any product or service, as part of an authorized activity. See 12 C.F.R. § 155.200. For example, the Office of Thrift Supervision explicitly permitted FSAs to invest in electronic funds transfer networks. See OTS Op. Ch. Couns. (Dec. 22, 1995); OTS Op. Ch. Couns. (Sept. 15, 1995).

20. See 12 C.F.R. § 7.5000 et seq; 12 C.F.R. § 155.200.

21. See, e.g., IL 890; IL 854.

22. See, e.g., IL 1157; IL 1140.

23. See, e.g., OCC Conditional Approval Letter 220; OCC Conditional Approval Letter 568; IL 737.

24. State of Illinois v. Continental Illinois National Bank, 536 F.2d 176, 178 (7th Cir. 1976) ("Any order to pay which is properly executed by a customer, whether it be check, card or electronic device, must be recognized as a routine banking function. . ."); Independent Bankers Association of America v. Smith, 534 F.2d 921, 944 (D.C. Cir. 1976) ("We conclude that Congress envisioned all account withdrawals when it used the shorthand phrase 'checks paid' in section 36(f). If future technological innovations render paper checks totally obsolete, section 36(f) will still include within its broad standard those facilities that permit bank customers to perform the traditional banking function of withdrawing funds from their accounts.").

with the fundamental principle that national bank powers "must be construed so as to permit new ways of conducting the very old business of banking."[25]

Using INVNs to facilitate payments transactions represents a new means of performing banks' permissible payments functions. At their core, payment activities involve transmitting instructions to transfer a specified sum from one account on a ledger to another account on the same or a different ledger (either at the same bank or at different banks). Established payment systems typically use a trusted, centralized entity to validate payments. Serving as nodes on INVNs is a new means of transmitting payment instructions and validating payments.[26] Rather than utilizing a centralized entity, nodes on the shared network validate the transfers. However, the basic functions are the same: transmitting payment instructions and validating payments. Accordingly, the same legal analysis applies, and a bank therefore may serve as a node on an INVN to facilitate payments transactions.

Likewise, a bank may use stablecoins to facilitate payment transactions for customers on an INVN, including by issuing a stablecoin,[27] and by exchanging that stablecoin for fiat currency.[28] In this context, stablecoins function as a mechanism of payment, in the same way that debit cards, checks, and electronically stored value (ESV) systems convey payment instructions. Banks have long used cashiers' checks, travelers' checks, and other bearer instruments as a means of facilitating cashless payments.[29]

---

25. M & M Leasing Corp. v. Seattle First Nat. Bank, 563 F.2d 1377, 1382 (9th Cir. 1977) cert. denied, 436 U.S. 956 (1978).

26. While the technology is new, the concept of using distributed ledgers to validate ownership and title is not. See e.g., Oliver Smith, Forbes, Blockchain's Secret 1,000 Year History (Mar 23, 2018), available at https://www.forbes.com/sites/oliversmith/2018/03/23/blockchains-secret-1000-year-history/#4484e42818d2; Kristin Sommer, Phys.org, Team puts an ancient spin on a new digital currency (June 11, 2019), available at https://phys.org/news/2019-06-team-ancient-digital-currency.htmlhttps://phys.org/news/2019-06-team-ancient- digital-currency.html; Sam Auch, rsmus.com, Blockchain and the Island of Yap, available at https://rsmus.com/what-we-do/services/blockchain-consulting/featured-topics/blockchain-basics/blockchain-and- the-island-of-yap.html.

27. Certain stablecoins may be securities. A bank's issuance of a stablecoin must comply with all applicable securities laws and regulations. Staff of the Securities and Exchange Commission (SEC) has issued a statement encouraging issuers of stablecoins of the type described in IL 1172 to contact the staff with any questions they may have to help ensure that such stablecoins are structured, marketed, and operated in compliance with the federal securities laws. The statement notes that the staff stands ready to engage with market participants, and, depending on the particular facts and circumstances, to assist them and consider providing, if appropriate, a "no-action" position regarding whether activities with respect to a specific stablecoin may invoke the application of the federal securities laws. See SEC FinHub Staff Statement on OCC Interpretation (Sept. 21, 2020), available at https://www.sec.gov/news/public-statement/sec-finhub-statement-occ-interpretation.

28. The OCC previously addressed the permissibility of a national bank holding reserves for stablecoins that are backed by fiat currency on at least a 1:1 basis. See IL 1172. In addition, the OCC has previously determined that a national bank may facilitate a customer's cryptocurrency and fiat currency exchange transactions. See IL 1170 n. 39.

29. See, e.g., Arnold Tours, Inc. v. Camp, 472 F.2d 427, 438 (1st Cir. 1972). National banks may cash and process checks; issue, collect, and process cashiers' checks and money orders; and sell

Twelve C.F.R. 7.5002(a)(3) expressly provides that a national bank may offer ESV systems. In an ESV system, cash is exchanged for ESV. That ESV is stored on a computer chip within a card. The cardholder makes payments by transferring that ESV to another party who may then redeem the ESV for cash. When codifying the authority of a national bank to offer ESV systems, the OCC noted that the "creation, sale, and redemption of [ESV] in exchange for dollars is part of the business of banking because it is the electronic equivalent of issuing circulating notes or other paper-based payment devices like travelers checks."[30] As the OCC had previously explained in Conditional Approval Letter No. 220, banks may engage in activities related to developing and operating an ESV system because ESV systems are an element of the payment system, and the issuance and redemption of ESV is a new way of conducting one aspect of payments: issuing and circulating notes.[31] The OCC further noted that ESV-related clearing and settlement activities are similar to those already being performed by banks in connection with the large volume of transactions using checks, drafts, travelers' checks, credit cards, debit cards, and electronic transfers of funds within and through the payments system.[32]

Like ESV, stablecoins can serve as electronic representations of those U.S. dollars. Instead of value being stored on an ESV card, the value is represented on the stablecoin. This distinction is technological in nature and does not affect the permissibility of the underlying activity. Banks may use new technologies that afford a new means of carrying out permissible banking functions, such as providing payments services and facilitating payments.[33] Using INVNs and related stablecoins to facilitate payments is merely a new means of performing that function.

---

travelers' checks and certified checks. 12 U.S.C. 24 (Seventh); 12 U.S.C. 4001 et seq; Conditional Approval No. 307 (April 1999). Banks may cash checks for non-customers. See OCC Interpretive Letter No. 1094 (Feb. 27, 2008); Interpretive Letter No. 932 (May 2002).

30. Electronic Activities, 67 FR 34,992, 34,966 (May 17, 2002).

31. See OCC Conditional Approval Letter No. 220. Specifically, the OCC permitted banks to invest, via operating subsidiaries, in a company (Mondex LLC) that created, sold, and redeemed ESV. The OCC also permitted banks to serve as members in the ESV system. As described in the letter, members would issue ESV cards to individuals in exchange for dollars. These cards were intended to become a new element of the payment system substituting ESV for cash and small checks in consumer transactions. Mondex LLC would create and sell ESV to members in exchange for dollars. Mondex LLC would invest the dollars in government securities, cash, and cash equivalents. If a member tendered ESV to Mondex LLC, Mondex LLC would redeem the ESV at par. Members would sell ESV to individuals and participating retailers in exchange for dollars. ESV would be loaded onto the individual's card or retailer or retailer's "purse carrier device." Members would also purchase ESV from retailers and individuals.

32. See *id.*

33. See, e.g., State of Ill. ex rel. Lignoul v. Cont'l Nat. Bank & Tr. Co. of Chicago, 536 F.2d 176, 178 (7th Cir. 1976) (concluding that debit cards constituted checks under the National Bank Act, despite technological differences between the two because "[t]he check is merely the means used by the bank to attain the desired objective, i.e., the payment of the money to its customer. The card serves the same purpose as the check. It is an order on the bank. Any order to pay which is properly executed by a customer, whether it be check, card or electronic device, must be recog-

Just as banks may buy and sell ESV as a means of converting the ESV into dollars (and vice versa) to complete customer payment transactions, banks may buy, sell, and issue stablecoin to facilitate payments.[34] For example, one entity (payer) may wish to remit a payment of U.S. dollars to a second entity (payee). Rather than using a centralized payment system, the payer converts the U.S. dollars to stablecoin and transfers the stablecoin to the payee via the INVN. The payee then converts the stablecoin back into U.S. dollars. In one common version of this fact pattern, the payment is a cross-border remittance. In certain circumstances, using INVNs and related stablecoins to facilitate the remittance may provide a cheaper, faster, and more efficient means of effecting the payment. The bank may serve several potential roles in this type of transaction: supporting the INVN by validating transactions as a node on the INVN, facilitating the conversion from U.S. dollars to stablecoin (and vice versa), and issuing the stablecoin.

Benefits and Risks III.

While the OCC neither encourages nor discourages banks from participating in and supporting INVNs and stablecoins, the recent adoption of INVNs and stablecoins by a major payment system operator,[35] coupled with the rapid market adoption of INVNs and stablecoins,[36] indicates that banks should evaluate the appropriateness of INVNs and stablecoin participation in order to ensure banks' continuing ability to provide payment services to their customers in a manner that reflects changing demand.

INVNs and stablecoins present both benefits and risks. Among the potential benefits is the fact that INVNs may enhance the efficiency, effectiveness, and stability of the provision of payments. For example, they may be more resilient than other payment networks because of the decentralized nature of INVNs. Rather than relying on a single entity (or a small number of parties) to verify payments, INVNs allow a comparatively large number of nodes to verify transactions in a trusted manner.

Simply put, these networks may be more resilient because they have no single point of failure and can continue to operate even if a number of nodes cease to func-

---

nized as a routine banking function when used as here. The relationship between the bank and its customer is the same."); Smith, 534 F.2d at 944 ("We conclude that Congress envisioned all account withdrawals when it used the shorthand phrase "checks paid" in section 36(f) [of the National Bank Act]. If future technological innovations render paper checks totally obsolete, section 36(f) will still include within its broad standard those facilities that permit bank customers to perform the traditional banking function of withdrawing funds from their accounts.").

34. Moreover, buying, selling, and issuing stablecoins to facilitate payments responds to customer demand and benefits customers by offering faster and more resilient payment mechanisms. In addition, providing payment services using INVNs and related stablecoins may allow banks to offer services to a more diverse customer base. Finally, the risks associated with buying, selling, and issuing stablecoins are similar to those that banks assume in other permissible payment activities, including the provision of ESV systems.

35. See supra n. 11.

36. See supra n. 12.

tion for some reason and may be more trusted because of their consensus mechanisms requiring more nodes to validate the underlying transactions. In addition, an INVN also acts to prevent tampering or adding inaccurate information to the database. Information is only added to the network after consensus is reached among the nodes confirming that the information is valid.

The use of stablecoins to facilitate payments allows banks to capture the advantages that INVNs may present in a manner that retains the stability of fiat currency.[37] INVNs can transfer multiple different cryptocurrencies including but not limited to stablecoins. Stablecoins serve as a means of representing fiat currency on an INVN. In this way, the stablecoin provides a means for fiat currency to have access to the payment rails of an INVN.

Although the use of INVNs may provide certain advantages over other technologies, it may also present new risks. Banks that seek to use these networks should ensure that they understand these risks, as well as the risks generally associated with the underlying activity.[38] In addition, banks seeking to use these networks must conduct the activities in a safe and sound manner. These banks should also conduct a legal analysis to ensure the activities will be conducted consistent with all applicable laws, including applicable anti-money laundering laws and regulations and consumer protection laws and regulations.

Payment activities involving cryptocurrencies could increase operational risks, including fraud risk. Depending on the nature of the payment activity, activities involving stablecoins could entail significant liquidity risks for banks.[39] Moreover, new technologies require sufficient technological expertise to ensure a bank can manage them in a safe and sound manner and otherwise conduct the activities in compliance with applicable law, including applicable consumer protection laws and regulations. Banks have experience developing such expertise in analogous areas. These risks are similar (though potentially greater in degree) to those of other electronic activities expressly permitted for banks, including providing electronic custody services,[40] acting as a digital certification authority[41] and providing data processing services.[42] Risk management should be commensurate with the complexity of the products and services offered. New activities should be developed and implemented consistently with sound risk management practices and should align with banks' overall business plans and strategies.[43]

---

37. See, e.g., Advancing Our Approach to Digital Currency: Visa's Outlook on New Digital Currency Payment Flows (July 22, 2020).

38. See, e.g., Comptroller's Handbook on Payment Systems and Fund Transfer Activities (March 1990); New, Modified, or Expanded Bank Products and Services: Risk Management Principles, OCC Bulletin 2017-43.

39. See IL 1172.

40. See Comptroller's Handbook on Custody Services at 70 (Jan. 2002).

41. 12 C.F.R. § 7.5005.

42. *Id.*

43. See OC Bulletin-2017-43.

Cryptocurrency payment activities could also raise heightened compliance risks. In particular, cryptocurrencies can present risks under anti-money laundering (AML) and countering the financing of terrorism requirements set forth in applicable laws, including the Bank Secrecy Act (BSA), because cryptocurrencies may be used by bad actors for the purposes of avoiding the financial system or engaging in other illicit activities. However, banks have significant experience with developing BSA/AML compliance programs to assure compliance with the reporting and recordkeeping requirements of the BSA and to prevent such usage of their systems by bad actors.[44] The OCC similarly would expect banks engaged in providing cryptocurrency services to customers to adapt and expand their BSA/AML compliance programs to assure compliance with the reporting and recordkeeping requirements of the BSA and to address the particular risks of cryptocurrency transactions.

A bank may validate, store, and record payments transactions by serving as a node on an INVN and use INVNs and related stablecoins to carry out other bank-permissible payment activities, consistent with applicable law and safe and sound banking practices. A bank should consult with OCC supervisors, as appropriate, prior to engaging in these payment activities. The OCC will review these activities as part of its ordinary supervisory processes.

Sincerely,

Jonathan V. Gould

Senior Deputy Comptroller & Chief Counsel

Discussion Points

1. *Distributed ledgers.* What are the advantages and disadvantages of distributed ledgers? Do you think distributed ledgers provide more security or less security than central databases? Does the ability of a distributed ledger to have nodes worldwide increase the risk of illicit activity? Why or why not?

2. *A risk that shouldn't be taken?* What are the risks of allowing banks to buy, sell, and issue stablecoins? Do you think that there should have been regulatory safeguards in place before banks should have been able to engage in these activities?

3. *What is the proper way to regulate bank involvement in digital asset custody?* Which federal regulatory agency do you think should have supervisory authority over banks that safeguard digital assets for customers? Should the SEC and OCC have concurrent authority to regulate banks' activities and custody of digital assets?

---

44. See, e.g., 12 U.S.C. § 1818(s); 12 C.F.R. § 21.21; 31 C.F.R. § 1020.210; see also FFIEC, FFIEC BSA/AML Examination Manual, available at https://bsaaml.ffiec.gov/manual (database of BSA/AML policies and procedures).

Chief Counsel's Interpretation Clarifying: (1) Authority of a Bank to Engage in Certain Cryptocurrency Activities; and (2) Authority of the OCC to Charter a National Trust Bank

Office of the Comptroller of the Currency, Interpretive Letter 1179

(November 18, 2021)

Introduction I.

The Chief Counsel issued three interpretive letters in 2020 and early 2021 addressing whether it is permissible for national banks and Federal savings associations (collectively referred to as "banks") to engage in certain cryptocurrency, distributed ledger, and stablecoin activities. The interpretive letters are:

- OCC Interpretive Letter 1170, addressing whether banks may provide cryptocurrency custody services;

- OCC Interpretive Letter 1172, addressing whether banks may hold dollar deposits serving as reserves backing stablecoin in certain circumstances; and

- OCC Interpretive Letter 1174, addressing (1) whether banks may act as nodes on an independent node verification network (*i.e.*, distributed ledger) to verify customer payments and (2) banks may engage in certain stablecoin activities to facilitate payment transactions on a distributed ledger. [1]

This letter clarifies that the activities addressed in those interpretive letters are legally permissible for a bank to engage in, *provided* the bank can demonstrate, to the satisfaction of its supervisory office, that it has controls in place to conduct the activity in a safe and sound manner. As discussed below and consistent with longstanding OCC precedent, a proposed activity cannot be part of the "business of banking" if the bank lacks the capacity to conduct the activity in a safe and sound manner. [2]

Specifically, as described further below, a bank should notify its supervisory office, in writing, of its intention to engage in any of the activities addressed in the interpretive letters. The bank should not engage in the activities until it receives written notification of the supervisory office's non-objection. In deciding whether to grant supervisory non-objection, the supervisory office will evaluate the adequacy of the bank's risk management systems and controls, and risk measurement

---

1. See Interpretive Letter 1170 (July 22, 2020), *available at* https://www.occ.gov/topics/charters-and-licensing/interpretations-and-actions/2020/int1170.pdf; Interpretive Letter 1172 (Sept. 21, 2020), *available at* https://www.occ.gov/topics/charters-and-licensing/interpretations-and-actions/2020/int1172.pdf; and Interpretive Letter 1174 (Jan. 4, 2021), *available at* https://www.occ.gov/news-issuances/news-releases/2021/nr-occ-2021-2a.pdf.

2. This letter is being issued as a result of the OCC's review of interpretive letters regarding cryptocurrencies and digital assets.

systems, to enable the bank to engage in the proposed activities in a safe and sound manner.[3]

This letter also clarifies OCC Interpretive Letter 1176, which addressed the OCC's authority to charter, or approve the conversion to, a national bank that limits its operations to those of a trust company and activities related thereto. In particular, this letter reiterates that Interpretive Letter 1176 addressed the OCC's chartering authority and did not expand or otherwise change existing banks' obligations under the OCC's fiduciary activities regulation, 12 C.F.R. Part 9.[4] This letter further clarifies that the OCC retains discretion in determining whether an activity is conducted in a fiduciary capacity for purposes of federal law.

II. Supervisory Process for Cryptocurrency Activities

On July 22, 2020, the OCC issued Interpretive Letter 1170, which concluded that banks may provide certain cryptocurrency custody services on behalf of customers, including by holding the unique cryptographic keys associated with cryptocurrency. In Interpretive Letter 1170, the OCC found that providing cryptocurrency custody services is a modern form of the traditional bank activities of custody and safekeeping, and that providing cryptocurrency custody services is a permissible form of a traditional banking activity that banks are authorized to perform via electronic means.[5]

On September 21, 2020, the OCC issued Interpretive Letter 1172, which recognized that stablecoin issuers may desire to place their cash reserves in a reserve account with a bank to provide assurance that the issuer has sufficient assets backing the stablecoin in certain situations. Interpretive Letter 1172 concluded that banks may hold deposits that serve as reserves for stablecoins that are backed on a 1:1 basis by a single fiat currency and held in hosted wallets.

---

3. Banks already engaged in cryptocurrency, distributed ledger, or stablecoin activities as of the date of publication of this letter do not need to obtain supervisory non-objection. However, consistent with the relevant interpretive letters, the OCC expects that a bank that has commenced such activity will have provided notice to its supervisory office. The OCC will examine these activities as part of its ongoing supervisory process. Banks engaged in such activities should have systems and controls in place consistent with those described in this letter to ensure that all activities are conducted in a safe and sound manner and consistent with all applicable law. *See, e.g.,* 12 U.S.C. § 1818.

4. See Interpretive Letter 1176 (Jan. 11, 2021), *available at* https://occ.gov/topics/charters-and - licensing/interpretations-and-actions/2021/int1176.pdf.

5. 12 C.F.R. § 7.5002(a) provides that a national bank may perform, provide, or deliver through electronic means and facilities any activity, function, product, or service that it is otherwise authorized to perform, provide, or deliver. This regulatory provision is based on the longstanding "transparency doctrine," under which the OCC looks through the means by which a product is delivered and focuses instead on the authority of the national bank to offer the underlying product or service. *See* 67 FR 34992, 34996 (May 17, 2002).

The OCC concluded that this activity is permissible for banks due to the express authority of banks to receive deposits.[6]

On January 4, 2021, the OCC issued Interpretive Letter 1174, which concluded that banks may use distributed ledgers and stablecoins to engage in and facilitate payment activities. In Interpretive Letter 1174, the OCC found that using independent node verification networks, such as distributed ledgers, to facilitate payments transactions for customers represents a new means of performing banks' permissible payments functions. In addition, Interpretive Letter 1174 concluded that, just as banks may buy and sell electronically stored value (ESV)[7] as a means of converting the ESV into dollars (and vice versa) to complete customer payment transactions, banks may buy, sell, and issue stablecoin to facilitate payments.

Consistent with OCC precedent, Interpretive Letters 1170, 1172, and 1174 indicated that banks must conduct the activities described in those letters consistent with safe and sound banking practices.[8] A longstanding corollary to this principle is that a proposed activity is not legally permissible if the bank lacks the capacity to conduct the activity in a safe and sound manner.[9] This letter explains the process by which a bank may demonstrate that it will engage in the activities in a safe and sound manner.[10] Specifically, before engaging in the activities addressed in the interpretive letters, a bank should notify its supervisory office, in writing, of the proposed activities and should receive written notification of the supervisory non-objection.

---

6. See 12 U.S.C. § 24 (Seventh); 12 U.S.C. § 1464(b).

7. See 12 C.F.R. § 7.5002(a)(3).

8. For example, Interpretive Letters 1170 and 1174 specifically stated that banks should consult with OCC supervisors, as appropriate, prior to engaging in the activities and that the OCC would review the activities as part of its ordinary supervisory processes.

9. In other words, a proposed activity cannot be part of the "business of banking" if the bank in question lacks the capacity to conduct the activity on a safe and sound basis. Courts have long recognized this linkage between qualifying activities and safety and soundness. *See, e.g., First National Bank v. Exchange National Bank,* 92 U.S. 122, 127 (1875); *Merchants National Bank v. Wehrmann,* 202 U.S. 295 (1906). In addition, the OCC considers safety and soundness issues when determining whether an activity is part of, or incidental to the business of banking. *See, e.g.,* OCC Interpretive Letter 1060 (Sept. 2018) (national bank may engage in customer-driven, perfectly-matched, cash-settled derivative transactions with payments based on reference assets, including plastics, petroleum products, and metals, only if the bank has controls in place to conduct the activity on a safe and sound basis); OCC Interpretive Letter 949 (Jan. 2003) (national bank may engage in cash-settled options and forwards on equity securities only if the bank has in place an appropriate risk measurement and management process); OCC Interpretive Letter 892 (Sept. 2000) (national bank may engage in equity hedging activities only if it has an appropriate risk management process in place).

10. The OCC, along with other federal financial regulatory agencies, recently committed to take action to address risks falling within each agency's jurisdiction given the significant and growing risks posed by stablecoins. *See* President's Working Group on Financial Markets, FDIC, and OCC, Report on Stablecoins (Nov. 1, 2021), *available at* https://home.treasury.gov/system/files/136/StableCoinReport_Nov1_508.pdf (PWG Report). The process described in this letter is the OCC's first complementary action to this commitment.

To obtain supervisory non-objection, the bank should demonstrate that it has established an appropriate risk management and measurement process for the proposed activities, including having adequate systems in place to identify, measure, monitor, and control the risks of its activities, including the ability to do so on an ongoing basis. For example, a bank should specifically address risks associated with cryptocurrency activities, including, but not limited to, operational risk (*e.g.*, the risks related to new, evolving technologies, the risk of hacking, fraud, and theft, and third party risk management), liquidity risk, strategic risk, and compliance risk (including but not limited to compliance with the Bank Secrecy Act, anti-money laundering, sanctions requirements, and consumer protection laws). This process is in addition to and does not replace the specific conditions, processes, and controls discussed in Interpretive Letters 1170, 1172, and 1174.

In deciding whether to grant supervisory non-objection, the supervisory office will evaluate the adequacy of a bank's risk measurement and management information systems and controls to enable the bank to engage in the proposed activities on a safe and sound basis. The supervisory office will also evaluate any other supervisory considerations relevant to the particular proposal, consulting with agency subject matter experts as appropriate. As part of that review, and in coordination with the Chief Counsel, as needed, the supervisory office will assess whether the bank has demonstrated that it understands and will comply with laws that apply to the proposed activities. After a bank has received supervisory non-objection, the OCC will review these activities as part of its ordinary supervisory processes.

To address compliance, the bank should demonstrate, in writing, an understanding of any compliance obligations related to the specific activities the bank intends to conduct, including, but not limited to, any applicable requirements under the federal securities laws, the Bank Secrecy Act, anti-money laundering, the Commodity Exchange Act, and consumer protection laws. For example, a bank should understand that there may be different legal and compliance obligations for stablecoin activities, depending on how the particular stablecoin is structured.[11] Prior to seeking supervisory non-objection, the bank should consider all applicable laws, ensure that the proposed structure of the activity is consistent with such laws, and that the compliance management system will be sufficient and appropriate to ensure compliance.

The OCC believes that this clarification will enhance prudential supervision by ensuring that banks demonstrate, before engaging in the activities, that they can conduct them in a safe and sound manner and in compliance with applicable law.

---

11. For example, certain stablecoins may be securities. A bank's issuance of a stablecoin that is a security must comply with all applicable securities laws and regulations. *See* PWG Report; SEC, Framework for "Investment Contract" Analysis of Digital Assets (Apr. 3, 2019), *available at* https://www.sec.gov/corpfin/framework-investment-contract-analysis-digital-assets; SEC FinHub Staff Statement on OCC Interpretation (Sept. 21, 2020), *available at* https://www.sec.gov/news/public-statement/sec-finhub-statement-occ-interpretation.

III. Standards for Chartering National Trust Banks

On January 11, 2021, the OCC issued Interpretive Letter 1176. This letter addressed the OCC's authority under the National Bank Act (12 U.S.C. § 27(a)) to charter, or approve the conversion to, a national bank that limits its operations to those of a trust company and activities related thereto. Interpretive Letter 1176 does not change the current obligations of national banks with existing fiduciary powers under Part 9.[12] The scope of Interpretive Letter 1176 is limited to how the OCC may view 12 U.S.C. § 27(a) in the context of a charter application.

Whether an institution may be chartered under 12 U.S.C. § 27(a) is a question of federal law. The OCC may look to state law to determine if an applicant's activities are limited to the operations "of a trust company and activities related thereto," but an applicant's activities will not automatically be deemed to be trust activities—or to be fiduciary activities—solely by virtue of state law.[13] The OCC retains discretion to determine if an applicant's activities that are considered trust or fiduciary activities under state law are considered trust or fiduciary activities for purposes of applicable federal law.

Importantly, and as described in Interpretive Letter 1176, for national banks that have already been granted fiduciary powers, the requirements of 12 C.F.R. Part 9 continues to apply to current activities of the banks, as they have in the past. Moreover, national banks currently conducting activities in a non-fiduciary capacity that are not subject to Part 9 have not, and will not, become subject to 12 C.F.R. Part 9 because of the letter.

/s/
Benjamin W. McDonough
Senior Deputy Comptroller and Chief Counsel

Discussion Points

1. *Supervisory process for cryptocurrency activities.* Interpretive Letter 1179 explains the process that a bank must demonstrate to engage in cryptocurrency activities in a safe manner. Discuss the strengths and weaknesses of

---

12. See Interpretive Letter 1176, fn. 15. Interpretive Letter 1176 did not change the definition of "fiduciary capacity" in 12 C.F.R. § 9.2(e) or authorize any additional fiduciary capacities under section 92a.

13. In the context of chartering, Interpretive Letter 1176 explained, "a bank performing in a fiduciary capacity for purposes of state law and operating consistent with the parameters provided for in relevant state laws and regulations *may be deemed to be* performing in a fiduciary capacity for purposes of 12 U.S.C. § 92a and subject to 12 C.F.R. Part 9." Interpretive Letter 1176 (emphasis added). When evaluating a charter or conversion application, the OCC may, in its discretion, consider the relevant state law to assess whether the specific activities in which the applicant is engaged are operations "of a trust bank and activities related thereto."

this Letter. Did the Letter fail to address anything that would be important to developing a strong framework regarding the custody of crypto assets?

2. *Standards for chartering national trust banks.* Should the Interpretative Letter have addressed custody of digital assets held in non-federally chartered banks? Does this Letter seem to be protective only of consumers whose assets are held in federally chartered banks?

3. *Unequal protection.* Does the stance taken by the OCC regarding digital asset custody in various financial institutions seem to suggest that privately chartered credit unions and banks will not receive the same protections as federally chartered, FDIC insured banks? How can this affect consumers?

III. Securities and Exchange Commission

The SEC has defined a digital asset as "an asset that is issued and transferred using distributed ledger or blockchain technology." The SEC released a commission statement requesting comments regarding custody of digital asset securities by broker-dealers in December 2020.

The statement proposes that for a period of 5 years, broker-dealers would not be subject to an enforcement action if it has "obtained and maintained physical possession or control of customer fully paid and excess margin digital asset securities."[61] The 5-year safe harbor rule is intended to permit "market participants with an opportunity to develop practices and processes that will enhance their ability to demonstrate possession or control over digital asset securities."[62] This will simultaneously offer the agency the opportunity to oversee the broker-dealers thereby developing some experience with the subject matter.[63] So long as all of the relevant laws, such as the Securities Exchange Act (SEA) and Bank Security Act (BSA), are complied with, the Commission's position is that the following scenarios would not be subject to enforcement action:

1. The broker-dealer has access to the digital asset securities and the capability to transfer them...;

2. The broker-dealer limits its business to... digital asset securities [trading]...;[64]

---

61. SEC, *Custody of Digital Asset Securities by Special Purpose Broker-Dealers*, Release No. 34-90788 Part IV (Dec. 23, 2020), https://www.sec.gov/rules/policy/2020/34-90788.pdf.

62. *Id.* at Part I.

63. *Id.*

64. "[P]rovided a broker-dealer may hold proprietary positions in traditional securities solely for the purposes of meeting the firm's minimum net capital requirements under Rule 15c3-1, or hedging the risks of its proprietary positions in traditional securities and digital asset securities." SEC, *Custody of Digital Asset Securities by Special Purpose Broker-Dealers*, Release No. 34-90788 (Dec. 23, 2020), https://www.sec.gov/rules/policy/2020/34-90788.pdf.

3. The broker-dealer establishes, maintains, and enforces reasonably designed written policies... [to ensure that registered or exempt digital assets are offered and sold];

4. The broker-dealer establishes, maintains, and enforces reasonably designed written policies... to conduct [due diligence] and document an assessment of the characteristics of a digital asset security's [blockchain] and associated network prior to undertaking to maintain custody of the digital asset security and at reasonable intervals thereafter;

5. The broker-dealer [cannot] maintain custody of a digital asset security if the firm is aware of any material security or operational problems or weaknesses with the [blockchain] or associated network...;

6. The broker-dealer establishes, maintains, and enforces reasonably designed written policies... that are consistent with industry best practices to demonstrate the broker-dealer has exclusive control over the digital asset securities it holds...;

7. The broker-dealer establishes, maintains, and enforces reasonably designed written policies [that]... specifically identify... the steps it will take in the event of a [breach or other event that would otherwise compromise the integrity of the blockchain], [] allow [] broker-dealer[s] to comply with a court-ordered freeze or seizure, and [] allow for the transfer of the digital asset securities held by the broker-dealer to another...;

8. The broker-dealer provides written disclosures to prospective customers [specifying] that the firm is deeming itself to be in possession or control of digital asset securities held for the customer for the purposes of paragraph (b)(1) of Rule 15c3-3 based on its compliance with this Commission position, and [] the risks of investing in or holding digital asset securities...; and

9. The broker-dealer enters into a written agreement with each customer that sets forth the terms and conditions with respect to receiving, purchasing, holding, safekeeping, selling, transferring, exchanging, [holding] custody [of], liquidating and otherwise transacting in digital asset securities on behalf of the customer.

See below for the SEC's rule on the custody of digital assets:

Securities and Exchange Commission: Custody of Digital Asset Securities by Special Purpose Broker-Dealers

86 FR 11627, 17 CFR Part 240 (April 27, 2021)

I. INTRODUCTION

The Commission is issuing this statement and request for comment to encourage innovation around the application of the Customer Protection Rule to digital asset securities.[1] The Commission envisions broker-dealers performing the full set of broker-dealer functions with respect to digital asset securities—including maintaining custody of these assets—in a manner that addresses the unique attributes of digital asset securities and minimizes risk to investors and other market participants.[2] Consequently, as discussed below, the Commission's position in this statement is premised on a broker-dealer limiting its business to digital asset securities to isolate risk and having policies and procedures to, among other things, assess a given digital asset security's distributed ledger technology and protect the private keys necessary to transfer the digital asset security. In this way, the Commission is cognizant of both investor protection and potential capital formation innovations that could result from digital asset securities.

Rule 15c3-3 under the Securities Exchange Act of 1934 (hereinafter the "Customer Protection Rule" or "Rule 15c3-3")[3] requires a broker-dealer to promptly obtain and thereafter maintain physical possession or control of all fully-paid and excess

---

1. For purposes of this statement, the term "digital asset" refers to an asset that is issued and/or transferred using distributed ledger or blockchain technology ("distributed ledger technology"), including, but not limited to, so-called "virtual currencies," "coins," and "tokens." The focus of this statement is digital assets that rely on cryptographic protocols. A digital asset may or may not meet the definition of a "security" under the federal securities laws. See, e.g., Report of Investigation Pursuant to Section 21(a) of the Securities Exchange Act of 1934: The DAO, Exchange Act Release No. 81207 (July 25, 2017). As used in this statement, a "digital asset security" means a digital asset that meets the definition of a "security" under the federal securities laws. A digital asset that is not a security is referred to herein as a "non-security digital asset."

2. See 17 CFR 240.15c3-3. The Commission staff has issued a joint statement with the Financial Industry Regulatory Authority on broker-dealer custody of digital asset securities ("Joint Statement"), as well as a no-action letter regarding the Joint Statement to broker-dealers operating alternative trading systems ("ATSs"). See Joint Staff Statement on Broker-Dealer Custody of Digital Asset Securities, dated July 8, 2019, available at https://www.sec.gov/news/public-statement/joint-staff-statement-broker-dealer-custody-digital-asset-securities. See also Letter to Ms. Kris Dailey, Financial Industry Regulatory Authority, ATS Role in the Settlement of Digital Asset Security Trades, dated September 25, 2020 (discussing a three-step process broker-dealers use when operating an alternative trading system for the purpose of trading digital asset securities), available at https://www.sec.gov/divisions/marketreg/mr-noaction/2020/finra-ats-role-in-settlement-of-digital-asset-security-trades-09252020.pdf. Staff statements represent the views of the staff. They are not rules, regulations, or statements of the Commission. The Commission has neither approved nor disapproved of their content. These staff statements, like all staff guidance, have no legal force or effect: they do not alter or amend applicable law, and they create new or additional obligations for any person.

3. See 17 CFR 240.15c3-3.

margin securities it carries for the account of customers.[4] Market participants have raised questions concerning the application of the Customer Protection Rule to the potential custody of digital asset securities for customers by broker-dealers. The Commission is requesting comment in this area to provide the Commission and its staff with an opportunity to gain additional insight into the evolving standards and best practices with respect to custody of digital asset securities. The Commission intends to consider the public's comments in connection with any future rulemaking or other Commission action in this area.

As an interim step, in addition to the request for comment, the Commission is issuing this statement. The Commission recognizes that the market for digital asset securities is still new and rapidly evolving. The technical requirements for transacting and custodying digital asset securities are different from those involving traditional securities. And traditional securities transactions often involve a variety of intermediaries, infrastructure providers, and counterparties for which there may be no analog in the digital asset securities market. The Commission supports innovation in the digital asset securities market to develop its infrastructure.

In particular, the Commission's position, which will expire after a period of five years from the publication date of this statement, is that a broker-dealer operating under the circumstances set forth in Section IV will not be subject to a Commission enforcement action on the basis that the broker-dealer deems itself to have obtained and maintained physical possession or control of customer fully paid and excess margin digital asset securities for the purposes of paragraph (b)(1) of Rule 15c3-3.[5] These broker-dealers will be subject to examination by the Financial Industry Regulatory Authority ("FINRA") and Commission staff to review whether the firm is operating in a manner consistent with the circumstances described in Section IV below.

The five-year period in which the statement is in effect is designed to provide market participants with an opportunity to develop practices and processes that will enhance their ability to demonstrate possession or control over digital asset securities. It also will provide the Commission with experience in overseeing broker-dealer custody of digital asset securities to inform further action in this area.

II. BACKGROUND

Customers who use broker-dealers registered with the Commission to custody their securities (and related cash) benefit from the protections provided by the federal securities laws, including the Customer Protection Rule and, in most cases, the Securities Investor Protection Act of 1970 ("SIPA").[6] Generally, the Commis-

---

4. See 17 CFR 240.15c3-3(b).

5. Pursuant to the Congressional Review Act, the Office of Information and Regulatory Affairs has designated this statement as a "major rule" as defined by 5 U.S.C. 804(2). See 5 U.S.C. 801 et seq.

6. 15 U.S.C. 78aaa, et seq. Under SIPA, customers securities held by a broker-dealer that is a member of the Securities Investor Protection Corporation and customers' cash on deposit at such a broker-dealer for the purpose of purchasing securities would be isolated and readily identifiable

sion's Customer Protection Rule requires a broker- dealer to segregate customer securities and related cash from the firm's proprietary business activities, other than those that facilitate customer transactions.[7] The rule requires the broker-dealer to maintain physical possession or control over customers' fully paid and excess margin securities.[8]

Broker-dealer custody of securities is an integral service provided to the securities markets. However, broker-dealer custody of digital assetsecurities raises certain compliance questions with respect to the Customer Protection Rule. More specifically, while paragraph (b)(1) of Rule 15c3-3 requires that a broker-dealer "control" customer fully paid and excess margin securities, it may not be possible for a broker-dealer to establish control over a digital asset security with the same control mechanisms used in connection with traditional securities. Moreover, there have been instances of fraud, theft, and loss with respect to the custodianship of digital assets, including digital asset securities.[9]

The risks associated with digital assets, including digital asset securities, are due in part to differences in the clearance and settlement of traditional securities and digital assets. Traditional securities transactions generally are processed and settled through clearing agencies, depositories, clearing banks, transfer agents, and issuers. A broker-dealer's employees, regulators, and outside auditors can contact these third parties to confirm that the broker-dealer is in fact holding the traditional securities reflected on its books and records and financial statements, thereby providing objective processes for examining the broker-dealer's compliance with the Customer Protection Rule. Also, the traditional securities infrastructure has established processes to reverse or cancel mistaken or unauthorized transactions. Thus, the traditional securities infrastructure contains checks and controls that can be used to verify proprietary and customer holdings of traditional securities by broker-dealers, as well as processes designed to ensure that both parties to a transfer of traditional securities agree to the terms of the transfer. Digital assets that are issued or transferred using distributed ledger technology may not be subject to the same established clearance and settlement process familiar to traditional securities market participants.[10] The

---

as "customer property" and, consequently, available to be distributed to customers ahead of other creditors in the event of the broker-dealer's liquidation. Id.

7. See Net Capital Requirements for Brokers and Dealers, Exchange Act Rel.No. 21651 (Jan. 11, 1985), 50 FR 2690, 2690 (Jan. 18, 1985) (Rule 15c3-3 is designed "to give more specific protection to customer funds and securities, in effect forbidding brokers and dealers from using customer assets to finance any part of their businesses unrelated to servicing securities customers; e.g., a firm is virtually precluded from using customer funds to buy securities for its own account").

8. See 17 CFR 240.15c3-3(b)(1).

9. See generally, Report of the Attorney General's Cyber Digital Task Force: Cryptocurrency Enforcement Framework (October 2020), at 15–16, available at https://www.justice.gov/ag/page/file/1326061/download.

10. The clearance and settlement of securities that are not digital assets are characterized by infrastructure whereby intermediaries such as clearing agencies and securities depositories serve

clearance and settlement of securities that are not digital assets are characterized by infrastructure whereby intermediaries such as clearing agencies and securities depositories serve as key participants in the process. The clearance and settlement of digital asset securities, on the other hand, generally rely on few, if any, intermediaries and remain evolving areas of practices and procedures.

The express language of the Customer Protection Rule includes cash and securities held at the broker-dealer. Therefore, customers holding digital assets that are not securities through a broker-dealer could receive less protection for those assets than customers holding securities. The potential liabilities caused by the theft or loss of non-securities property from a broker-dealer, including digital assets that are not securities, could cause the broker-dealer to incur substantial losses or even fail, impacting customers and other creditors. As a consequence, the broker-dealer may need to be liquidated in a proceeding under SIPA. SIPA protection does not extend to all assets that may be held at a broker-dealer. Consequently, in a SIPA liquidation of a broker-dealer that held non-security assets, including non-security digital assets, investors may be treated as general creditors, to the extent their claims involve assets that are not within SIPA's definition of "security."[11]

III. DISCUSSION

A broker-dealer that maintains custody of a fully paid or excess margin digital asset security for a customer must hold it in a manner that complies with Rule 15c3-3, including that the digital asset security must be in the exclusive physical possession or control of the broker-dealer.[12] A digital asset security that is not in the exclusive physical possession or control of the broker-dealer because, for example, an unauthorized person knows or has access to the associated private key (and therefore has the ability to transfer it without the authorization of the broker-dealer) would not be held in a manner that complies with the possession or control requirement of Rule 15c3-3 and thus would be vulnerable to the risks the rule seeks to mitigate.

---

as key participants in the process. The clearance and settlement of digital asset securities, on the other hand, generally rely on few, if any intermediaries and remain evolving areas of practices and procedures.

11. Generally, SIPA defines the term "security" to include, among other things, any note, stock, treasury stock bond, debenture, evidence of indebtedness, any investment contract or certificate of interest or participation in any profit-sharing agreement, provided that such investment contract or interest is the subject of a registration statement with the Commission pursuant to the Securities Exchange Act of 1933 (15 U.S.C. 77a et seq.), and any put, call, straddle, option, or privilege on any security, or group or index of securities. See 15 U.S.C. 78lll(14). Generally, in a SIPA liquidation, customers' claims receive priority to the estate of customer property (generally cash and securities received acquired or held by the broker-dealer for the securities accounts of customers) over other creditors. See 15 U.S.C. 78fff & 78fff-2(c). In addition, to the extent that the estate of customer property is insufficient to satisfy the net equity claims of customers, the trustee can advance up to $500,000 for each customer, of which up to $250,000 can be used for cash claims. See 15 U.S.C. 78fff-3(a) & (d).

12. See 17 CFR 240.15c3-3(b).

As noted above, the loss or theft of digital asset securities may cause the firm and its digital asset customers to incur substantial financial losses. This, in turn, could cause the firm to fail, imperiling its traditional securities customers as well as the broker-dealer's counterparties and other market participants. However, there are measures a broker-dealer can employ to comply with Rule 15c3-3 and mitigate these risks.

One step that a broker-dealer could take to shield traditional securities customers, counterparties, and market participants from the risks and consequences of digital asset security fraud, theft, or loss would be to limit its business exclusively to dealing in, effecting transactions in, maintaining custody of, and/or operating an alternative trading system for digital asset securities. Thus, to operate in a manner consistent with the Commission's position, the broker- dealer could not deal in, effect transactions in, maintain custody of, or operate an alternative trading system for traditional securities.

In addition, by limiting its activities exclusively to digital asset securities, the broker-dealer would shield its customers from the risks that could arise if the firm engaged in activities involving non-security digital assets, which are not expressly governed by the Customer Protection Rule. For example, to the extent that the requirements of the Customer Protection Rule do not apply to non-security digital assets, such assets could receive less protection than securities, which would increase the risk of theft or loss and could ultimately cause the broker-dealer to fail, impacting customers and other creditors.

A second step the broker-dealer could take is to establish, maintain, and enforce reasonably designed written policies and procedures to conduct and document an analysis of whether a digital asset is a security offered and sold pursuant to an effective registration statement or an available exemption from registration, and whether the broker-dealer has fulfilled its requirements to comply with the federal securities laws with respect to effecting transactions in that digital asset security, before undertaking to effect transactions in and maintain custody of such asset. Such policies and procedures should provide a reasonable level of assurance that any digital assets transacted in or held in custody by the broker-dealer are in fact digital asset securities. Utilizing such policies and procedures should help ensure that the broker-dealer is confining its business to digital asset securities and that such digital asset securities are being offered, sold, or otherwise transacted in compliance with the federal securities laws.

A third step the broker-dealer could take is to establish, maintain, and enforce reasonably designed written policies and procedures to conduct and document an assessment of the characteristics of a digital asset security's distributed ledger technology and associated network.[13] prior to undertaking to maintain custody of the

---

13. For the purposes of this statement, a digital asset security's distributed ledger technology and associated network includes the protocols and any smart contracts or applications integral to the operation of the digital asset security.

digital asset security and at reasonable intervals thereafter. The assessment could examine at least the following aspects of the distributed ledger technology and its associated network, among others: (1) performance (i.e., does it work and will it continues to work as intended); (2) transaction speed and throughput (i.e., can it process transactions quickly enough for the intended application(s)); (3) scalability (i.e., can it handle a potential increase in network activity); (4) resiliency (i.e., can it absorb the impact of a problem in one or more parts of its system and continue processing transactions without data loss or corruption); (5) security and the relevant consensus mechanism (i.e., can it detect and defend against malicious attacks, such as 51% attacks[14] or Denial-of-Service attacks, without data loss or corruption); (6) complexity (i.e., can it be understood, maintained, and improved); (7) extensibility (i.e., can it have new functionality added, and continue processing transactions without data loss or corruption); and (8) visibility (i.e., are its associated code, standards, applications, and data publicly available and well documented). The assessment also could examine the governance of the distributed ledger technology and associated network and how protocol updates and changes are agreed to and implemented. This would include an assessment of impacts to the digital asset security of events such as protocol upgrades, hard forks, airdrops, exchanges of one digital asset for another, or staking.[15] Such assessments would allow a broker- dealer to be able to identify significant weaknesses or other operational issues with the distributed ledger technology and associated network utilized by the digital asset security, or other risks posed to the broker-dealer's business by the digital asset security, which would allow a broker-dealer to take appropriate action to identify and reduce its exposure to such risks. Accordingly, if there are significant weaknesses or other operational issues with the distributed ledger technology and associated network, the broker-dealer would be able to determine whether it could or could not maintain custody of the digital asset security.

A fourth step the broker-dealer could take is to establish, maintain, and enforce reasonably designed written policies, procedures, and controls for safekeeping and demonstrating the broker-dealer has exclusive possession or control over digital asset securities that are consistent with industry best practices to protect against the theft, loss, and unauthorized and accidental use of the private keys necessary to access and transfer the digital asset securities the broker-dealer holds in custody. These policies, procedures, and controls could address, among other matters: (1)

---

14. For the purposes of this statement, a "51% attack" is an attack on a blockchain or distributed ledger in which an attacker or group of attackers controls a majority of the network's hash rate, mining or computing power, allowing the attacker or group of attackers to prevent new transactions from being confirmed.

15. For purposes of this statement, "hard forks" refer to backward-incompatible protocol changes to a distributed ledger that create additional versions of the distributed ledger, potentially creating new digital assets. "Airdrops" refer to the distribution of digital assets to numerous addresses, usually at no monetary cost to the recipient or in exchange for certain promotional services. "Staking" refers to the use of a digital asset in a consensus mechanism.

the on-boarding of a digital asset security such that the broker-dealer can associate the digital asset security to a private key over which it can reasonably demonstrate exclusive physical possession or control; (2) the processes, software and hardware systems, and any other formats or systems utilized to create, store, or use private keys and any security or operational vulnerabilities of those systems and formats; (3) the establishment of private key generation processes that are secure and produce a cryptographically strong private key that is compatible with the distributed ledger technology and associated network and that is not susceptible to being discovered by unauthorized persons during the generation process or thereafter; (4) measures to protect private keys from being used to make an unauthorized or accidental transfer of a digital asset security held in custody by the broker-dealer; and (5) measures that protect private keys from being corrupted, lost or destroyed, that back-up the private key in a manner that does not compromise the security of the private key, and that otherwise preserve the ability of the firm to access and transfer a digital asset security it holds in the event a facility, software, or hardware system, or other format or system on which the private keys are stored and/or used is disrupted or destroyed. These policies, procedures, and controls for safekeeping and demonstrating the broker-dealer has exclusive possession or control over digital asset securities should serve to protect against the theft, loss, and unauthorized and accidental use of the private keys and therefore the customers' digital asset securities.

A fifth step the broker-dealer could take is to establish, maintain, and enforce reasonably designed written policies, procedures, and arrangements to: (1) specifically identify, in advance, the steps it intends to take in the wake of certain events that could affect the firm's custody of the digital asset securities, including blockchain malfunctions, 51% attacks, hard forks, or airdrops; (2) allow the broker-dealer to comply with a court-ordered freeze or seizure; and (3) allow the transfer of the digital asset securities held by the broker-dealer to another special purpose broker- dealer, a trustee, receiver, liquidator, a person performing a similar function, or another appropriate person, in the event the broker-dealer can no longer continue as a going concern and self-liquidates or is subject to a formal bankruptcy, receivership, liquidation, or similar proceeding. These policies and procedures should include measures for ensuring continued safekeeping and accessibility of the digital asset securities, even if the broker-dealer is wound down or liquidated, and thus would provide a reasonable level of assurance that a broker-dealer has developed plans to address unexpected disruptions to the broker-dealer's control over digital asset securities.

A sixth step the broker-dealer could take is to provide written disclosures to prospective customers about the risks of investing in or holding digital asset securities. The disclosures could include, among other matters: (1) prominent disclosure explaining that digital asset securities may not be "securities" as defined in SIPA[16]—and in particular, digital asset securities that are "investment contracts"

---

16. 15 U.S.C. 78lll(14).

under the Howey test[17] but are not registered with the Commission are excluded from SIPA's definition of "securities"—and thus the protections afforded to securities customers under SIPA may not apply with respect to those securities; (2) a description of the risks of fraud, manipulation, theft, and loss associated with digital asset securities; (3) a description of the risks relating to valuation, price volatility, and liquidity associated with digital asset securities; and (4) a description of the processes, software and hardware systems, and any other formats or systems utilized by the broker-dealer to create, store, or use the broker-dealer's private keys and protect them from loss, theft, or unauthorized or accidental use (including, but not limited to, cold storage, key sharding, multiple factor identification, and biometric authentication). The purpose of such disclosures is to provide the prospective customers with sufficient and easily understandable information about the risks to enable them to make informed decisions about whether to invest in or hold digital asset securities through the broker-dealer.

A seventh step the broker-dealer could take is to enter into a written agreement with each customer that sets forth the terms and conditions with respect to receiving, purchasing, holding, safekeeping, selling, transferring, exchanging, custodying, liquidating, and otherwise transacting in digital asset securities on behalf of the customer.[18] This step would ensure documentation of the terms of agreement between the customer and the broker-dealer providing custody of the customer's digital asset security, which would provide greater clarity and certainty to customers regarding their rights and responsibilities under the agreement with the broker-dealer.

1. COMMISSION POSITION

The Commission's position[19] is expressly limited to paragraph (b) of Rule 15c3-3 under the Securities Exchange Act of 1934 ("Exchange Act"). Furthermore, the Commission's position does not modify or change any obligations of a broker-dealer, or other party, to otherwise comply with the federal securities laws, including the broker-dealer financial responsibility rules, obligations regarding proxy voting and beneficial ownership communications, as well as the broker-dealer's obligation to become a member of FINRA and to comply with applicable anti-money laundering and countering the financing of terrorism obligations under the Bank Secrecy Act.[20]

---

17. See SEC v. W.J. Howey Co., 328 U.S. 293 (1946).

18. The agreement should contain such provisions and disclosures as are required by applicable laws, rules, and regulations.

19. The Commission's position is an agency statement of general applicability with future effect designed to implement, interpret, or prescribe law or policy.

20. See Heath Tarbert, Chairman, U.S. Commodity Futures Trading Commission, Kenneth A. Blanco, Director, Financial Crimes Enforcement Network, and Jay Clayton, Chairman, Commission, Leaders of CFTC, FinCEN, and SEC Issue Joint Statement on Activities Involving Digital Assets, dated Oct. 11, 2019 (reminding persons engaged in activities involving digital assets of their anti-money laundering ("AML") and countering the financing of terrorism ("CFT") obligations under the Bank Secrecy Act, and stating that broker-dealers are required to implement reasonably-designed AML

All terms used in this Commission position will have the definitions set forth in Rule 15c3-3. Finally, the Commission's position, which will expire after a period of five years from the publication date of this statement, applies only to the exercise of its enforcement discretion with respect to compliance with paragraph (b)(1) of Rule 15c3-3 under the circumstances set forth below. During this period, the Commission will continue to evaluate its position, and the circumstances set forth below, on an ongoing basis as it considers responses to the request for comments as well as further action in this area, including any future rulemaking.

After considering the minimum steps that can be taken to mitigate the risks posed by broker-dealer custody of digital asset securities, for a period of five years, the Commission's position is that a broker-dealer in the following circumstances would not be subject to a Commission enforcement action on the basis that the broker-dealer deems itself to have obtained and maintained physical possession or control of customer fully paid and excess margin digital asset securities:

1. The broker-dealer has access to the digital asset securities and the capability to transfer them on the associated distributed ledger technology;

2. The broker-dealer limits its business to dealing in, effecting transactions in, maintaining custody of, and/or operating an alternative trading system for digital asset securities; provided a broker-dealer may hold proprietary positions in traditional securities solely for the purposes of meeting the firm's minimum net capital requirements under Rule 15c3-1,[21] or hedging the risks of its proprietary positions in traditional securities and digital asset securities.

3. The broker-dealer establishes, maintains, and enforces reasonably designed written policies and procedures to conduct and document an analysis of whether a particular digital asset is a security offered and sold pursuant to an effective registration statement or an available exemption from registration, and whether the broker-dealer meets its requirements to comply with the federal securities laws with respect to effecting transactions in the digital asset security, before undertaking to effect transactions in and maintain custody of the digital asset security;

4. The broker-dealer establishes, maintains, and enforces reasonably designed written policies and procedures to conduct and document an assessment of the characteristics of a digital asset security's distributed ledger technology and associated network prior to undertaking to maintain custody of the digital asset security and at reasonable intervals thereafter;

---

programs and report suspicious activity, and that such requirements are not limited in their application to activities involving digital assets that are "securities" under the federal securities laws), available at https://www.sec.gov/news/public-statement/cftc-fincen-secjointstatementdigitalassets.
   21. 17 CFR. 240.15c3-1.

5. The broker-dealer does not undertake to maintain custody of a digital asset security if the firm is aware of any material security or operational problems or weaknesses with the distributed ledger technology and associated network used to access and transfer the digital asset security, or is aware of other material risks posed to the broker-dealer's business by the digital asset security;

6. The broker-dealer establishes, maintains, and enforces reasonably designed written policies, procedures, and controls that are consistent with industry best practices to demonstrate the broker-dealer has exclusive control over the digital asset securities it holds in custody and to protect against the theft, loss, and unauthorized and accidental use of the private keys necessary to access and transfer the digital asset securities the broker-dealer holds in custody;

7. The broker-dealer establishes, maintains, and enforces reasonably designed written policies, procedures, and arrangements to: (i) specifically identify, in advance, the steps it will take in the wake of certain events that could affect the firm's custody of the digital asset securities, including, without limitation, blockchain malfunctions, 51% attacks, hard forks, or airdrops; (ii) allow for the broker-dealer to comply with a court-ordered freeze or seizure; and (iii) allow for the transfer of the digital asset securities held by the broker-dealer to another special purpose broker-dealer, a trustee, receiver, liquidator, or person performing a similar function, or to another appropriate person, in the event the broker-dealer can no longer continue as a going concern and self-liquidates or is subject to a formal bankruptcy, receivership, liquidation, or similar proceeding;

8. The broker-dealer provides written disclosures to prospective customers: (i) that the firm is deeming itself to be in possession or control of digital asset securities held for the customer for the purposes of paragraph (b)(1) of Rule 15c3-3 based on its compliance with this Commission position; and (ii) about the risks of investing in or holding digital asset securities that, at a minimum: (a) prominently disclose that digital asset securities may not be "securities" as defined in SIPA—and in particular, digital asset securities that are "investment contracts" under the Howey test but are not registered with the Commission are excluded from SIPA's definition of "securities"—and thus the protections afforded to securities customers under SIPA may not apply; (b) describe the risks of fraud, manipulation, theft, and loss associated with digital asset securities; (c) describe the risks relating to valuation, price volatility, and liquidity associated with digital asset securities; and (d) describe, at a high level that would not compromise any security protocols, the processes, software and hardware systems, and any other formats or systems utilized by the broker-dealer to create, store,

or use the broker-dealer's private keys and protect them from loss, theft, or unauthorized or accidental use; [22] and

9. The broker-dealer enters into a written agreement with each customer that sets forth the terms and conditions with respect to receiving, purchasing, holding, safekeeping, selling, transferring, exchanging, custodying, liquidating and otherwise transacting in digital asset securities on behalf of the customer. [23]

2. REQUEST FOR COMMENT

The Commission is seeking comment on the specific questions below. When responding to the request for comment, please explain your reasoning.

1. What are industry best practices with respect to protecting against theft, loss, and unauthorized or accidental use of private keys necessary for accessing and transferring digital asset securities? What are industry best practices for generating, safekeeping, and using private keys? Please identify the sources of such best practices.

2. What are industry best practices to address events that could affect a broker-dealer's custody of digital asset securities such as a hard fork, airdrop, or 51% attack? Please identify the sources of such best practices.

3. What are the processes, software and hardware systems, or other formats or systems that are currently available to broker-dealers to create, store, or use private keys and protect them from loss, theft, or unauthorized or accidental use?

4. What are accepted practices (or model language) with respect to disclosing the risks of digital asset securities and the use of private keys? Have these practices or the model language been utilized with customers?

5. Should the Commission expand this position in the future to include other businesses such as traditional securities and/or non-security digital assets? Should this position be expanded to include the use of non-security digital assets as a means of payment for digital asset securities, such as by incorporating a de minimis threshold for non-security digital assets?

6. What differences are there in the clearance and settlement of traditional securities and digital assets that could lead to higher or lower clearance and settlement risks for digital assets as compared to traditional securities?

---

22. The broker-dealer will need to retain these written disclosures in accordance with the broker-dealer record retention rule. See 17 CFR 240.17a-4(b)(4).

23. The broker-dealer will need to retain these written agreements in accordance with the broker-dealer record retention rule. See 17 CFR 240.17a-4(b)(7).

7. What specific benefits and/or risks are implicated in a broker-dealer operating a digital asset alternative trading system that the Commission should
consider for any future measures it may take?

> By the Commission.
> Dated: December 23, 2020
> Vanessa A. Countryman

Discussion Points

1. *What is a digital wallet?* Is a New York City Subway MetroCard, whether a
physical card or a digital card, a digital wallet? Are mobile payment processors, like Zelle or Venmo considered digital wallets? Why or why not? What
are the characteristics of digital wallets? If you do not maintain balances in
it, is it still a digital wallet?

2. *Private keys.* What are the security risks that could be associated with private keys? How should regulatory agencies respond to these risks?

IV. Federal Deposit Insurance Corporation

Advisory to FDIC-Insured Institutions Regarding FDIC
Deposit Insurance and Dealings with Crypto Companies
FDIC, FIL-35-2022 (July 29, 2022)

RISKS AND CONCERNS

- The FDIC is concerned about the risks of consumer confusion or harm
arising from crypto assets offered by, through, or in connection with insured depository institutions (insured banks). Risks are elevated when a
non-bank entity offers crypto assets to the non-bank's customers, while also
offering an insured bank's deposit products.

- Inaccurate representations about deposit insurance by non-banks, including crypto companies, may confuse the non-bank's customers and cause
those customers to mistakenly believe they are protected against any type
of loss. Moreover, non-bank customers may not understand the role of the
bank as it relates to the activities of the non- bank, or the speculative nature
of certain crypto assets as compared to deposit products.

- More broadly, customers can be confused about:
  - When FDIC deposit insurance applies. In the unlikely event of an insured-bank failure, the FDIC protects depositors of insured banks against the loss of their deposits, up to at least $250,000. The FDIC only pays deposit insurance after an *insured bank* fails. FDIC insurance does not protect a non-bank's customers against the default, insolvency, or bankruptcy of any non-bank entity, including crypto custodians, exchanges, brokers, wallet providers, or other entities that appear to mimic banks but are not, called "neobanks."
  - What products are FDIC insured. FDIC deposit insurance covers deposit products offered by insured banks, such as checking accounts and savings accounts. Deposit insurance does not apply to non-deposit products, such as stocks, bonds, money market mutual funds, securities, commodities, or crypto assets.
- In addition to potential consumer harm, customer confusion can lead to legal risks for banks if a crypto company, or other third-party partner of an insured bank with whom they are dealing, makes misrepresentations about the nature and scope of deposit insurance.
- Moreover, misrepresentations and customer confusion could cause concerned consumers with insured-bank relationships to move funds, which could result in liquidity risk to banks and in turn, could potentially result in earnings and capital risks.

RISK MANAGEMENT AND GOVERNANCE CONSIDERATIONS

- Insured banks need to be aware of how FDIC insurance operates and need to assess, manage, and control risks arising from all third-party relationships, including those with crypto companies.
- In their dealings with crypto companies, insured banks should confirm and monitor that these companies do not misrepresent the availability of deposit insurance in order to measure and control risks to the bank, and should take appropriate action to address such misrepresentations.
- Communications related to deposit insurance need to be clear and conspicuous. Non- bank entities, such as crypto companies, that advertise or offer FDIC-insured products in relationships with insured banks could reduce consumer confusion by clearly, conspicuously: (a) stating that they are not an insured bank; (b) identifying the insured bank(s) where any customer funds may be held on deposit; and (c) communicating that crypto assets are not FDIC-insured products and may lose value.
- Insured banks that are involved in relationships with non-bank entities that offer deposit products as well as non-deposit products, such as crypto assets, can help minimize customer confusion and harm by carefully re-

viewing and regularly monitoring the non- bank's marketing material and related disclosures to ensure accuracy and clarity.

- For safe and sound operation, the insured bank should have appropriate risk management policies and processes to ensure that any services provided by, or deposits received from any third-party, including a crypto company, are, and remain, in compliance with all laws and regulations.

- In addition, Part 328, Subpart B of the FDIC's Rules and Regulations titled *False Advertising, Misrepresentation of Insured Status, and Misuse of the FDIC's Name or Log,* can apply to non-banks, such as crypto companies. Accordingly, insured banks should determine if its third-party risk management policies and procedures effectively manage crypto-asset-related risks, including compliance risks related to Part 328 Subpart B.

ADDITIONAL RESOURCES

- The FDIC's website provides more information to help bankers understand deposit insurance coverage, including pass-through deposit insurance (https://www.fdic.gov/deposit/diguidebankers/fiduciary-accounts.html).

- The FDIC's website provides more information to help consumers understand deposit insurance coverage (https://www.fdic.gov/resources/deposit-insurance/).

- The FDIC maintains a portal for submission of complaints about suspected misrepresentations regarding deposit insurance (https://ask.fdic.gov/fdicinformationandsupportcenter/s/fdicdimcomplaintform/?language=en_US).

- The FDIC's regulations governing deposit insurance coverage are found at 12 C.F.R. Part 330 (https://www.ecfr.gov/current/title-12/chapter-III/subchapter-B/part-330).

- The FDIC's regulation relating to false advertising, misrepresentations about insured status, and misuse of the FDIC's name or logo is found at 12 C.F.R. Part 328 (https://www.ecfr.gov/current/title-12/chapter-III/subchapter-B/part-328).

- The FDIC's Fact Sheet: What the Public Needs to Know About FDIC Deposit Insurance and Crypto Companies is found at https://www.fdic.gov/news/fact-sheets/crypto-fact- sheet-7-28-22.pdf

For FDIC Supervised Institutions:

- The FDIC's Guidance For Managing Third-Party Risk is found at https://www.fdic.gov/news/financial-institution-letters/2008/fil08044a.html.

- The FDIC's Statement on Providing Banking Services is found at https://www.fdic.gov/news/financial-institution-letters/2015/fil15005.html.

V. FDIC at the State Level

At the state level, Wyoming has made great strides to accommodate the custody of digital assets. Wyoming is the first state that recognized the growing need to safe-keep digital assets in 2019 by passing regulations that permitted state-chartered banks to provide custodial services of digital assets.[66] This has resulted in the state becoming known as the "most crypto-friendly jurisdiction in the United States," which is evidenced by various high-profile companies that moved their operations to Cheyenne, Wyoming's capital.[67] One such company, Kraken Bank, told the media that the "company chose to domicile in Wyoming because it's the only state offering a banking charter that outlines exactly how bank regulators will supervise a bank that holds digital assets."[68]

At both the federal and state levels, digital banks have been on the rise. This can be attributed, in part, to the fact that there is a growing number of cryptocurrency users and that the industry is not regulated. A question naturally develops with the rise of digital banks: should the FDIC be involved? After all, people work hard for their money and they are accustomed to assurances that their money is protected when they make a deposit to a bank.[69] However, as recently as April 2020, the FDIC has referred to a digital wallet as it relates to online banking features and not as it relates to cryptocurrency.

This suggests that the FDIC is still not up to date on language that is now main-stream or, conversely, that the term digital wallet is still broad.[70] Specifically, FDIC insures up to $250,000 that is deposited into an account. Cryptocurrency is not USD, so the FDIC does not currently insure it, but the FDIC has recognized that "[d]ata is the new capital" through its FDiTech initiative.[71] FDiTech has implemented Rapid Phase Prototyping, a project that facilitates innovation for FDIC member banks. These efforts arguably fall short of recognizing cryptocurrency, because of their competing efforts, like modernizing bank financial reporting.[72]

In July of 2020, the FDIC issued the Request for Information on Standard Setting and Voluntary Certification for Models and Third-Party Providers of Technology and Other Services in the Federal Register to obtain information on fintech's opera-

---

66. WYO. STAT. ANN. § 34-29-104.

67. Chris Matthews, *How Wyoming Became the Promised Land for Bitcoin Investors*, MARKETWATCH, https://www.marketwatch.com/story/how-wyoming-became-the-promised-land-for-bitcoin -investors-11619201182 (last updated Apr. 24, 2021).

68. *Id.*

69. FDIC, *What We Do*, https://www.fdic.gov/about/what-we-do/ (last updated May 15, 2020).

70. *Is Digital Banking For Me?*, FDIC CONSUMER NEWS, https://www.fdic.gov/consumers/con-sumer/news/april2020.html (using the term "digital wallet" in the context of brick and mortar banks offering their services online).

71. FDiTech, *Why FDiTech*, https://www.fdic.gov/fditech/index.html (last visited Apr. 26, 2021).

72. *Id.*

tions.[73] The Blockchain Association responded to the request by explaining that, among other things, "tens of millions of Americans are not served by the existing banking system."[74] While the Blockchain Association focused its response on community banks using fintech third-parties to develop technology-based solutions, there was mention of the usefulness of cryptocurrency.[75]

Discussion Points

1. *The influence of states on federal bodies.* Does it seem that Wyoming may have influenced the OCC? Should states have regulatory authority over bank custody of digital assets?

2. *The impact of CBDC on banks.* Do you think the development of centrally backed digital currency (CDBC) will create more liabilities for banks? What possible legal implications could arise if banks issue CBDC? How should the regulatory framework of the banking industry respond to issues such as what the governing law will be in the event of a dispute involving CBDC?

3. *What is the FDIC to do?* Should the FDIC take more action to protect consumers from fraud and loss involving cryptocurrency? Should the FDIC insure against insolvency of a bank that holds crypto assets?

VI. Different Types of Custodians

Digital assets are stored through associating them with wallets. Wallets are stored on web servers, local hardware, jump drives, and mobile devices. The digital asset wallet takes the form of a cryptographic public key—a string of numbers and letters—matching a private key that is only known to the user. The public key is derived from the private key and must be paired with the correct and corresponding key for a transaction to be executed.

---

73. 85 FR 44890 (July 24, 2020), https://www.federalregister.gov/documents/2020/07/24/2020-16058/request-for-information-on-standard-setting-and-voluntary-certification-for-models-and-third-party.

74. Blockchain Association, Re: Request for Information on Standard Setting and Voluntary Certification for Models and Third-Party Providers of Technology and Other Services (RIN 3064–ZA18), Sept. 22, 2020, https://www.fdic.gov/regulations/laws/federal/2020/2020-request-for-info-standard-setting-3064-za18-c-020.pdf.

75. *Id.*

As discussed earlier, custodians safeguard digital assets by ensuring that investors' private keys are securely maintained. Digitals assets are securely maintained by storing them online, which is through a method called hot storage, or offline, known as cold storage. There are other ways to store digital assets—through hosted wallets, unhosted wallets, and smart contract wallets.

A. Hot Storage

Hot storage, also known as hot wallets, is online and can store as much or as little cryptocurrency as the consumer wishes. To access the wallet, a consumer would need to input their private key to gain access to their cryptocurrency. However, because the hot wallet must store the private key it is more vulnerable than the offline cold wallet to cyberattacks. For example, a hacker can gain access to the servers of the digital wallet. Nevertheless, the security of the consumer's hot wallet is largely dependent on them. If an online wallet is somehow hacked, then those coins are gone forever. A consumer will not get them back, which is different from the safeguards provided by the FDIC within the banking system that we are generally accustomed to.

The security of the third-party that hosts a consumer's wallet is particularly important because the consumer must hand over their private key as part of the terms of the user agreement. In 2017, a study revealed that 73% of wallets took custody of private keys. This may be alarming to those who want to retain custody of their own private keys, but perhaps not as much of a concern for institutional clients that want their representatives to invest on their behalf.

Hot wallets can be provided by digital exchanges or as downloadable software. When relying on downloaded software, the private keys are in the hands of the consumer, so the software is arguably safer than the digital wallet found on an exchange. However, digital exchanges generally have robust teams that are regularly updating the protection of its systems. Regardless, a hacker could still access a consumer's private key if the hacker specifically targets and successfully gains access to that consumer's wallet.

In 2017, the first sign of a hot wallet referred to in a court case is *United States v. Ulbricht*, 858 F.3d 71 (2d Cir. 2017), at footnote 51 where Circuit Judge Lynch explained the difference between hot and cold wallets. The terms hot wallet and cold wallet are derived from the more general terms hot storage and cold storage. Hot storage is online storage and cold storage is offline.

A hot wallet is a wallet for cryptocurrency in which the private keys are stored on a network-connected machine, whereas a cold wallet stores the private keys offline. This definition arose after the defendant, accused of creating a Silk Road, claimed that a witness's testimony did not properly describe what a hot wallet is, which proved to be immaterial to the case. Hot wallets made another appearance in 2018 in the unreported case *Symphony FS Limited v. Thompson*, 2018 U.S. Dist. LEXIS 214641 (E.D. Pa. Dec. 20, 2018); however, it was not defined as it was in *Ulbricht*. It is possible that it is because that court is familiar with the technology and how it operates. Regardless, the difference between a hot or cold wallet was also immaterial to the case. At the very least, another district court referred to this form of storage and will potentially encourage other districts to follow.

B. Cold Storage

All cold storage, also known as cold wallets, are non-custodial, meaning only the consumer holds the private key. Cold wallets are offline and typically come in the form of a USB. The cryptocurrency owner would transfer their cryptocurrency to the offline wallet then physically store it in a safe place. This is a safer method of storing one's coins, because it remedies the issue of storing the private key online. The private key of a cold wallet never contacts the server, so there is no real threat of a hacker obtaining that information.

Paper wallets are another form of cold wallets. They are what the name suggests: pieces of paper with the public and private key written, so they must be stored in a safe place. The only way a hacker could obtain this information is if they locate that specific piece of paper.

C. Smart Contract Wallet

Smart contract wallets are used for the custody of smart contract tokens, i.e., Ethereum. They are online custodianship and controlled by code and a master account private key. Unlike accounts, wallets are customizable.

D. Hosted Wallets

A provider of a hosted wallet is an account-based money transmitter that receives, stores, and transmits CVCs on behalf of the account holder. When using a hosted wallet, the money transmitter is the host, the account is the wallet, and the account holder is the wallet owner.

E. Unhosted Wallets

An unhosted wallet is software hosted on a person's phone, computer, or any other device that enables the person to store and conduct CVC transactions. The most important distinction from hosted wallets is that unhosted wallets do not require a third party to conduct transactions. If the person conducting the transaction, through the unhosted wallet, is doing so to purchase goods or services on the user's own behalf, they are not a money transmitter.

Discussion Points

1. *Comparing different types of wallets.* What are the differences between hosted and unhosted wallets? Which do you think is more advantageous to consumers? Why? Do hosted wallets provide consumers more protection than unhosted wallets? Why or why not? If third parties were not required to conduct any transaction, whether a consumer is using a hosted or unhosted wallet, would there be any fundamental difference between the two wallet types?

2. *Characterizing a hosted wallet.* Is a provider of a hosted wallet a money service business (MSB)? Why or why not? Should providers of hosted wallets be required to follow registration and licensing requirements similar to an MSB?

3. *Hot storage vs. cold storage.* What are the differences between hot storage and cold storage? Does one provide consumers more protection than the other? What happens if a cold wallet is lost? Conversely, are there any protections for consumers if their private key is hacked? How should lawmakers and regulators respond to these issues?

Six

Decentralized Finance

I. Introduction

Decentralized Finance (DeFi) is challenging the centralized financial system by disempowering intermediaries and empowering individuals to engage in peer to peer transactions. A centralized financial system is currently being used in almost every aspect of banking, lending, and trading, and is operated by intermediaries.

The appeal underlying DeFi is the idea that services are decentralized, transparent, and accessible. DeFi uses cryptocurrency and blockchain technology to manage financial transactions. Financial institutions make their products available on the blockchain to allow peer to peer interactions to occur between parties without the interference of a financial institution. By nature, DeFi does not offer custodial services, though its products have a similar look and feel to what consumers are accustomed to.

DeFi also has downfalls, such as being susceptible to hacking. Hackers are a threat to DeFi because of the software the financial products require. There is not any consumer protection in the DeFi space because the FDIC only protects centralized finance. Further, eligibility for certain transactions is limited because transactions require 100% collateral. Also of chief importance is that private keys are the only way to secure a digital wallet, and if a private key is lost, so are all the assets locked in that wallet.

There are also various legal implications with respect to DeFi. Such implications include the regulation of DeFi, the risk of class action suits, and patent-related litigation. Regarding the regulatory implication, both federal and state regulators have found it challenging to navigate through the world of cryptocurrencies, and DeFi is no different. While no state has taken a formal position on DeFi, New York has arguably taken the closest step to addressing the concept with its inception of BitLicense, because by adopting the BitLicense, New York acknowledged the validity of cryptocurrency. BitLicense may spur more regulation of virtual currencies, and of DeFi. In the meantime, absent any formal regulation, the private sector is left on its own to figure out how to comply with existing state and federal laws when pursuing DeFi.

II. Blockchain

Blockchain and cryptocurrency enable DeFi because they run on a decentralized system in which financial transactions are recorded in an encrypted code. This encryption allows users to remain anonymous, as well as removing the need for an intermediary to conduct the transaction.

A. Decentralized Apps

DeFi is being used today in the form of decentralized apps (DApps) or a program called "protocols." These two platforms handle transactions in Bitcoin and Ethereum. DApps and protocols are also used with traditional financial transactions and decentralized exchanges that facilitate peer to peer financial transactions, stablecoins, and e-wallets.

III. Regulatory Concerns

The Financial Stability Board ("FSB") clarified in its 2019 report on financial stability, regulatory, and governance implications, that distributed ledgers will pose new governance challenges. For example, distributed ledgers generally do not account for public policy objectives like anti-money laundering or financial stability.[76] The report also highlights jurisdictional uncertainties.[77] Traditional financial institutions are designed to reside in specific jurisdictions each with their own rules. However, the borderless nature of DeFi makes regulators face a new challenge.

People work hard for their money and need to have confidence that the financial institution or product of their choice will safeguard their assets. DeFi attacks the heart of traditional finance because it is the opposition to a centralized system. Our regulatory framework has only focused on the banking structure in existence, so there is no real guidance or requirements of compliance for decentralized financial institutions. DeFi is by nature non-custodial, whereas centralized financial platforms are custodial. Centralized platforms can fall within the purview of a regulatory body, whereas DeFi platforms currently do not. But, at the very least, if a DeFi app implicates any issues, such as with the Securities and Exchange Commission or Council of Economic Advisers, then the appropriate Act will kick in.

---

76. Financial Stability Board, *Decentralised Financial Technologies: Report on Financial Stability, Regulatory and Governance Implications* 22, (June 6, 2019), https://www.fsb.org/wp-content/uploads/P060619.pdf.
    77. *Id.* at 8.

U.S. Securities and Exchange Commission Statement on DeFi Risks, Regulations, and Opportunity

Commissioner Caroline A. Crenshaw,

1 INT' J. BLOCKCHAIN LAW 4 (Nov. 2021)

Whether in the news, social media, popular entertainment, and increasingly in people's portfolios, crypto is now part of the vernacular.[2] But what that term actually encompasses is broad and amorphous and includes everything from tokens, to non-fungible tokens, to Dexes to Decentralized Finance or DeFI. For those readers not already familiar with DeFi, unsurprisingly, definitions also vary. In general, though, it is an effort to replicate functions of our traditional finance systems through the use of blockchain-based smart contracts that are composable, interoperable, and open source.[3] Much of DeFi activity takes place on the Ethereum blockchain, but any blockchain that supports certain types of scripting or coding can be used to develop DeFi applications and platforms.

DeFi presents a panoply of opportunities. However, it also poses important risks and challenges for regulators, investors, and the financial markets. While the potential for profits attracts attention, sometimes overwhelming attention, there is also confusion, often significant, regarding important aspects of this emerging market. Social media questions like "who in the U.S. regulates the DeFi market?" and "Why are regulators involved at all?" abound. These are crucial questions, and the answers are important to lawyers and non-lawyers alike. This article attempts to provide a short background on the current regulatory landscape for DeFi, the role of the United States Securities and Exchange Commission ("SEC"), and highlights two important hurdles that the community should address.[4]

---

2. I am deeply grateful to my colleagues Robert Cobbs, Kathleen Gallagher, Micah Hauptman, Claire O'Sullivan, and Gosia Spangenberg, whose hard work made this submission possible. I would like to particularly thank my colleague David Hirsch, who has been instrumental not only to this submission, but also provides valuable support to my office's overall approach to digital assets. We are also grateful to a variety of industry experts and attorneys who generously shared their time and ideas, and helped deepen my understanding of these questions. And finally, thanks to Dr. Matthias Artzt, Sandra Ro, and all the editors of The International Journal of Blockchain Law. The views I express herein are my own and do not necessarily reflect the views of the Commission, my fellow Commissioners, or the SEC Staff.

3. Composable refers to the ability to link smart contracts and build on existing modular code, which leads some to refer to DeFi applications as money Legos. *See* Quantstamp Labs, DeFi's Composability: More Possibility, More Risk, (last visited Nov. 8, 2021). The term interoperable describes the ability to use DeFi protocols and applications across platforms and smart contracts. *See* Fabian Schär, *Decentralized Finance: On Blockchain and Smart Contract-Based Financial Markets*, Fed. Res. Bank St. Louis Rev. 153 (Feb. 5. 2021).

4. In addition to the securities law issues addressed in this article, regulators have also raised concerns about DeFi projects' failures to comply with rules relating to anti-money laundering, combating the financing of terrorism, tax compliance, the Commodity Exchange Act, and other issues. While not the primary focus of this article, I share some of those same concerns.

I. Many Investments Share Important Attributes

Many DeFi offerings and products closely resemble products and functions in the traditional financial marketplace.[5] There are decentralized applications, or dApps, running on blockchains, that enable people to obtain an asset or loan upon posting of collateral, much like traditional collateralized loans.[6] Others offer the ability to deposit a digital asset and receive a return. Both types of products offer returns, some directly, and some indirectly by enabling the use of borrowed assets for other DeFi investing opportunities. In addition, there are web-based tools that help users identify, or invest in, the highest-yielding DeFi instruments and venues.[7] Other applications let users earn fees in exchange for supplying liquidity or market making.[8] There are also tokens coded to track the prices of securities trading on registered U.S. national securities exchanges, and then can be traded and used in a variety of other DeFi applications. So while the underlying technology is sometimes unfamiliar, these digital products and activities have close analogs within the SEC's jurisdiction.

These similarities should come as a surprise to no one, considering finance is in the name. It should also come as a surprise to no one that investing is often at the core of DeFi activity. This movement is not about merely developing new digital asset tokens. Developers have also constructed smart contracts that offer individuals the ability to invest, to lever those investments, to take a variety of derivative positions, and to move assets quickly and easily between various platforms and protocols. And there are projects that show a potential for scalable increased efficiencies in transactions speed, cost, and customization.

These projects are evolving incredibly fast with new and interesting potential. Considering the relative infancy of blockchains that support the scripting needed for sophisticated smart contracts, DeFi development is particularly impressive. But these offerings are not just products, and their users are not merely consumers. DeFi, again, is fundamentally about investing. This investing includes speculative risks taken in pursuit of passive profits from hoped-for token price appreciation, or investments seeking a return in exchange for placing capital at risk or locking it up for another's benefit.

II. Unregulated Markets Suffer From Structural Limitations

Market participants who raise capital from investors, or provide regulated services or functions to investors, generally take on legal obligations. In what may be an

---

5. The DeFi market overall has grown dramatically. DeFi today has more than $101 billion in total value locked, representing rapid expansion since September 2020 when that figure stood at $19.5 billion. *See* Marketforces Africa, DeFi Market Soared 335% to $85 Billion, (last visited Nov. 8, 2021).

6. *See* Schär, *supra* note 3, at 164.

7. *Id.* at 165.

8. *Id.* at 162.

attempt to disclaim those legal obligations, many DeFi promoters disclose broadly that DeFi is risky and investments may result in losses, without providing the details investors need to assess risk likelihood and severity.[9] Others could accurately be characterized as simply advocating a "buyer beware" approach; by participating, investors assume the risk of any and all losses. Given this, many current DeFi participants recommend that new investors exercise caution, and many experts and academics agree there are significant risks.[10]

While DeFi has produced impressive alternative methods of composing, recording, and processing transactions, it has not rewritten all of economics or human nature. Certain truths apply with as much force in DeFi as they do in traditional finance:

- Unless required, there will be projects that do not invest in compliance or adequate internal controls;

- when the potential financial rewards are great enough, some individuals will victimize others, and the likelihood of this occurring tends to increase as the likelihood of getting caught and severity of potential sanctions decrease; and

- absent mandatory disclosure requirements,[11] information asymmetries will likely advantage rich investors and insiders at the expense of the smallest investors and those with the least access to information.

Accordingly, DeFi participants' current "buyer beware" approach is not an adequate foundation on which to build reimagined financial markets. Without a common set of conduct expectations, and a functional system to enforce those principles, markets tend toward corruption, marked by fraud, self-dealing, cartel-like activity, and information asymmetries. Over time that reduces investor confidence and investor participation.[12]

---

9. I listened to a recent podcast in which a young developer acknowledged that humans as a species are attracted to high returns, but are also bad at considering risk in choosing where to invest and at what price. He also said that people were mortgaging their homes to free up funds with which to invest in DeFi, and that he was concerned the outcome could be scary. Without reference to this specific person, it seems like common knowledge that some retail investors are taking on huge exposure in DeFi without understanding the risk or having the ability to price for it. Developers should build systems that are compliant with important regulatory and policy frameworks so that investors have all material information, including about the potential risks, and are protected from misconduct that puts them at a disadvantage.

10. *See* Nic Carter & Linda Jeng, *DeFi Protocol Risks: The Paradox of DeFi*, RiskBooks (forthcoming 2021).

11. For activity within the SEC's jurisdiction, compliance with the investor protections of the Securities Act of 1933 and the Securities and Exchange Act of 1934 requires important disclosures.

12. There is a great deal of academic research into network effects and how network adoption and engagement benefits the value of networks. I would be interested in research that studies how fraud and other violations of trust within a network impact that network's value by reducing adoption and engagement, and the potential for this impact to extend to competing networks.

Conversely, well-regulated markets tend to flourish, and I think our U.S. capital markets are prime examples. Because of their reliability and shared adherence to minimum standards of disclosure and conduct, our markets are the destination of choice for investors and entities seeking to raise capital. Our securities laws do not merely serve to impose obligations or burdens, they provide a critical market good. They help address the problems noted above, among others, and our markets function better as a result. But, in the brave new DeFi world, to date there has not been broad adoption of regulatory frameworks that deliver important protections in other markets.

III. Who Regulates DeFi?

In the United States, multiple federal authorities likely have jurisdiction over aspects of DeFi, including the Department of Justice, the Financial Criminal Enforcement Network, the Internal Revenue Service, the Commodity Futures Trading Commission, and the SEC.[13] State authorities likely have jurisdiction over aspects as well.[14] In spite of the number of authorities having some jurisdictional interest, DeFi investors generally will not get the same level of compliance and robust disclosure that are the norm in other regulated markets in the U.S. For example, a variety of DeFi participants, activities, and assets fall within the SEC's jurisdiction as they involve securities and securities-related conduct.[15] But no DeFi participants within the SEC's jurisdiction have registered with us, though we continue to encourage participants in DeFi to engage with the staff. If investment opportunities are offered completely outside of regulatory oversight, investors and other market participants must understand that these markets are riskier than traditional markets where participants generally play by the same set of rules.

---

13. The U.S. government has dedicated significant resources to providing feedback, supporting innovation, and developing in-house expertise to ensure regulatory approaches are based on an accurate understanding of the technology. For example, the SEC has a FinHub, and a number of other authorities have innovation initiatives that engage with market participants and study the technology.

14. *See* Melanie Waddell, *State Securities Regulators Report Tripling of Digital Asset Enforcement Actions*, ThinkAdvisor (last visited Nov. 8, 2021).

15. At the SEC we have existing laws and rules that guide our approach and are shaped by court interpretations. Rather than proactively labeling every investment vehicle as a security or not a security, we look at specific facts and circumstances and apply the law based on that analysis. We do not have a measuring box like at airports, where if a bag fits inside it can be carried on, and otherwise must be checked. That type of mechanical jurisdictional test might be easier to apply and yield a faster conclusion, but ultimately would require us to revise the test and adapt the rules every time a new type of investment is introduced or changes in form. Considering that we regulate capital markets exceeding $110 trillion, made up of tens of thousands of entities, that type of proactive "define everything" approach is too rigid, and markets are too large, for it to be workable. Our statutes recognize that and provide for a flexible, principles-based approach, but one that also inherently requires a more detailed analysis to determine whether specific conduct or assets are within the SEC's jurisdiction.

IV. The Role of the SEC

As an SEC Commissioner I have a duty to help ensure that market activity, whether new or old, operates fairly, and offers all investors a level playing field.[16] I would expect this goal to be one DeFi market participants also support.

To do this, the SEC has a variety of tools at its disposal ranging from rulemaking authority, to various exemptive or no action relief, to enforcement actions. Importantly, if DeFi development teams are not sure whether their project is within the SEC's jurisdiction, they should reach out to our Strategic Hub for Innovation and Financial Technology ("FinHub"), or our other Offices and Divisions, all of which have experts well-versed in issues relating to digital assets.[17] It is my understanding that FinHub has never refused a meeting, and their engagement is meaningful.[18] If a series of meetings is needed, they spend the necessary time. If a project does not fit neatly within our existing framework, *before proceeding to market*, that project team should come and talk to us.[19] The more the project team can lead that discussion with possible solutions, the better outcomes they can expect. Our staff cannot offer legal advice, but they stand ready to listen to ideas and provide feedback, as developers know their projects better than we ever could. If the project is seemingly constrained by our rules, it is critical for us to get specific ideas about how these new technologies can be integrated into our regulatory regime to ensure the market and investor protections afforded by the federal securities laws, while allowing innovations to flourish.

That being said, for non-compliant projects within our jurisdiction, we do have an effective enforcement mechanism. For example, the SEC recently settled an enforcement action with a purported DeFi platform and its individual promoters. The SEC alleged they failed to register their offering, which raised $30 million, and misled their investors while improperly spending investor money on themselves.[20] To

---

16. My responsibility extends to conduct within the SEC's jurisdiction, and my able colleagues at sibling agencies are responsible for other types of conduct.

17. *See* SEC Strategic Hub for Innovation and Financial Technology ("FinHub").

18. FinHub comprises representatives across the SEC's Divisions, and so those meetings includes access to a broad range of experts. FinHub is also an important resource to the Commission as it considers policy choices.

19. Coming in to speak with SEC staff does not provide amnesty for violative conduct. It is, however, an important path to help projects identify potential SEC regulatory compliance issues, discuss possible solutions, and develop a plan to operate legally. To the extent a project team has already been operating outside of compliance, working with staff to prevent future violations may also position it to more quickly and inexpensively resolve any potential enforcement action for related past violations. Our Division of Enforcement considers cooperation when determining what remedies to recommend for violative conduct and we have agreed to settle multiple cases with reduced or no penalties in response to self-reporting violations, including in the digital assets space. *See, e.g.,* In the Matter of Gladius Networks, Order Instituting Cease and Desist Proceedings, Securities Act Release No. 10608 (Feb. 20, 2019).

20. *See* In the Matter of Blockchain Credit Partners d/b/a DeFi Money Market, Gregory Keough, and Derek Acree, Order Instituting Cease and Desist Proceedings, Securities Act Release No. 10961 (Aug. 6, 2021).

the extent other offerings, projects, or platforms are operating in violation of securities laws, I expect we will continue to bring enforcement actions. But my preferred path is not through enforcement, and I do not consider enforcement inevitable. Broad non-compliance that necessitates numerous enforcement actions is not an efficient way to achieve what I believe are shared goals for DeFi. The more projects that voluntarily comply with regulations, the less frequently the SEC will have to pursue investigations and litigation.

V. Structural Hurdles

I recognize it is not the SEC's role to prevent all investment losses. It is also not my goal to restrict investor access to fair and appropriate opportunities. But it is my job to demand that investors have equal access to critical information so they can make informed decisions whether to invest and at what price. I am similarly committed to ensuring markets are fair and free from manipulation. Given this, it seems that there are two specific structural problems that the DeFi community needs to address.

A. Lack of Transparency

First, although transactions often are recorded on a public blockchain, in important ways, DeFi investing is not transparent. I am concerned that this lack of transparency contributes to a two tier market in which professional investors and insiders reap outsized returns while retail investors take more risks, get worse pricing, and are less likely to succeed over time.[21] Much of DeFi is funded by venture capital and other professional investors. It is unclear to me how well known this is in the DeFi retail investor community, but the underlying funding deals often grant professional investors equity, options, advisory roles, access to project team management, formal or informal say on governance and operations, anti-dilution rights, and the ability to distribute controlling interests to allies, among other benefits. Rarely are these arrangements disclosed, but they can have a significant impact on investment values and outcomes. Retail investors are already operating at a significant disadvantage to professional investors in DeFi,[22] and this information imbalance exacerbates the problem.

Some contend that DeFi is, in fact, more egalitarian and transparent because much of the activity is based on code that is publicly available.[23] However, only a rel-

---

21. I recognize that DeFi has experienced significant asset price appreciation, and that is part of what motivated me to write this. The impacts of the information disparities or market conduct on retail investors may not be easy to see until the next DeFi market downturn or crisis.

22. Joel Khalil, *Investing in DeFi is Seriously Risky But Maybe It Doesn't Have to Be*, Techradar. com (last visited Nov. 8, 2021) (describing "[h]igh transaction fees, market volatility and security incidents linked with vulnerabilities in smart contracts" as risks that are more pronounced for retail investors).

23. Kevin Werbach, *Finance 3.0: DeFi, Dapps, and the Promise of Decentralized Disruption*, The Reboot (last visited Nov. 8, 2021).

atively small group of people can actually read and understand that code, and even highly-qualified experts miss flaws or hazards. Currently the quality of that code can vary drastically, and has a significant impact on investment outcomes and security. If DeFi has ambitions of reaching a broad investing pool, it should not assume a significant portion of that population can or wants to run their own testnet to understand the risks associated with the code on which their investment prospects rely. It is not reasonable to build a financial system that demands investors also be sophisticated interpreters of complex code.

Put simply, if a retail investor has $2,000 to invest in a risky programmable asset, it is not cost effective for that investor to hire experts to audit the code to ensure it will behave as advertised. Instead, retail investors must rely on information available through marketing, advertising, word of mouth, and social media. Professional investors, on the other hand, can afford to hire technical experts, engineers, economists, and others, before making an investment decision. While this professional advantage exists historically in our financial markets, DeFi exacerbates it. DeFi removes intermediaries that perform important gatekeeping functions and operates outside the existing investor and market protection regime. That can leave retail investors without access to professional financial advisors or other intermediaries who help screen potential investments for quality and legitimacy. These provide meaningful fraud reduction and risk assessment assistance in traditional finance, but there are limited substitutes in DeFi.

B. Pseudonymity

A second foundational challenge for DeFi is that these markets are vulnerable to difficult to detect manipulation. DeFi transactions occur on a blockchain, and each transaction is recorded, immutable, and available for all to see. But that visibility extends only down to a certain identifier. Because of pseudonymity, the blockchain displays the blockchain address that sent or received assets, but not the identity of the person who controls it.

Without an efficient method for determining the actual identity of traders, or owners of smart contracts, it is very difficult to know if asset prices and trading volumes reflect organic interest or are the product of manipulative trading by, for example, one person using bots to operate multiple wallets, or a group of people trading collusively. There are specific U.S. securities laws prohibiting trading for the purpose of giving the false appearance of market activity or to manipulate the price of a security,[24] because successful investing depends on reliable information and market integrity. Pseudonymity makes it much easier to conceal manipulative activity and almost impossible for an investor to distinguish an individual engaging in manipulative trading from normal organic trading activity. In DeFi, because markets often turn on asset price, trading volumes, and momentum, investors are

---

24. See 15 U.S.C. § 78i (2018).

vulnerable to losses due to manipulative trading that makes those signals unreliable. To the extent transactions occur off public blockchains, it is even more difficult to assess whether trading is legitimate.

I recognize that in some ways DeFi is synonymous with pseudonymous. The use of alphanumeric strings that obscure real world identity was a core feature of Bitcoin and has been present in essentially all blockchains that have followed. But in the U.S., investors have long been comfortable with a compromise in which they give up some limited degree of privacy by sharing their identity with the entity through which they trade securities. In return, they benefit from regulated markets that are more fair, orderly, and efficient, with less manipulation and fraud.

In moving to DeFi, I suspect most retail investors are not doing so because they seek greater privacy; they are seeking better returns than they believe they can find from other investments. While some in DeFi believe in absolute financial privacy, I expect that projects that solve for pseudonymity are more likely to succeed, because investors can then be comfortable that asset prices reflect actual interest from real investors, not prices pumped by hidden manipulators. Projects that address this problem are also more likely to be able to comply with SEC regulations and other legal obligations, including requirements around anti-money laundering and countering the financing of terrorism imposed by the Bank Secrecy Act.

VI. Conclusion

My respect for innovation does not lessen my commitment to help ensure all our financial markets are sustainable and offer average investors a fair chance of success. DeFi is a shared opportunity and challenge. Some DeFi projects fit neatly within our jurisdiction, and others may struggle to comply with the rules as currently applied. It is not enough to just say it is too hard to regulate or to say it is too hard to comply with regulations.

It is a positive sign that many projects say they want to operate within DeFi in a compliant way. I credit their sincerity on this point, and hope they commit resources to collaborating with the SEC staff in the same spirit. For DeFi's problems, finding compliant solutions is something best accomplished together. Reimagining our markets without appropriate investor protections and mechanisms to support market integrity would be a missed opportunity, at best, and could result in significant harm, at worst. In conceiving a new financial system, I believe developers have an obligation to optimize for more than profitability, speed of deployment, and innovation. Whatever comes next, it should be a system in which all investors have access to actionable, material data, and it should be a system that reduces the potential for manipulative conduct. Such a system should lead capital to flow efficiently to the most promising projects, rather than being diverted by mere hype or false claims. It should also be designed to advance markets that are interconnected, but with sufficient safeguards to withstand significant shocks, including the potential for rapid deleveraging. In decentralized networks with diffuse control and disparate interests, regulations serve to create shared incentives aligned to benefit the entire system and ensure fair opportunities for its least powerful participants.

My staff and I have been actively engaged in helpful discussions with DeFi experts and my door remains open.[26] I can't promise an easy or quick process, unfortunately, but I can assure you of good faith consideration and a true desire to help promote responsible innovation.

Discussion Points

1. *The legal implications of DeFi.* What are some of the legal questions that need to be addressed regarding DeFi? Which federal regulatory agency do you think is best suited to regulate DeFi?

2. *Analysis.* What are the benefits of being able to trade, buy and sell assets without having to use an intermediary? Are there any disadvantages to this model?

3. *Is there a risk of fraud?* Do you think that DeFi could be used to perpetuate financial fraud against consumers? Should the FTC be involved in combating fraudulent activity involving DeFi?

4. *The SEC's possible effect on DeFi.* In 2022, the SEC undertook to increase the size of its cryptocurrency enforcement staff. Do you think this will cause DeFi platforms to be subject to greater enforcement? Should the SEC be involved in DeFi regulatory enforcement?

Illicit Finance Risk Assessment of Decentralized Finance
U.S. Department of the Treasury

April 2023

Executive Summary

This risk assessment explores how illicit actors are abusing what is commonly referred to as decentralized finance (DeFi) services as well as vulnerabilities unique to DeFi services. The findings will inform efforts to identify and address potential gaps in the United States' anti-money laundering and countering the financing of terrorism (AML/CFT) regulatory, supervisory, and enforcement regimes for DeFi.

---

26. In a recent speech I requested input from digital assets market participants. See Caroline Crenshaw, Commissioner, Sec. & Exch. Comm'n, Digital Asset Securities—Common Goals and a Bridge to Better Outcomes (Oct. 12, 2021). Unfortunately, that has not yet yielded much of a response from a community that often says it lacks necessary guidance from the SEC, among others. My door remains open, and I welcome your ideas. I've created a dedicated mailbox for this purpose: crenshaw-defi@sec.gov.

There is currently no generally accepted definition of DeFi, even among industry participants, or what characteristics would make a product, service, arrangement or activity "decentralized."[1] The term broadly refers to virtual asset protocols and services that purport to allow for some form of automated peer-to-peer (P2P) transactions, often through the use of self-executing code known as "smart contracts"[2] based on blockchain[3] technology.[4] This term is frequently used loosely in the virtual asset industry, and often refers to services that are not functionally decentralized. The degree to which a purported DeFi service is in reality decentralized is a matter of facts and circumstances, and this risk assessment finds that DeFi services often have a controlling organization that provides a measure of centralized administration and governance.

The assessment finds that illicit actors, including ransomware cybercriminals, thieves, scammers, and Democratic People's Republic of Korea (DPRK) cyber actors, are using DeFi services in the process of transferring and laundering their illicit proceeds. To accomplish this, illicit actors are exploiting vulnerabilities in the U.S. and foreign AML/CFT regulatory, supervisory, and enforcement regimes as well as the technology underpinning DeFi services. In particular, this assessment finds that the most significant current illicit finance risk in this domain is from DeFi services that are not compliant with existing AML/CFT obligations.

In the United States, the Bank Secrecy Act (BSA) and related regulations[5] impose obligations on financial institutions to assist U.S. government agencies in

---

1. U.S. Department of Justice (DOJ), *The Report of the Attorney General Pursuant to Section 5(b)(iii) of Executive Order 14067: The Role Of Law Enforcement In Detecting, Investigating, And Prosecuting Criminal Activity Related To Digital Assets*, (September 2022), https://www.justice.gov/d9/2022-12/The%20Report%20of%20the%20Attorney%20General%20Pursuant%20to%20Section.pdf, p. 10; this definition is for the purpose of the risk assessment and should not be interpreted as a regulatory definition under the Bank Secrecy Act (BSA) or other relevant regulatory regimes. Section 2.4 discusses several traits of virtual asset service providers (VASP) that may be more or less decentralized, often along a dynamic spectrum.

2. The term "smart contracts," as used in the Report, refers to code that is deployed on a blockchain and that, if activated by a transaction on the blockchain, "will be executed through the blockchain's network of computers and will produce a change in the blockchain's 'state.'" International Organization of Securities Commissions (IOSCO), *IOSCO Decentralized Finance Report*, (March 2022), https://www.iosco.org/library/pubdocs/pdf/IOSCOPD699.pdf.

3. Blockchain refers to a type of distributed ledger technology (DLT) that cryptographically signs transactions that are grouped into blocks. Since most virtual assets occur on blockchains, the assessment uses this term throughout, while recognizing that these assets and services could run on other forms of DLT.

4. DOJ, *The Report of the Attorney General Pursuant to Section 5(b)(iii) of Executive Order 14067: The Role Of Law Enforcement In Detecting, Investigating, And Prosecuting Criminal Activity Related To Digital Assets*, (September 2022), https://www.justice.gov/d9/2022-12/The%20Report%20of%20the%20Attorney%20General%20Pursuant%20to%20Section.pdf, p. 10.

5. The BSA is codified at 31 U.S.C. §§ 5311–5314, 5316–5336 and 12 U.S.C. §§ 1829b, 1951–1959. Regulations implementing the BSA are codified at 31 C.F.R. Chapter X.

detecting and preventing money laundering.[6] The BSA imposes such obligations on a wide range of financial institutions, and determining whether an entity, including purported DeFi services, is a covered financial institution will depend on specific facts and circumstances surrounding its financial activities. However, a DeFi service that functions as a financial institution as defined by the BSA, regardless of whether the service is centralized of decentralized, will be required to comply with BSA obligations, including AML/CFT obligations. A DeFi service's claim that it is or plans to be "fully decentralized" does not impact its status as a financial institution under the BSA.

Despite this, many existing DeFi services covered by the BSA fail to comply with AML/CFT obligations, a vulnerability that illicit actors exploit. A lack of a common understanding among industry participants of how AML/CFT obligations may apply to DeFi services exacerbates this risk. In some cases, industry providers may purposefully seek to decentralize a virtual asset service in an attempt to avoid triggering AML/CFT obligations, without recognizing that the obligations still apply so long as the provider continues to offer covered services. At the same time, some DeFi services developed with opaque organization structure may present critical challenges to supervision and, for cases in which DeFi services are not complying with their AML/CFT obligations, enforcement of applicable statutory and regulatory obligations.

This assessment recommends strengthening U.S. AML/CFT supervision and, when relevant, enforcement of virtual asset activities, including DeFi services, to increase compliance by virtual asset firms with BSA obligations. In tandem, federal regulators should conduct further engagement with industry, in line with previous guidance, public statements, and enforcement actions, to explain how relevant laws and regulations, including securities, commodities, and money transmission regulations, apply to DeFi services, and take additional regulatory actions and publish further guidance informed by this engagement as necessary.

The assessment also finds that to the extent a DeFi service falls outside the current definition of a financial institution under the BSA, referred to as "disintermediation" in this assessment, a vulnerability may exist due to the reduced likelihood that such DeFi services would choose to implement AML/CFT measures. In cases in which a DeFi service falls outside of the scope of the BSA, this can result in gaps in efforts by the DeFi service to identify and disrupt illegal activity and identify and report suspicious activity to law enforcement and other competent authorities. Globally, under the standards set by the Financial Action Task Force (FATF), the global standard setting body for AML/CFT, DeFi services that lack an entity with sufficient control

---

6. Financial Crimes Enforcement Network (FinCEN), *FinCEN Guidance*, (May 9, 2019), https://www.fincen.gov/sites/default/ files/2019-05/FinCEN%20Guidance%20CVC%20FINAL%20508 .pdf.

or influence over the service may not be explicitly subject to AML/CFT obligations,[7] which could lead to potential gaps for DeFi services in other jurisdictions. The assessment recommends enhancing the U.S. AML/CFT regulatory regime by closing any identified gaps in the BSA to the extent that they allow certain DeFi services to fall outside of the BSA's definition of financial institution.

Other identified vulnerabilities include the lack of implementation of international AML/CFT standards by foreign countries, which enables illicit actors to use DeFi services with impunity in jurisdictions that lack AML/CFT requirements. Additionally, poor cybersecurity practices by DeFi services, which enable theft and fraud of consumer assets, also present risks for national security, consumers, and the virtual asset industry. The assessment recommends stepping up engagements with foreign partners to push for stronger implementation of international AML/CFT standards and advocating for improved cybersecurity practices by virtual asset firms to mitigate these vulnerabilities.

The assessment highlights that the existing U.S. AML/CFT regulatory framework, coupled with the gradual implementation of global AML/CFT standards that apply to virtual assets, mitigates the identified vulnerabilities to a limited extent. This is in part due to DeFi services' current reliance on centralized virtual asset service providers (VASPs)[8] to access fiat currency. Centralized VASPs, which refer for the purpose of this report to VASPs that do not claim to be decentralized, tend to have simpler internal structures than DeFi services, are always covered within the regulatory perimeter of the FATF standards, and are more likely to implement AML/CFT measures than DeFi services.

The ability to use data from the public blockchain in addition to the development of industry- driven compliance solutions for DeFi services can also help mitigate some illicit finance risks. These measures and the transparency afforded by the public blockchain, however, do not sufficiently address the identified vulnerabilities on their own, and blockchain analytics cannot replace the importance of regulated financial intermediaries applying AML/CFT controls. Nonetheless, the U.S. government should also seek to further promote the responsible innovation of compliance tools for the industry, an avenue many in the private sector are already pursuing.

This assessment recognizes that the virtual asset ecosystem, including DeFi services, is changing rapidly. The U.S. government will continue to conduct research and engage with the private sector to support its understanding of developments in the DeFi ecosystem, and how such developments could affect the threats, vulnerabilities, and mitigation measures to address illicit finance risks. Lastly, the assess-

---

7. The FATF standards that apply to all individuals (like targeted financial sanctions) would still apply to DeFi services, regardless of structure.

8. Many centralized virtual asset exchanges operate off-chain, meaning that they record transactions internally rather than on the blockchain and can enable users to exchange virtual assets for fiat currency.

ment poses several questions that will be considered as part of the recommended actions of the assessment to address illicit finance risks, including related to treatment of DeFi services that fall outside of the BSA definition of financial institution and areas for additional regulatory clarity. The Department of the Treasury (Treasury) welcomes stakeholder input on these questions.

1. Introduction Context

In September 2022, Treasury, in line with Executive Order 14067 of March 9, 2022, "Ensuring Responsible Development of Digital Assets," published an Action Plan to Mitigate the Illicit Financing Risks of Digital Assets (Action Plan).[9] The Action Plan, building upon Treasury's 2022 National Risk Assessments for Money Laundering, Terrorist Financing, and Proliferation Financing (2022 NRAs),[10] identified illicit finance risks associated with virtual assets, including the misuse of what are commonly called DeFi services to launder illicit proceeds. There is currently no generally accepted definition of DeFi, even among industry participants, or a common understanding of what characteristics would make a product, service, arrangement, or activity "decentralized."[11] The term broadly refers to virtual asset protocols and services that purport to allow for some form of automated P2P transactions, often through the use of self-executing code known as smart contracts based on blockchain technology.

Risk Assessment Overview

This risk assessment explores how illicit actors abuse DeFi services and vulnerabilities unique to DeFi services to inform efforts to identify and address potential gaps in the United States' AML/CFT regulatory, supervisory, and enforcement regimes. This tailored assessment of DeFi services was prompted by the findings in the 2022 NRAs that illicit actors misused DeFi services and that many DeFi services lacked mitigation for illicit finance risks, as well as by rising concern globally related to DeFi risks.[12] Still, as previously noted in the 2022 NRAs, this risk assessment rec-

---

9. U.S. Department of the Treasury (Treasury), *Action Plan to Address Illicit Financing Risks of Digital Assets*, (September 2022), https://home.treasury.gov/system/files/136/Digital-Asset-Action-Plan.pdf.

10. Treasury, *Treasury Publishes National Risk Assessments for Money Laundering, Terrorist Financing, and Proliferation Financing*, (March 1, 2022), https://home.treasury.gov/news/press-releases/jy0619.

11. DOJ, *The Report of the Attorney General Pursuant to Section 5(b)(iii) of Executive Order 14067: The Role Of Law Enforcement In Detecting, Investigating, And Prosecuting Criminal Activity Related To Digital Assets*, (September 2022), https://www.justice. gov/d9/2022-12/The%20 Report%20of%20the%20Attorney%20General%20Pursuant%20to%20Section.pdf, p. 10.

12. *See* FATF, *Targeted Update On Implementation Of The FATF Standards On Virtual Assets And Virtual Asset Service Providers*, (June 2022), https://www.fatf-gafi.org/media/fatf/documents/recommendations/Targeted-Update-Implementation-FATF%20 Standards-Virtual%20Assets-VASPs. pdf; University of Toronto, *G20 Finance Ministers and Central Bank Governors Meetings Communique*, (February 18, 2022), http://www.g20.utoronto.ca/2022/220218-finance.html; Financial

ognizes that most money laundering, terrorist financing, and proliferation financing by volume and value of transactions occurs in fiat currency or otherwise outside the virtual asset ecosystem via more traditional methods. It also notes that the DeFi ecosystem is one element in the broader realm of "virtual assets," a term used by the FATF to cover digital representations of value that can be digitally traded or transferred, and can be used for payment or investment purposes, but do not include digital representations of fiat currencies, securities, and other financial assets.

The risk assessment begins with an overview of the market structure of the DeFi ecosystem and then demonstrates how threat actors misuse DeFi services to engage in and profit from illicit activity, in particular ransomware attacks, theft, fraud and scams, drug trafficking, and proliferation finance. It then considers vulnerabilities that enable the use of DeFi services for illicit purposes, including DeFi services non-compliant with AML/CFT and sanctions obligations, disintermediation, and a lack of implementation of the international AML/CFT standards in foreign countries, before highlighting mitigation measures that can address some of these vulnerabilities. The assessment includes several recommendations for the U.S. government to continue and strengthen efforts to mitigate illicit finance risks associated with DeFi services. Lastly, the assessment poses several questions that will be considered as part of the recommended actions of the assessment to address illicit finance risks.

2. Market Structure Definition and Scope

Frequently, DeFi services purport to run without the support of a central company, group, or person, despite having a controlling organization that provides a measure of centralized administration or governance (*e.g.*, through a decentralized autonomous organization (DAO),[13] concentrated ownership or governance rights, administrative keys, or otherwise).[14] In this sense, "decentralization" claims vary in their accuracy. At times, the use of the term reflects marketing more than reality. The degree to which a purported DeFi service is in reality decentralized is a matter of facts and circumstances.

This assessment discusses services, platforms, arrangements, and products that purport to be or are commonly referred to as "decentralized" or "DeFi" in order to assess the full spectrum of risks associated with DeFi. Additionally, the assessment uses the broad term "DeFi services" to capture providers of a variety of activities,

---

Stability Board, *Assessment of Risks to Financial Stability from Crypto-assets*, (February 16, 2022); https://www.fsb.org/2022/02/assessment-of-risks-to-financial-stability-from-crypto-assets/; European Central Bank, *A deep dive into crypto financial risks: stablecoins, DeFi and climate transition risk*, https://www.ecb.europa.eu/pub/financial-stability/macroprudential-bulletin/html/ecb.mpbu202207_1~750842714e.en.html.

13. DAOs can be described as a system of administration that aspires to operate, in part, according to a set of encoded and transparent rules or smart contracts.

14. Treasury, *Action Plan to Address Illicit Financing Risks of Digital Assets*, (September 2022), https://home.treasury.gov/system/ files/136/Digital-Asset-Action-Plan.pdf, p. 7.

including terms broadly used by industry to include a platform, exchange, application, organization, and others. This assessment also does not evaluate the relative merits of decentralization compared to centralization. As noted above, claims of decentralization may be overstated, and the degree of decentralization of a DeFi service could change over time.

Funds transfers between the holders of two unhosted wallets[15] that do not involve smart contracts or facilitation by a VASP[16] fall outside the scope of DeFi services for the purpose of this report.[17]

This assessment does not alter any existing legal obligations, issue any new regulatory interpretations, or establish any new supervisory expectations. The terms used in this report are intended to reflect the meanings commonly used by industry and market participants, with modifications and clarifications as appropriate. All definitions discussed in this assessment apply only within the scope of the assessment itself. They are intended only to facilitate an understanding of DeFi services and the attendant illicit finance risks.

DeFi Services and AML/CFT Regulatory Obligations

AML/CFT obligations in the United States are based on the activities in which a person engages. The BSA and its implementing regulations state that "financial institutions," such as banks, broker-dealers, mutual funds, money services businesses (MSBs), futures commission merchants (FCMs), and introducing brokers, have AML/CFT obligations.[18] These AML/CFT obligations include requirements to estab-

---

15. Many virtual assets can be self-custodied and transferred without the involvement of an intermediary financial institution. The use of wallets not hosted by any financial institution or other virtual asset service provider (VASP) is commonly known as an "unhosted" or "self-hosted" wallet. Users of unhosted wallets can retain custody and transfer their virtual assets without the involvement of a financial institution.

16. As defined by FATF, virtual asset service provider, often called VASP for short, means any natural or legal person who is not covered elsewhere under the FATF Recommendations, and as a business conducts one or more of the following activities or operations for or on behalf of another natural or legal person: (i.) exchange between virtual assets and fiat currencies; (ii.) exchange between one or more forms of virtual assets; (iii.) transfer of virtual assets; (iv.) safekeeping and/or administration of virtual assets or instruments enabling control over virtual assets; and (v.) participation in and provision of financial services related to an issuer's offer and/or sale of a virtual asset. VASPs in the United States qualify as money services businesses (MSBs), and some businesses that provide virtual asset services may be required to register with federal functional regulators, depending on the services that they are providing.

17. Direct P2P transfers do not include transfers involving P2P service providers, typically natural persons engaged in the business of buying and selling virtual assets rather than safekeeping virtual assets or engaging in P2P transfers on their own behalf. P2P service providers may have regulatory requirements depending on their precise business model; Treasury, *Action Plan to Address Illicit Financing Risks of Digital Assets*, (September 2022), https://home.treasury.gov/system/files/136/Digital-Asset-Action-Plan.pdf, p. 6.

18. 31 U.S.C. § 5312(a)(2); 31 C.F.R. § 1010.100(t).

lish and implement an effective anti-money laundering program (AML Program)[19] and recordkeeping and reporting requirements, including suspicious activity reporting (SAR) requirements.[20]

The nature of the activities in which a person engages is the key factor in determining whether and how that person must register with the Commodities Future Trading Commission (CFTC) (for FCMs and introducing brokers), the Financial Crimes Enforcement Network (FinCEN) (for MSBs), or the Securities and Exchange Commission (SEC) (for broker-dealers and mutual funds). While the degree to which a person is centralized could impact the service it provides, persons engaging in the activities of financial institutions as defined by the BSA, regardless of whether they are centralized or decentralized, will have these obligations. For example, if a DeFi service does business wholly or in substantial part in the United States and accepts and transmits virtual assets from one person to another person or location by any means, then it most likely would qualify as a money transmitter and have the same AML/CFT obligations as a money transmitter offering services in fiat currency.[21] The degree to which a service is decentralized has no bearing on these obligations so long as the service meets this definition.

Industry claims there is insufficient regulatory clarity in this space. Industry often states that there is a lack of clarity on what qualifies as a security, with which regulators they must register, and whether their DeFi services meet the definition of a financial institution under the BSA or other regulatory frameworks. Industry has also publicly engaged Treasury for additional clarity on when the deployment of software becomes covered activity under the BSA. CFTC, FinCEN, and SEC contest the perception that there is insufficient regulatory clarity, pointing to guidance they

---

19. *See* 31 C.F.R. § 1020.210 (banks); 31 C.F.R. § 1021.210 (casinos and card clubs); 31 C.F.R. § 1022.210 (MSBs); 31 C.F.R. § 1023.210 (brokers or dealers in securities); 31 C.F.R. § 1024.210 (mutual funds); 31 C.F.R. § 1026.210 (futures commission merchants and introducing brokers in commodities). An AML Program must include, at a minimum, (a) policies, procedures, and internal controls reasonably designed to achieve compliance with the provisions of the BSA and its implementing regulations; (b) independent testing for compliance; (c) designation of an individual or individuals responsible for implementing and monitoring the operations and internal controls; and (d) ongoing training for appropriate persons. Rules for some financial institutions refer to additional elements of an AML Program, such as appropriate risk- based procedures for conducting ongoing customer due diligence.

20. *See* 31 C.F.R. § 1020.320 (banks); 31 C.F.R. § 1021.320 (casinos and card clubs); 31 C.F.R. § 1022.320 (MSBs), 31 C.F.R. § 1023.320 (brokers or dealers in securities), 31 C.F.R. § 1024.320 (mutual funds), and 31 C.F.R. § 1026.320 (futures commission merchants and introducing brokers in commodities). A suspicious transaction must be reported if it is conducted or attempted by, at, or through the financial institution and the amount involved exceeds a certain threshold.

21. *See* 31 C.F.R. 1010.100(ff)(5)(i). When DeFi services perform money transmission, the definition of money transmitter will apply to the DeFi service, the owners/operators of the DeFi service, or both. FinCEN, *FinCEN Guidance*, (May 9, 2019), https://www.fincen.gov/sites/default/files/2019-05/FinCEN%20Guidance%20CVC%20FINAL%20508.pdf, p. 18.

have issued over the last 10 years[22] and, with respect to the CFTC and SEC, enforcement actions against purported DeFi services that failed to comply with regulatory obligations.[23] Through public statements, guidance, and enforcement actions, these agencies have made clear that the automation of certain functions through smart contracts or computer code does not affect the obligations of financial institutions offering covered services.[24]

Further, DeFi services that are U.S. persons, like all other U.S. persons, wherever located, are required to comply with economic sanctions programs administered and enforced by Treasury's Office of Foreign Assets Control (OFAC), while non-U.S. persons also have OFAC sanctions compliance obligations in some circumstances. Sanctions compliance obligations are the same regardless of whether a transaction is denominated in virtual assets or traditional fiat currency.[25] Additionally, in 2021 OFAC issued "Sanctions Compliance Guidance for the Virtual Currency Industry,"[26] outlining sanctions compliance obligations, reporting requirements, and best practices. OFAC subsequently has issued several Frequently Asked Questions[27] related to sanctions compliance obligations and virtual assets.

Market Overview

Building Blocks of DeFi

In DeFi, financial products and services often use smart contracts and involve various tiers of technologies that interact with one another. For the purpose of this report, DeFi technology is presented in four "layers":

---

22. *See*, e.g., SEC, *Strategic Hub for Innovation and Financial Technology (FinHub)*, https ://*www.sec.gov/finhub*; SEC, Crypto Assets, https://www.investor.gov/additional-resources/spotlight/crypto-assets; FinCEN, *FinCEN Guidance*, (May 9, 2019), https://www.fincen.gov/sites/default/files/2019-05/FinCEN%20Guidance%20CVC%20FINAL%20508.pdf; SEC, *Leaders of CFTC, FinCEN, and SEC Issue Joint Statement on Activities Involving Digital Assets*, (October 11, 2019), *https://www.sec. gov/news/public-statement/cftc-fincen-secjointstatementdigitalassets*; FinCEN, *Application of FinCEN's Regulations to Persons Administering, Exchanging, or Using Virtual Currencies*, (March 18, 2013), https://www.fincen.gov/sites/default/files/shared/ FIN-2013-G001.pdf.

23. SEC, *Crypto Assets and Cyber Enforcement Action*, *https://www.sec.gov/spotlight/cybersecurity -enforcement-actions*.

24. *See*, e.g., SEC, *SEC Issues Investigative Report Concluding DAO Tokens, a Digital Asset, Were Securities*, (July 25, 2017), https://www.sec.gov/news/press-release/2017-131.

25. OFAC, *Frequently Asked Questions: Questions on Virtual Currency: 560*, https://home.treasury.gov/policy-issues/financial- sanctions/faqs/560.

26. Treasury, *Sanctions Compliance Guidance for the Virtual Currency Industry*, (October 2021), https://home.treasury.gov/ system/files/126/virtual_currency_guidance_brochure.pdf.

27. *See* e.g., OFAC, *Frequently Asked Questions:560*, (March 19, 2018), https://home.treasury. gov/policy-issues/financial- sanctions/faqs/560; OFAC, *Frequently Asked Questions: 646*, (October 15, 2021), https://home.treasury.gov/policy-issues/ financial-sanctions/faqs/5646; OFAC, *Frequently Asked Questions: 1021*, (March 11, 2022), https://home.treasury.gov/ policy-issues/financial-sanctions /faqs/1021.

The settlement tier—blockchains, including both Layer 1[28] and Layer 2[29] solutions, where the consensus state of the blockchain is maintained, i.e., where transactions are recorded, and participants and smart contracts have addresses that can hold virtual assets and interact with other participants and smart contracts.

The asset tier—virtual assets (coins and tokens) utilized in a DeFi service, including native tokens.

The protocol tier—code deployed to and executed on a blockchain, including smart contracts; this may also include auxiliary software.

The application tier—front-end user interfaces, application programming interfaces (APIs), and other code that allow participants to interact with the smart contracts and are primarily hosted off-chain.[30]

Market Participants and How They Operate

DeFi services often provide customers with the same services and products as traditional financial institutions, such as lending, borrowing, purchasing, or trading virtual assets, including assets that function as financial products like securities, commodities, derivatives, or others (*e.g.,* insurance). However, services specific to the virtual asset ecosystem, such as mixers (which functionally obfuscate the source, destination, or amount involved in a virtual asset transaction) and cross-chain bridges (which allow users to exchange virtual assets or information from one blockchain to another) may also purport to be decentralized.

There are likely thousands of entities offering DeFi services, although only a small number experience significant user activity[31] or have registered with regulators. One frequently cited data aggregator reportedly tracks over 2,000 DeFi services worldwide with a combined reported "total value locked" (TVL)[32] of $39.77 billion as of

---

28. Layer 1 refers to the settlement-layer blockchain.

29. Layer 2 solutions are software on networks running on top of the settlement-layer blockchain and designed to be interoperable with the underlying Layer 1 blockchain. These Layer 2 solutions allow for transactions to occur on a separate network and eventually be recorded on the applicable blockchain. For example, Layer 2 solutions that operate with Ethereum are often marketed as cheaper and faster than Layer 1 transactions. IOSCO, *IOSCO Decentralized Finance Report*, (March 2022), https://www.iosco.org/library/pubdocs/pdf/IOSCOPD699.pdf, footnote 7.

30. IOSCO, *IOSCO Decentralized Finance Report*, (March 2022), https://www.iosco.org/library/pubdocs/pdf/IOSCOPD699.pdf.

31. Treasury, *Crypto-Assets: Implications for Consumers, Investors, and Businesses*, (September 2022), https://home.treasury.gov/ system/files/136/CryptoAsset_EO5.pdf, *p. 11.*

32. TVL, an industry reported metric, is the amount of user funds deposited or "locked" in a DeFi service and is used as a measure to gauge the size of the DeFi market or the degree of adoption or acceptance by users. TVL information is not audited or verified, may double-count funds, and therefore may not be a reliable metric. *See* IMF, *Global Financial Stability Report: COVID-19, Crypto, and Climate* (2021), https://www.imf.org/en/Publications/GFSR/Issues/2021/10/12/global - financial-stability-report-october-2021.

December 19, 2022.[33] The most prominent category of DeFi services is services that facilitate the trading of virtual assets, often called decentralized exchanges[34] (DEXs). There are reportedly 649 separate DEXs with a combined $15.85 billion in reported TVL operating as of December 19, 2022.[35] Following DEXs, lending and borrowing DeFi services reportedly have the greatest TVL at $10.85 billion across 197 separate services; there are also reportedly 60 protocols that pay users a reward for staking[36] virtual assets on the service—so-called "yield protocols"—with over $8.66 billion in reported TVL.[37] The remaining services include cross-chain bridges, liquid staking, and algorithmic stablecoins, among others, most of which are explained in the table below.

While these statistics indicate that DeFi services are an important part of the virtual asset ecosystem, they account for only a relatively small portion of total activity in virtual asset markets. According to a separate data aggregator, the 24-hour volume of total virtual asset activity in early January 2023 was $29.7 billion, with DEXs accounting for only 3 percent of the volume.[38]

Select types of DeFi services and the services they offer are illustrated in the graphic below.

---

33. Defi Llama, *TVL Rankings*, https://defillama.com.

34. The use of the term "exchange" in this assessment does not indicate registration as such or any legal status of any such platform. This definition is for the purpose of the risk assessment and should not be interpreted as a regulatory definition under the BSA or other relevant regulatory regimes.

35. Defi Llama, *TVL Rankings*, https://defillama.com.

36. Staking virtual assets refers to putting up virtual assets as collateral in a proof of stake block-chain consensus mechanism. Staked virtual assets can be destroyed as a penalty for adding invalid transactions to the blockchain, but users who stake virtual assets receive rewards for validating transactions to the blockchain.

37. *Id.*

38. CoinGecko, *Top Decentralized Exchanges Ranked by 24H Trading Volume*, accessed on January 10, https://www.coingecko. com/en/exchanges/decentralized.

Table 1

Service	Service Providers Examples	Description
Trading	DEXs	Facilitate the exchange of virtual assets through an order book exchange or liquidity pools; take deposits into liquidity pools and pay out accrued interest or other fees. [39]
Lending and borrowing	Lending and borrowing DeFi Services	Allow holders of virtual assets to earn a fixed or variable return on assets by depositing them in a pool that simultaneously allows other participants to borrow those assets for other financial activity. [40] Relatedly, some services provide "staking as a service" in which the service accepts and stakes virtual assets to participate in a proof-of-stake consensus mechanism. Some services provide "liquid staking," in which the service accepts and stakes virtual assets for users and typically issues a "liquid staking derivative" virtual asset in exchange for the staked virtual asset. Users earn a portion of staking rewards or transaction fees.
Access Across Blockchains	Cross-Chain Bridges	Facilitate network interoperability by allowing users to exchange virtual assets or information from one blockchain to another.
Mixing	Decentralized Mixers	Functionally obfuscate the source, destination, or amount involved in a virtual asset transaction. These types of services may involve centralized or decentralized mechanisms and may be effectuated using several techniques. [41]

39. IOSCO, *IOSCO Decentralized Finance Report*, (March 2022), https://www.iosco.org/library/pubdocs/pdf/IOSCOPD699. pdf, p. 14.

40. *Id.*

41. FinCEN, *Ransomware Trends in Bank Secrecy Act Data Between January 2021 and June 2021*, (October 2021), https://www. fincen.gov/sites/default/files/2021-10/Financial%20Trend%20Analysis_Ransomeware%20508%20FINAL.pdf, p. 13.

Service	Service Providers Examples	Description
Aggregation	Aggregators	Query a range of DeFi services to collate the best terms for a trade or other activity for users, often viewable in a single user interface; some aggregators can route transactions to fulfill desired parameters. [42]
Provision of Off-Chain Information	Oracles	Connect a smart contract to "off-chain" data, such as stock prices or off-chain collateral value, that may be an input for that smart contract's functionality. [43]
Purportedly Stable Virtual Assets	Algorithmic Stablecoin Protocols	Purport to maintain a stable value via protocols that provide for the increase or decrease of the supply of the stablecoin in response to changes in demand. [44]

In DeFi services, the activities defined above are often enabled by liquidity pools, whereby users pool and lock their assets in the service's smart contract,[45] from which the DeFi service can source virtual assets for trading, lending, borrowing, and other financial services.

In the case of a DEX, liquidity pools are funded by participants who may be incentivized by a portion of fees collected by the DEX. Liquidity providers may receive a separate virtual asset from the service in exchange for locking in their assets, often referred to as a "liquidity provider token" (LP token) that entitles them to their portion of the pool, including any accrued fees.[46] Other users, accessing the liquidity pool through the DEX, can then exchange a certain quantity of one virtual asset for a certain quantity of another virtual asset. For these types of DEXs, the exchange

---

42. IOSCO, *IOSCO Decentralized Finance Report*, (March 2022), https://www.iosco.org/library /pubdocs/pdf/IOSCOPD699. pdf, pp. 15–16.

43. *Id.*, pp. 8, 33.

44. Financial Stability Board, *Regulation, Supervision, and Oversight of 'Global Stablecoin' Arrangements*, (October 13, 2020); Available at https://www.fsb.org/wp-content/uploads/P131020-3 .pdf.

45. As discussed in the custody section below in section 2.5, when users lock up assets in smart contracts, they hand over management of those assets to the smart contract and the smart contract code dictates how the asset can be transacted.

46. IOSCO, *IOSCO Decentralized Finance Report*, (March 2022), https://www.iosco.org/library /pubdocs/pdf/IOSCOPD699. pdf, p. 14.

rate between tokens is typically set by an algorithm. [47] Users often pay a fee to use the service, which is shared with LP token holders. Similarly, with liquid staking, users stake virtual assets with a DeFi service and receive a separate virtual asset in return, which represents the staked virtual assets and any accrued fees from the staking service validating transactions on the blockchain. Since LP tokens and virtual assets representing staked assets can be exchanged between different persons, it is possible for a different person than the user who original staked the asset to redeem the LP or other tokens for the assets that were initially locked in the liquidity pool.

Users may choose to trade assets via a DeFi service rather than a centralized exchange for several reasons. DEXs may purport to offer some efficiencies, such as convenient access to other DeFi services, access to a wide variety of virtual assets, or arbitrage opportunities, although in some instances they may only be able to do so because of non-compliance with applicable laws and regulations, including U.S. AML/CFT obligations and sanctions regulations. For example, when using a DEX, users are often not required to provide personal information, as typically required by many centralized exchanges that have AML/CFT and sanctions compliance programs in place. Other DeFi service users say they value the transparency of DeFi services operating on public blockchains, citing the ability to view and confirm transactions and, in many cases, view the source code of DeFi services.

Elements of Centralization

Although many services claim to be "fully decentralized," in practice there is a wide range of activity that exists on the spectrum between fully "centralized" and fully "decentralized" services. Where a service falls on this spectrum may be affected by, among other things, the governance structure of the DeFi service, access points to the service, and the settlement layer upon which the service is built. Additionally, DeFi services may seek to become more decentralized over the course of their development; for example, DeFi services often start as centralized projects with the intent of becoming more decentralized over time, and the reverse evolution is also possible.

In line with previous U.S. government reports, this risk assessment finds that DeFi services are in many cases decentralized more in name than in fact. Still, for DeFi services developed with opaque organizational structures, it can be more challenging to identify natural or legal persons responsible for the DeFi service.

Governance

Many DeFi services claim not to rely on a formal centralized governance structure, and organizers of DeFi services often claim to operate autonomously. In prac-

---

47. Carapella, Dumas, Gerszten, Wwem, and Wall, *Decentralized Finance (DeFi): Transformative Potential & Associated Risks*, Federal Reserve Bank of Boston, Working Paper, SRA 22-02, (September 8, 2022), https://www.federalreserve.gov/econres/ feds/files/2022057pap.pdf, p. 12.

tice, however, many DeFi services continue to feature governance structures (*e.g.*, management functions, fixing problems with the code, or altering the functionality of the smart contracts to some degree).

In some cases, an owner or an operator of the DeFi service retains an administrative key, which may enable the holder to alter or disable a DeFi service's smart contracts, depending on how

"In practice, however, many DeFi services continue to feature governance structures (*e.g.*, management functions, fixing problems with the code, or altering the functionality of the smart contracts to some degree)."

the contracts are written. In other cases, governance purports to be managed by a DAO, which can be described as a system of administration that aims to operate, in part, according to a set of encoded and transparent rules or smart contracts. DAO participants often claim that there is no central authority in a DAO and that governance is distributed across the participants. A DAO's governance token[48]—and DeFi governance (or voting) tokens in general—purport to allow disparate participants to introduce and vote on proposals determining the function of a blockchain or protocols. Governance tokens typically are tradeable on DEXs or centralized exchanges in exchange for fiat currency or other digital assets.

Governance token holders' powers and authorities vary across DeFi services. For example, in some cases, governance token holders may be permitted to vote to alter a DeFi service's smart contract, while in others, votes are more limited, such as only having the ability to vote on the process by which token holders can propose or vote on decisions or the amount of fees accrued by LP token holders. The process by which governance token holders can introduce and vote on decisions may also vary. For certain DeFi services, all governance token holders may be permitted to vote on a proposal, but only token holders that hold a specified percentage of tokens can submit proposals for a vote. The percentage of votes that constitutes passage of a decision, and the manner in which a decision is implemented, also vary by DeFi service. In some cases, decisions voted upon and approved are enacted automatically by smart contracts, while in others, owners or operators with administrative keys implement the decisions.

Moreover, distribution and concentration of governance tokens and voting demonstrate control over decentralized applications. In some services, governance tokens or voting rights may be concentrated and held by a limited number of actors. Developers and early investors in a DeFi service may keep control of the service by allocating significant shares of governance tokens to themselves or otherwise maintaining de facto control.[49] Concentration of influence within a DeFi service can also

---

48. IOSCO, IOSCO Decentralized Finance Report, March 2022, https://www.iosco.org/library/pubdocs/pdf/IOSCOPD699.pdf, p. 24.
49. See, e.g., Danny Nelson & Tracy Wang, Master of Anons: How a Crypto Developer Faked a DeFi Ecosystem, Coindesk (August 4, 2022), https:// www.coindesk.com/layer2/2022/08/04/master-

result from a low level of participation by governance token holders in voting, providing outsized voting power to the minority of token holders that do participate. Separately, some services allow for the delegation of voting rights associated with governance tokens to other persons, called delegates, while the token holder retains the economic benefits of the token.[50] In some cases, delegates accumulate significant voting rights associated with a large number of governance tokens, and this model can result in a relatively small number of delegates holding a large portion of voting power for a DeFi service.[51] Within this framework, the use of governance tokens does not necessarily equate to decentralization in decision making for the services, and the ownership of voting rights for many governance tokens can be highly concentrated.[52] As a result, in many cases a small number of persons may be able to exercise a high degree of control even if the governance structure purports to be decentralized.

The case of The DAO, a venture capital fund deployed in April 2016, demonstrates how the use of a DAO and perceived distribution of voting power does not necessarily correlate with decentralized decision making and may be subject to regulatory obligations despite a claim of decentralization.[53] In this example, the core group who deployed The DAO chose "Curators," who reviewed proposals prior to a vote, had ultimate discretion as to whether or not to submit a proposal for DAO Token holders, and could make changes to the voting process. The core group also advertised that it would submit the first proposal to The DAO. In light of these and other salient facts, the SEC determined that The DAO's investors relied on the managerial and entrepreneurial efforts of the core group and the Curators to manage The DAO and put forth project proposals that could generate profits for The DAO's investors. The facts and circumstances of that case supported an SEC determination that DAO tokens were securities, and that The DAO was an issuer of securities and required to register the offer and sale of DAO tokens.

The CFTC enforcement actions against bZeroX, LLC, its founders, and its successor entity Ooki DAO allege that individuals who participate in DAO governance

---

of-anons-how-a-crypto-developer-faked-a-defi- ecosystem. For further discussion of governance in decentralized finance, see Sirio Aramonte, Wenqian Huang & Andreas Schrimpf, supra note 29, at 27–29. See also Igor Makarov & Antoinette Schoar, Cryptocurrencies and Decentralized Finance (DeFi), The Brookings Institution, (2022), https://www.brookings.edu/wpcontent/uploads/2022/03/SP22_BPEA_ MakarovSchoar_conf-draf.pdf.

50. IOSCO, IOSCO Decentralized Finance Report, (March 2022), https://www.iosco.org/library/pubdocs/pdf/IOSCOPD699. pdf, p. 41.

51. *Id.*

52. One recent analysis found that among several major DAOs, less than 1% of token holders controlled 90% of the voting power. See Chainalysis, Dissecting the DAO: Web3 Ownership is Surprisingly Concentrated, (June 27, 2022), https://blog. chainalysis.com/reports/web3-daos-2022. Also, the amount of governance tokens a user must either own or be delegated to raise new proposals may be extremely high.

53. SEC, Report of Investigation Pursuant to Section 21(a) of the Securities Exchange Act of 1934: The DAO, (July 25, 2017), https://www.sec.gov/litigation/investreport/34-81207.pdf.

processes may be deemed to be members of an unincorporated association who can potentially be held personally liable for the association's debts. As set forth in greater detail below, the CFTC in September 2022 issued an order simultaneously filing and settling charges against bZeroX, LLC and its two founders for various violations of the Commodity Exchange Act (CEA) and related CFTC Regulations and, at the same time, filed a federal court lawsuit against the Ooki DAO alleging the same violations. As part of that case, among other things, the CFTC's order found that the Ooki DAO was an unincorporated association of which the two founding members were actively participating members and thus personally liable for the Ooki DAO's violations.[54] Similarly, in a federal court action, in upholding the CFTC's service on the Ooki DAO, the U.S. District Court for the Northern District of California held that the Ooki DAO had the capacity to be sued as an unincorporated association under applicable law.[55]

Application Layer

While users of DeFi services can conduct activities by engaging directly with the smart contracts on a blockchain, users usually rely on applications or websites that make interacting with DeFi services more user-friendly and can include analytics that can be used to inform transactions. In most instances, application developers are critical to DeFi services' usability. Application developers can have meaningful effects on the degree to which users are able to use a DeFi service effectively, even if they purport not to exercise "control" over the DeFi service's smart contracts or are not necessarily token holders who play a role in its governance structure. As one example, Polymarket, an online trading platform offering event-based binary options,[56] deployed smart contracts to support operation of its markets.[57] While users could transact directly with the smart contracts, in order to do so they needed to interface with Polymarket's website, as the underlier to

---

54. CFTC, CFTC Imposes $250,000 Penalty Against bZeroX, LLC and Its Founders and Charges Successor Ooki DAO for Offering Illegal, Off-Exchange Digital-Asset Trading, Registration Violations, and Failing to Comply with Bank Secrecy Act, (September 22, 2022), https://www.cftc.gov/PressRoom/PressReleases/8590-22.

55. CFTC v. Ooki DAO, No. 3:22-cv-05416-WHO, 2022 WL 17822445, at *5–12 (N.D. Cal. December 20, 2022).

56. According to the order, through its website, Polymarket offered the public the opportunity to "bet on your beliefs" by buying and selling binary options contracts related to an event taking place in the future that are susceptible to a "yes" or "no" resolution, such as: "Will $ETH (Ethereum) be above $2,500 on July 22?"; "Will the 7-day average COVID-19 case count in the U.S. be less than 15,000 for the day of July 22"; "Will Trump win the 2020 presidential election?". See CFTC, CFTC Orders Event-Based Binary Options Markets Operator to Pay $1.4 Million Penalty, (January 3, 2022), https://www. cftc.gov/PressRoom/PressReleases/8478-22.

57. CFTC, Order Instituting Proceedings Pursuant To Section 6(C) And (D) Of The Commodity Exchange Act, Making Findings, And Imposing Remedial Sanctions, (January 3, 2022), https://www.cftc.gov/media/6891/ enfblockratizeorder010322/download; see section 4.1 of this report for additional information on the CFTC's order filing and settled charges against Polymarket.

every Polymarket binary option—whether a political event or the future price of Bitcoin—was only specifically identifiable through the Polymarket website. As this case indicates, information provided via applications can thus be integral to transactions using DeFi infrastructure.

Settlement Layer

Blockchains can also vary in degrees of decentralization. Most blockchains on which DeFi services operate are permissionless, meaning that users require no prior approval to participate in network activities.[58] However, some blockchains have a limited number of participants in their consensus mechanism, often referred to as validators, to confirm the transactions that have taken place and post them to the blockchain. While a blockchain with a small number of validators can enable faster settlement time to the blockchain and potentially lower fees, it can also concentrate decision making for approving transactions. This could enable a small group of persons to make decisions about the types of transactions that are supported by the blockchain, including the ability to approve certain transactions, or the order in which transactions are settled. For example, persons with sufficient mining power or staked virtual assets[59] could prioritize their own transactions over others'. Even blockchains with hundreds of thousands of validators can experience concentration if a small group of persons commands a large portion of mining power, staked virtual assets, proposed transaction blocks, or other means of controlling the consensus mechanism.

Custody

Some DeFi services purport to allow users to self-custody their virtual assets through their own digital wallets, claiming that users retain control over their virtual assets during interactions with the DeFi service. The retention of the virtual asset by a user will depend, however, on the type of DeFi service with which the participant is engaging. In many DeFi services, users are required to deposit or lock their virtual assets in a smart contract. In some cases, an individual, group of individuals, or entity will retain an administrative key, as noted above, to that smart contract or otherwise be able to change the smart contract and, as such, may have effective control over participant assets.[60] For example, in the case of bZx DAO/Ooki DAO

---

58. President's Working Group on Financial Markets, the Federal Deposit Insurance Corporation, and the Office of the Comptroller of the Currency, Report on Stablecoins, (November 2021), https://home.treasury.gov/system/files/136/ StableCoinReport_Nov1_508.pdf, p. 13.

59. Mining power refers to the ability of validators in a proof of work model to complete mathematical computations, which requires expensive computer equipment and energy, to record and validate transactions to the blockchain. Generally, the larger amount of mining power or staked virtual assets a validator has, the more often they will be responsible for approving transactions to the blockchain and accruing transaction fees.

60. IOSCO, *IOSCO Decentralized Finance Report*, (March 2022), https://www.iosco.org/library/pubdocs/pdf/IOSCOPD699. pdf, pp. 22–23.

described above, the DAO was able to access and control the operation of, and funds held in, the relevant bZx Protocol smart contracts.[61] The use of the administration keys was determined by votes of DAO token holders.

3. Illicit Finance Threats

Illicit actors, including cyber criminals and fraudsters, abuse DeFi services to launder illicit proceeds. They also take advantage of cybersecurity weaknesses, compromising DeFi services to steal virtual assets. In particular, the DPRK, under pressure from U.S., European, and United Nations (UN) sanctions regime, increasingly steals virtual assets from both centralized VASPs and DeFi services. DPRK and other actors' abuse of DeFi services is explored in more detail below. This assessment does not specifically address the possible role of DeFi services in terrorist financing.

This risk assessment draws extensively on case examples Treasury identified and analyzed in its research. However, final adjudication and public discussion of cases often takes years to complete. Given how recently the DeFi market has developed and expanded, there were relatively few case examples that this assessment could include. The number of case studies does not, however, reflect the level of risk identified in this assessment. The risk assessment was also informed by consultations with several U.S. government Departments and Agencies and the over 75 responses to Treasury's September 2022 Request for Comment, which was issued in conjunction with the publication of the Action Plan (see Annex A on methodology).

Money Laundering

There have been several instances of actors, including ransomware actors, thieves, scammers, and drug traffickers, using DeFi services to transfer and launder their illicit proceeds. These actors use a variety of techniques and services to accomplish this, including exchanging virtual assets for other virtual assets that are easier to use in the virtual asset industry or less traceable, sometimes using cross-chain bridges to exchange virtual assets for others that operate on other blockchains; sending virtual assets through mixers; and placing virtual assets in liquidity pools as a form of layering. Steps that criminals take involving DeFi services may not be for the specific purpose of obfuscation but could instead be to move illicit proceeds generated from thefts from DeFi services. For the purpose of this report, this is considered in the section on money laundering, as it is part of an overall process to enable criminals to profit from their crimes. While the objective of the money laundering process by malign actors using DeFi services remains the same, criminals may use new means to do so, for example through chain hopping.

In many cases, criminals use DeFi services for these purposes without being required to provide customer identification information. This can make DeFi services

---

61. Complaint at ¶ 41.d, CFTC v. Ooki DAO, No. 3:22-cv-05416, ECF #1, (N.D. Cal. September 22, 2022).

more appealing to criminals than centralized VASPs, which are more likely to implement AML/CFT measures.

These laundering methods can create challenges for investigators attempting to trace illicit proceeds, and many actors will use more than one of the techniques below. The level of sophistication will likely depend on the individual actor's technical experience and familiarity with virtual assets and DeFi services. However, law enforcement has observed even lesser-skilled actors using some of the techniques below.

- **DEXs and Cross-Chain Bridges**: Often, illicit actors will use DeFi services, such as a DEX, to convert one virtual asset into a different virtual asset. As described above, this could be done for a variety of reasons, including to exchange into a more liquid asset that has higher trading volumes and is easier to cash out into fiat currency. This is similar to how illicit actors may exchange stolen funds in a lesser-used fiat currency for U.S. dollars, which are more widely accepted, or into another currency that allows them to evade U.S. sanctions. Criminals may also use DEXs to exchange virtual assets into another virtual asset that is compatible with a cross-chain bridge, mixer, or other DeFi service; to exchange one virtual asset for another with weaker illicit finance mitigation or less centralized control; or to exchange for an asset that is less traceable. Actors may choose to exchange their illicit proceeds for several different assets, sometimes using different DEXs to obtain better conversion rates and diversify their laundering methods. Illicit actors can also chain-hop, exchanging virtual assets on one blockchain for virtual assets on another, which could be done through a DEX or aggregator or by interacting directly with a cross-chain bridge. Chain-hopping can make it more difficult for competent authorities to trace financial transactions or for service providers to detect if incoming funds are tied to illicit activity. This is especially true if actors are using specific assets or blockchains that are more difficult to trace given current limits on blockchain analysis.

- **Mixers**: Criminals also use virtual asset mixers to functionally obfuscate the source, destination, or amount involved in a transaction. Mixers can accomplish this through a variety of mechanisms, including: pooling or aggregating virtual assets from multiple individuals, wallets, or accounts into a single transaction or transactions; splitting an amount into multiple amounts and transmitting the virtual assets as a series of smaller independent transactions; or leveraging code to coordinate, manage, or manipulate the structure of the transaction; among other methods.[62] Mixing services

---

62. These descriptions are for the purpose of this risk assessment and should not be interpreted as a regulatory description under the BSA or other relevant regulatory regimes.

may be advertised as a way to evade AML/CFT requirements and rarely, if ever, include the capacity and willingness to provide upon request to regulators or law enforcement the resulting transactional chain or information collected as part of the transaction. [63] As such, mixers can functionally simulate a customer depositing funds from an anonymous account into a financial institution's omnibus account and withdrawing funds into a separate anonymous account.

- **Liquidity Pools:** Illicit actors can place criminals' proceeds in a DeFi service's liquidity pool, where the assets provide liquidity to support trades on the service. As noted above, liquidity providers typically lock their virtual assets into the liquidity pool and may receive a portion of fees or some other type of return or interest created through the DeFi service.[64] By placing funds into liquidity pools, actors may generate funds from trading fees.

After criminals have layered the funds or converted them to the desired virtual assets using DeFi services, they may use centralized VASPs to exchange virtual assets for fiat currency. Often, these VASPs have weak or non-existent AML/CFT controls and operate or are incorporated or headquartered in jurisdictions that have not effectively implemented international AML/CFT standards for virtual assets.[65] In other cases, rather than exchanging for fiat currency, launderers may let their virtual assets sit unused in liquidity pools or unhosted wallets or use the virtual assets to fund future criminal activity directly. For example, cybercriminals can in some cases use virtual assets to purchase technological tools, infrastructure, or services to enable additional attacks or exploits.

The sections below explain in detail several of the key threats for which criminals have used DeFi services to profit from their illicit activity. In many of the examples below, illicit actors use DeFi services not only to launder or exchange illicit proceeds, but also to commit underlying predicate crimes through hacks and heists of DeFi service.

---

63. See e.g., Treasury, U.S. Treasury Issues First-Ever Sanctions on a Virtual Currency Mixer, Targets DPRK Cyber Threats, (May 6, 2022), https://home.treasury.gov/news/press-releases/jy0768; FinCEN, First Bitcoin "Mixer" Penalized by FinCEN for Violating Anti-Money Laundering Laws, (October 19, 2020), https://www.fincen.gov/news/news-releases/first-bitcoin-mixer-penalized-fincen-violating-anti-money-laundering-laws.

64. IOSCO, *IOSCO Decentralized Finance Report*, (March 2022), https://www.iosco.org/library/pubdocs/pdf/IOSCOPD699.pdf, p. 14.

65. FATF, Targeted Update On Implementation Of The FATF Standards On Virtual Assets And Virtual Asset Service Providers, (June 2022), https://www.fatf-gafi.org/media/fatf/documents/recommendations/Targeted-Update-Implementation-FATF%20Standards-Virtual%20Assets-VASPs.pdf.

Ransomware

The severity and sophistication of ransomware attacks has risen in recent years. [66] Ransomware is a national security priority and an area of significant concern to the U.S. government in terms of potential loss of life, financial effects, and critical infrastructure vulnerability. [67] A FinCEN analysis of SAR data found that reported ransomware-related incidents more than doubled in 2021 compared to 2020, with ransomware-related filings in 2021 approaching $886 million in value. [68] Ransomware actors have increasingly targeted larger enterprises to demand larger payouts, with a median ransomware-related payment amount of $135,000, based on the same analysis. [69] Ransomware actors can use DeFi services to exchange virtual assets from ransomware-related payments for other virtual assets and decentralized mixers to obfuscate the movement of funds. [70] For example, one blockchain analytics firm identified that one cross-chain bridge was used to launder ransomware proceeds from over 13 ransomware strains. According to this report, ransomware actors laundered over $50 million through the cross-chain bridge in the first half of 2022. [71]

Cybercriminals often use remote desktop protocol endpoints [72] and phishing campaigns to harvest credentials or otherwise gain access to a victim's computer network. [73] Ransomware actors have also shared resources, such as exploit kits, [74] or

---

66. See Internet Crime Complaint Center, Annual Reports, with (1) 2021 IC3 Annual Report, (2) 2020 IC3 Annual Report, (3) 2019 IC3 Annual Report, and (4) 2018 IC3 Annual Report.

67. Treasury, *National Money Laundering Risk Assessment*, (February 2022), https://home.treasury.gov/system/files/136/2022- National-Money-Laundering-Risk-Assessment.pdf; Treasury, Treasury Continues Campaign to Combat Ransomware As Part of Whole-of-Government Effort, (Oct. 15, 2021), https://home.treasury.gov/news/press-releases/jy0410; DOJ, *U.S. Government Launches First One-Stop Ransomware Resource at StopRansomware.gov*, (Jul. 15, 2021), https://www.justice.gov/ opa/pr/us-government-launches-first-one-stopransomware-resource-stopransomwaregov; FinCEN, *Advisory on Ransomware and the Use of the Financial System to Facilitate Ransom Payments*, (November 8, 2021), https://www.fincen.gov/sites/default/ files/2021-11/FinCEN%20Ransomware%20Advisory_FINAL_508_.pdf.

68. FinCEN, *Financial Trend Analysis: Ransomware Trends in Bank Secrecy Act Data Between July 2021 and December 2021*, (November 2022), https://www.fincen.gov/sites/default/files/2022-11 /Financial%20Trend%20Analysis_Ransomware%20 FTA%202_508%20FINAL.pdf, p. 2.

69. *Id.* at p. 6.

70. FinCEN, *Ransomware Trends in Bank Secrecy Act Data Between January 2021 and June 2021*, (October 2021), https://www.fincen. gov/; FinCEN, *Ransomware Trends in Bank Secrecy Act Data Between January 2021 and June 2021*, (October 2021), https://www. fincen.gov/sites/default /files/2022-11/Financial%20Trend%20Analysis_Ransomware%20FTA%202_508%20FINAL.pdf.

71. Elliptic, *The State of Cross-Chain Crime*, (October 4, 2022), https://www.elliptic.co/resources/state-of-cross-chain-crime-report, p. 26–27.

72. Remote Desktop Protocol is a proprietary network protocol that allows an individual to control the resources and data of a computer over the Internet; Federal Bureau of Investigation (FBI), *Cyber Actors Increasingly Exploit the Remote Desktop Protocol to Conduct Malicious Activity*, (September 27, 2018), https://www.ic3.gov/Media/Y2018/PSA180927.

73. Treasury, *Action Plan to Address Illicit Financing Risks of Digital Assets*, (September 2022), https://home.treasury.gov/system/ files/136/Digital-Asset-Action-Plan.pdf.

74. Exploit kits are toolkits that automate the identification and exploitation of client-side vulnerabilities.

formed partnerships with other cybercriminals to enhance the effectiveness of their attacks. Some ransomware developers sell access to their malware to affiliates in a "ransomware-as-a-service" model, thereby decreasing the barrier to entry and level of technical expertise required to conduct ransomware attacks. In addition, ransomware actors increasingly employ double extortion tactics, where criminals steal confidential data before encrypting it and threaten to publish the data if the victim does not pay the ransom.

Theft

In 2022, illicit actors stole billions of dollars' worth of virtual assets from VASPs, including DeFi services. DeFi services have been particularly lucrative for cybercriminals, accounting for a majority of stolen virtual assets in 2022, according to one blockchain analytics company.[75] Cyber criminals are increasingly exploiting vulnerabilities in the smart contracts governing DeFi services to steal virtual assets, causing investors to lose money.[76] Cyber criminals have sought to take advantage of investors' increased interest in virtual assets, as well as the complexity of cross-chain functionality and the open source nature of DeFi services. After stealing funds, cyber criminals often use the techniques discussed above to exchange and move stolen assets to maximize profits from the theft. For example, criminals that have stolen platform-specific assets, like governance tokens of small DeFi services, may look to quickly exchange the stolen assets for more liquid virtual assets using DeFi services to avoid detection and a loss in price if other token holders also decide to sell as a result of a breach. Types of thefts in the virtual asset space include security breaches, code exploits, and flash loan attacks, described below.

- In a **security breach**, an attacker penetrates a victim's security controls to conduct unauthorized transactions, including sending funds from a victim's account to one controlled by the hacker. The victim may be an individual or the blockchain firm itself, whose credentials may be compromised through phishing, key logging, or social engineering.

- In **code exploits**, hackers find vulnerabilities in the code of smart contracts and leverage them to remove funds from DeFi services without authorization. Hackers can also use the discovered vulnerabilities to carry out attacks against the service. The exploitation of code vulnerabilities may trigger immediate copycat hacks, such as those conducted by automated trading bots.[77]

---

75. TRM Labs, *DeFi, Cross-Chain Bridge Attacks Drive Record Haul from Cryptocurrency Hacks and Exploits*, (December 16, 2022), https://www.trmlabs.com/post/defi-cross-chain-bridge-attacks-drive-record-haul-from-cryptocurrency-hacks-and-exploits.

76. FBI, *Cyber Criminals Increasingly Exploit Vulnerabilities in Decentralized Finance Platforms to Obtain Cryptocurrency, Causing Investors to Lose Money*, (August 29, 2022), https://www.ic3.gov/Media/Y2022/PSA220829.

77. *See* e.g. The Block, *Polychain-backed DFX Finance hacked for $7.5 million*, (November 11, 2022), https://www.theblock.co/post/185796/polychain-dfx-finance-hacked.

- In a **flash loan**[78] **attack,** the attacker manipulates the logic of the underlying smart contract's code so that all technical requirements are met, and the transaction is posted to the blockchain despite the attacker paying back only a small portion (or none) of the principal loan. In some cases, the attacker uses the temporary surge of funds obtained in a flash loan to manipulate prices of virtual assets, often through the interaction of multiple DeFi services. This enables attackers to take over the governance of a smart contract or protocol, change the code, and drain the treasury in a very compressed timeframe.[79]

Case Examples

- In January 2023, the CFTC filed a civil enforcement action charging Avraham Eisenberg with a scheme to unlawfully obtain over $110 million in digital assets from Mango Markets, a purported decentralized digital asset exchange, through a price inflation scheme using "oracle manipulation."[80] The CFTC alleged that to accomplish the scheme, Eisenberg created two anonymous accounts on Mango Markets, which he used to establish large leveraged positions in a swap contract based on the relative value of MNGO, the "native" token of Mango Markets, and USDC, a stablecoin. Eisenberg then allegedly artificially pumped up the price of MNGO by rapidly purchasing substantial quantities of MNGO on three digital asset exchanges that were the inputs for the "oracle," or data feed, used to determine the value of Eisenberg's swap positions, resulting in a temporary, artificial spike in the value of Eisenberg's swap positions on Mango Markets. The CFTC alleged that Eisenberg then cashed out his illicit profits by using the artificially inflated value of his swaps as collateral to withdraw over $110 million in digital assets from Mango Markets. In a separate indictment filed in January 2023, the U.S. Attorney's Office for the Southern District of New York charged Eisenberg with commodities fraud, commodities market manipu-

---

78. "Flash loans" enable users to borrow, use, and repay virtual assets in a single transaction that is recorded on the blockchain in the same data block. Because there is no default risk associated with flash loans, users can borrow without posting collateral and without risk of being liquidated; Treasury, *Crypto-Assets: Implications for Consumers, Investors, and Businesses,* (September 2022), https ://home.treasury.gov/system/files/136/CryptoAsset_EO5.pdf, footnote 118.

79. *Id.,* footnote 118; *see also* Shaurya Malwa, *Solana DeFi Protocol Nirvana Drained of Liquidity After Flash Loan Exploit,* Coindesk (July 28, 2022), https://www.coindesk.com/tech/2022/07/28 /solana-defi-protocol-nirvana-drained-of-liquidity-afer-flash-loan-exploit.

80. CFTC, *CFTC Charges Avraham Eisenberg with Manipulative and Deceptive Scheme to Misappropriate Over $110 million from Mango Markets, a Digital Asset Exchange,* (January 9, 2023) https://www.cftc.gov/PressRoom/PressReleases/8647- 23#:~:text=The%20complaint%20alleges%20 that%20on,Mango%20Markets%2C%20which%20he%20used.

lation, and wire fraud.[81] Eisenberg was also charged by the SEC in connection with his alleged manipulation of the MNGO token.[82]

- In November 2022, the Department of Justice (DOJ) announced that James Zhong pled guilty to committing wire fraud in September 2012 when he unlawfully obtained over 50,000 Bitcoin from the Silk Road dark web internet marketplace. In September 2012, Zhong executed a scheme to defraud Silk Road of its money and property by (a) creating a string of approximately nine Silk Road accounts in a manner designed to conceal his identity; (b) triggering over 140 transactions in rapid succession in order to trick Silk Road's withdrawal-processing system into releasing approximately 50,000 Bitcoin from its Bitcoin-based payment system into Zhong's accounts; and (c) transferring this Bitcoin into a variety of separate addresses also under Zhong's control, all in a manner designed to prevent detection, conceal his identity and ownership, and obfuscate the Bitcoin's source.[83] As part of this process, Zhong allegedly pushed approximately 750 Bitcoin of the Silk Road crime proceeds through a decentralized Bitcoin mixer.[84] In November 2021, law enforcement seized over 50,000 Bitcoin from Zhong's home, which was then the largest cryptocurrency seizure in DOJ history and was the Department's second- largest financial seizure ever as of November 2022.[85]

Fraud and Scams

Multiple U.S. government agencies track and publish virtual asset-related complaints by the public, which have indicated a sharp increase in losses related to virtual assets.[86] Federal agencies have also issued warnings related to their findings, including noting a material increase in virtual assets as a payment method for all types of scams.[87] In fact, in 2021, the Federal Bureau of Investigation (FBI) Inter-

---

81. DOJ, *Alleged Perpetrator Of $100 Million Crypto Market Manipulation Scheme To Make Initial Appearance In The Southern District Of New York*, (February 2, 2023), https://www.justice.gov/usao -sdny/pr/alleged-perpetrator-100-million-crypto- market-manipulation-scheme-make-initial.

82. SEC, *Manipulating Mango Markets' "Governance Token" to Steal $116 Million of Crypto Assets*, (January 20, 2023), https:// www.sec.gov/news/press-release/2023-13.

83. DOJ, *U.S. Attorney Announces Historic $3.36 Billion Cryptocurrency Seizure And Conviction In Connection With Silk Road Dark Web Fraud*, (November 7, 2022), https://www.justice.gov/usao-sdny /pr/us-attorney-announces-historic-336-billion-cryptocurrency-seizure-and-conviction.

84. DOJ, *Affidavit in Support of Government's Forfeiture Motion, s1 14 Cr. 68 (LGS)*, (November 7, 2022), https://www.justice.gov/usao-sdny/press-release/file/1549821/download, p. 17.

85. DOJ, *U.S. Attorney Announces Historic $3.36 Billion Cryptocurrency Seizure And Conviction In Connection With Silk Road Dark Web Fraud*, (November 7, 2022), https://www.justice.gov/usao-sdny /pr/us-attorney-announces-historic-336-billion-cryptocurrency-seizure-and-conviction.

86. Treasury, *Crypto-Assets: Implications for Consumers, Investors, and Businesses*, (September 2022), https://home.treasury.gov/system/files/136/CryptoAsset_EO5.pdf, p. 25–26; *see* summarized statistics from the FBI, Consumer Financial Protection Bureau, and the Federal Trade Commission.

87. United States Secret Service, *Combating the Illicit Use of Digital Assets*, https://www.secret service.gov/investigation/DigitalAssets.

net Crime Complaint Center (IC3) reported that while the number of complaints associated with virtual assets decreased by approximately 3 percent in 2021, the loss amount reported in virtual asset-related IC3 complaints increased by nearly 600 percent, from $246 million in 2020 to more than $1.6 billion in 2021.[88] These schemes often result in significant losses for the victims.

These scams are committed by a variety of actors and use an assortment of techniques, including "rug pulls" and "pig butchering" schemes.

- In a **"rug pull,"** a scammer raises investments funds in a seemingly legitimate project before ending the project and stealing invested funds. Rug pulls may involve scammers creating and contributing to a liquidity pool in a DeFi service in the form of a new virtual asset, often a stablecoin. One form of a rug pull is executed when, after a creator promotes the asset to investors to increase the demand and thereby increase the price of the virtual asset, the creator withdraws their contributions from the liquidity pool abruptly, causing the price of the new virtual asset to crash. Rug pulls may also involve restrictions on investors selling assets or may involve the coding of an explicit, malicious backdoor into a new virtual asset smart contract that enables the developer to pull out assets from a liquidity pool all at once.[89]

- **"Pig Butchering"** is where scammers initiate and develop relationships with victims and pressure them to invest in fake investment platforms that enable the scammer to steal invested funds.[90] These scammers encounter victims on dating apps, social media websites, or even text messages sent to appear inadvertently sent to the wrong number. After a scammer has developed trust with their target over a period of weeks or months, they will introduce the idea of making an investment using virtual assets and use confidence-building techniques to convince victims that they are investing in a legitimate virtual asset opportunity. A common iteration of the scam directs users to access fraudulent investment websites through virtual asset wallet applications where vulnerabilities are exploited to provide full access and control of victims' wallets to the scammers.

---

88. FBI, *2021 Internet Crime Report*, (2021), https://www.ic3.gov/Media/PDF/AnnualReport/2021_IC3Report.pdf.

89. Financial Stability Oversight Council (FSOC), *Report on Digital Asset Financial Stability Risks and Regulation*, (2022), https://home.treasury.gov/system/files/261/FSOC-Digital-Assets-Report-2022.pdf, p. 32.

90. DOJ, *Court Authorizes the Seizure of Domains Used in Furtherance of a Cryptocurrency "Pig Butchering" Scheme*, (November 21, 2022), https://www.justice.gov/usao-edva/pr/court-authorizes-seizure-domains-used-furtherance-cryptocurrency-pig- butchering-scheme; FINRA, Pig Butchering Scams: What They Are and How to Avoid Them," (December 13, 2022), https://www.finra.org/investors/insights/pig-butchering-scams.

Case Examples

- In June 2022, the DOJ and law enforcement partners announced that Le Anh Tuan, 26, a Vietnamese national, was charged with one count of conspiracy to commit wire fraud and one count of conspiracy to commit international money laundering in the Central District of California in connection with a scheme involving the "Baller Ape" non-fungible token (NFT).[91] Tuan allegedly was involved in the Baller Ape Club, an NFT investment project that purportedly sold NFTs in the form of various cartoon figures, often including the figure of an ape. According to the indictment, shortly after the first day Baller Ape Club NFTs were publicly sold, Tuan and his co-conspirators engaged in a "rug pull," ending the purported investment project, deleting its website, and stealing the investors' money. Based on blockchain analytics, shortly after the rug pull, Tuan and his co-conspirators allegedly laundered investors' funds through "chain-hopping," a form of money laundering in which one type of coin is converted to another type and funds are moved across multiple cryptocurrency blockchains and used decentralized cryptocurrency swap services to obscure the trail of Baller Ape Club investors' stolen funds. In total, Tuan and his co-conspirators allegedly obtained approximately $2.6 million from investors.

- In March 2022, the DOJ, Internal Revenue Service-Criminal Investigation, Department of Homeland Security, and the U.S. Postal Inspection Service announced that Ethan Nguyen and Andre Llacuna were charged in a criminal complaint with conspiracy to commit wire fraud and conspiracy to commit money laundering, in connection with an alleged million-dollar scheme to defraud purchasers of NFTs advertised as "Frosties." Rather than providing the benefits advertised to Frosties NFT purchasers, Nguyen and Llacuna allegedly transferred the cryptocurrency proceeds of the scheme to various cryptocurrency wallets under their control.[92] As alleged in the criminal complaint, after the Frosties NFT sale was publicly denounced as a fraud on social media, substantial amounts of Ether (ETH) were sent from wallets associated with the defendants to Tornado Cash smart contracts. Those smart contracts later transferred ETH to a wallet address that ultimately deposited the funds into wallets owned by the defendants.

---

91. DOJ, *Justice Department Announces Enforcement Action Charging Six Individuals with Cryptocurrency Fraud Offenses in Cases Involving Over $100 Million in Intended Losses*, (June 30, 2022), https://www.justice.gov/usao-cdca/pr/justice-department- announces-enforcement-action -charging-six-individuals-cryptocurrency.

92. DOJ, *Two Defendants Charged In Non-Fungible Token ("NFT") Fraud And Money Laundering Scheme*, (March 24, 2022), https://www.justice.gov/usao-sdny/pr/two-defendants-charged-non -fungible-token-nft-fraud-and-money-laundering-scheme-0; https://www.justice.gov/usao-sdny /press-release/file/1486846/download.

Drug Trafficking

Drug trafficking organizations are growing more comfortable with darknet markets[93] and the use of virtual assets generally to launder funds, including increased use of DeFi services, according to law enforcement assessments and analysis by blockchain analytic firms. For example, one blockchain analytics company identified that drug-focused darknet markets generated nearly $2 billion in virtual assets in 2021 through sales, representing a steady increase in revenue since 2018.[94] Still, the size and scope of drug proceeds generated on the darknet and laundered via virtual assets remain low in comparison to cash-based retail street sales.[95] In addition to darknet market sales in drugs, law enforcement assesses that certain drug traffickers are increasingly converting fiat currency proceeds into virtual assets for laundering.[96]

Proliferation Finance

Under pressure from robust U.S. and UN sanctions, the DPRK has resorted to illicit activities, including cyber-enabled heists from VASPs and other financial institutions, to generate revenue for its unlawful weapons of mass destruction (WMD) and ballistic missile programs.[97] The U.S. government has observed DPRK cyber actors targeting organizations in the virtual asset industry, including DeFi services (see text box below).[98] For example, on March 23, 2022, the Lazarus Group, a U.S.-sanctioned, DPRK state-sponsored cyber hacking group, carried out the largest virtual assets heist to date, worth almost $620 million, from a blockchain project linked to the online game Axie Infinity.[99] The group also stole $100 million worth

---

93. DOJ, *International Law Enforcement Operation Targeting Opioid Traffickers on the Darknet Results in 150 Arrests Worldwide and the Seizure of Weapons, Drugs, and over $31 Million*, (October 26, 2021), https://www.justice.gov/opa/pr/international- lawenforcement-operation-targeting-opioid-trafickers-darknet-results-p. 150.

94. Chainalysis, *The 2022 Crypto Crime Report*, p. 100.

95. DOJ, *International Law Enforcement Operation Targeting Opioid Traffickers on the Darknet Results in 150 Arrests Worldwide and the Seizure of Weapons, Drugs, and over $31 Million*, (October 26, 2021), https://www.justice.gov/opa/pr/international- lawenforcement-operation-targeting-opioid-trafickers-darknet-results-p. 150.

96. United Nations Office on Drugs and Crime, *World Drug Report 2021: Global Overview: Drug Demand Drug Supply*, (June 2021), https://www.unodc.org/res/wdr2021/field/WDR21_Booklet_2.pdf, p. 76.

97. Treasury, *U.S. Treasury Issues First-Ever Sanctions on a Virtual Currency Mixer, Targets DPRK Cyber Threats*, (May 6, 2022), https://home.treasury.gov/news/press-releases/jy0768.

98. CISA, *TraderTraitor: North Korean State-Sponsored APT Targets Blockchain Companies*, (April 18, 2022), https://www.cisa.gov/uscert/ncas/alerts/aa22-108a.

99. FBI, *FBI Statement on Attribution of Malicious Cyber Activity Posed by the Democratic People's Republic of Korea*, (April 14, 2022), https://www.fbi.gov/news/press-releases/fbi-statement-on-attribution-of-malicious-cyber-activity-posed-by-the-democratic-peoples-republic-of-korea; Treasury, *Treasury Designates DPRK Weapons Representatives*, (November 8, 2022), https://home.treasury.gov/news/press-releases/jy1087.

of virtual assets from a cross- chain bridge called Horizon.[100] In addition to heists, DPRK-linked actors are involved in other illicit activity related to virtual assets, including ransomware attacks[101] and the use of virtual asset applications modified to include malware to facilitate the theft of virtual assets.[102] DPRK has also dispatched thousands of highly skilled internet technology (IT) workers around the world who often take on projects involving virtual assets. These IT workers earn revenue for the DPRK that contributes to its weapons programs, and the privileged access these workers gain as contractors can enable DPRK's malicious cyber intrusions or support DPRK money laundering activities.[103] The U.S. government has observed DPRK actors using the techniques described above to launder the illicit proceeds from these activities.

---

100. Treasury, *U.S. Treasury Issues First-Ever Sanctions on a Virtual Currency Mixer,* Targets DPRK Cyber Threats, (May 6, 2022), https://home.treasury.gov/news/press-releases/jy0768; FBI, *FBI Confirms Lazarus Group Cyber Actors Responsible for Harmony's Horizon Bridge Currency Theft,* (January 23, 2023), https://www.fbi.gov/news/press-releases/fbi-confirms-lazarus-group-cyber-actors-responsible-for-harmonys-horizon-bridge-currency-theft.

101. Cybersecurity and Infrastructure Security Agency (CISA), *North Korean State-Sponsored Cyber Actors Use Maui Ransomware to Target the Healthcare and Public Health Sector,* (July 6, 2022), https://www.cisa.gov/uscert/ncas/alerts/aa22-187a.

102. CISA, *AppleJeus: Analysis of North Korea's Cryptocurrency Malware,* (February 17, 2021), https://www.cisa.gov/uscert/ncas/alerts/aa21-048a.

103. Department of State, Treasury, and FBI, *Guidance on the Democratic People's Republic of Korea Information Technology Workers,* (May 16, 2022), https://home.treasury.gov/system/files/126/20220516_dprk_it_worker_advisory.pdf.

> ### TraderTraitor: North Korean State-Sponsored Advanced Persistent Threat (APT) Targets Blockchain Companies, Including DeFi Protocols
>
> The FBI, the Cybersecurity and Infrastructure Security Agency (CISA), and Treasury issued a joint Cybersecurity Advisory (CSA) to highlight the cyber threat associated with virtual asset thefts and tactics used by a DPRK state-sponsored APT group[104] since at least 2020.[105] The U.S. government has observed DPRK cyber actors targeting a variety of organizations in the blockchain technology and virtual asset industry, including virtual asset exchanges, DeFi protocols, play-to-earn virtual asset video games, cryptocurrency trading companies, venture capital funds investing in virtual assets, and individual holders of large amounts of virtual assets or valuable NFTs. The activity described in the advisory involves social engineering of victims using a variety of communication platforms to encourage individuals to download trojanized virtual asset applications on Windows or Mac operating systems. The cyber actors then use the applications to gain access to the victim's computer, propagate malware across the victim's network environment, and steal private keys or exploit other security gaps. These activities enable additional follow-on activities that initiate fraudulent blockchain transactions.

Case Example

In November 2022, OFAC redesignated Tornado Cash under E.O. 13722 and E.O. 13694, as amended, for its role in enabling malicious cyber activities that ultimately support the DPRK's WMD program. Tornado Cash, an entity that provides virtual asset mixing services, obfuscated the movement of over $455 million worth of virtual assets stolen in March 2022 by the OFAC- designated, DPRK-controlled Lazarus Group, in the largest known virtual currency heist to date. Malicious cyber actors subsequently used the Tornado Cash smart contracts to launder more than $96 million of funds derived from the June 24, 2022 Harmony Bridge Heist and at least $7.8 million from the August 2, 2022 Nomad Heist.[106]

In connection with the November 2022 action, OFAC stated that sanctions were applied to the entity known as Tornado Cash and that Tornado Cash uses computer

---

104. [104] This group is commonly tracked by the cybersecurity industry as Lazarus Group, APT38, BlueNoroff, and Stardust Chollima.

105. [105] CISA, *TraderTraitor: North Korean State-Sponsored APT Targets Blockchain Companies*, (April 18, 2022), https://www.cisa. gov/uscert/ncas/alerts/aa22-108a.

106. [106] Treasury, *Treasury Designates DPRK Weapons Representatives*, (November 8, 2022), https://home.treasury.gov/news/press-releases/jy1087.

code known as "smart contracts" to implement its governance structure, provide mixing services, offer financial incentives for users, increase its user base, and facilitate the financial gain of its users and developers. OFAC also explained that Tornado Cash's organizational structure consists of: (1) its founders and other associated developers, who together launched the Tornado Cash mixing service, developed new Tornado Cash mixing service features, created the Tornado Cash DAO, and actively promoted the platform's popularity in an attempt to increase its user base; and (2) the Tornado Cash DAO, which is responsible for voting on and implementing new features created by the developers.[107]

4. Vulnerabilities

Non-Compliant DeFi Services in the United States

DeFi services at present often do not implement AML/CFT controls or other processes to identify customers, allowing layering of proceeds to take place instantaneously and pseudonymously, using long strings of alphanumeric characters rather than names or other personally identifying information. DeFi services engaged in activity covered by the BSA have AML/CFT obligations, and all DeFi services subject to U.S. jurisdiction have sanctions compliance obligations, regardless of their status as covered financial institutions. When these entities fail to register with the appropriate regulator, fail to establish and maintain sufficient AML/CFT controls, or do not comply with sanctions obligations, criminals are more likely to exploit their services successfully, including to circumvent U.S. and UN sanctions.

Despite these requirements, several DeFi projects have affirmatively touted a lack of AML/CFT controls as one of the primary goals of decentralization. For instance, one VASP announced in 2021 that it would transition from a traditional corporate structure into a DAO for the purpose of ceasing to collect customer information for AML/CFT compliance, although in practice this would not have impacted the service's BSA obligations.[108] Similarly, founders of an unregistered FCM argued that transitioning to a DAO would insulate the FCM from U.S regulatory oversight and accountability for compliance with U.S. law. These examples indicate that the lack of compliance may be due in part to gaps in common views between industry and regulators of how relevant laws and regulations, including securities, commodities, and money transmission regulations, apply to DeFi services. The assessment recog-

---

107. [107] OFAC, *Frequently Asked Questions: 1095*, (November 8, 2022), https://home.treasury .gov/policy-issues/financial-sanctions/faqs/added/2022-11-08.

108. [108] *See* Gary Silverman, *Cryptocurrency: Rise of Decentralized Finance Sparks 'Dirty Money' Fears*, Financial Times (September 15, 2021), https://www.ft.com/content/beeb2f8c-99ec-494b -aa76-a7be0bf9dae6; William Foxley, *ShapeShift Is Going Full DeFi to Lose KYC Rules*, Coindesk (January 6, 2021), https://www.coindesk.com/ business/2021/01/06/shapeshift-is-going-full-defi-to -lose-kyc-rules/; DOJ, *The Report of the Attorney General Pursuant to Section 5(b)(iii) of Executive Order 14067: The Role Of Law Enforcement In Detecting, Investigating, And Prosecuting Criminal Activity Related To Digital Assets*, (September 2022), https://www.justice.gov/d9/2022-12/The%20 Report%20 of%20the%20Attorney%20General%20Pursuant%20to%20Section.pdf, p. 10.

nizes that the public nature of the blockchain and the role of centralized VASPs in accessing fiat currency can partially mitigate this and other vulnerabilities. They are explored further with other mitigation measures in sections 5.2 and 5.3, respectively.

Regulators have pursued cases against DeFi services operating in the United States that failed to register with the appropriate regulators and failed to implement the requisite AML/CFT program for the services they provide.

Case Example

- As discussed above, the CFTC in September 2022 issued an order simultaneously filing and settling charges against a company, bZeroX LLC, and its two founders for illegally offering leveraged and margined retail commodity transactions in digital assets; engaging in activities only registered FCMs can lawfully perform; and failing to adopt a customer identification program as part of a BSA compliance program, as required of FCMs.[109] Simultaneously, the CFTC filed a federal civil enforcement action in the U.S. District Court for the Northern District of California charging a DAO—the successor to the original company that operated the same software protocol—with violating the same laws as the original company and founder. Neither the original company nor the DAO maintained a required customer identification program, and the lack of AML measures was explicitly advertised as a positive feature of the service.

  As part of the case, the CFTC's order found that bZeroX transferred control of the Protocol to the bZx DAO, which is now doing business as the Ooki DAO. By transferring control to a DAO, bZeroX's founders touted to bZeroX community members the operations would be enforcement-proof, allowing the Ooki DAO to violate the CEA and CFTC regulations with impunity, as alleged in the federal court action. The CFTC order found the DAO was an unincorporated association of which the two founding members were actively participating members and liable for the Ooki DAO's violations of the CEA and CFTC regulations. Similarly, in the federal court action, in upholding the CFTC's service on the Ooki DAO, the U.S. District Court for the Northern District of California held that the Ooki DAO had the capacity to be sued as an unincorporated association under applicable law.[110]

---

109. CFTC, *CFTC Imposes $250,000 Penalty Against bZeroX, LLC and Its Founders and Charges Successor Ooki DAO for Offering Illegal, Off-Exchange Digital-Asset Trading, Registration Violations, and Failing to Comply with Bank Secrecy Act*, (September 22, 2022), https://www.cftc.gov/PressRoom/PressReleases/8590-22.

110. *CFTC v. Ooki DAO*, No. 3:22-cv-05416-WHO, 2022 WL 17822445, at *5–12 (N.D. Cal. Dec. 20, 2022).

- The CFTC in January 2022 entered an order filing and simultaneously settling charges against a Delaware-registered company for offering off-exchange event-based binary options contracts and failure to obtain designation as a designated contract market or registration as a swap execution facility.[111] The company created, defined, and resolved the contracts for the event-based binary option markets offered through its website and recorded on the blockchain. Market participants could open accounts only with an email address and a username and fund their "Polymarket Wallets" for trading with an Ethereum-based "stablecoin" cryptocurrency pegged to the value of the U.S. dollar. To operate its markets, the company deployed smart contracts, which are programmable self-executing contracts hosted on a blockchain. While users could transact directly with the smart contracts, in order to understand the definition of the event market contract with which they are transacting, they needed to interface with Polymarket's website, which was owned and operated by the Delaware corporation with its headquarters in New York and made available to U.S. customers.

- In August 2021, the SEC charged two individuals and their Cayman Islands-based company for unregistered sales of more than $30 million in securities using smart contracts and so-called DeFi technology and for misleading investors concerning the operations and profitability of their business "DeFi Money Market."[112] The SEC's order found that the respondents used smart contracts to sell two types of digital tokens: one that could be purchased using specified digital assets and that paid a given percent interest, and another so-called "governance token" that purportedly gave holders certain voting rights, a share of excess profits, and the ability to profit from token resales in the secondary market. The order found that the two types of tokens were offered and sold as securities and that respondents had violated the registration and anti-fraud provisions of the federal securities laws. The order also found that the respondents misrepresented how the company was operating, violating the SEC's anti-fraud provisions, and publicly touted that they required no "Know Your Customer" documentation. Without admitting or denying the findings in the order, the respondents consented to a cease-and-desist order, including disgorgement totaling more than $12 million and penalties of $125,000 for each of the individual respondents.

In some cases, the lack of a clear organizational structure may make it difficult to identify any person, group of persons, or entity operating a DeFi service, whether

---

111. CFTC, *CFTC Orders Event-Based Binary Options Markets Operator to Pay $1.4 Million Penalty*, (January 3, 2022), https://www.cftc.gov/PressRoom/PressReleases/8478-22.

112. SEC, *SEC Charges Decentralized Finance Lender and Top Executives for Raising $30 Million Through Fraudulent Offerings*, (August 6, 2021), https://www.sec.gov/news/press-release/2021-145.

because no such person exists or because of distributed, poor, or purposefully confusing organization. This poses critical challenges for conducting supervision and, when appropriate, enforcement against DeFi services that are not fulfilling their AML/CFT obligations.[113] This challenge can be compounded by the fast pace of change in the virtual asset industry, the large and growing number of DeFi services, and limited resources at some regulatory agencies.[114]

Disintermediation

Many virtual assets can be self-custodied and transferred without the involvement of an intermediary financial institution, which can be referred to as disintermediation. For example, users of unhosted wallets can retain custody of and transfer their virtual assets without the involvement of a regulated financial institution. Many DeFi services claim to be disintermediated by enabling automated P2P transactions without the need for an account or custodial relationship. Whether an entity operating in the DeFi space is a covered financial institution under the BSA depends on specific facts and circumstances surrounding its financial activities. To the extent a DeFi service falls outside the current definition of a financial institution under the BSA, a vulnerability may exist due to the reduced likelihood that such DeFi services would choose to implement AML/CFT measures like assessing illicit finance risks, establishing an AML program, or reporting suspicious activity. In cases in which a DeFi service falls outside of the scope of the BSA, this can result in gaps in suspicious activity reporting and limit authorities' collection of and access to information critical to supporting financial investigations. A DeFi service's claim that it is or plans to be "fully decentralized" does not impact its status as a financial institution under the BSA.

Cross-Border Nature and Gaps in AML/CFT Regimes across Countries

The 2022 NRAs identified that the most significant illicit financing risk associated with virtual assets stemmed from VASPs operating abroad with substantially deficient AML/CFT programs, particularly in jurisdictions where AML/CFT standards for virtual assets are nonexistent or not effectively implemented. This remains a key vulnerability with DeFi services, as DeFi services may fall under the VASP definition established by the FATF.

---

113. DOJ, *The Report of the Attorney General Pursuant to Section 5(b)(iii) of Executive Order 14067: The Role Of Law Enforcement In Detecting, Investigating, And Prosecuting Criminal Activity Related To Digital Assets*, (September 2022), https://www. justice.gov/d9/2022-12/The%20 Report%20of%20the%20Attorney%20General%20Pursuant%20to%20Section.pdf, p. 10.

114. Treasury, *National Strategy for Combating Terrorist and Other Illicit Financing*, (May 2022), https://home.treasury.gov/ system/files/136/2022-National-Strategy-for-Combating-Terrorist-and-Other-Illicit-Financing.pdf, p. 14 ("Significant resource constraints at FinCEN, the IRS, and state and territorial financial regulators have materially affected their ability to effectively supervise and examine certain non-bank financial institutions, which may include those posing higher risk").

Uneven and often inadequate regulation and supervision internationally allows illicit actors to engage in regulatory arbitrage, which is compounded by the nearly instantaneous and borderless nature of virtual asset transfers. This potentially exposes the U.S. financial system to VASPs, including some DeFi services, with deficient or nonexistent AML/CFT controls operating abroad. VASPs may choose to operate in jurisdictions with minimal or nonexistent AML/CFT requirements, weak supervision of their legal frameworks, or both. Of 53 jurisdictions that FATF assessed as of June 2022, four years after the FATF amended the standards to apply to virtual assets and VASPs, the majority still require significant improvements on implementing these standards.[115] Of the assessed jurisdictions, 33 have received partially compliant ratings, and 8 have received non-compliant ratings. Additionally, less than half of jurisdictions that responded to a FATF-administered voluntary survey in March 2022 had introduced a licensing or registration regime for virtual assets and VASPs.

Given that many countries are still in the early stages of developing AML/CFT regimes for virtual assets and VASPs, few jurisdictions likely have assessed the risks associated with DeFi services, considered how they could fit into their regulatory regime, and allocated supervisory and enforcement resources for the virtual asset sector. In particular, jurisdictions have highlighted that they face challenges attempting to identify which DeFi entities should be regulated and how to consistently enforce national obligations that implement the FATF standards for such entities.[116]

Additionally, some VASPs claim not to have a headquarters or jurisdiction in which they are subject to regulatory obligations, including AML/CFT requirements. This is the case with several DeFi services that purport to have distributed governance models. Other VASPs have adopted a distributed organizational architecture under which they register in one country, have personnel in a second country, and offer services in several countries with different legal and regulatory approaches to virtual assets. For example, some countries' AML/CFT regimes apply if a DeFi service offers services to customers or operates within their jurisdiction. In other places, the key factor that triggers licensing or registration is whether the jurisdiction is the primary location in which business is performed, where business books or records physically reside, or otherwise. Differences and gaps in these approaches can complicate regulation, supervision, and enforcement, which often require considerable cooperation amongst authorities.

---

115. FATF, *Targeted Update On Implementation Of The FATF Standards On Virtual Assets And Virtual Asset Service Providers*, (June 2022), https://www.fatf-gafi.org/media/fatf/documents/recommendations/Targeted-Update-Implementation-FATF%20Standards-Virtual%20Assets-VASPs.pdf.

116. *Id.*, p. 20.

Cyber-Related Vulnerabilities

DeFi services are often particularly vulnerable to large-scale thefts due to a combination of factors, including aggregation of large amounts of funds, the lack of requirements for cybersecurity and audits in the DeFi space, concentrated administrator rights, and the availability of open-source code for DeFi services' smart contracts. As noted above, these vulnerabilities can be exploited by hackers through security breaches, code exploits, and flash loan attacks. The documented efforts of nation-state cyber groups or other illicit actors to steal or fraudulently acquire money, including virtual assets, present a national security concern. The noted cybersecurity gaps of DeFi services leave their operations vulnerable to theft and fraud, which also present risks for consumers and the virtual asset industry.

- Cross-chain bridges in particular can be attractive targets for hackers because they often feature a central storage point of funds that back the bridged assets on the receiving blockchain.[117] Regardless of how those funds are stored—locked up in a smart contract or with a centralized custodian—that storage point can become a target. For similar reasons, the treasuries and liquidity pools of DeFi services are also common targets.

- Secure code development is a difficult undertaking even in the best of circumstances, and large software firms may struggle to deploy secure products. Conversely, DeFi services are usually small enterprises that operate in a market without binding or normative requirements for cybersecurity. While some services perform code audits, there is a lack of standardization in audits, and several DeFi services have been exploited even after claiming successful audits. To educate users and DeFi service developers about these vulnerabilities, in August 2022 the FBI published a public service announcement recommending that users research DeFi services; ensure that the services have conducted audits; and be aware of risks posed by crowdsourced solutions to vulnerability identification and patching.[118] The announcement encouraged DeFi services to institute real-time analytics, monitoring, and rigorous testing of code to identify and respond to vulnerabilities and to develop and implement, when appropriate, an incident response plan. Per the text box above, the U.S. government issued a Cybersecurity Advisory in April 2022 about the DPRK targeting virtual asset

---

117. Chainalysis, *Vulnerabilities in Cross-chain Bridge Protocols Emerge as Top Security* Risk, (August 2, 2022), https://blog. chainalysis.com/reports/cross-chain-bridge-hacks-2022/; TRM Labs, DeFi, *Cross-Chain Bridge Attacks Drive Record Haul from Cryptocurrency Hacks and Exploits*, (December 16, 2022), https://www.trmlabs.com/post/defi-cross-chain-bridge-attacks-drive-record -haul-from-cryptocurrency-hacks-and-exploits.

118. FBI, *Cyber Criminals Increasingly Exploit Vulnerabilities in Decentralized Finance Platforms to Obtain Cryptocurrency, Causing Investors to Lose Money*, (August 29, 2022), https://www.ic3.gov /Media/Y2022/PSA220829.

firms, which provided information on tactics, techniques, and procedures and indicators of compromise to stakeholders in the virtual asset industry to identify and mitigate cyber threats.[119]

- As discussed above, the administration of a DeFi service's infrastructure may be more concentrated than advertised, enabling the targeting of an individual or small group with administrator rights to compromise the entire network.[120]

- Many DeFi services purport to make their code viewable to the public, which can increase transparency and users' confidence in the services and enable viewers to identify opportunities for code improvement. This can also, however, provide opportunities for cybercriminals to review the code and identify potential exploits to enable theft or other misuses.[121] This vulnerability can be compounded if the smart contracts are not written carefully or if they lack a mechanism for quick deactivation or alternations if a critical exploit is identified. As such, it is critical that the DeFi service identify and address vulnerabilities and potential exploits in open-source code. Depending on the particular factual circumstances, however, such code exploits may not always map neatly onto the elements of the criminal statutes used most often in fraud or computer intrusion cases, especially in instances where the code itself allows for the exploitation to take place.[122]

The public availability of many DeFi services' source code also presents the opportunity for other persons to reuse the code in smart contracts for a separate DeFi service. This could lead to widespread exploits if code reused in multiple DeFi services contains vulnerabilities. It also means that persons can "fork" the smart contracts, creating a clone of a DeFi services' source code, potentially with some modifications. As such, even if a DeFi service or related persons were subject to enforcement or law enforcement actions and required to cease operations, another person could simply "copy and paste" the code to re-constitute the DeFi service. Additionally, the original DeFi service source code could continue running and be

---

119. CISA, *TraderTraitor: North Korean State-Sponsored APT Targets Blockchain Companies*, (April 18, 2022), https://www.cisa. gov/uscert/ncas/alerts/aa22-108a.

120. To gain access to four out of the five validating nodes necessary to take control of the Ronin Bridge network and steal $620 million worth of cryptocurrency, DPRK-associated persons sent a PDF file containing malware to a single engineer; Cnet.com, A *Fake Job Offer Reportedly Led to Axie Infinity's $600 Million Hack*, (July 6, 2022), https://www.cnet.com/personal- finance/crypto/a-fake -job-offer-reportedly-led-to-axie-infinitys-600m-hack/.

121. DOJ, *The Report of the Attorney General Pursuant to Section 5(b)(iii) of Executive Order 14067: The Role Of Law Enforcement In Detecting, Investigating, And Prosecuting Criminal Activity Related To Digital Assets*, (September 2022), https://www.justice.gov/ d9/2022-12/The%20 Report%20of%20the%20Attorney%20General%20Pursuant%20to%20Section.pdf, p. 10.

122. *Id.*

available for use unless there is a person willing and able to deactivate it. The utility of the source code and re-constituted services, however, could be limited by a lack of liquidity or users.

5. Mitigation Measures

The U.S. government's assessments of risk take into consideration the effect of mitigating measures, including regulation, supervision, and enforcement. The below section explains regulatory frameworks at the global and domestic levels for DeFi services. It also explores the mitigating effects of elements specific to the virtual asset and DeFi ecosystem, including the transparency of public blockchains, the role of centralized VASPs to access fiat currency, and potential industry solutions. The assessment finds that these measures may partially mitigate illicit finance risks but do not sufficiently address the identified vulnerabilities.

Regulatory Frameworks

The AML/CFT regulatory framework in the United States, discussed above in section 2.2, is a foundational mitigation measure to address illicit finance risks associated with DeFi services that are operating in the United States. Additionally, work in international forums, in particular the FATF, can also play an important role in developing standards and promoting implementation of those standards to address illicit finance risks associated with DeFi services.

FATF

In 2018, the FATF revised its standards to apply similar rules for virtual assets and VASPs as those in existence for other kinds of financial services providers.

In 2019 and again in 2021 the FATF further elaborated on these standards in guidance. In its 2021 Updated Guidance for a Risk-based Approach for Virtual Assets and VASPs ("Updated Guidance"), FATF examined how virtual assets activities and VASPs, including some DeFi services, fall within the scope of the FATF Standards. With regards to DeFi services, the FATF clarified that the software programs themselves are not VASPs under the FATF Standards, meaning that the standards do not apply to underlying software or technology. However, the Updated Guidance highlighted that DeFi services often have a central party with some measure of involvement or control, such as creating and launching a virtual asset, developing service functions and user interfaces for accounts holding an administrative "key," or collecting fees. In such cases, DeFi services may fall under the FATF definition of a VASP and therefore have AML/CFT obligations. In particular, the Updated Guidance emphasizes that, since DeFi services are often not decentralized in practice, marketing terms or self-identification as a DeFi service or the specific technology involved do not determine if its owner or operator is a VASP. Still, under the FATF standards, DeFi services that lack an entity with sufficient control or influence over the service may not be explicitly subject to AML/

CFT obligations under the FATF standards,[123] which could lead to potential gaps for DeFi services in other jurisdictions.

Public Blockchain Transparency

As noted above, transactions involving DeFi services often occur on the public blockchain, which means that any person with access to the internet can view the pseudonymous transaction data in a public ledger for the blockchain. Because most DeFi services also conduct transactions using smart contracts that are settled on the blockchain rather than through an internal order book or ledger, the pseudonymous transaction information is viewable and traceable on a blockchain's public ledger.

Public ledgers can support investigations by competent authorities in tracing the movement of illicit proceeds. While the ledgers do not contain names or traditional account identifiers associated with any particular address, regulators and law enforcement can in some cases take viewable pseudonymous user and transaction information and pair it with other pieces of information to identify transaction participants. The transparency of blockchains can complicate attempts to move or obfuscate funds even pseudonymously.[124] For instance, a wallet address publicly identified with a hack may be the subject of intense public scrutiny, making it hard to launder proceeds in that wallet, even though its owner remains unknown. Financial institutions, regulatory agencies, and law enforcement may use multiple complementary third-party tools to identify, trace, and attribute virtual asset transactions on most virtual asset blockchains.[125] Currently, these tools support hundreds of virtual assets and use clustering algorithms, web scraping, scam database monitoring, and other methods to enable an investigator to link and attribute a wide range of transactions to real-world individuals and entities.[126] The tools can generate transaction graphs, which allow users to visualize and present complex associations. Records from the blockchain have been admitted as evidence in court cases, and blockchain analysis was determined to be a reliable foundation for probable cause for a search warrant application.[127] Blockchain analytics can also be a useful tool for the private sector to provide information on risk, support a risk-based approach

---

123. The FATF standards that apply to all individuals (like targeted financial sanctions) would still apply to DeFi services, regardless of structure.

124. Treasury, *Action Plan to Address Illicit Financing Risks of Digital Assets*, (September 2022), https://home.treasury.gov/system/ files/136/Digital-Asset-Action-Plan.pdf, p. 6.

125. DOJ, *The Report of the Attorney General Pursuant to Section 5(b)(iii) of Executive Order 14067: The Role Of Law Enforcement In Detecting, Investigating, And Prosecuting Criminal Activity Related To Digital Assets*, (September 2022), https://www.justice.gov/ d9/2022-12/The%20 Report%20of%20the%20Attorney%20General%20Pursuant%20to%20Section.pdf, p. 32

126. *Id.*

127. *In the Matter of the Search of Multiple Email Accounts Pursuant to 18 U.S.C. § 2703 for Investigation of Violation of 18 U.S.C. § 1956 et al.*, Case No. 20-sc-3310 (D.D.C.), (August 26, 2021), https://www.dcd.uscourts.gov/sites/dcd/ files/20sc3310-Opinion.pdf.

to compliance, and review customer activity at onboarding and on a periodic or event-triggered basis.[128]

However, there are some limitations to relying on public blockchain information and tracing to mitigate illicit finance risks in the DeFi space. First, as noted above, the data on the public blockchain is pseudonymous. While regulators, law enforcement, and public blockchain companies can in some cases identify transaction participants, they may in other cases only have the participants' wallet addresses without additional identifying information. Additionally, users can obfuscate the tracing of transactions on the public blockchain through the use of mixers, cross-chain bridges, or anonymity-enhanced cryptocurrencies (AECs), which can create challenges for blockchain tracing. Second, blockchain tracing and analytics often require an initial identified illicit transaction or address as a starting point, although new tools are able to identify potentially suspicious activity based on blockchain data. Third, critical activities in a DeFi service can occur off-chain and there are challenges to locating and obtaining this data.

Moreover, several virtual asset industry participants are exploring measures to increase privacy for virtual asset transactions, including the use of Layer 2 technology, or private blockchains, for which public ledgers will not be viewable and block-chain tracing will not be applicable. While the U.S. government supports privacy enhancing technologies that simultaneously allow for or even promote compliance with AML/CFT obligations, the use of non-public blockchains by entities that do not comply with AML/CFT obligations or services that may fall outside current regulations will heighten AML/CFT risks.

Finally, licenses to use blockchain for tracing are expensive and require extensive training, and as noted above, these blockchain tracing tools use methods for analyzing transaction data that may not apply to all blockchains or virtual assets, meaning the industry has a lack of visibility into transactions involving those blockchains or virtual assets.[129]

Use of Centralized VASPs as On- and Off-Ramps

While DeFi users may need to access centralized VASPs to exchange virtual assets for fiat currency to buy goods and services, reliance on AML/CFT programs of centralized VASPs only partially mitigates the risks associated with non-compliant

---

128. FinCEN, *Prepared Remarks of Alessio Evangelista, Associate Director, Enforcement and Compliance Division, During Chainalysis Links Conference,* (May 19, 2022), https://www.fincen.gov /news/speeches/prepared-remarks-alessio-evangelista-associate-director-enforcement-and -compliance; Treasury, *Sanctions Compliance Guidance for the Virtual Currency Industry,* (October 2021), https://home.treasury.gov/system/files/126/virtual_currency_guidance_brochure.pdf, p. 16.

129. DOJ, *The Report of the Attorney General Pursuant to Section 5(b)(iii) of Executive Order 14067: The Role Of Law Enforcement In Detecting, Investigating, And Prosecuting Criminal Activity Related To Digital Assets,* (September 2022), https://www.justice.gov/ d9/2022-12/The%20 Report%20of%20the%20Attorney%20General%20Pursuant%20to%20Section.pdf, pp. 43–44.

DeFi services. Many centralized VASPs are themselves non-compliant with international AML/CFT standards and often based in jurisdictions with weak or non-existent AML/CFT requirements. Additionally, there are identified cases of centralized VASPs that are subject to the requirements of the BSA yet fail to implement the requisite AML programs for the services they provide.[130] Moreover, even a centralized VASP with a strong AML program may face challenges in tracing virtual assets when users have leveraged DeFi services to obfuscate the source of funds.

While centralized VASPs are currently needed as on- and off-ramps for many transactions, further adoption of virtual assets may reduce this necessity in the future. At present, most merchants and businesses and many financial institutions do not accept virtual assets as a means of payment, and consumers often cannot use virtual assets to pay for goods and services. As such, virtual asset users often need to exchange virtual assets for fiat currency to buy goods and services, and DeFi service users frequently require centralized VASPs to access fiat currency. Still, the ability to use virtual assets to pay for goods and services is increasing.[131] While some merchants may use third-party services that have AML/CFT obligations, the growing use of virtual assets as payment for goods and services could decrease the role of centralized VASPs.

The U.S. government will continue efforts to improve implementation of international AML/CFT standards abroad and compliance by VASPs with AML/CFT and sanctions obligations in the United States and abroad. However, the present reliance on centralized VASPs to comply with AML/CFT and sanctions obligations is not likely to sufficiently mitigate illicit finance risks associated with DeFi services.

Potential Industry Solutions

Several entities in the virtual asset industry are developing AML/CFT and sanctions compliance solutions for DeFi services or other tools that could be used to mitigate illicit finance risks associated with DeFi. Technological innovation of this kind could potentially bolster the accessibility, transparency, and security of the U.S. financial system, but most tools remain too nascent for definitive conclusions on

---

130. *See* e.g., Treasury, *Settlement Agreement between the U.S. Department of the Treasury's Office of Foreign Assets Control and Payward, Inc. ("Kraken")*, https://home.treasury.gov/policy-issues/financial-sanctions/recent-actions/20221128; (November 28, 2022), Treasury, *Treasury Announces Two Enforcement Actions for over $24M and $29M Against Virtual Currency Exchange Bittrex, Inc.*, (October 11, 2022), https://home.treasury.gov/news/press-releases/jy1006; FinCEN, *First Bitcoin "Mixer" Penalized by FinCEN for Violating Anti-Money Laundering Laws*, (October 19, 2020), https://www.fincen.gov/ news/news-releases/first-bitcoin-mixer-penalized-fincen-violating-anti-money-laundering-laws.

131. Bitpay and PYMNTS.com, *Paying with Cryptocurrency: What Consumers and Merchants Expect from Digital Currencies*, (June 2022), https://www.pymnts.com/wp-content/uploads/2022/06/PYMNTS-Paying-With-Cryptocurrency-June-2022. pdf; Deloitte, *Merchants Getting Ready for Crypto: Merchant Adoption of Digital Currency Payments Survey*, (2022), https://www2.deloitte.com/content/dam/Deloitte/us/Documents/technology/us-cons-merchant-getting-ready-for-crypto.pdf.

their promise. Many potential solutions are designed to support various elements of compliance with AML/CFT obligations while maximizing user privacy, including through digital identity technology to support identity verification by DeFi services that can be informed by a user's transaction history on the public blockchain. Zero-knowledge proofs[132] can also enable a DeFi service user to confirm that their identity has been verified without revealing personal information. Industry solutions may also enable illicit finance risk mitigations to be integrated into smart contract code, such as restricting transaction frequency; placing threshold limits for certain customer types; or using oracles[133] to screen against virtual asset wallet addresses appearing on sanctions lists and to prevent sanctioned addresses from using a DeFi service. While some of these solutions may be applicable to the broader virtual asset ecosystem and financial system, DeFi services may provide an interesting use case given the use of smart contracts and the wealth of data available via the public blockchain. Such solutions could support compliance with BSA and sanctions obligations for obliged DeFi services but could also be used voluntarily by DeFi services not subject to AML/CFT obligations to mitigate risks.

It is important to note, however, that criminals likely will seek to take advantage of gaps in potential solutions, and many tools require further technical development and adjustments to meet AML/ CFT requirements. As such, it will be critical for relevant virtual asset entities to consider and address potential illicit finance risks before launch. Private sector firms and developers have raised questions—some of which are still to be addressed—about how to effectively meet AML/CFT and sanctions compliance obligations, and public-private sector engagement will play a critical role in the development of these solutions. Treasury is working to improve the overall effectiveness of the AML/CFT regulatory framework and sanctions compliance programs in the virtual asset space and will engage with the private sector to support responsible innovation in the DeFi space.

6. Conclusion, Recommended Actions, and Posed Questions

This risk assessment finds that criminals use DeFi services to profit from illicit activity, in particular ransomware, theft, scams, drug trafficking, and proliferation finance.

Key factors, such as non-compliant DeFi services, disintermediation, a lack of implementation of the international AML/CFT standards in foreign countries, and cybersecurity weaknesses in DeFi services, continue to pose vulnerabilities that enable criminal use of DeFi services to profit from illicit activity. While existing regulatory frameworks, transparency afforded by the public blockchain, the role of

---

132. A cryptographic scheme where a prover is able to convince a verifier that a statement is true, without providing any more information than that single bit (that is, that the statement is true rather than false); National Institute of Standards and Technology, *Glossary: Zero-Knowledge Proof*, https://csrc.nist.gov/glossary/term/zero_knowledge_proof.

133. *See* Table 1 for definition of "oracle."

centralized VASPs in the virtual asset ecosystem, and industry solutions can partially mitigate some of these vulnerabilities, the identified vulnerabilities still pose residual illicit finance risks associated with DeFi services. This report recognizes, however, that illicit activity is a subset of overall activity within the DeFi space and, at present, the DeFi space remains a minor portion of the overall virtual asset ecosystem. Moreover, money laundering, proliferation financing, and terrorist financing most commonly occur using fiat currency or other traditional assets as opposed to virtual assets.

Treasury has identified the following areas for further work to address these risks.

Recommended Actions

- **Strengthen U.S. AML/CFT Supervision of Virtual Asset Activities:** The U.S. government should work to strengthen existing supervisory and enforcement functions to increase and harmonize compliance with AML/CFT and other regulatory requirements, including for DeFi services with BSA obligations. As part of this effort, regulators should conduct additional outreach to industry to further explain how applicable regulations apply to DeFi services, in line with previously issued regulations and guidance. Based on feedback from industry, regulators should also consider taking additional regulatory actions and issuing additional guidance to provide further clarity.

- **Assess Possible Enhancements to the U.S. AML/CFT Regulatory Regime as Applied to DeFi Services:** Treasury will continue to evaluate the U.S. AML/CFT requirements to ensure that the U.S. framework effectively safeguards the U.S. financial system from all manner of threats and illicit financial activity, whether facilitated by fiat currency or virtual assets. The assessment recommends enhancing the U.S. AML/CFT regime as applied to DeFi services by closing any identified gaps in the BSA to the extent that they allow certain DeFi services to fall outside the scope of the BSA's definition of financial institutions.

- **Continue Research, Private Sector Engagement to Support Understanding of Developments in DeFi Ecosystem:** DeFi services have the potential to become more or less decentralized over the course of their evolution; for example, they often start out as centralized projects with decentralization as an end goal. The U.S. government should continue to monitor any changes in the DeFi ecosystem that could affect illicit finance risks or the application of AML/CFT obligations to entities in the space. The U.S. government should do this through research and engagement with the private sector.

- **Continue to Engage with Foreign Partners:** The U.S. government will continue working with foreign partners bilaterally and through multilateral fora to close gaps in implementation of the international standards with regards to virtual assets and VASPs. This will include sharing the findings of this report and encouraging partners to assess illicit finance risks associated with DeFi services and to develop and implement mitigation measures. Additionally, the United States at the FATF will press for immediate implementation of the FATF standards and advocate for FATF members to continue to monitor developments in DeFi and facilitate dialogue and mutual support on common AML/CFT implementation challenges, risk assessments, and good practices.

- **Advocate for Cyber Resilience in Virtual Asset Firms, Testing of Code, and Robust Threat Information Sharing**: The United States should continue to advocate for DeFi services to institute real time analytics, monitoring, and rigorous testing of code in order to more quickly identify vulnerabilities and respond to indicators of suspicious activity. The U.S. government should continue to, as available and appropriate, share information with virtual asset firms and the public about potential threats and mitigation measures that firms can take to improve defenses.

- **Promote Responsible Innovation of Mitigation Measures:** Several entities in the virtual asset industry are developing AML/CFT solutions for DeFi services or other tools that could be used by the virtual asset industry to mitigate illicit finance risks associated with DeFi. The U.S. government should engage with developers, including through tech sprints and potentially with research and development grants, to promote innovation that seeks to mitigate the illicit finance risks of DeFi services. Policymakers and regulators should also seek and assess necessary changes in regulation or guidance to support these developments.

Posed Questions

The questions posed below will be considered as part of the recommended actions above, and Treasury welcomes public input on these questions.

- What factors should be considered to determine whether DeFi services are a financial institution under the BSA?

- How can the U.S. government encourage the adoption of measures to mitigate illicit finance risks, such as those identified in Section 5.4 of the report, including by DeFi services that fall outside of the BSA definition of financial institution?

- The assessment finds that non-compliance by covered DeFi services with AML/CFT obligations may be partially attributable to a lack of understanding of how AML/CFT regulations apply to DeFi services. Are there additional recommendations for ways to clarify and remind DeFi services that fall under the BSA definition of a financial institution of their existing AML/CFT regulatory obligations?

- How can the U.S. AML/CFT regulatory framework effectively mitigate the risks of DeFi services that currently fall outside of the BSA definition of a financial institution?
- How should AML/CFT obligations vary based on the different types of services offered by DeFi services?

Annex A: Methodology

This report incorporates published and unpublished research and analysis, insights, and observations of managers and staff from U.S. government agencies. In drafting this assessment, the Treasury's Office of Terrorist Financing and Financial Crimes (TFFC) consulted with staff from the following U.S. government agencies, who also reviewed this report:

- Department of Homeland Security
  - Homeland Security Investigations
  - U.S. Secret Service
- Department of Justice
  - Criminal Division
    - Money Laundering and Asset Recovery Section
    - National Cryptocurrency Enforcement Team
    - Executive Office for U.S. Attorneys
  - Drug Enforcement Administration
  - Federal Bureau of Investigation
  - Virtual Asset Unit
- Department of State
  - Bureau of Economics and Business Affairs
- Department of the Treasury
  - Domestic Finance
  - Internal Revenue Service Criminal Investigations
  - International Affairs
  - Office of Terrorism and Financial Intelligence
    - FinCEN
    - OFAC
    - Office of Intelligence and Analysis
- Staff of the federal functional regulators[134]

---

134. This includes staff of the CFTC, the Office of the Comptroller of the Currency (OCC), and the SEC.

The authors of this report conducted several meetings with U.S. government operational agencies and used open-source reporting from Treasury's risk assessments, open-source reporting from the DOJ, and available court documentation.[135] The risk assessment was also informed by consultations with several U.S. government Departments and Agencies and the over 75 responses to Treasury's Request for Comment, which was issued in conjunction with the publication of the "Action Plan to Mitigate Illicit Finance Risks of Digital Assets"

The terminology and methodology of this risk assessment are based in part on the guidance of the FATF, the international standard-setting body for AML/CFT safeguards. The following concepts are used in this risk assessment:

- **Threats**: For purposes of this assessment, threats are the predicate crimes that are associated with money laundering as well as individuals or entities, or activity undertaken by those individuals and entities, with the potential to cause a defined harm. The environment in which predicate offenses are committed and the proceeds of crime are generated is relevant to understanding why, in some cases, specific crimes are associated with specific money laundering methods.

- **Vulnerabilities**: Vulnerabilities are what facilitate or create the opportunity for misuse of DeFi services to transfer or move funds to launder the proceeds of crime, finance terrorism, or acquire materiel or support revenue generation for WMD programs. They may relate to a specific financial sector or product or a weakness in law, regulation, supervision, or enforcement.

- **Consequences**: Consequences include harms or costs inflicted upon U.S. citizens and the effect on the U.S. economy, which provide further context on the nature of the threats.

- **Risk**: Risk is a function of threat, vulnerability, and consequence. It represents an overall assessment, taking into consideration the effect of mitigating measures including regulation, supervision, and enforcement.

Discussion Points

1. *DeFi.* How does the Department of Treasury define "decentralized finance"? Do you think DeFi companies fall under the Bank Secrecy Act's definition of a financial institution? Why or why not?

2. *Regulation.* Are DeFi companies currently regulated? How can a DeFi platform be regulated if it is completely decentralized? In your opinion, should

---

135. The charges contained in an indictment are merely allegations. All defendants are presumed innocent unless, and until, proven guilty beyond a reasonable doubt in a court of law.

a government agency regulate DeFi companies, or should Congress set forth laws to regulate them? Why?

3. Discuss the regulatory challenges and gaps identified in the report that relate to decentralized finance.

4. Analyze the role of decentralized exchanges (DEXs) in facilitating illicit finance and money laundering.

5. To what extent do the current regulatory frameworks address the illicit finance risks posed by decentralized finance?

Seven

Stablecoins

I. Introduction

Stablecoins are a form of digital currency whose value is pegged to the value of one or more other assets—the "stable" reserve assets. The type of asset can be anything from fiat, precious metals, another cryptocurrency, or even an algorithm. More often, the prices are pegged to a reserve asset like the U.S. dollar. Tying a coin to an asset like fiat or precious metals makes the coin more stable, less speculative, and much less volatile. An organization seeking to tie a coin to an asset must set up a reserve. The reserve acts as collateral for the coin and is directly tied to the coin so that one unit of the asset is represented by one coin.

There are four types of stablecoins: fiat-collateralized, crypto-collateralized, non-collateralized, and commodity-collateralized.

Fiat-collateralized. Fiat-collateralized stablecoins are attached to fiat-currency or real-world currency, like the U.S. dollar, Yen, Euro, Pound, etc. An example of this is Tether, which is backed by the US dollar, or Gemini, which is built on Ethereum and also backed by the U.S. dollar.

Crypto-collateralized. Crypto-collateralized stablecoins maintain the 1:1 ratio by being backed by other cryptocurrencies.

Commodity-collateralized. Commodity-collateralized stablecoins are backed by precious metals such as gold, or commodities, such as oil. One example is Digix, which is backed to gold. This means that 1 Digix is equal to 1 gram of gold on the ETH network.

Non-collateralized. Non-collateralized stablecoins are a type of stablecoin that is not backed by any asset, but uses an algorithm to adjust the supply or demand of the stablecoin.

Discussion Points

1. *Compare and contrast.* Compare the characteristics of stablecoins to Bitcoin. How are they different? How are they similar? Which do you think is better for consumers?

2. *Is it less volatile?* Does the fact that stablecoins are pegged to fiat currency make them less volatile than cryptocurrencies such as Bitcoin?

3. *Classification.* How should stablecoins be classified for regulatory purposes? Should stablecoins be considered bank deposits? Which regulatory agency should oversee stablecoins? The OCC? The CFTC? Why?

II. Centralized Reserves

Verification of an organization's reserve is exceedingly challenging. Establishing whether the reserve in fact exists and that it does contain the collateral necessary to back the coin is no easy feat because there is no real transparency.

In the Matter of Investigation by Letitia James, Attorney General of the State of New York, of iFinex Inc., BFXNA, Inc., Tether Holdings Limited, Tether Operations Limited, Tether Limited, Tether International Limited

Attorney General of the State of New York Investor Protection Bureau

SETTLEMENT AGREEMENT

1. The Office of the Attorney General of the State of New York ("OAG") commenced an investigation pursuant to New York General Business Law § 352 *et. seq.* (the "Martin Act") and Executive Law § 63(12) regarding fraud in connection with the Bitfinex trading platform and related matters. On April 24, 2019, the OAG filed a proceeding in Supreme Court, New York County pursuant to Section 354 of the Martin Act, seeking a court order to enjoin certain conduct by iFinex Inc., BFXNA Inc., BFXWW Inc. (collectively, "Bitfinex"), and Tether Holdings Limited, Tether Operations Limited, Tether Limited, and Tether International Limited (collectively, "Tether"), including the transfer of certain funds between the entities; enjoining the destruction of documents and communications relevant to the investigation; and ordering production of certain documents and information. That order was granted. *In re: James v. iFinex, et al.*, Index No. 450545/2019 (Apr. 24, 2019), *aff'd* 2020 N.Y. Slip Op. 03880 (July 9, 2020).

2. This Settlement Agreement contains the findings of the OAG's investigation and the relief agreed to by the OAG, Bitfinex, and Tether, whether acting through their respective directors, officers, employees, representatives, agents, affiliates, or subsidiaries (collectively, the "Parties").

3. The OAG finds that the conduct set forth herein violated the Martin Act and Executive Law § 63(12).

4. The OAG finds the relief and agreements contained in this Settlement Agreement appropriate and in the public interest. Therefore, the OAG is willing to accept this Settlement Agreement pursuant to Executive Law § 63(15), in lieu of commencing a statutory proceeding for violations of the Martin Act and Executive Law § 63(12), based on the conduct described below.

5. Bitfinex and Tether neither admit nor deny the OAG's findings set forth below.

OAG's FINDINGS

I. Bitfinex and Tether

6. Bitfinex operates an online platform for exchanging and trading virtual currency. Users access the Bitfinex trading platform and place orders through its website, available at www.bitfinex.com, through an associated Application Programming Interface ("API"), or via over-the-counter services. Bitfinex also provides users with the ability to store their virtual currency and transfer their holdings to a different trading platform. Bitfinex is one of the relatively few virtual currency trading platforms that allows traders to deposit and withdraw so- called "fiat" currency, including U.S. dollars, euros, pounds, and yen. Traders using the Bitfinex platform can deposit dollars with Bitfinex, convert them to virtual currency at the rates offered by Bitfinex, trade the virtual currency they have purchased, convert their virtual currency holdings back into dollars, and withdraw the funds. For that reason, it is important that Bitfinex has sufficient U.S. dollars on hand to fill withdrawal orders submitted by traders.

7. Prior to August 2017, Bitfinex had few geographical restrictions with respect to who could access its trading platform, meaning that New York-based users were able to create accounts, fund them with U.S. dollars, convert into virtual currency, trade, and withdraw funds. In August 2017, Bitfinex announced it would no longer permit U.S.-based users to access the trading platform, but U.S.-based business entities were still permitted to trade. In August 2018, Bitfinex's announced exclusion of U.S.-based individual users was expanded to include all U.S.- based entities, except those entities or organizations that maintained an incorporation address outside of the United States, and met other qualifications.

8. The primary function of Tether the company is as the issuer of a virtual currency also called "tether," a so-called "stablecoin," a term used to describe a virtual currency that is always supposed to have the same real-dollar value. In the case of tethers, one tether is always supposed to be valued at one U.S. dollar. Tethers are listed on at least several dozen virtual currency trading platforms around the world, trading under the symbol "USDT."

9. In order to signal to the market that each tether held by users is equal to one U.S. dollar, Tether has long represented that for every outstanding tether issued and trading in the market, the company holds one U.S. dollar ("USD") in reserve "backing" the tether. From its inception in 2014 until late February 2019, Tether

represented that every outstanding tether was "backed" by, and thus should be valued at, one U.S. dollar. For example, Tether represented to users that "Every tether is always backed 1-to-1, by traditional currency held in our reserves. So 1 USDT is always equivalent to 1 USD."

10. In late February 2019, Tether changed its representation, stating on its website that "[e]very tether is always 100% backed by our reserves, which include traditional currency and cash equivalents and, from time to time, may include other assets and receivables from loans made by Tether to third parties, which may include affiliated entities (collectively, 'reserves'). Every tether is also 1-to-1 pegged to the dollar, so 1 USDT is always valued by Tether at 1 USD."

11. Tether represents to users that any holder of tethers can redeem them from Tether the company at the rate of one tether for one U.S. dollar.

12. Tether is one of the most prominent and widely-traded virtual currencies. As of the date of this Settlement Agreement, Tether represents that over 31 billion tethers have been issued and are outstanding and traded in the market.

13. Bitfinex and Tether are owned and operated by a small group of executives and shareholders that are located around the world. During the time period relevant to the OAG's investigation, and as late as early-to-mid 2018, one of Bitfinex and Tether's senior executives lived in, and conducted his work from, New York.

II. In 2017, Bitfinex and Tether Misled the Market About Tether's U.S. Dollar Backing

14. Prior to 2017, Bitfinex and Tether used several Taiwan-based banks to send and receive wire transfers to fulfill client orders for U.S. dollars, and for other purposes. Wells Fargo acted as the correspondent bank. In late March 2017, Wells Fargo elected to no longer process U.S. dollar wire transfers from Bitfinex and Tether accounts, forcing the companies to find alternative banking arrangements.

15. At the time Wells Fargo stopped servicing the companies, approximately 50 million tethers had been issued and were circulating in the market. By May 31, 2017, over 108 million tethers had been issued and circulating.

16. In June 2017, Bitfinex opened an account at a Puerto Rico-based entity named Noble Bank International ("Noble Bank"). Noble Bank was a subsidiary of New York-based Noble Markets LLC.

17. However, Tether did not open an account at Noble Bank, or any other bank, until September 15, 2017. Tether deposited the vast majority of its cash holdings (ostensibly backing USDT) into a trust account at the Bank of Montreal in the name of its General Counsel. The Bank of Montreal account never had more than $61.5 million dollars on deposit.

18. Because Tether did not have a significant bank relationship in its name from at least March 2017 until September 15, 2017, it could not directly process any fiat

deposits for purchases of Tethers by customers on either the Tether website or via the Bitfinex trading platform. At the same time, neither the Tether website or the Bitfinex trading platform allowed for the direct purchase or exchange of tethers in exchange for any other virtual currency, including the two most popular virtual currencies, bitcoin and ether.

19. Between June 1, 2017 and September 15, 2017, Bitfinex's Noble Bank account received USD deposits from only two institutional trading firms, one of which was located in New York. Neither of those institutional trading firms purchased tethers directly from Bitfinex or Tether during this time period.

20. Because of Tether's inability to conduct significant banking activity during this time, it could not itself hold dollars sufficient to back the hundreds of millions of new tethers that had entered the market. Until September 15, 2017, the only U.S. dollars held by Tether ostensibly backing the approximately 442 million tethers in circulation was the approximately $61 million on deposit at the Bank of Montreal.

21. Between June 1, 2017 and September 15, 2017, Bitfinex held approximately $382 million of Tether's funds in a comingled account, which should have been held by Tether as "backing" for tethers then in circulation but was not. In certain documents Bitfinex and Tether produced to OAG during its investigation, Tether accounted for this amount as a "receivable" from Bitfinex. Between June 1, 2017 and September 15, 2017, the total number of tethers issued and circulating rose from approximately 108 million to 442 million.

22. In June 2017, Bitfinex and Tether engaged the U.S.-based firm Friedman LLP to complete an audit of both companies. Those audits were never completed.

23. By late summer 2017, online reports suggested that Tether did not have sufficient cash backing for the increasing numbers of tethers in circulation. To counter those suggestions, in early September 2017, Bitfinex and Tether requested that Friedman conduct a verification of the cash backing of tethers, which Bitfinex and Tether planned to release publicly in order to demonstrate to the market that tethers were fully backed.

24. Tether notified Friedman that the company did not have a bank account at Noble Bank (or any other institution) but were in the process of opening one.

25. Tether and Friedman agreed that Friedman would conduct the verification of Tether's assets as of September 15, 2017.

26. On the morning of September 15, 2017, Tether opened an account at Noble Bank. Later that day, Bitfinex transferred $382,446,847.71 from Bitfinex's account at Noble Bank into Tether's account at Noble Bank. Friedman conducted its verification of Tether's assets as of 8:00 p.m. EST.

27. On September 30, 2017, a post to the Tether website was made, entitled "Transparency Update," in which Tether represented the following:

Friedman LLP has been engaged to perform historical balance sheet audit procedures for Tether Limited. However, as the amount of Tethers in circulation has increased substantially in recent months, we have also asked Friedman to analyze our bank balances and our issued and outstanding token balance on an interim basis. Friedman agreed to perform consulting services for us in an effort to provide management with useful information concerning Tether's cash position and Tether tokens issued and outstanding as of an interim date. Friedman was able to provide consulting services for us on an expedited basis, using a procedures date of September 15, 2017. These consulting services do not constitute anaudit [sic] or attestation engagement, which would include a significantly expanded scope of procedures and take substantially more time to complete.

We hope that the community considers the attached memorandum for what it is: a good faith effort on our behalf to provide an interim analysis of our cash position and our issued and outstanding tokens, as part of ongoing efforts to further professionalize the transparency mechanisms of Tether Limited.

28. The attached memorandum from Friedman contained the following graphic, redacting the account holder's name, and redacting the names of Noble Bank and the Bank of Montreal:

29. The September 30, 2017 "Transparency Update" and the attached memorandum were misleading. At no point did Tether inform its clients or the market that from at least June 1, 2017 until September 15, 2017, tethers were not in fact not backed "1-to-1" by USD held by

Tether in a bank account. Rather, the funds ostensibly backing tethers had been held in an account under the control of its General Counsel, with the balance accounted for as a "receivable" from Bitfinex. No one reviewing Tether's representations would have reasonably understood that the $382,064,782 listed as cash reserves for tethers had only been placed in Tether's account as of the very morning that Friedman verified the bank balance.

III. In 2019, Bitfinex and Tether Misrepresented the Status of the Tether Reserves, After Bitfinex Suffered a Massive Loss of Funds

30. In 2017 and 2018, Bitfinex began to increasingly rely on third-party "payment processors" to handle customer deposits and withdrawals from the Bitfinex trading platform. The primary entity Bitfinex used was a purportedly Panama-based entity known as Crypto Capital Corp. ("Crypto Capital").

31. An individual known as "Oz Yosef," or "Oz Joseph," or simply "Oz" was Bitfinex's point of contact at Crypto Capital.

32. By mid-2018, Crypto Capital held over $1 billion of funds that emanated from customer deposits at Bitfinex.

33. In May 2018, Bitfinex asked "Oz" how Bitfinex could "move money efficiently out of Cryptocapital." That request came on the heels of a report in April 2018 that the government of Poland had frozen a Crypto Capital bank account holding at least $340 million. In response, "Oz" repeatedly stated that the account freeze was temporary. In the ensuing months, "Oz" would go on to provide a number of different excuses for why he could not return the funds to Bitfinex (or its clients), including tax complications, hurdles placed by various compliance personnel at various banks, bankers being on vacation, typos in wire instructions, and corruption in the Polish government.

34. At some point between April 2018 and July 2018, "Oz" informed Bitfinex that a Crypto Capital account in Portugal containing approximately $150 million of Bitfinex client funds had also been frozen.

35. In July 2018, Bitfinex told "Oz," that over eighty percent of Bitfinex's client deposits were held at bank accounts controlled by Crypto Capital.

36. Despite having nearly $500 million of customer deposits in Crypto Capital accounts purportedly "frozen," Bitfinex nevertheless continued to direct clients to utilize Crypto Capital to fund their accounts throughout the summer of 2018.

37. During this time period, Bitfinex began to look for ways to stave off what Bitfinex internally characterized as a "temporary liquidity crisis."

38. In the summer of 2018, Bitfinex borrowed $400 million from Tether. On or about August 21, 2018, and continuing through September 2018, Tether made at least four cash transfers from its account at Deltec Bank to Bitfinex's account at Deltec Bank. To offset those cash transfers, Bitfinex directed "Oz" to transfer funds from the Bitfinex account to the Tether account at Crypto Capital. In October 2018, Bitfinex redeemed 400 million tethers to repay the debt. Those transactions were not disclosed.

39. Despite efforts to stave off Bitfinex's "liquidity crisis," online reports continued to mount that Bitfinex was unable or unwilling to timely process client withdrawal requests. In response, Bitfinex issued the following statement to the market on October 7, 2018:

1. Bitfinex is not insolvent, and a constant stream of Medium articles claiming otherwise is not going to change this. As one of only a very few exchanges operating since 2013, with a small team and low operating costs, we do not entirely understand the arguments that purport to show us to be insolvent without providing any explanation about why. The wallets below represent a small fraction of Bitfinex cryptocurrency holdings and do not take into account fiat holdings of any kind.

   • Bitcoin cold wallet 1

   • Ethereum cold wallet 1

   • EOS cold wallet 1

How any rational party can claim insolvency when the opposite is there for all to see is interesting and, once again, perhaps indicative of a targeted campaign based on nothing but fiction.

2. Both fiat and cryptocurrency withdrawals are functioning as normal. Verified Bitfinex users can freely withdraw Euros, Japanese Yen, Pounds Sterling and U.S. Dollars. Complications continue to exist for us in the domain of fiat transactions, as they do for most cryptocurrency-related organisations. However, we continue to do our utmost to minimise any waiting times associated with fiat deposits and withdrawals.

3. Stories and allegations currently circulating mentioning an entity called Noble Bank have no impact on our operations, survivability, or solvency.

40. That statement was misleading. At the time this statement was made, Bitfinex had been beseeching "Oz" for months to process client withdrawals or return the money, which "Oz" was unable or unwilling to do. The statement also misleadingly implied that the company had little or no connection to "an entity called Noble Bank," which at that time had been Bitfinex's bank for over a year.

41. In October 2018, Bitfinex and Tether severed their relationship with Noble Bank.

42. On November 1, 2018, Tether made a public statement announcing that it had established a relationship with Deltec Bank & Trust Limited, headquartered in the Bahamas. In that announcement, Tether represented that "USDT in the market are fully backed by US dollars that are safely deposited in our bank accounts." The announcement also linked to a document on Deltec letterhead and addressed to Tether Limited, dated November 1, 2018, which stated:

Dear Sirs:

We hereby confirm that, at the close of business on October 31, 2018, the portfolio cash value of your account with our bank was US$1,831,322,828.

43. The next day, November 2, 2018, Tether made the first of five transfers ultimately totaling $475 million from its bank account at Deltec Bank to Bitfinex's account at Deltec Bank. At the same time, a corresponding transfer was made from Bitfinex's account at Crypto Capital to Tether's account at Crypto Capital via ledger entry Bitfinex also "purchased" 150 million tethers by transferring $150 million in funds held at Bitfinex's Crypto Capital account to Tether's account at Crypto Capital. These transfers were not disclosed.

44. And so, as of November 2, 2018, tethers were again no longer backed 1-to-1 by U.S. dollars in a Tether bank account, because a substantial portion of the backing in the Deltec account had been transferred to Bitfinex to make up for the funds taken by Crypto Capital, while the corresponding funds transferred from Bitfinex's

Crypto Capital account to Tether's Crypto Capital account were impaired by Crypto Capital's actions.

45. Tether's misrepresentation would continue until late February 2019, at which time Tether updated its website to note that "[e]very tether is always 100% backed by our reserves, which include traditional currency and cash equivalents and, from time to time, may include other assets and receivables from loans made by Tether to third parties, which may include affiliated entities (collectively, 'reserves')." Tether did not announce that it had changed its disclosure, and indeed there were no media reports about the change until several weeks later on March 14, 2019.

46. Throughout November, Bitfinex would continue to ask "Oz" to return the money, to no avail. For example, on November 1, 2018, Bitfinex told "Oz" that Bitfinex "urgently need liquidity to start paying out our small customer as your channel is stuck." On November 21, 2018, Bitfinex told "Oz" that "We have 860m with you. I can't believe we can't even get 20 or 30 M out…where is all the money, it doesn't sum up…350 in Poland, 150 in Portugal." On November 28, 2018, Bitfinex again messaged "Oz," stating that "we are at the end of the month and you haven't been sending out one wire, even 1 usd for the whole month."

47. Contrary to what was happening behind the scenes, Bitfinex issued a statement on November 11, 2018, stating that Bitfinex's "banking remained stable," while noting that in October 2018 alone Bitfinex "processed over 700 withdrawals representing more than $1 [billion]."

48. As set forth in further detail in the OAG's application for relief pursuant to Section 354 of the Martin Act, in late 2018 Bitfinex and Tether began to negotiate a line of credit transaction that would allow Bitfinex to further draw upon the Tether reserves. Ultimately, the line of credit transaction closed at the end of March 2019, allowing Bitfinex to draw up to $900 million from the Tether reserves. The $625 million that had been previously transferred from the Tether account in November 2018 was incorporated into the line of credit. Bitfinex collateralized the line of credit with shares of its parent company Digfinex.

49. At no time did Bitfinex or Tether disclose to the market that Tether had transferred at least $625 million to Bitfinex, or that Bitfinex had experienced critical liquidity issues because of loss of approximately $850 million to Crypto Capital.

50. On April 24, 2019, the OAG filed an application in Supreme Court, New York County for an order pursuant to Section 354 of the Martin Act, seeking court-ordered production of documents and information relevant to its ongoing investigation of Bitfinex and Tether, as well as seeking injunctive relief to prevent Bitfinex from further accessing Tether's reserves under the line of credit arrangement. As part of that application, the OAG disclosed to the market for the first time that Bitfinex had lost access to approximately $850 million, and that Bitfinex had made up for the shortfall by transferring hundreds of millions of dollars from Tether.

51. On April 26, 2019, Bitfinex issued a statement, which included a representation that "we have been informed that these Crypto Capital amounts are not lost but have been, in fact, seized and safeguarded."

52. That statement was misleading. At the time that statement was made, Bitfinex did not in fact know the whereabouts of all of the customer funds held by Crypto Capital, and so had no assurance that the funds might ever be made accessible again to Crypto Capital or Bitfinex.

53. As of the date of this Settlement Agreement, Bitfinex cannot represent whether, or when, any of the unrecovered funds might be returned to Bitfinex or its clients.

54. Based on the foregoing facts, OAG finds that Bitfinex and Tether violated New York General Business Law § 352 *et seq.* and Executive Law § 62(12).

RELIEF

IT IS HEREBY UNDERSTOOD AND AGREED, by and between the Parties:

55. Monetary Relief

> a. *Monetary Relief Amount*: Respondents shall pay to the State of New York a penalty in the amount of $18,500,000 (the "Monetary Relief Amount"). Respondents shall pay the Monetary Relief Amount no later than thirty (30) business days after the effective date of this Settlement Agreement.

> 2. Bitfinex and Tether agree that they will not claim, assert, or apply for a tax deduction or tax credit with regard to any foreign or U.S.-domestic tax, directly or indirectly, for any portion of the payment that it shall make pursuant to this Settlement Agreement.

> 3. Payments shall be made by attorney check, corporate or certified check, or bank draft, which shall be made payable to the "State of New York", and shall reference Settlement Agreement No. 21-012; payments shall be addressed to the attention of John D. Castiglione, Senior Enforcement Counsel, Investor Protection Bureau, 28 Liberty Street, New York, New York, 10005. Payments in excess of $50,000 shall be made by wire transfer, with instructions available upon request of Respondents.

Undertakings:

56. Within five (5) days of the receipt of the penalty set forth in paragraph 55, the OAG will move to voluntarily withdraw its application for relief pursuant to Section 354 of the Martin Act (*In re: James v. iFinex, et al.*, Docket No. 450545/2019) and agrees not to bring any claims or causes of action against Bitfinex or Tether, its present and former direct or indirect parents, subsidiaries, or affiliates, or any of its officers, directors, employees, managers or agents that are presently known to the OAG for matters relating to the conduct set forth in the Findings and the Petition (Whitehurst Aff.), *In re James v. iFinex, Inc.*, Index No. 450545/2019 (N.Y. Sup. Ct.

April 25, 2019), NYSCEF Doc. No. 1; arising out of Bitfinex or Tether's representations concerning the backing of tethers during the time period January 1, 2014 to the effective date of this Settlement Agreement; transfers of a portion of the cash reserves backing tethers to Bitfinex pursuant to the line of credit agreement; or representations concerning the location or status of funds transferred to Crypto Capital. This provision does not prevent the OAG from exercising its rights to enforce this Settlement Agreement pursuant to other provisions herein.

57. Bitfinex and Tether agree to undertake the following:

a. *Line of Credit Repayment*

The line-of-credit referenced in paragraphs 48–50, above, has been repaid in full as of January 2021.

b. *Mandated Reporting Regarding Bitfinex and Tether's Efforts to Exclude New York Clients*

1. Bitfinex and Tether have implemented, and during the time frame set forth in Paragraph 57(b)(2) will continue to implement, maintain, and improve internal controls and procedures in a manner reasonably designed to ensure the soundness of the companies' prohibitions against use of its products and services by New York persons and entities. For purposes of this Settlement Agreement, "New York persons" are defined as any person known or believed to reside in or regularly conduct trading activity from New York, and "New York entity" is defined as any entity that is incorporated in, has its headquarters in, regularly conducts trading activity in, or is directed or controlled from, New York.

2. Within ninety (90) days of the effective date of this Settlement Agreement, and on a quarterly basis thereafter for two (2) years following the effective date of this Settlement Agreement, Bitfinex and Tether will provide a written report to OAG regarding their compliance with Paragraph 57(b)(1), which will include, but not necessarily be limited to, discussion of platform policies, operations, investigations, and surveillance, concerning Bitfinex and Tether's prohibition of New York persons and entities.

3. Bitfinex and Tether may apply to the OAG for an extension of the deadlines described above before their expiration and, upon a showing of good cause by Bitfinex and Tether, the OAG may, in its sole discretion, grant such extensions for whatever time period it deems appropriate.

4. OAG may seek production of documents substantiating the existence and effectiveness of the measures set forth in paragraph 57(b)(1).

c. *Trading Activity with New York Persons and Entities*: Bitfinex and Tether shall discontinue any trading activity with any New York persons or entities (including any New York entity that holds a BitLicense or Trust Account from the New York Department of Financial Services) or is a broker/dealer registered with the State of New York. This prohibition does not include the provision of services from a company providing the following for Bitfinex or Tether: blockchain analysis or tracing services; Know Your Customer ("KYC") or Anti-Money Laundering ("AML") services; user risk-scoring or similar services, legal services located in New York related to virtual currency trading activity, or other commercial services unrelated to the purchase, sale, or exchange of virtual currencies.

d. Over the Counter Trading: Respondents agree not to conduct or facilitate over-the-counter trading activity with a New York person or entity.

e. Mandated Reporting on Certain Business Operations

Within ninety (90) days of the effective date of this Settlement Agreement, and on a quarterly basis thereafter for two (2) years following the effective date of this Settlement Agreement, Bitfinex and Tether will provide

i. documents substantiating Tether's reserve account(s), in a form substantially similar to what Tether has provided during OAG's investigation;

ii. verification that Bitfinex and Tether have appropriately segregated client, reserve, and operational accounts, including but not necessarily limited to verification that (a) Tether reserves are segregated from operational accounts; (b) Bitfinex and Tether maintain separate accounts; (c) virtual assets for customers and the companies are held at

2. Bitfinex and Tether may apply to the OAG for an extension of the deadlines described above before their expiration and, upon a showing of good cause by Bitfinex and Tether, the OAG may, in its sole discretion, grant such extensions for whatever time period it deems appropriate.

f. Publication of Tether's Reserves: On at least a quarterly basis for a period of two (2) years following the effective date of this Settlement Agreement, Tether will publish the categories of assets backing tether (*e.g.,* cash, loans, securities, etc.), specifying the percentages of each such category, and specifying whether any such category constituting a loan or receivable or similar is to an affiliated entity, in a form substantially similar to that previously presented to the OAG.

g. Transparency and Opt-Out of Payment Processors

1. Within ninety (90) days of the effective date of this Settlement Agreement, and on a quarterly basis thereafter for two (2) years following the effective date of this Settlement Agreement, Bitfinex and Tether will provide to OAG a list of payment processors whom they utilize, along with location and contact information for those entities, and information regarding ad-

ditional due diligence procedures the companies have implemented (or will implement) regarding the use of payment processors;

2. For the period set forth in Paragraph 57(g)(1), Bitfinex and Tether will provide a list of payment processors whom they utilize, along with location and contact information for those entities, to users upon request in connection with a deposit or withdrawal;

3. For the period set forth in Paragraph 57(g)(1), Bitfinex and Tether shall notify a user that Bitfinex or Tether intends to use a payment processor for that user's transaction(s), or to hold that user's funds, prior to the transaction. Users will be given the ability to opt-out of use of any (or all) payment processors, and will be permitted to use a different method of transfer or holding.

h. Future Activities in New York: In the event that Bitfinex or Tether should in the future seek to service New York persons or entities, they will do so in accordance with applicable law, including any applicable licensing requirements.

58. Respondent expressly agrees and acknowledges that a default in the performance of any obligation under the above paragraph is a violation of this Settlement Agreement, and that the OAG thereafter may commence a civil action or proceeding, in addition to any other appropriate investigation, action, or proceeding, and that evidence that the Settlement Agreement has been violated shall constitute prima facie proof of the statutory violations described in paragraph 54, pursuant to Executive Law § 63(15).

MISCELLANEOUS

Subsequent Proceedings:

59. Respondents expressly agree and acknowledge that the OAG may initiate a subsequent investigation, civil action, or proceeding to enforce this Settlement Agreement, for violations of the Settlement Agreement, or if the Settlement Agreement is voided pursuant to paragraph 68, and agrees and acknowledges that in such event:

a. any statute of limitations or other time-related defenses are tolled from and after the effective date of this Settlement Agreement;

b. the OAG may use statements, documents or other materials produced or provided by Bitfinex and Tether prior to or after the effective date of this Settlement Agreement;

c. any civil action or proceeding must be adjudicated by the courts of the State of New York, and that Bitfinex and Tether irrevocably and unconditionally waive any objection based upon personal jurisdiction, inconvenient forum, or venue;

d. evidence of a violation of this Settlement Agreement shall constitute prima facie proof of a violation of the applicable law pursuant to Executive Law §63(15).

60. If a court of competent jurisdiction determines that the Bitfinex or Tether has violated the Settlement Agreement, Bitfinex or Tether shall pay to the OAG the reasonable cost, if any, of obtaining such determination and of enforcing this Settlement Agreement, including without limitation legal fees, expenses, and court costs.

61. In the event the OAG believes that Respondents have violated this Settlement Agreement, the OAG agree to provide Respondents with written notice of such asserted violation prior to instituting any proceeding resulting from such violation. Within thirty (30) days of receipt of such notice, Respondents shall have the opportunity to respond to the OAG in writing to explain the nature and circumstances of such violation, as well as the actions Respondents have taken to address and remediate the situation, which explanation the OAG shall consider in determining whether to pursue enforcement or other proceedings.

Effects of Settlement Agreement:

62. Bitfinex and Tether shall not make or permit to be made any public statement denying, directly or indirectly the propriety of this Settlement Agreement or the OAG investigation. Nothing in this paragraph affects Bitfinex or Tether's (i) testimonial obligations or (ii) right to take positions in defense of litigation or other legal proceedings to which the OAG is not a party. This Agreement is not intended for use by any third party in any other proceeding.

63. All terms and conditions of this Settlement Agreement shall continue in full force and effect on any successor, assignee, or transferee of Bitfinex or Tether. Bitfinex and Tether shall include any such successor, assignment or transfer agreement a provision that binds the successor, assignee or transferee to the terms of the Settlement Agreement. No party may assign, delegate, or otherwise transfer any of its rights or obligations under this Settlement Agreement without the prior written consent of the OAG.

64. Nothing contained herein shall be construed as to deprive any person of any private right under the law.

65. This Settlement Agreement is not a final order of any court or governmental authority, and is made without trial or adjudication on any issue of fact or law.

66. Any failure by the OAG to insist upon the strict performance by Bitfinex or Tether of any of the provisions of this Settlement Agreement shall not be deemed a waiver of any of the provisions hereof, and the OAG, notwithstanding that failure, shall have the right thereafter to insist upon the strict performance of any and all of the provisions of this Settlement Agreement to be performed by Bitfinex or Tether.

Representations and Warranties:

68. The OAG has agreed to the terms of this Settlement Agreement based on, among other things, the representations made to the OAG by Bitfinex, Tether, and their counsel and the OAG's own factual investigation as set forth in Findings, paragraphs 6–54, above. Bitfinex and Tether represent and warrant that neither they nor their counsel have made any material representations of fact to the OAG that are false. If any material representations of fact by Bitfinex, Tether, or their counsel are later found to be false, this Settlement Agreement is voidable by the OAG in its sole discretion.

69. No representation, inducement, promise, understanding, condition, or warranty not set forth in this Settlement Agreement has been made to or relied upon by Bitfinex or Tether in agreeing to this Settlement Agreement.

70. Bitfinex and Tether represent and warrant, through the signatures below, that the terms and conditions of this Settlement Agreement are duly approved. Bitfinex and Tether further represent and warrant that the signatories to this Settlement Agreement are directors of Bitfinex and Tether.

General Principles:

71. Nothing in this Settlement Agreement shall relieve Bitfinex or Tether of other obligations imposed by any applicable state or federal law or regulation or other applicable law.

72. Nothing contained herein shall be construed to limit the remedies available to the OAG in the event that Bitfinex or Tether violate the Settlement Agreement after its effective date.

73. This Settlement Agreement may not be amended except by an instrument in writing signed on behalf of the Parties.

74. In the event that any one or more of the provisions contained in this Settlement Agreement shall for any reason be held by a court of competent jurisdiction to be invalid, illegal, or unenforceable in any respect, in the sole discretion of the OAG, such invalidity, illegality, or unenforceability shall not affect any other provision of this Settlement Agreement.

75. Bitfinex and Tether acknowledge that they have entered this Settlement Agreement freely and voluntarily and upon due deliberation with the advice of counsel.

76. This Settlement Agreement shall be governed by the laws of the State of New York without regard to any conflict of laws principles.

77. This Settlement Agreement and all its terms shall be construed as if mutually drafted with no presumption of any type against any party that may be found to have been the drafter.

78. This Settlement Agreement may be executed in multiple counterparts by the parties hereto. All counterparts so executed shall constitute one agreement binding upon all parties, notwithstanding that all parties are not signatories to the original or the same counterpart. Each counterpart shall be deemed an original to this Settlement Agreement, all of which shall constitute one agreement to be valid as of the effective date of this Settlement Agreement. For purposes of this Settlement Agreement, copies of signatures shall be treated the same as originals. Documents executed, scanned and transmitted electronically and electronic signatures shall be deemed original signatures for purposes of this Settlement Agreement and all matters related thereto, with such scanned and electronic signatures having the same legal effect as original signatures.

79. The effective date of this Settlement Agreement shall be February 18, 2021.

LETITIA JAMES

Attorney General of the State of New York

28 Liberty Street

New York, NY 10005

Discussion Points

1. *Did the OAG get it right?* Do you agree with the OAG's findings? Why or why not? Which particular findings, if any, do you disagree with and why?

2. *Deterring power.* Do you think the settlement agreement is enough to deter other entities from engaging in the same activities at Bitfinex and Tether? In your opinion, are federal agencies, such as the CFTC and OAG, doing enough to combat illicit activities and failure to follow regulatory guidelines?

3. *The role of states.* Do you think regulators at the state level should be more involved in cracking down on "unlicensed and unregulated individuals and entities"?

III. Regulations & Guidances

The United States is a global leader in regulating and adjusting to the emerging cryptocurrency industry. Before stablecoin can be regulated, regulations need to address cryptocurrency, generally. The current patchwork system makes it difficult to develop a cohesive regulatory approach among states.

Press Release: President's Working Group on Financial Markets Releases Report and Recommendations on Stablecoins

U.S. Department of Treasury (Nov. 1, 2021),

https://home.treasury.gov/news/press-releases/jy0454

Report Outlines Regulatory Framework for Stablecoins
and Pathways to Address Risks

WASHINGTON—Today, the President's Working Group on Financial Markets (PWG), joined by the Federal Deposit Insurance Corporation (FDIC) and the Office of the Comptroller of the Currency (OCC), released a report on stablecoins. Stablecoins are a type of digital asset generally designed to maintain a stable value relative to the U.S. dollar. While today stablecoins are primarily used to facilitate trading of other digital assets, stablecoins could be more widely used in the future as a means of payment by households and businesses.

"Stablecoins that are well-designed and subject to appropriate oversight have the potential to support beneficial payments options. But the absence of appropriate oversight presents risks to users and the broader system," said Secretary of the Treasury Janet L. Yellen. "Current oversight is inconsistent and fragmented, with some stablecoins effectively falling outside the regulatory perimeter. Treasury and the agencies involved in this report look forward to working with Members of Congress from both parties on this issue. While Congress considers action, regulators will continue to operate within their mandates to address the risks of these assets."

The potential for the increased use of stablecoins as a means of payments raises a range of concerns, related to the potential for destabilizing runs, disruptions in the payment system, and concentration of economic power. The PWG report highlights gaps in the authority of regulators to reduce these risks.

To address the risks of payment stablecoins, the agencies recommend that Congress act promptly to enact legislation to ensure that payment stablecoins and payment stablecoin arrangements are subject to a federal framework on a consistent and comprehensive basis. Such legislation would complement existing authorities with respect to market integrity, investor protection, and illicit finance, and would address key concerns:

- **To address risks to stablecoin users and guard against stablecoin runs,** legislation should require stablecoin issuers to be insured depository institutions.

- **To address concerns about payment system risk,** in addition to the requirements for stablecoin issuers, legislation should require custodial wallet providers to be subject to appropriate federal oversight. Congress should also provide the federal supervisor of a stablecoin issuer with the authority to require any entity that performs activities that are critical to the functioning of the stablecoin arrangement to meet appropriate risk-management standards.

- **To address additional concerns about systemic risk and concentration of economic power,** legislation should require stablecoin issuers to comply with activities restrictions that limit affiliation with commercial entities. Supervisors should have authority to implement standards to promote interoperability among stablecoins. In addition, Congress may wish to consider other standards for custodial wallet providers, such as limits on affiliation with commercial entities or on use of users' transaction data.

In the immediate term, the agencies are committed to taking action to address risks falling within each agency's jurisdiction, including efforts to ensure that stablecoins and related activities comply with   existing legal obligations, as well as to continued coordination and collaboration on issues of common interest. While Congressional action is urgently needed to address the risks inherent in payment stablecoins, in the absence of such action, the agencies recommend that the Financial Stability Oversight Council consider steps available to it to address the risks outlined in this report.

As discussed in the report, in addition to the risks noted above, stablecoins may also raise investor protection, market integrity, and illicit finance concerns. To the extent activity related to digital assets falls under the jurisdiction of the Securities and Exchange Commission (SEC) and Commodity Futures Trading Commission (CFTC), the SEC and CFTC have broad enforcement, rulemaking, and oversight authorities that may address certain of these concerns. To prevent misuse of stablecoins and other digital assets by illicit actors, Treasury will continue leading efforts at the Financial Action Task Force (FATF) to encourage countries to implement international AML/CFT standards and pursue additional resources to support supervision of domestic AML/CFT regulations.

While the scope of this report is limited to stablecoins, work on digital assets and other innovations related to cryptographic and distributed ledger technology is ongoing throughout the Administration. The Administration and the financial regulatory agencies will continue to collaborate closely on ways to foster responsible financial innovation, promote consistent regulatory approaches, and identify and address potential risks that arise from such innovation.

New York Department of Financial Services:
Virtual Currency Guidance

June 8, 2022

TO: Entities Licensed Under 23 NYCRR Part 200 or Chartered as Limited Purpose Trust Companies Under the New York Banking Law That Issue U.S. Dollar-Backed Stablecoins Under the Supervision of the New York State Department of Financial Services ("DFS")

FROM: Adrienne A. Harris, Superintendent of Financial Services

RE: Guidance on the Issuance of U.S. Dollar-Backed Stablecoins

*****

The adoption of stablecoins worldwide has grown substantially in recent years, and more regulators and policymakers are showing an interest in stablecoin arrangements and the rules that apply to them. Recent public policy discussions have addressed prudential authority over stablecoins generally, as well as specific prudential concerns with stablecoins, such as the existence of appropriate reserves backing the stablecoins and the possibility of "runs" on the stablecoins similar to bank runs.[1] As the prudential regulator of companies engaged in virtual currency business activity in New York,[2] DFS has imposed requirements, standards, and controls on the stablecoins issued by its regulated entities since 2018, when DFS approved the first issuance of stablecoins by its regulated virtual currency companies.[3]

When a company applies for a license to engage in virtual currency business activity (a "BitLicense")[4] or a charter as a limited purpose trust company under the New York Banking Law, DFS reviews the company's business plan and product offerings in detail, and any stablecoin-related aspects of the company's business model are thoroughly evaluated as part of DFS's determination of whether to grant the license or charter. After licensure, BitLicensees must obtain DFS's written approval before introducing a materially new product, service, or activity,[5] and this prior-approval requirement applies to the issuance of a stablecoin. DFS imposes analogous requirements on New York State limited purpose trust companies that engage in

---

1. See, e.g., President's Working Group on Financial Markets, et al. Report on Stablecoins (Nov. 2021) at 1–2.

2. See 23 NYCRR Part 200.

3. See DFS Continues to Foster Responsible Growth in New York's Fintech Industry With New Virtual Currency Product Approvals (Sept. 10, 2018).

4. See 23 NYCRR Part 200.

5. 23 NYCRR § 200.10.

virtual currency business activity and, accordingly, these companies also require DFS's written approval before they may issue a new stablecoin in New York.

The purpose of this Guidance on the Issuance of U.S. Dollar-Backed Stablecoins (this "Guidance") is to emphasize certain requirements that will generally apply to stablecoins backed by the U.S. dollar that are issued under DFS oversight. Specifically, this Guidance focuses on DFS requirements relating to:

i. the redeemability of such stablecoins;

ii. the asset reserves that back such stablecoins (the "Reserves"); and

iii. attestations concerning the backing by these Reserves.

Entities that issue stablecoins under DFS supervision, or that may be interested in doing so, can use this Guidance to better understand the baseline requirements in these three categories that they are expected to meet concerning U.S. dollar-backed stablecoins.

It is noted that, although stablecoins are a type of virtual currency that can be designed to maintain a stable value relative to any national currency or other reference asset, this Guidance applies only to stablecoins backed by the U.S. dollar, and only to stablecoins that are issued under DFS supervision by DFS-regulated virtual currency entities.

Baseline requirements for the issuance of U.S. dollar-backed stablecoins

DFS will generally impose the following conditions on all U.S. dollar-backed stablecoins whose issuance is subject to DFS approval.

1. Backing and redeemability

    a. The stablecoin must be fully backed by a Reserve of assets, meaning that the market value of the Reserve is at least equal to the nominal value of all outstanding units of the stablecoin as of the end of each business day.[6]

    b. The issuer of the stablecoin (the "Issuer") must adopt clear, conspicuous redemption policies, approved in advance by DFS in writing, that confer on any lawful holder of the stablecoin a right to redeem units of the stablecoin from the Issuer in a timely fashion at par—i.e., at a 1:1 exchange rate for the U.S. dollar, net of ordinary, well-disclosed fees—subject to reasonable, non-burdensome conditions including otherwise applicable legal or regulatory requirements, such as the ability of the stablecoin holder to onboard successfully with the Issuer before redeeming. These redemption policies shall clearly disclose the meaning of "redemption" and the required timing of "timely" redemption, or shall expressly adopt the following default terms:

---

6. In this Guidance, a "business day" is defined as a business day (9 a.m.–5 p.m.) in the United States, New York time.

i. Redemption in U.S. dollars is deemed to have occurred when the Issuer has fully processed and initiated the outgoing transfer of funds to the holder's financial or other institution, if and as requested by the holder, or has credited the funds to the holder's cash account with the Issuer, if requested by the holder. And,

ii. "Timely" redemption means redemption not more than two full business days ("T+2") after the business day on which the Issuer receives a "compliant redemption order," meaning the business day on which (A) the Issuer has received a redemption order and (B) the holder or the holder's designee has onboarded successfully with the Issuer and all other conditions necessary to permit compliant redemption have been met.[7]

iii. In extraordinary circumstances, where DFS concludes that timely redemption would likely jeopardize the Reserve's asset-backing requirement or the orderly liquidation of Reserve assets, DFS has the authority to require or allow redemption that would not qualify as timely under item 1(b), as it deems necessary.

2. Reserve

a. The assets in the Reserve must be segregated from the proprietary assets of the issuing entity, and must be held in custody with (i) U.S. state or federally chartered depository institutions with deposits insured by the Federal Deposit Insurance Corporation ("FDIC") and/or (ii) asset custodians, approved in advance in writing by DFS. The Reserve assets shall be held at these depository institutions and custodians for the benefit of the holders of the stablecoin, with appropriate titling of accounts.

b. The Reserve shall consist only of the following assets:

i. U.S. Treasury bills acquired by the Issuer three months or less from their respective maturities.

ii. Reverse repurchase agreements fully collateralized by U.S. Treasury bills, U.S. Treasury notes, and/or U.S. Treasury bonds on an overnight basis, subject to DFS-approved requirements concerning overcollateralization. Such reverse repurchase agreements shall be either (A) tri-party or (B) bilateral with a counterparty that the Issuer has found to be adequately creditworthy and whose identity has been submitted to DFS in writing, without objection, together with the Issuer's credit

---

7. A compliant redemption order received between the end of a business day and the start of the following business day shall be treated as having arrived during the following business day. Note that "receipt" of a redemption order shall be deemed to have occurred at the earlier of actual receipt and the time when actual receipt would have occurred but for Issuer negligence or willful ignorance.

assessment, at least 14 days prior to the Issuer's commencing to enter into contracts with such counterparty.

iii. Government money-market funds, subject to DFS-approved caps on the fraction of Reserve assets to be held in such funds and DFS-approved restrictions on the funds, such as a minimum percentage allocation to direct obligations of the Government of the United States and reverse repurchase agreements on such obligations. And,

iv. Deposit accounts at U.S. state or federally chartered depository institutions, subject to DFS-approved restrictions such as (A) percentage-of-Reserve or absolute-dollar-value caps on the assets to be deposited at any given depository institution and/or (B) limitations based on DFS's conclusions concerning the risk characteristics of particular depository institutions, taking into consideration the amounts reasonably needed to be held at depository institutions to meet anticipated redemption demands.

c. Issuers are expected to manage the liquidity risk of the Reserve in accordance with the redemption requirements discussed in paragraph 1 above.

3. Attestation

a. The Reserve must be subject to an examination of management's assertions, as set forth herein, at least once per month by an independent Certified Public Accountant ("CPA") licensed in the United States and applying the attestation standards of the American Institute of Certified Public Accountants ("AICPA"), where such CPA and such CPA's engagement letter shall have been approved in advance in writing by DFS. In each of these attestations, the CPA shall attest to management's assertions of the following as of the last business day of the period covered by the attestation and as of at least one randomly selected business day during the period: (i) the end-of-day market value of the Reserve, both in aggregate and broken down by asset class; (ii) the end-of-day quantity of outstanding stablecoin units; (iii) whether the Reserve was, at these times, adequate to fully back all outstanding stablecoin units as set forth in item 1(a) above, including reconciling items[8]; and (iv) whether all DFS-imposed conditions on the Reserve assets (whether set forth in paragraph 2 hereof or otherwise specified by DFS) have been met. For purposes of item 3(a)(iv), the CPA shall be entitled to rely on the DFS-imposed conditions on the Reserve assets that applied as of each day in the period covered by the attestation as reported to the CPA by

---

8. Reconciling items may exist, for example, in cases where the assets backing a newly minted stablecoin are in transit to the depository institutions and/or custodians.

the Issuer, together with the Issuer's certification that such conditions are being accurately reported. In all events, the specific conditions on the Reserve assets against which the attestation was performed shall be included in the CPA's attestation report.

b. In addition to attestations referred to in item 3(a), the Issuer shall obtain an annual attestation report by an independent CPA licensed in the United States and applying the attestation standards of the AICPA, attesting to management's assertions concerning the effectiveness of the internal controls, structure, and procedures for compliance with the requirements described in items 3(a)(i) through 3(a)(iv) hereof. Such CPA and such CPA's engagement letter shall have been approved in advance in writing by DFS.

c. For each attestation described in item 3(a), the Issuer must make the CPA's reports available to the public, and produce a copy to DFS in writing, not more than 30 days after the end of the period covered by the attestation.

d. For each annual attestation report described in item 3(b), the Issuer must produce a copy to DFS in writing, not more than 120 days after the end of the period covered by the report.

Please note that the above requirements as to redeemability, the Reserve, and attestations are not the only requirements DFS places or may place on the issuance of stablecoins, and the risks connected to these factors are not the only risks DFS considers. DFS looks at a range of potential risks before authorizing a regulated virtual currency entity to issue a stablecoin, including risks relating to cybersecurity and information technology; network design and maintenance and related technology and operational considerations; Bank Secrecy Act/anti-money-laundering ("BSA/AML") and sanctions compliance; consumer protection; safety and soundness of the issuing entity; and the stability/integrity of the payment system, as applicable. DFS may impose requirements on a stablecoin arrangement to address any of these risks, or any other risks, consistent with DFS's statutory mandate and the laws and regulations relevant to the circumstances.[9]

This Guidance is not intended to limit, and does not limit, any power of DFS or the scope or applicability of any law or regulation. DFS may, at any time and in its sole discretion, prohibit or otherwise limit a stablecoin's issuance or use before or after a DFS-regulated Issuer begins issuing the stablecoin, and may require that any such Issuer delist, halt, or otherwise limit or curtail activity with respect to any stablecoin.

---

9. See, e.g., New York Financial Services Law §§ 102 and 201; New York Banking Law § 10; 23 NYCRR Part 200; and 23 NYCRR Part 500.

This Guidance is not intended to, and does not, affect obligations of Issuers to submit audited financial statements to DFS pursuant to the New York Banking Law, the virtual currency business activity regulation, 23 NYCRR Part 200, the Issuer's Supervisory Agreement with DFS, or any other relevant law or regulation. DFS may update this Guidance from time to time, or withdraw it.

Each DFS-regulated issuer of a stablecoin is responsible for understanding and complying with all applicable laws and regulations, including any applicable legal and regulatory requirements imposed by other state or federal regulatory agencies. This Guidance is not intended to address and does not address such other state, federal, or other requirements.

Issuers that currently issue U.S. dollar-backed stablecoins under DFS supervision are expected to come into compliance with this Guidance within three months of the date hereof, except as to the requirements set forth in items 3(b) and 3(d), with which these Issuers shall come into compliance in a reasonable period as determined by DFS in its sole discretion.

Stablecoin Tethering and Bank Licensing Enforcement Act.

This is known as the STABLE Act, which is an effort for a singular approach to regulate stablecoins. The Act requires that companies which issue stablecoins must obtain a banking charter and comply with various rules and regulations.The organization would need to seek approval from the Federal Reserve and the U.S. Federal Deposit Insurance Corporation ("FDIC") at least six months in advance of issuing a stablecoin. Moreover, those organizations would need to maintain a reserve with the U.S. Federal Reserve, submit to regular audits, and obtain insurance through the FDIC.

The STABLE Act has been accused of undermining the purpose of cryptocurrency, which is to remain decentralized. The Act would lay the foundation for centralization of the underlying assets of stablecoins, which would further strengthen financial institutions thus weakening the people. Ironically, the Act purports to protect lay people from potentially harmful practices of stablecoin issuers, which is why the OCC would like to step in to regulate.

Discussion Points

1. *President's Working Group on Financial Markets.* On November 1, 2021, President Biden's Working Group on Financial Markets, along with the FDIC and the OCC, released a Report on Stablecoins. The Report recommends federal legislation that would require stablecoin issuers be insured depository institutions. Additionally, the Report summarizes risks presented by stablecoins, including loss of confidence in stablecoin val-

ue, payment system risks, systemic risk and concentration of economic power, and illicit finance concerns related to compliance with AML laws. Should the OCC and FDIC be involved in stablecoin regulation? In what ways? Should a new agency be created to oversee stablecoins and digital currencies in general?

2. *The FDIC's role.* Since companies issuing stablecoins need a bank charter, should they be FDIC insured for losses related to stablecoin transactions?

3. *Characterizing stablecoins.* Does the fact that stablecoins are pegged to fiat currency make them more akin to legal tender such as a U.S. dollar than to a virtual currency?

4. *In the Matter of James v. IFINEX, Inc.* Respondent IFINEX sought to terminate the Martin Act action due to lack of personal and subject matter jurisdiction of the court. The N.Y. Attorney General argued that it was too soon for the court to determine jurisdiction at this point in its investigation, but that IFINEX has activities affecting N.Y. and that N.Y. Gen. Bus. Law section 354 provides the Attorney General with the authority to make inquiries into the potentially fraudulent matter at hand. The court sided with the Attorney General by rejecting the respondent's attempts to limit the petitioner's investigation. Substantively and procedurally, the court believed the Attorney General has the authority to conduct its investigation and the court has the jurisdiction to preside over the matter. Specific to the Martin Act, the respondent argued that the underlying stablecoin, Tether, was neither a security nor a commodity that the Martin Act has defined. However, the judge disagreed because the Act's definition of a commodity is sufficient to capture Tether: "any foreign currency, any other good, article, or material."

5. *Securities.* Are stablecoins securities? The Chairman of the SEC, Gary Gensler, has stated on multiple occasions that certain stablecoins could become subject to SEC regulations. Charmain Gensler reasoned this by noting, "it doesn't matter whether it's a stock token, a stable value token backed by securities, or any other virtual product that provides synthetic exposure to underlying securities, these products are subject to the securities laws and must work within our securities regime."[78] Analyze his explanation. Do you agree? If not, why not?

---

78. Sean Anderson, Mark Chorazak, Donna Parisi & Le-el Sinai, *US Stablecoin Regulation: Bringing Stablecoins into the Regulatory Fold* (November 12, 2021).

In the Matter of Tether Holdings Limited, Tether Operations Limited, Tether Limited and Tether International Limited

CFTC Docket No. 22-04 (2021

* * *

II. FINDINGS

The Commission finds the following:

A. SUMMARY

Tether introduced the U.S. dollar tether token ("USDt" or "tether token") as a stablecoin in 2014. The USDt is a commodity as defined by the Act. At various times during the Relevant Period, Tether misrepresented to customers and the market that Tether maintained sufficient fiat reserves to back every USDt in circulation "one-to-one" with the "equivalent amount of corresponding fiat currency" held in reserves by Tether (the "Tether Reserves"), and that Tether would undergo routine, professional audits to demonstrate that it maintained "100% reserves at all times." In fact, during the majority of the Relevant Period, Tether failed to maintain fiat currency reserves in accounts in Tether's own name or in an account titled and held "in trust" for Tether (collectively the "Tether Bank Accounts") to back every USDt in circulation. While Tether represents that it maintained adequate reserves, some of the Tether Reserves were in accounts other than the Tether Bank Accounts, and at times included receivables and non-fiat assets among its counted reserves. In addition, at least until 2018, Tether utilized a manual process to track the Tether Reserves, which did not capture the real-time status of the Tether Reserves. Further, from at least 2018 through February 25, 2019, Tether failed to disclose that the Tether Reserves included unsecured receivables, commercial papers, funds held by third- parties, and other non-fiat assets. Finally, Tether Reserves were not routinely audited.

B. RESPONDENTS

Tether Holdings Limited was incorporated in the British Virgin Islands on September 5, 2014. Tether Holdings Limited owns 100% of Tether Operations Limited, Tether Limited, and Tether International Limited. Tether Holdings Limited has never been registered with the Commission in any capacity.

Tether Limited was incorporated in Hong Kong on September 8, 2014. Tether Limited operated Tether's website and token platform, tether.to from September 8, 2014 through March 15, 2017. Throughout the Relevant Period, Tether Limited was and continues to be registered with FinCEN as a non-bank financial institution known as a Money Services Business ("MSB"). Tether Limited has never been registered with the Commission in any capacity.

Tether Operations Limited was incorporated in the British Virgin Islands on March 15, 2017. Tether Operations Limited operates Tether's website and token platform, tether.to. Tether Operations Limited has never been registered with the Commission in any capacity.

Tether International Limited was incorporated in the British Virgin Islands on March 15, 2017. Tether International Limited has never been registered with the Commission in any capacity.

C. OTHER RELEVANT ENTITIES[2]

iFinex Inc. ("iFinex") is a privately-held financial technology company incorporated in the British Virgin Islands on May 21, 2013. iFinex operates the Bitfinex trading platform.

BFXNA Inc. ("BFXNA") was incorporated in the British Virgin Islands on November 4, 2014. BFXNA is a wholly-owned subsidiary of iFinex.

BFXWW Inc. ("BFXWW") was incorporated in the British Virgin Islands on April 28, 2015. BFXWW is a wholly-owned subsidiary of iFinex.

D. FACTS

1. The Tether Token

Since its launch in 2014, Respondents have represented that the tether token is a "stablecoin," a type of virtual currency whose value is pegged to fiat currency. At launch, Respondents announced, through their Facebook account, that: "Tether means a digital tie between a real-world asset and the digital assets backed by currencies." Although Respondents offer tether tokens in several national currencies, the dominant tether token is the U.S. dollar tether token, commonly referred to as "USDt." Throughout the Relevant Period, Respondents repeatedly represented that one USDt may always be redeemed for one U.S. dollar. Respondents' website represents the purpose and value of the USDt token as:

> Tether is a token backed by actual assets, including USD and Euros. One Tether equals one underlying unit of the currency backing it, e.g., the U.S. Dollar, and is backed 100% by actual assets in the Tether platform's reserve account. Being anchored or "tethered" to real world currency, Tether provides protection from the volatility of cryptocurrencies.

---

2. iFinex, BFXNA and BFXWW collectively did business as "Bitfinex" throughout the Relevant Period. Concurrently with this Order, the Commission is issuing an order against Bitfinex settling separate and distinct violations of Sections 4(a) and 4d(a)(1) of the Act, 7 U.S.C. §§ 6(a), 6d(a)(1) (2018), as well as BFXNA's violation of Part VII. A of the Commission's 2016 Order in In re BFXNA Inc. d/b/a Bitfinex, CFTC No. 16-19, 2016 WL 3137612 (June 2, 2016).

Beginning in January 2015, tether tokens have been used to deposit and withdraw funds on the Bitfinex platform. Tether tokens provide a medium of exchange across cryptocurrency trading platforms. For example, a trader may transfer USDt to Bitfinex or another cryptocurrency exchange and use the tether tokens to purchase or trade digital assets such as bitcoin. BTC/USDT is a frequently traded pair.

Before November 2017, customers could only acquire and redeem tether tokens directly from Respondents. To do so, typically, customers transferred the corresponding amount of U.S. dollars in order to acquire USDt from Respondents and received the corresponding amount of U.S. dollars in exchange for redeemed USDt, less any applicable fees. On or around

November 19, 2017, Respondents experienced a cyber-attack during which the attackers caused the unauthorized transfer of nearly 31 million USDt tokens that had been authorized but not issued (the "2017 Tether Hack"). No reserve funds were at risk or stolen during the 2017 Tether Hack. Following the 2017 Tether Hack, and continuing until on or about November 27, 2018, Respondents ceased directly issuing and redeeming tether tokens, and tether tokens could only be issued or redeemed through Bitfinex. Thereafter, beginning in or around November 27, 2018, customers could obtain USDt tokens from Bitfinex or Tether. Today, tether tokens can be obtained from dozens of cryptocurrency exchanges, including several operating in the U.S.

* * *

Discussion Points

1. *Tether Holdings Limited, Tether Limited, Tether Operations Limited, and Tether International Limited and the CFTC.* In 2014, Tether introduced the U.S. dollar tether token as a stablecoin. The CFTC, in its order against Tether, stated that digital assets such as bitcoin, Ethereum, Litecoin, and tether tokens are commodities, bringing them into the purview of the CFTC. Do you think the CFTC is the proper agency to regulate stablecoins? Why or why not?

2. *Applying the Howey test.* Are stablecoins securities? Apply the Howey test to stablecoins. Which element(s), if any, do stablecoins fail to meet?

Eight

Central Bank Digital Currency

I. Introduction

Americans have held money predominantly in digital form for quite some time. Common examples include bank accounts, payment apps, and the use of online transactions. Central Bank Digital Currency (CBDC) is a digital form of central bank money that is generally available for public use. CBDC, however, differs from the typical digital form of money. The key difference is that CDBC is considered a liability of the central bank, the Federal Reserve, instead of a liability of a commercial bank. In the United States, there are two types of central bank money. First, physical currency issued by the Federal Reserve. The second includes digital balances held by commercial banks at the Federal Reserve.

In January 2022, the Federal Reserve Board released a discussion paper titled, *Money and Payments: The U.S. Dollar in the Age of Digital Transformation*, which evaluates the pros and cons of a potential United States CBDC.[79] The discussion paper summarizes "the current state of the domestic payments system and discusses the different types of digital payment methods and assets that have emerged in recent years, including stablecoins and other cryptocurrencies. The paper concludes by examining the potential benefits and risks of a CBDC, and identifies specific policy considerations."[80]

Money and Payments: The U.S. Dollar in the
Age of Digital Transformation
Board of Governors of the Federal Reserve System (2022)

* * *

Central Bank Digital Currency

The Federal Reserve is considering how a CBDC might fit into the U.S. money and payments land- scape. A crucial test for a potential CBDC is whether it would

---

79. https://www.federalreserve.gov/publications/files/money-and-payments-20220120.pdf.

80. Press Release: Money and Payments: The U.S. Dollar in the Age of Digital Transformation, https://www.federalreserve.gov/publications/money-and-payments-discussion-paper.htm (May 23, 2022).

prove superior to other methods that might address issues of concern outlined in this paper.

As noted above, for the purposes of this discussion paper, CBDC is defined as a digital liability of the Federal Reserve that is widely available to the general public.[19] Today, Federal Reserve notes (i.e., physical currency) are the only type of central bank money available to the general public. Like existing forms of commercial bank money and nonbank money, a CBDC would enable the general public to make digital payments. As a liability of the Federal Reserve, however, a CBDC would not require mechanisms like deposit insurance to maintain public confidence, nor would a CBDC depend on backing by an underlying asset pool to maintain its value. A CBDC would be the safest digital asset available to the general public, with no associated credit or liquidity risk.

The Federal Reserve will continue to explore a wide range of design options for a CBDC. While no decisions have been made on whether to pursue a CBDC, analysis to date suggests that a potential U.S. CBDC, if one were created, would best serve the needs of the United States by being privacy-protected, intermediated, widely transferable, and identity-verified.

Privacy-protected: Protecting consumer privacy is critical. Any CBDC would need to strike an appropriate balance, however, between safeguarding the privacy rights of consumers and affording the transparency necessary to deter criminal activity.

Intermediated: The Federal Reserve Act does not authorize direct Federal Reserve accounts for individuals, and such accounts would represent a significant expansion of the Federal Reserve's role in the financial system and the economy. Under an intermediated model, the private sector would offer accounts or digital wallets to facilitate the management of CBDC holdings and payments. Potential intermediaries could include commercial banks and regulated nonbank financial service providers, and would operate in an open market for CBDC services. Although commercial banks and nonbanks would offer services to individuals to manage their CBDC holdings and payments, the CBDC itself would be a liability of the Federal Reserve. An intermediated model would facilitate the use of the private sector's existing privacy and identity-management frameworks; leverage the private sector's ability to innovate; and reduce the prospects for destabilizing disruptions to the well-functioning U.S. financial system.

---

19. Narrower-purpose CBDCs could also be developed, such as one designed primarily for large-value institutional payments and not widely available to the public. In this paper, the term "general purpose" includes such potential uses for a CBDC but is not limited to it. The Board welcomes comments that may address whether there is a potential more limited role for a CBDC for such uses. CBDC is formally and broadly defined as a type of digital money issued by the central bank, denominated in the same way as its currency, that is in some way different from traditional reserve bank balances or settlement accounts. See Committee on Payments and Market Infrastructures, *Central Bank Digital Currencies* (Basel: BIS, March 2018), https://www.bis.org/cpmi/publ /d174.pdf; Bank for International Settlements, *Central Bank Digital Currencies: Foundational Principles and Core Features* (Basel: BIS, October 2020), https://www.bis.org/publ/othp33.pdf.

Transferable: For a CBDC to serve as a widely accessible means of payment, it would need to be readily transferable between customers of different intermediaries. The ability to transfer value seamlessly between different intermediaries makes the payment system more efficient by allowing money to move freely throughout the economy.

Identity-verified: Financial institutions in the United States are subject to robust rules that are designed to combat money laundering and the financing of terrorism. A CBDC would need to be designed to comply with these rules. In practice, this would mean that a CBDC intermediary would need to verify the identity of a person accessing CBDC, just as banks and other financial institutions currently verify the identities of their customers.[20]

* * *

Discussion Points

1. *Characterizing CBDC.* Is CBDC a form of tender, or is it merely a payment and exchange instrument? Is CBDC a fiat? Why or why not?

2. *Policy considerations.* What legal and regulatory questions should federal agencies consider when drafting regulations that relate to CBDC?

3. *Effect on the payments industry.* How can CBDC be advantageous to the payments industry? Do you think CBDC can help facilitate peer to peer transactions without the use of an intermediary?

II. CBDC and Cryptocurrency

Cryptocurrency and CBDCs are both digital currencies, and the technologies behind them might sound like similar concepts. However, they are vastly different. CBDC is a digital representation of legal tender and is regulated by the government. It is different from traditional cryptocurrencies like Bitcoin and Ethereum because it is centralized and regulated. Similar to stablecoins, CBDCs are backed by a reserve of monetary assets including gold or foreign currency. Although no country has officially launched a CBDC, the conversations are happening, and the United States is trailing. The Bank of England, the People's Bank of China, the Bank of Canada, and more are seriously contemplating the application of the CBDC and how it could help their economy.

---

20. In this regard, a CBDC would differ materially from cash, which enables anonymous transactions. While central banks are unable to fully prevent cash from being used for illicit purposes, a CBDC could potentially be used at much greater scale and velocity than cash, so compliance with laws designed to combat money laundering and funding terrorism is particularly important for CBDC.

CBDC differs from a credit card because of the entity that backs the funds. Credit cards are backed by private financial institutions, whereas a CBDC is backed by the central government.[81] In the United States' case, the Federal Reserve. The Federal Reserve has gone as far as noting that COVID-19 has highlighted many of the inefficiencies in the current payments market especially as it related to the distribution of stimulus funds, which made the agency open its eyes to the benefits of CBDC as it relates to mass distribution. Congress even introduced various bills that would fundamentally change how current payment systems operate.[82]

The Federal Reserve is committed to retaining the long-standing principles of safety and efficacy in the nation's payment systems that have guided central banks for over 100 years. The Federal Reserve has also recognized the importance of keeping the stakeholders' goals in mind, such as the government bodies, end users, financial institutions, technology and infrastructure providers, and others like academic institutions and think tanks.[83]

With evolving technological advances in financial products and services, including mobile payment apps, cryptocurrencies, stablecoins, and digital wallets, the Federal Reserve must explore all potential benefits and risks of issuing a CBDC.

Discussion Points

1. *Distinguish.* Distinguish CBDC from Bitcoin. How are they different? How would you define CBDC in your own words?

2. *What will be the reaction?* Do you think payment processors are responding to the inception of a digital U.S. dollar? Why or why not? What concerns do you think major payment processors have regarding CBDC?

3. Identify and explain the legal and regulatory issues concerning the implementation of a CBDC in the context of privacy, consumer protection, and anti-money laundering.

4. What jurisdictional and governance issues arise in the issuance and operation of a CBDC?

5. Discuss the legal and policy considerations that arise when transitioning from the exchange of tangible cash to a digital currency. What are the legal implications for monetary sovereignty, legal tender laws, and the general public's trust in currency?

---

81. Jess Cheng et al., *Preconditions for a General-Purpose Central Bank Digital Currency*, Fed. Reserve (Feb. 24, 2021), https://www.federalreserve.gov/econres/notes/feds-notes/preconditions-for-a-general-purpose-central-bank-digital-currency-20210224.htm.

82. *Id.* at n.4 (citing the Financial Protections and Assistance for America's Consumers, States, Businesses, and Vulnerable Populations Act, the Banking for All Act, and the Automatic Boost to Communities Act).

83. *Id.*

III. Privacy

One major question underlying CBDCs is whether they would protect consumers' privacy. CBDC's primary objectives are to provide privacy, transferability, ease, accessibility and financial security to companies and consumers. A CBDC has the ability to provide businesses and households a convenient form of electronic central bank money.

Although CBDCs could mean convenience, lower-cost transactions, and greater access to the financial system for some consumers, privacy is an important aspect that could be threatened if CBDCs are introduced. Additionally, there needs to be transparency in a CBDC system to deter criminal activity, which further threatens consumers' privacy rights.

The advantages for, for example, physical cash is that it is issued by the Treasury Department and typically distributed to the public via commercial banks and ATMs. Once you are in possession of physical cash, there really is no direct visibility into how a consumer uses that cash, other than a transaction record or third-part receipt. CBDC, however, has the potential of being tracked by the federal government.

A. Recent Legislative Bills

In 2022, U.S. Senators Chuck Grassley (R-Iowa), Ted Cruz (R-Texas) and Mike Braun (R-Ind.) introduced a bill to prohibit the Federal Reserve from "issuing a digital dollar that could be sent straight to users." The bill was introduced due to fears that CBDC could be used as a financial surveillance tool by the federal government, which is a major fear regarding CBDC.

Democrat Congressman Stephen Lynch also introduced a digital-dollar related bill similarly focused on privacy concerns, intended to retain the privacy elements of cash in a digital dollar system. Congressman Lynch's bill dives into financial inclusion, arguing that any digital dollar must be accessible to all.

Press Release: Sen. Cruz Introduces Legislation Prohibiting Unilateral Fed Control of a U.S. Digital Currency

March 30, 2022

WASHINGTON, D.C.—U.S. Sen. Ted Cruz (R-Texas), member of the Senate Commerce Committee, today introduced legislation to prohibit the Federal Reserve from issuing a central bank digital currency (CBDC) directly to individuals. Sen. Cruz's bill was cosponsored by Sens. Braun (R-IN) and Grassley (R-IA).

Specifically, the legislation prohibits the Federal Reserve from developing a direct-to-consumer CBDC which could be used as a financial surveillance tool by the federal government, similar to what is currently happening in China. The bill aims to maintain the dollar's dominance without competing with the private sector.

As other countries, like China, develop CBDCs that omit the benefits and protections of cash, it is more important than ever to ensure the United States' digital currency policy protects financial privacy, maintains the dollar's dominance, and cultivates innovation. CBDCs that fail to adhere to these three basic principles could enable an entity like the Federal Reserve to mobilize itself into a retail bank, collect personally identifiable information on users, and track their transactions indefinitely. It is important to note that the Fed does not, and should not, have the authority to offer retail bank accounts.

Unlike decentralized digital currencies like Bitcoin, CBDCs are issued and backed by a government entity and transact on a centralized, permissioned blockchain. Not only would this CBDC model centralize Americans' financial information, leaving it vulnerable to attack, it could be used a direct surveillance tool into the private transactions of Americans.

Upon introducing the legislation, Sen. Cruz said:

"The federal government has the ability to encourage and nurture innovation in the cryptocurrency space, or to completely devastate it. This bill goes a long way in making sure big government doesn't attempt to centralize and control cryptocurrency so that it can continue to thrive and prosper in the United States. We should be empowering entrepreneurs, enabling innovation, and increasing individual freedom—not stifling it."

Discussion Points

1. *Pros and cons.* What are the advantages and disadvantages of CBDC? Should central bank laws authorize the issuance of CBDC to the public?

2. *Intermediated model.* Using an intermediated model, the private sector would offer digital wallets or accounts to maintain the CBDC holdings and payments, and facilitate the use of the private sector's existing privacy and identity-management frameworks. This model would mean that a CBDC intermediary would need to verify the identity of a person accessing the CBDC. Should this intermediate model be adopted? Does it counteract the purpose of CBDC to have an intermediary involved?

3. *Did Senator Cruz get it right?* Do you agree with the above proposal? Which parts of the proposal do you agree with and which do you disagree with? What did this proposal fail to address that you think it should before this legislation progresses?

Fact Sheet: White House Releases First-Ever Comprehensive Framework for Responsible Development of Digital Assets

The White House, September 16, 2022

Following the President's Executive Order, New Reports, Outline Recommendations to Protect Consumers, Investors, Businesses, Financial Stability, National Security, and the Environment

The digital assets market has grown significantly in recent years. Millions of people globally, including 16% of adult Americans, have purchased digital assets—which reached a market capitalization of $3 trillion globally last November. Digital assets present potential opportunities to reinforce U.S. leadership in the global financial system and remain at the technological frontier. But they also pose real risks as evidenced by recent events in crypto markets. The May crash of a so-called stablecoin and the subsequent wave of insolvencies wiped out over $600 billion of investor and consumer funds.

President Biden's March 9 Executive Order (EO) on Ensuring Responsible Development of Digital Assets outlined the first whole-of-government approach to addressing the risks and harnessing the potential benefits of digital assets and their underlying technology. Over the past six months, agencies across the government have worked together to develop frameworks and policy recommendations that advance the six key priorities identified in the EO: consumer and investor protection; promoting financial stability; countering illicit finance; U.S. leadership in the global financial system and economic competitiveness; financial inclusion; and responsible innovation.

The nine reports submitted to the President to date, consistent with the EO's deadlines, reflect the input and expertise of diverse stakeholders across government, industry, academia, and civil society. Together, they articulate a clear framework for responsible digital asset development and pave the way for further action at home and abroad. The reports call on agencies to promote innovation by kickstarting private-sector research and development and helping cutting-edge U.S. firms find footholds in global markets. At the same time, they call for measures to mitigate the downside risks, like increased enforcement of existing laws and the creation of commonsense efficiency standards for cryptocurrency mining. Recognizing the potential benefits and risks of a U.S. Central Bank Digital Currency (CBDC), the reports encourage the Federal Reserve to continue its ongoing CBDC research, experimentation, and evaluation and call for the creation of a Treasury-led interagency working group to support the Federal Reserve's efforts.

Protecting Consumers, Investors, and Businesses

Digital assets pose meaningful risks for consumers, investors, and businesses. Prices of these assets can be highly volatile: the current global market capitalization of cryptocurrencies is approximately one-third of its November 2021 peak.

Still sellers commonly mislead consumers about digital assets' features and expected returns, and non-compliance with applicable laws and regulations remains widespread. One study found that almost a quarter of digital coin offerings had disclosure or transparency problems—like plagiarized documents or false promises of guaranteed returns. Outright fraud, scams, and theft in digital asset markets are on the rise: according to FBI statistics, reported monetary losses from digital asset scams were nearly 600 percent higher in 2021 than the year before.

Since taking office, the Biden-Harris Administration and independent regulators have worked to protect consumers and ensure fair play in digital assets markets by issuing guidance, increasing enforcement resources, and aggressively pursuing fraudulent actors. As outlined in the reports released today, the Administration plans to take the following additional steps:

- The reports encourage regulators like the Securities and Exchange Commission (SEC) and Commodity Futures Trading Commission (CFTC), consistent with their mandates, to aggressively pursue investigations and enforcement actions against unlawful practices in the digital assets space.

- The reports encourage Consumer Financial Protection Bureau (CFPB) and Federal Trade Commission (FTC), as appropriate, to redouble their efforts to monitor consumer complaints and to enforce against unfair, deceptive, or abusive practices.

- The reports encourage agencies to issue guidance and rules to address current and emergent risks in the digital asset ecosystem. Regulatory and law enforcement agencies are also urged to collaborate to address acute digital assets risks facing consumers, investors, and businesses. In addition, agencies are encouraged to share data on consumer complaints regarding digital assets—ensuring each agency's activities are maximally effective.

- The Financial Literacy Education Commission (FLEC) will lead public-awareness efforts to help consumers understand the risks involved with digital assets, identify common fraudulent practices, and learn how to report misconduct.

Promoting Access to Safe, Affordable Financial Services

Today, traditional finance leaves too many behind. Roughly 7 million Americans have no bank account. Another 24 million rely on costly nonbank services, like check cashing and money orders, for everyday needs. And for those who do use banks, paying with traditional financial infrastructure can be costly and slow—particularly for cross-border payments.

The digital economy should work for all Americans. That means developing financial services that are secure, reliable, affordable, and accessible to all. To make payments more efficient, the Federal Reserve has planned the 2023 launch of Fed-

Now—an instantaneous, 24/7 interbank clearing system that will further advance nationwide infrastructure for instant payments alongside The Clearinghouse's Real Time Payments system. Some digital assets could help facilitate faster payments and make financial services more accessible, but more work is needed to ensure they truly benefit underserved consumers and do not lead to predatory financial practices.

To promote safe and affordable financial services for all, the Administration plans to take the following steps:

- Agencies will encourage the adoption of instant payment systems, like Fed-Now, by supporting the development and use of innovative technologies by payment providers to increase access to instant payments, and using instant payment systems for their own transactions where appropriate—for example, in the context of distribution of disaster, emergency or other government-to-consumer payments.

- The President will also consider agency recommendations to create a federal framework to regulate nonbank payment providers.

- Agencies will prioritize efforts to improve the efficiency of cross-border payments by working to align global payments practices, regulations, and supervision protocols, while exploring new multilateral platforms that integrate instant payment systems.

- The National Science Foundation (NSF) will back research in technical and socio-technical disciplines and behavioral economics to ensure that digital asset ecosystems are designed to be usable, inclusive, equitable, and accessible by all.

Fostering Financial Stability

Digital assets and the mainstream financial system are becoming increasingly intertwined, creating channels for turmoil to have spillover effects. Stablecoins, in particular, could create disruptive runs if not paired with appropriate regulation. The potential for instability was illustrated in May 2022 by the crash of the so-called stablecoin TerraUSD and the subsequent wave of insolvencies that erased nearly $600 billion in wealth. In October, the Financial Stability Oversight Council (FSOC) will publish a report discussing digital assets' financial-stability risks, identifying related regulatory gaps, and making additional recommendations to foster financial stability.

The Biden-Harris Administration has long recognized the need for regulation to address digital assets' stability risks. For example, in 2021, the President's Working Group on Financial Markets recommended steps for Congress and regulators to make stablecoins safer. Building on this work, the Administration plans to take the additional following steps:

- The Treasury will work with financial institutions to bolster their capacity to identify and mitigate cyber vulnerabilities by sharing information and promoting a wide range of data sets and analytical tools.

- The Treasury will work with other agencies to identify, track, and analyze emerging strategic risks that relate to digital asset markets. It will also collaborate on identifying such risks with U.S. allies, including through international organizations like the Organization for Economic Co-operation and Development (OECD) and the Financial Stability Board (FSB).

Advancing Responsible Innovation

U.S. companies lead the world in innovation. Digital asset firms are no exception. As of 2022, the United States is home to roughly half of the world's 100 most valuable financial technology companies, many of which trade in digital asset services.

The U.S. government has long played a critical role in priming responsible private-sector innovation. It sponsors cutting-edge research, helps firms compete globally, assists them with compliance, and works with them to mitigate harmful side-effects of technological advancement.

In keeping with this tradition, the Administration plans to take the following steps to foster responsible digital asset innovation:

- The Office of Science and Technology Policy (OSTP) and NSF will develop a Digital Assets Research and Development Agenda to kickstart fundamental research on topics such as next-generation cryptography, transaction programmability, cybersecurity and privacy protections, and ways to mitigate the environmental impacts of digital assets. It will also continue to support research that translates technological breakthroughs into market-ready products. Additionally, NSF will back social-sciences and education research that develops methods of informing, educating, and training diverse groups of stakeholders on safe and responsible digital asset use.

- The Treasury and financial regulators are encouraged to, as appropriate, provide innovative U.S. firms developing new financial technologies with regulatory guidance, best-practices sharing, and technical assistance through things like tech sprintsand Innovation Hours.

- The Department of Energy, the Environmental Protection Agency, and other agencies will consider further tracking digital assets' environmental impacts; developing performance standards as appropriate; and providing local authorities with the tools, resources, and expertise to mitigate environmental harms. Powering crypto-assets can take a large amount of electricity—which can emit greenhouse gases, strain electricity grids, and harm some local communities with noise and water pollution. Opportunities exist to align the development of digital assets with transitioning to a net-zero emissions economy and improving environmental justice.

- The Department of Commerce will examine establishing a standing forum to convene federal agencies, industry, academics, and civil society to exchange knowledge and ideas that could inform federal regulation, standards, coordinating activities, technical assistance, and research support.

Reinforcing Our Global Financial Leadership and Competitiveness

Today, global standard-setting bodies are establishing policies, guidance, and regulatory recommendations for digital assets. The United States is working actively with its partners to set out these policies in line with our goals and values, while also reinforcing the United States' role in the global financial system. Similarly, the United States has a valuable opportunity to partner with countries still developing their digital assets ecosystems, helping to ensure that countries' financial, legal, and technological infrastructures respect core values including data privacy, financial stability, and human rights.

To reinforce U.S. financial leadership and uphold U.S. values in global digital asset markets, the Administration will take the following steps outlined in the framework for international engagement released by the Treasury Department earlier this summer:

- U.S. agencies will leverage U.S. positions in international organizations to message U.S. values related to digital assets. U.S. agencies will also continue and expand their leadership roles on digital assets work at international organizations and standard-setting bodies—such as the G7, G20, OECD, FSB, Financial Action Task Force (FATF), and the International Organization for Standardization. Agencies will promote standards, regulations, and frameworks that reflect values like data privacy, free and efficient markets, financial stability, consumer protection, robust law enforcement, and environmental sustainability.

- The State Department, the Department of Justice (DOJ), and other U.S. enforcement agencies will increase collaboration with—and assistance to—partner agencies in foreign countries through global enforcement bodies like the Egmont Group, bilateral information sharing, and capacity building.

- The State Department, Treasury, USAID, and other agencies will explore further technical assistance to developing countries building out digital asset infrastructure and services. As appropriate, this assistance may include technical assistance on legal and regulatory frameworks, evidence-gathering and knowledge-sharing on the impacts, risks, and opportunities of digital assets.

- The Department of Commerce will help cutting-edge U.S. financial technology and digital asset firms find a foothold in global markets for their products.

Fighting Illicit Finance

The United States has been a leader in applying its anti-money laundering and countering the financing of terrorism (AML/CFT) framework in the digital asset ecosystem. It has published relevant guidance, engaged in regular public-private dialogue, used its enforcement tools, and led in setting international AML/CFT standards. While our efforts have strengthened the U.S. financial system, digital assets—some of which are pseudonymous and can be transferred without a financial intermediary—have been exploited by bad actors to launder illicit proceeds, to finance terrorism and the proliferation of weapons of mass destruction, and to conduct a wide array of other crimes. For example, digital assets have facilitated the rise of ransomware cybercriminals; narcotics sales and money laundering for drug trafficking organizations; and the funding of activities of rogue regimes, as was the case in the recent thefts by the Democratic People's Republic of Korea (DPRK)-affiliated Lazarus Group.

It is in the national interest to mitigate these risks through regulation, oversight, law enforcement action, and the use of other United States Government authorities. To fight the illicit use of digital assets more effectively, the Administration plans to take the following steps:

- The President will evaluate whether to call upon Congress to amend the Bank Secrecy Act (BSA), anti-tip-off statutes, and laws against unlicensed money transmitting to apply explicitly to digital asset service providers—including digital asset exchanges and nonfungible token (NFT) platforms. He will also consider urging Congress to raise the penalties for unlicensed money transmitting to match the penalties for similar crimes under other money-laundering statutes and to amend relevant federal statutes to let the Department of Justice prosecute digital asset crimes in any jurisdiction where a victim of those crimes is found.

- The United States will continue to monitor the development of the digital assets sector and its associated illicit financing risks, to identify any gaps in our legal, regulatory, and supervisory regimes. As part of this effort, Treasury will complete an illicit finance risk assessment on decentralized finance by the end of February 2023 and an assessment on non-fungible tokens by July 2023.

- Relevant departments and agencies will continue to expose and disrupt illicit actors and address the abuse of digital assets. Such actions will hold cybercriminals and other malign actors responsible for their illicit activity and identify nodes in the ecosystem that pose national security risks.

- Treasury will enhance dialogue with the private sector to ensure that firms understand existing obligations and illicit financing risks associated with digital assets, share information, and encourage the use of emerging technologies to comply with obligations. This will be supported by a Request for Comment published to the Federal Register for input on several items related to AML/CFT.

Informing the above recommendations, the Treasury, DOJ/FBI, DHS, and NSF drafted risk assessments to provide the Administration with a comprehensive view of digital assets' illicit-finance risks. The CFPB, an independent agency, also voluntarily provided information to the Administration as to risks arising from digital assets. The risks that agencies highlight include, but are not limited to, money laundering; terrorist financing; hacks that result in losses of funds; and fragilities, common practices, and fast-changing technology that may present vulnerabilities for misuse.

Exploring a U.S. Central Bank Digital Currency (CBDC)

A U.S. CBDC—a digital form of the U.S. dollar—has the potential to offer significant benefits. It could enable a payment system that is more efficient, provides a foundation for further technological innovation, facilitates faster cross-border transactions, and is environmentally sustainable. It could promote financial inclusion and equity by enabling access for a broad set of consumers. In addition, it could foster economic growth and stability, protect against cyber and operational risks, safeguard the privacy of sensitive data, and minimize risks of illicit financial transactions. A potential U.S. CBDC could also help preserve U.S. global financial leadership, and support the effectiveness of sanctions. But a CBDC could also have unintended consequences, including runs to CBDC in times of stress.

Recognizing the possibility of a U.S. CBDC, the Administration has developed Policy Objectives for a U.S. CBDC System, which reflect the federal government's priorities for a potential U.S. CBDC. These objectives flesh out the goals outlined for a CBDC in the E.O. A U.S. CBDC system, if implemented, should protect consumers, promote economic growth, improve payment systems, provide interoperability with other platforms, advance financial inclusion, protect national security, respect human rights, and align with democratic values. But further research and development on the technology that would support a U.S. CBDC is needed. The Administration encourages the Federal Reserve to continue its ongoing CBDC research, experimentation, and evaluation. To support the Federal Reserve's efforts and to advance other work on a potential U.S. CBDC, the Treasury will lead an interagency working group to consider the potential implications of a U.S. CBDC, leverage cross-government technical expertise, and share information with partners. The leadership of the Federal Reserve, the National Economic Council, the National Security Council, the Office of Science and Technology Policy, and the Treasury Department will meet regularly to discuss the working group's progress and share updates on and share updates on CDBC and other payments innovations.

Discussion Points

1. *Is this a good policy?* Do you think that the federal government is being pro-active in responding to the proliferation of digital currencies? Do you think the widespread adoption of national CBDC is possible? Why or why not?

2. *Which departments and agencies are "relevant"?* Which federal agencies and departments do you think should be at the forefront of overseeing the possible development of a national CBDC?

3. *Weighing the pros and cons.* What would be the advantages and disadvantages of adopting a U.S. CBDC? Would the FDIC have to expand its insurance coverage to include banks that hold custody of CBDC? Would the FDIC have to ensure all banks, regardless of whether they are federally or privately chartered?

Governor Michelle W. Bowman Speech on
Central Bank Digital Currency
April 18, 2023

Considerations for a Central Bank Digital Currency

At the Georgetown University McDonough School of Business Psaros Center for Financial Markets and Policy, Washington, DC

It is a pleasure to be with you today to discuss the evolving money and payments landscape in the United States, which is a topic of primary importance to the Federal Reserve. Technological innovation has changed this landscape in recent years, as we have seen the emergence of new financial services entrants offering payments services, new platforms designed to increase the speed of payments, clearing, and settlement, and new forms of digital money. Over the past several years, and as a direct result of these developments, we have seen a significant increase in attention on central bank digital currencies (CBDCs) from central banks around the world in addition to a great deal of international and domestic engagement on CBDC. A number of central banks have taken steps to begin exploring the potential uses of a CBDC in their home countries. A very small number have adopted a CBDC for their local jurisdictions. And of course, discussions of the purpose, design, and potential risks of a U.S. CBDC, and technical research about key design elements, continue here in the United States. While the Federal Reserve plays an important role in these ongoing discussions and technical research, the Fed would not implement a U.S. CBDC without the approval of Congress.

In broad terms, a CBDC is simply a new form of digital liability of a central bank. Because it is issued by a central bank, CBDC is typically thought of as being denominated in the currency of that central bank. One could imagine a digital U.S. dollar, a digital euro, or a digital pound. Beyond this baseline definition though, "what is a CBDC" defies a simple definition. A CBDC built on distributed ledger technology offers a wide range of design and potential use options, as well as potential risks. This variability complicates any discussion of a CBDC simply because we may not be talking about the same thing.

There are two threshold questions that a policymaker needs to ask before any decision to move forward with a CBDC. First, what problem is the policymaker trying to solve, and is a CBDC a potential solution? Second, what features and considerations--including unintended consequences—may a policymaker want to consider in deciding to design and adopt a CBDC? While it would be impossible for me to provide a comprehensive analysis of every issue surrounding CBDC, my goal today is to offer a perspective on these two threshold questions and to conclude with some thoughts about the imperative for future research on CBDCs and the potential future of CBDCs in the United States.

What Problem Could a CBDC Solve?

In my view, the fundamental question is: what problem could a CBDC solve?

CBDC and the Payment System

One issue being examined is whether a CBDC or even broader forms of digital money could make the payment system more efficient. Do these new technologies present opportunities to increase the speed of payments and/or lower costs and frictions within the payment system?

Of course, this question takes place in the context of the payments infrastructure in each jurisdiction, both for domestic payments and for cross-border payments. Many countries have launched faster payment systems and continue to investigate how central banks can support these payment systems. We have seen a wide range of motivations for this work, including addressing specific inefficiencies in the payment system, providing a CBDC if cash use were to decline, or promoting broader private-sector innovation for future generations of payments.[1]

---

1. For example, The Bank of England and HM Treasury have stated that they judge that it is likely a digital pound will be needed in the future and that further preparatory work is justified. See Bank of England and HM Treasury, *The Digital Pound: A New Form of Money for Households and Businesses? (PDF)* Consultation Paper (London: Bank of England, February 2023).

However, the UK parliament has previously expressed skepticism. See House of Lords, UK Parliament, *Central Bank Digital Currencies: A Solution in Search of a Problem?*, HL Paper 131, (London: House of Lords, UK Parliament, January 2022). Similarly, a government-appointed report in Sweden did not find a current need for a CBDC, though the Riksbank continues to investigate how an e-krona could work if a decision is taken in the future to issue digital central bank money. See Centralbanking.com, "Sweden Does Not Yet Need CBDC, Inquiry Finds," web article, https://www.centralbanking.com/fintech/cbdc/7957236/sweden-does-not-yet-need-cbdc-inquiry-finds and Sveriges Riksbank, *E-krona Pilot Phase 3* (Sweden: Riksbank, April 2023).

Improving the speed of payments, particularly retail payments, can be accomplished without the introduction of a CBDC. In the United States, beginning later this year, the Federal Reserve's FedNowSM Service will enable banks in the United States to offer their customers the ability to send and receive payments in real-time.[2]

Policymakers have also raised other arguments for why a CBDC may be suitable in their home countries. Some have argued that a CBDC would facilitate large-value transactions between financial institutions.[3] Others see CBDC as a vehicle to improve upon international payments. And still others view CBDCs as necessary to preserve the role of central bank money as a stabilizing force in the payments system and to safeguard monetary sovereignty,[4] or to ensure that digital money has a high degree of safety and uniformity to promote innovation and competition.[5]

CBDC and Financial Inclusion

Another issue that some have raised is whether innovation in money and payments, including a potential U.S. CBDC, could improve financial inclusion. We can all agree that financial inclusion is an important goal when considering improvements in access to financial services, banking, and the payment system. However, in the United States today, over 95 percent of households have a least one member of the household with a banking relationship holding a checking or savings account.[6] Of the remaining 4.5 percent who are not banked, nearly three-quarters have no interest in having a bank account, and approximately one-third cited a lack of trust in banks as the reason for not having a bank account. I think it is unlikely that this group would find the government somehow more trustworthy than highly regulated banks. Unbanked households are also less likely to own mobile phones or have access to the internet, which would present barriers to CBDC adoption. While there has been important research on these barriers to adoption, including consumer attitudes and technology requirements, policymakers also need to consider whether there are other means to improve financial

---

2. FedNow is expected to be available to financial institutions in July that are early adopters and have completed a program for customer certification and testing. See Board of Governors of the Federal Reserve System, "Federal Reserve Announces July Launch for the FedNow Service," news release, March 15, 2023.

3. Agustín Carstens, general manager of the Bank for International Settlements has discussed the idea of a "unified ledger" run by the central bank to fully realize the potential of new technologies developed by the private sector. See Agustín Carstens, "Innovation and the Future of the Monetary System," speech at the Monetary Authority of Singapore, Singapore, February 22, 2023.

4. Fabio Panetta, "Central Bank Digital Currencies: Defining the Problems, Designing the Solutions (PDF)," speech at U.S. Monetary Policy Forum, New York, February 18, 2022.

5. Jon Cunliffe, "The Digital Pound," speech at UK Finance, February 7, 2023.

6. 2021 FDIC National Survey of Unbanked and Underbanked Households (PDF).

inclusion, such as alternatives for making the distribution of government benefits more efficient and effective like promoting financial literacy.[7]

CBDC for Implementation of Policy Objectives

Another issue is whether the government should use new technologies, including a potential CBDC, to accomplish a variety of policy objectives beyond those directly related to the operating of an efficient and safe financial system. Imagine a scenario in which fiscal spending, in the form of government benefits or payments, could be transferred via CBDC and could include a limited timeframe in which they could be spent before expiring. Enabling this type of limit through a CBDC would stand in stark contrast to the flexibility and freedom embedded in physical currency or bank deposits and could serve to control or even harm consumers and businesses. There is also a risk that this type of control could lead to the politicization of the payments system and at its heart, how money is used. A CBDC that permitted this type of control not only has the potential to allow the government to limit certain types of private spending or limit access to banking accounts, it could also threaten the Federal Reserve's independence.

The Efficiency and Speed of the Payments System

CBDCs are often discussed in the context of providing fast or instant payments for a variety of transactions, whether consumer-to-business or person-to-person transactions. As I previously noted, the introduction of the FedNow Service in the United States and other instant payments platforms globally leads me to ask: What could a CBDC accomplish, if anything, over and above what instant payments platforms alone can accomplish? There are potential use cases in the context of certain interbank transactions in wholesale markets, where some transactions are slow and heavily resource-intensive to clear and settle. Participants in the wholesale financial markets have been considering innovative ways to address these frictions with newer technologies such as distributed ledger technology in which shared information across counterparties could be leveraged to increase speed and reduce back-office costs to reconcile transactions before they settle. In the public debate about CBDC, some have argued that the introduction of a wholesale version of a CBDC could fully unlock the benefits of these newer technologies for these financial market use cases. Similar to the questions noted for a retail level CBDC, policymakers must carefully consider the wholesale use cases, including whether there is added value of a wholesale version of CBDC in supporting new infrastructure to financial transactions over and above existing methods.

---

7. For additional discussion on CBDC design and financial inclusion, see Maniff, Jesse Leigh, "Inclusion by Design: Crafting a Central Bank Digital Currency to Reach All Americans."

Cross-Border Activities

In the international context, frictions and high costs are pain points often associated with cross-border payments. Many policymakers have discussed whether CBDCs could play a role in streamlining cross-border payments by using new technologies, introducing simplified distribution channels, and creating additional opportunities for cross-jurisdictional collaboration and interoperability. Of course, these opportunities may be limited by the regulatory and legal safeguards in place for payments between countries with different legal structures, including customer identification, customer due diligence, and sanctions screening for compliance with regulations and policies for Bank Secrecy Act/Anti-Money Laundering (BSA/AML). These competing priorities are challenging to reconcile. While cross-border payments are among the slowest and least efficient, they also raise substantial legal and regulatory compliance concerns that would apply equally to CBDCs.

International Role of the U.S. Dollar

Another consideration is whether a CBDC (or lack of it) would affect the role of the U.S. dollar in international trade.[8] In my view, the dollar serves this role because of the size of the U.S. economy, its deep and liquid financial markets, the strength of U.S. institutions, and its commitment to the rule of law. A CBDC, or lack of it, may not meaningfully change the existing incentives for people, firms, or countries to conduct business in the dollar. Therefore, maintenance of the dollar as a reserve global currency will require broad policies that foster economic growth, liquid markets, and an unwavering commitment to the rule of law. And we should have an imperative to research and experiment with new technological innovation. I will say more on that shortly.

Declining Cash Use and CBDC

In jurisdictions that have not adopted a CBDC, cash is generally the only central bank money available to the public, and it remains an important and popular means of payment.[9] In some countries, however, digital payments have rapidly supplanted the use of cash. As a result of this trend, many central banks have cited the importance of access to central bank money by the general public as a potential reason to issue a CBDC. For example, Sir Jon Cunliffe of the United Kingdom examined the central role money plays in social and economic stability and concluded that, because private money has been replacing the use of government money over time,

---

8. See Christopher J. Waller, "The U.S. Dollar and Central Bank Digital Currencies," speech at Digital Currencies and National Security Tradeoffs, a symposium presented by the Harvard National Security Journal, Cambridge, Massachusetts, October 14, 2022. ("I don't think there are implications... [on the adoption of a U.S. CBDC] for the role of the United States in the global economy and financial system.")

9. See Board of Governors of the Federal Reserve System, *Money and Payments: The U.S. Dollar in the Age of Digital Transformation (PDF)* (Washington: Board of Governors, January 2022).

at some point "a retail, general purpose digital currency ... will be needed in the U.K."[10] Because the Federal Reserve is committed to ensuring the continued safety and availability of cash, a CBDC could be considered as a means to *expand* safe payment options, not to reduce or replace them. So, an important issue for us to consider would be whether a CBDC could provide the public with a more attractive alternative to cash in a world that may be shifting away from cash-based payments. In probing this question, we need to also consider the privacy implications, and whether a CBDC would be a better alternative than private-sector solutions.

Stablecoins and CBDC

Some new private forms of money, often referred to as stablecoins, have emerged mainly to support trading in the crypto-asset ecosystem both as a means of payment and as a store of value. These stablecoins, which purport to have convertibility one-for-one with the dollar, have also been discussed as an alternative to traditional payments. However, stablecoins are less secure, less stable, and less regulated than traditional forms of money. and their structures and frameworks are opaque. To the extent stablecoins become widely used in day-to-day payments, these features could raise significant concerns. Of course, issuing a CBDC has been discussed as a potential alternative to stablecoins that could address some of these shortcomings. It is also possible that Congress could pass legislation to strengthen the regulation and oversight of stablecoins to mitigate some of these issues. I will be following developments in Congress closely on this and other digital assets. Regardless, it is important for us to continue to evaluate the evolving landscape of digital assets and understand whether and how well-regulated stablecoins or a CBDC would interact with each other and with the broader payments system.

Design Features and Policy Considerations The Fed's ongoing exploratory work helps us to think critically about a future shaped by innovations in payments and the broader economy, including instant payments and new potential forms of money and payment systems like CBDCs and other digital assets that could potentially play a larger role in the economy. While the investigation of CBDC raises many policy questions, for the purposes of today's discussion I will focus on a few key areas that are important from my perspective.

Privacy Considerations

As we consider these potential opportunities for improvements and innovation, we must also note that the introduction of a CBDC could present significant risks, challenges, and tradeoffs. First, in my view safeguarding privacy is a top concern and is also often identified as a top concern of consumers and other stakeholders. As a baseline, we need to think about how to protect the privacy of consumers and busi-

---

10. Jon Cunliffe, "The Digital Pound."

nesses, while also establishing an appropriate level of transparency that would deter criminal activity.

We must ensure that consumer data privacy protections embedded in today's payment systems continue and are extended into future systems. In thinking about the implications of CBDC and privacy, we must also consider the central role that money plays in our daily lives, and the risk that a CBDC would provide not only a window into, but potentially an impediment to, the freedom Americans enjoy in choosing how money and resources are used and invested. So, a central consideration must be how a potential U.S. CBDC could incorporate privacy considerations into its design, and what technology and policy options could support a robust privacy framework.

The issue of privacy may be less difficult to address in the case of wholesale use cases, in which a CBDC would only be used by traditional financial institutions to conduct a limited range of financial market transactions. As with many of these considerations, the purpose and intended function of a CBDC has a major impact on its policy and design considerations.

Interoperability and Innovation

Relatedly, one possible way to design a CBDC could be to focus on providing a foundational layer on top of which banks and other eligible institutions could build their own technology. In such an intermediated model, banks and other eligible institutions would build technology on top of a CBDC that could be offered to retail consumers and others to provide products and services that may not be available today. It would be important to understand how such a layer would connect or interact with existing and new payments infrastructures. It is useful to consider what types of innovations this could encourage. Some of the research on the design and functionality of CBDCs contemplates things like increased programmability—allowing the efficient transfer of money through the use of so-called smart contracts—that could improve upon existing, regulated forms of money and payments. These are important questions worth exploring, but they link back to the identification of "problems" that a CBDC would be designed to solve.

Unintended Effects on the U.S. Banking System

It is also necessary to consider the potential impacts of a CBDC on the banking sector. Today's banking system delivers important benefits to our economy and, as I noted earlier, is continuing to evolve through innovations, like the improved availability of instant payments already discussed.

There are significant risks in adopting a CBDC that cannibalizes rather than complements the U.S. banking system. The U.S. banking system is a mature, well-functioning, effective and efficient system. Banks provide consumers access to credit and other banking and payments services. Banks also support important public policies, including reporting on suspicious or criminal activity through their BSA/AML compliance and reporting.

More importantly, banks play an essential role in the transmission of monetary policy and supporting a well-functioning economy and financial system. If the Federal Reserve were to be authorized and directed to implement a U.S. CBDC, we would need to carefully consider how an intermediated CBDC, with private-sector service providers, could be designed in a way that maintains financial institution involvement and minimizes disruptions to the financial system. A CBDC, if not properly designed, could disrupt the banking system and lead to disintermediation, potentially harming consumers and businesses, and could present broader financial stability risks.[11] Consider the consequences of a CBDC that pays interest at comparable or better rates than commercial bank deposits and other low-risk assets. It seems likely that such a CBDC would reduce the funds available to lend and increase the cost of capital across the economy. Likewise, we need to consider the effect on bank stability, and the potential of even more rapid bank runs, in a world where there are fewer constraints on the volume and velocity of payments. The ongoing demand for private and public options to facilitate instant payments may exacerbate these concerns.

These are exactly the types of issues that policymakers must confront. It would be irresponsible to undermine the traditional banking system by introducing a CBDC without appropriate guardrails to mitigate these potential impacts on the banking sector and the financial system.

The Imperative of Continuing Research

The Federal Reserve's work continues to explore an array of CBDC design choices and the challenging consideration of policy tradeoffs that this multitude of choices presents. It is imperative that each of these tradeoffs is carefully evaluated and thoroughly understood. Where opportunities for improvements may exist, we should ask whether a U.S. CBDC is the most efficient and effective means to make such improvements, or are there better alternatives, such as enhancements to current payment infrastructures? Apart from focusing on payments alone, it is also worth considering whether other policies would more effectively target financial inclusion, including policies that are beyond the remit of the Federal Reserve. And in the absence of a CBDC, some of these risks I noted may still exist as the private sector continues to innovate, including the risk of substitution from commercial bank deposits to digital wallets, and the migration to less regulated digital assets, including stablecoins. With such significant potential opportunities, risks, and tradeoffs, it is essential that the Federal Reserve continue to thoroughly research and engage with

---

11. For discussion on CBDC implications for bank funding, lending, and resilience, see Bank for International Settlements, *"Central Bank Digital Currencies: Financial Stability Implications (PDF)* (Basel: BIS, September 2021); and Sebastian Infante, Kyungmin Kim, Anna Orlik, André F. Silva, and Robert J. Tetlow, "The Macrceconomic Implications of CBDC: A Review of the Literature," Finance and Economics Discussion Series 2022-076 (Washington: Board of Governors of the Federal Reserve System, October 2022).

stakeholders to further understand these issues. Future decisions about the implementation of technology innovations in money and payments, including a potential U.S. CBDC, must be informed by a deep and thorough understanding of potential intended and unintended consequences, as well as understanding whether a CBDC would be the most effective and efficient means to improve the payment system and address identified problems.

The Federal Reserve has continued its independent research and technical experimentation on digital innovations, including digital assets and CBDC. Specific to CBDC, the Federal Reserve established a program of work that aims to (1) carry out policy analysis to provide perspectives on issues articulated in the Board's January 2022 discussion paper; (2) conduct technology research and experimentation to inform potential CBDC designs; and (3) invest in engagement with the public, industry, academia, and the public sector to bring along stakeholders and obtain needed expertise.

Concluding Thoughts: The Potential Future of CBDC in the United States

Of course, as the evolution of money and payments continues, it is important for the Federal Reserve to continue looking ahead to anticipate potential changes to money and payments well into the future. With this in mind, our consideration of other potential innovations to money and payments, including a potential U.S. CBDC, must be viewed through the lens of whether and how the payment system would be improved beyond what instant payment services will achieve. We should ask "what current frictions exist or may emerge in the payment system that *only* a CBDC can solve, or that a CBDC can solve *most efficiently*?"

In my view, it is important that the Federal Reserve is a part of the ongoing conversations around CBDCs, whether or not a CBDC is ultimately created in the United States. As the Federal Reserve continues to monitor developments in other jurisdictions, we will work closely with international counterparts on payments innovation, CBDC, and other related topics. This includes work with multilateral institutions such as the Bank for International Settlements, the G7, and the Financial Stability Board, as well as bilateral engagements with other central banks.

From my perspective, there could be some promise for wholesale CBDCs in the future for settlement of certain financial market transactions and processing international payments. When it comes to some of the broader design and policy issues, particularly those around consumer privacy and impacts on the banking system, it is difficult to imagine a world where the tradeoffs between benefits and unintended consequences could justify a direct access CBDC for uses beyond interbank and wholesale transactions.

It is important that we thoughtfully examine the evolving money and payments landscape and digital innovations broadly, including a potential U.S. CBDC. In addition to understanding international approaches to these issues, the Federal Reserve's research, experimentation, and outreach to stakeholders help us to gain important input and perspective on these issues. Apart from these ongoing CBDC-related efforts, the Federal Reserve is committed to the successful implementation of Fed-Now, which is expected to support the broader adoption of instant payments in the U.S., meaningfully evolving and upgrading the U.S. payments infrastructure for consumers and businesses.

Thank you for the opportunity to share my thoughts on these important issues.

IV. Will a U.S. CBDC Replace Cash or Paper Currency?

Another major question underlying CBDCs is whether everything should be digital. The cash system also has the benefit of maintaining privacy and personal autonomy. Some may argue that society has undergone many technological updates and changes, and adopting a digital version of the dollar may better suit today's increasingly cashless world. On the contrary, others may argue that it could cause social and economic issues because not everyone has access to an electronic system. Many countries lack access to banking services. For example, in the United States, more than 5% of families do not utilize banks, about 7 million people.

The benefits of cash are that cash is a convenient means of payment, is safe, and preserves consumers' privacy. Many central banks are studying whether to adopt a CBDC that would stand alongside cash. A Bank of England discussion paper, in 2021, demonstrated that cash in England was the prominent means of transactions until 2016. They reasoned that the COVID-19 pandemic accelerated the trend of credit cards and other forms of payments.

The Federal Reserve has emphasized its commitment to ensuring the continued safety and availability of cash. Although the Federal Reserve is considering a CBDC, the objective would be to expand safe payment options, not reduce or replace them. However, there is fear that retailers and others will be reluctant to accept cash when digital currencies become mainstream. In the CBDC report discussed earlier in the chapter, Money and Payments: The U.S. Dollar in the Age of Digital Transformation, the Board acknowledges that further study would be helpful to determine how CBDC would affect financial inclusion, especially in underserved and lower-income communities.

Discussion Points

1. *The way of the future?* Do you think a U.S. digital dollar can replace paper money? Why or why not. What are the advantages and disadvantages of a cashless future? What ramifications would the use of solely digital money have on consumer privacy rights? Would consumers lose privacy protections if all transactions could be tracked and maintained using algorithms?

2. *Too much control?* From a regulatory perspective, what are the advantages of having a CBDC that is controlled by a central bank? From a legal perspective, what are the possible ramifications of this? In your opinion, what are the main legal questions that need to be answered as CBDC proliferates?

3. *Deterring criminal activity.* Do you think that CBDC is more or less prone to being used to facilitate money laundering? What attributes of CBDC make it more or less difficult for money laundering to occur? Does the algorithmic nature of transactions using CBDC make it easier for regulators to spot money laundering activity?

Nine

Anti-Money Laundering

I. Introduction

Money laundering affects both fiat and virtual currencies worldwide. Money laundering finances criminal activities that adversely impact the global economy, such as drug trafficking and terrorism. Money laundering is the practice of making illegally-obtained proceeds, i.e., "dirty money" appear legal and clean. The process of money laundering typically involves three steps: 1. Placement, 2. Layering, and 3. Integration. The first step, placement, is when the illegally-gained funds are secretly introduced into a legal financial system. The second step, layering, is when money is moved around to create confusion, i.e., through wiring or transferring through numerous accounts. The last step, integration, is when the illegally-gained funds are integrated into the financial system through more transactions until the "dirty money" appears "clean."

To combat the financing of these and other criminal activities, regulatory bodies have enacted anti-money laundering (AML) legislation. Particularly, the Financial Crimes Enforcement Network (FinCEN) bureau of the U.S. Department of Treasury focuses on safeguarding the financial system from illicit use and combatting money laundering. In 2001, in response to the September 11th terrorist attacks, Congress passed the USA Patriot Act, giving law enforcement agencies across the U.S., including FinCEN, a wide range of new investigative powers. These new powers comprise measures to address illicit financial crimes associated with terrorism, including money laundering and the financing of terrorism.

II. Anti-Money Laundering and Cryptocurrencies

FinCEN detects and deters money laundering in two ways: First, FinCEN works in alliance with the financial community. FinCEN requires that banks and other financial institutions report and keep a record of financial transactions by using anti-money laundering laws, like the Bank Secrecy Act. The second way that FinCEN detects and deters money laundering is through collaborating with law enforcement on local, state, and federal levels by providing intelligence and analytical support and increased information sharing. As technology evolves, FinCEN has to adapt its financial laws and regulations.

A. The Bank Secrecy Act

The BSA was the United States' first AML statute, enacted in 1970. FinCEN currently administers it and has become one of the most important tools in the fight against money laundering. The BSA requires financial institutions to assist the federal government in detecting and preventing money laundering and terrorism financing by meeting special program, recordkeeping, and reporting requirements. Those vulnerable institutions must file and report financial transactions that are suggestive of money laundering. These transactions include cash transactions over $10,000 and suspicious transactions.

The Patriot Act significantly changed the Bank Secrecy Act (BSA) because it expanded the legal requirements, including AML and Know Your Customer (KYC) provisions. Under the BSA, financial institutions must register with FinCEN, prepare a written anti-money laundering compliance program, and file BSA reports for suspicious activity and transactions. The reports required by the BSA help investigators create a financial trail to follow criminals and track their assets; however, for these reports to have a significant value, they must be accessible to law enforcement. The Patriot Act requires all financial institutions to develop and implement their own AML program and emphasizes a number of mandatory checks and screening capabilities. Every company should tailor their AML program to meet their company's particular vulnerabilities. The AML criteria states that a company must develop internal AML policies, procedures, and controls; an AML Compliance Officer must be appointed to oversee the AML program; employees must receive ongoing AML training; and the AML program must be independently audited regularly.

The AML program at a minimum, must:

- Incorporate policies, procedures and internal controls reasonably designed to assure ongoing compliance
- Designate an individual responsible for assuring day-to-day compliance with the program and BSA requirements
- Provide training for appropriate personnel, including training in the detection of suspicious transactions
- Provide for independent review to monitor and maintain an adequate program

B. The Anti-Money Laundering Act of 2020

Virtual currencies, like real currencies, are vulnerable to being manipulated, like for money laundering. Some virtual currencies have the power to fuel anonymous transactions, making money laundering a prime concern for regulators. AML in the cryptocurrencies space refers to the laws, regulations, and policies in place to prevent criminals from turning unlawfully obtained cryptocurrency into cash.

FinCEN was one of the first U.S. federal agencies to think about cryptocurrency regulation and the applicability of money transmitter laws and anti-money laundering laws on virtual currencies through the Bank Secrecy Act discussed earlier in this chapter. The agency has said for years that cryptocurrency and other digital assets fall within the scope of AML regulation. However, in January 2021, the Anti-Money Laundering Act of 2020 was introduced into law, codifying FinCEN's previous guidance related to digital currencies. The Act expands the Treasury Department's power to declare that cryptocurrency transactions must be reported to federal regulators because cryptocurrency is a monetary instrument, like other traditional currency transactions. By declaring this, certain cryptocurrency transactions must be reported to FinCEN's anti-money laundering program.

The AML Act revised the BSA to clearly include cryptocurrency and other digital assets within its regulatory scope. Although you will not find familiar phrases like, "bitcoin," "cryptocurrencies," "digital currency," or "virtual assets" anywhere in the AML Act, the statute, instead, uses language regarding "value that substitutes for currency." The AML Act, however, stays consistent with the BSA's stated mission. Trading and using virtual currencies are legal practices, but there is a risk that some terrorists and criminals seek to exploit vulnerabilities in the global financial system and increasingly rely on substitutes, like virtual currencies, to move illicit funds.

C. Financial Action Task Force

The Financial Action Task Force (FATF) is tasked with establishing global standards for anti-money laundering legislation. The FATF published cryptocurrency AML guidance in 2014, with many agencies codifying most of FATF's recommendations into law. Virtual asset service providers, including cryptocurrency exchanges, stablecoin issuers, and some DeFi protocols, are required to mandate KYC checks and regularly monitor transactions for suspicious activity.

In 2019, FATF issued "*Guidance for a Risk-Based Approach for Virtual Assets and Virtual Asset Service Providers*" that clarified the anti-money laundering and combatting the financing of terrorism (AML/CFT) space. The guidance provides:

- Clarification of the definitions of virtual assets and virtual asset service provider
- Categorization of non-fungible tokens (NFTs)
- Guidance on the travel rule
- Guidance on virtual asset service provider licensing and registration
- Recognition of the money laundering risks of peer to peer transactions

The guidance conveys the potential effect of prompting more countries to work towards strong regulation on cryptocurrency activity.

Discussion Points

1. *Considering current law.* Consider the above laws, specifically the BSA, Patriot Act and AML Act of 2020. In your opinion, are these three laws enough to effectively prevent and combat unlawful financial activities such as money laundering? Why or why not? Which regulatory agencies do you think are best suited to promulgate regulations to deal with these issues?

2. *FinCEN.* Do you think FinCEN should have concurrent authority over the regulation of cryptocurrencies with other federal agencies such as the CFTC or SEC? Why or why not? Should FinCEN be doing more to prevent financial crimes?

3. *Money laundering in P2P transactions.* Do you think that the algorithmic nature of blockchain transactions can help mitigate the risks of money laundering occurring via peer to peer transactions? Does the presence of an intermediary in financial transactions reduce the risk of money laundering? Why or why not?

Press Release: FinCEN Fines Ripple Labs Inc. in First Civil Enforcement Action Against a Virtual Currency Exchanger
May 5, 2015

WASHINGTON, DC —The Financial Crimes Enforcement Network (FinCEN), working in coordination with the U.S. Attorney's Office for the Northern District of California (USAO-NDCA), assessed a $700,000 civil money penalty today against Ripple Labs Inc. and its wholly-owned subsidiary, XRP II, LLC (formerly known as XRP Fund II, LLC). Ripple Labs willfully violated several requirements of the Bank Secrecy Act (BSA) by acting as a money services business (MSB) and selling its virtual currency, known as XRP, without registering with FinCEN, and by failing to implement and maintain an adequate anti-money laundering (AML) program designed to protect its products from use by money launderers or terrorist financiers. XRP II later assumed Ripple Labs' functions of selling virtual currency and acting as an MSB; however, like its parent company, XRP II willfully violated the BSA by failing to implement an effective AML program, and by failing to report suspicious activity related to several financial transactions.

"Virtual currency exchangers must bring products to market that comply with our anti-money laundering laws," said FinCEN Director Jennifer Shasky Calvery. "Innovation is laudable but only as long as it does not unreasonably expose our financial system to tech-smart criminals eager to abuse the latest and most complex products."

FinCEN's assessment is concurrent with the USAO-NDCA's announcement of a settlement agreement with Ripple Labs and XRP II. In that settlement, the companies resolved possible criminal charges and forfeited $450,000. The $450,000 forfeiture in that action will be credited to partially satisfy FinCEN's $700,000 civil money penalty. A Statement of Facts and Violations, describing the underlying activity and details of the BSA violations, is incorporated into FinCEN's assessment as well as the USAO-NDCA's settlement.

Both actions were accompanied by an agreement by Ripple and XRP II to engage in remedial steps to ensure future compliance with AML/CFT obligations, as well as enhanced remedial measures. Among these steps are agreements to only transact XRP and "Ripple Trade" activity through a registered MSB: to implement and maintain an effective AML program: to comply with the Funds Transfer and Funds Travel Rules: to conduct a three-year "look-back" to require suspicious activity reporting for prior suspicious transactions and a requirement for the companies to retain external independent auditors to review their compliance with the BSA every two years up to and including 2020. Pursuant to the agreement, Ripple Labs will also undertake certain enhancements to the Ripple Protocol to appropriately monitor all future transactions.

"By these agreements, we demonstrate again that we will remain vigilant to ensure the security of, and prevent the misuse of, the financial markets," said U.S. Attorney Melinda Haag. "Ripple Labs Inc. and its wholly-owned subsidiary both have acknowledged that digital currency providers have an obligation not only to refrain from illegal activity, but also to ensure they are not profiting by creating products that allow would–be criminals to avoid detection. We hope that this sets an industry standard in the important new space of digital currency."

"Federal laws that regulate the reporting of financial transactions are in place to detect and stop illegal activities, including those in the virtual currency arena," said Richard Weber, Chief, IRS Criminal Investigation. "Unregulated, virtual currency opens the door for criminals to anonymously conduct illegal activities online, eroding our financial systems and creating a Wild West environment where following the law is a choice rather than a requirement."

Ripple Labs Inc., headquartered in San Francisco, CA, facilitated transfers of virtual currency and provided virtual currency exchange transaction services. XRP II, LLC is a wholly-owned subsidiary of Ripple Labs that was incorporated as XRP Fund II, LLC in South Carolina on July 1, 2013; the company changed its name to XRP II in July 2014. As of 2015, Ripple is the second-largest cryptocurrency by market capitalization, after Bitcoin. On March 18, 2013, FinCEN released guidance clarifying the applicability of regulations implementing the BSA, and the requirement for certain participants in the virtual currency arena–namely, virtual currency exchangers and administrators–to register as MSBs with FinCEN pursuant to federal law.

Director Shasky Calvery expressed her appreciation to the U.S. Attorney's Office for the Northern District of California and to the Internal Revenue Service-Criminal Investigation Division for their contributions to the investigation and strong partnership with FinCEN.

FinCEN seeks to protect the U.S. financial system from being exploited by illicit activity. Its efforts are focused on compromised financial institutions and their employees; significant fraud; third-party money launderers; transnational organized crime and security threats; and cyber threats. FinCEN has a broad array of enforcement authorities to target both domestic and foreign actions affecting the U.S. financial system.

Discussion Points

1. *Is this enough?* Do you think the imposing of a $700,000 fine is enough to deter other bad actors? Should FinCEN have taken a more stringent approach? What do you think a proper penalty would be?

2. *Discussion.* How did Ripple Labs and its subsidiary XRP II willfully violate the Bank Secrecy Act? Do you think that "willfully" is the proper *mens rea* for a violation of the BSA? Should a negligent violation of the BSA be enough to trigger culpability? Why do you think this?

3. *Virtual currency providers.* Virtual currency providers that constitute MSBs are subject to FinCEN regulations and must develop, implement, and maintain an effective written AML program. Do you think that enforcement of these programs is enough to deter illicit money laundering activities?

4. *The role of state regulatory bodies.* Should states that have become more involved in regulating virtual currency activity, such as New York with the adoption of BitLicense, also be more heavily involved in regulating money laundering activities that occur intrastate or in interstate virtual currency transactions?

5. *Outlook.* Ripple Labs and its subsidiary XRP II made history as the first virtual currency provider to face a civil enforcement action, proving FinCEN's willingness to impose fines and remedial measures for MSBs that are at risk for exploitation through criminal activity. Do you think that the increased prevalence of CBDC and peer to peer exchanges that do not require intermediaries will increase the frequency of cases such as this one? Why or why not?

Press Release: FinCEN Announces $100 Million Enforcement Action Against Unregistered Futures Commission Merchant BitMEX for Willful Violations of the Bank Secrecy Act

August 10, 2021

WASHINGTON—The Financial Crimes Enforcement Network (FinCEN) has assessed a civil money penalty in the amount of $100 million against BitMEX, one of the oldest and largest convertible virtual currency derivatives exchanges, for violations of the Bank Secrecy Act (BSA) and FinCEN's implementing regulations.

BitMEX, which operated as an unregistered futures commission merchant (FCM) and provided money transmission services, willfully failed to comply with its obligations under the BSA. FinCEN's action is part of a global settlement with the U.S. Commodity Futures Trading Commission (CFTC).

"BitMEX's rapid growth into one of the largest futures commission merchants offering convertible virtual currency derivatives without a commensurate anti-money laundering program put the U.S. financial system at meaningful risk," FinCEN's Deputy Director AnnaLou Tirol said. "It is critical that platforms build in financial integrity from the start, so that financial innovation and opportunity are protected from vulnerabilities and exploitation."

For over 6 years, BitMEX failed to implement and maintain a compliant anti-money laundering program and a customer identification program, and it failed to report certain suspicious activity. These willful failures expose financial institutions to an increased risk of conducting transactions with money launderers and terrorist financiers, including noncompliant exchanges in high-risk jurisdictions, ransomware attackers, and darknet marketplaces. BitMEX conducted at least $209 million worth of transactions with known darknet markets or unregistered money services businesses providing mixing services. BitMEX also conducted transactions involving high-risk jurisdictions and alleged fraud schemes. BitMEX failed to file a Suspicious Activity Report (SAR) on at least 588 specific suspicious transactions.

From approximately 2014 through 2020, BitMEX allowed customers to access its platform and conduct derivative trading without appropriate customer due diligence – collecting only an email address and failing to verify customer identity. Despite BitMEX's public representation that its platform was not conducting business with U.S. persons, FinCEN found that BitMEX failed to implement appropriate policies, procedures, and internal controls to screen for customers that use a virtual private network to access the trading platform and circumvent internet protocol monitoring. In some instances, BitMEX senior leadership altered U.S. customer information to hide the customer's true location.

In addition to paying a civil money penalty, BitMEX has agreed to engage an independent consultant to conduct a historical analysis of its transaction data, sometimes referred to as a "SAR lookback," to determine whether BitMEX must file additional SARs on this activity. BitMEX will also engage an independent consultant to conduct two reviews, including relevant testing, to ensure that appropriate policies, procedures, and controls are in place that are effective and reasonably designed and implemented to ensure that BitMEX is not operating wholly or in substantial part in the United States.

This is FinCEN's first enforcement action against an FCM. FinCEN appreciates the close collaboration with its partners at the CFTC on this matter. The CFTC and BitMEX have separately agreed to a <u>Consent Order</u> requiring the payment of a civil money penalty with additional equitable relief. FinCEN's $100 million assessment will be satisfied by immediate payments totaling $80 million to FinCEN and the CFTC, with $20 million suspended pending the successful completion of the SAR lookback and independent consultant reviews.

Discussion Points

1. *U.S. regulators.* Regulators in the United States have made it evident that they expect digital asset market participants to abide by the same standards of conduct that have been applied to more traditional market participants.

2. *Analyzing due diligence.* What do you think would have constituted proper "due diligence" before BitMEX allowed customers to conduct derivative trading?

3. *The issue.* What was FinCEN's argument? Do you agree or disagree with FinCEN's determination?

4. *Willful failure to maintain a compliance AML program.* What do you think are the necessary components of an AML program BitMEX should have adopted?

Complaint: United States of America v. BTC-e, a/k/a/ Canton Business Corp., and Alexander Vinnik

Case 3:19-cv-04281 (N.D. Cal. 2019)

The United States of America alleges as follows:

I. NATURE OF ACTION

1. The United States brings this action against BTC-e a/k/a Canton Business Corporation ("BTC-e") and Alexander Vinnik ("Vinnik") (collectively "Defendants"), to recover civil money penalties imposed under the Currency and Foreign Transactions Reporting Act of 1970, 31 U.S.C. §§ 5311–5314 and 5316–5332, which is commonly referred to as the Bank Secrecy Act ("BSA").

II. JURISDICTION AND VENUE

2. This Court has jurisdiction over the subject matter of this action pursuant to 28 U.S.C. §§ 1331 and 1345. The Court may exercise personal jurisdiction over Defendants because they transact business in this District.

3. Venue is proper in the Northern District of California under 28 U.S.C. §§ 1391(b) and (c) because Defendants transact business in this District.

III. PARTIES

4. The United States brings this action on behalf of the Department of the Treasury.

5. Defendant BTC-e is a corporation organized under the laws of either Cyprus and/or the Seychelles Islands. BTC-e operated in Bulgaria, the Seychelles Islands, and other jurisdictions, including the Northern District of California. At all times relevant to this complaint, BTC-e was a money services business providing services subject to the BSA in the Northern District of California and elsewhere.

6. Defendant Alexander Vinnik is a Russian national who is currently incarcerated in Greece. At all times relevant to this complaint, Vinnik occupied a senior leadership position within BTC-e.

IV. THE BANK SECRECY ACT

7. The Financial Crimes Enforcement Network ("FinCEN"), a bureau within the United States Department of the Treasury, administers the BSA pursuant to authority delegated by the Secretary of the Treasury. *See* Treasury Order 180-01 (July 1, 2014). The BSA requires the filing of reports and the maintenance of records useful in criminal, tax, or regulatory investigations or proceedings, or in the conduct of intelligence or counterintelligence activities to protect against international terrorism. Regulations implementing the BSA appear at 31 C.F.R. Chapter X. Rules issued under the BSA require the registration of money services businesses ("MSBs"), the filing of Suspicious Activity Reports ("SARs"), the implementation of anti-money laundering ("AML") programs, and the maintenance of records related to transmittals of funds.

8. FinCEN may impose a civil monetary penalty "at any time before the end of the 6-year period beginning on the date of the transaction with respect to which the penalty was assessed," and may commence an action to recover the civil money penalty at any time before the end of the 2-year period beginning on the date the penalty was imposed. *See* 31 U.S.C. §§ 5321(b)(1) and 5330(e)(3).

9. MSBs are "financial institutions" for purposes of the BSA and its implementing regulations. *See* 31 U.S.C. § 5312(a)(2)(J), (K) and (R); 31 C.F.R. § 1010.100(t)(3). A "money services business" is defined in regulations implementing the BSA to include persons who are engaged as a business in providing money transmission services "wholly or in substantial part within the United States." *See* 31 C.F.R. § 1010.100(ff) (5). Exchangers of convertible virtual currency provide "money transmission ser-

vices" for purposes of regulations implementing the BSA and may therefore qualify as MSBs. *See* FIN-2013-G001, "Application of FinCEN's Regulations to Persons Administering, Exchanging, or Using Virtual Currencies" (March 18, 2013).

10. FinCEN may impose on any person who owns or controls an unregistered MSB a civil money penalty for each day that the MSB remains unregistered. *See* 31 U.S.C. § 5330(e)(2); 31 C.F.R. § 1022.380(e). For MSB registration violations occurring on or before November 2, 2015, FinCEN may assess a penalty of up to $7,954 for each violation. 31 C.F.R. § 1010.821. Violations occurring after November 2, 2015, may be assessed in an amount up to $8,084 for each violation. *Id.* Each day a violation continues constitutes a separate violation. 31 C.F.R. § 1022.380(e).

11. FinCEN may impose a civil money penalty on a domestic financial institution that willfully violates the BSA by failing to establish or maintain an adequate AML program and for failing to file SARs as appropriate, and on any partner, director, officer or employee who willfully participates in the violation. *See* 31 U.S.C. § 5321(a)(1); 31 C.F.R. § 1010.820. The term "domestic" refers to "the doing of business within the United States" or the performance of functions within the United States. 31 C.F.R. § 1010.100(o); *see also* 31 U.S.C. § 5312(b)(1). For violations occurring on or before November 2, 2015, FinCEN may impose a penalty of $25,000 to $100,000 for willful violations of BSA program requirements. 31 U.S.C. § 5321(a)(1); 31 C.F.R. § 1010.820(f). For AML program violations after November 2, 2015, FinCEN may impose a penalty of $54,789 to $219,156. 31 C.F.R. § 1010.821. For violations of the requirement to implement an adequate AML program, "a separate violation occurs for each day that the violation continues." *See* 31 U.S.C. § 5321(a)(1) and 31 C.F.R. §1010.821.

V. FACTUAL ALLEGATIONS

A. Bitcoin and Digital Currencies

12. Bitcoin is a form of decentralized, convertible digital currency that exists through the use are many others, including litecoin, ether, worldcoin, and dogecoin; however, bitcoin has the largest market capitalization of any present form of decentralized digital currency. While bitcoin is an internet-based form of currency, it is possible to "print out" the necessary bitcoin information and exchange it via physical media. Bitcoin is not issued by any government, bank, or company, but rather is generated and controlled through computer software operating via a decentralized network. To acquire bitcoin, a typical user will purchase it from a bitcoin seller or "exchanger."

13. Bitcoin exchangers typically accept payments of fiat currency (currency which derives its value from government regulation or law), or other convertible digital currencies. When a user wishes to purchase bitcoin from an exchanger, the user will typically send payment in the form of fiat currency, often via bank wire or automated clearing house ("ACH") transfer, for the corresponding quantity of bit-

coin, based on a fluctuating exchange rate. The exchanger, often for a commission, will then attempt to broker the purchase with another user of the exchange that is trying to sell bitcoin, or, in some instances, will act as the seller itself.

14. When a user acquires bitcoin, ownership of the bitcoin is transferred to the user's bitcoin address. The bitcoin address is somewhat analogous to a bank account number and is compromised of a case-sensitive string of letters and numbers amounting to a total of 26 to 35 characters. The user can then conduct transactions with other bitcoin users by transferring bitcoin to their bitcoin addresses via the internet.

15. Little to no personally identifiable information about the payer or payee is transmitted in a bitcoin transaction itself. Bitcoin transactions occur using a public key and a private key. A public key is used to receive bitcoin, and a private key is used to allow withdrawals from a bitcoin address. Only the bitcoin address of the receiving party and the sender's private key are needed to complete the transaction. These two keys by themselves rarely reflect any information identifying the payer or payee.

16. All bitcoin transactions are recorded on what is known as the Blockchain. The Blockchain is a distributed public ledger that maintains all bitcoin transactions, incoming and outgoing. The Blockchain records every bitcoin address that has ever received a bitcoin and maintains records of every transaction for each bitcoin address. In some circumstances, bitcoin payments may be effectively traced by analyzing the Blockchain.

B. BTC-e Operations

17. BTC-e was a digital currency exchange that allowed users to buy and sell bitcoin, and other digital currencies, anonymously through its web domain btc-e.com. Since its founding, BTC-e has served approximately 700,000 users worldwide, including numerous customers in the United States and in the Northern District of California. BTC-e was used by cybercriminals worldwide and was one of the principal entities used to launder and liquidate criminal proceeds, converting them from digital currencies, including bitcoin, to fiat currencies, including U.S. Dollars, Euros, and Rubles.

18. To use BTC-e, a user created an account by accessing BTC-e's website, www.btc-e.com. To create an account, a user did not need to provide even the most basic identifying information, such as name, date of birth, address, or other identifiers. All BTC-e required to create a user account was a self-created username, password, and an email address. Unlike legitimate digital currency exchangers, BTC-e did not require its users to validate their identity by providing official identification documents. When a customer attempted to use bank wires to transfer funds to or from BTC-e's exchange, BTC-e at times did request identifying documentation, such as a driver's license or passport. BTC-e did not request such documents for all transactions involving bank wires or for other types of transactions.

19. BTC-e's business model obscured and anonymized transactions and sources of funds. A BTC-e user did not fund an account by directly transferring money to BTC-e itself, but rather users were instructed to wire funds to one of BTC-e's "front" companies that, although nominally separate from BTC-e were, in fact, controlled by and operated for the benefit of BTC-e. Nor could BTC-e users withdraw funds from their accounts directly, such as through an ATM withdrawal. Instead, BTC-e users were required to make withdrawals through the use of third-party "exchangers" or other processors, thus enabling BTC-e to avoid collecting any information about its users that would leave a centralized financial paper trail. Thus, a user could create a BTC-e account with nothing more than a username and email address, which often bore no relationship to the actual identity of the user.

20. BTC-e accounts received criminal proceeds directly from various cybercrimes, including numerous hacking incidents, ransomware payments, identity theft schemes, embezzlement by corrupt public officials, and narcotics distribution. A significant portion of BTC-e's business was derived from suspected criminal activity.

21. Messages on BTC-e's own forum openly and explicitly reflected some of the criminal activity in which the users on the platform were engaged and how they used BTC-e to launder funds. BTC-e users established accounts under monikers suggestive of criminality, including user names such as "ISIS," "CocaineCowboys," "blackhathackers," "dzkillerhacker," and "hacker4hire." Despite these suspicious usernames, BTC-e did nothing to identify these customers or to investigate whether these or any of its other customers were using its services to conduct, conceal, or facilitate illegal activity.

22. BTC-e's structure allowed criminals to conduct financial transactions with high levels of anonymity and thereby avoid apprehension by law enforcement or seizure of funds. This aspect of BTC-e contributed to its customers' willingness to accept BTC-e's unfavorable exchange rates compared to other legitimate digital currency exchangers that registered with FinCEN and that had appropriate and effective anti-money laundering and "Know-Your-Customer" policies in place.

23. Customers located within the United States used BTC-e to conduct at least 21,000 bitcoin transactions worth over $296,000,000 and tens of thousands of transactions in other convertible virtual currencies.

24. BTC-e made no effort to register with FinCEN, maintain any elements of an AML program, or report suspicious activity.

C. Vinnik

25. Vinnik occupied a senior leadership position within BTC-e and participated in the direction and supervision of BTC-e's operations and finances. Vinnik controlled multiple BTC-e administrative accounts used to process BTC-e's transactions.

26. The owners and administrators of BTC-e, including Vinnik, were aware BTC-e functioned as a money laundering enterprise. Vinnik sent emails claiming to be an owner of BTC-e and used the site to personally conduct transactions with illegal proceeds.

27. Vinnik operated several administrative, financial, operational, and support accounts at BTC-e, including accounts that have been tied to thefts from other virtual currency exchanges such as Mt. Gox. Furthermore, withdrawals from these accounts were deposited directly into bank accounts tied to Vinnik. These accounts granted Vinnik the ability to observe transactions coming to and leaving from BTC-e, as well as specific customer activity and profiles. Vinnik made no efforts to ensure that BTC-e registered with FinCEN, maintained any elements of an AML program, or reported suspicious transactions.

D. Indictment

28. On May 31, 2016, a grand jury sitting in the Northern District of California returned a two-count indictment charging BTC-e and Alexander Vinnik with operation of an Unlicensed Money Services Business, in violation of 18 U.S.C § 1960, and Conspiracy to Commit Money Laundering, in violation of 18 U.S.C. § 1956(h).

29. On January 17, 2017, the grand jury issued a twenty-one count superseding indictment charging BTC-e and Vinnik with Operation of an Unlicensed Money Services Business, in violation of 18 U.S.C § 1960; Conspiracy to Commit Money Laundering, in violation of 18 U.S.C. § 1956(h); Money Laundering, in violation of 18 U.S.C. § 1956(a)(1)(A)(i) and (a)(1)(B)(i); and Engaging in Unlawful Monetary Transactions, in violation of 18 U.S.C. § 1957.

E. FinCEN's Civil Monetary Penalty

30. As detailed in the Assessment of Civil Money Penalty issued on July 26, 2017 (attached 24 hereto as Exhibit 1), FinCEN assessed monetary penalties against BTC-e and Vinnik for the following conduct:

Failure to Register as an MSB

31. A Money Services Business ("MSB") is any person or entity that receives something of value (including currency or value that substitutes for currency) from one person and transmits either the same or a different form of value to another person or location by any means. 31 C.F.R. §1010.100(ff); 2011 MSB Final Rule, 76 FR 43585, at 43596. An MSB is required to register with FinCEN within 180 days of beginning operation and to renew such registration every two years. 31 U.S.C. § 5330; 31 C.F.R. § 1022.380(b)(2). Foreign-located MSBs that conduct business within the United States must register and must also appoint an agent within the United States to accept legal process in BSA-related matters. 31 U.S.C. § 5330; 31 C.F.R. § 1022.380(a)(2).

32. The BTC-e website (btc-e.com) Terms and Conditions contained the following information, "BTC-e provides an online tool that allows users to freely trade Bitcoins for a number of different currencies worldwide." Thus, BTC-e's business model was to transfer something of value – bitcoin and other cryptocurrency – between entities and individuals and between locations. As such, BTC-e was an MSB. At no point in its existence did BTC-e register as an MSB with FinCEN. In March of 2013, FinCEN issued guidance clarifying and affirming its July 2011 Final Rules establishing that exchangers and administrators that transmitted virtual currency and operated in the United States were subject to FinCEN requirements, including registration as an MSB. Nevertheless, BTC-e continued to fail to register.

Failure to Establish AML Programs and Procedures

33. Under the BSA, an MSB must develop, implement, and maintain an effective AML program that is reasonably designed to prevent the MSB from being used to facilitate money laundering and the financing of terrorist activities. 31 U.S.C. §§ 5318(a)(2) and (h); 31 C.F.R. § 1022.210(a). The collect even the most basic customer information needed to comply with the BSA. BTC-e allowed its customers to open accounts and conduct transactions with only a username, password, and e-mail address. BTC-e collected only this limited information no matter how large the transaction or how many transactions the customer conducted. When BTC-e finally implemented policies to verify customer identification in May of 2017, it made those procedures "optional."

34. At no point in time did BTC-e have any AML policies or procedures, let alone an effective program for detecting and preventing suspicious transactions. To the contrary, BTC-e's lax policies encouraged persons engaged in criminal activity to use its services, and BTC-e became the virtual currency exchange of choice for criminals looking to launder their illegal proceeds.

35. BTC-e had no policies or procedures to verify customer identification. BTC-e failed to collect even the most basic customer information needed to comply with the BSA. BTC-e allowed its customers to open accounts and conduct transactions with only a username, password, and e-mail address. BTC-e collected only this limited information no matter how large the transaction or how many transactions the customer conducted. When BTC-e finally implemented policies to verify customer identification in May of 2017, it made those procedures "optional."

36. In fact, BTC-e processed digital currency transactions with features that restricted its ability to identify its customers and detect suspicious activity. For example, BTC-e processed millions of dollars' worth of transactions using bitcoin "mixers." Instead of transmitting bitcoin directly between two users, the "mixer" created layers of temporary bitcoin addresses operated by the mixer itself to complicate any attempt to analyze the flow of the transaction.

37. Moreover, BTC-e had no policies or procedures for conducting due diligence or monitoring transactions for suspicious activity. On some occasions, BTC-e customers contacted BTC- e's administration with questions regarding how to process and access proceeds obtained from the sale of illegal drugs and from transactions on known "darknet" illegal markets, including Silk Road. In addition, BTC-e's customers openly discussed using BTC-e to facilitate illegal activity on BTC-e's own internal messaging system, as well as on its public user chat system. Nevertheless, BTC-e did not implement any policies or procedures to monitor its platform for suspect activity.

Failure to File SARs

38. Under the BSA, an MSB must report transactions that the MSB "knows, suspects, or has reason to suspect" are suspicious where those transactions involve the MSB and aggregate to at least $2,000 in value. 31 U.S.C. § 5318(g)(1); 31 C.F.R. § 1022.320(a)(2). A transaction is "suspicious" if it (a) involves funds derived from illegal activity; (b) is designed to evade reporting requirements; (c) has no business or apparent lawful purpose; or (d) involves the use of the MSB to facilitate illegal activity. 31 U.S.C. § 5318(g)(1); 31 CFR. §§ 1022.320(a)(2)(i)-(iv).

39. Despite the rampant evidence of illegal activity on its platform, BTC-e did not file a single SAR, including for the specific activities identified in the Assessment.

40. On July 26, 2017, FinCEN imposed on BTC-e and Alexander Vinnik civil monetary penalties in the amounts of $88,596,314 and $12,000,000, respectively, for the conduct described above. AML program must: contain written policies, procedures and internal controls; designate an individual responsible for BSA compliance; provide training, including on how to detect suspicious transactions; and provide for independent review of the AML program. 31 U.S.C. §§ 5318(a)(2) and (h); 31 C.F.R. §§ 1022.210(c) and (d).

FIRST CAUSE OF ACTION:
RECOVERY OF CIVIL MONETARY PENALTY

41. Plaintiff hereby incorporates by reference each and every allegation set forth in the foregoing paragraphs.

42. The July 26, 2017, Assessment of Civil Money Penalty constitutes a lawful administrative sanction against BTC-e and Vinnik for failure to comply with the BSA's requirements under 31 U.S.C. §§ 5321(b)(1) and 5330(e)(3).

43. BTC-e is liable to the United States for a civil penalty in the amount of $88,596,314, plus interest and costs.

44. Vinnik is liable to the United States for a civil penalty in the amount of $12,000,000, plus interest and costs.

PRAYER FOR RELIEF

WHEREFORE, Plaintiff respectfully requests that the Court reduce Plaintiff's claims against BTC-e and Alexander Vinnik to judgment, award Plaintiff judgments against BTC-e and Alexander Vinnik in the amounts of $88,596,314 and $12,000,000, respectively, plus interest as provided by law, and award such other relief as the Court deems just and proper, including Plaintiff's costs.

———————————————

Dated: July 25, 2019

Respectfully submitted,

DAVID L. ANDERSON

United States Attorney

KIRSTIN M. AULT

Assistant United States Attorney

Attorneys for United States of America

Exhibit 1

UNITED STATES OF AMERICA
DEPARTMENT OF THE TREASURY
FINANCIAL CRIMES ENFORCEMENT NETWORK

IN THE MATTER OF:

BTC-E a/k/a Canton Business Corporation and Alexander Vinnik

Number 2017-03

ASSESSMENT OF CIVIL MONEY PENALTY

I. INTRODUCTION

The Financial Crimes Enforcement Network (FinCEN) has determined that grounds exist to assess civil money penalties against BTC-E a/k/a Canton Business Corporation (BTC-e) and Alexander Vinnik, pursuant to the Bank Secrecy Act (BSA) and regulations issued pursuant to that Act.[1]

———————————————

1. The Bank Secrecy Act is codified at 12 U.S.C. §§ 1829b, 1951–1959 and 31 U.S.C. §§ 5311–5314, 5316–5332. Regulations implementing the Bank Secrecy Act currently appear at 31 C.F.R. Chapter X.

FinCEN has the authority to impose civil money penalties on money services businesses (MSBs) and individuals involved in the ownership or operation of MSBs.[2] Rules implementing the BSA state that "[o]verall authority for enforcement and compliance, including coordination and direction of procedures and activities of all other agencies exercising delegated authority under this chapter" has been delegated by the Secretary of the Treasury to FinCEN.[3]

BTC-e and Alexander Vinnik have been indicted in the Northern District of California under 18 U.S.C. §§ 1956, 1957, and 1960 for money laundering, conspiracy to commit money laundering, engaging in unlawful monetary transactions, and the operation of an unlicensed money transmitting business.[4]

II. JURISDICTION

BTC-e operates as an "exchanger" of convertible virtual currencies, offering the purchase and sale of U.S. dollars, Russian Rubles, Euros, Bitcoin, Litecoin, Namecoin, Novacoin, Peercoin, Ethereum, and Dash.[5] BTC-e also offered "BTC-e code," which enabled users to send and receive fiat currencies, including U.S. dollars, with other BTC-e users. Since 2011, BTC-e has served approximately 700,000 customers worldwide and is associated with bitcoin wallet addresses that have received over 9.4 million bitcoin. Alexander Vinnik participated in the direction and supervision of BTC-e's operations and finances and controlled multiple BTC-e administrative accounts used in processing transactions.

Exchangers of convertible virtual currency are "money transmitters" as defined at 31 C.F.R § 1010.100(ff)(5) and "financial institutions" as defined at 31 C.F.R § 1010.100(t). A foreign-located business qualifies as an MSB if it does business as an MSB "wholly or in substantial part within the United States."[6] Customers located within the United States used BTC-e to conduct at least 21,000 bitcoin transactions worth over $296,000,000 and tens of thousands of transactions in other convertible virtual currencies. The transactions included funds sent from customers located within the United States to recipients who were also located within the United States. In addition, these transactions were processed through servers located in the United States. BTC-e attempted to conceal the fact that it provided services to customers located within the United States. BTC-e instructed customers to make use of correspondent accounts held by foreign financial institutions or services provided by affiliates of BTC-e located abroad.

---

2. 12 U.S.C. §§ 1829b(j) and 1955; 31 U.S.C. §§ 5321(a)(1) and 5330(e); 31 C.F.R. § 1010.820.

3. 31 C.F.R. § 1010.810(a).

4. *United States v. BTC-e a/k/a Canton Business Corporation and Alexander Vinnik*, CR 16-00227 SI (N.D. CA. Jan. 17, 2017).

5. FIN-2013-G001, "Application of FinCEN's Regulations to Persons Administering, Exchanging, or Using Virtual Currencies," March 18, 2013.

6. 31 U.S.C. §§ 5312(a)(6), 5312(b), and 5330(d); 31 C.F.R. § 1010.100(ff).

III. DETERMINATIONS

FinCEN has determined that, from November 5, 2011 through the present: (a) BTC-e and Alexander Vinnik[7] willfully violated MSB registration requirements; (b) BTC-e willfully violated[8] the requirement to implement an effective anti-money laundering (AML) program, the requirement to detect suspicious transactions and file suspicious activity reports (SARs), and the requirement to obtain and retain records relating to transmittals of funds in amounts of $3,000 or more; and (c) Alexander Vinnik willfully participated[9] in violations of AML program and SAR requirements.[10]

A. Registration as a Money Services Business

The BSA and its implementing regulations require the registration of an MSB within 180 days of beginning operations and the renewal of such registration every two years.[11] A foreign-located MSB must appoint an agent who will accept legal process in matters related to compliance with the BSA.[12] The agent must reside within the United States.

At no point in its operations was BTC-e registered with FinCEN. Notably, BTC-e went unregistered even after FinCEN issued guidance pertaining to exchangers and administrators of virtual currency in March 2013. BTC-e never appointed an agent for service of process.

B. Violations of AML Program Requirements

The BSA and its implementing regulations require an MSB to develop, implement, and maintain an effective written AML program that is reasonably designed

---

7. 31 U.S.C. § 5330(a)(1) ("Any person who owns or controls a money transmitting business shall register the business…"); 31 U.S.C. 5330(e)(1) ("Any person who fails to comply with any requirement of [31 U.S.C. § 5330] or any regulation prescribed under [31 U.S.C. § 5330] shall be liable…for a civil penalty…"); 31 C.F.R. § 1022.380(c) ("[A]ny person who owns or controls a money services business is responsible for registering the business…"); 31 C.F.R. § 1022.380(e) ("Any person who fails to comply with any requirement of [31 U.S.C. § 5330 or 31 C.F.R. § 1022.380] shall be liable for a civil penalty…").

8. 12 U.S.C. § 1829b(j); 31 U.S.C. § 5321(a)(1); 31 C.F.R. § 1010.820(f).

9. 31 U.S.C. § 5321(a)(1); 31 C.F.R. § 1010.820(f) (For any willful violation…of any reporting requirement for financial institutions…, the Secretary may assess upon any domestic financial institution, and upon any partner, director, officer, or employee thereof who willfully participates in the violation, a civil penalty…).

10. In civil enforcement of the Bank Secrecy Act under 31 U.S.C. § 5321(a)(1), to establish that a financial institution or individual acted willfully, the government need only show that the financial institution or individual acted with either reckless disregard or willful blindness. The government need not show that the entity or individual had knowledge that the conduct violated the Bank Secrecy Act, or that the entity or individual otherwise acted with an improper motive or bad purpose.

11. 31 U.S.C. § 5330 and 31 C.F.R. § 1022.380(b)(2).

12. 31 U.S.C. § 5330 and 31 C.F.R. § 1022.380(a)(2). *See generally* FIN-2012-A001, "Foreign-Located Money Services Businesses," February 15, 2012.

to prevent the MSB from being used to facilitate money laundering and the financing of terrorist activities.[13] BTC-e was required to implement a written AML program that, at a minimum: (a) incorporates policies, procedures and internal controls reasonably designed to assure ongoing compliance; (b) designates an individual responsible to assure day to day compliance with the program and BSA requirements; (c) provides training for appropriate personnel, including training in the detection of suspicious transactions; and (d) provides for independent review to monitor and maintain an adequate program.[14]

BTC-e lacked basic controls to prevent the use of its services for illicit purposes. Through their operation of BTC-e, Alexander Vinnik and other individuals occupying senior leadership positions within the virtual currency exchange attracted and maintained a customer base that consisted largely of criminals who desired to conceal proceeds from crimes such as ransomware, fraud, identity theft, tax refund fraud schemes, public corruption, and drug trafficking. BSA compliance was compromised by revenue interests. BTC-e quickly became the virtual currency exchange of choice for criminals looking to conduct illicit transactions or launder illicit proceeds, all of which BTC-e failed to report both to FinCEN and law enforcement.

1. Internal Controls

BTC-e failed to implement policies, procedures, and internal controls reasonably designed to prevent the MSB from facilitating money laundering. The BSA requires MSBs to implement policies and procedures to verify customer identification, file BSA reports, create and maintain BSA records, and respond to law enforcement requests. BTC-e lacked adequate controls to verify customer identification, to identify and report suspicious activity, and to prevent money laundering and the financing of terrorist activities. BTC-e offered a variety of convertible virtual currencies internationally and operated as one of the largest volume virtual currency exchanges. The BSA and its implementing regulations require an MSB to implement internal controls that are commensurate with the risks posed by its clientele, the nature and volume of the financial services it provides, and the jurisdictions in which the MSB provides its services.

BTC-e failed to collect and verify even the most basic customer information needed to comply with the BSA. BTC-e allowed its customers to open accounts and conduct transactions with only a username, password, and an email address. The minimal information collected was the same regardless of how many transactions were processed for a customer or the amount involved. BTC-e implemented policies to verify customer identification in May 2017 but stated that compliance with those policies was "optional."

---

13. 31 U.S.C. §§ 5318(a)(2) and (h); 31 C.F.R. § 1022.210(a).
14. 31 U.S.C. §§ 5318(a)(2) and (h)(1); 31 C.F.R. §§ 1022.210(c) and (d).

BTC-e processed transactions with digital currency features that restricted its ability to verify customer identification or monitor for suspicious activity. BTC-e allowed over $40 million in transfers on its platform from bitcoin mixers. Mixers anonymize bitcoin addresses and obscure bitcoin transactions by weaving together inflows and outflows from many different users. Instead of directly transmitting bitcoin between two bitcoin addresses, the mixer disassociates connections. Mixers create layers of temporary bitcoin addresses operated by the mixer itself to further complicate any attempt to analyze the flow of bitcoin. BTC-e lacked adequate internal controls to mitigate the risks presented by bitcoin mixers.

BTC-e also lacked adequate internal controls to mitigate the risks presented by virtual currencies with anonymizing features. BTC-e facilitated transfers of the convertible virtual currency Dash, which has a feature called "PrivateSend." PrivateSend provides a decentralized mixing service within the currency itself in an effort to enhance user anonymity. BTC-e and Alexander Vinnik failed to conduct appropriate risk-based due diligence to address the challenges anonymizing features would have on compliance with BSA reporting and recordkeeping requirements.

BTC-e lacked adequate procedures for conducting due diligence, monitoring transactions, and refusing to consummate transactions that facilitated money laundering or other illicit activity. Users of BTC-e openly and explicitly discussed conducting criminal activity through the website's internal messaging system and on BTC-e's public "Troll Box," or user chat. This resulted in no additional scrutiny from Alexander Vinnik or BTC-e's other operators and senior leadership. BTC-e received inquiries from customers on how to process and access proceeds obtained from the sale of illegal drugs on darknet markets, including Silk Road, Hansa Market, and AlphaBay.

BTC-e processed transactions involving funds stolen from the Mt.Gox exchange between 2011 and 2014. BTC-e processed over 300,000 bitcoin of these proceeds, which were sent and held at three separate but linked BTC-e accounts. BTC-e failed to conduct any due diligence on the transactions or on the accounts in which the stolen bitcoin were held. Moreover, BTC-e failed to file any SARs on these transactions even after the thefts were publicly reported in the media.

C. Failure to File Suspicious Activity Reports

The BSA and its implementing regulations require an MSB to report transactions that the MSB "knows, suspects, or has reason to suspect" are suspicious, if the transactions are conducted or attempted by, at, or through the MSB, and the transactions involve or aggregate to at least $2,000 in funds or other assets.[15] A transaction is "suspicious" if the transaction: (a) involves funds derived from illegal activity; (b) is designed to evade reporting requirements; (c) has no business or apparent lawful

---

15. 31 U.S.C. § 5318(g)(1) and 31 C.F.R. § 1022.320(a)(2).

purpose, and the MSB knows of no reasonable explanation for the transaction after examining the available facts, including background and possible purpose; or (d) involves use of the money services business to facilitate criminal activity.[16]

BTC-e processed thousands of suspicious transactions without ever filing a single SAR. Unreported transactions included those conducted by customers who were widely reported as associated with criminal or civil violations of U.S. law. For example, from November 14, 2013 through July 21, 2015, BTC-e processed over 1,000 transactions for the unregistered U.S.-based virtual currency exchange Coin.MX. Coin.MX's operator, Anthony R. Murgio, pled guilty to charges that included conspiracy to operate an unlicensed money transmitting business.[17] Coin.MX processed over $10 million in bitcoin transactions derived from illegal activity throughout its operations, including a substantial number that involved funds from ransomware extortion payments. Even after the conviction of Coin.MX's operator, BTC-e failed to conduct reviews of the transactions that BTC-e processed for Coin.MX and failed to file any SARs.

Criminals, and cybercriminals in particular, used BTC-e to process the proceeds of their illicit activity. This was particularly the case for some of the largest ransomware purveyors, which used BTC-e as a means of storing, distributing, and laundering their criminal proceeds. FinCEN has identified at least $800,000 worth of transactions facilitated by BTC-e tied to the ransomware known as "Cryptolocker," which affected computers in 2013 and 2014. Further, over 40 percent of all bitcoin transactions, over 6,500 bitcoin, associated with the ransomware scheme known as "Locky" were sent through BTC-e. Despite readily available, public information identifying the bitcoin addresses associated with Locky, BTC-e failed to conduct any due diligence on the recipients of the funds and failed to file SARs.

BTC-e also failed to file SARs on transactions that involved the money laundering website Liberty Reserve. Liberty Reserve was a Costa Rica-based administrator of virtual currency that laundered approximately $6 billion in criminal proceeds. Liberty Reserve's website was seized by the U.S. government and shut down when its owner and six other individuals were charged with conspiracy to commit money laundering and operating an unlicensed money transmitting business. FinCEN issued a finding under Section 311 of the USA PATRIOT Act that Liberty Reserve was a financial institution of primary money laundering concern.[18] Not only did BTC-e share customers with Liberty Reserve, "BTC-e code" was redeemable for Liberty

---

16. 31 U.S.C. § 5318(g)(1) and 31 C.F.R. §§ 1022.320(a)(2)(i)-(iv).

17. "Operator Of Unlawful Bitcoin Exchange Pleads Guilty In Multimillion-Dollar Money Laundering And Fraud Scheme," Department of Justice, U.S. Attorney's Office for the Southern District of New York, January 9, 2017, https://www.justice.gov/usao-sdny/pr/operator-unlawful-bitcoin -exchange-pleads-guilty-multimillion-dollar-money- laundering.

18. "Treasury Identifies Virtual Currency Provider Liberty Reserve as a Financial Institution of Primary Money Laundering Concern under USA Patriot Act Section 311," Department of the Treasury, May 28, 2013, https://www.treasury.gov/press-center/press-releases/Pages/jl1956.aspx.

Reserve virtual currency. BTC-e failed to file SARs even after the public shutdown of Liberty Reserve in May 2013.

D. Recordkeeping Requirements

The BSA and its implementing regulations require MSBs and other non-bank financial institutions to obtain and retain records related to transmittals of funds in amounts of $3,000 or more.[19] BTC-e failed to collect even the most basic customer information and lacked adequate procedures for conducting due diligence and monitoring transactions. Transactional records maintained by BTC-e lacked critical information such as name, address, and account numbers.

IV. CIVIL MONEY PENALTY

FinCEN has determined that BTC-e willfully violated the BSA and its implementing regulations, as described in this ASSESSMENT, and that grounds exist to assess civil money penalties for these violations. FinCEN has determined that the proper penalties in this matter are a penalty of $110,003,314 imposed on BTC-e and a penalty of $12,000,000 imposed on Alexander Vinnik.

By:

_____ /s/_____7/26/2017

Jamal El-Hindi Date:

Acting Director

FINANCIAL CRIMES ENFORCEMENT NETWORK

U.S. Department of the Treasury

Discussion Points

1. *BTC-e.* How did the BTC-e digital currency exchange operate?
2. *FinCEN.* What were the penalties sought against BTC-e and Vinnik? Do you think this was a proper outcome?
3. *Regulating MSBs.* Should FinCEN and other federal regulators take more enforcement action against unregistered MSBs?

---

19. 12 U.S.C. § 1829b and 31 C.F.R. § 1010.410(e).

In the Matter of: Larry Dean Harmon d/b/a Helix

United States of America Financial Crimes Enforcement Network

(Number 2020-2)

I. INTRODUCTION

The Financial Crimes Enforcement Network (FinCEN) has determined that grounds exist to assess a civil money penalty against Larry Dean Harmon, as the primary operator of Helix, and as the Chief Executive Officer (CEO) and primary operator of Coin Ninja LLC (Coin Ninja), pursuant to the Bank Secrecy Act (BSA) and regulations issued pursuant to that Act.[1]

FinCEN has the authority to investigate and impose civil money penalties on money services businesses (MSBs) that willfully violate the BSA and on current and former employees who willfully participate in such violations.[2] Rules implementing the BSA state that "[o]verall authority for enforcement and compliance, including coordination and direction of procedures and activities of all other agencies exercising delegated authority under this chapter" has been delegated by the Secretary of the Treasury to FinCEN.[3] At all relevant times, both Mr. Harmon, doing business as Helix, and Coin Ninja were "money transmitters" as defined at 31 C.F.R § 1010.100(ff)(5) and a "financial institutions" as defined at 31 C.F.R § 1010.100(t).

Mr. Harmon has been indicted in the District of Columbia under related criminal charges pursuant to 18 U.S.C. §§ 1956 and 1960 for conspiracy to launder monetary instruments and the operation of an unlicensed money transmitting business.[4]

II. JURISDICTION

Mr. Harmon, doing business as Helix, operated as an "exchanger" of convertible virtual currencies, accepting bitcoin and transmitting bitcoin to another person or location by a variety of means.[5] Beginning on or about June 6, 2014, through on or about December 16, 2017, Mr. Harmon doing business as Helix, conducted over 1,225,000 transactions for customers and is associated with virtual currency wallet addresses that have sent or received over $311 million. FinCEN has identified at least 356,000 bitcoin transactions through Helix between June 2014 and December 2017. Beginning on or about July 13, 2017 through the present, Mr. Harmon served as CEO of Coin Ninja, a Delaware-incorporated and Ohio-located money transmitter that operates as an exchanger of convertible virtual currencies. Mr. Harmon willfully participated

---

1. The BSA is codified at 12 U.S.C. §§ 1829b, 1951–1959 and 31 U.S.C. §§ 5311–5314, 5316–5332. Regulations implementing the BSA appear at 31 C.F.R. Chapter X.

2. Treasury Order 180-01 (July 1, 2014); 31 U.S.C. § 5321(a); 31 C.F.R. § 1010.810(a).

3. 31 C.F.R. § 1010.810(a).

4. *United States of America v. Larry Dean Harmon*, 19-cr-00395, (D.C. DC, Dec. 3, 2019).

5. FIN-2013-G001, "Application of FinCEN's Regulations to Persons Administering, Exchanging, or Using Virtual Currencies," March 18, 2013.

in the direction and supervision of Coin Ninja's operations and finances. Exchangers of convertible virtual currency are "money transmitters" as defined at 31 C.F.R § 1010.100(ff)(5) and "financial institutions" as defined at 31 C.F.R § 1010.100(t).

III. DETERMINATIONS

FinCEN has determined that, from on or about June 6, 2014 through December 3, 2019, Mr. Harmon, doing business as Helix, willfully violated the BSA's registration, program, and reporting requirements.[6] Mr. Harmon, doing business as Helix, willfully (a) failed to register as a money services business;[7] (b) failed to implement and maintain an effective anti-money laundering (AML) program;[8] and (c) failed to report certain suspicious activity.[9] In addition, FinCEN has determined that on or about July 13, 2017 through December 3, 2019, Mr. Harmon willfully participated in Coin Ninja's failure to register as a money services business.[10]

These violations, and the governing facts and law surrounding the violations, are described more fully in the Statement of Facts (Attachment A), which is fully incorporated here by reference.

IV. CIVIL MONEY PENALTY

FinCEN determined that Mr. Harmon, in his roles with Helix and Coin Ninja, willfully violated the BSA and its implementing regulations, as described in this ASSESSMENT and Attachment A, and that grounds exist to assess a civil money penalty for these violations.[11] FinCEN determined that the maximum penalty in this matter is **$209,144,554**.[12]

FinCEN may impose a civil money penalty of $57,317 for each willful violation of AML program requirements assessed on or after October 10, 2019.[13] The BSA states that a "separate violation" of the requirement to establish and implement an effective AML program occurs "for each day that the violation continues."[14] The authorized penalty for each violation of MSB registration requirements assessed on or after

---

6. In civil enforcement of the BSA under 31 U.S.C. § 5321(a)(1), to establish that a financial institution or individual acted willfully, the government need only show that the financial institution or individual acted with either reckless disregard or willful blindness. The government need not show that the entity or individual had knowledge that the conduct violated the BSA, or that the entity or individual otherwise acted with an improper motive or bad purpose.

7. 31 U.S.C. § 5330 and 31 C.F.R. § 1022.380.

8. 31 U.S.C. § 5318(h) and 31 C.F.R. § 1022.210.

9. 31 U.S.C. § 5318(g)(1) and 31 C.F.R. § 1022.320.

10. 31 U.S.C. § 5330 and 31 C.F.R. § 1022.380.

11. 31 U.S.C. §§ 5321 and 5330(e); 31 C.F.R. §§ 1010.820 and 821.

12. Pursuant to the Federal Civil Penalties Inflation Act of 2015 (Pub. L. 114-74) ("the 2015 Act"), increased civil money penalties apply only with respect to underlying violations occurring after the enactment of the 2015 Act, i.e., after November 2, 2015.

13. 31 U.S.C. § 5321(a)(1); 31 C.F.R. §§ 1010.820(i) and 821.

14. 31 U.S.C. § 5321(a)(1).

October 10, 2019 is $8,457.[15] The BSA states that "each day" a violation of the failure to register as a MSB continues "constitutes a separate violation."[16] FinCEN may impose a penalty not to exceed the greater of the amount involved in the transaction (but capped at $229,269) or $57,317 for each willful violation of SAR requirements assessed on or after October 10, 2019.[17]

V. CONSIDERATION OF PENALTY FACTORS

On February 6, 2020, FinCEN provided Helix with a written pre-assessment notice that included a draft ASSESSMENT and Statement of Facts (the "PAN package"). The PAN package provided Helix with FinCEN's charges outlining violations of the BSA and its implementing regulations, the factors taken into consideration in determining whether to assess a civil money penalty and the proposed civil money penalty amount, and instructions on how to respond to these charges. Helix responded, through counsel, on March 6, 2020 denying that it operated as a MSB and requesting more time to respond to FinCEN's Statement of Facts. FinCEN provided Helix with multiple opportunities to respond to the PAN package. To date, over eight months since FinCEN issued its PAN package, Helix has not provided any additional information or documentation responding to the allegations or considerations contained in FinCEN's PAN package. As such, FinCEN concludes that Helix has decided not to submit any new facts or explanations for consideration. In light of this, FinCEN has considered the following factors in determining the disposition of this matter:

1. <u>Nature and seriousness of the violations and harm to the public</u>. The violations outlined in this ASSESSMENT are considered by FinCEN to be of a serious and egregious nature. The BSA and its implementing regulations require MSBs and money transmitters such as Helix to develop and implement a risk-based AML program designed to deter illicit financial activity and report suspicious activity, among other things, in order to assist law enforcement in detecting crimes. In this instance, Helix operated as a MSB in a high-risk industry that deals in convertible virtual currencies without developing an AML program and, in fact, provided its services in such a manner that it assisted and facilitated illicit financial activity. As a sophisticated enterprise, Helix worked in conjunction with darknet marketplaces to launder illicit bitcoin proceeds and actively marketed its services as an anonymity-enhancing service to launder bitcoin from illicit activity. For example, FinCEN observed bitcoin transactions equal to $121,511,877 transferred to darknet-associated addresses by, through, or to Helix.

---

15. 31 U.S.C. § 5330(e)(1); 31 C.F.R. §§ 1022.380(e) and 1010.821.
16. 31 U.S.C. § 5330 and 31 C.F.R. § 1022.380(e).
17. 31 U.S.C. § 5321(a)(1); 31 C.F.R. §§ 1010.820(i) and 821.

2. <u>Impact of violations on FinCEN's mission to safeguard the financial system</u>. Helix was totally and completely deficient in its compliance with the BSA and its implementing regulations during the entire course of Helix's operation. FinCEN analysis evidenced that Helix failed to maintain all required elements of an AML program. During the lifespan of the MSB, Helix developed no AML program and was vulnerable to illicit use. In addition to having no AML program, Helix further failed to designate a compliance officer, conduct any AML training for employees, and never conducted an independent test required under law. Rather than collect customer data as part of a viable AML program, Helix asserted that it deleted even the minimal customer information it did collect for all transactions it facilitated. Helix also failed to conduct appropriate suspicious activity monitoring from 2014 through 2017, making it difficult to completely ascertain the number of specific reporting violations that exist. Independent FinCEN analysis of Helix's public records and analysis of convertible virtual currency blockchains identified at least 245,817 instances in which suspicious transactions took place. Yet, Helix failed to file a single SAR throughout the corresponding time period.

3. <u>Pervasiveness of wrongdoing within the financial institution</u>. Helix openly flaunted existing regulatory requirements and went out its way to create ways for darknet customers and vendors to avoid law enforcement detection. Helix purposefully created a system to facilitate illicit activity, which was recognized by darknet drug vendors like AlphaBay—a marketplace that integrated Helix into its platform. Rather than institute policies and procedures to comply with the BSA, Helix instead instituted policies and procedures that allowed customers of darknet marketplaces to launder bitcoin through Helix.

4. <u>History and duration of violations</u>. Helix operated for over three years, from April 2014 to December 2017, without appropriate AML policies and procedures in place. Helix did not implement even basic AML program requirements and specifically sought to launder bitcoin from illegal activity.

5. <u>Failure to terminate the violations</u>. After Helix closed operations in December 2017, Helix continued to operate another unregistered MSB by creating, controlling, and operating the money transmitter Coin Ninja LLC in 2017, which operated through February 6, 2020.

6. <u>Financial gain or other benefit as a result of violation</u>. Helix made a significant financial gain in administrator fees from its facilitation of transactions with darknet marketplaces, ransomware, child exploitation websites, and unregistered MSBs. Helix did not expend any resources on compliance with the BSA and its implementing regulations.

7. <u>Cooperation</u>. Helix agreed to two statute of limitations tolling agreements with FinCEN.

8. <u>Systemic nature of violations</u>. Helix's systemic failure to report potentially suspicious activity led to shortcomings that denied potentially critical information to the BSA database for at least a three-year period. FinCEN's independent investigation found that Helix conducted numerous potentially suspicious transactions with darknet marketplaces, ransomware, unregistered MSBs, and other mixing platforms offering similar money laundering services.

9. <u>Timely and Voluntary Disclosure of Violations</u>. FinCEN did not consider this as an aggravating or mitigating factor in this matter.

10. <u>Penalties by Other Government Entities</u>. FinCEN is the sole government regulator with authority to pursue civil violations of the BSA and its implementing regulations for MSBs.[18] FinCEN has considered Helix's indictment in the District of Columbia under 18 U.S.C. §§ 1956 and 1960 for conspiracy to launder monetary instruments and the operation of an unlicensed money transmitting business.[19]

As a result of the analysis described above, FinCEN hereby imposes a penalty in the amount of **$60,000,000.**

Kenneth A. Blanco

Director

Financial Crimes Enforcement Network U.S. Department of the Treasury

Attachment to In the Matter of: Larry Dean Harmon d/b/a Helix

A Statement of Facts

I. Background

A. Larry Dean Harmon and Coin Ninja

1. Larry Dean Harmon (Mr. Harmon) is a U.S. person residing in Akron, Ohio. Mr. Harmon was the creator, administrator, and primary operator of Grams, a darknet website that operated on the onion router (Tor) network and advertised itself as the "Google of the Darkweb" from in or about April 2014 through on or about December 16, 2017. Grams served as a search engine and content aggregator allowing users to search for illicit goods sold on

---

18. 31 C.F.R. § 1010.810(a); Treasury Order 180-01 (July 1, 2014).

19. *United States of America v. Larry Dean Harmon*, 19-cr-00395, (D.C. DC, Dec. 3, 2019).

darknet markets. Grams also indexed darknet .onion pages for vendors of illicit goods such as narcotics, illegal firearms, and stolen Personally Identifiable Information (PII).

2. On or about June 2014, Mr. Harmon began operating and administrating a convertible virtual currency exchanger called Helix through the Grams darknet .onion site.[1] Mr. Harmon was the primary administrator and operator of Helix. Helix was a service linked to and affiliated with Grams, and the two services were sometimes referred to collectively as "Grams-Helix." Helix operated what is commonly referred to as a "mixer" or "tumbler" of the convertible virtual currency bitcoin—charging customers a fee to send bitcoin to a designated address in a manner designed to conceal and obfuscate the source or owner of the bitcoin. Mr. Harmon offered customers two options to transmit "tumbled" bitcoin: Helix and Helix Light. Helix was built as a function into customer's Grams "account" and operated in the following manner:

   a. Customers would send bitcoin to a wallet associated with their Grams account;

   b. Customers would then complete a Helix withdrawal form, which included the amount to withdraw, a destination address, and the ability to set a time delay for the transactions;

   c. Helix would transmit the bitcoin deposited into their wallet to one of numerous accounts held at different exchangers of convertible virtual currency;

   d. Helix would take bitcoin from a different account it held and transmit that bitcoin to a different bitcoin address;

   e. From this bitcoin address, Helix would then transmit bitcoin to the customer, minus a fee, into the previously provided customer destination address;

   f. Helix asserted that it deleted customer information after seven days, or allowed customers to delete their logs manually after a withdrawal.

3. Helix Light was a service of Helix that allowed individuals to transact without creating a Grams "account." Helix Light conducted transactions in the following manner:

   a. Customers were asked to provide a destination address to receive bitcoins;

   b. Helix Light would provide an address to which the customer would send the desired amount of bitcoin between .02 and 6 bitcoins;

---

1. "Introducing Grams Helix: Bitcoin Cleaner," DeepDotWeb, June 22, 2014, Accessed January 24, 2018.

    c. Helix Light would transmit the bitcoin deposited into their wallet to one of numerous accounts held at different exchangers of convertible virtual currency;

    d. Helix Light would take bitcoin from a different account it held and transmit that bitcoin to a different bitcoin address;

    e. From this bitcoin address, Helix Light would then transmit bitcoin to the customer, minus a fee, into the previously provided customer destination address;

4. On or about July 13, 2017, Mr. Harmon, through his legal representative, registered Coin Ninja LLC (Coin Ninja) in Delaware. Mr. Harmon later filed a corporate registration in Ohio on November 8, 2017.[2] Mr. Harmon is the Chief Executive Officer of Coin Ninja, which operates as a money services business. Mr. Harmon willfully participated in the direction and supervision of Coin Ninja's operations and finances. Coin Ninja has stated on its Frequently Asked Questions (FAQ) page that it also provided a "mixing" service including an "FAQ" titled "Why should I mix my bitcoins?"[3] Coin Ninja offers a service called DropBit, which describes itself as "like Venmo for Bitcoin" allowing customers to accept and transmit bitcoin through text messages or Twitter handles.[4] Mr. Harmon has advertised Coin Ninja's DropBit service on Reddit, under the moniker "doolbman," as a service that helps circumvent know your customer procedures.[5]

B. The Financial Crimes Enforcement Network

5. The Financial Crimes Enforcement Network (FinCEN) is a bureau within the Department of Treasury. Pursuant to 31 C.F.R. § 1010.810, FinCEN has "[o]verall authority for enforcement and compliance, including coordination and direction of procedures and activities of all other agencies exercising delegated authority" under the Bank Secrecy Act (BSA) and its implementing regulations. FinCEN regulates money services businesses and other financial institutions under the BSA.[6]

C. Mixers and Tumblers Status as Money Transmitters Under the BSA

6. Providers of anonymizing services, commonly referred to as "mixers" or "tumblers," are either persons that accept convertible virtual currencies and

---

2. Registration of Foreign for Profit Limited Liability Company Document Number 201731201776, State of Ohio Secretary of State, November 8, 2017.

3. "Frequently Asked Questions," https://coinninja.io/faq, February 14, 2018.

4. @dropbitapp, Twitter, https://twitter.com/dropbitapp, accessed November 20, 2019.

5. doolbman, "Send Bitcoin instead of Venmo or PayPal. Spread the wealth," https://www.reddit.com/r/Bitcoin/

6. *See* Treasury Order 180-01 (July 1, 2014).

retransmit them in a manner designed to prevent others from tracing the transmission back to its source (anonymizing services provider). An anonymizing services provider is a money transmitter under FinCEN regulations because it accepts and transmits convertible virtual currencies.[7]

II. Anti-Money Laundering/Bank Secrecy Act Violations A. Failure to Register as a Money Services Business

7. The BSA and its implementing regulations require the registration of an MSB within 180 days of beginning operations and the renewal of such registration every two years.[8]

8. Mr. Harmon began operating Helix in June 2014 and ceased operations in December 2017 and never registered as an MSB with FinCEN.

9. Before closing Helix, Mr. Harmon began operating Coin Ninja on or about July 13, 2017. Neither Coin Ninja, nor its DropBit service, have ever registered as an MSB with FinCEN.

B. Failure to Implement an Anti-Money Laundering Program

10. Since July 24, 2002, MSBs have been required to "develop, implement, and maintain an effective anti-money laundering (AML) program."[9] The program must be in writing and commensurate with the risks posed by the location and size of, and the nature and volume of the financial services provided by the MSB.[10] An effective AML program is one that is reasonably designed to prevent the MSB from being used to facilitate money laundering and the financing of terrorist activities.[11] MSBs must, "[i]ncorporate policies, procedures, and internal controls reasonably designed to assure compliance…."[12] An MSB is also required to designate a person to assure day to day compliance with its AML program.[13] An MSB must provide for training of personnel, including training in the detection of suspicious transactions and provide for independent review to monitor and maintain an adequate program.[14] Mr. Harmon never implemented any type of AML program related to Helix and failed to comply with all of the aforementioned requirements.

---

7. "Application of FinCEN's Regulations to Certain Business Models Involving Convertible Virtual Currencies," (FIN- 2019-G001)," May 9, 2019, p.19–20.
  8. 31 U.S.C. § 5330 and 31 C.F.R. §§ 1022.380(b)(2) and (3).
  9. 31 C.F.R. § 1022.210(a).
  10. 31 C.F.R. § 1022.210(b).
  11. 31 C.F.R. § 1022.210(a).
  12. 31 C.F.R. § 1022.210(d)(1).
  13. 31 C.F.R. § 1022.210(d)(2).
  14. 31 C.F.R. § 1022.210(d)(3)-(4).

i. Policies, Procedures, and Internal Controls

11. An MSB is required to have a compliance program that includes "[a] system of internal controls to assure ongoing compliance."[15] Mr. Harmon failed to establish and maintain appropriate internal controls to ensure compliance with the BSA's reporting requirements during the operation of his business. In fact, Mr. Harmon actively aided cybercriminals and other threat actors in circumventing the policies, procedures, and internal controls in place at U.S.-based convertible virtual currency exchanges. Through his services Mr. Harmon promoted unlawful online activities by concealing the nature, the location, the source, the ownership, and the control of the proceeds of online drug sales, amongst other illegal online activities.

12. Mr. Harmon publicly advertised Helix on Reddit forums dedicated to darknet marketplaces, actively seeking out and facilitating high-risk transactions directly through customer service and feedback. On December 7, 2014, Mr. Harmon, using the online moniker "gramsadmin," posted, "Helix does exactly what it says it does, breaks the blockchain taint so a transaction can't be followed through the blockchain. Helix gives you new bitcoins [sic] from a different pool, that have never been on the darkweb."[16] On November 24, 2014, Mr. Harmon, using the same online moniker and forum, identified transactions passing from a specific darknet marketplace through Helix, stating "Since Helix uses expiring addresses and all the Agora withdrawals just started coming[.] I have a bunch of unclaimed bitcoins."[17]

13. Despite requiring account creation for transactions through Helix, Mr. Harmon chose not to collect information on any of the over 809,500 unique addresses sending and receiving bitcoin. In addition, Mr. Harmon developed Helix Light so that customers could conduct transactions without even creating the accounts required by the Helix service offered through his Grams platform. As a result, Mr. Harmon failed to collect and verify customer names, addresses, or any other related customer identifiers on over 1.2 million transactions between June 2016 and December 2017 alone.

14. In fact, during its entire operational period, Mr. Harmon openly advertised Helix as a service that did not conduct customer due diligence, stating "My goals with Helix light [and] Regular helix [have] always and will always work to perfection for tumbling bitcoins and keeping a user anonymous."[18]

---

15. 31 C.F.R. § 1022.210(b)(2)(i).

16. gramsadmin, "Helix : Agora bitcoin claim process?," https://www.reddit.com/r/DarkNet-Markets/comments/2oi5jh/ helix_deanonymization_the_response/, December 7, 2014. gramsadmin, "Helix : Agora bitcoin claim process?,"

17. gramsadmin, "Helix : Agora bitcoin claim process?," https://www.reddit.com/r/DarkNet Markets/comments/2nanzl/helix_agora_bitcoin_claim_process/Reddit, November 24, 2014.

18. gramsadmin, "Helix : Agora bitcoin claim process?," https://www.reddit.com/r/DarkNet Markets/comments/2nanzl/helix_agora_bitcoin_claim_process/Reddit, November 24, 2014.

During the operational period, Mr. Harmon conducted over $311 million worth of transactions in convertible virtual currencies without performing appropriate due diligence on transactions or customers.

15. Mr. Harmon also failed to implement policies and procedures to file reports required by the BSA and to create and retain appropriate records.[19] In public fora, Mr. Harmon advertised that "All logs are deleted after 7 days, but you can deleted the logs off the server manually after the helix withdraw is complete."[20] Mr. Harmon asserted that he deleted any customer information Helix had after a period of seven days.[21] Mr. Harmon also claimed to allow customers to delete their own customer information at will. Such a policy made it impossible for Mr. Harmon to comply with the requirements of the BSA. During its operations over 1.2 million transactions passed through Helix.

16. More specifically, Mr. Harmon failed to implement appropriate policies, procedures, and internal controls to detect and report potentially suspicious transactions. FinCEN identified a significant volume of transactions that bore indicia of money laundering and other illicit activity. These included transactions supporting illegal narcotics and controlled substances, drug paraphernalia, counterfeit and fraud-related goods and services, child exploitation websites, and white nationalist/neo-Nazi groups. As detailed in Section II. C (below), potentially suspicious activity going through sites controlled and operated by Mr. Harmon totaled over $121 million.

17. Mr. Harmon failed to mitigate risks associated with Tor-enabled browsers. While use of Tor in and of itself is not suspicious, the many transactions that take place through an anonymizing internet browser, such as darknet marketplaces, may be a strong indicator of potential illicit activity when no additional due diligence is conducted. Because of this, Mr. Harmon failed to determine customer identity and whether or not the funds were derived from illegal activity.

18. Mr. Harmon failed to apply due diligence measures proportionate to the risks arising to any jurisdictions with AML/CFT deficiencies.[22] These deficiencies were exacerbated by Mr. Harmon's failure to implement appropriate due diligence over transactions occurring through Tor-enabled browsers. For example, according to FinCEN's analysis, from June 2014 through December 2017 Mr. Harmon accepted and processed multiple transactions

---

19. 31 C.F.R. § 1022.210(d)(1)(i)(B) and (C).

20. gramsadmin, "New Grams' Helix," https://www.reddit.com/r/onions/comments/28t66t/new_grams_helix/, June 22, 2014.

21. Introducing Grams Helix: Bitcoins Cleaner, DeepDotWeb, June 22, 2014.

22. *See* "Advisory on the Financial Action Task Force-Identified Jurisdictions with AML/CFT Deficiencies (FIN- 2015-A002)," July 17, 2015; "Advisory on the Financial Action Task Force-Identified Jurisdictions with AML/CFT Deficiencies (FIN-2016-A001)," January 19, 2016.

with Iran-affiliated accounts. Mr. Harmon failed to implement policies, procedures, and internal controls to review for potential suspicious activity occurring by, through, or to jurisdictions with a heightened risk for money laundering and terrorist finance.

ii. Compliance Officer

19. An MSB is also required to designate a person to assure day to day compliance with their compliance program and the BSA. This person is responsible for assuring that the MSB files reports, and creates and retains records, that the compliance program is updated as necessary to reflect the current requirements of the BSA, and provides appropriate training.[23] At no point in its operations did Mr. Harmon designate a person to assure day to day compliance with their compliance program and the BSA.

iii. Training

20. An MSB must provide for training of personnel, including training in the detection of suspicious transactions.[24] Mr. Harmon failed to train appropriate personnel in BSA recordkeeping and reporting requirements and failed to train personnel in identifying, monitoring, and reporting suspicious activity.

iv. Independent Testing

21. An MSB must provide for independent review to monitor and maintain an adequate program.[25] At no point in its operations did Mr. Harmon conduct an independent test.

C. Failure to File Suspicious Activity Reports

22. The BSA and its implementing regulations require an MSB to report a transaction that the MSB "knows, suspects, or has reason to suspect" is suspicious, if the transaction is conducted or attempted by, at, or through the MSB, and the transaction involves or aggregates to at least $2,000 in funds or other assets.[26] A transaction is "suspicious" if the transaction: (a) involves funds derived from illegal activity; (b) is intended or conducted in order to hide or disguise funds or assets derived from illegal activity, or to disguise the ownership, nature, source, location, or control of funds or assets derived from illegal activity; (c) is designed, whether through structuring or other means, to evade any requirement in the BSA or its implementing

---

23. 31 C.F.R. § 1022.210(d)(2)(i)-(iii).
24. 31 C.F.R. § 1022.210(d)(3).
25. 31 C.F.R. § 1022.210(d)(4).
26. 31 C.F.R. § 1022.320.

regulations; (d) has no business or apparent lawful purpose or is not the sort in which the particular customer would normally be expected to engage, and the casino knows of no reasonable explanation for the transaction after examining the available facts, including the background and possible purpose of the transaction; or (e) involves use of the MSB to facilitate criminal activity. An MSB must file a SAR no later than 30 calendar days after initially detecting facts that may constitute a basis for filing a suspicious activity report.[27]

23. FinCEN has identified at least 2,464 instances in which Mr. Harmon failed to file a SAR for transactions involving Helix.

i. Darknet and other Illicit Markets

24. Helix addresses were found to interact directly with 39 darknet marketplaces and other illicit markets where individuals bought and sold illicit goods and services. Bitcoin is the most common medium of exchange on these marketplaces. FinCEN observed 241,594 direct bitcoin transactions worth $39,074,476.47 with darknet and other illicit marketplace-associated addresses, not including indirect transactions. At least 2,097 of these direct transactions were for an amount over $2,000. Mr. Harmon failed to file a SAR on all darknet and other illicit market transactions.

25. **Abraxas Market.** Abraxas Market was a Tor-network based darknet market in operation from in and around December 2014 to around November 2015 that sold illegal narcotics and controlled substances, drug paraphernalia, counterfeit and fraud-related goods and services, and other illegal contraband. FinCEN observed Helix conducting 776 bitcoin transactions worth $308,077.74 directly with the Abraxas darknet marketplace. At least 25 of these direct transactions were for an amount over $2,000. Mr. Harmon failed to file a SAR on these transactions.

26. **Agora Market.** Agora Market was a Tor-network based darknet market in operation from in and around January 2014 to around August 2015 that sold illegal narcotics and controlled substances, drug paraphernalia, counterfeit and fraud-related goods and services, and other illegal contraband. FinCEN observed Helix conducting 3,978 bitcoin transactions worth $1,725,338.13 directly with the Agora darknet marketplace. At least 131 of these direct transactions were for an amount over $2,000. Mr. Harmon failed to file a SAR on these transactions.

27. **AlphaBay Market.** AlphaBay Market was a Tor-network based darknet market in operation from in and around December 2014 to July 2017, when

---

27. 31 C.F.R. §§ 1022.320(a)(2)(i) – (iv).

the site was seized by law enforcement.[28] At the time of the seizure, Alpha-Bay was the largest Darknet marketplace in operation, offering a platform for customers to purchase a variety of illegal drugs, guns, and other illegal goods. In or about November 2016, the AlphaBay website recommended to its customers that they use a bitcoin tumbler service to "erase any trace of [their] coins coming from AlphaBay," and provided an embedded link to the Tor website for Helix. FinCEN observed Helix conducting 191,988 bitcoin transactions worth $27,066,798 directly with the AlphaBay darknet marketplace. At least 1,201 of these direct transactions were for an amount over $2,000. Mr. Harmon failed to file a SAR on these transactions.

28. **Aviato Market.** Aviato Market was a Tor-network based darknet market in operation from in and around April 2016 to around December 2017 that sold illegal narcotics and controlled substances, drug paraphernalia, counterfeit and fraud-related goods and services, and other illegal contraband. FinCEN observed Helix conducting 406 bitcoin transactions worth $32,439 directly with the Aviato darknet marketplace. Mr. Harmon failed to file a SAR on these transactions.

29. **Black Bank Market.** Black Bank Market was a Tor-network based darknet market in operation from in and around March 2015 to around June 2015 that sold illegal narcotics and controlled substances, drug paraphernalia, counterfeit and fraud-related goods and services, and other illegal contraband. FinCEN observed Helix conducting 453 bitcoin transactions worth $179,681 directly with the Black Bank darknet marketplace. At least nine of these direct transactions were for an amount over $2,000. Mr. Harmon failed to file a SAR on these transactions.

30. **Doctor D Market.** Doctor D Market was a Tor-network based darknet market in operation from in and around March 2015 to around August 2016 that sold illegal narcotics and controlled substances, drug paraphernalia, counterfeit and fraud-related goods and services, and other illegal contraband. FinCEN observed Helix conducting 101 bitcoin transactions worth $43,945 directly with the Doctor D darknet marketplace. At least two of these direct transactions were for an amount over $2,000. Mr. Harmon failed to file a SAR on these transactions.

31. **Dream Market.** Dream Market was a Tor-network based darknet market in operation from in and around November 2013 to April 2019 that sold illegal narcotics and controlled substances, drug paraphernalia, counterfeit and fraud-related goods and services, and other illegal contraband. FinCEN observed Helix conducting 20,724 bitcoin transactions worth $3,544,497 directly with the Dream darknet marketplace. At least 250 of these direct

---

28. "AlphaBay, the Largest Online 'Dark Market,' Shut Down," U.S. Department of Justice, https://www.justice.gov/opa/ pr/alphabay-largest-online-dark-market-shut-down, July 20, 2017.

transactions were for an amount over $2,000. Mr. Harmon failed to file a SAR on these transactions.

32. **DutchDrugz Market.** DutchDrugz Market was a Tor-network based darknet market in operation from in and around January 2017 to around January 2018 that sold illegal narcotics and controlled substances, and drug paraphernalia. FinCEN observed Helix conducting 19 bitcoin transactions worth $29,366 directly with the DutchDrugz darknet marketplace. At least five of these direct transactions were for an amount over $2,000. Mr. Harmon failed to file a SAR on these transactions.

33. **Evolution Market.** Evolution Market was a Tor-network based darknet market in operation from in and around January 2014 to around March 2015 that sold illegal narcotics and controlled substances, drug paraphernalia, counterfeit and fraud-related goods and services, and other illegal contraband. FinCEN observed Helix conducting 295 bitcoin transactions worth $114,670 directly with the Evolution darknet marketplace. At least nine of these direct transactions were for an amount over $2,000. Mr. Harmon failed to file a SAR on these transactions.

34. **Flugsvamp Market 2.0.** Flugsvamp Market 2.0 was a Tor-network based darknet market in operation from in and around April 2015 to around September 2018 that sold illegal narcotics and controlled substances, drug paraphernalia, counterfeit and fraud-related goods and services, and other illegal contraband. FinCEN observed Helix conducting 758 bitcoin transactions worth $161,774 directly with the darknet marketplace. At least 22 of these direct transactions were for an amount over $2,000. Mr. Harmon failed to file a SAR on these transactions.

35. **Hansa Market.** Hansa Market was a Tor-network based darknet market in operation from in and around August 2015 to around July 2017 that sold illegal narcotics and controlled substances, drug paraphernalia, counterfeit and fraud-related goods and services, and other illegal contraband. Dutch and US law enforcement seized the market and arrested the site owners in 2017.[29] FinCEN observed Helix conducting 4,885 bitcoin transactions worth $635,685 directly with the darknet marketplace. At least 26 of these direct transactions were for an amount over $2,000. Mr. Harmon failed to file a SAR on these transactions.

36. **Hydra Market.** Hydra Market was a Tor-network based darknet market in operation since at least 2014 that sells illegal narcotics and controlled substances, drug paraphernalia, counterfeit and fraud-related goods and services, and other illegal contraband. FinCEN observed Helix conducting

---

29. "Massive Blow to Criminal Dark Web Activities after Globally Coordinated Operation," Europol, July 20, 2017, https://www.europol.europa.eu/newsroom/news/massive-blow-to-criminal-dark-web-activities-after-globally-coordinated-operation.

297 bitcoin transactions worth $77,983 directly with the darknet marketplace. At least seven of these direct transactions were for an amount over $2,000. Mr. Harmon failed to file a SAR on these transactions.

37. **Joker's Stash Market.** Joker's Stash Market was an illicit market in operation from in and around October 2014 to around July 2017 that sold stolen credit card numbers and fraud- related goods and services. FinCEN observed Helix conducting 33 bitcoin transactions worth $2,279 directly with the marketplace. Mr. Harmon failed to file a SAR on these transactions.

38. **Middle Earth Marketplace.** Middle Earth Marketplace was a Tor-network based darknet market in operation from in and around July 2014 to in and around November 2015 that sold illegal narcotics and controlled substances, drug paraphernalia, counterfeit and fraud-related goods and services, and other illegal contraband. FinCEN observed Helix conducting 353 bitcoin transactions worth $105,231 directly with the darknet marketplace. At least 11 of these direct transactions were for an amount over $2,000. Mr. Harmon failed to file a SAR on these transactions.

39. **Nucleus Market.** Nucleus Market was a Tor-network based darknet market in operation from in and around November 2014 to in and around April 2016 that sold illegal narcotics and controlled substances, drug paraphernalia, counterfeit and fraud-related goods and services, and other illegal contraband. FinCEN observed Helix conducting 6,405 bitcoin transactions worth $3,480,201 directly with the darknet marketplace. At least 306 of these direct transactions were for an amount over $2,000. Mr. Harmon failed to file a SAR on these transactions.

40. **Oasis Market.** Oasis Market was a Tor-network based darknet market in operation from in and around March 2016 to around September 2016 that sold illegal narcotics and controlled substances, drug paraphernalia, counterfeit and fraud-related goods and services, and other illegal contraband. FinCEN observed Helix conducting 452 bitcoin transactions worth $102,481 directly with the darknet marketplace. At least 12 of these direct transactions were for an amount over $2,000. Mr. Harmon failed to file a SAR on these transactions.

41. **Russian Anonymous Marketplace.** Russian Anonymous Marketplace (RAMP) was a Tor-network based darknet market in operation from in and around November 2014 to around July 2017 that sold illegal narcotics and controlled substances, drug paraphernalia, counterfeit and fraud-related goods and services, and other illegal contraband. FinCEN observed Helix conducting 256 bitcoin transactions worth $120,047 directly with the darknet marketplace. At least 19 of these direct transactions were for an amount over $2,000. Mr. Harmon failed to file a SAR on these transactions.

42. **Silk Road 2 Market.** Silk Road 2 Market was a Tor-network based dark-net market in operation from in and around November 2013 to around November 2014 that sold illegal narcotics and controlled substances, drug paraphernalia, counterfeit and fraud-related goods and services, and other illegal contraband. US law enforcement shutdown the market and arrested the site owner on November 6, 2014.[30] FinCEN observed Helix conducting 17 bitcoin transactions worth $5,881 directly with the darknet marketplace. Mr. Harmon failed to file a SAR on these transactions.

43. **TradeRoute Market.** TradeRoute Market was a Tor-network based dark-net market in operation from in and around September 2016 to around September 2017 that sold illegal narcotics and controlled substances, drug paraphernalia, counterfeit and fraud-related goods and services, and other illegal contraband. FinCEN observed Helix conducting 6,871 bitcoin transactions worth $884,507 directly with the darknet marketplace. At least 34 of these direct transactions were for an amount over $2,000. Mr. Harmon failed to file a SAR on these transactions.

44. **Unicc.** Unicc was an illicit market in operation from in and around July 2015 to around January 2018 that sold stolen credit card numbers and other fraud-related goods and services, and other illegal contraband. FinCEN observed Helix conducting 134 bitcoin transactions worth over $31,846 directly with the marketplace. FinCEN traced 0.91898767 bitcoin, worth $2,172.51, directly exchanged with Helix from a Unicc associated wallet on June 15, 2017. Mr. Harmon failed to file a SAR on this transaction.

45. **Valhalla Market (Silkkitie).** Valhalla Market (Silkkitie) was a Tor-network based darknet market in operation from in and around July 2015 to around June 2017 that sold illegal narcotics and controlled substances, drug paraphernalia, counterfeit and fraud-related goods and services, and other illegal contraband. Finnish law enforcement seized the market and arrested the site administrators in 2019.[31] FinCEN observed Helix conducting 1,934 bitcoin transactions worth $388,581 directly with the darknet marketplace. At least 27 of these direct transactions were for an amount over $2,000. Mr. Harmon failed to file a SAR on these transactions.

46. **Wall Street Market.** Wall Street Market was a Tor-network based darknet market in operation from in and around November 2016 until May 2019. Wall Street Market was one of the world's largest dark web marketplaces that allowed vendors to sell a wide variety of contraband, including an ar-

---

30. "Operator of Silk Road 2.0 Website Charged in Manhattan Federal Court," FBI, November 6, 2014, https://www.fbi.gov/contact-us/field-offices/newyork/news/press-releases/operator-of-silk-road-2.0-website-charged-in-manhattan-federal-court.

31. "Double Blow To Dark Web Marketplaces," Europol, May 3, 2019, https://www.europol.europa.eu/newsroom/news/double-blow-to-dark-web-marketplaces.

ray of illegal narcotics, counterfeit goods, and malicious computer hacking software. German and US law enforcement seized the market and arrested three administrators on May 3, 2019.[32] Wall Street Market functioned like a conventional e-commerce website. FinCEN observed Helix conducting 279 bitcoin transactions worth $23,964 directly with the darknet marketplace. Mr. Harmon failed to file a SAR on these transactions.

ii. Convertible Virtual Currency Mixing Services

47. Other providers of anonymizing services were found to frequently interact with Helix. Darknet marketplaces actively promote these additional mixers as the primary method for obfuscating bitcoin transactions. FinCEN observed bitcoin transactions equal to $55,617,653 transferred with other mixing service-associated addresses. Of these, FinCEN observed 2,423 direct bitcoin transactions—not including indirect transactions—equal to $2,118,476.43 between Helix and unregistered bitcoin mixing services. At least 261 of these direct transactions were for an amount over $2,000. Mr. Harmon failed to file a SAR on these transactions.

48. **CVC Mixer 1.** FinCEN observed Helix conducting 1,126 direct bitcoin transactions worth $1,622,807 with CVC Mixer 1. At least 209 of these direct transactions were for amounts over $2,000. Mr. Harmon failed to file SARs on these transactions.

49. **CVC Mixer 2.** FinCEN observed Helix conducting 92 direct bitcoin transactions worth $287,548 with CVC Mixer 2. At least 27 of these direct transactions were for amounts over $2,000. Mr. Harmon failed to file SARs on these transactions.

50. **CVC Mixer 3.** FinCEN observed Helix conducting 52 direct bitcoin transactions worth $42,219 with CVC Mixer 3. At least seven of these direct transactions were for amounts over $2,000. Mr. Harmon failed to file SARs on these transactions.

51. **CVC Mixer 4.** FinCEN observed Helix conducting 1,149 direct bitcoin transactions worth $164,943 with CVC Mixer 4. At least 17 of these direct transactions were for amounts over $2,000. Mr. Harmon failed to file SARs on these transactions.

---

32. "3 Germans Who Allegedly Operated Dark Web Marketplace with Over 1 Million Users Face U.S. Narcotics and Money Laundering Charges," Department of Justice, May 3, 2019, https ://www.justice.gov/usao-cdca/pr/3-germans-who- allegedly-operated-dark-web-marketplace-over -1-million-users-face-us.

iii. Darknet Child Exploitation Site

52. Mr. Harmon failed to file a SAR on transactions of convertible virtual currency to a darknet child exploitation site. Users were allowed to send convertible virtual currency into Helix to obfuscate origins of these illicit purchases.

53. **Welcome to Video.** Welcome to Video was a Tor-network based child pornography website, which began operating in or about June 2015 and was shut down by law enforcement on October 16, 2019.[33] Welcome to Video had over 200,000 unique video files, which totaled approximately eight terabytes of data. FinCEN observed Helix conducting at least 73 bitcoin transactions worth over $2,000 directly with Welcome to Video. Mr. Harmon failed to file a SAR on these transactions.

iv. Additional Illicit Proceeds

54. FinCEN observed Helix accepting and transmitting convertible virtual currency for wallets containing the proceeds of various acts of cybercrime. FinCEN traced convertible virtual currencies passing through Helix from these cybercriminal wallets holding value from large scale hacks, account takeovers, criminal organizations and businesses. Many of these transactions contained values greater than or cumulative to $2,000. Mr. Harmon failed to file a SAR on these transactions.

55. **BTC-e.** BTC-e was an unregistered exchanger of convertible virtual currencies that operated from 2011 to July 27, 2017, before it was shut down by a coordinated U.S. government action for alleged money laundering and operating an as unlicensed money transmitter. Concurrently, FinCEN assessed a $110 million dollar civil money penalty against BTC-e and a $12 million dollar civil money penalty against one of its operators, Alexander Vinnik, for failing to register as a money services business, failing to maintain an AML program, and for facilitating millions of dollars of suspicious transactions without filing a SAR. FinCEN observed Helix conducting 1,723 direct bitcoin transactions worth over $904,637 with BTC-e. At least 107 of these direct transactions were for amounts over $2,000. Mr. Harmon failed to file SARs on these transactions.

---

33. "South Korean National and Hundreds of Others Charged Worldwide in the Takedown of the Largest Darknet Child Pornography Website, Which was Funded by Bitcoin," Department of Justice, Oct. 16, 2019, https://www.justice.gov/opa/pr/south-korean-national-and-hundreds-others -charged-worldwide-takedown-largest-darknet-child.

Discussion Points

1. *Helix.* Helix was a darknet-based cryptocurrency mixer that partnered with darknet marketplaces to provide bitcoin money laundering services for darknet market consumers. What preventative measures can the law take to prevent similar Helix activities from happening? Do you think that the darknet will provide a new route for money laundering?

2. *Is cryptocurrency "safe"?* Do you think that virtual currencies are more or less susceptible to money laundering activity? Does the use of blockchain technology provide regulators enhanced ability to prevent financial crimes before they occur?

3. *Setting precedent.* Do you think this case is good precedent for how similar future cases should be decided? Do you agree with FinCEN's determinations? What, if anything, should FinCEN have decided differently?

4. *Do you agree with FinCEN?* Do you think FinCEN should have done more than impose a penalty? Should FinCEN have taken more action against Helix?

5. *Consider the factors.* Do you think FinCEN's analysis was comprehensive enough? What other factors, if any, should FinCEN have considered in determining a penalty?

FinCEN Advisory: Advisory on Illicit Activity Involving Convertible Virtual Currency

FIN-2019-A003 (May 9, 2019)

The Financial Crimes Enforcement Network (FinCEN) is issuing this advisory to assist financial institutions in identifying and reporting suspicious activity concerning how criminals and other bad actors exploit convertible virtual currencies (CVCs) for money laundering, sanctions evasion, and other illicit financing purposes, particularly involving darknet marketplaces, peer-to- peer (P2P) exchangers, foreign-located Money Service Businesses (MSBs), and CVC kiosks. Virtual currencies, particularly CVCs, are increasingly used as alternatives to traditional payment and money transmission systems. As with other payment and money transmission methods, financial institutions should carefully assess and mitigate any potential money laundering, terrorist financing, and other illicit financing risks associated with CVCs. This advisory highlights prominent typologies and red flags associated with such activity and identifies information that would be most valuable to law enforcement, regulators, and other national security agencies in the filing of suspicious activity reports (SARs).[1]

---

1. Many business models of entities dealing with CVC operate as money transmitters. As money transmitters, persons accepting and transmitting CVC are required, like any money transmitter, to

The Risks Posed by Virtual Currencies

CVCs may create illicit finance vulnerabilities due to the global nature, distributed structure, limited transparency, and speed of the most widely utilized virtual currency systems. New types of anonymity-enhanced CVCs have emerged that further reduce the transparency of transactions and identities as well as obscure the source of the CVC through the incorporation of anonymizing features, such as mixing and cryptographic enhancements.[2] Some CVCs appear to be designed with the express purpose of circumventing anti-money laundering/countering the financing of terrorism (AML/CFT) controls. All of these factors increase the difficulty for law enforcement and other national security agencies' efforts to combat money laundering, terrorist financing, and other financial crimes facilitated through CVC.

A financial institution that fails to comply with its AML/CFT program, recordkeeping and reporting obligations, as well as other regulatory obligations, such as those administered by the Office of Foreign Assets Control (OFAC), risks exposing the financial system to greater illicit finance risks. This is particularly true among unregistered MSBs that may be attempting to evade supervision and fail to implement appropriate controls to prevent their services from being leveraged in money laundering, terrorist financing, and other related illicit activities. Without sufficient controls in place, financial institutions cannot reasonably assess and mitigate the potential risks posed by a customer's source of funds or a customer's counterparty, and criminals can exploit the U.S. financial system by engaging in illicit transactions. Individuals engaged in illicit activity will continue to exploit these vulnerabilities as long as the perceived risk of detection is less than that of using traditional financial institutions.

The prevalence of unregistered CVC entities without sufficient AML/CFT controls and the limited transparency of CVC transactions makes CVCs an attractive method of money transmission by those engaged in illicit conduct and other criminal acts that threaten U.S. national security. According to FinCEN's analysis of BSA and other data, illicit actors have used CVCs to facilitate criminal activity such as human trafficking, child exploitation, fraud, extortion, cybercrime, drug trafficking, money laundering, terrorist financing, and to support rogue regimes and facilitate sanctions evasion. Additionally, the increased use of CVC has made legitimate users

---

register with FinCEN as MSBs and comply with anti-money laundering/countering the financing of terrorism (AML/CFT) program, recordkeeping, and reporting requirements. These requirements apply equally to domestic and foreign-located CVC money transmitters doing business in whole or substantial part within the United States, even if the foreign-located entity has no physical presence in the United States. For more detail on how FinCEN regulations apply to varying business models involving virtual currency, *see* FinCEN Guidance FIN-2019-G001, "Application of FinCEN's Regulations to Certain Business Models Involving Convertible Virtual Currencies," May 9, 2019 ("2019 CVC Guidance").

2. Mixing or tumbling involves the use of mechanisms to break the connection between an address sending CVC and the addresses receiving CVC.

and financial intermediaries the target of sophisticated cyber intrusions aimed at theft of CVC. Of particular concern is that CVC has come to be one of the principal payment and money transmission methods used in online darknet marketplaces that facilitate the cybercrime economy.[3]

Virtual Currency Abuse Typologies

FinCEN and U.S. law enforcement have observed unregistered entities being exploited or wittingly allowing their platforms to be utilized by criminals in the United States and abroad to further illicit activity, including through darknet marketplaces, P2P exchangers, foreign-located MSBs, and CVC kiosks.[4]

Darknet Marketplaces

Darknet marketplaces are websites that are only available in anonymized overlay networks that require specific software to access.[5] Some require additional vetting or configurations to access. These marketplaces frequently include offers for the sale of illicit goods and services and specify virtual currency as a method—sometimes the sole method—of payment. The use of CVC in conjunction with darknet market activity may indicate drug purchases or sales, child exploitation, cybercrime, or other criminal activity. Accordingly, detectable darknet marketplace linkages, such as through a customer's online behavior, may indicate CVC use in support of illicit activity. Additionally, darknet marketplaces often directly facilitate transactions denominated in CVC to facilitate purchases of goods or services. Entities facilitating the transmission of CVCs are required to register with FinCEN as an MSB. If such an entity has not registered with FinCEN, it may be operating illegally as an unregistered MSB.

---

3. Darknet marketplace content is not indexed by traditional search engines and requires unique software or authorization to access. *See* Federal Bureau of Investigation, "A Primer on DarkNet Marketplaces: What They Are and What Law Enforcement is Doing to Combat Them," Nov. 1, 2016; *see also* U.S. Department of Homeland Security, U.S. Immigration and Customs Enforcement, "ICE Investigators Expose Darknet Criminals to the Light," last updated Nov. 2017.

4. The typologies and red flags discussed in this advisory apply to any decentralized ledger-based currency or CVC.

5. An overlay network is a telecommunications network that is built on top of another network and is supported by its infrastructure. The Onion Router (Tor) network, accessible through specialized software, is an example of an overlay network.

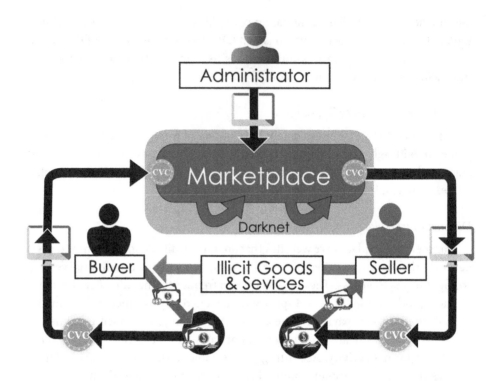

Darknet Marketplace—AlphaBay and Alexandre Cazes (a.k.a. Alpha02, Admin): In July 2017, U.S. law enforcement agencies announced a multi-national effort that dismantled AlphaBay, the largest criminal darknet market in operation at the time. On July 5, 2017, Thai authorities, on behalf of the United States, arrested Alexandre Cazes for his role as the creator and administrator of AlphaBay on charges that included conspiracy to commit identity theft, distribution of narcotics, and money laundering conspiracy. AlphaBay operated as a hidden service on the Tor network to hide the locations of its underlying servers and the identities of its administrators, moderators, and users. In a two-year span, AlphaBay was used by hundreds of thousands of people to buy and sell illegal drugs (e.g., fentanyl and heroin), in addition to other illicit products, often through transactions denominated in CVCs such as bitcoin, monero, and ether.[6] U.S. law enforcement authorities worked with international partners to freeze and preserve millions of dollars' worth of CVC-denominated proceeds of AlphaBay's illegal activities that were subject to forfeiture counts in the indictment.[7]

---

6. AlphaBay had approximately 200,000 users, 40,000 vendors, 250,000 listings, and facilitated more than $1 billion in CVC transactions between 2015 and 2017. *See* U.S. Department of Justice Press Release, "AlphaBay, the Largest Online 'Dark Market,' Shut Down," July 20, 2017.

7. *See* U.S. Department of Justice Press Release, "AlphaBay, the Largest Online 'Dark Market,' Shut Down," July 20, 2017.

Unregistered Peer-to-Peer (P2P) Exchangers

P2P exchangers are individuals or entities offering to exchange fiat currencies for virtual currencies or one virtual currency for another virtual currency. P2P exchangers usually operate informally, typically advertising and marketing their services through online classified advertisements, online forums, social media, and through word of mouth. P2P exchangers may provide their services online, or may arrange to meet prospective customers in person to purchase or sell virtual currency.

As explained in FinCEN's recent Guidance issued on May 9, 2019, in undertaking these activities, P2P exchangers function as MSBs and, therefore, must comply with all requirements for MSBs under the Bank Secrecy Act (BSA) and its implementing regulations.[8] FinCEN is aware of cases in which unregistered entities fraudulently represent themselves as individual account holders or misrepresent the nature of their business to conceal their money transmission activity and avoid MSB AML/CFT requirements.

Some P2P exchangers employ techniques, such as mixing or the use of money mules, to further conceal or anonymize transactions. Mixing refers to mechanisms that allow a CVC user to mask their identity through blending the proceeds of their transaction with those of other users. Money mules refer to third parties used to carry out transactions on behalf of another individual.[9]

Financial institutions may identify P2P exchangers through perceived funnel account activity, as many of the P2P exchangers' clients deposit funds into the P2P exchanger's account.[10] Financial institutions may be able to distinguish P2P exchangers from traditional funnel account activity by identifying frequent interactions with CVC-focused MSBs.

P2P exchangers are distinct from online P2P trading platforms that match potential virtual currency buyers and sellers with one another in order to facilitate in-person, direct exchanges between individuals. Some buyers and sellers also engage in ongoing, repeated exchange transactions, thereby operating as small-scale unregistered CVC exchangers. Recent cases suggest that CVC buyers and sellers involved in small-volume exchanges are increasingly used for money laundering purposes, possibly without their knowledge, such as to launder proceeds from drug trafficking.[11]

---

8. *See* 2019 CVC Guidance, at 14–15.

9. *See also supra*, at 2 n.2.

10. For a detailed description of funnel accounts, *see* FinCEN Advisory, FIN-2014-A005, "Update on U.S. Currency Restriction in Mexico: Funnel Accounts and TBML," May 28, 2014.

11. For examples of cases involving P2P trading platforms, *see* U.S. Department of Justice Press Release, U.S. Attorney's Office Western District of New York, "Rochester Man Pleads Guilty in Case Involving Bitcoins," April 27, 2017; *see also* U.S. Department of Justice Press Release, U.S. Attorney's Office District of Arizona, "Arizona-Based Peer-to-Peer Bitcoin Trader Convicted of Money Laundering, Mar. 29, 2018."

Unregistered P2P Exchanger—Eric Powers: On April 18, 2019, FinCEN assessed a $35,350 civil money penalty against Eric Powers for willfully violating the BSA's registration, program, and reporting requirements during his operations as a P2P exchanger of CVC. The action included an industry bar that prohibits him from providing money transmission services or engaging in any other activity that would make him a "money services business" for purposes of FinCEN regulations. This was FinCEN's first enforcement action against a P2P CVC exchanger. Powers failed to register as an MSB, had no written policies or procedures for ensuring compliance with the BSA, and failed to report suspicious transactions and currency transactions. He advertised his intent to purchase and sell bitcoin on the Internet and completed transactions by either physically delivering or receiving currency in person, sending or receiving currency through the mail, or coordinating transactions by wire through a depository institution. Powers processed numerous suspicious transactions without ever filing a SAR, including doing business related to the illicit darknet marketplace "Silk Road," as well as servicing customers through Tor without taking steps to determine customer identity and whether funds were derived from illegal activity. Powers conducted over 200 transactions involving the physical transfer of more than $10,000 in currency, yet failed to file a single CTR.[12]

P2P Exchangers Facilitating Malicious Cyber Activity—Ali Khorashadizadeh and Mohammad Ghorbaniyan: On November 28, 2018, OFAC took action against two Iranian individuals operating as digital currency[13] P2P exchangers, Ali Khorashadizadeh and Mohammad Ghorbaniyan, helped exchange bitcoin ransom payments into Iranian rial on behalf of malicious Iranian cyber actors involved with the SamSam ransomware scheme that targeted over 200 known victims. As part of these designations, OFAC identified two digital currency addresses associated with these designated Iranian financial facilitators. This marked OFAC's first public attribution of digital currency addresses to designated individuals.[14]

Unregistered Foreign-Located MSBs

Foreign-located MSBs, like P2P exchangers, offer to exchange fiat and CVCs. They may also accept one type of CVC and transmit the same or a different type of CVC to a different person or location. A foreign-located business qualifies as an MSB if

---

12. *See* FinCEN Press Release, "FinCEN Penalizes Peer-to-Peer Virtual Currency Exchanger for Violations of Anti-Money Laundering Laws," April 18, 2019.

13. For the purposes of OFAC sanctions programs, "digital currency" includes sovereign cryptocurrency, virtual currency, and digital representations of fiat currency. *See* U.S. Department of the Treasury Resource Center, "OFAC FAQs: Sanctions Compliance—Questions on Virtual Currency."

14. *See* Treasury Press Release, "Treasury Designates Iran-Based Financial Facilitators of Malicious Cyber Activity and for the First Time Identifies Associated Digital Currency Addresses," Nov. 28, 2018.

it does business as an MSB "wholly or in substantial part within the United States."[15] Foreign-located MSBs seeking to avoid regulatory coverage generally choose to operate in jurisdictions that lack or have limited AML/CFT laws governing the use of CVC. These foreign-located MSBs often do not comply with the AML/CFT regime of the United States, despite doing business wholly or in substantial part within the United States. Foreign-located MSBs that do not adhere to AML/CFT requirements and standards are popular among illicit users of CVC seeking to move funds in and out of the United States and represent a significant money laundering vulnerability. Further, the absence of effective AML/CFT regulatory and supervisory frameworks for CVC activities across jurisdictions can exacerbate illicit financing risks and may create opportunities for legal and regulatory arbitrage.

Unregistered Foreign-Located MSB—BTC-e (a.k.a. Canton Business Corporation) and Alexander Vinnik: In January 2017, BTC-e and its alleged owner and operator, Alexander Vinnik, were indicted in the U.S. District Court for the Northern District of California for operating an unlicensed MSB, conspiracy to commit money laundering, money laundering, and engaging in unlawful monetary transactions. Further, FinCEN simultaneously imposed civil money penalties on BTC-e and Alexander Vinnik of $110,003,314 and $12,000,000 respectively for willful violations of the BSA and its implementing regulations.[16] BTC-e was a foreign- located money transmitter doing business in the United States that exchanged fiat currency as well as CVCs such as bitcoin, litecoin, namecoin, novacoin, peercoin, ether, and dash. It was among the largest virtual currency exchanges by volume in the world. In addition to being an unlicensed MSB, BTC-e and Vinnik failed to comply with their AML program, reporting, and recordkeeping obligations, including the obligation to know your customer (KYC). BTC-e and Vinnik provided users and transactions anonymity by allowing users to access their services indirectly through a system of BTC-e shell companies and affiliate entities. The structure of BTC-e and its business dealings made it a leading outlet for money laundering among criminals, including cybercriminals. BTC-e facilitated transactions involving ransomware, computer hacking, identity theft, tax refund fraud schemes, public corruption, and drug trafficking. From 2011 through 2017, BTC-e processed several billion dollars in exchanges.[17]

CVC Kiosks

CVC kiosks (also called bitcoin Automated Teller Machines (ATMs) or crypto ATMs) are ATM- like devices or electronic terminals that allow users to exchange cash and virtual currency. CVC kiosks generally facilitate money transmission be-

---

15. 31 U.S.C. §§ 5312(a)(6), 5312(b), and 5330(d); 31 C.F.R. § 1010.100(ff).

16. *See* FinCEN Assessment of Civil Money Penalty, "Assessment of Civil Money Penalty In the matter of BTC-E a/k/a Canton Business Corporation and Alexander Vinnik," July 2017.

17. *See* U.S. v. BTC-e, A/K/A Canton Business Corporation and Alexander Vinnik (Jan. 2017).

tween a CVC exchange and a customer's wallet or operate as a CVC exchange themselves. While some kiosk operators have registered and implemented AML/CFT controls, other kiosks have operated in ways that suggest a willful effort to evade BSA requirements. For example, some kiosk operators have assisted in structuring transactions, failed to collect and retain required customer identification information, or falsely represented the nature of their business—for instance by claiming involvement in cash intensive activities—to their CVC exchange and depository institutions.

CVC Kiosks—Khalil Wright: In 2017, the U.S. District Court for the District of Maryland sentenced Khalil Wright to two years' imprisonment for possession with intent to distribute a controlled substance. During the course of the investigation underlying the conviction, law enforcement obtained evidence that Wright purchased at least $112,797 of bitcoin from a bitcoin kiosk in Baltimore, Maryland and sent the bitcoin purchased at the kiosk directly to AlphaBay, a now-defunct darknet marketplace that facilitated drug sales.[18]

Red Flag Indicators of the Abuse of Virtual Currencies

CVC-focused MSBs and other financial institutions can play key roles in identifying unregistered MSB activity and suspicious virtual currency purchases, transfers, and transactions through the application of certain red flags or indicators of illicit conduct. As no single red flag is necessarily indicative of CVC activity linked to illicit conduct, institutions should consider additional contextual information and the surrounding facts and circumstances, such as a customer's historical financial activity and whether the customer exhibits multiple indicators before determining that CVC activity is suspicious. When evaluating potential suspicious activity, institutions should be mindful that some red flags might be more readily observable during general transactional screening, while others may be more readily observable during transaction- specific reviews.

Darknet Marketplaces

- A customer conducts transactions with CVC addresses that have been linked to darknet marketplaces or other illicit activity.

- A customer's CVC address appears on public forums associated with illegal activity. A customer's transactions are initiated from IP addresses associated with Tor.

- Blockchain analytics indicate that the wallet transferring CVC to the exchange has a suspicious source or sources of funds, such as a darknet marketplace.

---

18. *See* United States v. Khalil Wright, No. 1:16-mj-02987 (Nov. 2016).

- A transaction makes use of mixing and tumbling services, suggesting an intent to obscure the flow of illicit funds between known wallet addresses and darknet marketplaces.

Unregistered or Illicitly Operating P2P Exchangers

- A customer receives multiple cash deposits or wires from disparate jurisdictions, branches of a financial institution, or persons and shortly thereafter uses such funds to acquire virtual currency.

- A customer receives a series of deposits from disparate sources that, in aggregate, amount to nearly identical aggregate funds transfers to a known virtual currency exchange platform within a short period of time.

- Customer's phone number or email address is connected to a known CVC P2P exchange platform advertising exchange services.

Unregistered Foreign-Located MSBs

- A customer transfers or receives funds, including through traditional banking systems, to or from an unregistered foreign CVC exchange or other MSB with no relation to where the customer lives or conducts business.

- A customer utilizes a CVC exchanger or foreign-located MSB in a high-risk jurisdiction lacking, or known to have inadequate AML/CFT regulations for CVC entities, including inadequate KYC or customer due diligence measures.

- A customer directs large numbers of CVC transactions to CVC entities in jurisdictions with reputations for being tax havens.

- A customer that has not identified itself to the exchange, or registered with FinCEN, as a money transmitter appears to be using the liquidity provided by the exchange to execute large numbers of offsetting transactions, which may indicate that the customer is acting as an unregistered MSB.

Unregistered or Illicitly Operating CVC Kiosks

- A customer operates multiple CVC kiosks in locations that have a relatively high incidence of criminal activity.

- Large numbers of transactions from different customers sent to and from the same CVC wallet address but not operating as a known CVC exchange.

Illicit Activity Leveraging CVC Kiosks
- Structuring of transactions just beneath the CTR threshold or the CVC kiosk daily limit to the same wallet address either by using multiple machines (i.e., smurfing) or multiple identities tied to the same phone number.

Other Potentially Illicit Activity

- A customer conducts transactions with CVC addresses that have been linked to extortion, ransomware, sanctioned CVC addresses, or other illicit activity.

- A customer's transactions are initiated from non-trusted IP addresses, IP addresses from sanctioned jurisdictions, or IP addresses previously flagged as suspicious.

- Use of virtual private network (VPN) services or Tor to access CVC exchange accounts.

- A customer initiates multiple rapid trades between multiple virtual currencies with no related purpose, which may be indicative of attempts to break the chain of custody on the respective blockchains or further obfuscate the transaction.

- A customer provides identification or account credentials (e.g., non-standard password, IP address, or flash cookies) shared by another account.

- A customer conducts transactions or rapidly executes multiple conversions between various types of different CVCs below relevant due diligence, recordkeeping, or reporting thresholds and then transfers the value off of the exchange.

- Discrepancies arise between IP addresses associated with the customer's profile and the IP addresses from which transactions are being initiated.

- A customer significantly older than the average age of platform users opens an account and engages in large numbers of transactions, suggesting their potential role as a CVC money mule or a victim of elder financial exploitation.

- A customer shows limited knowledge of CVC despite engagement in CVC transactions or activity, which may indicate a victim of a scam.

- A customer declines requests for "know your customer" documents or inquiries regarding sources of funds.

- A customer purchases large amounts of CVC not substantiated by available wealth or consistent with his or her historical financial profile, which may indicate money laundering, a money mule, or a victim of a scam.

- A common wallet address is shared between accounts identified as belonging to two different customers.

- Deposits into an account or CVC address significantly higher than ordinary with an unknown source of funds, followed by conversion to currency of legal tender, which may indicate theft of funds.

- Multiple changes to email address and other contact information for an account or customer which may indicate an account takeover against a customer.

- Use of language in CVC message fields indicative of the transactions being conducted in support of illicit activity or in the purchase of illicit goods, such as drugs or stolen credit card information.

Valuable Information in Reporting Suspicious Activity Involving CVC

CVC transactions generate a significant variety of information elements that may be extremely useful to law enforcement and other national security agencies in investigating potential illicit conduct involving CVC transactions. Specifically, the following information is particularly helpful to law enforcement:

- virtual currency wallet addresses

- account information

- transaction details (including virtual currency transaction hash and information on the originator and the recipient)

- relevant transaction history

- available login information (including IP addresses)

- mobile device information (such as device IMEI)

- information obtained from analysis of the customer's public online profile and communications.

When filing a SAR, financial institutions should provide all pertinent available information in the SAR form and narrative.

Suspicious Activity Reporting

A financial institution is required to file a SAR if it knows, suspects, or has reason to suspect a transaction conducted or attempted by, at, or through the financial institution involves funds derived from illegal activity, or attempts to disguise funds derived from illegal activity; is designed to evade regulations promulgated under the BSA; lacks a business or apparent lawful purpose; or involves the use of the financial institution to facilitate criminal activity.[19] Suspicious activity involving CVC may be observable by financial institutions specializing in commerce related to CVC, financial institutions servicing such businesses, or financial institutions with customers actively involved in the use of CVC.

---

19. *See generally* 31 CFR §§ 1010.320, 1020.320, 1021.320, 1022.320, 1023.320, 1024.320, 1025.320, 1026.320, 1029.320, and 1030.320.

Because some red flags associated with abuse of CVC may reflect legitimate financial activities, financial institutions should evaluate indicators of potential CVC misuse in combination with other red flags and the expected transaction activity before determining that a particular transaction is suspicious. Due to the technical nature of blockchain analysis and other frameworks of analyzing CVC activity, FinCEN encourages communication within financial institutions among AML, fraud and information technology departments, as appropriate. FinCEN also encourages communication among financial institutions under the auspices of Section 314(b) of the USA PATRIOT Act in determining transactions' potential suspiciousness related to terrorist financing or money laundering activities, and in filing SARs, as appropriate.

Discussion Points

1. *Understanding CVC.* What is CVC? How should CVC be regulated? Should both federal and state regulators be involved in regulating CVC kiosks? Should CVC kiosks be regulated in the same manner MSBs are regulated?

2. *The value of SAR Reports.* Do you think that SAR reports are helpful in combating illicit financial activity? Are regulators placing too much trust in entities to report violations of the BSA? Should regulators have more control over financial institutions? Why or why not?

3. *Combating money laundering.* Do you think federal regulators are doing enough to tackle money laundering in the virtual currency market? Should the legal community be more actively involved in creating AML laws and policies?

SAR Filing Instructions

FinCEN requests that financial institutions reference this advisory by including the key term:

"CVC FIN-2019-A003"

in the SAR narrative to indicate a connection between the suspicious activity being reported and possible illicit activity involving CVC. Using the new, mandatory SAR Form that took effect on January 1, 2019, financial institutions should reference this advisory using the above key term in SAR field 2 ("Filing Institution Note to FinCEN").

OFAC Obligations[1]

U.S. individuals and institutions involved in digital currency use or transactions should be aware of their responsibilities for ensuring that they do not engage in unauthorized transactions prohibited by OFAC. OFAC sanctions requirements include not only screening against OFAC's Specially Designated Nationals (SDN) list, but also undertaking appropriate steps to prohibit persons in sanctioned countries and jurisdictions from opening accounts and trading in digital currency. Businesses and entities dealing in digital currency should implement policies and procedures that allow them to: block IP addresses associated with a sanctioned country or region; disable the accounts of all holders identified from a sanctioned country or region; install a dedicated Compliance Officer with authority to ensure compliance with all OFAC- administered sanctions programs; screen all prospective users to ensure they are not from geographic regions subject to U.S. sanctions; and ensure OFAC compliance training for all relevant personnel.

For Further Information

Questions or comments regarding the contents of this advisory should be addressed to the FinCEN Regulatory Support Section at frc@fincen.gov.

Financial institutions wanting to report suspicious transactions that may potentially relate to terrorist activity should call the Financial Institutions Toll-Free Hotline at (866) 556-3974 (7 days a week, 24 hours a day). The purpose of the hotline is to expedite the delivery of this information to law enforcement. Financial institutions should immediately report any imminent threat to local- area law enforcement officials.

Financial institutions or virtual currency providers having questions concerning OFAC sanctions should either call OFAC's Toll-Free Hotline at 1-800-540-6322 or email OFAC's Feedback Account at OFAC_Feedback@treasury.gov

The mission of the Financial Crimes Enforcement Network is to safeguard the financial system from illicit use, combat money laundering, and promote national security through the strategic use of financial authorities and the collection, analysis, and dissemination of financial intelligence.

---

1. U.S. persons, including U.S. financial institutions, have other regulatory obligations as well, including the obligation to comply with U.S. sanctions. The Office of Foreign Assets Control issued guidance specific to digital currency, including CVCs, in March 2018 (*see* Treasury Resource Center, "OFAC FAQs: Sanctions Compliance – Questions on Virtual Currency").

Discussion Points

1. *Risks.* What are some virtual currency abuse typologies utilized by criminals in furtherance of illicit schemes? How can regulators prevent these crimes from occurring, and how should the courts respond to these crimes? How can similar criminal activities be prevented?

2. *One and the same.* Should CVCs be treated similar to MSBs and be required to implement AML programs and comply with reporting requirements? Should all CVCs be required to register as MSBs? What are the implications of treating CVCs and MSBs the same? Should they be viewed the same? Why or why not? What differentiates an MSB from a CVC? Compare the characteristics of both.

3. *The BSA and CVCs.* How should the BSA be applied to CVCs? Should CVCs be required to satisfy all BSA requirements or only select requirements? Which ones? If CVCs should not be subject to all BSA requirements, why not?

Leaders of CFTC, FinCEN, and SEC Issue Joint Statement on Activities Involving Digital Assets

(October 11, 2019)

Washington, DC—The leaders of the U.S. Commodity Futures Trading Commission, the Financial Crimes Enforcement Network, and the U.S. Securities and Exchange Commission (the "Agencies") today issued the following joint statement to remind persons engaged in activities involving digital assets of their anti-money laundering and countering the financing of terrorism (AML/CFT) obligations under the Bank Secrecy Act (BSA).[1]

AML/CFT obligations apply to entities that the BSA defines as "financial institutions," such as futures commission merchants and introducing brokers obligated to register with the CFTC, money services businesses (MSBs) as defined by FinCEN, and broker-dealers and mutual funds obligated to register with the SEC. Among those AML/CFT obligations are the requirement to establish and implement an effective anti-money laundering program (AML Program)[2] and re-

---

1. The BSA is codified at 31 U.S.C. §§ 5311–5314; 5316–5332 and 12 U.S.C. §§ 1829b, 1951–1959.

2. *See* 31 C.F.R. § 1022.210 (MSBs); 31 C.F.R. § 1023.210 (brokers or dealers in securities); 31 C.F.R. § 1024.210 (mutual funds); 31 C.F.R. § 1026.210 (futures commission merchants and introducing brokers in commodities). An AML Program must include, at a minimum, (a) policies, procedures, and internal controls reasonably designed to achieve compliance with the provisions of the BSA and its implementing regulations; (b) independent testing for compliance; (c) designation of an individual or individuals responsible for implementing and monitoring the operations and internal controls; and (d) ongoing training for appropriate persons. Rules for some financial institutions refer

cordkeeping and reporting requirements, including suspicious activity reporting (SAR) requirements.[3]

For the purpose of this joint statement, "digital assets" include instruments that may qualify under applicable U.S. laws as securities, commodities, and security- or commodity-based instruments such as futures or swaps. We are aware that market participants refer to digital assets using many different labels.[4] The label or terminology used to describe a digital asset or a person engaging in or providing financial activities or services involving a digital asset,[5] however, may not necessarily align with how that asset, activity or service is defined under the BSA, or under the laws and rules administered by the CFTC and the SEC. For example, something referred to as an "exchange" in a market for digital assets may or may not also qualify as an "exchange" as that term is used under the federal securities laws. As such, regardless of the label or terminology that market participants may use, or the level or type of technology employed, it is the facts and circumstances underlying an asset, activity or service, including its economic reality and use (whether intended or organically developed or repurposed), that determines the general categorization of an asset, the specific regulatory treatment of the activity involving the asset, and whether the persons involved are "financial institutions" for purposes of the BSA.[6]

---

to additional elements of an AML Program, such as appropriate risk-based procedures for conducting ongoing customer due diligence.

3. *See* 31 C.F.R. § 1022.320 (MSBs), 31 C.F.R. § 1023.320 (brokers or dealers in securities), 31 C.F.R. § 1024.320 (mutual funds), and 31 C.F.R. § 1026.320 (futures commission merchants and introducing brokers in commodities). A suspicious transaction must be reported if it is conducted or attempted by, at, or through the financial institution and the amount involved exceeds a certain threshold.

4. Digital assets may be referred to in the industry by labels such as "virtual assets," "crypto-assets," "digital tokens," "digital coins," "digital currencies," "cryptocurrencies," and "convertible virtual currencies." Financial activities involving digital assets may also be referred to as "initial coin offerings" or "ICOs."

5. The Financial Action Task Force (FATF), for example, refers to such persons as "virtual asset service providers."

6. *See United Housing Foundation, Inc. v. Forman*, 421 U.S. 837, 848 (1975) (quoting *Tcherepnin v. Knight*, 389 U.S. 332, 336 (1967)) ("[I]n searching for the meaning and scope of the word 'security' in the [U.S. securities laws], form should be disregarded for substance and the emphasis should be on economic reality."); *SEC v. W.J. Howey Co.*, 328 U.S. 293, 298 (1946) ("Form was disregarded for substance and emphasis was placed upon economic reality."); *United Housing*. 421 U.S. at 849 ("Because securities transactions are economic in character, Congress intended the application of these statutes to turn on the economic realities underlying a transaction, and not on the name appended thereto."); *Haekal v. Refco, Inc.*, CFTC No. 93-109, 2000 WL 1460078, at *4 (Sept. 29, 2000) ("[T]he labels that parties apply to their transactions are not necessarily controlling. Because such labels are often illusory, a decision maker must evaluate those labels in the context of the parties' actual conduct."); *In re Stovall*, CFTC No. 75-7, 1979 WL 11475, at *5 (Dec. 6, 1979) (holding that the CFTC "will not hesitate to look behind whatever label the parties may give to the instrument"); *see also* FIN-2019-G001, "Application of FinCEN's Regulations to Certain Business Models Involving Convertible Virtual Currencies" (May 9, 2019) (available at https://www.fincen.gov/resources/statutes-regulations/guidance/application-fincens-regulations-certain-business-models) (discussing the distinction between

The nature of the digital asset-related activities a person engages in is a key factor in determining whether and how that person must register with the CFTC, FinCEN, or the SEC. For example, certain "commodity"-related activities may trigger registration and other obligations under the Commodity Exchange Act (CEA), while certain activities involving a "security" may trigger registration and other obligations under the federal securities laws. If a person falls under the definition of a "financial institution," its AML/CFT activities will be overseen for BSA purposes by one or more of the Agencies (and potentially others). For example, the AML/CFT activities of a futures commission merchant will be overseen by the CFTC, FinCEN, and the National Futures Association (NFA); those of an MSB will be overseen by FinCEN; and those of a broker-dealer in securities will be overseen by the SEC, FinCEN and a self-regulatory organization, primarily the Financial Industry Regulatory Authority (FINRA).

Certain BSA obligations that apply to a broker-dealer in securities, mutual fund, futures commission merchant, or introducing broker, such as developing an AML Program or reporting suspicious activity, apply very broadly and without regard to whether the particular transaction at issue involves a "security" or a "commodity" as those terms are defined under the federal securities laws or the CEA.

****

Additional Comments by the U.S. Commodity Futures Trading Commission Chairman

The mission of the CFTC is to promote the integrity, resilience, and vibrancy of the U.S. derivatives markets through sound regulation. In advancing that mission, the CFTC regulates key participants in the derivatives markets, including boards of trade, futures commission merchants, introducing brokers, swaps dealers, major swap participants, retail foreign exchange dealers, commodity pool operators, and commodity trading advisors pursuant to the CEA. An "introducing broker" or "futures commission merchant" is defined in BSA regulations as a person that is registered or required to register as an introducing broker or futures commission merchant under the CEA.[7] Introducing brokers and futures commission merchants are required to report suspicious activity and implement reasonably-designed AML Programs.[8] These requirements are not limited in their application to activities in which digital assets qualify as commodities or are used as derivatives. The rules would also apply to activities that are not subject to regulation under the CEA.

****

"business models" and "labels"); *see also* https://www.sec.gov/corpfin/framework-investment-contract-analysis-digital-assets (Framework for "Investment Contract" Analysis of Digital Assets).

7. 31 C.F.R. §§ 1010.100(x), 1010.100(bb), 1026.100(f), and 1026.100(g).

8. 31 C.F.R. §§ 1026.210 and 1026.320.

Additional Comments by the Financial Crimes
Enforcement Network Director

As a bureau of the Department of the Treasury, FinCEN is the administrator of and lead regulator under the BSA—the nation's first and most comprehensive AML/ CFT statute. FinCEN's mission is to protect our financial system from illicit use, ensure our national security, and protect our people from harm. FinCEN has supervisory and enforcement authority over U.S. financial institutions to ensure the effectiveness of the AML/CFT regime. As such FinCEN mandates certain controls, reporting, and recordkeeping obligations for U.S. financial institutions. The BSA and its implementing regulations set forth the regulatory obligations that generally apply to financial institutions,[9] including AML Program, recordkeeping, and reporting requirements.

FinCEN regulates, among other persons, money transmitters and other MSBs.[10] FinCEN's BSA regulations define a "money transmitter" as a person engaged in the business of providing money transmission services or any other person engaged as a business in the transfer of funds.[11] The term "money transmission services" means "the acceptance of currency,[12] funds, or other value that substitutes for currency from one person and the transmission of currency, funds, or other value that substitutes for currency to another location or person by any means."[13]

In May 2019, FinCEN issued interpretive guidance (2019 CVC Guidance) to remind persons subject to the BSA how FinCEN regulations relating to MSBs apply to certain business models involving money transmission denominated in value that substitutes for currency, specifically, convertible virtual currencies.[14] The 2019 CVC Guidance consolidated current FinCEN regulations, and related administrative rulings and guidance issued since 2011, and applied these rules and interpretations to other common business models involving CVC engaging in the same underlying patterns of activity. Covered persons and institutions are strongly encouraged to review the 2019 CVC Guidance.

---

9. The BSA and its implementing regulations list a number of businesses that qualify as "financial institutions." *See generally* 31 U.S.C. § 5312(a)(2); 31 CFR § 1010.100(t).

10. *See generally* 31 CFR § 1010.100(ff). An MSB includes a money transmitter, a dealer in foreign exchange, a check casher, an issuer or seller of traveler's checks or money orders, or a seller or provider of prepaid access.

11. 31 CFR § 1010.100(ff)(5).

12. "Currency" is defined at 31 CFR § 1010.100(m) as "[t]he coin and paper money of the United States or of any other country that is designated as legal tender and that circulates and is customarily used and accepted as a medium of exchange in the country of issuance."

13. 31 CFR § 1010.100(ff)(5)(i)(A).

14. *See* Application of FinCEN's Regulations to Certain Business Models Involving Convertible Virtual Currencies, FIN-2019-G001 (May 9, 2019) (available at https://www.fincen.gov/resources/statutes-regulations/guidance/application- fincens-regulations-certain-business-models) (summarizing FinCEN guidance interpreting the term "value that substitutes for currency")

As set forth in the 2019 CVC Guidance, a number of digital asset-related activities qualify a person as an MSB that would be regulated by FinCEN. FinCEN's BSA regulations also provide that any person "registered with, and functionally regulated or examined by, the SEC or the CFTC,"[15] would not be subject to the BSA obligations applicable to MSBs, but instead would be subject to the BSA obligations of such a type of regulated entity. Accordingly, even if an introducing broker, futures commission merchant, broker-dealer or mutual fund acts as an exchanger of digital assets and provides money transmission services for the purposes of the BSA, it would not qualify as a money transmitter or any other category of MSB and would not be subject to BSA requirements that are applicable only to MSBs. Instead, these persons would be subject to FinCEN's regulations applicable to introducing brokers, futures commission merchants, broker-dealers and mutual funds, respectively. These obligations include the development of an AML program and suspicious activity reporting requirements, as well as requirements under applicable CFTC or SEC rules. Furthermore, regardless of federal functional regulator, all financial institutions dealing in digital assets meeting the definition of "securities" under federal law must comply with federal securities law.

****

Additional Comments by the U.S. Securities and Exchange Commission Chairman

The statutory mission of the SEC is to protect investors, maintain fair, orderly, and efficient markets, and facilitate capital formation. In general, the SEC has jurisdiction over securities and securities-related conduct. Persons engaged in activities involving digital assets that are securities have registration or other statutory or regulatory obligations under the federal securities laws.[16]

The SEC oversees the key participants in the securities markets, some of which may engage in digital asset activities.[17] Key participants in the securities markets in-

---

15. 31 CFR § 1010.100(ff)(8)(ii).

16. *See, e.g.,* https://www.sec.gov/news/public-statement/statement-clayton-2017-12-11 (Statement on Cryptocurrencies and Initial Coin Offerings); https://www.sec.gov/corpfin/framework-investment-contract-analysis-digital-assets (Framework for "Investment Contract" Analysis of Digital Assets); https://www.sec.gov/news/public-statement/enforcement-tm-statement-potentially-unlawful-online-platforms-trading (Statement on Potentially Unlawful Online Platforms for Trading Digital Assets); https://www.sec.gov/news/public-statement/digital-asset-securites-issuuance-and-trading (Statement on Digital Asset Securities Issuance and Trading). SEC staff statements represent the views of the SEC staff. They are not rules, regulations, or statements of the SEC. The SEC has neither approved nor disapproved their content. SEC staff statements, like all SEC staff guidance, have no legal force or effect: they do not alter or amend applicable law, and they create no new or additional obligations for any person.

17. Issuers of securities are required to register the offer and sale of securities pursuant to the Securities Act of 1933 unless an exemption from registration is available. *See* 15 U.S.C. 77e. To the extent the issuer meets certain thresholds related to size or has a class of securities listed on a national

clude but are not limited to national securities exchanges, securities brokers and dealers, investment advisers, and investment companies. Market participants receiving payments or engaging in other transactions in digital assets should consider such transactions to present similar or additional risks, including AML/CFT risks, as are presented by transactions in cash and cash equivalents. With regard to SEC regulated entities, broker-dealers and mutual funds are defined as "financial institutions" in rules implementing the BSA. A "broker-dealer" is defined in rules implementing the BSA as a person that is registered or required to register as a broker or dealer under the Securities Exchange Act,[18] while a "mutual fund" is defined as an investment company that is an "open-end company" and that is registered or required to register under the Investment Company Act of 1940.[19] Broker-dealers and mutual funds are required to implement reasonably-designed AML Programs and report suspicious activity.[20] These rules are not limited in their application to activities involving digital assets that are "securities" under the federal securities laws.[21]

Discussion Points

1. *AML/CFT.* AML/CFT obligations apply to entities defined as "financial institutions" per the BSA. What qualifies as a financial institution per the BSA's iteration? Are money transmitters financial institutions? Are payment processors financial institutions? Why or why not? Will the definition of "financial institution" change as the use of CBDC, digital wallets and peer to peer transactions becomes more prevalent?

2. *Getting AML/CFT priorities straight.* Should the FinCEN's AML/CFT priorities shift toward placing a greater emphasis on combating crimes financed by virtual currency? In your opinion, is FinCEN doing enough to address criminal activity in the virtual currency sector?

---

securities exchange, that issuer is required to file reports pursuant to the Securities Exchange Act of 1934 ("Exchange Act") with the Commission, under Section 13(a) of the Exchange Act. *See* 15 U.S.C. 78m. Generally, an issuer of securities is not, solely by virtue of offering or selling securities, or solely by registering a class of securities, "a person registered with, and functionally regulated or examined by, the SEC...," such that the issuer would fall within the exemption from MSB status contained in 31 CFR 1010.100(ff)(8)(ii).

18. 31 CFR §§ 1010.100(h), 1023.100(b).

19. 31 C.F.R. § 1010.100(gg).

20. 31 C.F.R. §§ 1023.210 and 1023.320 (broker-dealers); 31 C.F.R. §§ 1024.210 and 1024.320 (mutual funds). For a compilation of key laws, rules, and guidance applicable to broker-dealers and mutual funds, *see* https://www.sec.gov/about/offices/ocie/amlsourcetool.htm (Anti-Money Laundering (AML) Source Tool for Broker-Dealers) and https://www.sec.gov/about/offices/ocie/amlmf sourcetool.htm (Anti-Money Laundering (AML) Source Tool for Mutual Funds).

21. Broker-dealers have other obligations, such as financial responsibility rules, that are relevant to digital assets. *See* https://www.sec.gov/news/public-statement/joint-staff-statement-broker-dealer-custody-digital-asset-securities (Joint Staff Statement on Broker-Dealer Custody of Digital Asset Securities).

3. *Public policy considerations.* How does requiring CVCs, MSBs and other entities to follow registration and reporting requirements promote public policy? Do these measures benefit consumers? In what ways?

In the Matter of Bittrex, Inc.

United States of America

Financial Crimes Enforcement Network Department of the Treasury

Number 2022-03, October 11, 2022

CONSENT ORDER IMPOSING
CIVIL MONEY PENALTY

The Financial Crimes Enforcement Network (FinCEN) has conducted a civil enforcement investigation and determined that grounds exist to impose a Civil Money Penalty against Bittrex, Inc. (Bittrex) for violations of the Bank Secrecy Act (BSA) and its implementing regulations.[1] Bittrex admits to the Statement of Facts and Violations set forth below and consents to the issuance of this Consent Order.

I. JURISDICTION

Overall authority for enforcement and compliance with the BSA lies with the

Director of FinCEN, and the Director may impose civil penalties for violations of the BSA and its implementing regulations.[2] At all times relevant to this Consent Order, Bittrex was a "domestic financial institution," specifically, a "money services business" (MSB) as defined by the BSA and its implementing regulations.[3] As such, Bittrex was required to comply with applicable BSA regulations.

II. STATEMENT OF FACTS

The conduct described below took place from on or about February 13, 2014, through on or about December 7, 2018 (Relevant Time Period), unless otherwise indicated.

A. Bittrex

Throughout the Relevant Time Period, Bittrex owned and operated a convertible virtual currency (CVC) trading platform known as "Bittrex." The platform was primarily operated from offices located in Bellevue, Washington, and included a hosted digital wallet service for storing and transferring CVCs. Bittrex also operat-

---

1. The BSA is codified at 31 U.S.C. §§ 5311–5314, 5316–5336 and 12 U.S.C. §§ 1829b, 1951–1959. Regulations implementing the BSA appear at 31 C.F.R. Chapter X.

2. 31 U.S.C. § 5321(a); 31 C.F.R. §§ 1010.810(a), (d); Treasury Order 180-01 (July 1, 2014).

3. 31 C.F.R. § 1010.100(ff) (defining "money services business").

ed as an "exchanger" of over 250 different CVCs,[4] including bitcoin, ether, monero, zcash, and dash.[5] During the Relevant Time Period, Bittrex facilitated almost 546 million trades on its platform in the United States and at times averaged over 20,000 transactions (deposits and withdrawals) through its hosted wallets daily during the Relevant Time Period, including transactions involving over $17 billion worth of bitcoin during the Relevant Time Period.

B. Bank Secrecy Act Requirements

The term "money services business" is defined in 31 C.F.R. §1010.100(ff) as any of the following categories of business: (1) dealers in foreign exchange; (2) check cashers; (3) issuers or sellers of traveler's checks or money orders; (4) providers of prepaid access; (5) money transmitters; (6) U.S. Postal Service; or (7) sellers of prepaid access.[6] The regulations define the term "money transmitter" as a person that either "provides money transmission services" or who is otherwise "engaged in the transfer of funds."[7]

"Money transmission services" are defined in FinCEN's regulations as "the acceptance of currency, funds, or other value that substitutes for currency from one person and the transmission of currency, funds, or other value that substitutes for currency to another location or person by any means."[8] Given these definitions and Bittrex's activities within the United States, Bittrex was a "domestic financial institution," specifically a "money services business," operating in the United States.[9] As a result, Bittrex was required to comply with FinCEN's regulations applicable to MSBs during the Relevant Time Period.

The BSA and its implementing regulations require an MSB, including a "money transmitter" like Bittrex, to develop, implement, and maintain an effective Anti-Money Laundering (AML) program that is reasonably designed to prevent the

---

4. *See* FIN-2013-G001, "Application of FinCEN's Regulations to Persons Administering, Exchanging, or Using Virtual Currencies," March 18, 2013 (explaining that exchangers of CVC are money transmitters under FinCEN's regulations).

5. *See* 31 U.S.C. §5312(a)(2)(R).

6. 31 C.F.R. §1010.100(ff). The definition also includes any "person wherever located doing business, whether or not on a regular basis or as an organized or licensed business concern, wholly or in substantial part within the United States, in one or more of the capacities listed [above].... This includes but is not limited to maintenance of any agent, agency, branch, or office within the United States."

7. 31 C.F.R. §1010.100(ff)(5).

8. 31 C.F.R. §1010.100(ff)(5).

9. *See* 31 U.S.C. §5312(b)(1) (defining domestic financial institution); 31 C.F.R. §§1010.100(ff) (defining "money services business") and 1010.100(ff)(5) (defining "money transmitter"). FinCEN has issued interpretive guidance explaining why CVC exchangers are money transmitters. See FIN-2013-G001, "Application of FinCEN's Regulations to Persons Administering, Exchanging, or Using Virtual Currencies," March 18, 2013; FIN-2019-G001, "Application of FinCEN's Regulations to Certain Business Models Involving Convertible Virtual Currencies," May 9, 2019.

MSB from being used to facilitate money laundering and the financing of terrorist activities.[10]

As of May 14, 2014, Bittrex was required to develop, implement and maintain an effective, written AML program that, at a minimum: (a) incorporates policies, procedures and internal controls reasonably designed to assure ongoing compliance with the BSA and its implementing regulations; (b) designates an individual responsible to assure day-to-day compliance with the MSB's AML program and all BSA regulations; (c) provides education and/or training for appropriate personnel, including training in the detection of suspicious transactions; and (d) provides for independent review to monitor and maintain an adequate program.[11]

C. Bittrex Failed to Develop, Implement and Maintain an Effective AML Program

Bittrex was aware of its obligations under the BSA and its implementing regulations as an MSB, yet it failed to develop, implement, and maintain an effective AML program during the Relevant Time Period. In particular, Bittrex was required to develop and implement internal controls that were reasonably designed to assure compliance with the BSA's suspicious activity reporting requirements, but it failed to do so. For example, in 2016, Bittrex averaged 11,000 transactions (deposits and withdrawals) per day on its platform, with a daily value of approximately $1.54 million. Instead of utilizing widely available transaction monitoring software tools to screen the transactions for suspicious activity, the company relied on two employees with minimal AML training and experience to manually review all of the transactions for suspicious activity. These manual transaction monitoring responsibilities were in addition to their other duties. Later in 2017, Bittrex's transaction volume and values increased to an average of 23,800 transactions per day with a daily value of approximately $97.9 million, yet the company continued to rely on the same two employees to manually review all of its transactions for suspicious activity. The manual transaction monitoring process utilized by Bittrex was demonstrably ineffective. Bittrex did not file a single suspicious activity report (SAR) from its founding in 2014 through May 2017.

Bittrex did not take any steps to begin addressing its inadequate and ineffective transaction monitoring process until April 2017 when the company hired additional employees to help the two existing employees manually review thousands of transactions per day for suspicious activity. The new and existing employees were overwhelmed and the program remained highly ineffective throughout the Relevant Time Period. For example, Bittrex filed only one SAR between May 2017 and November 2017.

---

10. 31 U.S.C. § 5318(h); 31 C.F.R. § 1022.210(a).

11. 31 U.S.C. § 5318(h)(1); 31 C.F.R. § 1022.210(d) and (e) ("A [MSB] must develop and implement an [AML] program that complies with the requirements of this section on or before ... the end of the 90- day period beginning on the day following the date the business is established.").

FinCEN's investigation revealed that Bittrex failed to detect suspicious transactions through its platform, in addition to the thousands of transactions that were prohibited by the U.S. Department of the Treasury's Office of Foreign Assets Control (OFAC) as discussed below, during the Relevant Time Period. The suspicious transactions involved various types of illicit activity, including direct transactions with online darknet marketplaces such as AlphaBay, Agora, and the Silk Road 2. These markets are used to buy and sell contraband such as stolen identification data, illegal narcotics, and child pornography. The company also failed to detect, investigate and report transactions connected to ransomware attacks against individuals and small businesses in the United States during the relevant time period.

D. Internal Revenue Service Examination

In October 2017, the Internal Revenue Service (IRS) notified Bittrex that it intended to examine the company for compliance with the BSA and its implementing regulations.[12] A month later, Bittrex filed 119 SARs with FinCEN. Bittrex also hired additional compliance staff and began improving the development and implementation of its AML policies, procedures, and internal controls in late 2017. For example, in December 2017, Bittrex paused the opening of new customer accounts and used the pause to begin improving its Know Your Customer procedures in compliance with the BSA. Bittrex also hired its first qualified BSA officer in late 2017 to manage day-to-day compliance with the BSA. Despite these improvements and investments, the company's AML program remained seriously under-resourced and it continued to manually review tens of thousands of transactions per day for suspicious activity through December 2018.

Bittrex's failure to develop, implement, and maintain an effective AML program from February 2014 until December 2018 left its platform open to abuse by bad actors, including money launderers, terrorist financiers, and sanctions evaders.

E. OFAC-Prohibited Transactions

As described above, Bittrex was required to develop, implement, and maintain an effective AML program that was reasonably designed to prevent the MSB from being used to facilitate money laundering and the financing of terrorist activities. In 2015, and again in 2017, Bittrex adopted a written AML program that identified various money laundering risks stemming from its operations as well as policies, procedures, and controls that the company could use to mitigate those risks. One of the risks that the company identified was geographic risk, including the risk that its platform would be used to facilitate transactions subject to U.S. sanctions administered OFAC, as well as high-risk and non-cooperative jurisdictions identified by the Financial Action Task Force. In some cases, transactions that violate OFAC sanctions

---

12. Authority to examine MSBs to determine compliance with the BSA and its implementing regulations is delegated to the IRS pursuant to 31 C.F.R. § 1010.810(b)(8).

also constitute suspicious activity that must be reported to FinCEN.[13] From February 2014 through February 2016, Bittrex knew that it was required to ensure that it did not process transactions that violated OFAC sanctions, but the company failed to do so. In February 2016, Bittrex hired a third-party vendor to install and integrate software into its platform that automatically screened transactions for compliance with OFAC sanctions. However, the vendor's software only screened transactions to identify potential matches on the OFAC's List of Specially Designated Nationals and Blocked Persons (the "SDN List") and other lists. The vendor's software did not begin screening some customers or transactions for a nexus to sanctioned jurisdictions until at least October 2017.

As a result, Bittrex conducted over 116,000 transactions, valued at over $260 million, with entities and individuals located in jurisdictions subject to comprehensive OFAC sanctions during the Relevant Time Period, including transactions with entities and individuals operating openly from OFAC-sanctioned jurisdictions such as Iran, Cuba, Sudan, Syria, and the Crimea region of Ukraine. The transactions should have been investigated, blocked and reported to OFAC, or rejected, and potentially reported to FinCEN. For example, Bittrex processed transactions with parties located in sanctioned jurisdictions that were hundreds of times larger than typical transactions for certain customers or for the customers on the platform as a whole, yet Bittrex took no action whatsoever with regard to these atypical transactions.

F. Bittrex Lacked Proper Risk-Based Controls for Certain High Risk CVCs

Effective AML programs must be risk-based and reasonably designed to address the nature and volume of the financial services provided by an MSB.[14] During the Relevant Time Period, Bittrex facilitated the purchase, trade, and sale of over 250 different CVCs on its platform. CVCs vary greatly and have different features that increase or decrease transparency and traceability. Certain Anonymity-Enhanced Cryptocurrencies (AECs) present unique money laundering risks and challenges for MSBs and other financial institutions seeking to comply with the BSA and its implementing regulations. Bittrex was aware of the risks and challenges presented by the AECs that were exchanged on its platform, such as monero, zcash, pivx, and dash, but the company failed to fully address the risks in practice or in the company's written AML compliance program. While Bittrex disabled privacy-enhancing features for most of the AECs it transacted in, Bittrex did not implement any other controls to manage the risks presented by AECs for which it was impossible to disable privacy-enhancing features until after the Relevant Time Period. Bittrex also failed to implement appropriate policies, procedures, and internal controls to

---

13. *See* 18 U.S.C. § 1956(a)(1)(A) (money laundering); 18 U.S.C. § 1956(a)(2)(A) (international money laundering). See also infra note 18.
14. 31 C.F.R. § 1022.210(b).

effectively mitigate the risks associated with particularly challenging AECs, such as monero, until several years after the Relevant Time Period.[15]

G. Bittrex Failed to File Suspicious Activity Reports

The BSA and its implementing regulations require MSBs to report transactions that the MSB "knows, suspects, or has reason to suspect" are suspicious, if the transactions are conducted or attempted by, at, or through the MSB, and the transactions involve or aggregate to at least $2,000 in funds or other assets.[16]

A transaction is "suspicious" and requires the filing of a SAR if the MSB knows, suspects, or has reason to suspect it: (a) involves funds derived from illegal activity; (b) is designed to evade reporting requirements; (c) has no business or apparent lawful purpose, and the MSB knows of no reasonable explanation for the transaction after examining the available facts, including background and possible purpose; or (d) involves use of the MSB to facilitate criminal activity.[17]

As discussed above, during the Relevant Time Period, Bittrex failed to develop and implement policies, procedures, and internal controls that were reasonably designed to assure compliance with its suspicious activity reporting obligations. Despite Bittrex's substantial increase in transaction volume and value in 2017, Bittrex failed to develop or install widely available software tools to monitor its transactions for indicia of suspicious activity until September 2018, relying instead on a few employees with insufficient training to manually review thousands of transactions per day for suspicious activity. Bittrex's inadequate procedures and controls, and its ineffective and under-resourced transaction monitoring process, compromised its ability to identify, enhance, integrate, and analyze available and relevant information, including traceable CVC activity on public blockchains. This further undermined Bittrex's ability to make appropriate and timely determinations regarding the suspicious nature of transactions and file SARs when appropriate.

As a result, Bittrex failed to file SARs on a significant number of transactions involving sanctioned jurisdictions. Bittrex opened hundreds of accounts on behalf of individuals located in jurisdictions subject to comprehensive OFAC sanctions programs including Iran, Syria and the Crimea region of Ukraine. Through these

---

15. Monero's protocol includes features that prevent tracking by using advanced programming to purposefully insert false information into every transaction on its private blockchain. The false information is impossible to separate from the valid payment details, effectively concealing sender data and completely hiding all transaction amounts. The Monero network ultimately sends funds to an auto-generated, one time use only, wallet known only to the transacting parties. It is designed to make supervisory transaction monitoring virtually impossible. Moreover, wallet addresses on monero's private blockchain are selectively visible only when an observer has obtained a private "view key." *See* The Monero Project, *Moneropedia: View Key* (last visited Sept. 30, 2022), https://www .getmonero.org/resources/moneropedia/viewkey.html.

16. 31 U.S.C. § 5318(g)(1); 31 C.F.R. § 1022.320(a)(2).

17. 31 U.S.C. § 5318(g)(1); 31 C.F.R. §§ 1022.320(a)(2)(i)-(iv).

accounts, some individuals conducted transactions that were suspicious above and beyond the fact that they involved a comprehensively sanctioned jurisdiction. For example, Bittrex processed more than 200 transactions that involved $140,000 worth of CVC—nearly 100 times larger than the average withdrawal or deposit on the Bittrex platform—and 22 transactions involving over $1 million worth of CVC each. Bittrex's failure to implement adequate procedures or controls led to its failure to identify and report these transactions to FinCEN.[18]

III. VIOLATIONS

FinCEN has determined that Bittrex willfully violated the BSA and its implementing regulations during the Relevant Time Period with regard to its AML program and reporting of suspicious transactions.[19] Specifically, FinCEN has determined that Bittrex failed to develop, implement and maintain an effective AML program that was reasonably designed to prevent its CVC trading platform and hosted wallet service from being used to facilitate money laundering and the financing of terrorist activities, in violation of 31 U.S.C. § 5318(h)(1) and 31 C.F.R. § 1022.210. Additionally, FinCEN has determined that Bittrex failed to accurately, and timely, report suspicious transactions to FinCEN, in violation of 31 C.F.R. § 1022.320.

---

18. In some cases, FinCEN will deem reports filed with OFAC as sufficient to satisfy the financial institution's SAR filing obligation. As FinCEN has explained in interpretive guidance, "reports filed with [OFAC] of blocked transactions with Specially Designated Global Terrorists, Specially Designated Terrorists, Foreign Terrorist Organizations, Specially Designated Narcotics Trafficker Kingpins, and Specially Designated Narcotics Traffickers will be deemed by FinCEN to fulfill the requirement to file [SARs] on such transactions for purposes of FinCEN's suspicious activity reporting rules." FinCEN, Interpretive Release 2004-02—Unitary Filing of Suspicious Activity and Blocking Reports, 69 Fed. Reg. 76,847, 76, 848 (Dec. 23, 2004). However, as FinCEN has also explained, "this interpretation does not affect a financial institution's obligation to identify and report suspicious activity beyond the fact of the OFAC match. To the extent that the financial institution is in possession of information not included on the blocking report filed with OFAC, a separate [SAR] should be filed with FinCEN including that information. This interpretative guidance also does not affect a financial institution's obligation to file a [SAR], even if it has filed a blocking report with OFAC, to the extent that the facts and circumstances surrounding the OFAC match are independently suspicious—and are otherwise required to be reported under existing FinCEN regulations. In those cases, the OFAC blocking report would not satisfy a financial institution's [SAR] filing obligation."

19. In civil enforcement of the BSA under 31 U.S.C. § 5321(a)(1), to establish that a financial institution acted willfully, the government need only show that the financial institution or individual acted with either reckless disregard or willful blindness. The government need not show that the entity or individual had knowledge that the conduct violated the BSA, or that the entity or individual otherwise acted with an improper motive or bad purpose.

IV. ENFORCEMENT FACTORS

FinCEN has considered all of the factors outlined in its Statement on Enforcement of the Bank Secrecy Act issued August 18, 2020.[20] The following factors were particularly relevant to FinCEN's evaluation of the appropriate disposition of this matter, including the decision to impose a Civil Money Penalty and the size of that Civil Money Penalty.

- Nature and seriousness of the violations, including extent of possible harm to the public and systemic nature of the violations. Bittrex's violations were serious and exposed the public to a significant risk of possible harm. Bittrex's CVC platform was facilitating thousands of high-risk transactions, yet it failed to implement appropriate policies, procedures, and internal controls to effectively manage that risk. FinCEN's investigation showed that Bittrex failed to detect, investigate, and report suspicious transactions, including transactions with sanctioned jurisdictions and darknet marketplaces. Bittrex failed to hire and train appropriate personnel to assure compliance with the BSA, and instead relied on an ineffective manual transaction review process that could not keep pace with the volume of transactions conducted through its platform. Moreover, Bittrex operated for almost three years as an MSB before filing its first SAR in May 2017, depriving law enforcement and others of critical financial intelligence used to protect national security and safeguard the financial system from illicit use. Further, because of its inadequate manual review process, the majority of SARs filed by Bittrex were filed well after the transaction dates.

- Pervasiveness of wrongdoing within the financial institution. From the beginning of Bittrex's operations in February 2014 until late 2017, Bittrex designated its Chief Executive Officer as the AML compliance officer responsible for complying with Bittrex's statutory and regulatory obligations under the BSA. This appointment was not commensurate with Bittrex's risk profile based on the volume and scope of its activity. Bittrex failed to adopt a written AML compliance program until August 2015, almost a year and half after it began operations as an MSB. The written AML program, while thorough and rigorous in many ways, did not adequately address Bittrex's overall risk environment, including the unique risks presented by some of the over 250 CVCs traded on its platform. It also failed to adequately address the geographic risks posed by its customer base, and the program was not fully implemented until December 2018. Bittrex processed tens of thousands of transactions every day, yet the company's management failed

---

20. FinCEN, Statement on Enforcement of the Bank Secrecy Act (Aug. 18, 2020), https://www.fincen.gov/ sites/default/files/shared/FinCEN%20Enforcement%20Statement_FINAL%20508.pdf

to utilize an appropriate transaction monitoring process resulting in the failure to file a significant number of SARs in a timely manner.

- <u>History of similar violations or misconduct in general.</u> Bittrex has not been the subject of any prior criminal, civil, or regulatory enforcement action.

- <u>Financial gain or other benefit resulting from the violations.</u> Bittrex increased revenue and grew its business without investing in appropriate resources, tools, and personnel to develop, implement, and maintain an effective AML compliance program. This gave the company an unfair competitive advantage in the marketplace as compared to other companies offering similar products and services that were investing in appropriate technology and personnel to comply with the BSA. The financial benefit resulting from the violations was more limited after Bittrex paused the opening of new customer accounts in December 2017 and began dedicating more resources to its compliance program.

- <u>Presence or absence of prompt, effective action to terminate the violations upon discovery, including self-initiated remedial measures.</u> In late 2017, after receiving notification of an upcoming federal compliance examination, but prior to the issuance of the examination results, Bittrex began taking corrective actions to address its compliance failures. In December 2017, Bittrex hired a qualified AML compliance officer with significant BSA/AML experience. That same month, Bittrex paused new customer registrations for four months and used the pause to bolster its AML compliance program. To date, Bittrex has continued to increase compliance staffing and training, and it continues to develop and implement new policies and procedures, including the purchase and integration of several automated transaction monitoring systems. The company has also undergone independent audits by experienced auditing firms and significantly increased and improved its SAR filing quality and timeliness. After the Relevant Time Period, Bittrex compliance employees were required to take specialized training, including event driven training corresponding to regulatory changes, changes in technology, and/or the results of significant investigations. Bittrex has updated its SAR evaluation and filing procedures. The company has also contracted with a vendor to perform automated transaction monitoring for fiat currency transactions. Bittrex also added automated CVC transaction monitoring and customer account surveillance capabilities. Bittrex also updated its OFAC blocking, rejection, and reporting procedures. Bittrex has updated its customer identification and verification processes, including a tool used to verify the authenticity of government-issued identification documents, among other enhancements. Additionally, Bittrex proactively works with U.S. government agencies on ways to improve BSA/AML compliance by virtual asset service providers. Due to the substantial investments and improvements to its compliance program after the Relevant Time Period, FinCEN is not requiring additional remedial measures as part of this Consent Order.

- <u>Timely and voluntary disclosure of the violations to FinCEN.</u> Bittrex did not voluntarily disclose its compliance failures to FinCEN.

- <u>Quality and extent of cooperation with FinCEN and other relevant agencies.</u> Bittrex has been responsive to requests for information from the IRS and FinCEN throughout the course of the IRS's examination and FinCEN's investigation. Bittrex agreed to waive any defense related to the statute of limitations for conduct occurring during the Relevant Time Period. The company's cooperation and significant investment and efforts to design and build an effective AML compliance program have led FinCEN to impose a significantly lower Civil Money Penalty than it would have otherwise imposed for Bittrex's serious and systemic violations.

- <u>Whether another agency took enforcement action for related activity.</u> Following a separate but parallel investigation by OFAC, Bittrex has agreed to pay approximately $24 million to resolve OFAC's investigation into apparent violations of the Cuban Assets Control Regulations, 31 C.F.R. Part 515; the Sudanese Sanctions Regulations, 31 C.F.R. Part 538; the Syrian Sanctions

V. CIVIL PENALTY

Regulations, 31 C.F.R. Part 542; Iranian Transactions and Sanctions Regulations, 31 C.F.R. Part 560; and the Crimea region of Ukraine-related sanctions under Executive Order 13685. FinCEN will credit payments made by Bittrex to resolve OFAC's enforcement investigation because FinCEN's violations stem from some of the same underlying conduct.

FinCEN may impose a Civil Money Penalty of $25,000 per day for willful violations of the requirement to implement and maintain an effective AML program occurring on or before November 2, 2015, and $62,689 per day for violations occurring after that date. [21]

For each willful violation of a SAR reporting requirement occurring on or before November 2, 2015, FinCEN may impose a Civil Money Penalty not to exceed the greater of the amount involved in the transaction (capped at $100,000) or $25,000. [22] The per-violation cap increases to $250,759, and the floor increases to $62,689, for violations occurring after November 2, 2015. [23]

After considering all the facts and circumstances in this case, as well as the enforcement factors discussed above, FinCEN has decided to impose a Civil Money

---

21. 31 U.S.C. § 5321(a)(1); 31 C.F.R. § 1010.821.
22. 31 U.S.C. § 5321(a)(1).
23. 31 C.F.R. § 1010.821.

Penalty of $29,280,829.20 in this matter. As discussed above, FinCEN will credit the $24,280,829.20 Bittrex has agreed to pay for the OFAC violations. Accordingly, Bittrex shall make a payment of $5,000,000 to the U.S. Department of the Treasury pursuant to payment instructions that will be transmitted to Bittrex upon execution of this Consent Order.

VI. CONSENT AND ADMISSIONS

To resolve this matter and only for that purpose, Bittrex admits to the Statement of Facts and Violations set forth in this Consent Order and admits to willfully violating the BSA and its implementing regulations. Bittrex consents to the use of the Statement of Facts, and any other findings, determinations, and conclusions of law set forth in this Consent Order in any other proceeding brought by or on behalf of FinCEN, or to which FinCEN is a party or claimant, and agrees they shall be taken as true and correct and be given preclusive effect without any further proof. Bittrex understands and agrees that in any administrative or judicial proceeding brought by or on behalf of FinCEN against it, including any proceeding to enforce the Civil Money Penalty imposed by this Consent Order or for any equitable remedies under the BSA, Bittrex shall be precluded from disputing any fact or contesting any determinations set forth in this Consent Order.

To resolve this matter, Bittrex agrees to and consents to the issuance of this Consent Order and all terms herein and agrees to make a payment of $5,000,000 to the U.S. Department of the Treasury pursuant to the payment instructions that will be transmitted to Bittrex upon execution of this Consent Order. If timely payment is not made, Bittrex agrees that interest, penalties, and administrative costs will accrue.[24] If Bittrex fails to pay the $24,280,829.20 settlement arising out of its apparent OFAC violations, it must pay the entire $ $29,280,829.20 penalty imposed by this Consent Order within thirty days of default.

Bittrex understands and agrees that it must treat the Civil Money Penalty paid under this Consent Order as a penalty paid to the government and may not claim, assert, or apply for a tax deduction, tax credit, or any other tax benefit for any payments made to satisfy the Civil Money Penalty. Bittrex understands and agrees that any acceptance by or on behalf of FinCEN of any partial payment of the Civil Money Penalty obligation will not be deemed a waiver of Bittrex's obligation to make further payments pursuant to this Consent Order, or a waiver of FinCEN's right to seek to compel payment of any amount assessed under the terms of this Consent Order, including any applicable interest, penalties, or other administrative costs.

Bittrex affirms that it agrees to and approves this Consent Order and all terms herein freely and voluntarily and that no offers, promises, or inducements of any nature whatsoever have been made by FinCEN or any employee, agent, or represen-

---

24. 31 U.S.C. § 3717; 31 C.F.R. § 901.9.

tative of FinCEN to induce Bittrex to agree to or approve this Consent Order, except as specified in this Consent Order.

Bittrex understands and agrees that this Consent Order implements and embodies the entire agreement between Bittrex and FinCEN, and its terms relate only to this enforcement matter and any related proceeding and the facts and determinations contained herein. Bittrex further understands and agrees that there are no express or implied promises, representations, or agreements between Bittrex and FinCEN other than those expressly set forth or referred to in this Consent Order and that nothing in this Consent Order is binding on any other law enforcement or regulatory agency or any other governmental authority, whether foreign, Federal, State, or local.

Bittrex understands and agrees that nothing in this Consent Order may be construed as allowing Bittrex, its subsidiaries, affiliates, Board, officers, employees, or agents to violate any law, rule, or regulation.

Bittrex consents to the continued jurisdiction of the courts of the United States over it and waives any defense based on lack of personal jurisdiction or improper venue in any action to enforce the terms and conditions of this Consent Order or for any other purpose relevant to this enforcement action. Solely in connection with an action filed by or on behalf of FinCEN to enforce this Consent Order or for any other purpose relevant to this action, Bittrex authorizes and agrees to accept all service of process and filings through the Notification procedures below and to waive formal service of process.

VII. COOPERATION

Bittrex shall fully cooperate with FinCEN in any and all matters within the scope of or related to the Statement of Facts, including any investigation of its current or former directors, officers, employees, agents, consultants, or any other party. Bittrex understands that its cooperation pursuant to this paragraph shall include, but is not limited to, truthfully disclosing all factual information with respect to its activities, and those of its present and former directors, officers, employees, agents, and consultants. This obligation includes providing to FinCEN, upon request, any document, record or other tangible evidence about which FinCEN may inquire of Bittrex. Bittrex's cooperation pursuant to this paragraph is subject to applicable laws and regulations, as well as valid and properly documented claims of attorney-client privilege or the attorney work product doctrine.

VIII. RELEASE

Execution of this Consent Order and compliance with all of the terms of this Consent Order, settles all claims that FinCEN may have against Bittrex for the conduct described in this Consent Order during the Relevant Time Period. Execution of this Consent Order, and compliance with the terms of this Consent Order, does not release any claim that FinCEN may have for conduct by Bittrex other than the conduct described in this Consent Order during the Relevant Time Period, or any claim that FinCEN may have against any current or former director, officer, owner, or employee of Bittrex, or any other individual or entity other than those named in this Consent Order. In addition, this Consent Order does not release any claim or provide any other protection in any investigation, enforcement action, penalty assessment, or injunction relating to any conduct that occurs after the Relevant Time Period as described in this Consent Order.

IX. WAIVERS

Nothing in this Consent Order shall preclude any proceedings brought by, or on behalf of, FinCEN to enforce the terms of this Consent Order, nor shall it constitute a waiver of any right, power, or authority of any other representative of the United States or agencies thereof, including but not limited to the Department of Justice.

In consenting to and approving this Consent Order, Bittrex stipulates to the terms of this Consent Order and waives:

a. Any and all defenses to this Consent Order, the Civil Money Penalty imposed by this Consent Order, and any action taken by or on behalf of FinCEN that can be waived, including any statute of limitations or other defense based on the passage of time;

b. Any and all claims that FinCEN lacks jurisdiction over all matters set forth in this Consent Order, lacks the authority to issue this Consent Order or to impose the Civil Money Penalty, or lacks authority for any other action or proceeding related to the matters set forth in this Consent Order;

c. Any and all claims that this Consent Order, any term of this Consent Order, the Civil Money Penalty, or compliance with this Consent Order, or the Civil Money Penalty, is in any way unlawful or violates the Constitution of the United States of America or any provision thereof;

d. Any and all rights to judicial review, appeal or reconsideration, or to seek in any way to contest the validity of this Consent Order, any term of this Consent Order, or the Civil Money Penalty arising from this Consent Order;

e. Any and all claims that this Consent Order does not have full force and effect, or cannot be enforced in any proceeding, due to changed circumstances, including any change in law;

f. Any and all claims for fees, costs, or expenses related in any way to this enforcement matter, Consent Order, or any related administrative action, whether arising under common law or under the terms of any statute, including, but not limited to, under the Equal Access to Justice Act. Bittrex agrees to bear its own costs and attorneys' fees.

X. VIOLATIONS OF THIS CONSENT ORDER

Determination of whether Bittrex has failed to comply with this Consent Order, or any portion thereof, and whether to pursue any further action or relief against Bittrex shall be in FinCEN's sole discretion. If FinCEN determines, in its sole discretion, that a failure to comply with this Consent Order, or any portion thereof, has occurred, or that Bittrex has made any misrepresentations to FinCEN or any other government agency related to the underlying enforcement matter, FinCEN may void any and all releases or waivers contained in this Consent Order; reinstitute administrative proceedings; take any additional action that it deems appropriate; and pursue any and all violations, maximum penalties, injunctive relief, or other relief that FinCEN deems appropriate. FinCEN may take any such action even if it did not take such action against Bittrex in this Consent Order and notwithstanding the releases and waivers herein. In the event FinCEN takes such action under this paragraph, Bittrex specifically agrees to toll any applicable statute of limitations and to waive any defenses based on a statute of limitations or the passage of time that may be applicable to the Statement of Facts in this Consent Order, until a date 180 days following Bittrex's receipt of notice of FinCEN's determination that a misrepresentation or breach of this agreement has occurred, except as to claims already time barred as of the Effective Date of this Consent Order.

In the event that FinCEN determines that Bittrex has made a misrepresentation or failed to comply with this Consent Order, or any portion thereof, all statements made by or on behalf of Bittrex to FinCEN, including the Statement of Facts, whether prior or subsequent to this Consent Order, will be admissible in evidence in any and all proceedings brought by or on behalf of FinCEN. Bittrex agrees that it will not assert any claim under the Constitution of the United States of America, Rule 408 of the Federal Rules of Evidence, or any other law or federal rule that any such statements should be suppressed or are otherwise inadmissible. Such statements shall be treated as binding admissions, and Bittrex agrees that it shall be precluded from disputing or contesting any such statements. FinCEN shall have sole discretion over the decision to impute conduct or statements of any director, officer, employee, agent, or any person or entity acting on behalf of, or at the direction of Bittrex in determining whether Bittrex has violated any provision of this Consent Order.

XI. PUBLIC STATEMENTS

Bittrex agrees that it shall not, nor shall its attorneys, agents, partners, directors, officers, employees, affiliates, or any other person authorized to speak on its behalf or within its authority or control, take any action or make any public statement, directly or indirectly, contradicting its admissions and acceptance of responsibility or any terms of this Consent Order, including any fact finding or determination in this Consent Order.

FinCEN shall have sole discretion to determine whether any action or statement made by Bittrex, or by any person under the authority, control, or speaking on behalf of Bittrex contradicts this Consent Order, and whether Bittrex has repudiated such statement.

XII. RECORD RETENTION

In addition to any other record retention required under applicable law, Bittrex agrees to retain all documents and records required to be prepared or recorded under this Consent Order or otherwise necessary to demonstrate full compliance with each provision of this Consent Order, including supporting data and documentation. Bittrex agrees to retain these records for a period of 6 years after creation of the record, unless required to retain them for a longer period of time under applicable law.

XIII. SEVERABILITY

Bittrex agrees that if a court of competent jurisdiction considers any of the provisions of this Consent Order unenforceable, such unenforceability does not render the entire Consent Order unenforceable. Rather, the entire Consent Order will be construed as if not containing the particular unenforceable provision(s), and the rights and obligations of FinCEN and Bittrex shall be construed and enforced accordingly.

XIV. SUCCESSORS AND ASSIGNS

Bittrex agrees that the provisions of this Consent Order are binding on its owners, officers, employees, agents, representatives, affiliates, successors, assigns, and transferees to whom Bittrex agrees to provide a copy of the executed Consent Order. Should Bittrex seek to sell, merge, transfer, or assign its operations, or any portion thereof, that are the subject of this Consent Order, Bittrex must, as a condition of sale, merger, transfer, or assignment obtain the written agreement of the buyer, merging entity, transferee, or assignee to comply with this Consent Order.

XV. MODIFICATIONS AND HEADINGS

This Consent Order can only be modified with the express written consent of FinCEN and Bittrex. The headings in this Consent Order are inserted for convenience only and are not intended to affect the meaning or interpretation of this Consent Order or its individual terms.

XVI. AUTHORIZED REPRESENTATIVE

Bittrex's representative, by consenting to and approving this Consent Order, hereby represents and warrants that the representative has full power and authority to consent to and approve this Consent Order for and on behalf of Bittrex, and further represents and warrants that Bittrex agrees to be bound by the terms and conditions of this Consent Order.

XVII. NOTIFICATION

Unless otherwise specified herein, whenever notifications, submissions, or communications are required by this Consent Order, they shall be made in writing and sent via first-class mail and simultaneous email, addressed as follows:

To FinCEN: Associate Director, Enforcement and Compliance Division, Financial Crimes Enforcement Network
P.O. Box 39
Vienna, Virginia 22183

To Bittrex: Head of Litigation and Regulatory Affairs Bittrex, Inc.
701 5th Avenue, Suite 4200
Seattle, WA 98104-3100

Notices submitted pursuant to this paragraph will be deemed effective upon receipt unless otherwise provided in this Consent Order or approved by FinCEN in writing.

XVIII. COUNTERPARTS

This Consent Order may be signed in counterpart and electronically.

Each counterpart, when executed and delivered, shall be an original, and all of the counterparts together shall constitute one and the same fully executed instrument.

XIX. EFFECTIVE DATE AND CALCULATION OF TIME

This Consent Order shall be effective upon the date signed by FinCEN.

Calculation of deadlines and other time limitations set forth herein shall run from the effective date (excluding the effective date in the calculation) and be based on calendar days, unless otherwise noted, including intermediate Saturdays, Sundays, and legal holidays.

By Order of the Director of the Financial Crimes Enforcement Network.

/s/

Himamauli Das
Acting Director
Consented to and Approved By:

/s/

Richie Lai
Chief Executive Officer Bittrex, Inc

Discussion Points

1. *Money Transmission Services.* Do you agree that Bittrex's conduct falls within the BSA's definition of "money transmission services"? Why or why not?

2. *Bank Secrecy Act.* FinCEN concluded that Bittrex failed to implement and maintain an effective AML program. What additional measures should Bittrex have taken to monitor their transactions for suspicious activities? Do you think a virtual currency transmitter needs to adopt an AML program that differs from traditional financial institutions?

3. Discuss the role of MSBs in the context of combating money laundering and other financial crimes.

4. Analyze the potential implications of the Bittrex case on the broader cryptocurrency industry and regulatory oversight.

5. Explain the specific compliance failures or deficiencies highlighted in the case and their impact on Brittrex's operations.

Ten

IRS and CFBP

I. IRS

The International Revenue Service provides American taxpayers with services to understand and comply with their tax responsibilities. Digital assets are treated as property per federal taxes; thus, individuals may be required to report digital asset activity on their tax returns. The IRS has defined digital assets as any "digital representation of value which is recorded on a cryptographically secured distributed ledger or any similar technology as specified by the Secretary."[84] Some examples include convertible virtual currency and cryptocurrency, stablecoins, and non-fungible tokens—also known as NFTs.

Subject: Applicability of Section 1031 to Exchanges of Bitcoin (BTC) for Ether (ETH), Bitcoin for Litecoin (LTC), and Ether for Litecoin

IRS Chief Counsel Advice (CCA) 202114020

June 18, 2021

Memorandum
CC:ITA:B04:JYu
PRENO-112294-21
UILC: 1031.00-00, 1031.02-00
Date: June 08, 2021

To: Michael Fiore
Area Counsel
(Small Business/Self-Employed)

From: Ronald J. Goldstein
Senior Technician Reviewer, Branch 4 (Income Tax & Accounting)

Subject: Applicability of Section 1031 to Exchanges of Bitcoin (BTC) for Ether (ETH), Bitcoin for Litecoin (LTC), and Ether for Litecoin

---

84. https://www.irs.gov/businesses/small-businesses-self-employed/digital-assets.

This responds to your request for non-taxpayer specific advice regarding the applicability of § 1031 of the Internal Revenue Code ("Code") to exchanges of certain cryptocurrencies completed prior to January 1, 2018.

ISSUE

If completed prior to January 1, 2018, does an exchange of (i) Bitcoin for Ether, (ii) Bitcoin for Litecoin, or (iii) Ether for Litecoin qualify as a like-kind exchange under § 1031 of the Code?

CONCLUSION

No. If completed prior to January 1, 2018, an exchange of (i) Bitcoin for Ether, (ii) Bitcoin for Litecoin, or (iii) Ether for Litecoin does not qualify as a like-kind exchange under § 1031 of the Code.

BACKGROUND

Virtual currency is a digital representation of value that functions as a medium of exchange, a unit of account, or a store of value other than a representation of the U.S. dollar or a foreign currency. Notice 2014-21; Rev. Rul. 2019-24. Virtual currency that has an equivalent value in real currency, or acts as a substitute for real currency, such as Bitcoin, is referred to as "convertible" virtual currency and is considered property for federal income tax purposes. Notice 2014-21. Accordingly, general tax principles applicable to property transactions apply to transactions involving convertible virtual currency. *Id.*

Bitcoin, Ether, and Litecoin are all forms of cryptocurrency, a type of virtual currency that utilizes cryptography to secure transactions that are digitally recorded on a distributed ledger, such as a blockchain. Rev. Rul. 2019-24 at 2. Distributed ledger technology uses independent digital systems to record, share, and synchronize transactions, the details of which are recorded in multiple places at the same time with no central data store or administration functionality. *Id.* Cryptocurrencies may be used as a method of payment; however, many taxpayers transact in cryptocurrency for investment or other purposes.

Cryptocurrency exchanges are digital platforms that allow users to trade one cryptocurrency for another cryptocurrency, as well as for fiat currencies such as the U.S. dollar. The possible combinations supported by the exchange are known as trading pairs. Major cryptocurrencies like Bitcoin and Ether typically may be traded for any other cryptocurrency and vice versa. However, some cryptocurrencies on a cryptocurrency exchange can be traded for only a limited number of other cryptocurrencies and cannot be traded for fiat currency at all. For example, one popular cryptocurrency exchange supported more than 30 different cryptocurrencies, but almost all of them could be acquired with or traded for only Bitcoin, Ether, or fiat currency. In 2017, there were more than 1,000 different cryptocurrencies in existence.

DISCUSSION

Section 1031(a)(1) of the Code provides that no gain or loss shall be recognized on the exchange of property held for productive use in a trade or business or for investment if such property is exchanged solely for property of like-kind which is to be held either for productive use in a trade or business or for investment. The nonrecognition of gain or loss under § 1031 is intended to apply to transactions where the taxpayer's economic situation following the exchange is essentially the same as it had been before the transaction. H. Rept. 704, 73d Cong., 2d Sess. (1934), 1939-1 C.B. (Part 2) 554, 564. The Tax Cuts and Jobs Act, P.L. 115-97, amended § 1031 to limit like-kind exchange treatment after December 31, 2017, to exchanges of real property. Prior to 2018, section 1031 also applied to certain exchanges of personal property.

Treas. Reg. § 1.1031(a)-1(b) defines "like kind" to mean the nature or character of the property and not the grade or quality. One kind or class of property may not be exchanged for property of a different kind or class. For example, an investor who exchanged gold bullion for silver bullion was required to recognize gain in part because silver is primarily used as an industrial commodity while gold is primarily used as an investment. Rev. Rul. 82-166. Similarly, an investor who exchanged one kind of gold coin for another kind of gold coin was required to recognize a gain because one coin's value was derived from its collectability while the other's value was derived from its metal content. Rev. Rul. 79-143.

BTC/LTC and ETH/LTC

In 2016 and 2017, Bitcoin, and to a lesser extent Ether, held a special position within the cryptocurrency market because the vast majority of cryptocurrency-to-fiat trading pairs offered by cryptocurrency exchanges had either Bitcoin or Ether as part of the pair. In other words, an individual seeking to invest in a cryptocurrency other than Bitcoin or Ether, such as Litecoin, would generally need to acquire either Bitcoin or Ether first. Similarly, an individual seeking to liquidate his or her holdings in a cryptocurrency other than Bitcoin or Ether, such as Litecoin, generally would need to exchange those holdings for Bitcoin or Ether first. In contrast, Litecoin's trading pair availability at the time was substantially more limited.

Thus, Bitcoin and Ether played a fundamentally different role from other cryptocurrencies within the broader cryptocurrency market during 2016 and 2017. Unlike other cryptocurrencies, Bitcoin and Ether acted as an on and off-ramp for investments and transactions in other cryptocurrencies. Because of this difference, Bitcoin and Ether each differed in both nature and character from Litecoin. Therefore, Bitcoin and Litecoin (BTC/LTC) do not qualify as like-kind property for purposes of section 1031; nor do Ether and Litecoin (ETH/LTC).

BTC/ETH

As discussed above, Bitcoin and Ether shared a special role in the cryptocurrency market that made them fundamentally different from Litecoin during the relevant years. However, while both cryptocurrencies share similar qualities and uses, they are also fundamentally different from each other because of the difference in over-all design, intended use, and actual use. The Bitcoin network is designed to act as a payment network for which Bitcoin acts as the unit of payment. The Ethereum blockchain, on the other hand, was intended to act as a payment network and as a platform for operating smart contracts and other applications, with Ether working as the "fuel" for these features. Thus, although Ether and Bitcoin may both be used to make payments, Ether's additional functionality differentiates Ether from Bitcoin in both nature and character. Therefore, Bitcoin and Ether do not qualify as like-kind property under section 1031.

CONCLUSION

If completed prior to January 1, 2018, an exchange of (i) Bitcoin for Ether, (ii) Bit-coin for Litecoin, or (iii) Ether for Litecoin does not qualify as a like-kind exchange under § 1031.

This chief counsel advice is limited to the exchanges involving Bitcoin, Ether, or Litecoin discussed above. This chief counsel advice does not address any other cryptocurrencies, or any other analyses not discussed in this advice. Accordingly, no inferences should be made based on this chief counsel advice that are not explicitly set forth in this advice.

This chief counsel advice may not be used or cited as precedent. Please contact James Yu at (202) 317-4718 if you have any further questions.

Internal Revenue Service
Notice 2014-21

SECTION 1. PURPOSE

This notice describes how existing general tax principles apply to transactions using virtual currency. The notice provides this guidance in the form of answers to frequently asked questions.

SECTION 2. BACKGROUND

The Internal Revenue Service (IRS) is aware that "virtual currency" may be used to pay for goods or services, or held for investment. Virtual currency is a digital representation of value that functions as a medium of exchange, a unit of account, and/or a store of value. In some environments, it operates like "real" currency—i.e., the coin and paper money of the United States or of any other country that is designated as legal tender, circulates, and is customarily used and accepted as a medium of exchange in the country of issuance—but it does not have legal tender status in any jurisdiction.

Virtual currency that has an equivalent value in real currency, or that acts as a substitute for real currency, is referred to as "convertible" virtual currency. Bitcoin is one example of a convertible virtual currency. Bitcoin can be digitally traded between users and can be purchased for, or exchanged into, U.S. dollars, Euros, and other real or virtual currencies. For a more comprehensive description of convertible virtual currencies to date, see Financial Crimes Enforcement Network (FinCEN) Guidance on the Application of FinCEN's Regulations to Persons Administering, Exchanging, or Using Virtual Currencies (FIN-2013-G001, March 18, 2013).

SECTION 3. SCOPE

In general, the sale or exchange of convertible virtual currency, or the use of convertible virtual currency to pay for goods or services in a real-world economy transaction, has tax consequences that may result in a tax liability. This notice addresses only the U.S. federal tax consequences of transactions in, or transactions that use, convertible virtual currency, and the term "virtual currency" as used in Section 4 refers only to convertible virtual currency. No inference should be drawn with respect to virtual currencies not described in this notice.

The Treasury Department and the IRS recognize that there may be other questions regarding the tax consequences of virtual currency not addressed in this notice that warrant consideration. Therefore, the Treasury Department and the IRS request comments from the public regarding other types or aspects of virtual currency transactions that should be addressed in future guidance.

Comments should be addressed to:

Internal Revenue Service
Attn: CC:PA:LPD:PR (Notice 2014-21) Room 5203
P.O. Box 7604
Ben Franklin Station
Washington, D.C. 20044

or hand delivered Monday through Friday between the hours of 8 A.M. and 4 P.M. to:

Courier's Desk
Internal Revenue ServiceAttn: CC:PA:LPD:PR (Notice 2014-21)
1111 Constitution Avenue, N.W. Washington, D.C. 20224

Alternatively, taxpayers may submit comments electronically via e-mail to the following address: Notice.Comments@irscounsel.treas.gov. Taxpayers should include "Notice 2014-21" in the subject line. All comments submitted by the public will be available for public inspection and copying in their entirety.

For purposes of the FAQs in this notice, the taxpayer's functional currency is assumed to be the U.S. dollar, the taxpayer is assumed to use the cash receipts and disbursements method of accounting and the taxpayer is assumed not to be under common control with any other party to a transaction.

SECTION 4. FREQUENTLY ASKED QUESTIONS

Q-1: How is virtual currency treated for federal tax purposes?

A-1: For federal tax purposes, virtual currency is treated as property. General tax principles applicable to property transactions apply to transactions using virtual currency.

Q-2: Is virtual currency treated as currency for purposes of determining whether a transaction results in foreign currency gain or loss under U.S. federal tax laws?

A-2: No. Under currently applicable law, virtual currency is not treated as currency that could generate foreign currency gain or loss for U.S. federal tax purposes.

Q-3: Must a taxpayer who receives virtual currency as payment for goods or services include in computing gross income the fair market value of the virtual currency?

A-3: Yes. A taxpayer who receives virtual currency as payment for goods or services must, in computing gross income, include the fair market value of the virtual currency, measured in U.S. dollars, as of the date that the virtual currency was received. See Publication 525, Taxable and Nontaxable Income, for more information on miscellaneous income from exchanges involving property or services.

Q-4: What is the basis of virtual currency received as payment for goods or services in Q&A-3?

A-4: The basis of virtual currency that a taxpayer receives as payment for goods or services in Q&A-3 is the fair market value of the virtual currency in U.S. dollars as of the date of receipt. See Publication 551, Basis of Assets, for more information on the computation of basis when property is received for goods or services.

Q-5: How is the fair market value of virtual currency determined?

A-5: For U.S. tax purposes, transactions using virtual currency must be reported in U.S. dollars. Therefore, taxpayers will be required to determine the fair market value of virtual currency in U.S. dollars as of the date of payment or receipt. If a virtual currency is listed on an exchange and the exchange rate is established by market supply and demand, the fair market value of the virtual currency is determined by converting the virtual currency into U.S. dollars (or into another real currency which in turn can be converted into U.S. dollars) at the exchange rate, in a reasonable manner that is consistently applied.

Q-6: Does a taxpayer have gain or loss upon an exchange of virtual currency for other property?

A-6: Yes. If the fair market value of property received in exchange for virtual currency exceeds the taxpayer's adjusted basis of the virtual currency, the taxpayer has taxable gain. The taxpayer has a loss if the fair market value of the property received is less than the adjusted basis of the virtual currency. See Publication 544, Sales and Other Dispositions of Assets, for information about the tax treatment of sales and exchanges, such as whether a loss is deductible.

Q-7: What type of gain or loss does a taxpayer realize on the sale or exchange of virtual currency?

A-7: The character of the gain or loss generally depends on whether the virtual currency is a capital asset in the hands of the taxpayer. A taxpayer generally realizes capital gain or loss on the sale or exchange of virtual currency that is a capital asset in the hands of the taxpayer. For example, stocks, bonds, and other investment property are generally capital assets. A taxpayer generally realizes ordinary gain or loss on the sale or exchange of virtual currency that is not a capital asset in the hands of the taxpayer. Inventory and other property held mainly for sale to customers in a trade or business are examples of property that is not a capital asset. See Publication 544 for more information about capital assets and the character of gain or loss.

Q-8: Does a taxpayer who "mines" virtual currency (for example, uses computer resources to validate Bitcoin transactions and maintain the public Bitcoin transaction ledger) realize gross income upon receipt of the virtual currency resulting from those activities?

A-8: Yes, when a taxpayer successfully "mines" virtual currency, the fair market value of the virtual currency as of the date of receipt is includible in gross income. See Publication 525, Taxable and Nontaxable Income, for more information on taxable income.

Q-9: Is an individual who "mines" virtual currency as a trade or business subject to self-employment tax on the income derived from those activities?

A-9: If a taxpayer's "mining" of virtual currency constitutes a trade or business, and the "mining" activity is not undertaken by the taxpayer as an employee, the net earnings from self-employment (generally, gross income derived from carrying on a trade or business less allowable deductions) resulting from those activities constitute self- employment income and are subject to the self-employment tax. See Chapter 10 of Publication 334, Tax Guide for Small Business, for more information on self- employment tax and Publication 535, Business Expenses, for more information on determining whether expenses are from a business activity carried on to make a profit.

Q-10: Does virtual currency received by an independent contractor for performing services constitute self-employment income?

A-10: Yes. Generally, self-employment income includes all gross income derived by an individual from any trade or business carried on by the individual as other than an employee. Consequently, the fair market value of virtual currency received for services performed as an independent contractor, measured in U.S. dollars as of the date of receipt, constitutes self-employment income and is subject to the self-employment tax. See FS-2007-18, April 2007, Business or Hobby? Answer Has Implications for Deductions, for information on determining whether an activity is a business or a hobby.

Q-11: Does virtual currency paid by an employer as remuneration for services constitute wages for employment tax purposes?

A-11: Yes. Generally, the medium in which remuneration for services is paid is immaterial to the determination of whether the remuneration constitutes wages for employment tax purposes. Consequently, the fair market value of virtual currency paid as wages is subject to federal income tax withholding, Federal Insurance Contributions Act (FICA) tax, and Federal Unemployment Tax Act (FUTA) tax and must be reported on Form W-2, Wage and Tax Statement. See Publication 15 (Circular E), Employer's Tax Guide, for information on the withholding, depositing, reporting, and paying of employment taxes.

Q-12: Is a payment made using virtual currency subject to information reporting?

A-12: A payment made using virtual currency is subject to information reporting to the same extent as any other payment made in property. For example, a person who in the course of a trade or business makes a payment of fixed and determinable income using virtual currency with a value of $600 or more to a U.S. non-exempt recipient in a taxable year is required to report the payment to the IRS and to the payee. Examples of payments of fixed and determinable income include rent, salaries, wages, premiums, annuities, and compensation.

Q-13: Is a person who in the course of a trade or business makes a payment using virtual currency worth $600 or more to an independent contractor for performing services required to file an information return with the IRS?

A-13: Generally, a person who in the course of a trade or business makes a payment of $600 or more in a taxable year to an independent contractor for the performance of services is required to report that payment to the IRS and to the payee on Form 1099- MISC, Miscellaneous Income. Payments of virtual currency required to be reported on Form 1099-MISC should be reported using the fair market value of the virtual currency in U.S. dollars as of the date of payment. The payment recipient may have income even if the recipient does not receive a Form 1099-MISC. See the Instructions to Form 1099-MISC and the General Instructions for Certain Information Returns for more information. For payments to non-U.S. persons, see Publication 515, Withholding of Tax on Nonresident Aliens and Foreign Entities.

Q-14: Are payments made using virtual currency subject to backup withholding?

A-14: Payments made using virtual currency are subject to backup withholding to the same extent as other payments made in property. Therefore, payors making reportable payments using virtual currency must solicit a taxpayer identification number (TIN) from the payee. The payor must backup withhold from the payment if a TIN is not obtained prior to payment or if the payor receives notification from the IRS that backup withholding is required. See Publication 1281, Backup Withholding for Missing and Incorrect Name/TINs, for more information.

Q-15: Are there IRS information reporting requirements for a person who settles payments made in virtual currency on behalf of merchants that accept virtual currency from their customers?

A-15: Yes, if certain requirements are met. In general, a third party that contracts with a substantial number of unrelated merchants to settle payments between the merchants and their customers is a third party settlement organization (TPSO). A TPSO is required to report payments made to a merchant on a Form 1099-K, Payment Card and Third Party Network Transactions, if, for the calendar year, both (1) the number of transactions settled for the merchant exceeds 200, and (2) the gross amount of payments made to the merchant exceeds $20,000. When completing Boxes 1, 3, and 5a-1 on the Form 1099-K, transactions where the TPSO settles payments made with virtual currency are aggregated with transactions where the TPSO settles payments made with real currency to determine the total amounts to be reported in those boxes. When determining whether the transactions are reportable, the value of the virtual currency is the fair market value of the virtual currency in U.S. dollars on the date of payment.

See The Third Party Information Reporting Center, http://www.irs.gov/Tax- Professionals/Third-Party-Reporting-Information-Center, for more information on reporting transactions on Form 1099-K.

Q-16: Will taxpayers be subject to penalties for having treated a virtual currency transaction in a manner that is inconsistent with this notice prior to March 25, 2014?

A-16: Taxpayers may be subject to penalties for failure to comply with tax laws. For example, underpayments attributable to virtual currency transactions may be subject to penalties, such as accuracy-related penalties under section 6662. In addition, failure to timely or correctly report virtual currency transactions when required to do so may be subject to information reporting penalties under section 6721 and 6722. However, penalty relief may be available to taxpayers and persons required to file an information return who are able to establish that the underpayment or failure to properly file information returns is due to reasonable cause.

SECTION 5. DRAFTING INFORMATION

The principal author of this notice is Keith A. Aqui of the Office of Associate Chief Counsel (Income Tax & Accounting). For further information about income tax issues addressed in this notice, please contact Mr. Aqui at (202) 317-4718; for further information about employment tax issues addressed in this notice, please contact Mr. Neil D. Shepherd at (202) 317- 4774; for further information about information reporting issues addressed in this notice, please contact Ms. Adrienne E. Griffin at (202) 317- 6845; and for further information regarding foreign currency issues addressed in this notice, please contact Mr. Raymond J. Stahl at (202) 317-6938. These are not toll-free calls.

II. CFPB

The Consumer Financial Protection Bureau (CFPB) is an independent bureau within the Federal Reserve System. CFPB's mission is to promote fairness and transparency for consumer financial products and services, including mortgages and credit cards. The Bureau sets forth clear and consistent rules, allowing banks and other consumer financial service providers to compete fairly and consumers to plainly see the costs and features of products and services. In November 2022, the CFPB released a new complaint bulletin, which underlined complaints that the Bureau has received related to crypto-assets. Most consumers complained about being victimized by frauds, theft, hacks, and scams.

Consumer Financial Protection Bureau
Complaint Bulletin—An Analysis of Consumer Complaints
Related to Crypto-assets
November 2022

Executive summary

Crypto-assets are increasingly offered and marketed to consumers, including being incorporated into other products such as credit, debit, and prepaid cards offering rewards in crypto -assets, crypto-asset product offerings by person-to-person (P2P) payments platforms. Even large financial firms have begun offering and marketing crypto-asset custodial services to certain customers. As these offerings have increased, so too have consumers' complaints to the Consumer Financial Protection Bureau (CFPB) related to crypto-assets.

The majority of the more than 8,300 complaints related to crypto-assets submitted to the CFPB from October 2018 to September 2022 have been submitted in the last two years with the greatest number of complaints coming from consumers in California. In these complaints, the most common issue selected was fraud and scams (40%), followed by transaction issues (with 25% about the issue of "Other transaction problem," 16% about "Money was not available when promised," and 12% about "Other service problem"). In addition, analyses suggest that complaints related to crypto-assets may increase when the price of Bitcoin and other crypto-assets increase.

This report finds that fraud, theft, hacks, and scams are a significant problem in crypto-asset markets:

- **The top issue across all crypto-asset complaints was "Fraud or scam."** This issue appears to be getting worse, as fraud and scams make up more than half of "virtual currency" complaints received thus far in 2022. Some consumers stated that they have lost hundreds of thousands of dollars due to unauthorized account access. The prevalence of fraud and scam complaints raises the question of whether crypto-asset platforms are effectively identifying and stopping fraudulent transactions.

- **Consumers report many different scam types, including romance scams, "pig butchering," and scammers posing as influencers or customer service.** Crypto-assets are often targeted in romance scams, where scammers play on a victim's emotions to extract money. According to the FTC, of all romance scam payment types, crypto-asset romance scams accounted for the highest median individual reported losses at $10,000.[1] Some of these scammers employ a technique law enforcement refers to as "pig butchering," where fraudsters pose as financial successes and spend time gaining the victim's confidence and trust, coaching victims through setting up crypto-asset accounts.[2] Some scammers try to use social media posts by crypto-asset influencers and celebrities to trick victims. Finally, lack of customer service options for many crypto-asset platforms and wallets creates opportunities for social media scams where attackers pretend to be customer service representatives to gain access to customers' wallets and steal crypto-assets.

- **Crypto-assets are a common target for hacking.** Consumers reported "SIM-swap" hacks, where an attacker intercepts SMS messages to exploit two-factor authentication, and phishing attacks, social engineering, or both. Companies often responded to these complaints by stating that consumers are responsible for the security of their accounts. Crypto platforms are a frequent target of hacks by malicious actors, including certain nation-state actors. Hackers affiliated with one nation state have stolen over $2 billion in crypto-assets total[3], including more than $1 billion from Jan 2022 – July 2022 alone[4], and their hacks have included several prominent crypto platforms, including a "play to earn" crypto-asset game.[5]

---

1. Fed. Trade Comm'n, Data Spotlight: Reports show scammers cashing in on crypto craze (June2022), http://www.ftc.gov/system/files/ftc_gov/pdf/Crypto%20Spotlight%20FINAL%20 June%202022.pdf.

2. *See* FBI Miami Field Office and the Internet Crime Complaint Center (IC3), *Cryptocurrency Investment Schemes* (Oct. 3, 2022), https://www.ic3.gov/Media/Y2022/PSA221003.

3. *See, e.g.,* Elliptic Connect, The $100 Million Horizon Hack: Following the Trail Through Tornado Cash to North Korea (June 6, 2022), https://hub.elliptic.co/analysis/the-100-million-horizon -hack-following-the-trail-through- tornado-cash-to-north-korea/.

4. *See, e.g.,* Choe Sang-Hun and David Yaffe-Bellany, *How North Korea Used Crypto to Hack Its Way Through the Pandemic*, NYTimes (Jul. 2022), https://www.nytimes.com/2022/06/30/business /north-korea-crypto-hack.html.

5. *See* Statement, Fed. Bureau of Investigation, *FBI Statement on Attribution of Malicious Cyber Activity Posed by the Democratic People's Republic of Korea* (Apr. 14, 2022), https://www.fbi. gov/news/press-releases/press-releases/fbi-statement-on-attribution-of-malicious-cyber-activity -posed-by-the-democratic-peoples-republic-of- korea. *See also* Aaron Schaffer, *North Korean hackers linked to $620 million Axie Infinity crypto heist*, Washington Post (Apr. 14, 2022), https://www .washingtonpost.com/technology/2022/04/14/us-links-axie- crypto-heist-north-korea/.

- **There are signs that older consumers are also impacted by crypto-asset frauds and scams.** Older consumers report a higher rate of crypto-asset related frauds and scams compared to complaints overall: 44% versus 40%.

- **Complaints suggest that service members are facing issues with crypto-asset scams.** Servicemembers have submitted complaints about "SIM-swap" hacks, identity theft, and romance scams. Servicemembers have also submitted complaints about transaction problems and poor customer service at crypto-asset platforms.

- Complaints about frauds or scams continue to rise, making up more than half of all total crypto-asset complaints received by the CFPB thus far in 2022. Crypto-asset complaints and fraud reports have also been increasing at other federal agencies: The SEC has received over 23,000 tips, complaints, and referrals regarding crypto-assets since fiscal year 2019, with a particularly sharp increase in the last two years,[6] while crypto-asset losses reported to the FTC in 2021 were nearly sixty times more than in 2018.[7]

Consumer complaints describe a wide range of account access and dispute resolution issues, including platform bankruptcies where their assets are indefinitely frozen, weeks-long waits due to account access problems, hours-long platform outages, difficulty executing transactions, and poor customer service.

- **Frozen accounts, platform bankruptcies, and consumer losses.** Several large crypto-asset platforms have recently either frozen customers' account withdrawals, filed for bankruptcy protection, or both. These failures have impacted millions of consumers.[8] The CFPB has received several complaints about crypto-asset platforms that froze consumers' assets before filing for bankruptcy protection. Some consumers report losing six figures or more due to the platform's failures. Consumers describe companies that misled them, refused or ignored requests to withdraw the U.S. dollars consumers deposited with these platforms, and contradicted their disclosures. Similar

---

6. Fin. Stability Oversight Council, Report on Digital Asset Financial Stability Risks and Regulation (Oct 3, 2022), https://home.treasury.gov/system/files/261/FSOC-Digital-Assets-Report-2022 .pdf ("FSOC Report on Digital Assets").

7. Fed. Trade Comm'n, *supra* note 1.

8. *See, e.g.,* Cision PR Newswire, *Voyager Digital Reports Revenue Of US$102.7 Million For The Quarter Ended March 31, 2022* (May 16, 2022), https://www.prnewswire.com/news-releases/voyager -digital-reports-revenue-of-us102-7-million-for-the-quarter-ended-march-31--2022--301547719 .html ("Total funded accounts reached 1,190,000 as of March 31, 2022") *See also* Vicky Ge Huang, *Big Crypto Lender Celsius Freezes All Account Withdrawals,* WallStreetJournal(June13,2022),https://www .wsj.com/articles/big-crypto-lender-celsius-freezes-all-account-withdrawals-11655096584;VickyGe Huang,*Crypto Broker Voyager Digital Suspends Withdrawals,* Wall Street Journal (July 1, 2022), https://www.wsj.com/articles/crypto-broker-voyager-digital-suspends-withdrawals-11656705822.

claims have been raised in letters filed in certain crypto-asset bankruptcy proceedings.[9]

- **Consumers report difficulty obtaining restitution for hacks or frauds.** In situations where consumers had assets stolen or their account hacked, they are often told there is nowhere to turn for help. Consumers reported losing their life savings in a scam, while the companies stated their assets were not recoverable.

- **Poor customer service is a recurring issue in complaints about crypto-assets.** Consumers described hard to reach, non-responsive, or non-existent customer service. Some consumers reported being unable to get their problem resolved because they cannot reach a human at the company, and that the failure to provide timely customer service exposed them to unnecessary risks.

Consumers also submitted complaints about a series of other issues, including problems with crypto-asset credit, prepaid, and debit cards, unexpected fees or hidden costs, and platforms trying to hide behind terms and conditions.

- **Consumers reported a range of issues with products that have been marketed to them as crypto-asset credit, prepaid, and debit cards.** Consumers reported problems including the inability to make purchases, issues closing their account, rejecting their claims for reimbursement on fraudulent charges, or failing to receive advertised rewards.

- **Undisclosed or unexpected fees costs.** Some consumers complained about undisclosed or unexpected costs on crypto-asset platforms, or claims there were no fees when, in reality, the consumer noticed a large difference between the price the crypto- asset could be purchased and the price it could be sold (the "spread").

1. Introduction

The term "crypto-assets" describes various digital financial assets and their associated products and services, and is the term used in several reports published in response to President Biden's Executive Order on Ensuring Responsible Development of Digital Assets.[10] In its narrowest sense, the term crypto-asset refers specifically to a

---

9. Excerpts from letters to the judge in the Voyager Digital bankruptcy case, Molly White.com (July 23, 2022), https://blog.mollywhite.net/voyager-letters/;Excerptsfromletterstothejudgeinthe CelsiusNetwork bankruptcy case, MollyWhite.com (July 22, 2022), https://blog.mollywhite.net/celsius-letters/.

10. *See, e.g.,* FSOC Report on Digital Assets, *supra* note 6. *See also* U.S. Dep't of the Treasury, Crypto-Assets: Implications for Consumers, Investors, and Businesses (Sept. 2022), https://home.treasury.gov/system/files/136/CryptoAsset_EO5.pdf.

private sector digital asset that depends primarily on cryptography and a distributed ledger (such as a blockchain) or similar technology.[11] The term "digital assets" refers to two categories of products: central bank digital currencies (CBDCs) and crypto-assets.[12] Other alternative terms to crypto-assets—such as "virtual currencies," "cryptocurrencies," "crypto tokens," "crypto coins," or simply "crypto"—are often used by market participants as a catch-all to describe these assets. These assets can be purchased, sold, loaned, borrowed, stored, sent, and received via accounts and/ or digital wallets on crypto-asset platforms or services, though platforms typically require first funding these accounts through a connection to a bank or a purchase from a credit card (which may be facilitated by a third-party payment provider).

Crypto-assets can and often experience significant volatility. For example, in the last year, Bitcoin is down more than 70% as of October 3, 2022, from its November 2021 high, and the market value of all crypto-assets have fallen by as much as 68% as of July 2022.[13]

Crypto-assets can be stored via accounts, digital wallets, or both. Wallets can either be custodied with a crypto-asset platform or service or kept in a software or hardware wallet (on a device such as a USB drive) that is sometimes referred to as "unhosted" wallets.

Over the past decade, the sheer number of crypto-assets has vastly expanded. One estimate puts the count of total crypto-assets at more than 1.8 million.[14] A non-trivial percentage of all outstanding crypto-asset tokens are estimated to be scams (such as tokens where a so-called "rug pull" has occurred[15], or tokens explicitly coded to be able to be purchased, but not sold[16]). Nearly all these tokens are available (or at one point were available) on the so-called "decentralized finance" or "DeFi" part of the crypto-asset ecosystem. While there is no generally accepted definition of "DeFi," or what makes a product, service, arrangement or activity "decentralized,"[17] DeFi commonly refers to the provision of financial products, services, and arrangements that use systems built on top of public permissionless blockchains,[18] smart contracts,

---

11. FSOC Report on Digital Assets, *supra* note 6.

12. *Id.*

13. *See, e.g.,* Yahoo Finance, Bitcoin USD (BTC-USD), https://finance.yahoo.com/quote/BTC -USD/ (last visited Oct. 3, 2022). *See also* Olga Kharif, *Why Another 'Crypto Winter' Is Test for Digital Money,* Bloomberg (July 27, 2022), https://www.bloomberg.com/news/articles/2022-07-27/why -another-crypto-winter-is-test-for-digital-money- quicktake.

14. Token Sniffer, https://tokensniffer.com (last visited Nov. 3, 2022).

15. FSOC Report on Digital Assets, *supra* note 6 at 32.

16. Chris Stokel-Walker, *How a Squid Game Crypto Scam Got Away With Millions,* Wired (Nov. 2, 2021), https://www.wired.com/story/squid-game-coin-crypto-scam/.

17. The Bd. of the Int'l Org. of Sec. Comm'n, IOSCO Decentralized Finance Report (Mar. 2022), https://www.iosco.org/library/pubdocs/pdf/IOSCOPD699.pdf.

18. NIST describes a blockchain as a distributed digital ledger of cryptographically-signed transactions that are grouped into blocks. Each block is cryptographically linked to the previous one

software applications, and end-user applications, such as web interfaces, which simplify interacting with blockchains.[19]

Once tokens become sufficiently popular on DeFi and/or attract sufficient liquidity, some are listed on large crypto-asset platforms. Estimates of the number of individual crypto-assets available on large crypto-asset platforms range from 16,000[20] to more than 20,000.[21] This estimated range of crypto-assets trading on large platforms is over twice the amount of publicly traded stocks in U.S. markets.[22]

As crypto-asset platforms and services have become more commonplace, the risks may have become more salient among consumers, and the CFPB has noted a sharp increase in the number of complaints received related to these assets.[23] Consumers typically submit complaints about crypto-assets in the *virtual currency* product category, which has been an available on the CFPB's complaint form since August 2014.[24] Over the past two years, complaint volumes for total virtual currency

---

(making it tamper evident) after validation and undergoing a consensus decision. As new blocks are added, older blocks become more difficult to modify (creating tamper resistance). New blocks are replicated across copies of the ledger within the network, and any conflicts are resolved automatically using established rules. *See* Nat'l Inst. of Standards and Tech., Blockchain Technology Overview (Oct. 2018), https://nvlpubs.nist.gov/nistpubs/ir/2018/NIST.IR.8202.pdf.

19. The Bd. of the Int'l Org. of Sec. Comm'n, *supra* note 17 at 1 ("DeFi products, services, arrangements and activities rely upon systems built on top of public permissionless smart contract platforms, such as the Ethereum blockchain. DeFi involves a multi-layered technology "stack." In summary, at the base, or settlement layer, is the underlying blockchain. On top of the settlement layer, multiple systems of smart contracts (and auxiliary software) create financial products and services (protocols)…these smart contract and software applications may include, among others, activities that are or are akin to offering, trading, lending, borrowing, and asset management activities. End-user applications, such as web interfaces, are built on top of the smart contract layer. Often, end-user applications may aggregate multiple protocols to provide access and interoperability.")

20. Susannah Hammond and Todd Ehret, *Cryptocurrency Regulations by Country*, Thomson Reuters (2022), https://www.thomsonreuters.com/en-us/posts/wp-content/uploads/sites/20/2022/04/Cryptos-Report- Compendium-2022.pdf.

21. CoinMarketCap, *Today's Cryptocurrency Prices by Market Cap* (Sep. 7, 2022), https://web.archive.org/web/20220907050505/https://coinmarketcap.com/.

22. Securities and Exchange Comm'n Chair Gary Gensler, *Testimony at Hearing before the Subcommittee on Financial Services and General Government U.S. House Appropriations Committee* (May. 17, 2022),

23. *See* Consumer Fin. Prot. Bureau, Consumer Response Annual Report (Mar. 2022) at Section 4.6, https://files.consumerfinance.gov/f/documents/cfpb_2021-consumer-response-annual-report_2022-03.pdf.

24. The list of product and service categories and subcategories on the CFPB's complaint form are intended to enhance usability for the consumer, rather than to reflect a legal determination by the CFPB. *See* Consumer Fin. Prot. Bureau, Note on user experience, https://portal.consumerfinance.gov/consumer/s/login/. Moreover, consumers who submit complaints related to crypto-assets may not know or self-report the details needed to determine which categories of consumer financial products or services may be implicated by the experiences described in their complaints.

complaints have increased from their levels in 2019 with sharp upticks in 2021 (Figure 1).[25]

FIGURE 1: WEEKLY COUNT OF VIRTUAL CURRENCY COMPLAINTS, OCT. 2018 TO SEPT. 2022

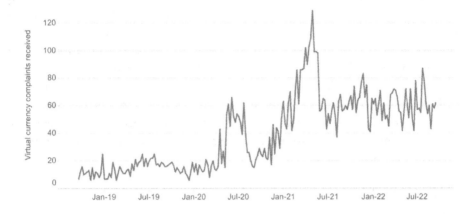

In addition, analyses suggest that complaints about virtual currency may increase when the price of Bitcoin (and crypto-assets generally[26]) increases (Figure 2).[27]

FIGURE 2: WEEKLY COUNT OF VIRTUAL CURRENCY COMPLAINTS AND BITCOIN PRICE, OCT. 2018 TO SEPT. 2022

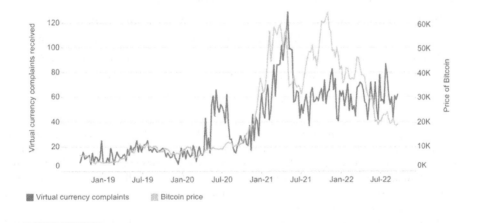

---

25. *See* discussion *infra* Section 2.

26. Crypto-assets overall, and Ether in particular, appear to be highly correlated with Bitcoin. *See, e.g.,* Erik Norland, *The Differences in Bitcoin and Ethereum Performance Drivers*, CME Group (June 9, 2022),

27. *See* Consumer Fin. Prot. Bureau, Digital Payments Conversation (Apr. 2022), https://files .consumerfinance.gov/f/documents/cfpb_digital-payments-conversation_slides_2022-04.pdf.

Increasingly crypto-assets are being offered to consumers, including through consumer products such as credit, debit, and prepaid cards that offer rewards in crypto -assets and through crypto-asset products offered by person-to-person (P2P) payment platforms. Even large financial firms now offer and market crypto-asset custodial services to certain customers.

Given the growth in complaints related to crypto-assets, the CFPB is publishing this complaint report to share preliminary findings about the types of issues consumers face when using crypto-assets and the platforms in which they are stored, bought, sold, sent, received, loaned, and borrowed. This report describes complaints submitted to the CFPB about crypto-assets (Section 2), the issues consumers raise in their complaints (Section 3), and how these issues affect and pose specific risks to older consumers and servicemembers (Section 4). This report also discusses how the complaints the Bureau receives reflect on the marketplace (Section 5) and outlines some common risks consumers should consider when using crypto-assets and associated platforms (Section 6).

2. Complaint data

This report analyzes complaints submitted to the CFPB from October 2018 to September 2022.[28] When consumers submit complaints, the CFPB asks them to identify the consumer financial product or service with which they have a problem, the issue that best describes the problem, and the company to which they want to direct their complaint.[29] The CFPB then routes consumers' complaints directly to financial companies and works to get consumers a timely response. When the CFPB cannot send the complaint to a company, it refers the complaint to other federal agencies, such as the Federal Trade Commission (FTC).

The CFPB also makes a subset of this data publicly available in the Consumer Complaint Database (Database).[30] Complaints sent to companies for response are eligible to be published in the Database and are only published after 15 days or after the company responds, confirming a commercial relationship, whichever comes first.

---

28. Complaint data in this report are current as of October 1, 2022. This report excludes some complaints that the Bureau received, including multiple complaints submitted by a given consumer on the same issue (i.e., duplicates), whistleblower tips, and complaints in which the CFPB discontinued processing because it had reason to believe that a submitter did not disclose their involvement in the complaint process. Complaint numbers are rounded throughout the report; therefore, numbers and percentages may not sum to 100%.

29. *See generally,* Consumer Fin. Prot. Bureau, *Learn how the complaint process works,* https ://www.consumerfinance.gov/complaint/process/. *See also* Consumer Fin. Prot. Bureau, *supra* note 23 at Section 1.

30. *See* Consumer Fin. Prot. Bureau, Consumer Complaint Database, https://www.consumer finance.gov/data-research/consumer-complaints/. *See also* Disclosure of Consumer Complaint Narrative Data, 80 FR 15572 (Mar. 24, 2015), https://www.federalregister.gov/documents /2015/03/24/2015-06722/disclosure-of-consumer- complaintnarrative-data.

There are two considerations researchers should keep in mind when analyzing complaints about crypto-assets:

1. When submitting complaints, consumers select the product or service that best describes the one that is the subject of their complaint.[31] Consumers generally select one of two categories when submitting complaints about crypto-assets: *virtual currency* and *mobile or digital wallet*. Consumers also submit complaints in other categories where crypto-assets have converged with more traditional banking products, such as credit cards offered by crypto-asset platforms.

2. Many virtual currency complaints are not published in the Database because they could not be sent to a company for response and thus do not meet the CF-PB's publication criteria.[32] Instead, these complaints are referred to other regulatory agencies for handling, where appropriate. Last year, for example, about one quarter of virtual currency complaints were referred to other regulatory agencies. No matter if a complaint receives a company response, the CFPB shares complaint data with the FTC for inclusion in its Sentinel Network database and makes them available to federal and state agencies via the CFPB's secure Government Portal.[33] These complaints are also available to CFPB staff for review and analysis.[34]

Virtual currency complaints

From October 2018 to September 2022, the CFPB received more than 8,300 virtual currency complaints—the majority in the last two years. Consumers from all 50 states and the District of Columbia submitted complaints to the CFPB about virtual currency with the greatest number of complaints coming from California (Figure 3). In these complaints, the most common consumer-selected issue was fraud and scams, followed by transaction issues (Figure 4). Within the "Fraud or scam" complaints, consumers often report fraudulent transactions, theft, account hacks, and scams (Section 3).

---

31. *See* Consumer Fin. Prot. Bureau, Consumer Complaint Form Product and Issue Options (Apr. 24, 2017), https://files.consumerfinance.gov/f/documents/201704_cfpb_Consumer_Complaint_Form _Product_and_Issue _Options.pdf (listing the current product and issue options available for consumers to select).

32. *See* Disclosure of Consumer Complaint Narrative Data, 80 FR 15572 (Mar. 24, 2015), https:// www.federalregister.gov/documents/2015/03/24/2015-06722/disclosure-of-consumer-complaint narrative-data.

33. 12 U.S.C. 5493(b)(3)(D).

34. *See* Consumer Fin. Prot. Bureau, *supra* note 23 at Section 1 (How the CFPB uses complaint information).

FIGURE 3: VIRTUAL CURRENCY COMPLAINT SUBMISSIONS BY STATE, OCT. 2018 TO SEP. 2022

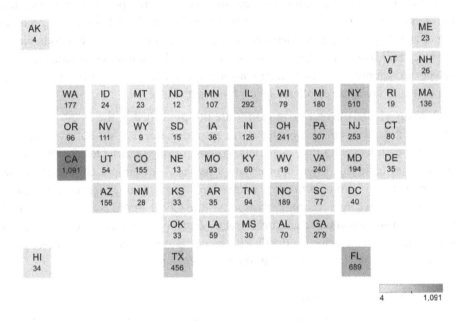

FIGURE 4: VIRTUAL CURRENCY COMPLAINTS BY ISSUE, OCT. 2018 TO SEP. 2022

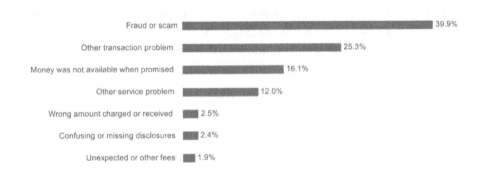

Complaint volume related to fraud and scams has been increasing over time (Figure 5).

FIGURE 5: VIRTUAL CURRENCY COMPLAINTS BY ISSUE BY MONTH, OCT. 2018 TO SEP. 2022

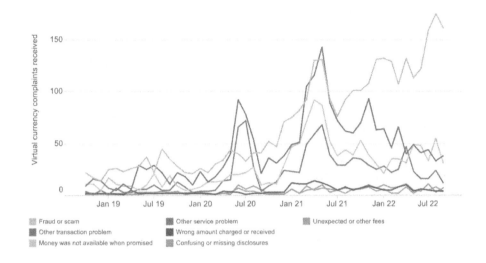

Indeed, complaints about fraud and scams make up more than half of virtual currency complaints received thus far in 2022 (Figures 6 and 7).

FIGURE 6: VIRTUAL CURRENCY COMPLAINTS BY ISSUE, OCT. 2018 TO SEP. 2022

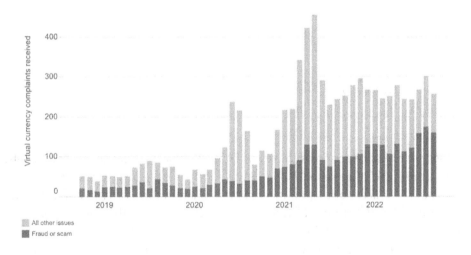

FIGURE 7: PERCENTAGE OF MONTHLY COMPLAINT VOLUME BY ISSUE, OCT. 2018 TO SEP. 2022

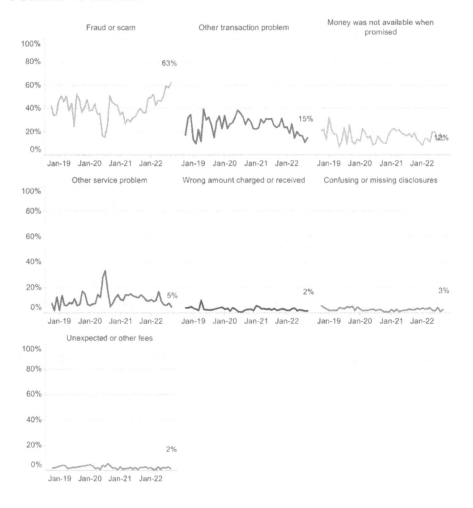

3. Consumer issues

Several broad issues predominate in CFPB complaints related to crypto-assets. First, consumers often report being victimized by frauds, theft, hacks, and scams.[35] Second, many users of crypto- asset platforms and wallets complain about issues resulting from the timing of transactions such as trades, the ability to execute transactions, and the ability to transfer assets between platforms. Third, many complaints are submitted by consumers who have trouble accessing accounts or assets held within accounts because of identity verification issues, security holds,

---

35. Throughout this report, the CFPB highlights consumer narratives. The CFPB is sharing these narratives to better illustrate how consumers currently describe this market and the issues they experience. Inclusion of narrative s in this report are for illustrative purposes only and do not represent a determination made by the CFPB about its legal authorities. *See also* discussion *supra* note 24.

or because of technical issues with platforms. Additionally, consumers having trouble getting help from a company's customer service is a common theme running through these issues.

Taken together, issues commonly identified in these complaints strongly suggest that consumers are at risk when seeking to acquire or transact with crypto-assets.

Complaints suggest that consumers that use or hold crypto-assets need to be aware of two distinct kinds of risk. First, crypto-assets are subject to the expected financial risk of loss associated with speculative assets. Second, crypto-assets are vulnerable to risks of cyber and data security vulnerabilities, transaction processing issues, technical platform issues, and other kinds of non-financial loss. In addition, these distinct risks have spillover effects; for example, discovery and exploitation of cyber and data security risks in a crypto -asset can result in price changes as market sentiment adjusts to these risks. Technical problems at platforms can also impact asset prices.

3.1 Fraud, theft, hacks, and scams

Complaints suggest that crypto-asset platforms and wallets are often a direct target of fraud and theft. For example, some technically sophisticated thefts have been perpetrated by intercepting SMS messages using a so-called "SIM-swap" to exploit two-factor authentication at crypto-asset platforms. For example, one consumer stated:

> I got SIM hacked on [date], i.e., Hackers took over my phone temporarily via SIM transfer and my Gmail permanently. After I got my phone number back from [cell phone provider] I instantly tried locking my account on [crypto-asset platform]. When I couldn't get in, I finally found a phone number where you can do that, even though it's just a bot. I also wrote an email to [crypto -asset platform] support and they only responded with a generic email about security and mentioned reinstalling the account via email (which just had been hacked and is still compromised!?!).
>
> I have not received any updates if the hackers were successful in transferring any crypto out (I'm afraid so) or if they are locked out or what the actual damage is, etc. And I read in many forums like [social media site] that [crypto-asset platform] often takes their sweet time to respond, up to weeks and months! How is that possible for such a big company with a huge IPO to ignore their customer safety this badly? This contributes to the bad image crypto has as enabling criminals...[36]

In its response, the company stated that those transactions were irreversible.

---

36. Consumer Complaint 4356993, https://www.consumerfinance.gov/data-research/consumer -complaints/search/detail/4356993.

Other fraudulent behavior aimed at crypto-assets involves phishing, social engineering, or both to gain access to personal and account information. This personal information is then used to gain access to a consumer's crypto wallet and crypto-assets. As was the case in the above example, companies often responded to these complaints by telling consumers that these transfers are not reversible because of the nature of the crypto-asset that was stolen, and by noting that consumers are responsible for the security of their accounts. Some consumers state d that they have lost hundreds of thousands of dollars due to unauthorized account access.

For example, one consumer shared:

> [On date] I clicked a phishing link saying my [crypto-asset platform] account was compromised. I reset my password on the internet browser link and then logged in on the app where I saw different tokens being converted into [crypto-asset]. I called [crypto-asset platform] to freeze my account and did it virtually as there are no live people. I got an email saying my funds were frozen. Then I got an email saying all of my funds were transferred out into a different wallet. I did not do any two-factor authentication as I am supposed to. I did not authorize any funds transferring out. I also did not authorize any computer besides my phone to complete any transaction ever. Someone took around 10,000 from me, which [crypto-asset platform] shouldn't have allowed within seconds of a password being changed. They also could have reversed or stopped this as I was on the phone within seconds of changing my password. I have contacted them repeatedly, but it has been over two weeks now without any personalized response or acknowledgement. They said they transferred my case to a specialist and are not responding to any more emails.[37]

In its response, the company stated it was unable to reverse the transaction. Indeed, many crypto-asset firms reference the immutability of many blockchain transactions to tell consumers there is no way for fraudulent transactions to be reversed or, in some cases, for the consumer to be compensated.

Scams that use crypto-assets as a premise are also common. In many of these complaints, consumers are victimized by individuals that frequently offer promises of large returns that never materialize. Often these scams involve advertising, outreach, or other marketing on social media platforms like Facebook, Instagram, and YouTube. Some consumers claimed that advertisements on these platforms directly promoted scams.[38]

In one complaint, a consumer reported one such scam:

---

37. Consumer Complaint, 4317161, https://www.consumerfinance.gov/data-research/consumer-complaints/search/detail/4317161.

38. Tech Transparency Project, Google Helps Scammers Target Americans Seeking Student Loan Relief (July13, 2022), https://www.techtransparencyproject.org/articles/google-helps-scammers-target-americans-seeking- student-loan-relief.

[H]ere was a YouTube video saying free [crypto-asset] if you send it to a certain wallet address: [URL]…

Amount: [about 4,000] [crypto-asset] ([about 5,000] USD)…

I sent the [crypto-asset] not knowing it was a scam. I would like my money back. I saved it for years and was investing it. I didn't know this was a scam.[39]

In its response, the company stated that it would be impossible to recover the lost assets.

According to the FTC, the most common type of crypto-asset scams is "investment scams," similar to the example above.[40] Another common type of scam involves a person or entity impersonating a business or government.

In other complaints, crypto-assets were targeted in romance scams or merchant scams. Like prepaid cards and cash, the ability to obscure the transfer of assets[41] makes crypto-assets a useful target for scammers in many cases.[42] In fact, many hackers looking to exploit vulnerable technical systems have recently shifted their focus to crypto-asset markets.[43]

According to the FTC, romance scams—where scammers play on a victim's emotions to extract money—are also increasingly common.[44] Some of these scammers combine romance scams with a technique law enforcement refers to as "pig butchering," where fraudsters pose as financial successes and spend time gaining the victim's

---

39. Consumer Complaint 4323561, https://www.consumerfinance.gov/data-research/consumer -complaints/search/detail/4323561.

40. Fed. Trade Comm'n, *supra* note 1.

41. There are a number of techniques for obscuring crypto-asset transfers, including chain hopping, utilizing opaque "Layer 2" protocols, the use of mixers and tumblers, and converting one crypto-asset to an anonymity-enhanced crypto-asset, also known as "privacy coins." *See* FSOC Report on Digital Assets, *supra* note 6 at 68.

42. Relatedly some median reports suggest that the availability of crypto-assets has enabled more sophisticated ransomware attacks on business. *See* Greg Myre, How Bitcoin Has Fueled Ransomware Attacks (June 10, 2021), https://www.npr.org/2021/06/10/1004874311/how-bitcoin-has-fueled-ran-somware-attacks.

43. *See, e.g.,* Ruholamin Haqshanas, *Hackers Stole USD 670M from DeFi Projects in Q2, Up by 50% from Q2 2021*, CryptoNews (July 6, 2022), https://cryptonews.com/news/hackers-stole-usd -670m-from-defi-projects-in-q2-up- by-50-from-q-2021.htm ("Hackers and fraudsters stole a total of USD 670.7m from various crypto protocols during the second quarter of the year, according to a report by major bug bounty and security services platform Immunefi…The report claimed that the bulk majority of the losses (almost 97%) happened as a result of hacks. It added that black hat hackers are now primarily targeting and exploiting DeFi projects, as 49 out of 50 instances involved DeFi protocols…Glassnode also noted that hackers have recently shifted their focus from crypto exchanges and centralized crypto platforms toward DeFi projects mainly because they are open-source, meaning their code is publicly visible.").

44. Emily Fletcher, *Data Spotlight: Reports of romance scams hit record highs in 2021*, Federal Trade Comm'n (Feb. 10, 2022), https://www.ftc.gov/news-events/data-visualizations/data-spotlight /2022/02/reports-romance-scams- hit-record-highs-2021.

confidence and trust, coaching victims through setting up crypto-asset accounts.[45] Data from the CFPB shows that romance scams are particularly common among older consumers.[46] One older consumer told the CFPB:

> I connected with someone on [social media] who had a profile as an instructor at the [a military school] in [location] and who later went on to say that he was being sent overseas again by the CIA on an undercover assignment for our country. He also said he had made me his sole contact and that his "handler" would text me information to send to him once he was in Kazakhstan so that he could access the ASA/FMC account and send money through to my credit cards so I could take out cash advances and send them to him via bitcoins for him to conduct the project he was sent on assignment to do. Money started showing up in some of my credit card accounts and I was eventually sent a "promissory agreement" on what appeared to be real CIA letterhead, so I went forward sending bitcoins to him thinking I was helping not only him but our country. Eventually it became clear that it was a scam after all of the money sent through to my credit card accounts was sucked back out after I sent him the funds...I am stuck with approximately $100,000 in debt...[47]

In its response, the company said it was unable to help the consumer recover the lost assets. Section 4.1 discusses issues facing older consumers further.

3.2 Transactions issues

Another common set of issues identified in complaints involve transaction issues when buying and selling crypto-assets, or when attempting to withdraw assets or U.S. dollars from crypto platforms. Consumer complaints suggest that many consumers have trouble executing transactions, especially during times of increasing crypto-asset prices (Section 1, Figure 2). These consumers often complain that they cannot complete transactions promptly, resulting in losses or the inability to realize profits. As one consumer stated:

> [On date] [crypto-asset platform] app shut down around 10am with all my cash and cryptocurrency in it. Has been having 'technical difficulties' for the past 6 hours, causing me to be unable to buy/sell cryptocurrency. As a result, I have not been able even see my account and have lost a lot of money since I am not able to access or trade during a downturn in the cryptocurrency market.[48]

---

45. *See* FBI Miami Field Office and the Internet Crime Complaint Center (IC3), *Cryptocurrency Investment Schemes* (Oct. 3, 2022), https://www.ic3.gov/Media/Y2022/PSA221003.

46. Consumer Fin. Prot. Bureau, *supra* note 27.

47. Consumer Complaint 4255326, https://www.consumerfinance.gov/data-research/consumer-complaints/search/detail/4255326.

48. Consumer Complaint 4160391, https://www.consumerfinance.gov/data-research/consumer-complaints/search/detail/4160391.

In its response to the consumer, the company cited its terms and conditions, which state in part "that you acknowledge and agree that we will not be liable, and you will not hold or seek to hold us liable for any technical problems, system failures and malfunctions, communication line failures, equipment or software failures or malfunctions, system access issues, system capacity issues, high internet traffic demand, security breaches and unauthorized access, and other similar computer problems and defects."

Other consumers had issues with compatibility between crypto -assets they owned, and those that could be used on a specific crypto-asset platform. For example, some consumers stated that they could not sell assets after learning that they would be de-listed by a platform (so that the consumer is no longer able to transact in that particular asset). Other consumers experienced losses when attempting to transfer incompatible assets between different wallets or crypto -asset platforms. Because several major crypto-assets have been "forked," or split off into separate blockchains, consumers are often unaware of the incompatibility between their assets until attempting to make a transfer. In these situations, consumers complain about difficulty recovering their transferred assets. As one consumer stated:

> Hello, I have problem with [crypto-asset platform] company about a crypto transaction. I tried to contact the company, but they don't answer my email and they don't have a number to call. On the [date] in my [crypto -asset platform] wallet I sent some 20,000 [crypto-asset] from [crypto-asset platform] wallet to my [crypto-asset] Wallet in [URL]. the transaction was approved but the funds never arrived. They told me that I can't send swap different currency. So, I gently asked them to reverse the transaction, but they told [me] that they can't, and my money are lost. The value of these funds now is [over $15,000].[49]

In its response, the company stated that the consumer had been given warning messages not to attempt the transfer, and that it was unable to help recover the assets.

3.2.1 Undisclosed or unexpected costs

Some consumers complained about undisclosed or unexpected costs on crypto -asset platforms, or claims there were no fees when, in reality, the consumer noticed a large cost in the form of a large spread.[50] One consumer mentioned misleading terms indicating that converting from one crypto to another would be "free":

---

49. Consumer Complaint 4203691, https://www.consumerfinance.gov/data-research/consumer -complaints/search/detail/4203691.

50. The spread refers to the difference between two prices, commonly, the gap between the price an asset can be purchased at (the bid) and the price an asset can be sold at (the ask).

[Under] the guise of "Free" conversion from crypto to crypto [crypto-asset platform] charges a huge spread when making these "Free" [conversions]. They need to disclose the spread and the cost of that crypto to crypto transfer. [51]

Another consumer complained about discrepancies between listed prices and the amounts they received when selling an asset or the high fees for completing transactions:

On [date], I executed a trade of [crypto tokens] using the [crypto-asset platform] App. At this time the spot price on [the platform] was ~.46-.47 USD. As communicated through the [platform's] App, when I agreed to sell my tokens, my portfolio was valued at ~42,XXX.XX USD. As the transaction was completed moments later, my portfolio, then in USD, was valued at [under $32,000] - an evaporation of ~11,XXX USD...I fully understand slippage is to be expected while trading crypto-assets, especially on [the app], however a delta of north of 20% is not slippage but an error (at best) and one that hopefully is corrected swiftly. [52]

In its response, the company stated that this resulted from the difference between the "spot" price and the price locked in when the trade is executed, and that the amount the consumer received from the sale was accurate.

Another consumer described extremely large spreads and price discrepancies:

On 10/29/2021, I had total 61259495 [crypto -asset] coins in my account. When I looked at the home screen on [crypto-asset platform] it was showing current value 4879.85$ and checked [crypto-asset] current market price 0.00007827$.

Then I tried to sell some coins so went into trade -> selected [crypto-asset] and selected max (coins) for sale and went on confirm screen and it was showing sale price 0.00007127$ and total value 4366.01$...

For next 2 weeks, I tried same thing for about 7–8 times and noticed that when I try to see coins it is showing higher price when I initiate the sale and it suddenly changes at the final confirmation page. It is almost 20% less...This seems like a software trick to make money and scam people.

I raised this issue multiple times with [crypto-asset platform] but have not received satisfactory response. [53]

---

51. Consumer Complaint 5154181, https://www.consumerfinance.gov/data-research/consumer-complaints/search/detail/5154181.

52. Consumer Complaint 4345742, https://www.consumerfinance.gov/data-research/consumer-complaints/search/detail/4345742.

53. Consumer Complaint 5510377, https://www.consumerfinance.gov/data-research/consumer-complaints/search/detail/5510377.

In its response, the company stated that "a price increase or decrease from the reference price to the execution price could be due to volatility in the value of the digital asset being bought or sold."

Finally, another consumer complained that a crypto-asset platform would not let them close an account until their balance was zero, but the fee to withdraw the remaining U.S. dollars exceeded the amount in the account, so the consumer could not close their account. The consumer describes also being unable to sell their crypto-assets due to needing to verify their account through a wire transfer, which also incurred a fee:

> Created an account...and deposited $100, bought 18+ [crypto-asset] coin and have approximately $9 dollars in [crypto-asset]. Want to close account and they require zero balance, but I can't sell anything because they want a wire transfer from my bank (deposit more money) which costs $25 both ways which is crazy and unfair since they let me in without a wire transfer.[54]

In its response, the company stated it had requested a wire transfer to verify the bank account was controlled by the consumer. After a discussion with the consumer, the company refunded the consumer's initial debit card deposit and closed the account.

3.2.2 Account access and verification

Consumers also often complained about account issues related to verifying their identity or confirming account ownership, which led to them being locked out of their accounts. Some consumers pointed to specific large transactions that resulted in these issue s. Others claimed that they were asked for additional identity verification documents after using a platform for some time. Consumers reported multiple attempts to resolve issues by uploading documents, such as a driver's license. These customers often complained about poor or non-existent customer service. Some consumers claimed that accounts remained frozen for weeks or months. For example, according to a consumer:

> I was asked to verify again in December and provided them with a passport photo which was accepted and got the account unrestricted but then a few months later I received an email telling me my account would be restricted again as my account was under review, a process that they said would take a few days. I don't mind having my buy and sell capabilities suspended but I can't even send my assets to a different exchange. They ignore my emails, customer support requests and tweets and it seems like my money is gone forever, they have taken it with no route to get it back. [The crypto-asset platform] are doing this to many people and it's unacceptable...I just want some clarity, why is

---

54. Consumer Complaint 5047875, https://www.consumerfinance.gov/data-research/consumer -complaints/search/detail/5047875.

my account under review? Is there any document I can provide to resolve this issue? In an ideal world I would like my account back, able to buy, sell and send my cryptocurrency but at this point I have lost all trust in [the crypto-asset platform] so I would just like to move my funds to a better exchange that have never treated me like this. [55]

In its response, the company apologized for the experience, reported that the issue had been resolved, and offered about twenty dollars as a gesture of apology.

3.3 Customer service issues

Poor customer service is a common theme across complaints. [56] It is also a re-curring issue in complaints about crypto-assets generally. Consumers sometimes complained about the difficulties they face in getting in touch with customer service representatives at crypto-asset platforms and getting the help they need. For exam-ple, one consumer complained:

I'd like to submit a formal complaint about [a crypto-asset platform], their customer service and the quality of their service in general.

Ever since I created an account with [a crypto-asset platform] approximately six months ago, I have encountered number of issues. Even though I went through all the required steps of verification, I would experience the issues with [the crypto - asset platform's] system that would not allow me to purchase cryptocurrency, or sell cryptocurrency, or transfer the money from my check-ing account to USD wallet on [the crypto-asset platform] or it would not allow me to plug in my debit card.

When I would write a message to customer service, it would take them days to respond. It would be weeks before they do anything. And they would ask me to email them very sensitive personal financial information even though I already submitted that information before, even though everything was veri-fied by their system, even though I have already made purchases and money transfers before. But they would be asking to email them more information like banking statements for the last few months etc. And then they would say that they had to do that to white-list my account. I don't even know what that means. When I would ask them questions why my account still didn't work even though I went through all the proper notification steps, and why they are requesting more of the sensitive documents, they would not answer questions, and they would be kind of rude in their email response. [57]

---

55. Consumer Complaint 4137827, https://www.consumerfinance.gov/data-research/consumer -complaints/search/detail/4137827.

56. *See generally* Consumer Fin. Prot. Bureau, *supra* note 23.

57. Consumer Complaint 3992322, https://www.consumerfinance.gov/data-research/consumer -complaints/search/detail/3992322.

In its response, the company stated it would try to be more responsive in the future.

Some consumers reported being unable to get their problem resolved because they cannot reach a human at the company. For example, one consumer stated:

> My family and I have 4 accounts with [crypto-asset platform]. All of a sudden, we are still able to log into our accounts, but the accounts are "restricted" and it is NOT possible to make any transactions or close the account. There is NO one at the company to talk to... only website inquiries. There are NO options to choose from regarding a "restricted account." I have used other forms on their website to submit an inquiry but for the last 4 weeks NO one has responded. I need someone at your office to either, (1) contact [crypto-asset platform] for me, (2) email the a [sic] phone number at [crypto-asset platform] where I can actually speak to someone.[58]

Because of the price volatility of the underlying crypto-assets, consumer soften pointed out that failure to provide timely customer service exposed them to unnecessary risks. One consumer stated:

> I have an account with [crypto-asset platform] (for 3 years) where I buy and trade [crypto-asset] as an investment opportunity. I have funds locked in a [crypto -asset] Vault that need to be moved to my [crypto-asset] wallet (part of their normal security process). There are multiple layers of security, and 2 email addresses are required. One of my old email addresses is no longer active so this is preventing me from receiving an authentication email to get my funds. [The crypto-asset platform] no longer has a phone line for customer service (I assume due to covid) so email is the only customer service available. I first emailed them about this problem Dec.3, receiving a generic email thanking me for contacting them and someone would be in touch soon. I waited one week, heard nothing, email—same generic response back. Emailed again every day from the 11–18. Finally on Dec 19th I get a response saying the only way to fix this is to have them move the funds to my wallet, delete the vault, and then I could create a new vault and be back in shape. They sent a link asking me to verify my ID... which I did. On the 21st I get the same email asking me to verify again which I did and got confirmation that it was verified. Today (12/28) they email me saying if they don't hear from me my case will be closed due to no action on my part. BEYOND FRUSTRATING that my investment money is locked with no access and their lack of customer service is causing

---

58. Consumer Complaint 4133656, https://www.consumerfinance.gov/data-research/consumer-complaints/search/detail/4133656.

me to lose money every day as the [crypto-asset] market fluctuates like a stock price...[59]

In its response, the company apologized for the experience, reported that the issue had been resolved, and offered ten dollars as a gesture of apology.

3.3.1 Scammers impersonating customer service representatives

Lack of customer service options for many crypto-asset platforms and wallets creates opportunities for social media scams where attackers pretend to be customer service representatives to gain access to customers' wallets and steal crypto-assets.[60] For example, on certain social media sites, merely mentioning certain crypto-asset wallet names in a post often leads to many bot-type accounts responding with (false) offers to help.[61] In actuality, these are attempts to scam a user out of their crypto-assets. The lack of dedicated support for one wallet provider may be contributing to a plethora of scams, enough that the provider itself posted tips on avoiding these scams on social media,[62] and the parent company of the provider wrote an entire blog post devoted to explaining how to avoid these scams.[63] Impersonation of customer service representatives are not limited to companies with no customer service divisions; scammers impersonate customer service representatives even from companies that have such a division.

For example, in a complaint to the Bureau, a consumer reported being at risk of losing nearly $40,000 when they were contacted by a scammer who claimed to be an employee of a crypto - asset platform who needed to help them unlock their account.[64]

In another complaint, one consumer complained about losing tens of thousands of dollars to someone that the crypto-asset platform later determined was a scammer impersonating a customer service representative for that platform:

---

59. Consumer Complaint 4033764, https://www.consumerfinance.gov/data-research/consumer-complaints/search/detail/4033764.

60. See Will Gendron, *Scammers are impersonating MetaMask tech support on Twitter*, Input Mag (Jan. 21, 2022), https://www.inputmag.com/tech/beware-of-scammers-impersonating-metamask-support-on-twitter.

61. Lawrence Abrams, *Twitter bots pose as support staff to steal your cryptocurrency*, Bleeping Computer (Dec. 7, 2021), https://www.bleepingcomputer.com/news/security/twitter-bots-pose-as-support-staff-to-steal-your- cryptocurrency/.

62. @MetaMask, Twitter (May. 2, 2022, 9:33 PM), https://twitter.com/MetaMask/status/1389030423611658241 ("An easy easy way to avoid this kind of phishing attack is to ONLY seek support from WITHIN the app you want help on!").

63. Joel Willmore, *Spoofing, Sweepers, and Clipboard Hacks: How To Stay Safe From Scams*, Consensys (Jan. 13, 2022), https://consensys.net/blog/metamask/spoofing-sweepers-and-clipboard-hacks-how-to-stay-safe-from- scams/.

64. Consumer Complaint 4716709, https://www.consumerfinance.gov/data-research/consumer-complaints/search/detail/4716709.

I'm filing a complaint against [a crypto-asset platform]. $20,000+ of my digital assets were stolen from the [the platform]. [The platform] is not taking responsibility for the gross negligence on their part. My account was initially hacked in August 2021 and I immediately informed them about it. They failed to protect my account and did not respond to my concerns until nothing was left in my portfolio... zero, zilch, nada! I could not even access my account to withdraw the remaining funds. [The platform] kept reiterating that transactions on the blockchain are irreversible. But I informed them of the initial incident when I still had around 90% of my funds left. If transactions are irreversible, they should have protected or froze my account after I first found out it was hacked. I asked [the platform] to secure my account before the hacker took out the remaining funds in my account. They did not protect my account. They ignored my emails. When they finally responded, I was left with ZERO balance in my account...[65]

In its response, the company agreed to reimburse the consumer for their lost funds.

3.3.2 Scammers impersonating influencers on social media

Some scammers try to use social media posts by crypto -asset influencers and celebrities to trick victims. For example, a scammer may impersonate a celebrity, influencer, or prominent crypto-asset developer or development team using verified (sometimes stolen) social media accounts or promotional videos to promote giveaways or "double your crypto" scams.[66]

A consumer complained about losing over ten thousand dollars' worth of crypto-assets to a scammer impersonating a crypto-asset development team:

Commencing on or about November 15, 2021, I fell victim to a multilayered scam operation orchestrated by Fake Representatives of [crypto-asset] Giveaway (the "Scammer"), using web address (the "Scam Website"), all of which aim at contributing to the goal of robbing and defrauding clients, through a predetermined cycle of the client's losses to their gains. The equivalent of 10,177.70 USD (5000.18 [crypto-asset]) was transferred from my wallet utilizing [crypto- asset platform] services.[67]

The CFPB has also received complaints from consumers about scams being promoted by scammers impersonating crypto-asset developers and founders on other

---

65. Consumer Complaint 5191424, https://www.consumerfinance.gov/data-research/consumer -complaints/search/detail/5191424.

66. Molly White, *'Double your money' scammers capitalize on Ethereum merge*, Web3 is Going Great (Sep. 14, 2022), https://web3isgoinggreat.com/single/double-your-money-scammers-capitalize -on-ethereum-merge.

67. Consumer Complaint 5868008, https://www.consumerfinance.gov/data-research/consumer -complaints/search/detail/5868008.

websites such as YouTube. Another form of this scam is impersonating the official accounts of governments or nation states. In March 2022, the FTC warned of scammers soliciting crypto-asset donations to allegedly help people in Ukraine; instead, donations go to the scammer's crypto-asset wallet.[68]

3.4 Frozen accounts and platform bankruptcies

Several large crypto-asset platforms have recently either frozen customers' account withdrawals, filed for bankruptcy protection, or both. These failures have impacted millions of consumers.[69] At least one of the firms repeatedly misrepresented through official channels the nature of its Federal Deposit Insurance Corporation (FDIC) insurance, leading to confusion among consumers and, ultimately, a cease-and-desist order by other agencies.[70] Other crypto-asset websites and platforms have since received cease-and-desist orders from the FDIC regarding misleading language about FDIC insurance.[71]

The CFPB has received complaints from consumers related to their inability to access U.S. dollars in their account. A consumer's complaint highlighted that the company's actions contradict the disclosures it had made to consumers:

> I have an account with [crypto-asset platform]. They have recently froze my account and they are not allowing me any withdrawals at the moment. According to the disclosure these should not be affecting me. I have provided a copy of the disclosure to complete the research of this complaint.[72]

Another consumer complained about their inability to withdraw funds:

> I deposited $65k into [a digital] wallet and they just froze my account for withdrawing money. This is hard earned money I need to pay for medical expenses.[73]

Another consumer described how the company was unresponsive to their request for a wire transfer:

---

68. Rosario Méndez, *Donating with crypto? Watch out for scams*, Fed. Trade Comm'n (Mar. 25, 2022), https://consumer.ftc.gov/consumer-alerts/2022/03/donating-crypto-watch-out-scams.

69. *See, e.g.,* Cision PR Newswire, *supra* note 8 ("Total funded accounts reached 1,190,000 as of March 31, 2022") *See also* Vicky Ge Huang, *supra* note 8; Vick yGe Huang, *supra* note 8.

70. *See, e.g.,* Fed. Deposit Ins. Corp., Joint Letter Regarding Potential Violations of Section 18(a)(4) of the Federal Deposit Insurance Act (July 28, 2022), https://www.fdic.gov/news/press-releases/2022/pr22056a.pdf. *See also* Press Release, Fed. Bd. of Governors of the Fed. Rsrv. Sys., FDIC and Federal Reserve Board issue letter demanding Voyager Digital cease and desist from making false or misleading representations of deposit insurance status (July 28, 2022), https://www.federalreserve.gov/newsevents/pressreleases/bcreg20220728a.htm.

71. Press Release, Fed. Deposit Ins. Corp., FDIC Issues Cease and Desist Letters to Five Companies For Making Crypto- Related False or Misleading Representations about Deposit Insurance (Aug. 19, 2022), https://www.fdic.gov/news/press-releases/2022/pr22060.html.

72. Consumer Complaint (on file with author).

73. Consumer Complaint (on file with author).

I have around $150,000 worth of USD and digital currency there (mostly USD which they claim is FDIC insured…) - I want to withdraw all of my USD as quickly as possible because I am worried they will freeze withdrawals soon, the way the [another crypto-asset platform] did. I have been withdrawing $10,000 / day for 6 days now, but I decided early yesterday to open a support ticket requesting a wire transfer because their website says they offer wire transfers for $50 per. They have not responded to this ticket and a friend of mine opened a ticket days ago requesting the same thing and got no response.[74]

Still another consumer reported the same issue with a wire transfer:

On [date and time] I provided instructions for an outgoing wire in the amount of [over $200,000]. I then emailed the company and have not received the wire nor response from the company since that time. The wire was coming to a personal bank account of mine. I also do know that they got my emails because they responded to other mails.[75]

The CFPB also received complaints about another crypto-asset platform that froze consumers' assets and recently filed for bankruptcy protection. For example, a consumer described how the company had misled them:

I am a customer with [a crypto-asset platform] that recently froze withdrawals. I had no loan products and only bought a stablecoin, [crypto-asset], which is pegged to the US dollar and has not been depegged. [The crypto-asset platform] misled me when I deposited approximately $5000 USD into their exchange with the promise that it could be withdrawn at will. My most recent balance is approximately $5300 [crypto-asset].[76]

3.5 Crypto-asset card complaints

Many crypto-asset platforms offer products marketed by companies as credit, debit, or prepaid cards with various features, including offering rewards in crypto-assets. Consumers submitted complaints about credit cards and prepaid cards in which they reported several problems using these crypto-asset cards, including the inability to make purchases, issues closing their account, rejecting their claims for reimbursement on fraudulent charges, or failing to receive advertised rewards. A consumer stated that they would like "my credit card to work when I use it, or to know why a certain retailer or transaction was blocked," and was not receiving this resolution from their crypto-asset reward card:

---

74. Consumer Complaint (on file with author).

75. Consumer Complaint (on file with author).

76. Consumer Complaint 5675592, https://www.consumerfinance.gov/data-research/consumer-complaints/search/detail/5675592.

I have the [crypto-asset platform] card, it regularly gets rejected, or stops working for no reason. I have opened up multiple tickets, and there is never any resolution, they just say that 'a fraud prevention algorithm prevented the transaction'. And this is after multiple support calls, where they are completely unable to tell me why my card isn't working. [77]

A consumer complained about not receiving rewards from their credit card, and then having trouble closing their account once they were told they will not receive the advertised crypto- asset rewards feature:

I obtained the [crypto-asset platform] card because they allowed your rewards to be used to buy Crypto... Now they say that they don't know why the feature is not working and there is nothing they can do about it. Now, I asked them to close the account and they are giving me the run around saying I need to contact a third-party bank?! [78]

Another consumer complained that they failed to receive an advertised sign-up bonus after meeting the terms specified by the rewards card. The company replied that its offer may be redeemed only by the eligible participant and that "such eligibility to be determined by [company] in its sole discretion." [79]

4. Impact on special populations

The use of crypto-assets varies across different communities, and some reports have noted concerns about risks crypto-assets pose to younger populations[80] and Black and Latino communities. [81] Older consumers and servicemembers are just two populations of special interest to the CFPB, as they can be disproportionately impacted by problems with financial products and services and can also face special

---

77. Consumer Complaint 5787938, https://www.consumerfinance.gov/data-research/consumer-complaints/search/detail/5787938.

78. Consumer Complaint 5029504, https://www.consumerfinance.gov/data-research/consume-complaints/search/detail/5029504.

79. Consumer Complaint 5566854, https://www.consumerfinance.gov/data-research/consumer-complaints/search/detail/5566854.

80. *See, e.g.*, Cheyenne DeVon, "Only about 30% of millennials are comfortable investing in crypto, down from about 50% in 2021: 'The shine has come off these coins'", CNBC (Sep. 29, 2022), https://www.cnbc.com/2022/09/29/millennial-investors-are-getting-less-comfortable-with-crypto currency.html.

81. *See, e.g.*, Terri Bradford, *The Cryptic Nature of Black Consumer Cryptocurrency Ownership*, Federal Reserve Bank of Kansas City (Jun.1,2022), https://www.kansascityfed.org/research/payments-system-research-briefings/the-cryptic-nature-of-black-consumer-cryptocurrency-ownership; Paulina Cachero, *Crypto Collapse Threatens to Leave Black, Hispanic Investors Further Behind*, Bloomberg (Jul. 7, 2022), https://www.bloomberg.com/news/articles/2022-07-07/crypto-collapse-threatens-to-leave-black-hispanic- investors-further-behind.

concerns and constraints on solving these problems.[82] For these populations, crypto-assets are no exception.

4.1 Older consumers

Cybercrime losses in general among older consumers are increasing steeply, in general. A 2021 report from the FBI states, "[i]n 2021, over 92,000 victims over the age of 60 reported losses of $1.7 billion to the [Internet Crime Complaint Center] IC3. This represents a 74 percent increase in losses over losses reported in 2020."[83] The CFPB has observed an increase in complaints about crypto-assets submitted by older consumers (Figure 8), especially complaints involving

frauds and scams (Figure 9). Other research also indicates that older consumers' losses as a result of crypto-asset scams are larger than any other age group.[84]

FIGURE 8: COUNT OF VIRTUAL CURRENCY COMPLAINTS SUBMITTED BY OLDER CONSUMERS, OCT. 2018 TO SEPT. 2022

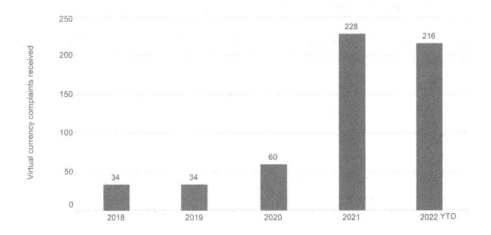

---

82. "Service members" and "older consumers" are both self-identified. Servicemembers refers to servicemembers, veterans, and military families. "Older consumers" refers to consumers who voluntarily reported their age as 62 or older.

83. Fed. Bureau of Investigation, Elder Fraud Report (2021), https://www.ic3.gov/Media/PDF/AnnualReport/2021_IC3ElderFraudReport.pdf.

84. *See, e.g.,* Fed. Trade Comm'n, *supra* note 1 ("median individual reported losses have tended to increase with age, topping out at $11,708 for people in their 70s").

FIGURE 9: VIRTUAL CURRENCY COMPLAINTS SUBMITTED BY OLDER CONSUMERS BY ISSUE OVER TIME, OCT. 2018 TO SEPT. 2022

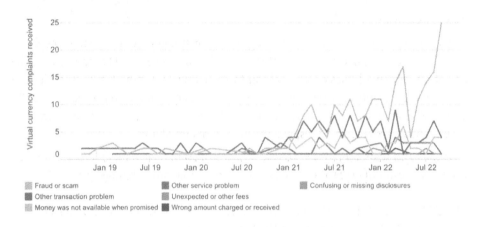

Of the total virtual currency complaints submitted by older consumers since October 2018, more than 44% were about fraud and scams (Figure 10).

FIGURE 10: VIRTUAL CURRENCY COMPLAINTS SUBMITTED BY OLDER CONSUMERS BY ISSUE, OCT. 2018 TO SEPT. 2022

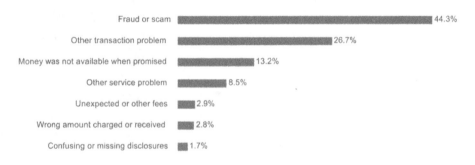

In one instance, a consumer lost their life savings after two fake customer support scams:

> I have a [crypto-asset] account I have or had over 162,000.00 in it. I was seeking help for a problem [withdrawing crypto-assets from another platform and] the support team there sent me to [a] chat where I was scammed for 5 [crypto-asset] out of my [crypto-asset platform] account...I contacted [the crypto-asset platform support and] I got a case number. Then right after that a thing called Official Support pops up I asked if they were from [the platform], and they said they handle [problems with that platform]...I told them about the scam on the [crypto-asset] and he or she said for me to send them a copy of the withdraw address. I did and they said the [crypto-asset] hasn't made it

to the scammer's wallet yet, so I said great can you get it back and they said yes. Well, they even sent me a [official documents from the platform] I had to e-sign saying they could lose the [crypto- asset] in the process. I signed [and] they asked some personal questions. I said I don't know if I should answer, but they keep saying we are the official [platform] support…so I answered them so after a while things goes south they froze my account but keep assuring me it's a part of the process…

Well [in March 2021] I get a email from the bank saying I'm overdrawn on my checking…sure enough someone tried to withdraw 17,900.00 out of my checking [but] the bank stop all but 2500.00 cause that's what I had in it. Anyhow now I felt scammed out of my life savings. I'm 67 and not tech savvy. I don't understand how this could happen…

Anyhow if you ever dealt with [the platform's customer support, it] is very bad to say the least. After a couple more tries on [date] they answered my account was still frozen I told them the story and I need to check my account they told me its locked cause I owe them money so that told me the scammer took all my money and now I owe [because the platform] has a thing where if you commit to a withdraw from your bank which means a deposit to them you can have the money right away so that's how the scammers got the money from my checking account and since the bank stopped the withdraw cause I couldn't cover it…so now I owe [the platform] money.

So, all I did was went to [the platform's] customer service and put my trust in them [and] I'm out 162,000 plus 17,900 owed to [the platform]. That's 179,900.00. Now I'm 67 with a heart condition and within less than a week I'm broke. Please I'm begging help me I feel [the platform] failed to keep my account secure as no one should go to [the platform] support and have someone help them that's a scammer… [85]

In response, the company stated that the consumer was a victim of a scam, and that the funds were not recoverable.

4.2 Servicemembers

Hundreds of servicemember complaints to the CFPB involved crypto-assets or crypto platforms in the last several years (Figure 11), and complaints include reports of scams targeting servicemembers through identity theft or romance scams.

---

85. Consumer Complaint 4252242, https://www.consumerfinance.gov/data-research/consumer-complaints/search/detail/4252242.

FIGURE 11: COUNT OF VIRTUAL CURRENCY COMPLAINTS SUBMITTED BY SERVICEMEMBERS, OCT. 2018 TO SEPT. 2022

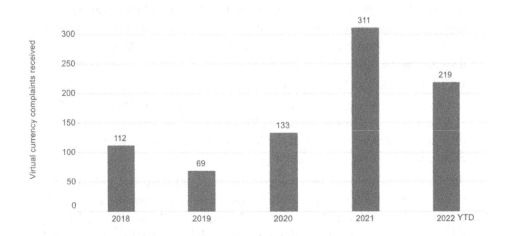

Of the total virtual currency complaints submitted by servicemembers since October 2018, more than 37% were about fraud and scams (Figure 12).

FIGURE 12: VIRTUAL CURRENCY COMPLAINTS SUBMITTED BY SERVICE-MEMBERS BY ISSUE, OCT. 2018 TO SEPT. 2022

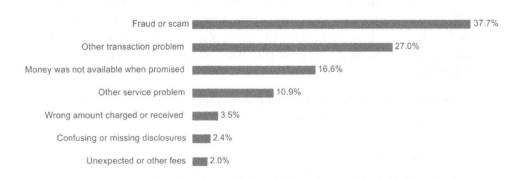

The CFPB has seen a significant increase in complaints about fraud and scams submitted in the past 12 months (Figure 13). From October 2021, to September 1, 2022, approximately 42% of total virtual currency complaints from servicemembers were about as frauds or scams.

FIGURE 13: VIRTUAL CURRENCY COMPLAINTS SUBMITTED BY SERVICE-MEMBERS BY ISSUE OVER TIME, OCT. 2018 TO SEPT. 2022

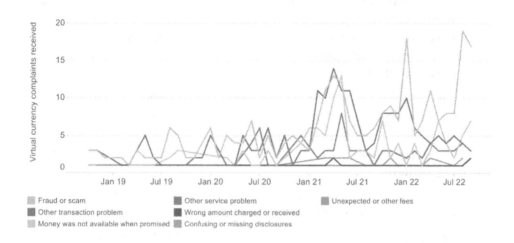

In one complaint, a servicemember stated that they had lost crypto-assets as the result of identity theft, despite taking extensive steps to stop the fraudulent transactions from taking place:

> I would like to report unauthorized transactions made on my [crypto-asset platform] account. This is to ensure [crypto-asset platform] is advised of all steps taken by me, in an effort to work with [crypto-asset platform] to resolve this matter and regain access to my [crypto-asset platform] account.

> [Date]: Text came that my [mobile] password was reset. On [my cell phone], I get text that [crypto-asset platform] password was reset. Asked [cell phone company] for SIM Lock & Port Freeze. [Cell phone company] rep reset my PIN, changed password.

> [Date]: Called Internet Service Provider...to change password on email used to login to the T-Mobile and [crypto-asset platform].

> [Date]: Received emails from [crypto-asset platform] for following four unauthorized transactions: 1) $104.79, 2) $400.00, 3) $80.63, 4) $35,000.00. I called [crypto-asset platform]...to deactivate my account and completed online form providing details. I received [crypto-asset platform] email...with directions to take security precautions and reply back when ready to restore access to my account. On 4/13/21, I completed all precautions and replied to [crypto-asset platform] to restore access to account.

[Date]: [Bank] shows 2 transactions pending; stop payment on both $400 and $35,000. Changed all banking and credit card passwords.

[Date]: Called [cell phone company]. [Customer service representative] said someone accessed [my] account on 4/12/21, reset password, changed SIM card number within T-[my] account. That allowed criminal to make unauthorized transactions remotely from a new SIM card and phone. [Customer service representative] put port freeze and SIM lock on account.

[Date]: Email response from [crypto-asset platform] state they are working with a specialist to address this issue; to follow-up as soon as they have update.

[Date]: Email from [crypto-asset platform] stated the $35,000.00 and the $400.00 transactions failed. If I don't take action, in 5 days they initiate automatic recovery.

[Date]: I Email [crypto-asset platform] with additional information and request status of their investigation of this issue.

[Date]: I sent online inquiry to [crypto-asset platform] for status update and request account access. They replied by email and have passed all my info on to an account specialist reviewing the case; state it generally takes 4–5 business days.

[Date]: I sent email inquiry to [crypto-asset platform] asking for account specialist to respond with update and help me restore access to my [crypto-asset platform] account.

[Date]: [Officer from county] Sheriff's Department took info and documentation to share with investigators in his office and file police report regarding the unauthorized transactions reported to [crypto-asset platform].

[Date]: I filed identity theft report with the Federal Trade Commission regarding the unauthorized transactions reported to [crypto -asset platform].

[Date]: I sent email inquiry to [crypto-asset platform] asking for account specialist to respond with update and help me restore access to my [crypto-asset platform] account...[86]

In response, the company stated that the consumer was a victim of a SIM swap hack. The company also stated that it could not reimburse the consumer, and that the consumer also would need to repay the company over $3500 as a result of the reversed transaction.

---

86. Consumer Complaint 4358006, https://www.consumerfinance.gov/data-research/consumer-complaints/search/detail/4358006.

5. Discussion

Common among the issues described by consumers in their complaints as discussed in the preceding sections challenges holding companies accountable when consumers experience a problem.

Issue resolution

Consumer complaint outcomes vary widely. In situations where a consumer is facing a technical issue or a problem accessing their account or crypto-assets, they are often able to get the help they need to reestablish access, or at least beginning the process—although as discussed, the wait may be long.

But in situations where consumers have had assets stolen, or had their account hacked, they are often told there is nowhere to turn for help. In one complaint, a consumer reported a loss of their life savings in a scam, which the company stated was not recoverable:

> On [Date], my cell phone, email & [crypto-asset platform] wallet were all hacked.
>
> At around 9:00 PM I turned on my cell phone and realized it wasn't working- I couldn't make any calls and wasn't receiving any messages. When I got in contact with [wireless company] (using my wife's phone), they had advised someone earlier in the day asked to switch the SIM from my iPhone 13 Pro to their iPhone 7...
>
> While on the phone with [wireless company], I had also called [crypto-asset platform] to lock my account. However, the damage was already done. A day later, when I regained access to my [crypto-asset platform] account, I was able to see all the trades this scammer had done... [H]e had sent fractions of the total [crypto- asset] holdings & in 1,000+ (clear fraud & suspicious) transactions sent it all to unknown addresses/ wallets...
>
> Around $70,000 was stolen. The scammer offloaded all the Bitcoin in hundreds of transactions, $15.28 at a time. Isn't it suspicious?? Who would do so many transactions to the same wallet? Isn't it obvious a fraud occurred?
>
> Below is 1 of 1,000+ transactions [the crypto-asset platform] allowed a scammer to withdraw from my [crypto-asset platform] wallet/ my entire life savings....
>
> [Crypto-asset platform] refuses to help and there's no one to call, "sorry, we can only interact via email." I've sent multiple emails and all they say is "we are looking into it", "there's nothing we can do once the money has left your wallet" and "to call the authorities". I went to the authorities, and they need me to provide the hashtags/ transactions to where the crypto was sent. I asked [crypto-asset platform] to investigate this for me, as I tried every way to do it myself on [crypto-asset platform], and they responded, "that's going to be very

hard to do." As to how they let clear fraud and suspicious activity happen is beyond me. But maybe they don't care, as they made a lot of money on these transaction fees. They really need to [be] investigated and held responsible. They do not have proper measures in place and soon enough it's going to happen to many more people...[87]

Fraudulent transactions and platform responses

The complaint above also raises the question of whether crypto-asset platforms are effectively identifying and stopping fraudulent transactions. The pattern mentioned above—hundreds of small transactions to the same wallet—suggests that scammers may be aware of existing controls and purposefully avoiding them. There are Anti-Money Laundering (AML) and Countering the Financing of Terrorism (CFT) obligations under the Bank Secrecy Act required for financial institutions. These obligations include requirements to establish and implement effective, risk-based anti-money laundering programs and recordkeeping and reporting requirements, including the filing of suspicious activity reports (SARs).[88] But as noted by the Department of Justice, there remain significant vulnerabilities: "criminals continue to take advantage of noncompliant actors—including noncompliant cryptocurrency exchanges, peer-to-peer exchangers, or automated cryptocurrency kiosks—to exchange their cryptocurrency for cash or other digital assets without facing rigorous AML/CFT scrutiny."[89]

Some crypto-asset platforms appear only to be taking steps to verify the authority of a person to act on behalf of a customer after receiving a complaint from that customer, and often only after several escalations by that customer.

Crypto-asset platforms sometimes hide behind terms and conditions

In situations where consumers are having problems with a crypto -asset platform or wallet that does not involve fraud or technical issues, companies sometimes cite boilerplate user agreement language to absolve themselves of responsibility.

---

87. Consumer Complaint 5545300, https://www.consumerfinance.gov/data-research/consumer -complaints/search/detail/5545300.

88. *See* Joint Statement of Commodity Futures Trading Comm'n, Fin. Crimes Enforcement Network, & U.S. Sec. and Exchange Comm'n, *Leaders of CFTC, FinCEN, and SEC Issue Joint Statement on Activities Involving Digital Assets* (Oct. 11, 2019), https://www.sec.gov/news/public-statement /cftc-fincen-secjointstatementdigitalassets. *See also* Fin. Crimes Enforcement Network, Application of FinCEN's Regulations to Certain Business Models Involving Convertible Virtual Currencies (May 9, 2019), https://www.fincen.gov/resources/statutes- regulations/guidance/application-fincens -regulations-certain-business-models.

89. U.S. Dep't of Just., The Role Of Law Enforcement In Detecting, Investigating, And Prosecuting Criminal Activity Related To Digital Assets (Sept. 6, 2022), https://www.justice.gov/ag/page /file/1535236/download.

For example, one consumer complained that their crypto-asset lender blocked access to $18,000 of the consumer's assets due to "liquidity issues." In its response, the company cited its terms of use, which stated in part "that [the company] may experience extreme market conditions which could result in the pausing of withdrawals and transfers between accounts from the user's [account]." The company also directed the consumer to a blog post which stated that the company had "paused all withdrawals and transfers between accounts due to extreme market conditions until further notice."[90] At this writing, withdrawals and transfers are still unavailable at this crypto-asset platform.

Consumers have also submitted complaints, reporting that some crypto-asset platforms have incorporated arbitration clauses into their terms and conditions that requires consumer to resolve disputes through arbitration. For example, according to a consumer:

> Prior to the end of January 2022, I enrolled as a member of a class action lawsuit against [crypto-asset platform] for charging undisclosed transaction fees while advertising no fee transactions. . . . At the end of January 2022, [crypto-asset platform] updated its terms of service to require anyone using their site agree to binding arbitration for any disputes between them and a user, past, present, or future. As such, users who are party to the class action are rendered unable to access their accounts in order to download data necessary for income tax reporting without first agreeing to the updated terms of service. This is a flagrantly unconscionable and abusive practice.[91]

Some consumers are bringing actions that are challenging these arbitration clauses.[92]

6. Consumer risks and resources

Generally, providers of consumer financial products and services offering crypto-assets and related services, and consumers who want to use crypto-assets should remember some key facts and risks. There are also some steps consumers can take to protect themselves.

Key facts and risks

- **Crypto-assets are a common target for hacking.** Crypto platforms are a frequent target of hacks by malicious actors, including certain nation-state actors. Hackers affiliated with one nation state have stolen over $2 billion

---

90. Consumer Complaint 5687115, https://www.consumerfinance.gov/data-research/consumer-complaints/search/detail/5687115.

91. Consumer Complaint (on file with author).

92. *See* Bielski v. Coinbase, Inc., No. C 21-07478 WHA, 2022 WL 1062049 (civil action against a crypto-asset platform in which the court denied the platform's motion to compel arbitration).

in crypto-assets total,[93] including more than \$1 billion from Jan 2022 to July 2022 alone,[94] and their hacks have included several prominent crypto platforms, including a "play to earn" crypto-asset game.[95] The top 10 crypto-asset hacks alone have amounted to over \$2.5 billion in losses from August 2021 to November 2022 according to one industry report.[96]

- **Important terms and clarifications are often buried in the Terms and Conditions:** It is important that consumers read the agreement between them and their wallet provider and crypto-asset platform (often found under "Terms and Conditions" sections). If questions arise as to what rights you may have under the agreement, reach out to the wallet provider or crypto-asset platform for a written answer.

- **Arbitration clauses and class action bans may limit dispute options.** Many crypto-asset platforms and associated service providers use dispute resolution mechanisms such as mandatory arbitration clauses and class action bans that inhibit consumers' and investors' ability to pursue legal claims.[97]

- **The value of crypto-assets have and will likely continue to fluctuate greatly.** It is important that consumers be aware of the risk of financial loss when acquiring crypto-assets. Consumers have reported losing their savings after acquiring crypto-assets because the value decreased significantly.

- **Transactions may not be as private as imagined.** Many crypto-asset transactions are recorded on publicly accessible blockchains, and those transactions are associated with a crypto-asset address. People with the correct knowledge and motivation maybe be able to link those transactions and the crypto address with a consumer's identity or their other transactions. In addition, in the bankruptcy proceeding of one crypto-asset platform, the names and recent transactions of all customers were published.[98]

- **The use of crypto-assets may violate sanctions.** On certain blockchains, a consumer's transaction may be validated by an anonymous entity and/ or a sanctioned person, as blockchain users cannot choose their miner or validator.[99]

Steps consumers can take to protect themselves

---

93. *See, e.g.,* Elliptic Connect, *supra* note 3.

94. *See, e.g.,* Choe Sang-Hun and David Yaffe-Bellany, *supra* note 4.

95. *See* Statement, Fed. Bureau of Investigation, *supra* note 5. *See also* Aaron Schaffer, *supra* note 5.

96. Rekt News, Leaderboard, https://rekt.news/leaderboard/.

97. U.S. Dep't of the Treasury, *supra* note 10 at 33.

98. *See, e.g.,* Matt Novak, *Celsius Execs Cashed out at Least \$17 Million in Crypto Before Halting Withdrawals for Customers*, Gizmodo (Oct. 6, 2022), https://gizmodo.com/celsius-execs-cashed-out-bitcoin-price-crypto-ponzi- 1849623526.

99. Fin. Stability Oversight Council, *supra* note 6 at 44.

- **Watch out for signs of a scam.** Beware of claims promising huge rates of return. No legitimate government or business will require a consumer to buy crypto-assets. If they do, it is a scam.[100]

- **Don't mix crypto-assets and romance.** Consumers should be very careful if a new love interest, especially one they have never met in person, wants to show them how to invest in crypto-assets or asks them to send crypto. It is probably a scam.[101]

- **Know who you are dealing with.** Consumers should make sure they know how to contact the platform if something goes wrong with a crypto-asset transaction. Some crypto-asset platforms do not identify their owners, their phone numbers and addresses, or even the countries where they are located.

- **Understand what the actual costs will be.** Know there levantex change rate and how it was determined. Find out in advance about mark-ups to the exchange rate or other fees. Find out how long the transaction will take to complete.

- **Access resources.** Both the CFPB and the FTC offer online resources to help consumers spot and avoid crypto-asset scams and theft. The FTC has published an online guide titled "What to Know About Cryptocurrency and Scams," while the CFPB released the consumer advisory "Risks to consumers posed by virtual currencies."

- **Report any suspicious claims of FDIC insurance.** If crypto-asset or other firms misuse the name or logo of the FDIC or engage in false advertising or make misrepresentations to consumers about deposit insurance, it likely violates the Consumer Financial Protection Act's prohibition on deception, whether or not such conduct is engaged in knowingly.[102] If consumers suspect a platform may be making false claims about FDIC insurance, they can submit a complaint to the CFPB.

- **Submit a complaint to the CFPB.** If consumers have a problem with a consumer financial product or service, they can submit a complaint online or by calling (855) 411-2372.

---

100. *See, e.g.,* Consumer Fin. Prot. Bureau, Fraud and scams, https://www.consumerfinance.gov/consumer-tools/fraud/.

101. *See, e.g.,* Consumer Fin. Prot. Bureau, Money Smart for Older Adults: avoid financial exploitation, https://www.consumerfinance.gov/consumer-tools/educator-tools/resources-for-older-adults/money-smart-for- older-adults.

102. Consumer Fin. Prot. Bureau, Consumer Financial Protection Circular 2022-02: Deceptive representations involving the FDIC's name or logo or deposit insurance, https://www.consumerfinance.gov/compliance/circulars/circular-2022-02-deception-representations-involving-the-fdics-name-or-logo-or-deposit-insurance/.

Discussion Points

1. *Consumer Financial Protection Bureau (CFPB).* Why do you think the CFPB has received an uptick in complaints related to crypto-related assets? What role do you think the CFPB should have in preventing fraud, theft, and other scams related to crypto-assets? How can it offer greater protection to consumers?

2. *CFPB Regulation.* Should the CFPB implement regulations concerning crypto-asset platforms? If so, what kinds of regulations do you think would deter illicit activity? Should the CFPB organize a committee to monitor suspicious activity that poses a threat to consumers? Why or why not?

3. Describe the main types of consumer complaints discussed in the bulletin as it relates to crypto-assets and the types of specific issues consumers seem to encounter in these complaints.

4. How does the bulletin address the importance of consumer education and awareness regarding the risks and characteristics of crypto-assets?

5. Identify and explain any emerging trends or developments in the crypto-asset industry that may have contributed to consumer complaints.

Eleven

International Laws

I. Introduction

The cryptocurrency space was complicated even before governments started getting involved in its regulation. As the use of cryptocurrency increases and cryptocurrency exchanges become more prevalent, so do regulations and policies. The cryptocurrency space is constantly evolving and keeping up with the regulations of different global jurisdictions is challenging as rules can vary significantly among countries. This chapter will explore various regulatory approaches of different countries.

II. The United Kingdom

In the United Kingdom, cryptocurrency regulations have grown in the post-Brexit financial landscape. Previously enacted cryptocurrency regulations had already been in place once the United Kingdom left the European Union in 2020. However, the Bank of England and Financial Conduct Authority ("FCA") have issued warnings about the usage of cryptocurrency. To combat the many issues that come with cryptocurrencies, the United Kingdom government created a Cryptoassets Taskforce in 2018. His Majesty's Treasury, Bank of England (BoE), and the Financial Conduct Authority (FCA) work collaboratively to initiate policy responses to the impact of crypto assets and distributed ledger technology (DLT). The government of the United Kingdom has also published a Cryptoassets Manual which contains guidance on the tax liabilities that are associated with cryptocurrency holders.

Crypto asset firms that provide services to U.K. residents, or have a presence or market in the U.K., must be registered with the FCA. FCA guidance also requires that any entity engaging in cryptocurrency assets must comply with the Money Laundering, Terrorist Financing and Transfer of Funds Regulations (MLRSs).

In 2021, the FCA banned retail cryptocurrency derivatives to protect consumers from market volatility. Unregulated transferable crypto assets are tokens, such as Bitcoin and Ether, which are not "specified investments" that can be traded. The FCA estimates that because of this ban, retail consumers will save around £53 million a year. The FCA banned the sale of cryptocurrency derivatives because the FCA believes the products are "ill-suited for retail consumers due to the harm they pose."

Financial Conduct Authority (FCA): Prohibiting the Sale to Retail Clients of Investment Products That Reference Cryptoassets

Policy Statement PS2/10 (October 2020)

1 Summary

In July 2019, we published Consultation Paper (CP)19/22—Prohibiting the sale to retail clients of investment products that reference cryptoassets. We consulted on rules to ban the marketing, distribution and sale of derivatives and exchange traded notes (ETNs) that reference certain types of cryptoassets to retail consumers. References to 'retail consumers' refers to 'retail clients' as in COBS 3.4.

The consultation fulfilled our commitment in the Cryptoassets Task Force Report, published in October 2018. The Task Force (CATF) consisted of the Treasury, the FCA and the Bank of England.

This Policy Statement (PS) summarises the consultation feedback we received. It sets out our final policy position and Handbook rules that will come into force on 28 October 2020.

Having considered the feedback, we are confirming the rules as consulted on, subject to some minor, technical amendments.

The rules will come into force on 6 January 2021 after the end of the transition period which has operated since the UK's departure from the EU on 31 January 2020. We have therefore amended the rules to reflect the end of the transition period and to ensure that the rules continue to apply to the same firms as would have been subject to the rules before that point. Due to a delay in publishing this Policy Statement, we amended the coming-into-force date of the rules after the rules were made to give firms more time to prepare for them.

Who this affects

Our proposals will directly affect:

- firms issuing or creating products referencing cryptoassets
- firms distributing products referencing cryptoassets, including brokers, investment platforms, and financial advisers
- firms marketing products referencing cryptoassets
- operators of trading venues and platforms
- retail consumers and consumer organisations

This is not a complete list, and the PS is likely to be relevant to other stakeholders, both regulated and unregulated.

The wider context of this policy statement

Our consultation

The concerns we outlined in CP19/22 are consistent with the CATF report. We consider that retail consumers cannot reliably assess the value and risks of derivatives and exchange traded notes that reference certain cryptoassets. This is due to the:

- nature of the underlying assets, which have no inherent value and so differ from other assets that have physical uses, promise future cash flows or are legally accepted as money

- presence of market abuse and financial crime (including cyberthefts from cryptoasset platforms) in cryptoasset markets

- extreme volatility in cryptoasset prices

- inadequate understanding of cryptoassets by retail consumers and the lack of a clear investment need for investment products referencing them

As a result, we think that retail consumers will suffer harm from potentially sudden and unexpected losses if they buy these products.

How it links to our objectives

This prohibition advances our objective of ensuring an appropriate degree of protection for consumers and supports our objective of protecting and enhancing the integrity of the UK financial system.

What we are changing and what outcomes we are seeking

We are prohibiting the marketing, distribution and sale in or from the UK to all retail clients, of derivatives and ETNs that reference certain types of unregulated, transferable cryptoassets.

Covid-19

Covid-19 is having a significant impact on firms and the wider economy and we have considered whether this is the right time to bring in the prohibition given the current circumstances. The risk of harm which the prohibition intends to address has not gone away as a result of COVID-19 and we think there is still a need to make the rules to protect consumers. We have, however, delayed publication of this Policy Statement and the implementation date so as to avoid imposing additional implementation work during the period when firms have been most impacted by Covid-19.

Since March 2020 we have continued to see extreme volatility in cryptoasset markets in line with other periods of price movements for cryptoassets. Our analysis of the harms from unregulated transferable cryptoassets has not changed.

Measuring success

Our intervention will be successful if we reduce the harm to retail consumers from buying crypto-derivatives.

We have updated our cost benefit analysis (CBA) to include additional data on client outcomes obtained since CP19/22. We now estimate that a ban on the sale, marketing and distribution of crypto-derivatives to retail consumers could reduce overall consumer losses by between £19m and £101m per year. Based on additional client data, in response to feedback and over a longer period, expected benefits are lower than our estimates of a reduction of consumer losses of between £75m to £234.3m in CP19/22. This reduction in losses is in large part because of leverage limits imposed on CFD trading by ESMA and the FCA.

Summary of feedback and our response

The consultation closed on 3 October 2019. We received 527 responses. These responses were from firms, trade bodies, retail consumers and EU national competent authorities (NCAs).

Respondents focused on:

- our argument that cryptoassets do not have intrinsic value, and that retail consumers are unable to value them reliably
- how proportionate a prohibition is and whether other, less restrictive measures would achieve our policy objectives
- our supporting CBA

Chapter 2 of this PS summarises the feedback we received and our response. Appendix 1 sets out our final rules.

Equality and diversity considerations

One individual commented on our equality impact assessment. They argued that because cryptoasset investors, not derivative investors, are mostly male and between the ages of 20 and 44, the policy will disproportionately affect younger, male consumers.

Even though age and sex are relevant protected characteristics under the Equalities Act, this information has not changed our assessment. The prohibition of crypto-derivatives is designed to protect all retail investors, and will apply to all investors regardless of their protected characteristics.

Our assessment of the impact of these changes on groups with protected characteristics remains unchanged from Consultation Paper CP19/22. We do not consider that this policy adversely impacts any of the groups with protected characteristics ie age, disability, sex, marriage or civil partnership, pregnancy and maternity, race, religion and belief, sexual orientation and gender reassignment.

Next steps

If your firm carries out marketing, distribution or selling activities in, or from, the UK of the relevant products to retail clients, you are required to cease these activities by 6 January 2021.

Retail consumers with existing holdings can remain invested following the prohibition, until they choose to disinvest. There is no time limit on this, and we do not require or expect firms to close out retail consumers' positions unless consumers ask for this.

The rules apply to:

- MiFID investment firms, including Capital Requirements Directive (CRD) credit institutions as appropriate, who are marketing, distributing or selling crypto-derivatives in, or from, the UK to retail clients.

- MiFID optional exemption firms who are marketing, distributing or selling crypto-derivatives in, or from, the UK to retail clients.

- UK branches of third-country investment firms who are marketing, distributing or selling crypto-derivatives in, or from, the UK to retail clients.

- EEA MiFID investment firms which currently passport into the UK and which continue operating in the UK after 6 January 2021 under the temporary permissions regime or the financial services contracts regimes. The UK left the EU on 31 January 2020 with a Withdrawal Agreement. It has entered a transition period which is due to operate until 31 December 2020. When the transition period ends, EEA firms which currently passport into the UK and wish to continue operating in the UK will be subject to the temporary permissions regime or the financial services contracts regime (which covers supervised run-off firms and contractual run-off firms). We intend that our rules will apply to those firms in the same way that they apply to other firms.

We remind UK and third-country investment firms that the FCA regulates certain activities, such as dealing, arranging, advising, when carried on in relation to derivative instruments which reference or are backed by cryptoassets ('crypto-derivatives'). Carrying on these regulated activities in the UK generally requires authorisation.

What we will do next

We expect firms to comply with the prohibition. Our supervision in this area will focus on:

- attempts to avoid the effect of our new Handbook rules by:

  - inappropriately 'opting up' retail clients to become elective professional clients

  - moving retail consumers to associated non-UK entities

- the conduct of inward passporting firms operating under the Temporary Permissions Regime

We will keep this prohibition under review in line with Article 42(6) of the Market in Financial Instruments Regulation (MiFIR). We will consider whether there is a need to review the prohibition if we see robust evidence indicating that the cryptoasset market has changed in ways which materially tackle the drivers of the harms we have identified.

2 Our response to consultation feedback

In CP19/22, we asked for views on our proposal to prohibit the sale, marketing and distribution of crypto-derivatives in, or from, the UK to retail consumers because of our concerns about the actual and potential harm these investments cause.

We received 527 responses to the consultation from a range of stakeholders including:

- firms that sell crypto-derivatives
- firms that issue crypto-ETNs
- exchanges that offer crypto-derivatives and unregulated cryptoassets
- firms involved in cryptoassets
- trade bodies representing cryptoasset firms
- trade bodies representing regulated exchanges
- an association representing law firms
- National Competent Authorities (NCAs)
- individuals, including retail consumers, a legal professional, and an academic

Most respondents (97%) opposed our proposal arguing that:

- cryptoassets have intrinsic value
- retail consumers are capable of valuing cryptoassets
- a prohibition was disproportionate and other measures could achieve our objectives
- our CBA did not represent accurately the costs and benefits of banning crypto-derivatives sold to retail consumers

Our response to the consultation feedback only applies to products referencing unregulated transferable cryptoassets that are within scope of our proposed ban.

It does not relate to security tokens (ie those that qualify as specified investments), which are within our regulatory remit. Derivatives referencing security tokens are not within scope of our ban.

Cryptoassets' intrinsic value

In CP19/22, we outlined why we think unregulated cryptoassets have no inherent value. They differ from other assets that have physical uses, promise future cash flows or are legally accepted as money.

We concluded that cryptoassets are opaque, complex and unreliable as reference assets for investments for retail consumers.

Some respondents argued that some cryptoassets have intrinsic value because they are:

- accepted as a means of payment for goods and services, highlighting that Starbucks and Microsoft accept bitcoin through a service offered by Bakkt (a US cryptoasset company backed by Intercontinental Exchange (ICE))
- readily exchanged for fiat currency on numerous exchanges
- limited in supply and can act as a potential store of value, like gold

Our Response

We recognise that some companies accept cryptoassets as a means of payment. These companies price their goods and services in fiat currency and convert the price into bitcoin at the time of sale. In effect, fiat currency remains the underlying medium of exchange. The Bank for International Settlements (BIS) states that cryptoassets cannot reliably provide the standard functions of money because they are currently too volatile to become accepted as a standard of value. Lower volatility is necessary for them to be widely accepted for purchasing goods and services.

We do not think that cryptoassets being exchanged for fiat currency equates to intrinsic value. We remain of the view that the price of cryptoassets is determined by sentiment and speculative behaviour. As a result, future valuations are highly subjective. We provide below our analysis of data supporting this view. This is because cryptoassets do not commonly have consistent valuations based on assumptions on dividends/coupons, or use of materials in production or consumption.

We recognise the argument that some cryptoassets could potentially act as a store of value in the future. To act as a genuine and reliable store of value, we think those cryptoassets would need to demonstrate that they are not prone to the same level of volatility that existing exchange tokens, such as bitcoin and ethereum, currently exhibit. Cryptoassets do not currently benefit from the same social, economic, cultural and physical-usage related factors that have established other assets as a store of value, such as gold.

We recognise that retail consumers may assign a subjective value to cryptoassets. However, this does not mean that they can value cryptoassets reliably or consistently, or the derivatives that reference them.

Businesses that have tested cryptoasset products in a controlled environment in the FCA's Sandbox have demonstrated that some cryptoassets (not their derivatives), can reduce costs and transaction times, particularly for cross-border payments. We recognise that cryptoassets can, in some circumstances, be beneficial to consumers. We will continue to help firms through our Innovate support functions, like 'Direct Support' and the Sandbox, where cryptoassets can potentially bring benefits to consumers and markets. We will also continue to consider whether our regulatory framework enables the legitimate use of cryptoassets, while managing the harms associated with some cryptoassets. These potential benefits do not, however, mean that unregulated cryptoassets are currently an appropriate underlying asset from which to price derivatives intended for sale to retail consumers.

The valuation of cryptoassets

We said that retail consumers cannot value cryptoassets reliably because they have no intrinsic value, and the valuation model inputs are subjective and vary significantly, which results in significant differences in valuations. Without a reliable model on which to base value, it is impossible for retail consumers reliably to value crypto-derivatives. This makes the risk of unexpected losses high.

CP19/22 contained analysis supporting our view that retail consumers are unable accurately to price cryptoassets and derivatives referencing them, including:

- price dislocation across exchanges—exchange data showing significant differences in bitcoin prices between exchanges over a 14-day period

- correlation between different cryptoassets—data showing a high correlation between different cryptoasset prices, supporting our view that cryptoasset prices are driven by speculative behaviour and sentiment rather than economic factors such as use or technological developments

- data demonstrating speculative behaviour—Google trends data (used as a proxy for retail consumers' interest in cryptoassets), showing a strong correlation between the prices of bitcoin and ethereum, and the number of Google searches for these cryptoassets.

Industry bodies, exchanges, and manufacturers of crypto-derivatives and ETNs said we had not considered valuation models adequately. They disagreed with us, believing that retail consumers are able to value cryptoassets accurately. To demonstrate this, they provided various examples of cryptoasset research and valuation methodologies. They argued these show cryptoassets can be valued like other assets that are the reference point for derivatives we allow to be sold to retail consumers.

The same respondents said that the volatility of cryptoassets does not mean that retail consumers cannot value them. They also said we should not ban crypto-derivatives on the grounds of volatility, as we allow firms to sell products to retail consumers with the same or higher levels of volatility. If cryptoassets can be reliably valued, then crypto-derivatives should be treated the same as other 'high risk' assets. That is, require leverage limits and enhanced disclosures.

One firm said that retail consumers are just as capable at valuing cryptoassets as institutional investors. Respondents also said that retail consumers are unable to value foreign exchange derivatives reliably.

Some firms argued that the data we relied on to demonstrate that cryptoassets cannot be valued reliably and are driven by speculative behaviour, was inaccurate and unrepresentative, and so misleading. They cited:

- Price dislocation across exchanges—the data we used to demonstrate divergence in cryptoasset prices across exchanges were not representative because the exchanges whose data we relied on were not reputable. They said we should not rely on data from a sample of exchanges that were suspected of publishing inaccurate trading volumes. One respondent said that the 14-day period (10 to 24 December 2017) was too short to be representative of the performance of cryptoasset markets.

- Correlation between cryptoasset prices—showing correlation between markets within the same general industry, does not demonstrate that markets are driven by speculative behaviour rather than economic factors. They said, for example, that equity indices (eg FTSE 100 and S&P 500) are also highly correlated.

- Demonstrate speculative behaviour—3 firms said that Google Trends data do not demonstrate that cryptoasset prices are driven by speculative behaviour, as we cannot demonstrate causality. These respondents said it was not clear whether higher prices led to higher search volumes on Google, or whether higher search volumes on Google led to higher prices. Another respondent argued that speculative behaviour is normal in well-functioning financial markets, and leads to price discovery.

Our Response

We analysed and considered the alternative valuation models provided (see Technical Annex). The models use a variety of techniques and factors to value cryptoassets, including different subjective inputs, suggesting there are no clear indicators to predict the price of cryptoassets reliably. The models produced a wide range of valuations from US$0 to US$50,000 for the same cryptoasset. As a result, the models provided by respondents support our conclusion that cryptoassets cannot be reliably valued.

We recognise that professional clients will face the same difficulties as retail consumers in reliably valuing cryptoassets. However, as stated in CP19/22, we think that professional clients and institutional investors may, in general, have greater understanding of the risks and greater capacity to absorb potential investment losses. So we are not extending the prohibition to professional clients.

We recognise that foreign exchange derivatives are difficult for retail consumers to value. But there are a set of objective valuation factors, such as interest rates, trade flows and economic growth, that inform their valuation. These factors do not apply in the same way to cryptoassets.

We have considered the feedback on the data we used to demonstrate that cryptoassets cannot be reliably valued. We then conducted the following additional analysis.

- Price dislocation across exchanges—in response to the feedback, we undertook further analysis of other exchanges to assist in our considerations around price dislocation, using data from a set of exchanges that respondents suggested better reflected actual trading values. We undertook additional analysis to examine the spreads across 5 different exchanges from January 2016 to December 2019. We chose these exchanges as they are all verified by the Blockchain Transparency Institute (BTI) which tests the accuracy of data collected from exchanges and monitors instances of wash-trading.

  This additional analysis reinforces our conclusions in CP19/22 that there is a wide dispersion between the spreads at the highest price on a given day. Between January 2016 and November 2019, we observe similar periods of sustained price dislocation between the sampled exchanges with spreads of over $1,500 across exchanges (see Technical Annex for further detail). The significant differences in prices across exchanges supports our conclusion that cryptoassets cannot be reliably valued.

- Correlation between cryptoasset prices—We analysed data from the 5 exchanges listed above over a longer period of time (January 2016 to December 2019). These show a high correlation between cryptoassets over a rolling 30-day period, and that the correlation increases over time (see Technical Annex for further detail).

We do not think the high correlation between equity indices (eg FTSE 100 and the S&P 500) is an appropriate comparison, as it does not explain the correlation between cryptoassets. Equity indices will be highly correlated partly because their rise and fall will be a function of common economic factors, eg interest rates and growth prospects. However, individual shares may diverge because of factors particular to each company, such as demand for their products and their relative competitiveness. As cryptoassets are differentiated by their underlying technology, yet compete in the same market, we would expect, if valuation was based on economic factors, to see a greater level of variation between cryptoasset prices based on how widely they are used.

On the use of Google data to demonstrate that cryptoasset prices are driven by speculative behaviour, we think it is reasonable to conclude that:

- Google trends data are an appropriate proxy for retail investors' interest in bitcoin. A Google search shows consumer engagement which may take the form of background research, price information or looking for an exchange to buy the cryptoasset.

- Retail investor interest, evidenced by Google searches for Bitcoin, is correlated to increases in the price and trading volumes of bitcoin. An 'investment mania' as the Financial Times called it, where price increases and reports of gains encouraged more retail participation.

- Higher prices and higher investor returns for bitcoin generated more media exposure and increased retail interest, which contributed to the price bubble in December 2017. The data shows a rapid rise in searches for bitcoin then a sharp decline once prices began to fall.

Our conclusions, based on the use of google data to show speculative behaviour, are supported by the analysis of professor Frode Kjærland's of the NTNU Business School. He concluded that, 'based on our full and reduced model, past price performance, optimism, and Google search volume all play significant roles in explaining Bitcoin prices.'

We think that, taken together, the Google data and the wider evidence cited in CP19/22 paragraphs 3.15 and 3.16 support our view that cryptoassets prices are driven by speculation, which makes it difficult for consumers to value them reliably.

This is supported by our recently published consumer research that found that 47% of consumers surveyed bought cryptoassets 'as a gamble that could make or lose money,' compared with only 31% in the 2019 consumer research. While 22% of respondents bought cryptoassets due to a fear of missing out. This shows that the majority of retail clients are not investing in cryptoassets for a legitimate investment need.

Risks from financial crime, market abuse and operational issues

CP19/22 said that the integrity of and confidence in the cryptoasset market affects retail consumers holding crypto-derivatives because their value is directly affected by any sudden devaluation or price dislocation in underlying token prices.

We recognised that the Fifth Anti-Money Laundering Directive ('5AMLD') will help reduce money laundering risks from the anonymity of cryptoassets, but will not mitigate other financial crime risks such as abusive trading or cyber-thefts of unregulated tokens.

Industry bodies, exchanges and manufacturers of these products questioned our claims around financial crime, arguing that:

- instances of financial crime have reduced over time, which is due partly to improvements in market oversight by cryptoasset exchanges

- trading volumes associated with wash trading (where misleading and artificial activity in the marketplace occurs) are decreasing

- the evidence presented does not support our conclusions that financial crime affects the value of cryptoassets

Our Response

We have considered the feedback that financial crime and market abuse is reducing. Reported hacks and thefts have decreased by 66% from 2018 to 2019. However, cryptocurrency user and investor losses due to fraud and misappropriation increased by 533% over the same period according to a report by CipherTrace. Industry commentators suggest that wash trading is increasing in cryptocurrency markets and, irrespective of the actual trend, remains significant. We think that our analysis evidences that financial crime, such as exchanges being hacked, effects cryptoasset prices. For example, the hack of Bitstamp, made public on 3 January 2015, resulted in a 15% decrease in the value of Bitcoin. More recently, in August 2019, the price of bitcoin decreased by 5% following the hack of Binance when around US$40m of bitcoin were stolen. These sudden changes in the price of the underlying tokens will be reflected in related changes in the value of the derivatives that reference them.

Crypto-derivatives do not serve a legitimate investment need

CP19/22 said that crypto-derivatives do not meet a legitimate investment need and most retail consumers lose money trading them.

Consultation respondents highlighted potential legitimate uses of crypto-derivatives, including:

- hedging—investors who invest directly in underlying cryptoassets use crypto- derivatives to hedge against volatility

- bypassing custody issues—crypto-derivatives offer exposure to the underlying without the custody issues associated with third parties. This removes the risk of scams and theft and exchange-traded notes also reduce the counterparty risk by transacting with an authorised firm

- access to more liquid markets—derivative markets are often more liquid than underlying cryptoasset markets

- <u>access to leverage</u>—CFDs and futures provide retail consumers with leverage that they otherwise would not have in the spot market

A regulated exchange and an individual respondent also said that crypto-derivative markets play a critical role in the effective price formation process for cryptoasset markets. Banning the retail crypto-derivatives market will undermine this.

Individual investors said that volatility and the prospects of high returns attract investors, and the prohibition would remove their ability to trade on these markets. This implies that they use crypto-derivatives to speculate on price movements in the hope of achieving a profit.

Our Response

We continue to think that crypto-derivatives do not meet a legitimate investment need. We have considered and set out our response below.

- <u>Hedging</u>—We recognise that some retail consumers will use crypto- derivatives to hedge their exposure to the underlying cryptoasset market, but this is not common. Feedback from retail investors suggest that crypto-derivatives are primarily used for speculative purposes akin to gambling.

- <u>Bypassing custody issues</u>—We recognise that crypto-derivatives allow consumers to avoid the risk exposure of cryptoassets being stolen, or losing their encrypted key, that comes with investing in the underlying cryptoassets. We do not think this benefit outweighs our analysis of harm and the expected benefits to retail consumers from a ban (see our updated CBA). We continue to view unregulated cryptoassets as very risky and discourage consumers from viewing them as 'investments'.

- <u>Access to more liquid markets</u>—We recognise that some derivatives markets may be more liquid than underlying spot markets. However, improved liquidity does not address retail consumers' inability to value crypto-derivatives, or reduce the losses we have demonstrated that, on average, they will make trading these products.

- <u>Access to leverage</u>—While leverage will sometimes lead to increased profits, it will at other times make losses worse. Our analysis of the impact of leverage on retail consumers in CP18/38 – Restricting contract for difference products sold to retail clients and a discussion of other retail derivative products concludes that lower leverage reduces trading losses. This is further supported by our analysis of client data for crypto-CFDs and crypt ETNs (see our updated CBA).

- <u>Price formation</u>—We recognise that derivatives may play a limited role in the price formation of cryptoassets. This does not change our view that cryptoassets have no intrinsic value and cannot be valued reliably.

The proportionality of a ban

CP19/22 explained that we do not think that existing regulatory requirements sufficiently address the harms from crypto-derivatives. Having considered other, less restrictive policy measures, e.g. restricting marketing, we concluded that a prohibition is necessary to address the harm.

We also considered all of the applicable conditions in Article 42 of MiFIR and Article 21(2) of the Delegated Regulation of MiFIR and determined that the marketing, distribution and sale of crypto-derivatives to retail consumers gives rise to significant investor protection concerns and that the other relevant conditions are met (paragraphs 3.4 to 3.6 in CP19/22).

We consulted on applying the prohibition to all derivatives (ie CFDs, options and futures) and ETNs that reference unregulated transferable cryptoassets. We thought that all crypto-derivatives were harmful to retail consumers because of retail consumers' inability to value them. We also thought that crypto-ETNs pose similar risks to derivatives, although the risks are reduced because they are typically sold without leverage. We had also seen poor outcomes from the limited number of products currently available on EU trading venues.

Arguments that existing regulation addresses the harm

Several respondents, including an NCA, trade associations and firms offering crypto- derivatives, said that current regulations provide adequate consumer protections. Current regulations include applicable Markets in Financial Instruments Directive (MiFID) II conduct rules, including product governance and disclosure requirements, as well as the listing rules under the Prospectus Regulation, and the EU Benchmark Regulation (BMR).

One responding firm commented that the EU Benchmark Regulation is intended to ensure that authorised benchmarks have appropriate methodologies, systems and controls to ensure that they provide reliable prices. They said derivative instruments referencing authorised cryptocurrency benchmarks should not be captured by the proposed ban.

A trade association and 2 CFD providers argued that we had not considered the impact of 2:1 leverage limits for CFDs referencing cryptoassets, which came into force in August 2018. They argued that our CBA analysis should therefore include a longer timeframe to capture the impact of the leverage limits.

An NCA, firms that offer crypto-derivatives and an individual respondent said that a prohibition would harm retail consumers by reducing choice. They also argued retail consumers would lose existing regulatory protections by encouraging them to trade crypto-derivatives with third country firms on their own initiative, and trade cryptoassets with unregulated entities.

Our Response

We still view the prohibition as proportionate to the harm, and do not think that existing regulatory requirements address our significant investor protection concerns, as set out below.

- Adequacy of existing protections—Existing conduct and disclosure regulations are intended to address the risk from regulated products (e.g. derivatives and transferable securities) rather than harm from the underlying assets that regulated products reference. Many of the rules referred to, such as product governance, appropriateness assessments, and suitability, are intended to improve the distribution of products that are suitable for a subset of retail consumers.

  We do not think that crypto-derivatives are suitable for any retail consumer. We recognise that the Benchmark Regulation (BMR) seeks to improve the quality of market pricing and settlement by ensuring that benchmark methodologies and input data are sufficiently robust to represent accurately and reliably represent the market that the benchmark seeks to measure. However, this does not address our concerns about the integrity of the underlying cryptoasset market, and does not allow retail consumers to value crypto-derivatives reliably.

- Impact assessment of 2:1 leverage limits for CFDs—The timing of our original CBA meant that we were unable to consider the impact of 2:1 leverage limits over a longer period. In response to CP feedback, we have analysed additional client data from January 2019 to September 2019. This allowed us to assess client outcomes over a 13-month period when crypto-CFDs were subject to 2:1 leverage limits. These data show that leverage limits have reduced harm by reducing retail consumer losses, but most retail consumers still lost money trading crypto-CFDs and losses remained significant (see Chapter 3: Cost Benefit Analysis for further detail). We do not think leverage limits will adequately address the harm as they do not address the concerns we have with the underlying cryptoassets and retail consumers' inability to value these derivatives reliably.

- A ban will drive consumers to unregulated exchanges or third country firms—We recognise the risk that by banning crypto- derivatives for retail investors, consumers may choose to trade unregulated cryptoassets or look to trade crypto-derivatives with firms in third country jurisdictions. Despite this, we think that a prohibition will protect most consumers and will help inform retail consumers of the risks and harms of trading these products. Lower standards in other jurisdictions are not a reason for us to compromise our own investor protection standards.

In response to feedback on proportionality, we have also reconsidered all the applicable criteria in Article 42 of MiFIR and Article 21(2) of the Delegated Regulation of MiFIR. We remain of the view that the relevant criteria are met and that the marketing, distribution and sale of all crypto-derivatives to retail consumers creates significant investor protection concerns and that a prohibition is necessary and proportionate. As part of feedback we have examined a range of alternative options and these do not address the harms we have identified.

Arguments that other, less restrictive measures would address the harm

Some respondents suggested we consider the following alternative, product-specific measures to address the harm:

- limiting leverage to 1:1 for derivatives products
- limiting marketing, and/or their sale and distribution, to high-net worth and self- certified sophisticated investors
- requiring a suitability test and/or requiring consumers to demonstrate they have adequate knowledge and understanding
- requiring enhanced disclosures
- excluding retail consumers who are using these products for hedging
- permitting crypto-derivatives on the 'top 20' cryptoassets

Some respondents suggested other measures to address the harm:

- requiring firms to hold specific permissions to offer crypto-derivatives
- restricting the firms that can offer crypto-derivatives to 730k firms
- conduct a review of trading fees
- requiring firms to use established and recognised exchanges when pricing derivative contracts
- prohibiting the use of cryptoassets as margin for trading

One CFD provider said that we should apply other, less restrictive measures first and assess whether those measures address the harm before imposing a ban. They argued this would reduce the costs to retail consumers and maintain the competitiveness of the UK market.

Firms offering crypto-derivatives to retail consumers said that a prohibition would be significantly more restrictive than the policy approach of other EEA and third country jurisdictions.

A large number of individual respondents said that we should not proceed with imposing a ban, as they would be forced to assume losses.

A trade association representing cryptoasset firms said that we should introduce a code of conduct to address our concerns about the underlying market by ensuring they are more transparent and efficient.

An NCA agreed with our analysis of the key risks and harm posed by these products, and agreed with our proposal to prohibit the sale, marketing and distribution of derivatives and ETNs referencing relevant cryptoassets to retail consumers.

Our Response

We have considered whether other, less restrictive measures would address the harm. We do not think they would, for the following reasons:

- 1:1 leverage limits—Similar to the impact of applying 2:1 leverage limits to CFDs that reference cryptoassets, we expect that retail consumers would lose less money if they were unable to trade with leverage. However, most retail consumers would probably still make losses. Our updated CBA (see Chapter 3: Cost Benefit Analysis) shows that the majority of retail consumers lost money trading crypto-ETNs, which are not leveraged, during a representative data period outside the cryptoasset bubble.

- Restricting crypto-derivatives to high-net worth and self- certified sophisticated investors—Client data suggest that wealthier consumers are more likely to experience higher losses and higher profits from trading. We do not have any evidence to suggest that wealthier retail consumers are more capable of valuing these crypto-derivatives. We recognise that these consumers are more capable of absorbing losses, but do not think this alters our assessment of the drivers of harm we have identified, or justifies applying less restrictive measures for these consumers. We do not consider crypto-derivatives to be suitable for any retail consumers. Firms that offer crypto-ETNs also indicated that it would be costly to restrict these products to a sub-set of wealthier consumers.

- Applying a suitability test and/or requiring consumers to demonstrate knowledge and understanding—Our analysis concludes that cryptoassets cannot be reliably valued so we do not think that retail consumers would be able to demonstrate adequate knowledge and understanding of crypto-derivatives.

- Enhanced disclosure requirements—This would potentially improve retail consumers' understanding of the product risks. But disclosure would not alter the lack of intrinsic value and would not improve retail consumers' ability to value them reliably.

- Permit crypto-derivatives for hedging—We believe that only a small minority of retail consumers use crypto derivatives for legitimate hedging purposes. While we acknowledge that these clients could benefit from a hedging exemption if consumers use it to hedge effectively, we think that overall this will still lead to net harm. It is also difficult for firms to implement and for us to supervise.

- <u>Permit crypto-derivatives on the top 20 cryptoassets</u>—We do not think this is appropriate as the 'top 20' cryptoassets pose the same harms to retail consumers and we have not seen evidence that these cryptoassets can be valued more reliably than any other unregulated cryptoassets.

We have also considered whether applying measures to firms offering cryptoassets to retail consumers would address the harm. We think that the harms from crypto-derivatives are due to the risks of the underlying assets rather than the way that these products are offered. So, we do not think it is effective or more proportionate to apply firm-specific measures.

We recognise that our prohibition is more restrictive than other EEA and most third country jurisdictions at the current time. But our analysis demonstrates that crypto-derivatives are harmful to retail consumers and the prohibition meets the relevant product intervention criteria (Article 42 of MiFIR). We consider it appropriate and proportionate to prohibit crypto-derivatives to protect retail consumers.

We welcome market-based initiatives to improve the transparency, efficiency and effectiveness of the underlying cryptoasset markets. In compliance with Article 42(6) of MiFIR, we will keep the prohibition under review in light of any evidence of significant market improvements that appropriately mitigate the drivers of the harms we have identified.

Some firms suggested that we prohibit firms from accepting cryptoassets as collateral for margin when trading CFDs. We remind firms that only cash can be accepted as margin for CFD trading involving retail consumers (per COBS 22.5.10R).

Less restrictive measures would not address our significant concerns about investor protection. So we remain of the view that a retail prohibition is necessary to address the harms.

We have considered potential costs to consumers with existing positions. As indicated in CP19/22, retail consumers with existing holdings can remain invested following the ban, until they choose to disinvest. We do not require or expect firms to close out consumers' positions unless consumers ask for this.

Relative harm of crypto-ETNs

Firms that distribute exchange-traded products argued that ETNs should not be prohibited because they benefit from protections that derivatives do not. ETNs are listed and traded on a regulated exchange, for example, and require a prospectus. They are not leveraged, and typically charge lower trading fees compared with CFDs. As such, some respondents argued that these products have lower risks and they should be subject to less restrictive measures. These respondents suggested this was supported by our CBA, which showed most retail consumers profiting from crypto- ETNs over the period we examined, while consumers suffered losses from crypto- CFDs and crypto-futures. They also suggested that we consider a longer data period (before June 2017) as this would show retail consumers experiencing even higher profits from trading crypto-ETNs.

Our Response

In response to feedback, we have considered whether to exclude crypto- ETNs from our prohibition or to apply less restrictive measures to them. To do so, we considered whether the features of these products reduced the risk of consumer harm compared with crypto-CFDs, options and futures (see table below).

Table 1: Comparison of crypto-ETNs, CFDs, futures and options

Product	ETNs	CFDs	Futures	Options
Provides exposure to cryptoassets	√	√	√	√
Leveraged	X	√	√	X
Limit losses to their initial investment	√	X Losses are limited to cash in the client's trading account	X	√
Subject to MiFID- derived conduct rules	√	√	√	√
Subject to an appropriateness assessment	X	√	√	√
Sold with a prospectus that complies with the Prospectus Directive	√	X	X	X
Traded on a trading venue	√	X Most commonly traded over-the-counter (OTC)	√ Some crypto-futures are traded OTC	√ Not currently offered in the UK, but can be traded on trading venues or OTC

We recognise that derivatives and ETNs have different features and that crypto-ETNs do not share all of the riskier features of derivatives. For example, they are not leveraged products. We also recognise that crypto-ETNs have to meet some additional regulatory requirements because of the way that they are structured. Specifically:

- ETNs are sold with a prospectus in compliance with the Prospectus Directive. This will potentially help retail consumers understand how the product is structured and appreciate the risks associated with crypto-ETNs. But this will not allow retail consumers to value crypto- ETNs reliably.

- ETNs are always traded on a traded venue. It is argued that exchange-traded products generally receive better prices when compared with OTC derivatives. However, retail consumers are still unable reliably to predict potential price impacts caused by issues in the underlying cryptoasset markets. As a result, these consumers cannot value them or the ETN reliably.

- ETNs are not leveraged. As discussed above, the lack of leverage is likely to reduce consumer losses but will not address the harm from retail consumers' inability to value crypto-derivatives.

Despite the differences between crypto-ETNs and crypto-derivatives, we think that these products have the same key risk features in common. As crypto-ETNs' value is derived from cryptoassets that cannot be reliably valued, they expose retail consumers to the same harms. This is evidenced by the additional analysis of client data that we conducted since CP19/22. Our data show that a majority of retail consumers trading crypto-ETNs lose money, which is similar to outcomes from trading crypto-CFDs and futures (see Chapter 3: Cost benefit analysis). We conclude that crypto-derivatives and crypto- ETNs should be subject to the prohibition due to our significant concerns about investor protection.

Arguments that a prohibition is contrary to our policy objectives

An NCA, a trade body, a trading venue and a manufacturer of these products said that a prohibition was contrary to our policy objectives, including:

- consumers having responsibility for their own investment decisions

- our approach to other, highly volatile derivative products, eg EU carbon credits

- our wider objective to promote innovation and entrepreneurship as part of our competition

Our Response

We believe that a prohibition is consistent with our wider policy objectives for the following reasons.

- The general principle that consumers should take responsibility for their decisions—We are prohibiting crypto-derivatives because we believe that the information asymmetries retail consumers face when choosing whether to invest are too great. We have concluded that retail consumers cannot value these products reliably, meaning they are not able to make informed investment decisions.

- Promoting effective competition—Our policy proposal seeks to ensure that UK firms compete in the interests of consumers. This is as opposed to lowering conduct standards and/or offering products or services to retail consumers for whom they are inappropriate, and who may suffer harm as a result. We have considered the competition impacts of the prohibition and whether alternative measures would address the harms and provide appropriate protections for consumers. We have not identified any alternative approaches which better promote competition while addressing the significant investor harms identified.

- Promoting innovation in support of our competition objective—We support innovation that is in the interests of consumers. We do not believe that crypto-derivatives sold to retail consumers meet this test, as our analysis indicates that these products are harmful to retail consumers. We continue to welcome innovation that supports competition, improves the effective functioning of markets and is in the interests of consumers, including through the FCA Sandbox. This includes innovation based on distributed ledger technology, or using cryptoassets to benefit markets and consumers, for example, increasing efficiency of existing processes like cross-border money remittance. We note the following:

  - A third of all tests in the sandbox are based on distributed ledger technology, and many of these tests have involved the use of cryptoassets. We will continue to support sandbox tests involving cryptoassets where the proposition is truly innovative, provides a genuine consumer benefit, is within scope of the sandbox, there's a need to test and the firm is ready.

  - Firms testing cryptoasset-based propositions in the sandbox have benefited from FCA support in developing and testing compliant products. These tests have also helped us learn more about market developments and to ensure our approach supports legitimate innovation.

Keeping a prohibition under review

A large number of respondents said that our prohibition should be kept under review.

Our Response

We agree that our prohibition should be kept under review. This is in line with Article 42(6) of MiFIR. We will reconsider our position if there is robust evidence that the cryptoasset market is sufficiently changing to address the drivers of the harms we have identified.

Scope of products caught

In CP19/22 we proposed prohibiting the sale, marketing and distribution to retail consumers of all derivatives (i.e. CFDs, options and futures) and exchange traded notes referencing unregulated transferable cryptoassets.

Our proposed definition of unregulated transferable cryptoassets was intended to capture derivatives referencing cryptoassets that we called transferable exchange and utility tokens in CP19/3: Guidance on Cryptoassets.

We also explained that we did not intend to capture:

- security tokens—because these tokens already qualify as specified investments and do not pose the same risks as exchange and comparable utility tokens since they will have a basis for valuation according to the legal rights or promise of payment they will provide

- tokens that are not widely transferable (eg tokens used on a private network that can only be redeemed with the issuer)

- e-money tokens

A law firm and an association representing law firms said that our proposed rules would capture products that we did not intend to capture. The law firm said our rules would prohibit derivatives referencing commodities, such as gold, where ownership of the underlying commodity was recorded on the blockchain and that this was inconsistent with our policy objectives.

These same respondents said that we should define the scope of our crypto- derivatives ban by specifying the key features of cryptoassets that we think should be within scope. For example, we should consider using the definition of virtual currencies used in the Fifth Anti Money Laundering Directive (5AMLD).

Our Response

We recognise that the definition of unregulated transferable cryptoassets that we proposed could have captured crypto-derivatives we did not intend to be subject to our rules. These are:

- commodities where ownership is recorded on the blockchain (crypto-commodities)

- currencies issued or guaranteed by a central bank or public authority, commonly known as central bank digital currencies (CBDCs)

We agree that derivatives referencing crypto-commodities and CBDCs should not be subject to our prohibition because they do not pose the same harms. For example, a crypto-commodity could be reliably valued as it represents ownership of a commodity that is used as a raw material for an industrial process, is a commercial good or is a recognised store of value. To our knowledge, these products are not available today. However, capturing these products would unnecessarily undermine innovation and competition in financial markets by discouraging firms from applying new technology to existing financial products and services.

In response to feedback, we are amending the definition of unregulated transferable cryptoassets that are within scope of the prohibition to exclude crypto-commodities and CBDCs.

We do not think that there are any other cryptoassets that should be excluded from our prohibition for derivatives or ETNs referencing them. But, we will consider amending the scope of our prohibition if products become available that do not pose the same harms.

We will consider amending the scope of the prohibition if we find new products that are not within the current scope cause similar harms to crypto-derivatives and ETNs referencing cryptoassets.

3 Changes to Final Rules

We are making amendments to final rules that were made (but did not come into effect) by the Board in July 2020 without consultation. This is because the publication of the policy statement was delayed following the approval by the Board. These amendments change the:

- final rules to deal with deficiencies arising from EU exit; and
- coming into force date of final rules.

We are publishing both the original instrument (FCA 2020/34) and amending instrument (FCA 2020/46) on the FCA Handbook website.

Dealing with deficiencies arising from EU Exit

We said in CP19/22 that when the UK leaves the EU the rules we were consulting on would continue to apply to the same firms after exit as were covered by the rules before exit. The changes described below ensure that our rules will apply to the firms the rules would have applied to, had the rules come into force before 31 December 2020. They also deal with deficiencies in the rules arising from the UK's withdrawal from the European Union.

Territorial Scope

The rules will not apply to EEA firms unless they have temporary permission, are in the financial services contracts regime as a supervised run-off firm, are a contractual run-off firm, or they have a Part 4A permission.

As a result of the changes, EEA firms operating outside the temporary regimes will be treated in the same way as third country firms. This is due to changes being made to the glossary terms used in the application provisions. The rules will apply to temporary permission firms, supervised run-off firms and contractual run-off firms.

Passporting

We have also made some consequential changes to reflect the assumption that UK firms will lose passporting rights after exit day.

We are also deleting COBS 22.6.1R(2) and COBS 22.6.2 G., These rules contain a carve- out which provides that where another Member State has adopted more stringent rules covering the same products, then firms must comply with those instead.

The reason for this deletion is that the rules and guidance are premised on the assumption that UK firms can sell crypto-derivatives to consumers in other EEA states under a passport. If we assume no passporting in future (in line with the HMT baseline), then the carve-out becomes redundant. Hence, the deletion is consistent with the HMT baseline.

Changes to the Coming into Force Date

We are also amending the coming into force date of the instrument that was approved by the FCA Board in July 2020. This is because the publication of the PS was delayed. As we want to provide the industry with time to prepare for the new rules, we have amended the coming into force date to 6 January 2021.

4 Cost benefit analysis

In CP19/22, we conducted a CBA to assess the proportionality of our proposed intervention and its likely effects on retail consumers and market participants.

As mentioned in the CP, we are relying on our powers under Article 42 MiFIR as well as our rule-making powers under the Financial Services and Markets Act 2000 (FSMA) to make these rules. We set out our CBA in the CP to fulfil the requirements of FSMA and to assess the proportionality of the proposed prohibition in line with MiFIR. Specifically, section 138I of FSMA requires us to publish a CBA of proposed rules, defined as 'an analysis of the costs, together with an analysis of the benefits that will arise if the proposed rules are made'. MiFIR does not specifically require a CBA, however, we are required under Article 42(2)(c) of MiFIR to consider the proportionality of our proposed intervention including its likely effects on investors and market participants. We undertook a CBA for that purpose as well.

Benefits to consumers

In CP19/22 we considered the prohibition would likely benefit most retail consumers investing in derivatives and ETN products referencing cryptoassets.

We estimated expected benefits to retail consumers based on data requested from seven firms that make up a large proportion of the CFD, futures and ETN market in the UK during the collection period.

The data collection period covered a 19-month period from June 2017 to December 2018. This period captures important stages in the price evolution of cryptoassets (including periods of price increases and decreases as well as periods of relatively low volatility). When requesting data from firms we asked them to provide data for all products referencing cryptoassets that they offered to retail consumers.

Using this methodology, we concluded that our proposals would benefit most consumers by protecting them from future losses. We estimated potential benefits to be in a range from £75m to £234.3m annually (Table 2). This figure is obtained by using fees paid by retail consumers as a lower bound and total losses experienced by retail consumers (including fees) as an upper bound. We use this value to avoid short-term periods of (high) net profits and a small number of large profitable retail ETN clients distorting the performance of an average consumer. We do not consider a positive outcome over time is likely to be sustained and have found net losses to be £53.3m for all clients in the updated CBA (Table 3).

We recognised that some retail consumers made a profit over the period. However, we consider the significant variance in retail consumer outcomes to be consistent with our policy analysis. That is, the value of these products in the short run is highly unpredictable and prone to extreme volatility due to the nature of the underlying assets. While we cannot forecast future prices in this market, it is reasonable to base our proposals on a central scenario in which a bubble of the magnitude of the one experienced in 2017–18 is not repeated.

Table 2: CBA in CP19/22

Product	Net outcomes from trading* (Jun 2017-Dec 2018)	Total Losses from trading* Jun 2017-Dec 2018)	Total Losses from trading (per annum)*	Fees (per annum)
CFDs	(£55m)	(£245m)	(£155m)	(£68.5m)
Futures	(£36.5m)	(£87.3m)	(£55.1m)	(£2.3m)
ETNs	£117m	(£38.3m)	(£24.2m)	(£5.7m)
Total	£25.5m	(£370.6m)	(£234.3m)	(£75m)

*All figures are inclusive of fees

ETNs

Based on client data from June 2017 to December 2018, we estimated the total benefits of prohibiting crypto-ETNs to retail consumers to be in the range of £5.7m to £24.2m annually. We do however, recognise that some retail consumers made a profit over the period. We explained this in more detail in the CBA in CP19/22.

We also observed that the net aggregate outcome from trading crypto-ETNs by retail consumers was a profit of £117m (across all four crypto-ETNs offered). We concluded that client outcomes over this period were not a reliable indicator of likely future returns because:

- The period November 2017 to February 2018, a subset of the original data request used in the CBA, accounted for £116m (out of £141m profits). This suggests that that the large profits were the result of a large number of early buy-and-hold investors in the Bitcoin ETN, and a small number of clients investing very large amounts in the run up to the bubble.

- In the second half of 2018 most retail consumers made a loss. Between March 2018 to December 2018, we observed client outcomes from trading were an aggregate loss of £16.8m.

A provider of cryptoasset investment products questioned the validity of the CBA in relation to crypto-ETNs because:

- The CBA showed that retail consumers made profits from trading crypto-ETNs.
- The timeframe we used (June 2017 to December 2018) was not representative of expected client outcomes. They said we should have assessed retail consumer benefits based on client data over the entire period that the crypto-ETN was available and that this longer data period would have shown that retail consumers made more profits from trading crypto-ETNs.

Our Response

In response to feedback on our assessment of benefits in relation to crypto-ETNs we collected additional client data for the same instruments from firms that provided data for the original CBA. These additional data covered the period from June 2015—when the crypto-ETN was made available—to April 2019—the latest month that we could have reasonably requested data from firms before publishing CP19/22 in July 2019. One firm was unable to provide data prior to January 2016.

Client outcomes from trading crypto-ETNs between June 2015 and April 2019 are as follows:

- 60% of retail consumer accounts made a profit and median outcomes were positive.
- The net aggregate outcome from trading was a profit of £122.5m. This compares with a profit of £117m over the period covered in CP19/22.
- Profits were highly concentrated as the top 1% of retail consumer accounts (256 retail consumers) made £111m in profits or 71% of the £143m in total profits from profit-making accounts. Profits were also concentrated over the period analysed in CP19/22.
- Loss-making retail consumer accounts made a loss of £20.5m, which is less than retail consumer losses in the period covered by CP19/22 (£38.3m).

Client outcomes over the longer data period are not significantly different from client outcomes over the period covered in our assessment of client outcomes in CP19/22.

We still think that client outcomes between June 2015 to the peak of the bubble in December 2017, when prices rose by 8,700% (see Figure 1 below) are unlikely to be repeated. It is reasonable to base our proposals on a scenario which avoids the bubble seen in 2017.

Figure 1: Bitcoin prices between June 2015 and April 2019

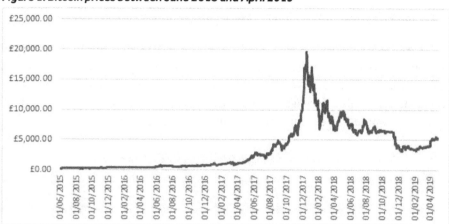

We also tested our conclusion that retail consumer outcomes over the data period in the original CBA (June 2017 to December 2018) were not a reliable indicator of future returns.

We analysed client outcomes from trading using client data from 1 April 2018 to 31 December 2019. We chose this period because it does not cover the period where we see large increases and decreases in the price of cryptoassets which could distort outcomes. We think this period reflects market conditions that are less affected by extreme volatility (see Figure 2 below and Technical Annex), and therefore better estimates the expected benefits from a prohibition. We have used this data to calculate our revised CBA for ETNs.

Figure 2: Bitcoin prices between 1 April 2018 and 31 December 2019

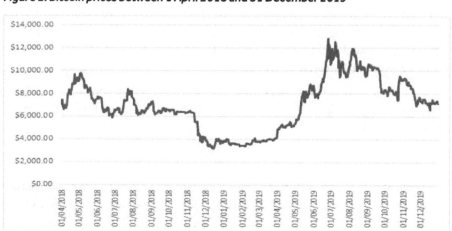

Client outcomes from trading crypto-ETNs between April 2018 and December 2019 were as follows:

- 57% of retail consumer accounts made a loss and median outcomes were negative

- aggregate outcomes from trading was a loss of £2.7m

- total losses from loss-making retail consumer accounts was £14.3m.

These data support our view that retail consumers are unlikely to experience sustained profits from trading outside the historical cryptoasset bubble (Q3 and Q4 2017). This analysis, we believe, supports that retail consumers cannot value cryptoassets reliably because the majority of retail consumers lost money despite the significant increases in the price of the underlying assets.

Table 3: Clients outcomes from trading ETNs across three data periods

	June 2017 to December 2018 (Original CBA)	June 2015 to April 2019	April 2018 to December 2019 (Updated CBA)
Loss-making client accounts	41%*	40%	57%
Net outcomes from trading	£117m	£122m	(£2.7m)
Gross Profits[1]	£141m	£143m	£11.6m
Gross Losses[2]	(£24m)	(£21m)	(£14.3m)

*　This figure is based on a different methodology to the percentage of loss-making client accounts over other period (ie it is calculated on an instrument-by-instrument basis), but we think it reasonably estimates the percentage of profitable client accounts. Due to rounding, numbers presented may not add up precisely to the totals indicated.

1,2　Gross Profits and Gross Losses are the sum of all the profits and losses made by profit-making and loss-making clients. This is not calculated on an annualised basis in contrast to Table 3.

All 3 data sets show that a significant amount of retail clients lost money and that for the updated CBA a majority (57%) of clients lost money, with a net loss of £2.7m.

CFDs

Based on client data from June 2017 to December 2018, we estimated the total benefits of prohibiting crypto-CFDs to retail consumers to be in the range of £68.5m and £155m annually. We also observed that net aggregate client outcomes from trading crypto-CFDs was a loss of £55m.

A range of respondents including CFD providers, retail consumers and trade associations argued that we had not fully considered the impact of 2:1 leverage on cryptoasset CFDs.

Our Response

For crypto-CFDs, we collected additional client data covering the period between August 2018 and September 2019. This provided 14 months of data to assess the impact of 2:1 leverage limits on client outcomes when trading crypto-CFDs.

These additional crypto-CFD data show that:

- annualised net aggregate losses were £37.2m per annum compared to £155m in the original CBA
- fees were lower, with retail consumers incurring fees of £13.9m compared with £68.5m

The reduction in client losses is explained by:

- the impact of 2:1 leverage limits and fewer consumers trading crypto- CFDs after the bubble, which resulted in lower trading volumes
- CFD providers lowered their fees after the bubble

This is unsurprising and we would expect the intervention to have this effect.

The additional analysis shows that although ESMA's product intervention imposing 2:1 leverage limits reduced harm, we still see harm from crypto-CFDs traded at lower leverage levels. The crypto- ETN data (as these products are unleveraged) also suggest that reducing leverage further (eg to 1:1) would not sufficiently address the harm as the majority of retail consumers would still make losses, as seen by the updated CBA. So, we think that prohibiting crypto-CFDs remains appropriate and proportionate.

Futures

Based on client data from June 2017 to December 2018, we estimated the total benefits of prohibiting crypto-futures to retail consumers to be in the range of £2.3 and £55.1m annually. We also observed that client outcomes from trading crypto-CFDs was a loss of £36.5m.

We did not receive feedback on our assessment of benefits in relation to crypto-futures.

Costs to firms

In CP19/22, we said that firms would not incur any ongoing costs from implementing our proposals and will face minimal costs from withdrawing products from retail consumers and ceasing marketing activities to retail consumers. This also leads to minimal familiarisation costs for firms. Our proposal would, however, lead to a loss of revenue for UK firms from fees and charges of around £75m per annum across all products.

One cryptoasset firm stated that we had not considered the loss of revenues from future product offerings. The same respondent and an individual respondent said that our proposed prohibition would reduce the attractiveness of the UK to cryptoasset firms and that this would result in a loss of tax revenue for the UK Government.

Our Response

We do not have any evidence to suggest that firms will soon significantly expand their crypto-derivative offerings. As indicated in our assessment of consumer benefits (see above), consumer demand for crypto-derivatives has declined significantly. Furthermore, any loss of revenue for firms will form an equal and offsetting part of the benefits to retail consumers.

Again, we have no evidence that business will expand their offerings which would increase profits and tax revenues. In response to feedback regarding the loss of tax revenue for the UK Government, loss of tax revenue is already accounted for in the CBA through the loss of revenue to firms and consumers for those that experienced profits (as tax is transferred from their profit to the government).

Based on our additional analysis of client outcomes we have lowered our estimates of costs to firms because revenues from fees and charges have decreased after demand for crypto-derivatives fell following the cryptoasset bubble and the introduction of 2:1 leverage limits for crypto-CFDs. Based on our revised estimate, our prohibition will cost firms around £19m through lost revenue.

Updated cost benefit analysis

The tables below display our revised CBA based upon additional client data (as explained above). Our methodology for calculating the costs and benefits of a prohibition remains unchanged.

We remain of the view that our proposals will ultimately benefit the majority of consumers by protecting them from future losses.

We estimate that expected range of benefits to be between £19 and £101m on an annualised basis. The lower range benefit of £19m represents the annualised figure of retail consumer losses from fees incurred from trading across the three product types. The estimated upper range benefit of £101m represents the annualised total losses experienced by retail consumers for all products. We estimate that the annualised net benefits to consumers will be towards the middle of this range at £53m.

We remain of the view that we do not expect firms to incur any ongoing costs from implementing our proposals, and will face minimal costs from withdrawing products from retail consumers and ceasing marketing activities to retail consumers.

We do not consider the costs and benefits of the prohibition for crypto-options, even though they are in scope of the prohibition, because these products are not currently available in the UK.

Table 3: Revised CBA following additional client data

Product	Net Aggregate Outcomes from trading*	Total Losses*	Fees*
CFDs	(£18.1m)	(£37.2m)	(£13m)
Futures	(£33.7m)	(£55.1m)	(£2.3m)
ETNs	(£1.5m)	(£8.2m)	(£3.7m)
Total	**(£53.3m)**	**(£100.5m)**	**(£19m)**

* All figures are calculated on an annualised basis. Aggregate outcomes from trading and total losses are inclusive of fees.

Discussion Points

1. *Setback.* Some say the ban is a setback for the U.K. in maintaining its dominant position as a global fintech hub. Do you agree with that assertion? Why or why not?

2. *Benefits.* Others say that this ban is good for retail consumers, the financial services market, and for the U.K. Do you agree with that assertion? Why or why not?

3. *Will consumers really be protected?* Do you agree with the sentiment above that these proposals will protect consumers? Compare and contrast the consumer protection mechanisms of U.S. regulators with that of the U.K. Should the U.K. adopt AML laws similar to the U.S.?

III. Malta

Although cryptocurrency is not a legal tender in Malta, Malta is still a global leader in cryptocurrency regulation. Malta has established cryptocurrency as a "medium of exchange, a medium of the unit, or a store of value." Many large cryptocurrency exchanges are establishing their headquarters in Malta, such as OKEx and Binance. Malta's government has also established policies and regulations concerning cryptocurrencies, such as the Virtual Financial Assets Act ("VFA"), which regulates crypto exchanges, Brokers, wallet providers, ICOS, advisers, and asset managers.

Malta has been incredibly receptive to virtual assets and earned its nickname as "The Blockchain Island." Malta has essentially poised itself as being at the forefront of cryptocurrency regulation. The Maltese government acknowledges cryptocurrencies as a medium of exchange, store of value, or unit of account, but not legal tender.

In July 2018, Malta became the first country to pass explicit regulations on blockchain, cryptocurrency and distributed ledger technology (DLT). This was accomplished when Malta passed the Virtual Financial Asset Act (VFAA), the Malta Digital Innovation Authority Act (MDIA), and the Innovative Technological Arrangement and Services Act (ITAS). These Acts set up a cryptocurrency framework and cover various AML/CTF issues. Further, Malta has also established the Malta Digital Innovation Authority (MDIA) to promote government policies that support digital innovation in Malta. MDIA implements ethical standards regarding cryptocurrency and blockchain, as well as certifies DLT platforms.

Cryptocurrency exchanges are legal in Malta, and are regulated by the VFAA. The VFAA regulates the tendering of virtual assets to the public and virtual financial asset services. The VFAA also provides cryptocurrency users financial investment protection. The VFAA governs cryptocurrency exchanges, wallet rovers, ICOs, brokers, asset managers and similar bodies. Entities looking to provide VFAA services need to complete a VFAA Services licence application. ITAS provides for innovative technology arrangements or service providers. It creates stricter rules through its audit requirements, and mostly oversees the establishment of exchanges and similar entities.

Despite moves to encourage licensing and set deadlines, Malta has faced limited uptake on this front. At the end of the VFAA transitory period to apply for licensing in October 2019, companies operating under VFAA and providing VFA services had failed to apply for a VFA Service License, nor had they ceased operations.

The Malta Financial Services Authority (MFSA) regulates financial services in Malta and regulates the crypto asset space. MFSA developed a Virtual Financial Assets Framework to encourage innovation and development for financial services in the crypto asset space. The regulatory developments are mostly guided by technology as opposed to a strictly financial or legal approach. This allows for more flexibility in the scope of the regulations, and more likely accommodates newer technological developments in the space.

The laws help promote legal certainty in the crypto asset space, and makes it more welcoming to similar technologies. In terms of tax, there is no targeted tax legislation for crypto assets, and the exchange of fiat for crypto does not bear any VAT consequences.

Press Release: Malta Financial Services Authority: The Virtual Financial Assets Act Comes into Force
Chapter 590 (November 1, 2018)

1 Background

The Virtual Financial Assets Act (Chapter 590 of the Laws of Malta) (the 'Act') came into force today, 1 November 2018.

2 Submissions of Applications under the Virtual Financial Assets Act

Requests for applications, authorisations and approvals under the Act will be accepted by the MFSA from today onwards through the designated online portal. Initially, the MFSA will be processing applications only in relation to persons seeking to be registered as VFA Agents under the Act. In the Act, the registration of the whitepaper for an offer to the public and/ or admission to trading of the issuer's Virtual Financial Assets ('VFAs') on an exchange, as well as an application for a licence to provide any service falling within the Second Schedule to the Act in relation to VFAs ('VFA Service'), shall all be made solely through a VFA Agent duly registered with the MFSA. The registered VFA Agents will be listed in the MFSA Financial Services Register, in due course.

3 Persons seeking registration under Articles 7 and/or 14 of the Act

3.1 *Submitting an Application*

Prior to proceeding with the submission of an application for registration, Applicants are required to submit a statement of intent in terms of R1-2.3.3.2.1 and R1-2.3.3.2.2 of *Chapter 1 of the Virtual Financial Assets Rulebook: Virtual Financial Assets Rules for VFA Agents.* The statement of intent should be submitted to the MFSA via email through fintech@mfsa.com.mt and in original to the attention of the Fintech Team at the MFSA.

Applicants seeking registration as a VFA Agent to exercise the functions specified in terms of Article 7 and/or Article 14 of the Act shall submit their application to the MFSA through the designated online portal. The VFA Agent Application Form shall be submitted in accordance with the provisions of the Act and the relevant sections of Chapter 1 of the Virtual Financial Assets Rulebook. Applicants are expected to read the *Guidance Note to the VFA Agent Application* to be in a position to successfully complete the

3.2 *Preparation of Application Form*

Applicants are required to prepare and submit an online Personal Questionnaire for persons who are being proposed to hold a position which requires the MFSA's prior approval before submitting an application. Prior to completing a Personal Questionnaire, Applicants are expected to read the *Guidelines to the Personal Questionnaire* and the corresponding *Glossary.* For the purposes of all applications under the VFA Framework, only digitised Personal Questionnaire submissions will be considered as valid. Paper-based submissions will not be accepted for this purpose. The Authority wishes to clarify that individuals that have previously submitted a Personal Questionnaire to the Authority shall be required to submit a new digitised Personal Questionnaire for the purposes of the application for registration as a VFA Agent. Further information on the launch of the digitised Personal Questionnaire can be found on the *Circular to Licence Holders and Applicants who are being proposed to hold a position which requires the MFSA's prior approval.*

Before submitting an online application, the Applicant should have finalised its commercial and regulatory business plan, decided on which approval is necessary, organised its resources, and be in a position to complete and submit the online Application Form.

3.3 *Incomplete Application Form Submissions*

During the completion of the online VFA Agent Application Form, the online system will contain a number of validations verifying the correctness of the information inserted or otherwise, at each stage. This notwithstanding, if, following the full submission of the online Application Form for the purposes of registration as a VFA Agent, the MFSA considers, at any time during the assessment period, that the information contained in the online Application Form is lacking and incomplete, the MFSA will inform the Applicant accordingly, in writing, together with the reasons for rejecting the online Application Form. In such an eventuality, the MFSA will consider the Application Form as invalid and thus the Applicant would need to submit a new online Application Form.

4 Transitory Period

Furthermore, as from 1 November 2018, persons who, prior to the said date started performing the activity under Articles 7 and, or 14 of the Act, may avail themselves of the transitory period under Article 62 of the Act, subject to a notification requirement to the MFSA, through the *Notification Form*, as outlined in the *Circular to Persons Involved in DLT Asset Activity and Services*. Information on the Transitory Period can be found in *Circular to the Industry on the Transitory Provision under Article 62 of the VFA Act*.

Whilst persons availing themselves of the transitory period may continue providing certain services to clients, it is only VFA Agents who are registered under the Act who will be permitted to submit applications to the MFSA for the purposes of registration of a whitepaper or an application for a licence to provide VFA Service/s under the Act.

The Notification under Article 62 of the Act and the statement of intent in terms of R1-2.3.3.2.1 and R1-2.3.3.2.2 of Chapter 1 of the Virtual Financial Assets Rulebook are different requirements, which should be cumulatively satisfied by existing operators that are going to apply for registration. The statement of intent should be submitted to the MFSA via email through fintech@mfsa.com.mt and in original to the attention of the Fintech Team at the MFSA.

5 Contact and Updates

Any queries are to be addressed to fintech@mfsa.com.mt. Further updates and developments on the Virtual Financial Assets Framework will be made public on: www.mfsa.com.mt/vfa.

Communications Unit
Malta Financial Services Authority

Discussion Points

1. *Registration requirements.* Do you agree with Malta's registration requirements? Which components of the above VFA do you agree with? Do you find the VFA's requirements to be too stringent? Is there anything the VFA should address that the above text does not mention?

2. *The transitory period.* In your opinion, what is the benefit of the "transitory period"? Should U.S. regulators adopt something similar? Why or why not?

IV. Bermuda

Similar to Malta, Bermuda is also considered a global leader in cryptocurrency regulatory space. Bermuda became one of the first countries in the world to regulate cryptocurrencies and blockchain technology. The Bermuda government, specifically the Bermuda Monetary Authority (BMA), established The Digital Asset Business Act (DABA), which introduced the need for a license for any entity incorporated or formed in Bermuda and carries on a digital asset business and to any entity that conducts digital asset business in or from within Bermuda.

The BMA offers three types of DAB licenses that enable entities to conduct activities that fall under the Digital Asset Business Act 2018: the Test "T" License are for those seeking to test their proof of concept; the Modified "M" License for those seeking to expand operations for a limited period; and the Full "F" License for companies seeking to provide DAB activities, including issuing, selling or redeeming virtual coins, tokens or any other form of digital asset, operating as a digital asset exchange, and providing custodial wallet services.[85]

In 2021, Bermuda's government announced that it will launch a blockchain-based stimulus token for Bermuda's retail market. The stimulus token will be a Bermuda dollar-backed stablecoin and will be regulated under the DABA.

Discussion Points

1. *Licensing requirements.* Do you think that DABA's requirement for entities that carry on a "digital asset business" necessarily includes MSBs? Should DABA define "MSBs" and "digital asset businesses" differently? In your opinion, what are the differences between general digital asset businesses and MSBs? Should they be considered the same?

2. *Bermuda at the beginning.* Why would Bermuda, a comparatively small country, want to be among the first countries to regulate cryptocurrencies? What do you think are the advantages for a small country having a regulatory framework for cryptocurrencies? Do you think the economies of smaller countries could be more susceptible to economic downturns if cryptocurrencies are unregulated?

---

85. Bermuda Monetary Authority, *Digital Asset Business*, https://www.bma.bm/digital-asset -business (Last visited on August 1, 2022).

Bermuda Monetary Authority: Digital Asset Business
Supervision and Regulation

The Digital Asset Business Act 2018 (the Act) is the statutory basis for regulating Digital Asset Business (DAB) in Bermuda. The Act provides for a licensing regime for any person or undertaking (unless otherwise exempted) which carries out any of the following activities:

- issuing, selling or redeeming virtual coins, tokens or any other form of digital assets
- operating as a payment service provider business utilising digital assets
- includes the provision of services for the transfer of funds
- operating as an electronic exchange
- providing custodial wallet services
- operating as a digital assets services vendor

WHAT IS A DIGITAL ASSET?

According to the Act, "digital asset" means anything that exists in binary format and comes with the right to use it and includes a digital representation of value that—

- is used as a medium of exchange, unit of account, or store of value and is
- not legal tender, whether or not denominated in legal tender
- is intended to represent assets such as debt or equity in the promoter
- is otherwise intended to represent any assets or rights associated with such assets; or

but does not include—

- a transaction in which a person grants value as part of an affinity or rewards programme, which value cannot be taken from or exchanged with the person for legal tender, bank credit or any digital asset; or a
- digital representation of value issued by or on behalf of the publisher and used within an online game, game platform, or family of games sold by the same publisher or offered on the same game platform

V. Japan

Japan has not yet taken an official stance as to whether cryptocurrency is a currency or commodity, but Japan does accept cryptocurrency as a valid method of payment. Instead, the Japanese government seems to endorse cryptocurrency at arms-length. The government backs cryptocurrency through an official liaison and does not directly intervene in the cryptocurrency market. Consequently, the government defers to technology experts to advise on relevant matters.

In 2014, the Japanese Authority of Digital Assets ("JADA"), a self-regulatory authority, was founded by cryptocurrency operators that advocated for the cryptocurrency industry by advising on various best practices. In 2016, the JADA became the Japan Blockchain Association ("JBA"), which allows them to also focus on the technology that underlies cryptocurrency: blockchain. In 2020, two more self-regulatory blockchain associations were later approved by Japan's version of the SEC known as the Financial Services Agency (FSA): the Japan Security Token Offering Association ("JSTOA"), and the Japan Virtual Currency Exchange Business Association ("JVCEA") now known as the Japan Crypto Asset Trading Business Association. The JSTOA supports fundraising through token offerings by bringing together experts in the field to opine on and comply with various laws while protecting investors, and the Trading Business Association has rule-making authority for digital currency exchanges. The government has also taken the position that they will protect an investor of cryptocurrency should something egregious go awry. In 2014, MtGox, the famed cyptocurrency exchange platform, declared bankruptcy after it lost approximately 850,000 bitcoins after various cyberattacks, and the courts intervened to protect investors. A few years after MtGox declared bankruptcy, the Japanese parliament approved a bill that amended the Payment Services Act that defined cryptocurrency (i.e., "virtual currency"), required cryptocurrency exchanges to register, subjected cryptocurrency transactions to money laundering regulations, and offered protections for cryptocurrency users, which took effect on April 1, 2017.

In early 2018, hackers got away with nearly 500 million in the NEM altcoin from another exchange, Coincheck, Inc. Several months later, another cryptocurrency exchange, Zaif, was hacked, losing approximately $60 million worth of cryptocurrency. At the time, the JVCEA was set up to assess the security of exchanges, but the various cyberattacks and damage felt by exchanges and investors alike led the FSA to officially approve the JVCEA as a self-regulatory organization allowing them to promulgate rules and enforce compliance.

Separately, while profits earned from selling cryptocurrency is taxed as miscellaneous income rather than capital gains, purchases made with cryptocurrency are not subject to a consumption tax. The Japanese government recognizes the need for proper reporting of cryptocurrency, but has removed the onus from the consumer and has instead placed the burden of accountability onto the cryptocurrency exchanges.

FSA Study Group on Digital and Decentralized Finance Interim Report

November 17, 2021

* * *

3. Legal and Regulatory Framework related to Stablecoins

(1) Types of Stablecoins and Existing Digital Money

Although there is no clear definition of so-called stablecoins, it is generally considered to be a digital asset that aims to stabilize value in relation to a specific asset and uses a distributed ledger technology (or similar technology).

Building on the existing legal and regulatory framework, stablecoins aiming at stabilizing value in relation to a fiat currency can be classified as follows according to the stabilizing mechanism.

(a) Digital assets issued at a price pegged to the value of a fiat currency (e.g., 1 coin = 1 yen) while promising redemption at par (the same price as the issue price) (and other digital assets with equivalent features) (digital-money-type stablecoins)

(b) Digital assets other than (a), including those using algorithms in an attempt to stabilize value (crypto-asset-type stablecoins)

The current use cases of stablecoins are as followed:

(i) Digital-money-type stablecoins have been experimented with to see if they could be commercialized in payment and settlement services, including those related to securities settlement and inter-company settlement. Some of them could evolve to function as the existing digital money that is widely used in the economy as a means of payment and settlement.

(ii) Both digital-money type and crypto-asset-type stablecoins are used as a part of crypto assets trading. Various risks and issues are pointed out with regard to digital-money-type stablecoins, which relate to underlying assets held by issuers and include the risk of failing to fulfill redemption promises and opaque disclosure.

Digital-money-type stablecoins and crypto-asset-type stablecoins differ presumably in terms of their functions to be fulfilled in the economy, their legal interests to be protected, and the issues in financial regulation and supervision. Therefore, the extension of their different treatment in the existing legal and regulatory frameworks is considered appropriate. In considering regulatory responses, issues related to user protection should be addressed properly.

(2) Digital-Money-Type Stablecoins and Existing Digital Money

Digital-money-type stablecoins in general are currently provided in a manner in which the issuer and intermediary are separated using distributed ledgers or an equivalent system. However, as described above, it can evolve to function as digital money that is widely used in the economy as an electronic instrument of payment and settlement services.

On the other hand, existing digital money services are currently provided, with the issuer being accountable for the entire service. In the future, however, a new business model separating the issuer from intermediary could emerge.

Based on the principle of "same business, same risk, and same rule," the revision of the existing legal and regulatory frameworks should be considered. It should allow the separation between the issuer and intermediary, while being applied holistically to digital money and its equivalent as a whole, including the existing digital money, and not limited to digital-money-type stablecoins.

(3) Considerations on the Separation between Issuer and Intermediary

The functionalities of electronic payment and settlement services can be broadly divided into the following three elements, if focusing on the ones performed by service providers.

(i) Providing mechanisms for issuance, redemption and stabilization of value (which usually include management of underlying assets and custody services);

(ii) Providing services to transfer the rights of users, (which usually include transaction verification mechanisms);

(iii) Providing services related to customer contacts for management and transactions (which typically include wallet services to manage customers' private keys and business applications to enable coin transactions);

The existing legal framework for digital money in Japan is predicated on the underlying assumption that the single entity is accountable for performing the functions of (i) to (iii) above. The following points were raised on this framework.

- The requirements of the financial regulation and supervision are different in terms of (i) the functionalities of issuance and related operations (the main function is to receive and manage funds from users) and (ii) the functionalities of transfer and management (the main function is customer management including compliance with AML/CFT regulations and system management).

- Digital money legislation of the European Union (EU) separates (i) the functionalities of issuance from (ii) the functionalities of transfer and management. Stablecoins prevailing in the United States and other countries also take similarly separate forms.

- The use of distributed ledgers makes it easier for multiple entities to share ledgers while providing functions (i) and (ii) separately.

- Where functions (i) and (ii) are separated in providing services, the application of the Payment Service Act to the related parties is not necessarily clear. For instance, it is not clear whether appropriate regulations for user protection, AML/CFT and the stability of settlement are consistently applied to the relevant parties—including those who promise redemption at par but whose possibility of redemption is questionable—or stablecoins arrangements that enable trading in the same manner as crypto assets.

It is appropriate to explore the establishment of a legal and regulatory framework that is flexible and sufficient but not overly stringent, which enables payment and settlement services separating (i) the functions of issuance from (ii) the functions of intermediary. Such a framework should take into account the use of distributed ledgers (or similar ones) and strike a right balance between promoting innovation and protecting users.

The framework should require the clear redemption rights of users and the establishment of a comprehensive governance framework to clarify the accountability of relevant parties involved, taking into account the high level recommendations for the global stablecoin arrangement published by the FSB.

(4) Legal and Regulatory Framework related to Issuer and Intermediary

1. Issuer

Under the current legal framework, issuing and redeeming electronic instruments of payment and settlement services, including digital-money-type stablecoins, falls under the act of fund transfer that requires a bank license or registration as a fund transfer business company.

Regarding the issuer's functions (i) (issuance, redemption, and provision of a value stabilization mechanism), the user's right to claim redemption against the issuer should be clearly secured and appropriately protected, including in the event of the insolvency of the issuer or intermediary.

The following schemes, while not exhaustive, could satisfy the requirements related to the redemption right of users, assuming the separation of the issuer and intermediary and building on the existing legal frameworks and prevalent business practices.

- Based on the current business practice of fund transfer using a bank deposit account, a scheme in which an intermediary, who has been granted the authority of representation by the bank, administrates the transfer of funds between individual users' bank accounts (so-called joint-named bank deposits in which the intermediary administers the share of individual users' bank deposits among the total of joint-name bank deposits)

- As a scheme to which the existing Trust Law applies, a scheme in which an intermediary sells or transfers the trust beneficiary rights, for which all the trust assets are managed with demand deposits at banks

Electronic instruments of payment and settlement services could be issued through various schemes other than those described above. Any stablecoins arrangement which lacks a sufficient level of user protection should not be permitted.

2. Intermediary

The regulatory framework to be introduced for intermediaries dealing with digital- money-type stablecoins, who (i) transfer and (ii) act as points of contact with customers for management and transactions as a business, should determine its perimeter – the scope of actions that require registration and accompanied supervision. It should properly cover not only the current transactions and trading practices of stablecoins prevailing overseas, taking into account their similarities to those of crypto assets, but also the so-called joint-named bank deposit and trust schemes mentioned above.

Considering its functions, an intermediary should take enough measures to provide appropriate information to users on electronic instruments of payment and settlement services and to comply with AML/CFT requirements. Such measures should include appropriate IT system development. These requirements have been applied to registered crypto-asset exchange service providers. Moreover, no intermediaries to be registered should deal with electronic instruments of payment and settlement services that lack a sufficient level of user protection, including those issued overseas, as registered crypto-asset service providers have been required to do.

2. Discipline Covering Both Issuer and Intermediary

Furthermore, payment and settlement services should be provided properly as a whole. Sufficient measures should be taken to achieve appropriate coordination between the issuer and intermediary and clarify their respective roles and responsibilities for users.

(5) Regulatory Discipline on Global Stablecoins

Electronic instruments of payment and settlement services used on a large scale or used for cross-border settlement can have a significant impact on financial stability, including the impact of their issuance and redemption on the financial market. A higher level of regulatory discipline is required.

The regulatory disciplines discussed in (4)1 through 3 for digital-money-type stablecoins are in line with the high level recommendations for global stablecoins published by the FSB. Risk-based supervision under these disciplines could address the potential additional risks posed by global stablecoins, including the impact on financial markets. Risk-based supervision on stablecoins should be calibrated, taking into account their structure and scale of operations.

Discussion Points

1. *Restricting the issuance of stablecoins.* In 2022, Japan's upper house of parliament passed a law to regulate stablecoins. The law imposed a mandatory link with the yen and enshrined the right to redeem them at face value. The issuance of stablecoins will now be restricted only to banks, licensed money transfer agents, and trust companies. Do you think that this restriction will stifle cross-border transactions using cryptocurrencies? How would such a restriction impact consumers?

2. *Compare.* Compare the way the U.K. seems to view consumers' use of cryptocurrency to the way Japan seems to view consumers' use of cryptocurrency. What are the differences between the ways in which each country has gone about regulating cryptocurrency? Do you agree with the regulatory framework of cryptocurrency that one country has more than that of the other? If so, why?

3. *The implications of "miscellaneous income" tax.* Do you agree with Japan's classification of cryptocurrency (earning over a certain amount) as "miscellaneous income"? Do you think that cryptocurrency should be taxed the same as other income? Why or why not? Do you think this encourages or discourages individuals from using cryptocurrency?

VI. China

The Chinese government has not directly banned cryptocurrency, but it has aggressively restricted the use of cryptocurrency. Since 2013, the Chinese government has prohibited financial institutions from transacting using Bitcoin. These efforts were furthered in 2014 with the inception of a new requirement on commercial banks to close down Bitcoin trading accounts. Such restrictive measures continued in 2017 when China prohibited initial coin offerings ("ICOs"). The government even went as far as shutting down three of the largest exchanges that dealt with Bitcoin. It may be the case that the Chinese government was antagonistic in their approach to cryptocurrency because of the growing number of Bitcoin users within its borders.

Prior to the ban on transacting in Bitcoin in 2013, One Foundation, a Chinese charity, had accepted donations in Bitcoin, receiving 230 Bitcoins within 48 hours (approximately $30,000). This could have accidentally helped to legitimize cryptocurrency as a currency or method of payment in the eyes of Chinese citizens, which led to the government turning its attention to the technology. Some experts have estimated that 85% of the global Bitcoin transactions occurred in China for 2017. This was likely a concerning figure for regulators since cryptocurrency could be used to circumvent the authorities for various reasons. These restrictions make it clear that the government does not view cryptocurrency as a form of money. Instead, it seems that the Chinese government views cryptocurrency as a virtual commodity since it cannot be circulated by financial institutions.

The restrictive efforts of the Chinese government started shortly after Satoshi Nakamoto's white paper that disrupted the way the world views currency. In 2009, the government banned online "gold farming," which occurred not as the result of mining bitcoin, but instead happened from popular gaming sites such as World of Warcraft. Virtual gold was created within the game then sold for money that could be used in the real world. This may have laid the foundation for the restrictions that have evolved over time. Nowhere in the Chinese marketplace can Bitcoin be legally transacted. Such actions taken by the Chinese government implies a disdain for cryptocurrency. Perhaps such contempt is due to the government's political views. Communism is predicated on government control, but the decentralized nature of cryptocurrency disregards the notion of centralized control.

However, China may be shifting their views as implied by their endorsement of stablecoins, which are different from cryptocurrency, because stablecoins are pegged to an acceptable form of currency. In April 2020, China launched their own digital currency that is pegged with China's national currency at a rate of 1:1. The digital currency mimics what we know as cashless payments. Digitizing the yuan has allowed the Chinese government to monitor transactions through a private, government-managed distributed ledger, as distinguished from its decentralized counterpart: Bitcoin.

Unlike Bitcoin, the digital yuan is designed to be a risk-free and government-backed currency, which makes it stable. This signals a willingness of the Chinese government to recognize a digital coin when it is pegged to a national currency (i.e., a stablecoin). Other countries are also attempting to create their own central bank digital currency ("CBDC"); however, China's pilot is the most advanced attempt to date. Some commentators believe that this may encourage persons (individual or entity) located outside of China to use the yuan through its digital equivalent.

In 2021, the most powerful regulators in China banned all cryptocurrency transactions and mining, which targeted Bitcoin and other major cryptocurrencies. The People's Bank of China, the central bank of China, stated that cryptocurrencies are illegal and that they "cannot be circulated as currency in the market." Because of China's low electricity rates and the vast availability for computer hardware, it was one of the main hubs for cryptocurrency mining. The energy that is needed to mine the cryptocurrency transactions are harming the climate, according to these Chinese regulators.

Discussion Points

1. *In the name of public policy.* Do you think that Chinese regulators chose to ban cryptocurrency for public policy reasons, or for a different reason? How could this decision to ban cryptocurrency negatively impact China's economy?

2. *The digital yuan.* What are the key differences between the digital yuan and Bitcoin? How are they different, if at all? Is the yuan a stablecoin? If so, how?

VII. Switzerland

Cryptocurrencies and blockchain technology have been ushered into the mainstream in Switzerland. Both cryptocurrencies and cryptocurrency exchanges are legal in Switzerland. For tax purposes, the Swiss Federal Tax Administration categorizes cryptocurrencies as assets to be declared on annual returns. Switzerland aims to be blockchain friendly and has institutions like the Swiss Blockchain Federation to further its aim of promoting Switzerland as a preferred location for blockchain-based activities and to create a secure legal framework. Cryptocurrency uptake and development is encouraged at various levels in the country, and in the Swiss town of Zug in 2016, Bitcoin could be used to pay city fees.

Switzerland's Financial Market Supervisory Authority (FINMA) is an independent financial markets regulator. FINMA is Switzerland's financial regulatory authority which oversees the financial markets and providers. Cryptocurrency exchanges in Switzerland are legal as long as they are licensed by FINMA. In 2019, FINMA granted two financial institutions licenses to conduct cryptocurrency trading and custody activities—Maerki Baumann and Income Bank. Additionally, the Swiss Federal Tax Administration ("SFTA") classifies Bitcoin and Ethereum as assets covered by Switzerland's Wealth Tax, which must be declared yearly on tax returns.

After noting an uptake in initial coin offerings (ICOs), in September 2017, FINMA issued guidance and only conducts legal assessments of ICOs within the financial market legislation sphere, and companies launching ICOs must comply with relevant financial market laws. The Anti-Money Laundering Act governs payment transaction services like wallet services used to transfer or store crypto assets. In terms of banking law, where virtual currencies are stored separately on the blockchain for each customer and there is a direct link and easy identification of the individual customer making a deposit, a banking license is not necessary. Cryptocurrency exchanges must be registered and licensed by FINMA.

FINMA analyzes stablecoins with a neutral viewpoint, and mainly focuses on the economic objective and function of the stablecoins. For payments on the blockchain, FINMA applies Swiss regulations to the sending of information in payment transactions on the blockchain. The same strict anti-money laundering rules are applied to blockchain payments.

In January 2020, the Swiss Financial Services Act (FinSA) was enacted and serves to regulate financial services in Switzerland. Its ambit covers companies providing Fintech services in Switzerland, Swiss clients or the provision of asset management or similarly regulated services in Switzerland. For Anti-Money Laundering legislation, blockchain applications, cryptocurrencies, and other similar mediums qualify as intermediaries and are subject to AML and KYC obligations.

In summer 2020, Swiss parliamentarians passed the "Blockchain Act" with law reforms that could further decentralize finance and create digital company shares. The legislation provides clarity on the exchange of digital-only securities and provides a framework for cryptocurrency exchanges.

Discussion Points

1. *The Blockchain Act.* Do you think the increased decentralization of financial transactions can promote economic growth? If so, how? How, if at all, do you think a financial system that requires intermediaries to facilitate transactions among consumers stifles economic growth?

2. *Comparison to Japan.* Japan considers cryptocurrency of a certain amount to be "miscellaneous income" for tax purposes. In Switzerland, the Swiss Federal Tax Administration categorizes cryptocurrencies as assets to be declared on annual tax returns. Which view of cryptocurrency as a taxable income do you think is better? Why?

3. *Registration required.* Should cryptocurrency exchanges be required to register and be licensed with FINMA? Why or why not?

Fact Sheet: Blockchain and Cryptoassets in the Financial Sector: Switzerland's Pioneering Role on the International Stage

Switzerland State Secretariat for International Financial Matters (January 24, 2022)

* * *

What are cryptoassets?

- **Cryptoassets** is a collective term for digital assets that are usually recorded on a blockchain. These include not only the so-called cryptocurrencies that are often the focus of attention and have no backing (e.g. bitcoin) or are linked to a fiat currency in order to reduce their volatility (so-called stable-coins), but also so-called asset tokens that represent rights (e.g. shares) or physical assets (e.g. wine).

The **blockchain** and **distributed ledger technology** behind cryptoassets harbours great potential. It allows the encrypted, decentralised storage and transfer of values. This can create an end-to-end digital value chain, which promises innovative applications and greater efficiency, not least in the area of asset tokens.

- The global **market capitalisation** of all cryptoassets totalled over USD 2 trillion in 2021. This corresponds to around 1% of all financial assets or 0.5% of all financial and real economic assets. The largest cryptoassets by market capitalisation are the cryptocurrencies bitcoin (around USD 1 trillion) and Ethereum (around USD 500 billion), although the value of such cryptocurrencies is subject to extremely large fluctuations that can hardly be predicted.

What are the implications for Switzerland?

1. Consolidating its status as an innovative financial centre

- **The Swiss financial centre** is one of the world's most important centres and has a strong international focus. It is also one of the most advanced in the field of **fintech** and blockchain. For Switzerland, it is essential that the legal framework enables **innovation** and that the potential of new technologies can be realised.

  - Among other things, the innovation-friendly **framework conditions** and the **legal certainty** created by the authorities (clarification of legal issues through guidelines, creation of regulatory frameworks) have allowed the emergence of a dynamic **Swiss blockchain ecosystem** made up of developers, service providers and advisers. Switzerland does not regulate the technology, but rather, where necessary, the activities carried out with the help of the technology (technology neutrality principle).

  - The establishment of the **Ethereum Foundation** in the so-called **Crypto Valley** in Zug was likewise decisive for the development of the ecosystem. Switzerland was also open to providing a serious regulatory framework for innovative projects as part of the **Diem project** (formerly **Libra**), which originally wanted to be located in Switzerland. The close collaboration with foreign supervisory authorities before the project was even ready for approval was widely acknowledged.

- Like all financial centres, Switzerland faces **risks** of abuse and **vulnerabilities**, including in relation to cryptoassets. Switzerland is determined to minimise the risks posed by cryptoassets in terms of money laundering and terrorist financing, financial stability, taxation, and investor and consumer protection. Since their emergence, it has been committed to controlling and reducing these risks, adapting **national law** where necessary, and actively participating in the development of **international standards.**

- In 2021, the **Federal Act on the Adaptation of Federal Law to Developments in Distributed Electronic Register Technology (DLT)** and the associated blanket ordinance came into force. Among other things, this legislation improves the conditions for companies using blockchain in Switzerland (introduction of security rights registered on a blockchain), increases legal certainty in the event of bankruptcy (segregation of cryptoassets), creates a new licence category for DLT/blockchain-based trading systems within the framework of financial market supervision, and provides a proportionate response to the risks identified in the area of money laundering and terrorist financing.

- FINMA supervises the implementation of financial market regulation by financial intermediaries. Since 2019, it has published, among other things, a practical guide for authorisation enquiries and a position statement on stablecoins. The legal certainty provided by the above-mentioned regulations also enabled it to grant a banking licence to financial service providers specialising in DLT/blockchain in 2019, and to approve the first Swiss cryptofund in 2021.

- The Federal Council is closely monitoring the latest developments in blockchain, such as **non-fungible tokens** (NFTs) and **decentralised finance** (DeFi), which have not been the subject of an international consensus on how they should be regulated to date.

2. Safeguarding the integrity of the financial centre by taking proactive action against crime

- The Federal Council attaches great importance to preserving the integrity and good reputation of the Swiss financial centre. The Anti-Money Laundering Act applies to financial intermediary activities involving cryptoassets. A Swiss financial intermediary that holds or helps to transfer cryptocurrencies for third parties is therefore subject to the same obligations as if the currency used were fiat money, e.g., Swiss Francs. FINMA also published guidance on payments on the blockchain.

- Switzerland thus goes beyond the international standards of the Financial Action Task Force (FATF). It was one of the first two countries to be assessed in this area, and with good results. In a globalized world where cybercrime is on the rise, this reduces the risk of ransom payments being transferred to wallets managed by Swiss financial intermediaries.

- Many other countries have not yet implemented these standards, which increases the risk of money laundering at the international level. The vulnerabilities associated with transactions conducted without a financial intermediary or through intermediaries located in jurisdictions without legislation comparable to Switzerland's (e.g. via cryptocurrency exchange platforms located abroad) can be minimized solely through international cooperation.

- Switzerland actively advocates the rapid global implementation of the FATF standards in order to avoid legal loopholes and havens for criminals.

3. Continuing to ensure the stability of the financial centre

- The Federal Council is monitoring developments in the area of cryptoassets that could have an impact on **financial stability**. Due to the global dimension of these projects, international cooperation is essential. For this reason, Switzerland actively participates in the work of the relevant **international bodies**, such as the Financial Stability Board (FSB), the Basel Committee on Banking Supervision (BCBS), the International Organization of Securities Commissions (IOSCO) and the Committee on Payments and Market Infrastructures (CPMI), which are continuing to develop international standards for cryptoassets.

- To date, **no material risk** to financial stability has been identified by the FSB. However, developments happen quickly and could have consequences in the future. Consequently, these analyses are **regularly repeated**.

4. Clear taxation of cryptoassets

- Developments in the financial markets require international tax assistance to be adapted in order to ensure global **tax transparency**. Currently, the OECD is working on an extension of the global standard for the international **automatic exchange of information** on financial accounts (AEOI standard) to include cryptoassets and providers of services with cryptoassets. Switzerland is actively involved in this work.

- Switzerland is also actively involved in international work on the **taxation of cryptoassets**. Domestically, the Federal Council acknowledged an FDF report on a possible need to adapt tax law to the developments in DLT/blockchain in 2020. The report concluded that there is no need to change the existing legal framework. The Federal Tax Administration regularly publishes information on the practice followed in the area of cryptoassets based on current tax law.

Discussion Points

1. *Is Switzerland getting it right?* Do you think that Switzerland is taking appropriate measures to prevent criminal activity involving virtual currencies? If so, how? Do you think that the requirement that intermediaries that hold or help transfer cryptocurrencies for third parties be subject to the same obligations as intermediaries transferring fiat currency is justified? Is it too rigid a requirement? Why or why not?

2. *Should the U.S. revamp its regulatory framework for virtual currencies?* Should the U.S. establish entities and task forces on the federal level to develop policies and regulations, and to monitor various aspects of virtual currency development and usage? Given the way federal agencies are created in the U.S., do you think it is within the executive or congressional power to create new agencies that deal solely with the virtual currency space?

Appendix

New York Bit License Statutes

New York Codes, Rules and Regulations
Title 23—Financial Services
Chapter I - Regulations of the Superintendent of Financial Services
Part 200—Virtual Currencies

23 CRR-NY I 200 Notes

(Statutory authority: Financial Services Law, §§ 102, 104, 201, 206, 301, 302, 309, 408)

Current through May 31, 2021

200.1 Introduction.

This Part contains regulations relating to the conduct of business involving virtual currency, as defined herein, in accordance with the superintendent's powers pursuant to the above-stated authority.

Current through May 31, 2021

200.2 Definitions.

For purposes of this Part only, the following definitions shall apply:

(a) *affiliate* means any person that directly or indirectly controls, is controlled by, or is under common control with, another person;

(b) *cyber security event* means any act or attempt, successful or unsuccessful, to gain unauthorized access to, disrupt, or misuse a licensee's electronic systems or information stored on such systems;

(c) *department* means the New York State Department of Financial Services;

(d) *exchange service* means the conversion or exchange of fiat currency or other value into virtual currency, the conversion or exchange of virtual currency into fiat currency or other value, or the conversion or exchange of one form of virtual currency into another form of virtual currency;

(e) *fiat currency* means government-issued currency that is designated as legal tender in its country of issuance through government decree, regulation, or law;

(f) *licensee* means any person duly licensed by the superintendent pursuant to this Part;

(g) *New York* means the State of New York;

(h) *New York resident* means any person that resides, is located, has a place of business, or is conducting business in New York;

(i) *person* means an individual, partnership, corporation, association, joint stock association, trust, or other entity, however organized;

(j) *prepaid card* means an electronic payment device that:

(1) is usable at a single merchant or an affiliated group of merchants that share the same name, mark, or logo, or is usable at multiple, unaffiliated merchants or service providers;

(2) is issued in and for a specified amount of fiat currency;

(3) can be reloaded in and for only fiat currency, if at all;

(4) is issued and/or reloaded on a prepaid basis for the future purchase or delivery of goods or services;

(5) is honored upon presentation; and

(6) can be redeemed in and for only fiat currency, if at all;

(k) *principal officer* means an executive officer of an entity, including, but not limited to, the chief executive, financial, operating, and compliance officers, president, general counsel, managing partner, general partner, controlling partner, and trustee, as applicable;

(l) *principal stockholder* means any person that directly or indirectly owns, controls, or holds with power to vote 10 percent or more of any class of outstanding capital stock or other equity interest of an entity or possesses the power to direct or cause the direction of the management or policies of the entity;

(m) *principal beneficiary* means any person entitled to 10 percent or more of the benefits of a trust;

(n) *qualified custodian* means a bank, trust company, national bank, savings bank, savings and loan association, Federal savings association, credit union, or Federal credit union in the State of New York, subject to the prior approval of the superintendent. To the extent applicable, terms used in this definition shall have the meaning ascribed by the Banking Law;

(o) *transmission* means the transfer, by or through a third party, of virtual currency from a person to a person, including the transfer from the account or storage repository of a person to the account or storage repository of a person;

(p) *virtual currency* means any type of digital unit that is used as a medium of exchange or a form of digitally stored value. virtual currency shall be broadly construed to include digital units of exchange that: have a centralized repository or administrator; are decentralized and have no centralized repository or administrator; or may be created or obtained by computing or manufacturing effort. *Virtual currency* shall not be construed to include any of the following:

(1) digital units that:

(i) are used solely within online gaming platforms;

(ii) have no market or application outside of those gaming platforms;

(iii) cannot be converted into, or redeemed for, fiat currency or virtual currency; and

(iv) may or may not be redeemable for real-world goods, services, discounts, or purchases;

(2) digital units that can be redeemed for goods, services, discounts, or purchases as part of a customer affinity or rewards program with the issuer and/ or other designated merchants or can be redeemed for digital units in another customer affinity or rewards program, but cannot be converted into, or redeemed for, fiat currency or virtual currency; or

(3) digital units used as part of prepaid cards;

(q) *virtual currency business activity* means the conduct of any one of the following types of activities involving New York or a New York resident:

(1) receiving virtual currency for transmission or transmitting virtual currency, except where the transaction is undertaken for non-financial purposes and does not involve the transfer of more than a nominal amount of virtual currency;

(2) storing, holding, or maintaining custody or control of virtual currency on behalf of others;

(3) buying and selling virtual currency as a customer business;

(4) performing exchange services as a customer business; or

(5) controlling, administering, or issuing a virtual currency.

The development and dissemination of software in and of itself does not constitute virtual currency business activity.

Current through May 31, 2021

200.3 License.

(a) License required.

No person shall, without a license obtained from the superintendent as provided in this Part, engage in any virtual currency business activity. Licensees are not authorized to exercise fiduciary powers, as defined under section 100 of the Banking Law.

(b) Unlicensed agents prohibited.

Each licensee is prohibited from conducting any virtual currency business activity through an agent or agency arrangement when the agent is not a licensee.

(c) Exemption from licensing requirements.

The following persons are exempt from the licensing requirements otherwise applicable under this Part:

(1) persons that are chartered under the New York Banking Law and are approved by the superintendent to engage in virtual currency business activity; and

(2) merchants and consumers that utilize virtual currency solely for the purchase or sale of goods or services or for investment purposes.

Current through May 31, 2021

200.4 Application.

(a) Application for a license required under this Part shall be in writing, under oath, and in a form prescribed by the superintendent, and shall contain the following:

(1) the exact name of the applicant, including any doing business as name, the form of organization, the date of organization, and the jurisdiction where organized or incorporated;

(2) a list of all of the applicant's affiliates and an organization chart illustrating the relationship among the applicant and such affiliates;

(3) a list of, and detailed biographical information for, each individual applicant and each director, principal officer, principal stockholder, and principal beneficiary of the applicant, as applicable, including such individual's name, physical and mailing addresses, and information and documentation regarding such individual's personal history, experience, and qualification, which shall be accompanied by a form of authority, executed by such individual, to release information to the department;

(4) a background report prepared by an independent investigatory agency acceptable to the superintendent for each individual applicant, and each principal officer, principal stockholder, and principal beneficiary of the applicant, as applicable;

(5) for each individual applicant; for each principal officer, principal stockholder, and principal beneficiary of the applicant, as applicable; and for all individuals to be employed by the applicant who have access to any customer funds, whether denominated in fiat currency or virtual currency:

(i) a set of completed fingerprints, or a receipt indicating the vendor (which vendor must be acceptable to the superintendent) at which, and the date when, the fingerprints were taken, for submission to the State Division of Criminal Justice Services and the Federal Bureau of Investigation;

(ii) if applicable, such processing fees as prescribed by the superintendent; and

(iii) two portrait-style photographs of the individuals measuring not more than two inches by two inches;

(6) an organization chart of the applicant and its management structure, including its principal officers or senior management, indicating lines of authority and the allocation of duties among its principal officers or senior management;

(7) a current financial statement for the applicant and each principal officer, principal stockholder, and principal beneficiary of the applicant, as applicable, and a projected balance sheet and income statement for the following year of the applicant's operation;

(8) a description of the proposed, current, and historical business of the applicant, including detail on the products and services provided and to be provided, all associated website addresses, the jurisdictions in which the applicant is engaged in business, the principal place of business, the primary market of operation, the projected customer base, any specific marketing targets, and the physical address of any operation in New York;

(9) details of all banking arrangements;

(10) all written policies and procedures required by, or related to, the requirements of this Part;

(11) an affidavit describing any pending or threatened administrative, civil, or criminal action, litigation, or proceeding before any governmental agency, court, or arbitration tribunal against the applicant or any of its directors, principal officers, principal stockholders, and principal beneficiaries, as applicable, including the names of the parties, the nature of the proceeding, and the current status of the proceeding;

(12) verification from the New York State Department of Taxation and Finance that the applicant is compliant with all New York State tax obligations in a form acceptable to the superintendent;

(13) if applicable, a copy of any insurance policies maintained for the benefit of the applicant, its directors or officers, or its customers;

(14) an explanation of the methodology used to calculate the value of virtual currency in fiat currency; and

(15) such other additional information as the superintendent may require.

(b) As part of such application, the applicant shall demonstrate that it will be compliant with all of the requirements of this Part upon licensing.

(c) Notwithstanding subdivision (b) of this section, the superintendent may in his or her sole discretion and consistent with the purposes and intent of the Financial Services Law and this Part approve an application by granting a conditional license.

(1) A conditional license may be issued to an applicant that does not satisfy all of the regulatory requirements upon licensing.

(2) A licensee that holds a conditional license may be subject to heightened review, whether in regard to the scope and frequency of examination or otherwise.

(3) Unless the superintendent removes the conditional status of or renews a conditional license, said license shall expire two years after its date of issuance.

(i) The superintendent may in his or her sole discretion and consistent with the purposes and intent of the Financial Services Law and this Part:

(a) renew a conditional license for an additional length of time; or

(b) remove the conditional status from a conditional license.

(4) A conditional license may be suspended or revoked pursuant to section 200.6 of this Part.

(5) A conditional license may impose any reasonable condition or conditions, as determined by the superintendent in his or her sole discretion.

(6) The superintendent may remove any condition or conditions from a conditional license that has been issued.

(7) In determining whether to issue a conditional license, renew or remove the conditional status of a conditional license, or impose or remove any specific conditions on a conditional license, the superintendent may consider any relevant factor or factors. Relevant factors may include but are not limited to:

(i) the nature and scope of the applicant's or licensee's business;

(ii) the anticipated volume of business to be transacted by the applicant or licensee;

(iii) the nature and scope of the risks that the applicant's or licensee's business presents to consumers, virtual currency markets, financial markets, and the general public;

(iv) the measures which the applicant or licensee has taken to limit or mitigate the risks its business presents;

(v) whether the applicant or licensee is registered with FinCEN;

(vi) whether the applicant or licensee is licensed, registered, or otherwise authorized by any governmental or self-regulatory authority to engage in financial services or other business activities;

(vii) the applicant's or licensee's financial services or other business experience; and

(viii) the licensee's history as a holder of a conditional license issued by the superintendent.

(d) The superintendent may permit that any application for a license under this Part, or any other submission required by this Part, be made or executed by electronic means.

Current through May 31, 2021

200.5 Application fees.

As part of an application for licensing under this Part, each applicant must submit an initial application fee, in the amount of $5,000, to cover the cost of processing the application, reviewing application materials, and investigating the financial condition and responsibility, financial and business experience, and character and general fitness of the applicant. If the application is denied or withdrawn, such fee shall not be refunded. Each licensee may be required to pay fees to the department to process additional applications related to the license.

Current through May 31, 2021

200.6 Action by superintendent.

(a) Generally.

Upon the filing of an application for licensing under this Part, payment of the required fee, and demonstration by the applicant of its ability to comply with the provisions of this Part upon licensing, the superintendent shall investigate the financial condition and responsibility, financial and business experience, and character and general fitness of the applicant. If the superintendent finds these qualities are such as to warrant the belief that the applicant's business will be conducted honestly, fairly, equitably, carefully, and efficiently within the purposes and intent of this Part, and in a manner commanding the confidence and trust of the community, the superintendent shall advise the applicant in writing of his or her approval of the application, and shall issue to the applicant a license to conduct virtual currency business activity, subject to the provisions of this Part and such other conditions as the superintendent shall deem appropriate; or the superintendent may deny the application.

(b) Approval or denial of application.

The superintendent shall approve or deny every application for a license hereunder within 90 days from the filing of an application deemed by the superintendent to be complete. Such period of 90 days may be extended at the discretion of the superintendent for such additional reasonable period of time as may be required to enable compliance with this Part. A license issued pursuant to this Part shall remain in full force and effect until it is surrendered by the licensee, is revoked or suspended, or expires as provided in this Part.

(c) Suspension or revocation of license.

The superintendent may suspend or revoke a license issued under this Part on any ground on which the superintendent might refuse to issue an original license, for a violation of any provision of this Part, for good cause shown, or for failure of the licensee to pay a judgment, recovered in any court, within or without this State, by a claimant or creditor in an action arising out of, or relating to, the licensee's virtual currency business activity, within 30 days after the judgment becomes final or within 30 days after expiration or termination of a stay of execution thereon; provided, however, that if execution on the judgment is stayed, by court order or operation of law or otherwise, then proceedings to suspend or revoke the license (for failure of the licensee to pay such judgment) may not be commenced by the superintendent during the time of such stay, and for 30 days thereafter. "Good cause" shall exist when a licensee has defaulted or is likely to default in performing its obligations or financial engagements or engages in unlawful, dishonest, wrongful, or inequitable conduct or practices that may cause harm to the public.

(d) Hearing.

No license issued under this Part shall be revoked or suspended except after a hearing thereon. The superintendent shall give a licensee no less than 10 days' written notice of the time and place of such hearing by registered or certified mail addressed to the principal place of business of such licensee. Any order of the superintendent suspending or revoking such license shall state the grounds upon which it is based and be sent by registered or certified mail to the licensee at its principal place of business as shown in the records of the department.

(e) Preliminary injunction.

The superintendent may, when deemed by the superintendent to be in the public interest, seek a preliminary injunction to restrain a licensee from continuing to perform acts that violate any provision of this Part, the Financial Services Law, Banking Law, or Insurance Law.

(f) Preservation of powers.

Nothing in this Part shall be construed as limiting any power granted to the superintendent under any other provision of the Financial Services Law, Banking Law, or Insurance Law, including any power to investigate possible violations of law, rule, or regulation or to impose penalties or take any other action against any person for violation of such laws, rules, or regulations.

Current through May 31, 2021

200.7 Compliance.

(a) Generally.

Each licensee is required to comply with all applicable Federal and State laws, rules, and regulations.

(b) Compliance officer.

Each licensee shall designate a qualified individual or individuals responsible for coordinating and monitoring compliance with this Part and all other applicable Federal and State laws, rules, and regulations.

(c) Compliance policy.

Each licensee shall maintain and enforce written compliance policies, including policies with respect to anti-fraud, anti-money laundering, cyber security, privacy and information security, and any other policy required under this Part, which must be reviewed and approved by the licensee's board of directors or an equivalent governing body.

Current through May 31, 2021

200.8 Capital requirements.

(a) Each licensee shall maintain at all times such capital in an amount and form as the superintendent determines is sufficient to ensure the financial integrity of the licensee and its ongoing operations based on an assessment of the specific risks applicable to each licensee. In determining the minimum amount of capital that must be maintained by a licensee, the superintendent may consider a variety of factors, including but not limited to:

(1) the composition of the licensee's total assets, including the position, size, liquidity, risk exposure, and price volatility of each type of asset;

(2) the composition of the licensee's total liabilities, including the size and repayment timing of each type of liability;

(3) the actual and expected volume of the licensee's virtual currency business activity;

(4) whether the licensee is already licensed or regulated by the superintendent under the Financial Services Law, Banking Law, or Insurance Law, or otherwise subject to such laws as a provider of a financial product or service, and whether the licensee is in good standing in such capacity;

(5) the amount of leverage employed by the licensee;

(6) the liquidity position of the licensee;

(7) the financial protection that the licensee provides for its customers through its trust account or bond;

(8) the types of entities to be serviced by the licensee; and

(9) the types of products or services to be offered by the licensee.

(b) Each licensee shall hold capital required to be maintained in accordance with this section in the form of cash, virtual currency, or high-quality, highly liquid, investment-grade assets, in such proportions as are acceptable to the superintendent.

Current through May 31, 2021

200.9 Custody and protection of customer assets.

(a) Each licensee shall maintain a surety bond or trust account in United States dollars for the benefit of its customers in such form and amount as is acceptable to the superintendent for the protection of the licensee's customers. To the extent a licensee maintains a trust account in accordance with this section, such trust account must be maintained with a qualified custodian.

(b) To the extent a licensee stores, holds, or maintains custody or control of virtual currency on behalf of another person, such licensee shall hold virtual currency of the same type and amount as that which is owed or obligated to such other person.

(c) Each licensee is prohibited from selling, transferring, assigning, lending, hypothecating, pledging, or otherwise using or encumbering assets, including virtual currency, stored, held, or maintained by, or under the custody or control of, such licensee on behalf of another person except for the sale, transfer, or assignment of such assets at the direction of such other person.

Current through May 31, 2021

200.10 Material change to business.

(a) Each licensee must obtain the superintendent's prior written approval for any plan or proposal to introduce or offer a materially new product, service, or activity, or to make a material change to an existing product, service, or activity, involving New York or New York residents.

(b) A "materially new product, service, or activity" or a "material change" may occur where:

(1) the proposed new product, service, or activity, or the proposed change may raise a legal or regulatory issue about the permissibility of the product, service, or activity;

(2) the proposed new product, service, or activity, or the proposed change may raise safety and soundness or operational concerns; or

(3) a change is proposed to an existing product, service, or activity that may cause such product, service, or activity to be materially different from that previously listed on the application for licensing by the superintendent.

(c) The licensee shall submit a written plan describing the proposed materially new product, service, or activity, or the proposed material change, including a detailed description of the business operations, compliance policies, and the impact on the overall business of the licensee, as well as such other information as requested by the superintendent.

(d) If a licensee has any questions about the materiality of any proposed new product, service, or activity, or of any proposed change, the licensee may seek clarification from the department prior to introducing or offering that new product, service, or activity or making that change.

Current through May 31, 2021

200.11 Change of control; mergers and acquisitions.

(a) Change of control.

No action shall be taken, except with the prior written approval of the superintendent, that may result in a change of control of a licensee.

(1) Prior to any change of control, the person seeking to acquire control of a licensee shall submit a written application to the superintendent in a form and substance acceptable to the superintendent, including but not limited to detailed information about the applicant and all directors, principal officers, principal stockholders, and principal beneficiaries of the applicant, as applicable.

(2) For purposes of this section, the term *control* means the possession, directly or indirectly, of the power to direct or cause the direction of the management and policies of a licensee whether through the ownership of stock of such licensee, the stock of any person that possesses such power, or otherwise. Control shall be presumed to exist if a person, directly or indirectly, owns, controls, or holds with power to vote 10 percent or more of the voting stock of a licensee or of any person that owns, controls, or holds with power to vote 10 percent or more of the voting stock of such licensee. No person shall be deemed to control another person solely by reason of his being an officer or director of such other person.

(3) The superintendent may determine upon application that any person does not or will not upon the taking of some proposed action control another person. Such determination shall be made within 30 days or such further period as the superintendent may prescribe. The filing of an application pursuant to this subdivision in good faith by any person shall relieve the applicant from any obligation or liability imposed by this section with respect to the subject of the application until the superintendent has acted upon the application. The superintendent may revoke or modify his or her determination, after notice and opportunity to be heard, whenever in his or her judgment revocation or modification is consistent with this Part. The superintendent may consider the following factors in making such a determination:

(i) whether such person's purchase of common stock is made solely for investment purposes and not to acquire control over the licensee;

(ii) whether such person could direct, or cause the direction of, the management or policies of the licensee;

(iii) whether such person could propose directors in opposition to nominees proposed by the management or board of directors of the licensee;

(iv) whether such person could seek or accept representation on the board of directors of the licensee;

(v) whether such person could solicit or participate in soliciting proxy votes with respect to any matter presented to the shareholders of the licensee; or

(vi) any other factor that indicates such person would or would not exercise control of the licensee.

(4) The superintendent shall approve or deny every application for a change of control of a licensee hereunder within 120 days from the filing of an application deemed by the superintendent to be complete. Such period of 120 days may be extended by the superintendent, for good cause shown, for such additional reasonable period of time as may be required to enable compliance with the requirements and conditions of this Part.

(5) In determining whether to approve a proposed change of control, the superintendent shall, among other factors, take into consideration the public interest and the needs and convenience of the public.

(b) Mergers and acquisitions.

No action shall be taken, except with the prior written approval of the superintendent, that may result in a merger or acquisition of all or a substantial part of the assets of a licensee.

(1) Prior to any such merger or acquisition, an application containing a written plan of merger or acquisition shall be submitted to the superintendent by the entities that are to merge or by the acquiring entity, as applicable. Such plan shall be in form and substance satisfactory to the superintendent, and shall specify each entity to be merged, the surviving entity, or the entity acquiring all or substantially all of the assets of the licensee, as applicable, and shall describe the terms and conditions of the merger or acquisition and the mode of carrying it into effect.

(2) The superintendent shall approve or deny a proposed merger or a proposed acquisition of all or a substantial part of the assets of a licensee within 120 days after the filing of an application that contains a written plan of merger or acquisition and is deemed by the superintendent to be complete. Such period of 120 days may be extended by the superintendent, for good cause shown, for such additional reasonable period of time as may be required to enable compliance with the requirements and conditions of this Part.

(3) In determining whether to so approve a proposed merger or acquisition, the superintendent shall, among other factors, take into consideration the public interest and the needs and convenience of the public.

Current through May 31, 2021

200.12 Books and records.

(a) Each licensee shall, in connection with its virtual currency business activity, make, keep, and preserve all of its books and records in their original form or native file format for a period of at least seven years from the date of their creation and in a condition that will allow the superintendent to determine whether the licensee is complying with all applicable laws, rules, and regulations. The books and records maintained by each licensee shall, without limitation, include:

(1) for each transaction, the amount, date, and precise time of the transaction, any payment instructions, the total amount of fees and charges received and paid to, by, or on behalf of the licensee, and the names, account numbers, and physical addresses of:

(i) the party or parties to the transaction that are customers or accountholders of the licensee; and

(ii) to the extent practicable, any other parties to the transaction;

(2) a general ledger containing all asset, liability, ownership equity, income, and expense accounts;

(3) bank statements and bank reconciliation records;

(4) any statements or valuations sent or provided to customers and counterparties;

(5) records or minutes of meetings of the board of directors or an equivalent governing body;

(6) records demonstrating compliance with applicable State and Federal anti-money laundering laws, rules, and regulations, including customer identification and verification documents, records linking customers to their respective accounts and balances, and a record of all compliance breaches;

(7) communications and documentation related to investigations of customer complaints and transaction error resolution or concerning facts giving rise to possible violations of laws, rules, or regulations;

(8) all other records required to be maintained in accordance with this Part; and

(9) all other records as the superintendent may require.

(b) Each licensee shall provide the department, upon request, immediate access to all facilities, books, records, documents, or other information maintained by the licensee or its affiliates, wherever located.

(c) Records of non-completed, outstanding, or inactive virtual currency accounts or transactions shall be maintained for at least five years after the time when any such virtual currency has been deemed, under the Abandoned Property Law, to be abandoned property.

Current through May 31, 2021

200.13 Examinations.

(a) Each licensee shall permit and assist the superintendent to examine the licensee whenever in the superintendent's judgment such examination is necessary or advisable, but not less than once every two calendar years, including, without limitation, to determine:

(1) the financial condition of the licensee;

(2) the safety and soundness of the conduct of its business;

(3) the policies of its management;

(4) whether the licensee has complied with the requirements of laws, rules, and regulations; and

(5) such other matters as the superintendent may determine, including, but not limited to, any activities of the licensee outside the State of New York if in the opinion of the superintendent such activities may affect the licensee's virtual currency business activity.

(b) Each licensee shall permit and assist the superintendent at any time to examine all of the licensee's books, records, accounts, documents, and other information.

(c) Each licensee shall permit and assist the superintendent to make such special investigations as the superintendent shall deem necessary to determine whether a licensee has violated any provision of the applicable laws, rules, or regulations and to the extent necessary shall permit and assist the superintendent to examine all relevant facilities, books, records, accounts, documents, and other information.

(d) For the purpose of determining the financial condition of the licensee, its safety and soundness practices, or whether it has complied with the requirements of laws, rules, and regulations, the licensee shall permit and assist the superintendent, when in the superintendent's judgment it is necessary or advisable, to examine an affiliate of the licensee.

Current through May 31, 2021

200.14 Reports and financial disclosures.

(a) Each licensee shall submit to the superintendent quarterly financial statements within 45 days following the close of the licensee's fiscal quarter in the form, and containing such information, as the superintendent shall prescribe, including without limitation, the following information:

(1) a statement of the financial condition of the licensee, including a balance sheet, income statement, statement of comprehensive income, statement of change in ownership equity, cash flow statement, and statement of net liquid assets;

(2) a statement demonstrating compliance with any financial requirements established under this Part;

(3) financial projections and strategic business plans;

(4) a list of all off-balance sheet items;

(5) a chart of accounts, including a description of each account; and

(6) a report of permissible investments by the licensee as permitted under this Part.

(b) Each licensee shall submit audited annual financial statements, together with an opinion and an attestation by an independent certified public accountant regarding the effectiveness of the licensee's internal control structure. All such annual financial statements shall include:

(1) a statement of management's responsibilities for preparing the licensee's annual financial statements, establishing and maintaining adequate internal controls and procedures for financial reporting, and complying with all applicable laws, rules, and regulations;

(2) an assessment by management of the licensee's compliance with such applicable laws, rules, and regulations during the fiscal year covered by the financial statements; and

(3) certification of the financial statements by an officer or director of the licensee attesting to the truth and correctness of those statements.

(c) Each licensee shall notify the superintendent in writing of any criminal action or insolvency proceeding against the licensee or any of its directors, principal stockholders, principal officers, and principal beneficiaries, as applicable, immediately after the commencement of any such action or proceeding.

(d) Each licensee shall notify the superintendent in writing of any proposed change to the methodology used to calculate the value of virtual currency in fiat currency that was submitted to the department in accordance with section 200.4 of this Part.

(e) Each licensee shall submit a report to the superintendent immediately upon the discovery of any violation or breach of law, rule, or regulation related to the conduct of activity licensed under this Part.

(f) Each licensee shall make additional special reports to the superintendent, at such times and in such form, as the superintendent may request.

Current through May 31, 2021

200.15 Anti-money laundering program.

(a) All values in United States dollars referenced in this section must be calculated using the methodology to determine the value of virtual currency in fiat currency that was provided to the department under this Part.

(b) Each licensee shall conduct an initial risk assessment that will consider legal, compliance, financial, and reputational risks associated with the licensee's activities, services, customers, counterparties, and geographic location and shall establish, maintain, and enforce an anti-money laundering program based thereon. The licensee shall conduct additional assessments on an annual basis, or more frequently as risks change, and shall modify its anti-money laundering program as appropriate to reflect any such changes.

(c) The anti-money laundering program shall, at a minimum:

(1) provide for a system of internal controls, policies, and procedures designed to ensure ongoing compliance with all applicable anti-money laundering laws, rules, and regulations;

(2) provide for independent testing for compliance with, and the effectiveness of, the anti-money laundering program to be conducted by qualified internal personnel of the licensee, who are not responsible for the design, installation, maintenance, or operation of the anti-money laundering program, or the policies and procedures that guide its operation, or a qualified external party, at least annually, the findings of which shall be summarized in a written report submitted to the superintendent;

(3) designate a qualified individual or individuals in compliance responsible for coordinating and monitoring day-to-day compliance with the anti-money laundering program; and

(4) provide ongoing training for appropriate personnel to ensure they have a fulsome understanding of anti-money laundering requirements and to enable them to identify transactions required to be reported and maintain records required to be kept in accordance with this Part.

(d) The anti-money laundering program shall include a written anti-money laundering policy reviewed and approved by the licensee's board of directors or equivalent governing body.

(e) Each licensee, as part of its anti-money laundering program, shall maintain records and make reports in the manner set forth below.

(1) Records of virtual currency transactions. Each licensee shall maintain the following information for all virtual currency transactions involving the payment, receipt, exchange, conversion, purchase, sale, transfer, or transmission of virtual currency:

(i) the identity and physical addresses of the party or parties to the transaction that are customers or accountholders of the licensee and, to the extent practicable, any other parties to the transaction;

(ii) the amount or value of the transaction, including in what denomination purchased, sold, or transferred;

(iii) the method of payment;

(iv) the date or dates on which the transaction was initiated and completed; and

(v) a description of the transaction.

(2) Reports on transactions. When a licensee is involved in a virtual currency to virtual currency transaction or series of virtual currency to virtual currency transactions that are not subject to currency transaction reporting requirements under Federal law, including transactions for the payment, receipt, exchange, conversion, purchase, sale, transfer, or transmission of virtual currency, in an aggregate amount exceeding the United States dollar value of $10,000 in one day, by one person, the licensee shall notify the department, in a manner prescribed by the superintendent, within 24 hours.

(3) Monitoring for suspicious activity. Each licensee shall monitor for transactions that might signify money laundering, tax evasion, or other illegal or criminal activity.

(i) Each licensee shall file suspicious activity reports ("SARs") in accordance with applicable Federal laws, rules, and regulations.

(ii) Each licensee that is not subject to suspicious activity reporting requirements under Federal law shall file with the superintendent, in a form prescribed by the superintendent, reports of transactions that indicate a possible violation of law or regulation within 30 days from the detection of the facts that constitute a need for filing. Continuing suspicious activity shall be reviewed on an ongoing basis and a suspicious activity report shall be filed within 120 days of the last filing describing continuing activity.

(f) No licensee shall structure transactions, or assist in the structuring of transactions, to evade reporting requirements under this Part.

(g) No licensee shall engage in, facilitate, or knowingly allow the transfer or transmission of virtual currency when such action will obfuscate or conceal the identity of an individual customer or counterparty. Nothing in this section, however, shall be construed to require a licensee to make available to the general public the fact or nature of the movement of virtual currency by individual customers or counterparties.

(h) Each licensee shall also maintain, as part of its anti-money laundering program, a customer identification program.

(1) Identification and verification of account holders. When opening an account for, or establishing a service relationship with, a customer, each licensee must, at a minimum, verify the customer's identity, to the extent reasonable and practicable, maintain records of the information used to verify such identity, including name, physical address, and other identifying information, and check customers against the Specially Designated Nationals ("SDNs") list maintained by the Office of Foreign Asset Control ("OFAC"), a part of the U.S. Treasury Department. Enhanced due diligence may be required based on additional factors, such as for high risk customers, high-volume accounts, or accounts on which a suspicious activity report has been filed.

(2) Enhanced due diligence for accounts involving foreign entities. licensees that maintain accounts for non-U.S. persons and non-U.S. licensees must establish enhanced due diligence policies, procedures, and controls to detect money laundering, including assessing the risk presented by such accounts based on the nature of the foreign business, the type and purpose of the activity, and the anti-money laundering and supervisory regime of the foreign jurisdiction.

(3) Prohibition on accounts with foreign shell entities. licensees are prohibited from maintaining relationships of any type in connection with their virtual currency business activity with entities that do not have a physical presence in any country.

(4) Identification required for large transactions. Each licensee must require verification of the identity of any accountholder initiating a transaction with a value greater than $3,000.

(i) Each licensee shall demonstrate that it has risk-based policies, procedures, and practices to ensure, to the maximum extent practicable, compliance with applicable regulations issued by OFAC.

(j) Each licensee shall have in place appropriate policies and procedures to block or reject specific or impermissible transactions that violate Federal or State laws, rules, or regulations.

(k) The individual or individuals designated by the licensee, pursuant to paragraph (c)(3) of this section, shall be responsible for day-to-day operations of the anti-money laundering program and shall, at a minimum:

(1) monitor changes in anti-money laundering laws, including updated OFAC and SDN lists, and update the program accordingly;

(2) maintain all records required to be maintained under this section;

(3) review all filings required under this section before submission;

(4) escalate matters to the board of directors, senior management, or appropriate governing body and seek outside counsel, as appropriate;

(5) provide periodic reporting, at least annually, to the board of directors, senior management, or appropriate governing body; and

(6) ensure compliance with relevant training requirements.

Current through May 31, 2021

200.16 Cyber security program.

(a) Generally.

Each licensee shall establish and maintain an effective cyber security program to ensure the availability and functionality of the licensee's electronic systems and to protect those systems and any sensitive data stored on those systems from unauthorized access, use, or tampering. The cyber security program shall be designed to perform the following five core cyber security functions:

(1) identify internal and external cyber risks by, at a minimum, identifying the information stored on the licensee's systems, the sensitivity of such information, and how and by whom such information may be accessed;

(2) protect the licensee's electronic systems, and the information stored on those systems, from unauthorized access, use, or other malicious acts through the use of defensive infrastructure and the implementation of policies and procedures;

(3) detect systems intrusions, data breaches, unauthorized access to systems or information, malware, and other cyber security events;

(4) respond to detected cyber security events to mitigate any negative effects; and

(5) recover from cyber security events and restore normal operations and services.

(b) Policy.

Each licensee shall implement a written cyber security policy setting forth the licensee's policies and procedures for the protection of its electronic systems and customer and counterparty data stored on those systems, which shall be reviewed and approved by the licensee's board of directors or equivalent governing body at least annually. The cyber security policy must address the following areas:

(1) information security;

(2) data governance and classification;

(3) access controls;

(4) business continuity and disaster recovery planning and resources;

(5) capacity and performance planning;

(6) systems operations and availability concerns;

(7) systems and network security;

(8) systems and application development and quality assurance;

(9) physical security and environmental controls;

(10) customer data privacy;

(11) vendor and third-party service provider management;

(12) monitoring and implementing changes to core protocols not directly controlled by the licensee, as applicable; and

(13) incident response.

(c) Chief information security officer.

Each licensee shall designate a qualified employee to serve as the licensee's chief information security officer ("CISO") responsible for overseeing and implementing the licensee's cyber security program and enforcing its cyber security policy.

(d) Reporting.

Each licensee shall submit to the department a report, prepared by the CISO and presented to the licensee's board of directors or equivalent governing body, at least annually, assessing the availability, functionality, and integrity of the licensee's electronic systems, identifying relevant cyber risks to the licensee, assessing the licensee's cyber security program, and proposing steps for the redress of any inadequacies identified therein.

(e) Audit.

Each licensee's cyber security program shall, at a minimum, include audit functions as set forth below.

(1) Penetration testing. Each licensee shall conduct penetration testing of its electronic systems, at least annually, and vulnerability assessment of those systems, at least quarterly.

(2) Audit trail. Each licensee shall maintain audit trail systems that:

(i) track and maintain data that allows for the complete and accurate reconstruction of all financial transactions and accounting;

(ii) protect the integrity of data stored and maintained as part of the audit trail from alteration or tampering;

(iii) protect the integrity of hardware from alteration or tampering, including by limiting electronic and physical access permissions to hardware and maintaining logs of physical access to hardware that allows for event reconstruction;

(iv) log system events including, at minimum, access and alterations made to the audit trail systems by the systems or by an authorized user, and all system administrator functions performed on the systems; and

(v) maintain records produced as part of the audit trail in accordance with the recordkeeping requirements set forth in this Part.

(f) Application security.

Each licensee's cyber security program shall, at minimum, include written procedures, guidelines, and standards reasonably designed to ensure the security of all applications utilized by the licensee. All such procedures, guidelines, and standards shall be reviewed, assessed, and updated by the licensee's CISO at least annually.

(g) Personnel and intelligence.

Each licensee shall:

(1) employ cyber security personnel adequate to manage the licensee's cyber security risks and to perform the core cyber security functions specified in paragraphs (a)(1)-(5) of this section;

(2) provide and require cyber security personnel to attend regular cyber security update and training sessions; and

(3) require key cyber security personnel to take steps to stay abreast of changing cyber security threats and countermeasures.

Current through May 31, 2021

200.17 Business continuity and disaster recovery.

(a) Each licensee shall establish and maintain a written business continuity and disaster recovery ("BCDR") plan reasonably designed to ensure the availability and functionality of the licensee's services in the event of an emergency or other disruption to the licensee's normal business activities. The BCDR plan, at minimum, shall:

(1) identify documents, data, facilities, infrastructure, personnel, and competencies essential to the continued operations of the licensee's business;

(2) identify the supervisory personnel responsible for implementing each aspect of the BCDR plan;

(3) include a plan to communicate with essential persons in the event of an emergency or other disruption to the operations of the licensee, including employees, counterparties, regulatory authorities, data and communication providers, disaster recovery specialists, and any other persons essential to the recovery of documentation and data and the resumption of operations;

(4) include procedures for the maintenance of back-up facilities, systems, and infrastructure as well as alternative staffing and other resources to

enable the timely recovery of data and documentation and to resume operations as soon as reasonably possible following a disruption to normal business activities;

(5) include procedures for the back-up or copying, with sufficient frequency, of documents and data essential to the operations of the licensee and storing of the information off site; and

(6) identify third parties that are necessary to the continued operations of the licensee's business.

(b) Each licensee shall distribute a copy of the BCDR plan, and any revisions thereto, to all relevant employees and shall maintain copies of the BCDR plan at one or more accessible off-site locations.

(c) Each licensee shall provide relevant training to all employees responsible for implementing the BCDR plan regarding their roles and responsibilities.

(d) Each licensee shall promptly notify the superintendent of any emergency or other disruption to its operations that may affect its ability to fulfill regulatory obligations or that may have a significant adverse effect on the licensee, its counterparties, or the market.

(e) The BCDR plan shall be tested at least annually by qualified, independent internal personnel or a qualified third party, and revised accordingly.

Current through May 31, 2021

200.18 Advertising and marketing.

(a) Each licensee engaged in virtual currency business activity shall not advertise its products, services, or activities in New York or to New York Residents without including the name of the licensee and the legend that such licensee is "licensed to engage in virtual currency business activity by the New York State Department of Financial Services."

(b) Each licensee shall maintain, for examination by the superintendent, all advertising and marketing materials for a period of at least seven years from the date of their creation, including but not limited to print media, internet media (including websites), radio and television advertising, road show materials, presentations, and brochures. Each licensee shall maintain hard copy, website captures of material changes to internet advertising and marketing, and audio and video scripts of its advertising and marketing materials, as applicable.

(c) In all advertising and marketing materials, each licensee shall comply with all disclosure requirements under Federal and State laws, rules, and regulations.

(d) In all advertising and marketing materials, each licensee and any person or entity acting on its behalf, shall not, directly or by implication, make any false, misleading, or deceptive representations or omissions.

Current through May 31, 2021

200.19 Consumer protection.

(a) Disclosure of material risks.

As part of establishing a relationship with a customer, and prior to entering into an initial transaction for, on behalf of, or with such customer, each licensee shall disclose in clear, conspicuous, and legible writing in the English language and in any other predominant language spoken by the customers of the licensee, all material risks associated with its products, services, and activities and virtual currency generally, including at a minimum, the following:

(1) virtual currency is not legal tender, is not backed by the government, and accounts and value balances are not subject to Federal Deposit Insurance Corporation or Securities Investor Protection Corporation protections;

(2) legislative and regulatory changes or actions at the State, Federal, or international level may adversely affect the use, transfer, exchange, and value of virtual currency;

(3) transactions in virtual currency may be irreversible, and, accordingly, losses due to fraudulent or accidental transactions may not be recoverable;

(4) some virtual currency transactions shall be deemed to be made when recorded on a public ledger, which is not necessarily the date or time that the customer initiates the transaction;

(5) the value of virtual currency may be derived from the continued willingness of market participants to exchange fiat currency for virtual currency, which may result in the potential for permanent and total loss of value of a particular virtual currency should the market for that virtual currency disappear;

(6) there is no assurance that a person who accepts a virtual currency as payment today will continue to do so in the future;

(7) the volatility and unpredictability of the price of virtual currency relative to fiat currency may result in significant loss over a short period of time;

(8) the nature of virtual currency may lead to an increased risk of fraud or cyber attack;

(9) the nature of virtual currency means that any technological difficulties experienced by the licensee may prevent the access or use of a customer's virtual currency; and

(10) any bond or trust account maintained by the licensee for the benefit of its customers may not be sufficient to cover all losses incurred by customers.

(b) Disclosure of general terms and conditions.

When opening an account for a new customer, and prior to entering into an initial transaction for, on behalf of, or with such customer, each licensee shall disclose in clear, conspicuous, and legible writing in the English language and in any other predominant language spoken by the customers of the licensee, all relevant terms and conditions associated with its products, services, and activities and virtual currency generally, including at a minimum, the following, as applicable:

(1) the customer's liability for unauthorized virtual currency transactions;

(2) the customer's right to stop payment of a preauthorized virtual currency transfer and the procedure to initiate such a stop-payment order;

(3) under what circumstances the licensee will, absent a court or government order, disclose information concerning the customer's account to third parties;

(4) the customer's right to receive periodic account statements and valuations from the licensee;

(5) the customer's right to receive a receipt, trade ticket, or other evidence of a transaction;

(6) the customer's right to prior notice of a change in the licensee's rules or policies; and

(7) such other disclosures as are customarily given in connection with the opening of customer accounts.

(c) Disclosures of the terms of transactions.

Prior to each transaction in virtual currency, for, on behalf of, or with a customer, each licensee shall furnish to each such customer a written disclosure in clear, conspicuous, and legible writing in the English language and in any other predominant language spoken by the customers of the licensee, containing the terms and conditions of the transaction, which shall include, at a minimum, to the extent applicable:

(1) the amount of the transaction;

(2) any fees, expenses, and charges borne by the customer, including applicable exchange rates;

(3) the type and nature of the virtual currency transaction;

(4) a warning that once executed the transaction may not be undone, if applicable; and

(5) such other disclosures as are customarily given in connection with a transaction of this nature.

(d) Acknowledgement of disclosures.

Each licensee shall ensure that all disclosures required in this section are acknowledged as received by customers.

(e) Receipts.

Upon completion of any transaction, each licensee shall provide to a customer a receipt containing the following information:

(1) the name and contact information of the licensee, including a telephone number established by the licensee to answer questions and register complaints;

(2) the type, value, date, and precise time of the transaction;

(3) the fee charged;

(4) the exchange rate, if applicable;

(5) a statement of the liability of the licensee for non-delivery or delayed delivery;

(6) a statement of the refund policy of the licensee; and

(7) any additional information the superintendent may require.

(f) Each licensee shall make available to the department, upon request, the form of the receipts it is required to provide to customers in accordance with subdivision (e) of this section.

(g) Prevention of fraud.

Licensees are prohibited from engaging in fraudulent activity. Additionally, each licensee shall take reasonable steps to detect and prevent fraud, including by establishing and maintaining a written anti-fraud policy. The anti-fraud policy shall, at a minimum, include:

(1) the identification and assessment of fraud-related risk areas;

(2) procedures and controls to protect against identified risks;

(3) allocation of responsibility for monitoring risks; and

(4) procedures for the periodic evaluation and revision of the anti-fraud procedures, controls, and monitoring mechanisms.

Current through May 31, 2021

200.20 Complaints.

(a) Each licensee shall establish and maintain written policies and procedures to fairly and timely resolve complaints.

(b) Each licensee must provide, in a clear and conspicuous manner, on its website or websites, in all physical locations, and in any other location as the superintendent may prescribe, the following disclosures:

(1) the licensee's mailing address, email address, and telephone number for the receipt of complaints;

(2) a statement that the complainant may also bring his or her complaint to the attention of the Department;

(3) the Department's mailing address, website, and telephone number; and

(4) such other information as the superintendent may require.

(c) Each licensee shall report to the superintendent any change in the licensee's complaint policies or procedures within seven days.

Current through May 31, 2021

200.21 Transitional period.

A person already engaged in virtual currency business activity must apply for a license in accordance with this Part within 45 days of the effective date of this regulation. In doing so, such applicant shall be deemed in compliance with the licensure requirements of this Part until it has been notified by the superintendent that its application has been denied, in which case it shall immediately cease operating in this State and doing business with New York State residents. Any person engaged in virtual currency business activity that fails to submit an application for a license within 45 days of the effective date of this regulation shall be deemed to be conducting unlicensed virtual currency business activity.

Current through May 31, 2021

200.22 Severability.

If any provision of this Part or the application thereof to any person or circumstance is adjudged invalid by a court of competent jurisdiction, such judgment shall not affect or impair the validity of the other provisions of this Part or the application thereof to other persons or circumstances.

Current through May 31, 2021

Part 500 - Cybersecurity Requirements for Financial Services Companies

23 CRR-NY I 500 Notes

(Statutory authority: Financial Services Law; §§ 102, 201, 202, 301, 302, 408)

Current through May 31, 2021

500.0 Introduction.

The New York State Department of Financial Services (DFS) has been closely monitoring the ever-growing threat posed to information and financial systems by nation-states, terrorist organizations and independent criminal actors. Recently, cybercriminals have sought to exploit technological vulnerabilities to gain access to sensitive electronic data. Cybercriminals can cause significant financial losses for DFS regulated entities as well as for New York consumers whose private information may be revealed and/or stolen for illicit purposes. The financial services industry is a significant target of cybersecurity threats. DFS appreciates that many firms have proactively increased their cybersecurity programs with great success.

Given the seriousness of the issue and the risk to all regulated entities, certain regulatory minimum standards are warranted, while not being overly prescriptive so that cybersecurity programs can match the relevant risks and keep pace with technological advances. Accordingly, this regulation is designed to promote the protection of customer information as well as the information technology systems of regulated entities. This regulation requires each company to assess its specific risk profile and design a program that addresses its risks in a robust fashion. Senior management must take this issue seriously and be responsible for the organization's cybersecurity program and file an annual certification confirming compliance with these regulations. A regulated entity's cybersecurity program must ensure the safety and soundness of the institution and protect its customers.

It is critical for all regulated institutions that have not yet done so to move swiftly and urgently to adopt a cybersecurity program and for all regulated entities to be subject to minimum standards with respect to their programs. The number of cyber events has been steadily increasing and estimates of potential risk to our financial services industry are stark. Adoption of the program outlined in these regulations is a priority for New York State.

Current through May 31, 2021

500.1 Definitions.

For purposes of this Part only, the following definitions shall apply:

(a) *Affiliate* means any person that controls, is controlled by or is under common control with another person. For purposes of this subdivision, *control* means the possession, direct or indirect, of the power to direct or cause the direction of the management and policies of a person, whether through the ownership of stock of such person or otherwise.

(b) *Authorized user* means any employee, contractor, agent or other person that participates in the business operations of a covered entity and is authorized to access and use any information systems and data of the covered entity.

(c) *Covered entity* means any person operating under or required to operate under a license, registration, charter, certificate, permit, accreditation or similar authorization under the Banking Law, the Insurance Law or the Financial Services Law.

(d) *Cybersecurity event* means any act or attempt, successful or unsuccessful, to gain unauthorized access to, disrupt or misuse an information system or information stored on such information system.

(e) *Information system* means a discrete set of electronic information resources organized for the collection, processing, maintenance, use, sharing, dissemination or disposition of electronic information, as well as any specialized system such as industrial/process controls systems, telephone switching and private branch exchange systems, and environmental control systems.

(f) *Multi-factor authentication* means authentication through verification of at least two of the following types of authentication factors:

(1) knowledge factors, such as a password;

(2) possession factors, such as a token or text message on a mobile phone; or

(3) inherence factors, such as a biometric characteristic.

(g) *Nonpublic information* shall mean all electronic information that is not publicly available information and is:

(1) business related information of a covered entity the tampering with which, or unauthorized disclosure, access or use of which, would cause a material adverse impact to the business, operations or security of the covered entity;

(2) any information concerning an individual which because of name, number, personal mark, or other identifier can be used to identify such individual, in combination with any one or more of the following data elements:

(i) social security number;

(ii) drivers' license number or non-driver identification card number;

(iii) account number, credit or debit card number;

(iv) any security code, access code or password that would permit access to an individual's financial account; or

(v) biometric records;

(3) any information or data, except age or gender, in any form or medium created by or derived from a health care provider or an individual and that relates to:

(i) the past, present or future physical, mental or behavioral health or condition of any individual or a member of the individual's family;

(ii) the provision of health care to any individual; or

(iii) payment for the provision of health care to any individual.

(h) *Penetration testing* means a test methodology in which assessors attempt to circumvent or defeat the security features of an information system by attempting penetration of databases or controls from outside or inside the covered entity's information systems.

(i) *Person* means any individual or any non-governmental entity, including but not limited to any non-governmental partnership, corporation, branch, agency or association.

(j) *Publicly available information* means any information that a covered entity has a reasonable basis to believe is lawfully made available to the general public from: Federal, State or local government records; widely distributed media; or disclosures to the general public that are required to be made by Federal, State or local law.

(1) For the purposes of this subdivision, a covered entity has a reasonable basis to believe that information is lawfully made available to the general public if the covered entity has taken steps to determine:

(i) that the information is of the type that is available to the general public; and

(ii) whether an individual can direct that the information not be made available to the general public and, if so, that such individual has not done so.

(k) *Risk assessment* means the risk assessment that each covered entity is required to conduct under section 500.9 of this Part.

(l) *Risk-based authentication* means any risk-based system of authentication that detects anomalies or changes in the normal use patterns of a person and requires additional verification of the person's identity when such deviations or changes are detected, such as through the use of challenge questions.

(m) *Senior officer(s)* means the senior individual or individuals (acting collectively or as a committee) responsible for the management, operations, security, information systems, compliance and/or risk of a covered entity, including a branch or agency of a foreign banking organization subject to this Part.

(n) Third party service provider(s) means a person that:

(1) is not an affiliate of the covered entity;

(2) provides services to the covered entity; and

(3) maintains, processes or otherwise is permitted access to nonpublic information through its provision of services to the covered entity.

Current through May 31, 2021

500.2 Cybersecurity program.

(a) Cybersecurity program.

Each covered entity shall maintain a cybersecurity program designed to protect the confidentiality, integrity and availability of the covered entity's information systems.

(b) The cybersecurity program shall be based on the covered entity's risk assessment and designed to perform the following core cybersecurity functions:

(1) identify and assess internal and external cybersecurity risks that may threaten the security or integrity of nonpublic information stored on the covered entity's information systems;

(2) use defensive infrastructure and the implementation of policies and procedures to protect the covered entity's information systems, and the nonpublic information stored on those information systems, from unauthorized access, use or other malicious acts;

(3) detect cybersecurity events;

(4) respond to identified or detected cybersecurity events to mitigate any negative effects;

(5) recover from cybersecurity events and restore normal operations and services; and

(6) fulfill applicable regulatory reporting obligations.

(c) A covered entity may meet the requirement(s) of this Part by adopting the relevant and applicable provisions of a cybersecurity program maintained by an affiliate, provided that such provisions satisfy the requirements of this Part, as applicable to the covered entity.

(d) All documentation and information relevant to the covered entity's cybersecurity program shall be made available to the superintendent upon request.

Current through May 31, 2021

500.3 Cybersecurity policy.

Cybersecurity policy. Each covered entity shall implement and maintain a written policy or policies, approved by a senior officer or the covered entity's board of directors (or an appropriate committee thereof) or equivalent governing body, setting forth the covered entity's policies and procedures for the protection of its information systems and nonpublic information stored on those information systems. The cybersecurity policy shall be based on the covered entity's risk assessment and address the following areas to the extent applicable to the covered entity's operations:

(a) information security;

(b) data governance and classification;

(c) asset inventory and device management;

(d) access controls and identity management;

(e) business continuity and disaster recovery planning and resources;

(f) systems operations and availability concerns;

(g) systems and network security;

(h) systems and network monitoring;

(i) systems and application development and quality assurance;

(j) physical security and environmental controls;

(k) customer data privacy;

(l) vendor and third party service provider management;

(m) risk assessment; and

(n) incident response.

Current through May 31, 2021

500.4 Chief information security officer.

(a) Chief information security officer.

Each covered entity shall designate a qualified individual responsible for overseeing and implementing the covered entity's cybersecurity program and enforcing its cybersecurity policy (for purposes of this Part, chief information security officer or CISO). The CISO may be employed by the covered entity, one of its affiliates or a third party service provider. To the extent this requirement is met using a third party service provider or an affiliate, the covered entity shall:

(1) retain responsibility for compliance with this Part;

(2) designate a senior member of the covered entity's personnel responsible for direction and oversight of the third party service provider; and

(3) require the third party service provider to maintain a cybersecurity program that protects the covered entity in accordance with the requirements of this Part.

(b) Report.

The CISO of each covered entity shall report in writing at least annually to the covered entity's board of directors or equivalent governing body. If no such board of directors or equivalent governing body exists, such report shall be timely presented to a senior officer of the covered entity responsible for the covered entity's cybersecurity program. The CISO shall report on the covered entity's cybersecurity program and material cybersecurity risks. The CISO shall consider to the extent applicable:

(1) the confidentiality of nonpublic information and the integrity and security of the covered entity's information systems;

(2) the covered entity's cybersecurity policies and procedures;

(3) material cybersecurity risks to the covered entity;

(4) overall effectiveness of the covered entity's cybersecurity program; and

(5) material cybersecurity events involving the covered entity during the time period addressed by the report.

Current through May 31, 2021

500.5 Penetration testing and vulnerability assessments.

The cybersecurity program for each covered entity shall include monitoring and testing, developed in accordance with the covered entity's risk assessment, designed to assess the effectiveness of the covered entity's cybersecurity program. The monitoring and testing shall include continuous monitoring or periodic penetration testing and vulnerability assessments. Absent effective continuous monitoring, or other systems to detect, on an ongoing basis, changes in information systems that may create or indicate vulnerabilities, covered entities shall conduct:

(a) annual penetration testing of the covered entity's information systems determined each given year based on relevant identified risks in accordance with the risk assessment; and

(b) bi-annual vulnerability assessments, including any systematic scans or reviews of information systems reasonably designed to identify publicly known cybersecurity vulnerabilities in the covered entity's information systems based on the risk assessment.

Current through May 31, 2021

500.6 Audit trail.

(a) Each covered entity shall securely maintain systems that, to the extent applicable and based on its risk assessment:

(1) are designed to reconstruct material financial transactions sufficient to support normal operations and obligations of the covered entity; and

(2) include audit trails designed to detect and respond to cybersecurity events that have a reasonable likelihood of materially harming any material part of the normal operations of the covered entity.

(b) Each covered entity shall maintain records required by paragraph (a)(1) of this section for not fewer than five years and shall maintain records required by paragraph (a)(2) of this section for not fewer than three years.

Current through May 31, 2021

500.7 Access privileges.

As part of its cybersecurity program, based on the covered entity's risk assessment each covered entity shall limit user access privileges to information systems that provide access to nonpublic information and shall periodically review such access privileges.

Current through May 31, 2021

500.8 Application security.

(a) Each covered entity's cybersecurity program shall include written procedures, guidelines and standards designed to ensure the use of secure development practices for in-house developed applications utilized by the covered entity, and procedures for evaluating, assessing or testing the security of externally developed applications utilized by the covered entity within the context of the covered entity's technology environment.

(b) All such procedures, guidelines and standards shall be periodically reviewed, assessed and updated as necessary by the CISO (or a qualified designee) of the covered entity.

Current through May 31, 2021

500.9 Risk assessment.

(a) Each covered entity shall conduct a periodic risk assessment of the covered entity's information systems sufficient to inform the design of the cybersecurity program as required by this Part. Such risk assessment shall be updated as reasonably necessary to address changes to the covered entity's information systems, nonpublic information or business operations. The covered entity's risk assessment shall allow for revision of controls to respond to technological developments and evolving threats and shall consider the particular risks of the covered entity's business operations related to cybersecurity, nonpublic information collected or stored, information systems utilized and the availability and effectiveness of controls to protect nonpublic information and information systems.

(b) The risk assessment shall be carried out in accordance with written policies and procedures and shall be documented. Such policies and procedures shall include:

(1) criteria for the evaluation and categorization of identified cybersecurity risks or threats facing the covered entity;

(2) criteria for the assessment of the confidentiality, integrity, security and availability of the covered entity's information systems and nonpublic information, including the adequacy of existing controls in the context of identified risks; and

(3) requirements describing how identified risks will be mitigated or accepted based on the risk assessment and how the cybersecurity program will address the risks.

Current through May 31, 2021

500.10 Cybersecurity personnel and intelligence.

(a) Cybersecurity personnel and intelligence.

In addition to the requirements set forth in section 500.4(a) of this Part, each covered entity shall:

(1) utilize qualified cybersecurity personnel of the covered entity, an affiliate or a third party service provider sufficient to manage the covered entity's cybersecurity risks and to perform or oversee the performance of the core cybersecurity functions specified in section 500.2(b)(1)-(6) of this Part;

(2) provide cybersecurity personnel with cybersecurity updates and training sufficient to address relevant cybersecurity risks; and

(3) verify that key cybersecurity personnel take steps to maintain current knowledge of changing cybersecurity threats and countermeasures.

(b) A covered entity may choose to utilize an affiliate or qualified third party service provider to assist in complying with the requirements set forth in this Part, subject to the requirements set forth in section 500.11 of this Part.

Current through May 31, 2021

500.11 Third party service provider security policy.

(a) Third party service provider policy.

Each covered entity shall implement written policies and procedures designed to ensure the security of information systems and nonpublic information that are accessible to, or held by, third party service providers. Such policies and procedures shall be based on the risk assessment of the covered entity and shall address to the extent applicable:

(1) the identification and risk assessment of third party service providers;

(2) minimum cybersecurity practices required to be met by such third party service providers in order for them to do business with the covered entity;

(3) due diligence processes used to evaluate the adequacy of cybersecurity practices of such third party service providers; and

(4) periodic assessment of such third party service providers based on the risk they present and the continued adequacy of their cybersecurity practices.

(b) Such policies and procedures shall include relevant guidelines for due diligence and/or contractual protections relating to third party service providers including to the extent applicable guidelines addressing:

(1) the third party service provider's policies and procedures for access controls, including its use of multi-factor authentication as required by section 500.12 of this Part, to limit access to relevant information systems and nonpublic information;

(2) the third party service provider's policies and procedures for use of encryption as required by section 500.15 of this Part to protect nonpublic information in transit and at rest;

(3) notice to be provided to the covered entity in the event of a cybersecurity event directly impacting the covered entity's information systems or the covered entity's nonpublic information being held by the third party service provider; and

(4) representations and warranties addressing the third party service provider's cybersecurity policies and procedures that relate to the security of the covered entity's information systems or nonpublic information.

(c) Limited exception.

An agent, employee, representative or designee of a covered entity who is itself a covered entity need not develop its own third party information security policy pursuant to this section if the agent, employee, representative or designee follows the policy of the covered entity that is required to comply with this Part.

Current through May 31, 2021

500.12 Multi-factor authentication.

(a) Multi-factor authentication.

Based on its risk assessment, each covered entity shall use effective controls, which may include multi-factor authentication or risk-based authentication, to protect against unauthorized access to nonpublic information or information systems.

(b) Multi-factor authentication shall be utilized for any individual accessing the covered entity's internal networks from an external network, unless the covered entity's CISO has approved in writing the use of reasonably equivalent or more secure access controls.

Current through May 31, 2021

500.13 Limitations on data retention.

As part of its cybersecurity program, each covered entity shall include policies and procedures for the secure disposal on a periodic basis of any nonpublic information identified in section 500.1(g)(2)-(3) of this Part that is no longer necessary for business operations or for other legitimate business purposes of the covered entity, except where such information is otherwise required to be retained by law or regulation, or where targeted disposal is not reasonably feasible due to the manner in which the information is maintained.

Current through May 31, 2021

500.14 Training and monitoring.

As part of its cybersecurity program, each covered entity shall:

(a) implement risk-based policies, procedures and controls designed to monitor the activity of authorized users and detect unauthorized access or use of, or tampering with, nonpublic information by such authorized users; and

(b) provide regular cybersecurity awareness training for all personnel that is updated to reflect risks identified by the covered entity in its risk assessment.

Current through May 31, 2021

500.15 Encryption of nonpublic information.

(a) As part of its cybersecurity program, based on its risk assessment, each covered entity shall implement controls, including encryption, to protect nonpublic information held or transmitted by the covered entity both in transit over external networks and at rest.

(1) To the extent a covered entity determines that encryption of nonpublic information in transit over external networks is infeasible, the covered entity may instead secure such nonpublic information using effective alternative compensating controls reviewed and approved by the covered entity's CISO.

(2) To the extent a covered entity determines that encryption of nonpublic information at rest is infeasible, the covered entity may instead secure such nonpublic information using effective alternative compensating controls reviewed and approved by the covered entity's CISO.

(b) To the extent that a covered entity is utilizing compensating controls under subdivision (a) of this section, the feasibility of encryption and effectiveness of the compensating controls shall be reviewed by the CISO at least annually.

Current through May 31, 2021

500.16 Incident response plan.

(a) As part of its cybersecurity program, each covered entity shall establish a written incident response plan designed to promptly respond to, and recover from, any cybersecurity event materially affecting the confidentiality, integrity or availability of the covered entity's information systems or the continuing functionality of any aspect of the covered entity's business or operations.

(b) Such incident response plan shall address the following areas:

(1) the internal processes for responding to a cybersecurity event;

(2) the goals of the incident response plan;

(3) the definition of clear roles, responsibilities and levels of decision-making authority;

(4) external and internal communications and information sharing;

(5) identification of requirements for the remediation of any identified weaknesses in information systems and associated controls;

(6) documentation and reporting regarding cybersecurity events and related incident response activities; and

(7) the evaluation and revision as necessary of the incident response plan following a cybersecurity event.

Current through May 31, 2021

500.17 Notices to superintendent.

(a) Notice of cybersecurity event.

Each covered entity shall notify the superintendent as promptly as possible but in no event later than 72 hours from a determination that a cybersecurity event has occurred that is either of the following:

(1) cybersecurity events impacting the covered entity of which notice is required to be provided to any government body, self-regulatory agency or any other supervisory body; or

(2) cybersecurity events that have a reasonable likelihood of materially harming any material part of the normal operation(s) of the covered entity.

(b) Annually each covered entity shall submit to the superintendent a written statement covering the prior calendar year. This statement shall be submitted by April 15th in such form set forth as Appendix A of this Title, certifying that the covered entity is in compliance with the requirements set forth in this Part. Each covered entity shall maintain for examination by the department all records, schedules and data supporting this certificate for a period of five years. To the extent a covered entity has identified areas, systems or processes that require material improvement, updating or redesign, the covered entity shall document the identification and the remedial efforts planned and underway to address such areas, systems or processes. Such documentation must be available for inspection by the superintendent.

Current through May 31, 2021

500.18 Confidentiality.

Information provided by a covered entity pursuant to this Part is subject to exemptions from disclosure under the Banking Law, Insurance Law, Financial Services Law, Public Officers Law or any other applicable State or Federal law.

Current through May 31, 2021

500.19 Exemptions.

(a) Limited exemption.

Each covered entity with:

(1) fewer than 10 employees, including any independent contractors, of the covered entity or its affiliates located in New York or responsible for business of the covered entity;

(2) less than $5,000,000 in gross annual revenue in each of the last 3 fiscal years from New York business operations of the covered entity and its affiliates; or

(3) less than $10,000,000 in year-end total assets, calculated in accordance with generally accepted accounting principles, including assets of all affiliates, shall be exempt from the requirements of sections 500.4, 500.5, 500.6, 500.8, 500.10, 500.12, 500.14, 500.15 and 500.16 of this Part.

(b) An employee, agent, representative or designee of a covered entity, who is itself a covered entity, is exempt from this Part and need not develop its own cybersecurity program to the extent that the employee, agent, representative or designee is covered by the cybersecurity program of the covered entity.

(c) A covered entity that does not directly or indirectly operate, maintain, utilize or control any information systems, and that does not, and is not required to, directly or indirectly control, own, access, generate, receive or possess nonpublic information shall be exempt from the requirements of sections 500.2, 500.3, 500.4, 500.5, 500.6, 500.7, 500.8, 500.10, 500.12, 500.14, 500.15 and 500.16 of this Part.

(d) A covered entity under article 70 of the Insurance Law that does not and is not required to directly or indirectly control, own, access, generate, receive or possess non-public information other than information relating to its corporate parent company (or affiliates) shall be exempt from the requirements of sections 500.2, 500.3, 500.4, 500.5, 500.6, 500.7, 500.8, 500.10, 500.12, 500.14, 500.15 and 500.16 of this Part.

(e) A covered entity that qualifies for any of the above exemptions pursuant to this section shall file a Notice of Exemption in the form set forth as Appendix B of this Title within 30 days of the determination that the covered entity is exempt.

(f) The following persons are exempt from the requirements of this Part, provided such persons do not otherwise qualify as a covered entity for purposes of this Part: persons subject to Insurance Law section 1110; persons subject to Insurance Law section 5904; and any accredited reinsurer or certified reinsurer that has been accredited or certified pursuant to 11 NYCRR Part 125.

(g) In the event that a covered entity, as of its most recent fiscal year end, ceases to qualify for an exemption, such covered entity shall have 180 days from such fiscal year end to comply with all applicable requirements of this Part.

Current through May 31, 2021

500.20 Enforcement.

This regulation will be enforced by the superintendent pursuant to, and is not intended to limit, the superintendent's authority under any applicable laws.

Current through May 31, 2021

500.21 Effective date.

This Part will be effective March 1, 2017. Covered entities will be required to annually prepare and submit to the superintendent a certification of compliance with New York State Department of Financial Services Cybersecurity Regulations under section 500.17(b) of this Part commencing February 15, 2018.

Current through May 31, 2021

500.22 Transitional periods.

(a) Transitional period.

Covered entities shall have 180 days from the effective date of this Part to comply with the requirements set forth in this Part, except as otherwise specified.

(b) The following provisions shall include additional transitional periods. Covered entities shall have:

(1) one year from the effective date of this Part to comply with the requirements of sections 500.4(b), 500.5, 500.9, 500.12 and 500.14(b) of this Part;

(2) eighteen months from the effective date of this Part to comply with the requirements of sections 500.6, 500.8, 500.13, 500.14(a) and 500.15 of this Part;

(3) two years from the effective date of this Part to comply with the requirements of section 500.11 of this Part.

Current through May 31, 2021

500.23 Severability.

If any provision of this Part or the application thereof to any person or circumstance
is adjudged invalid by a court of competent jurisdiction, such judgment shall not
affect or impair the validity of the other provisions of this Part or the application
thereof to other persons or circumstances.

Current through May 31, 2021

Part 504 - Banking Division Transaction Monitoring and Filtering Program Requirements and Certifications

3 CRR-NY III C 504 Notes

(Statutory authority: Banking Law, §§ 37[3][4], 17; Financial Services Law, § 302)

Current through May 31, 2021

3 CRR-NY 504.1

504.1 Background.

The Department of Financial Services (the department) has been involved in investigations into compliance by regulated institutions, as defined below, with applicable
Bank Secrecy Act/Anti-Money Laundering laws and regulations[1] (BSA/AML) and
Office of Foreign Assets Control of the Treasury Department (OFAC)[2] requirements
implementing Federal economic and trade sanctions.[3] As a result of these investigations, the department identified shortcomings in the transaction monitoring and
filtering programs of these institutions attributable to a lack of robust governance,
oversight, and accountability at senior levels. Based on not only this experience, but
also its regular examinations for safety and soundness, along with other factors, the
department has reason to believe that financial institutions have shortcomings in
their transaction monitoring and filtering programs. As a result, the department
has determined to clarify the required attributes of a Transaction Monitoring and
Filtering Program and to require that the board of directors or senior officer(s),
as applicable, of each regulated institution submit to the superintendent annually

---

1. With respect to Federal laws and regulations, see 31 U.S.C. § 5311, *et seq.* and 31 CFR Chapter
X. For New York State regulations, see Part 115 (3 NYCRR 115), Part 116 (3 NYCRR 116), Part 416
(3 NYCRR 416) and Part 417 (3 NYCRR 417).

2. 31 CFR part 501 *et seq.*

3. For information regarding the *Unites States Code*, the *Code of Federal Regulations* and the
Federal Register, see Supervisory Policy G-1.

a board resolution or compliance finding, as defined in this Part, confirming the steps taken to ascertain compliance by the regulated institution with this Part. This regulation implements these requirements.

Current through May 31, 2021

504.2 Definitions.

The following definitions apply in this Part:

(a) *Annual board resolution* or *senior officer compliance finding* means a board resolution or senior officer(s) finding in the form set forth in section 504.7 of this Title.

(b) *Bank regulated institutions* means all banks, trust companies, private bankers, savings banks, and savings and loan associations chartered pursuant to the New York Banking Law (the Banking Law) and all branches and agencies of foreign banking corporations licensed pursuant to the Banking Law to conduct banking operations in New York.

(c) *Board of directors* means the governing board of every regulated institution or the functional equivalent if the regulated institution does not have a board of directors.

(d) *Nonbank regulated institutions* shall mean all check cashers and money transmitters licensed pursuant to the Banking Law.

(e) *Regulated institutions* means all bank regulated institutions and all nonbank regulated institutions.

(f) *Risk assessment* means an on-going comprehensive risk assessment, including an enterprise wide BSA/AML risk assessment, that takes into account the institution's size, staffing, governance, businesses, services, products, operations, customers, counterparties, other relations and their locations, as well as the geographies and locations of its operations and business relations.

(g) *Senior officer(s)* shall mean the senior individual or individuals responsible for the management, operations, compliance and/or risk of a regulated institution including a branch or agency of a foreign banking organization subject to this Part.

(h) *Suspicious activity reporting* means a report required pursuant to 31 U.S.C. section 5311 *et seq.* that identifies suspicious or potentially suspicious or illegal activities.

(i) *Transaction Monitoring Program* means a program that includes the attributes specified in section 504.3(a), (c) and (d) of this Part.

(j) *Filtering Program* means a program that includes the attributes specified in section 504.3(b), (c) and (d) of this Part.

(k) *Transaction Monitoring and Filtering Program* means a Transaction Monitoring Program, and a Filtering Program, collectively.

Current through May 31, 2021

504.3 Transaction Monitoring and Filtering Program requirements.

(a) Each regulated institution shall maintain a Transaction Monitoring Program reasonably designed for the purpose of monitoring transactions after their execution for potential BSA/AML violations and suspicious activity reporting, which system may be manual or automated, and which shall include the following attributes, to the extent they are applicable:

(1) be based on the risk assessment of the institution;

(2) be reviewed and periodically updated at risk-based intervals to take into account and reflect changes to applicable BSA/AML laws, regulations and regulatory warnings, as well as any other information determined by the institution to be relevant from the institution's related programs and initiatives;

(3) appropriately match BSA/AML risks to the institution's businesses, products, services, and customers/counterparties;

(4) BSA/AML detection scenarios with threshold values and amounts designed to detect potential money laundering or other suspicious or illegal activities;

(5) end-to-end, pre-and post-implementation testing of the Transaction Monitoring Program, including, as relevant, a review of governance, data mapping, transaction coding, detection scenario logic, model validation, data input and program output;

(6) documentation that articulates the institution's current detection scenarios and the underlying assumptions, parameters, and thresholds;

(7) protocols setting forth how alerts generated by the Transaction Monitoring Program will be investigated, the process for deciding which alerts will result in a filing or other action, the operating areas and individuals responsible for making such a decision, and how the investigative and decision-making process will be documented; and

(8) be subject to an on-going analysis to assess the continued relevancy of the detection scenarios, the underlying rules, threshold values, parameters, and assumptions.

(b) Each regulated institution shall maintain a Filtering Program, which may be manual or automated, reasonably designed for the purpose of interdicting transactions that are prohibited by OFAC, and which shall include the following attributes, to the extent applicable:

(1) be based on the risk assessment of the institution;

(2) be based on technology, processes or tools for matching names and accounts,[4] in each case based on the institution's particular risks, transaction and product profiles;

---

4. The technology used in this area may be based on automated tools that develop matching algorithms, such as those that use various forms of so-called "fuzzy logic" and culture-based name

(3) end-to-end, pre- and post-implementation testing of the Filtering Program, including, as relevant, a review of data matching, an evaluation of whether the OFAC sanctions list and threshold settings map to the risks of the institution, the logic of matching technology or tools, model validation, and data input and program output;

(4) be subject to on-going analysis to assess the logic and performance of the technology or tools for matching names and accounts, as well as the OFAC sanctions list and the threshold settings to see if they continue to map to the risks of the institution; and

(5) documentation that articulates the intent and design of the Filtering Program tools, processes or technology.

(c) Each Transaction Monitoring and Filtering Program shall require the following, to the extent applicable:

(1) identification of all data sources that contain relevant data;

(2) validation of the integrity, accuracy and quality of data to ensure that accurate and complete data flows through the Transaction Monitoring and Filtering Program;

(3) data extraction and loading processes to ensure a complete and accurate transfer of data from its source to automated monitoring and filtering systems, if automated systems are used;

(4) governance and management oversight, including policies and procedures governing changes to the Transaction Monitoring and Filtering Program to ensure that changes are defined, managed, controlled, reported, and audited;

(5) vendor selection process if a third party vendor is used to acquire, install, implement, or test the Transaction Monitoring and Filtering Program or any aspect of it;

(6) funding to design, implement and maintain a Transaction Monitoring and Filtering Program that complies with the requirements of this Part;

(7) qualified personnel or outside consultant(s) responsible for the design, planning, implementation, operation, testing, validation, and on-going analysis of the Transaction Monitoring and Filtering Program, including automated systems if applicable, as well as case management, review and decision making with respect to generated alerts and potential filings; and

(8) periodic training of all stakeholders with respect to the Transaction Monitoring and Filtering Program.

---

conventions to match names. This regulation does not mandate the use of any particular technology, only that the system or technology used must be reasonably designed to identify prohibited transactions.

(d) To the extent a regulated institution has identified areas, systems, or processes that require material improvement, updating or redesign, the regulated institution shall document the identification and the remedial efforts planned and underway to address such areas, systems or processes. Such documentation must be available for inspection by the superintendent.

Current through May 31, 2021

504.4 Annual board resolution or senior officer(s) compliance finding.

To ensure compliance with the requirements of this Part, each regulated institution shall adopt and submit to the superintendent a board resolution or senior officer(s) compliance finding in the form set forth in section 504.7 of this Part by April 15th of each year. Each regulated institution shall maintain for examination by the department all records, schedules and data supporting adoption of the board resolution or senior officer(s) compliance finding for a period of five years.

Current through May 31, 2021

504.5 Penalties/enforcement actions.

This regulation will be enforced pursuant to, and is not intended to limit, the superintendent's authority under any applicable laws.

Current through May 31, 2021

504.6 Effective date.

This Part shall be effective January 1, 2017. Regulated Institutions will be required to prepare and submit to the superintendent annual board resolutions or senior officer(s) compliance findings under section 504.4 of this Part commencing April 15, 2018.

Current through May 31, 2021

504.7 Attachment A.

_____

(Regulated Institution Name)

APRIL 15, 20___

Annual Board Resolution or Senior Officer(s) Compliance Finding For Bank Secrecy Act/Anti-Money Laundering and Office of Foreign Asset Control Transaction Monitoring and Filtering Program

Whereas, in compliance with the requirements of the New York State Department of Financial Services (the department) that each Regulated Institution maintain Transaction Monitoring and Filtering Program in compliance with section 504.3 of this Part; and

Whereas, section 504.4 of this Part requires that the board of directors or a senior officer(s), as appropriate, adopt and submit to the superintendent a board resolution or senior officer compliance finding confirming its or such individual's findings that the regulated institution is in compliance with section 504.3 of this Part;

NOW, THEREFORE, the board of directors or senior officer certifies:

(1) The board of directors (or name of senior officer[s]) has reviewed documents, reports, certifications and opinions of such officers, employees, representatives, outside vendors and other individuals or entities as necessary to adopt this board resolution or senior officer compliance finding;

(2) The board of directors or senior officer(s) has taken all steps necessary to confirm that (name of regulated institution) has a Transaction Monitoring and Filtering Program that complies with the provisions of section 504.3 of this Part; and

(3) To the best of the (board of directors) or (name of senior officer[s]) knowledge, the Transaction Monitoring and the Filtering Program of (name of regulated institution) as of _____ (date of the board resolution or senior officer(s) compliance finding) for the year ended ___ (year for which board resolution or compliance finding is provided) complies with section 504.3 of this Part.

Signed by each member of the board of directors or senior officer(s)

Name:_____

Date:

Current through May 31, 2021

Index